ESSAYS ON THE
MAHĀBHĀRATA

ESSAYS ON THE MAHĀBHĀRATA

Edited by

ARVIND SHARMA

MOTILAL BANARSIDASS PUBLISHERS
PRIVATE LIMITED • DELHI

Reprint: Delhi, 2011
First Indian Edition: Delhi, 2007
(First Published by E.J. Brill under the series of Brill's Indological Library,
Edited by Johannes Bronkhorst as Vol. I)

Acknowledgements
Permission by The University of Chicago Press to cite pp. 276-282 from the *Mahābhārata: The Book of the Beginning,* translated and edited by J.A.B. van Buitenen, and published in 1973, is gratefully acknowledged.

Chapters 1-10 of this book appeared originally in *The Journal of South Asian Literature* (Vol. XX, No. 1, Part I:1-168; Winter, Spring, 1985) and are included here with slight modifications. Permission to include them in this volume is gratefully acknowledged.

ISBN: 978-81-208-2738-7

MOTILAL BANARSIDASS
41 U.A. Bungalow Road, Jawahar Nagar, Delhi 110 007
8 Mahalaxmi Chamber, 22 Bhulabhai Desai Road, Mumbai 400 026
203 Royapettah High Road, Mylapore, Chennai 600 004
236, 9th Main III Block, Jayanagar, Bangalore 560 011
Sanas Plaza, 1302 Baji Rao Road, Pune 411 002
8 Camac Street, Kolkata 700 017
Ashok Rajpath, Patna 800 004
Chowk, Varanasi 221 001

Printed in India

By Jainendra Prakash Jain at Shri Jainendra Press,
A-45 Naraina, Phase-I, New Delhi 110 028
and Published by Narendra Prakash Jain for
Motilal Banarsidass Publishers Private Limited,
Bungalow Road, Delhi 110 007

This book is dedicated to
Prof. Dr. Jan Gonda

CONTENTS

PREFACE

This volume, like the epic it deals with, passed through several stages before assuming its present form. Originally some of these essays appeared in the *Journal of South Asian Literature* (XX:1:1–168). I would like to take this opportunity to thank Professor Carlo Coppola for inviting me to edit the section of that issue devoted to the *Mahābhārata* and for permitting me to incorporate it in this volume.

Not everyone who wanted to write could do so in time for the issue, and so the idea of a book emerged. In due course the alchemy of patience (and repeated requests) gradually transformed promises into finished products. Thus, after several years of a merely notional existence the book is now in your hands. But then some things are worth waiting for—a sentiment I hope the appearance of this volume will confirm.

Arvind Sharma

MANUSCRIPTS USED IN THE CRITICAL EDITION OF THE *MAHĀBHĀRATA*: A SURVEY AND DISCUSSION

JOHN DUNHAM

There has never been a census of manuscripts of the *Mahābhārata*, and there is never likely to be. Such a census, significant as it could be in providing more information about the magnitude of the number of copies made of that enormous literary work, could never pretend to complete comprehensiveness. It might, to forestall such criticism, be limited to the Indian subcontinent, putting aside the other parts of Asia in which the *Mahābhārata* was, at one time or another, copied and recited. It could also ignore the libraries and private collections in more remote parts of the world where manuscripts were acquired in relatively recent times as a concomitant of colonial rule or the European historical and literary interest in ancient India. Yet it would still be doomed to failure because of the intractable complexities of locating, describing and comparing old manuscripts within India and its neighboring countries today.

The most extensive search undertaken for manuscripts of the *Mahābhārata* was that of the Bhandarkar Oriental Research Institute, which was begun soon after the institute's founding in 1917 and continued for almost fifty years after that date. The purpose of that search was to acquire manuscripts in order to prepare a critical edition of the text, using manuscripts in various scripts and of the oldest period possible. It was not a census as such, and many manuscripts were passed over in the selection of others which the institute felt fulfilled its purposes better.

Nevertheless it has uncovered unexpected and hitherto unnoticed branches of the *Mahābhārata*'s textual tradition and has produced exciting possibilities for futher research. These results have as yet been incompletely recorded and analyzed, mainly because the critical edition (C.E.) was not completed until 1966, and it was impossible until then to consider the critical apparatus as a whole. Editors of the particular *parvans* have limited their discussion, more or less, to the manuscripts which they had used for their own work. The time has now come when a more comprehensive discussion can properly be undertaken.

In this paper a start has been made on this wider analysis. Necessarily this has involved, at the beginning, a complete enumeration of the manuscripts used in the entire C.E. with details of their dates and locations of copying and copyists involved. It has also included reference to instances where the same codex has been used for different *parvans*, although in many circumstances this information is not given in the details of the critical apparatus of those *parvans* which were completed before others, using the same codices, had begun. In some cases these omissions were not the fault of the editors so much as of the cataloging policies of the libraries holding the manuscripts. Some libraries have cataloged as separate codices manuscripts which are by the same copyist but are of different *parvans* of the *Mahābhārata*. When editors of the C.E. were not able to see the manuscripts for themselves, relying instead on collation sheets alone, it was impossible to describe the contents of some codices fully. Incompleteness of this kind is not at all uncommon in the critical apparatus of most *parvans* of the C.E., and it now requires a very considerable familiarity with the critical apparatus of the entire C.E. before a reader is able to make a fully informed assessment of the usefulness of some manuscripts.

A more important consequence of this analysis is to show quite plainly the pattern of the foundations on which the C.E. has been erected and to suggest under what stresses and strains these have been placed. The manuscripts have been grouped in the list according to the script in which they are written, with the important exception of the category I(B), "Transcripts of Śāradā Manuscripts". This category was the original idea of V.S. Sukthankar and accords with his view of the importance of Kashmir as the home of the "purest" version of the *Mahābhārata*. It is almost exclusively a category of Devanāgarī manuscript, but it does include two manuscripts which were not written in this script. The other groupings are regular ones.

The scripts of manuscripts of the *Mahābhārata* used in the C.E. do not exhaust the number of those identified as having been used in India during the past five hundred years. Among the most significant omissions would appear to be Uriyā, Kannaḍa and Nandināgarī. Why manuscripts in these scripts were not used is not stated in the C.E. It may have been that old manuscripts in these scripts are very rare, or that the manuscripts turned out to contain versions which were "eclectic on no recognizable principles".

What follows is a summary of the main features of each of the categories of manuscript, followed by a discussion of some of the methodological problems to be confronted by the historian in his use of the C.E. as a source of *Mahābhārata* tradition.

I(A). *Śāradā Manuscripts*

The manuscripts written in this script are rare. There were only six located for use in the C.E.[1] These six do not provide a complete coverage of the *Mahābhārata*, as no Śāradā manuscript of the *Anuśāsanaparvan*, *Mausalaparvan*, *Mahāprasthānikaparvan*, and *Svargārohaṇaparvan* have been found to date.[2] Second Śāradā manuscripts are available for the whole, or part, of six *parvans*, with one *parvan* (*Āraṇyakaparvan*) having a third, fragmentary Śāradā codex.

The extant manuscripts are not especially old. The earliest possibly belongs to the later half of the sixteenth century. It was written in Himalayan birchbark (*būrjapatra*) and is quite unique. The others are dated and belong to the late seventeenth century or the early eighteenth century, or are not dated but appear to belong to the same period or later.

The manuscripts are not heavily annotated. There are, instead, occasional variant readings, usually entered interlinearly, which serve to demonstrate that manuscripts were compared with others. That this practice of comparison applied to manuscripts that had originated in centers far removed from Kashmir is shown by a marginal note in the Telugu script in S2 at 7.24.24.

In quite a few instances it is possible to see how marginal notes, glosses and variant readings were absorbed into the text itself through this practice of comparison. The explanation of a word, *kṣamā*, once a marginal gloss, has become part of the text after 4.27.26ab in S1, for example. A passage from Nīlakaṇṭha's commentary has been absorbed into the same Śāradā manuscript after 4.27.22 (254*). One copyist of the commentary of Arjunamiśra, who was adding it to a text of the *Mahābhārata* which was not the version followed by the commentator, has attempted to correct the text in the light of the commentary, though this was done marginally and interlinearly in S1 of the *Śāntiparvan* (p. xxi).

There is evidence, though, that the copyists of these Śāradā manuscripts were, on the whole, conservative in regard to additional passages and readings from non-Śāradā sources. While it is difficult to make precise comparisons it is nonetheless generally true that the Śāradā manuscripts present shorter versions of all the *parvans* for which they are extant. It was this characteristic of the manuscripts above any other which

---

[1] This figure does not include the Śāradā manuscripts used in the supplementary apparatus for the *Bhagavadgītā* alone (*Bhīṣmaparvan*, pp. lvi–lviii). The Raghunath Temple Library in Jammu held Śāradā manuscripts of the *Virāṭaparvan*, but Raghu Vira said these had to be rejected from the critical apparatus of that *parvan* because, on detailed examination, they "turned out to be recent copies of Nīlakaṇṭha's text and hence of no value as Śāradā codices" (*Virāṭaparvan*, pp. ix–x).

[2] Only the first two *adhyāyas* and two stanzas of the third *adhyāya* of the *Āśramavāsikaparvan* are extant in a Śāradā manuscript. See *Āśramavāsikaparvan*, p. xii.

encouraged V.S. Sukthankar to declare the Śāradā version the *textus simplicior* in the C.E., and to regard it as "the best Northern version, and probably, taken as a whole, the best extant version" (*Ādiparvan*, pp. xlviii, lvi).

I(B). *Transcripts of Śāradā Manuscripts*

That transcripts of the *Mahābhārata* were made from Śāradā exemplars is evidenced by both the appearance of some manuscripts and the close correlation of their contents with those of the Śāradā manuscripts. In describing K1, *Ādiparvan*, V.S. Sukthankar has drawn attention to both these characteristics. Of the former he wrote:

> The lines of writing, as in Śāradā (bhūrjapatra) manuscripts, run parallel to the narrow side of the folio. The signatures in the margin are like those found in Kaśmīrī books. The numerous clerical errors, which disfigure every page, betray the writer to be a professional scribe, not thoroughly familiar with the awkward Śāradā script, and still less so with the language of the text, easily misled by the deceptive similarity between certain letters of the Śāradā and Devanāgarī alphabets.[3]

Others editors in the C.E. have noted information about the copyist or the place of copying given in the colophons which indicated a northern (even Kashmiri), or at least northwestern origin of these manuscripts.[4] In making these observations they support V.S. Sukthankar's suggestion that "the Mss comprising this version . . . may in part represent the version of a province or a region adjoining the Śāradā zone which it has not been possible to localize more precisely".[5]

Not all manuscripts grouped under this heading in the C.E. display their connection with the Śāradā manuscripts superficially. This is especially so in the case of the manuscripts in the Bengali and Telugu scripts—K4 *Bhīṣmaparvan*, T2 *Śāntiparvan* (see pp. clxix-clxx), K5 *Āśvamed*-where the outward appearance of the manuscript gives no hint of its primary affiliation. With these, as with all the other manuscripts included in the K version, it was the appearance of characteristically S readings in the text, the inclusion of "additional passages" peculiar to S, transpositions of passages into an order that follows S, and the omission of passages

---

[3] *Ādiparvan*, p. xi. V.S. Sukthankar also refers to a typical style of Kashmiri handwriting (e.g. *Āraṇyakaparvan*, p. iii). Raghu Vira gives examples of mislections of the Śāradā script, *Virāṭaparvan*, p. iv).

[4] For example, *Āraṇyakaparvan*, p. iii; *Anuśāsanaparvan*, p. xviii; *Āśramavāsikaparvan*, p. xxxiv; *Mausalaparvan*, p. xxiv, etc.

[5] *Āraṇyakaparvan*, p. xxi.

that were likewise omitted by S, that determined for the editors a manuscript's basic relationship.

Devanāgarī manuscripts of the Kashmiri type were found to be relatively common, and editors of the C.E. were usually able to use five or more K manuscripts in the critical apparatus of each *parvan*.[6] Some forty-eight manuscripts were used in this way, though this figure can only be taken as notional since there are instances where different editors have used the same manuscript as a K and a D manuscript in editing different *parvans* of the *Mahābhārata*.[7]

The vast majority of dated manuscripts (nineteen out of a total of twenty-three) were copied in the seventeenth and eighteenth centuries. They are most often copies of a single *parvan* or a part thereof. Only four of the K manuscripts survive now as almost complete texts of the *Mahābhārata*, and in only one of these instances has an editor in the C.E. drawn attention to the likelihood of the manuscript having been written by a single hand (K2, *Udyogaparvan*).

The manuscripts are sometimes accompanied by marginal glosses, marginal and interlinear variant readings (sometimes in the same hand, sometimes in another), and corrections. In one case, K4 of the *Ādiparvan*, the manuscript includes supplementary folios at five places which give additional episodes to be fitted into the text at the appropriate places. In one place in the manuscript at least (1.1.53), there is a marginal note to indicate where the episode is to be inserted. Another manuscript, K4 *Udyogaparvan*, has a commentary which is not written in the usual manner (above and below the text in the margins) but is "imbedded" in the text itself.

Being for the most part Devanāgarī copies of Śāradā exemplars, the K manuscripts are much more susceptible to the inclusion of passages from other manuscripts written in Devanāgarī than those written in the less accessible Śāradā script. Nevertheless the editors of the C.E. usually found one or two of their K manuscripts to be very close to the Śāradā text. The editor of the *Karṇaparvan*, for example, concluded that his K1 and K2 were "Devanāgarī transcripts probably from one and the same codex, of which our S1 and S2 are copies".[8] In the *Virāṭaparvan* the editor

---

[6] The editor of the *Anuśāsanaparvan* did not classify any manuscripts as K on the grounds that there was no Śāradā manuscripts for that *parvan* extant, and therefore it was hypothetical to suggest that any manuscript was a transcript of such. See *Anuśāsanaparvan*, p. xvii.

[7] See II (ii), (v), (vi), (xviii), (xx), (xxx), (xlviii) in manuscript enumeration and description.

[8] *Karṇaparvan*, p. xxxvii.

found that he could not separate the two: "Our S and K are equally good Kaśmīrī Mss. They do not form separate categories".[9]

At the other extreme some manuscripts have been very heavily influenced by other Devanāgarī, Bengali, and southern texts. Such influences have been readily detected in such manuscripts as K4 in the *Udyogaparvan*, *Āraṇyakaparvan*, *and Bhīṣmaparvan*, to give but a few examples. It was with such disparity before him that V.S. Sukthankar wrote of this class of manuscript that it "cannot be said to be quite homogeneous".[10]

II. *Nepālī Manuscripts*

Nepālī manuscripts were found for only four *parvans* of the *Mahābhārata*: *Ādiparvan*, *Sabhāparvan*, *Sauptikaparvan*, and *Strīparvan*. The five manuscripts located were written in Newārī characters and appear to be older, as a group, than any other manuscripts used in the C.E., though only one of the manuscripts actually gave a date in the colophon. The manuscripts are not described in detail in the C.E. because they were mostly collated, not at the Bhandarkar Oriental Research Institute, but by local pandits in Nepal. The Nepālī manuscripts are closely related to the Maithilī, Bengali, and Devanāgarī (except K) manuscripts rather than the Śāradā or Śāradā transcript manuscripts.[11]

V.S. Sukthankar drew attention to the fact that despite their age and the distance of Nepal from south India there were numerous instances where these manuscripts shared interpolations common in southern manuscripts.[12] In the *Sabhāparvan* such borrowings were not found among what Franklin Edgerton called "common secondary insertions".[13] Instead, these passages (which were fewer in number than for any other class of manuscript other than the Śāradā) were exclusively drawn from Maithilī, Bengali or Devanāgarī sources, or were peculiar to the Nepālī manuscripts.

III. *Maithilī Manuscripts*

The five manuscripts written in this script of northern Bihar each contain a single *parvan*. Four are dated in the Lakṣmaṇa era, and belong either to

---

[9] *Virāṭaparvan*, p. xvi.

[10] *Āraṇyakaparvan*, p. xxii.

[11] Cf. *Ādiparvan*, p. lix, *Sabhāparvan*, p. xli, *Sauptikaparvan*, p. xxvi.

[12] *Ādiparvan*, p. lix. H.D. Velankar also draws attention to the influence of the "versions of the S recension" in reference to manuscript III (iii). He concluded that this manuscript's "agreement with the Śāradā or the Kashmirian version is very rare" (*Sauptikaparvan*, p. xxvi).

[13] *Sabhāparvan*, p. xlii.

the second half of the fifteenth century or the early part of the sixteenth century. This means that, in company with the Nepālī manuscripts, they form the oldest stratum of the manuscript tradition and are of special interest for this reason among others.

Three of the five manuscripts were collated in Nepal, and there are few details given in the C.E. about the appearance of these manuscripts. The fourth, the manuscript in the possession of the Bihar and Orissa Research Society, has occasional marginal corrections and additions made by the same writer of the manuscript. It is a manuscript which has been "normalized and carefully prepared" in view of its special purpose in a coronation ceremony.[14] This has meant that the copyist has excluded all "additional" passages which did not have other textual precedents in the manuscripts available to him (and to the editor of the C.E.). On the other hand, he appears to have been extraordinarily zealous in including as many "additional" passages for which he had authority. There are 239 of these passages out of a total of 901 found in the critical apparatus of the *Śāntiparvan* as a whole.

IV. *Bengali Manuscripts*

The editors of the C.E. selected predominantly eighteenth-century manuscripts (thirty out of a total of forty-five dated manuscripts) that usually contained only a single *parvan*. There were no manuscripts of the complete *Mahābhārata* in this script used in the C.E., though this omission may only be apparent, and due to a tendency found in the C.E.'s description of Bengali manuscripts which frequently overlooks the full extent of a manuscript.[15]

Although the Bengali manuscripts are often described in the C.E. as a very homogeneous group, they contain few passages which are exclusive to themselves. In the *Śāntiparvan* there are only two such passages, and in the *Bhīṣmaparvan* it is only two omissions which they share in common. Elsewhere editors seem to have come to much the same conclusion as Raghu Vira when he wrote: "There are no such things as *specific* B[engali] or D[evanāgarī] passages, i.e. passages found in the whole of B or the whole of D, but nowhere else".[16]

Once again V.S. Sukthankar has drawn attention to the influence of south India on manuscripts in this script. He wrote that "sporadic

---

[14] *Śāntiparvan*, p. xlvi.

[15] See, for example, this tendency in regard to (viii). It is not fully described in the *Virāṭaparvan* (p. iv) or the *Karṇaparvan* (p. xiv).

[16] *Virāṭaparvan*, p. xxi. Compare *Droṇaparvan*, p. xxiii, and *Udyogaparvan*, p. xxxix.

contamination between B and S, as a whole, cannot be altogether denied and that there are, as a matter of fact, some Bengali manuscripts that stand, palpably, under the influence of the Southern tradition, even in the matter of minor readings . . . "[17]

V(A). *Devanāgarī Manuscripts (with Commentaries)*

Manuscripts of the *Mahābhārata* are often accompanied by commentaries which are usually written in strips on either side of the text. The six commentators whose works accompany texts of the *Mahābhārata* used in the C.E. are Arjunamiśra (c. 1450–1500 A.D.), Caturbhujamiśra (c. 1350–1550 A.D.), Nīlakaṇṭha (c. 1700 A.D.), Ratnagarbha (?), Sarvajña-Nārāyaṇa (c. 1100–1300 A.D.) and Vidyāsāgara (c. 1350 A.D.). The commentaries of Arjunamiśra (*Bhāratārthapradīpikā*) and Nīlakaṇṭha (*Bhāratabhāvadīpa*) are attached to the largest number of texts used in the C.E., while those with Ratnagarbha's were used only in three instances, and then only for two *adhyāyas* of the *Ādiparvan*.[18] In addition to the use of the text of the *Mahābhārata* found in conjunction with these commentaries, extensive use was made of the commentaries themselves in the C.E. as testimonia.

The text of the *Mahābhārata* used by these commentators is closely related to the part of India in which they lived. Arjunamiśra and Caturbhujamiśra were both from the eastern part of India and their text follows closely other manuscripts from this part of the country. Similarly Nīlakaṇṭha and Vidyāsāgara, both westerners, shared a text that had much in common with the Devanāgarī manuscripts from there.[19]

In general this kind of manuscript is well written, with few corrections and only occasional marginal notes.[20]

V(B). *Devanāgarī Manuscripts*

The total numbers of Devanāgarī manuscripts used in the C.E. was 230, though this figure would be reduced somewhat if manuscripts belonging to a single codex were properly counted as such. Nevertheless this approximation gives some idea of the dominance of Devanāgarī manuscripts in the

[17] *Ādiparvan*, p. lxii.

[18] These manuscripts are not included in the brief descriptions that follow.

[19] On the more complex relationships of the text which accompanies the commentary of Sarvajña-Nārāyaṇa, see the comments of S.K. De, *Udyogaparvan*, pp. xvi–xvii.

[20] A manuscript like Dn3, *Araṇyakaparvan*, is quite exceptional from this point of view.

textual tradition sampled in the C.E. It is a dominance which is seen in the fact that Devanāgarī manuscripts are greater in number than the total of manuscripts in all other scripts.

Despite their number there have been very few old manuscripts discovered in this script. The oldest dated manuscript is D1, *Virāṭaparvan* (dated V. Saṁvat 1493 = c. 1437 A.D.), which is considerably more recent than the dated Nepalese manuscripts (N1, *Ādiparvan*) and the dated Bengali manuscripts (B1, *Āraṇyakaparvan*). The majority of Devanāgarī manuscripts which carry a date were copied in the seventeenth and eighteenth centuries A.D.

Manuscripts in this script, unlike those in other scripts, were found in many parts of India. The largest collections drawn upon for the C.E. were those of the Sarasvati Mahal Library, Thanjavur, and the Bombay Government Collection; but important manuscripts were found in collections as separated from one another as the Dayanand Anglo-Vedic College Library in Lahore and the Adyar Library, Madras.

The variations between Devanāgarī manuscripts are almost as vast as these distances. It was V.S. Sukthankar's view that "a Devanāgarī manuscript of the Mahābhārata may, in fact, contain any version or combination of version".[21] They were likely to swing from following a southern tradition to a northern without reason, and he specifically mentioned the *Mahābhārata* collection in the Sarasvati Mahal Library as an example of manuscripts which from his point of view were of little value in the C.E.[22]

The Devanāgarī manuscripts described above usually contain only a single *parvan*, with the exception of the shorter, later *parvans* where it appears to have been usual to copy four or more together.

VI. *Telugu Manuscripts*

Although a minimum of two Telugu manuscripts were used in each *parvan* of the C.E. the total number of manuscripts described there is not large. This was partly due to the fact that many of the manuscripts used contained more than one *parvan*, a feature of the Telugu manuscripts which distinguishes them, to some degree, from the other groups of manuscripts. Another reason for the small number may have been the low estimate which V.S. Sukthankar placed on their value so far as the textual criticism of the *Mahābhārata* was concerned. They were, in his view, probably of less

[21] *Ādiparvan*, p. lxii.
[22] *Ādiparvan*, p. lxxii.

value for the C.E. than the Devanāgarī manuscripts because, like this group, they were "eclectic" without a recognizable principle, and had little to offer in the way of passages shared by themselves exclusively.[23] Other editors confirmed this view by showing how very few passages the Telugu version had to itself, and how closely it followed other Grantha manuscripts.[24]

Only two of the manuscripts are dated, but one of these dates cannot be properly read. The other is dated *śaka* 1974(c. 1973 A.D.), which makes it the most recently copied manuscript used in the critical apparatus of the C.E. A third Telugu manuscript can be taken to indicate that it was copied at some time in the period 1684–1710 A.D.

VI. *Grantha Manuscripts*

Copies of all the *parvans* of the *Mahābhārata* written in the Grantha script were available for the C.E. and a minimum of three such manuscripts was used for each *parvan*. Very few of the Grantha manuscripts are dated. Those that do have dates have ones for which it is difficult to find equivalents. Libraries have hesitated to estimate the age of the manuscripts, and this practice has been adopted by the editors of the C.E. However, there is no indication that these Grantha manuscripts are older than, or even as old as, the northern manuscripts.

Some twenty-nine of the forty-nine manuscripts in the Grantha script contain only a single *parvan* or part thereof. There were no complete or nearly complete manuscripts of the *Mahābhārata* located for use in the C.E. Only four of the manuscripts give the name of the copyist, and none gives the place of copying.

That the Grantha manuscripts were not the product of an isolated development is shown by the large measure of agreement that is found between their texts and those of the Telugu and Malayālam manuscripts. It is significant, though, that there are relatively few Grantha manuscripts which include any number of "additional" passages common in northern manuscripts.

VIII. *Malayālam Manuscripts*

The Malayālam manuscripts used in the C.E. were located, with only four exceptions, in collections in Kerala. It was this location in the extreme

---

[23] *Ādiparvan*, p. lxxii.

[24] See, for example, *Sabhāparvan*, p. xliv, *Bhīṣmaparvan*, p. cx, *Droṇaparvan*, p. xxviii.

south west of the Indian subcontinent which helped to preserve the "purity" of the text as it is found in these manuscripts, according to the editors of the C.E. "Indeed, the M[alayālam] version may, in a sense, be regarded as being in relation to S[outhern Recension] what Ś[āradā version] is in relation to N[orthern Recension]", Professor R.N. Dandekar suggested.[25] The Malayālam manuscripts do not share abundantly in the "additional" passages of the Telugu and Grantha manuscripts. Instead, they tend to remain apart, maintaining a textual tradition of their own "which shows little alliance with T[elugu version], G[rantha version] and not very much with N."[26]

The Malayālam manuscripts are not without their record of comparison with other manuscripts as is shown by the large number of interlinear variant readings in such manuscripts as M4, *Virāṭaparvan*, and M1, *Udyogaparvan*. These additions to the manuscripts have not come directly from the north but can be shown to have percolated through T or TG (cf. *Udyogaparvan*, p. xlvii).

Those Malayālam manuscripts which are dated were all copied in the nineteenth century, with only one exception, a manuscript dating from the first half of the eighteenth century. They form, therefore, the most recent of the dated manuscripts in the critical apparatus of the C.E.

The collection and comparison of a large number of manuscripts from a wide area of the subcontinent in the preparation of the C.E. of the *Mahābhārata* has contributed substantially to the knowledge of the nature of the processes of preservation and growth of that literary tradition.[27] It has conclusively demonstrated that all the extant manuscripts, whatever their place or origin and whatever the version or recension to which they might be assigned, have been subject to a process of addition and alteration that has occurred for the entire period for which there is manuscript

---

[25] *Salyaparvan*, p. xlix.

[26] *Bhīṣmaparvan*, p. cxiii.

[27] *The Souvenir of the Completion of the Critical Edition of the Mahābhārata* (Pune: 1966) gives the figures 1,259 and 734 as the total numbers of manuscripts examined for, and actually used in the C.E. respectively. The latter figure, in particular, should be treated with caution in the light of comments made on p. 2 above. Franklin Edgerton believed that as a result of the search for *Mahābhārata* manuscripts "in most parts of India . . . the chances are that they [V.S. Sukthankar and his colleagues] have included within their purview examples of all important streams of tradition" and added that "the search should of course be continued, especially in out-of-the-way regions, such as Nepal . . . Kashmir, too, may yield important results" (*JAOS*, vol. 48 [1928], 186). After V.S. Sukthankar's death in 1943 the interest in the search for old manuscripts in these areas, which he had stimulated, seems to have extinguished. There were no futher *Nepālī* manuscripts used in *parvan* of the C.E. published after that date, and the only other *Śāradā* manuscript was obtained from the Bibliothèque Nationale in Paris (S1, *Śāntiparvan*).

evidence at least.[28] There is no such thing as a static branch of the manuscript tradition anywhere in India. There is no "pure" version of the *Mahābhārata*, a version that has steadfastly resisted the inclusion of new material from manuscripts or other sources, a perfect copy of the first text. Instead most manuscripts show a complex pattern of affiliations which makes it extremely difficult to classify them into clearly demarcated versions.[29]

The explanation for this circumstance has hardly anything to do with a lack of integrity or skill on the part of the copyists, though there is evidence of this to some degree in the manuscript material now available.[30]

---

[28] V.S. Sukthankar described the situation thus:

> We have unfortunately no single thread to guide us out of the maze, but rather a collection of strands intertwined and entangled and leading along divergent paths. With the epic text as preserved in the extant Mahābhārata manuscripts, successive syntheses of divergent texts, carried out—providentially—in a haphazard fashion, through centuries of diaskeuastic activities; and that with the *possible exception of the Śāradā* (*Kaśmīrī*) *version*, which appears to have been protected by its largely unintelligible script and by the difficulties of access to the province, *all versions are indiscriminately conflated.* (*Ādiparvan*, p. lxxxii)

An opposite point of view is represented by Professor P.P.S. Sastri. He wrote:

> It will . . . be clear that the main text-tradition of the Mahābhārata is one that has been preserved with remarkable accuracy and that the whole work as we have it now in 18 Parvans is the work of a single author, Vyāsa, though it may be permissible to assume that some of the preliminary chapters of the Ādiparvan are in their very nature connecting links supplied by Vaiśampāyana and Sūta to suit the occasion when each in his turn was called upon to narrate the story . . . we are driven to the irresistible conclusion that the Mahābhārata text-tradition, as we have it now in the Southern Recension, is quite authentic and reliable, that the final reduction of the story from the beginning of the first chapter as narrated by Sūta is equally trustworthy and the extent and scope of the Mahābhārata even during Sūta's time consisted of eighteen main parvans with one hundred subparvans, divided into two thousand chapters and comprising one hundred thousand stanzas (*The Mahābhārata* [*Southern Recension*] [Madras, 1931], vol. 2, Ādi Parvan—part II, xxi–xxii).

For V.S. Sukthankar's discussion of these views see *Ādiparvan*, pp. xcvii note, *Āranyakaparvan*, pp. xxix, xxx, xxxiii–xxxv. See also Raghu Vira, *Virātaparvan*, p. xxiv; Franklin Edgerton, *Sabhāparvan*, pp. xxx–xxxi; S.K. De, *Udyogaparvan*, pp. xlviii-xlix; P.L. Vaidya, *Karṇaparvan*, pp. xxxiii–xxxv.

[29] Franklin Edgerton was quite prepared to admit this. He wrote:

> It is . . . a question fundamentally of more or less, when we undertake to decide which "recension" a particular manuscript belongs to. And having once decided, we must be prepared for all sorts of qualifications of our answer. Even different parts of the same Ms may suggest different groupings. (*Sabhāparvan*, p. xxxiii).

[30] An example of error of this kind is noted in relation to 1.85.20 of the C.E. where the copyist of K1 has mistakenly made a transposition in the text by copying the reverse of the folio in place of the obverse and vice versa.

The copyist's duty, as he saw it, was to keep the tradition as completely intact as possible:

> If a reciter or commentator came across, in another manuscript, an additional passage, there was every chance of his copying it down somewhere, either in the margin of his own copy, or in a supplementary folio; for there would be, in his mind, always present the possibility that the passage in question was some part of the original that his own manuscript had unaccountably lost. How else, forsooth, could the passage get into the other manuscripts?[31]

Libraries containing multiple copies in manuscripts of the one title are, no doubt, a recent phenomenon in India.[32] More usually an individual or a family could only hope to own a single, complete manuscript of a work of the dimensions of the *Mahābhārata*. See, for example, the manuscripts which belonged to, and in some cases were written by, various members of the Daśaputra family of *brāhmaṇas*. D1 of *Śalyaparvan* belonged to Gaṇeśa Daśaputra (c. 1592 A.D.); D3 of *Karṇaparvan* belonged to Govinda Daśaputra (c. 1603 A.D.), D1 of *Bhīṣmaparvan* belonged to, and was written by, Gaṇeśa, the son of Viṭṭhala (c. 1640 A.D.), while Daśaputra's son, Sundarapanta, is said to have been the copyist of D2 of *Droṇaparvan* (*c.* 1684 A.D.). Even in the more extensive hereditary libraries of rulers and patrons of literature where it was possible for a large number of copyists to be employed over long periods of time, it is hard to imagine that there would have been any deeply felt need for more than replacement copies of the *Mahābhārata*.[33] So the opportunity for comparing manuscripts of the widest

---

[31] *Ādiparvan*, p. lv. The copyist was not the only one to feel this responsibility. Very frequently manuscripts were corrected and annotated by their owners and those who used them professionally. For examples of a later copyist making "corrections" to a number of manuscripts (even when these were written in different scripts), see D2–4, T2, C1–2 of *Udyogaparvan*. Marginal notes were added " presumably for expository discourses" in K3, *Āśramavāsikaparvan*, for example. In his article "A Sanskrit Deed of Sale concerning a Kaśmīrian Mahābhārata Manuscript" (*JRAS*, 1900, pp. 187–194), M.A. Stein drew attention to the work of a Kaśmirian "glossator", Takaḍe Bhaṭṭa Haraka, who "annotated and revised not only the archetypus of the Rājataraṅgiṇī, but also a considerable number of other manuscripts which Ratnakaṇṭha ("the scholarly scribe of the codex archetypus") had copied evidently for his own use" (p. 191). Bhaṭṭa Haraka was the writer of the Sanskrit deed of sale referred to in the title of M.A. Stein's article.

[32] There were, of course, cities in which many copies of the one title could have been obtained. Places like Vārāṇasī and Thanjavur feature often as the place where manuscripts were copied (e.g., D1 of *Sauptikaparvan*, D1 of *Strīparvan*, *T3 of Ādiparvan*). There must have been instances, too, like that of V1 of *Śāntiparvan*, where quite a number of manuscripts were used as exemplars in order for some special purpose to be satisfied.

[33] In the manuscripts used in the critical appartus of the C.E. there is no case of a patron requesting more than one copy, though this does not guarantee that such a practice was not usual. That a copy of the complete *Mahābhārata* took considerable time to produce is shown by the dates given in K2 and Dn2 of *Bhīṣmaparvan*. (The editor of that *parvan* calculated that

possible variation did not generally exist, as far as can be judged.[34]

A great many commentators and copyists of the *Mahābhārata*, perhaps even the majority, did work from more than one exemplar and they were able to select and substitute what they regard as the best readings, if not at the time of copying then later in the manuscript's existence.[35] This kind of "limited" comparison and editing of texts acted to restrain the growth of the manuscript tradition. Its place in the overall history of the text is a relatively small one and is easily outweighed by the profusion of growth that was the result of less selective comparisons.

The initial source of change was not in the written records of versions of the *Mahābhārata*. It was in the oral tradition and then as a result of the interaction between reciters, their learned versions of the tradition, and their many and varied audiences.[36] Only secondarily, and at a later date, was the *Mahābhārata* a textual tradition to which alterations could be made as a result of the comparison of manuscripts. The oral tradition, with its own capacities for growth, has always been the impulse for many changes to the textual tradition. When trying to characterize the earliest history of the textual tradition, V.S. Sukthankar rightly emphasized the formative influence of the oral tradition:

> Whenever and wherever the text was then written down—and it was probably written down independently in different epochs and under different circumstances—these transmissions by word of mouth must have contaminated the written text and introduced innumerable variations in it. The assumption of some such complicated derangement, beyond the normal vicissitudes of transmission, is necessary to account for the abnormal discrepancies and strange vagaries of the Mahābhārata manuscript tradition.

---

the six copyists took three months to complete the codex, No. 246 BORI Collection, and that in the case of the manuscript Dn2, the copyist was able to complete 112 stanzas per day of the *Āraṇyakaparvan*.) The cost of complete texts of the *Mahābhārata* must have been very considerable. See, for example, the evidence of M.A. Stein, p. 192ff. The existence of so many "composite" manuscripts probably indicates that there was a common practice of renewing parts of *parvans* (as well as whole *parvans*) by employing a copyist to replace the damaged or missing part. These "patched up" manuscripts would further indicate that the *Mahābhārata*, or even parts of it, was not usually held by the one owner in multiple copies.

[34] Compare above, p. 3.

[35] Nīlakaṇṭha, for example, compared manuscripts of the *Mahābhārata* collected from different parts of India, as well as the scholia of other authorities, in preparing his commentary. His stated intention was to make the text about which he wrote "a thesaurus of all excellences" (*Ādiparvan*, p. lxvff.), a motive that was not always conducive to the restraint mentioned below.

[36] "Le même rapsode variait sans doute d'une récitation à l'autre, soit defaillance de memoire, soit confusion entre passages ou formules analogures, soit goût d'innover, soit encore bien d'autres raisons", Sylvain Lévi wrote in reference to this tradition of the *Mahābhārata* (*Journal Asiatique*), vol. 215 (1929), 348).

> In other words, we are compelled to assume that even in its early phases the Mahābhārata textual tradition must have been not uniform and simple, but multiple and polygenous.[37]

It follows from this understanding of the textual tradition that any attempt to restore it to what it was at some period in the past would not be able to reduce the variety in that tradition to a single version, one text. If this were possible then it would have suggested that there had been a time in history when the *Mahābhārata* tradition had been static and not subject to the textual or oral dynamics suggested above. Yet it is certain that such a situation never existed in India at any time in the past. There was no agency, religious or political, which could have imposed this conformity or would have desired it.

The C.E. is an attempt at restoring the *Mahābhārata* on historical lines. It is claimed to be "*the oldest form of the text which it is possible to reach, on the basis of the manuscript material available*".[38] The editor, V.S. Sukthankar, did not claim that the C.E. was the "Ur-Mahābhārata" or "Vyāsa's Bhārata" and made it quite clear that he believed that it was "useless to think of reconstructing a fluid text in a literally original shape, on the basis of an archetype and a *stemma codicum*.".[39]

Even if this "*original* shape" could not be reconstructed by this approach, V.S. Sukthankar believed that the "oldest form of the text . . . on the basis of the manuscript material available" could. He grouped manuscripts into nine versions and made up a pedigree in which each version was shown to have descended from either a northern (N) or a southern (S) source via, in most cases, lost archetypes.[40]

This procedure, together with its results, can be criticized on a number of grounds. First, the manuscripts which V.S. Sukthankar grouped under the headings "Śāradā", "K," "Nepālī," etc., are not homogeneous, nor has it been established that the manuscripts chosen for the critical apparatus are

---

[37] *Ādiparvan*, p. lxxix.

[38] *Ādiparvan*, p. lxxxvi.

[39] Ibid. Madelaine Biardeau has argued that the C.E. of the *Mahābhārata* represents an attempt to employ western scientific method for purposes which are not really scientific but religious. See her "Some more considerations about textual criticism", *Purāṇa*, vol. X (1968), 115–123.

[40] *Ādiparvan*, p. xxx; *Āraṇyakaparvan*, p. xiii. See also *Virāṭaparvan*, p. xvi, *Udyogaparvan*, p. xxiv. In *Bhīṣmaparvan*, p. cxv, the Pedigree of Manuscripts shows each manuscript and gives its secondary affiliation. Franklin Edgerton, alone among editors of the C.E., assumed the existence of *three* independent recensions—Western (W), Eastern (E), Southern (S)—instead of N and S. "For this book", he wrote, "I do not regard 'N' as a historic reality. I do not believe that W and E are descended from a common secondary archetype" (*Sabhāparvan*, p. xlviii).

representative examples of their groups.[41] The lack of homogeneity is most manifest among the *Devanāgarī* (including K) and *Telugu* manuscripts, while it is less apparent in the *Malayālam* and *Bengali* groups. However all groups contain manuscripts which show complex affiliations and in no group is there any one manuscript which can be said to contain the "pure" type of that text. To some extent this heterogeneity is a deliberate result of editorial policy, where manuscripts were selected for the critical apparatus because they were thought to reveal the extremes of variation within the version.[42] But by adopting this criterion of selection without a complete survey of all extant manuscripts, it has been impossible to assert with complete certainty that the manuscripts chosen are fully representative, or for that matter, of the way in which they are representative.

Nor can the groups of manuscripts be properly claimed to derive from archetypes. An archetype is, after all, "the exemplar from which the first split originated"[43] and an assumption that is usually made in stemmatics is that "copies made since the primary split in the tradition each reproduce one examplar only, i.e. that no scribe has combined several exemplars (*contaminatio*)".[44] Without this assumption "the science of stemmatics in the strict sense breaks down".[45] There are few, if any, manuscripts or groups of manuscripts of the *Mahābhārata* of which this assumption can safely be made. That V.S. Sukthankar was himself aware of this criticism there can be no doubt. He wrote in the Foreword to Fascicule 1 that

> ... it is impossible to apply to the Mahābhārata the special canons of textual criticism which are derived from a study of classical (Greek and Latin) texts and which depend ultimately upon their being a more or less complete concatenation of copies and exemplars reaching finally back to a single authentic (written) archetype.[46]

---

[41] Policy differed between editors in the C.E. over the number of manuscripts they selected to represent a version and even on the classification of the manuscripts as belonging to one or other version, as has been shown in Appendix 1. In some unfortunate circumstances editors had to use a single extant manuscript to "represent" a version.

[42] *Ādiparvan*, p. vi.

[43] Paul Maas, *Textual Criticism* (Oxford: 1958), p. 2.

[44] Ibid., p. 3.

[45] Ibid., p. 48.

[46] *Mahābhārata*, *Ādiparvan*, Fasc. 1, p. ii. In "Epic Studies III. Dr. Ruben on the Critical Edition of the *Mahābhārata*", *ABORI*, vol. 11 (1930), 261, V.S. Sukthankar quoted with approval the paper delivered by Maurice Winternitz at the XVIIth International Congress of Orientalists (Oxford: 1928):

> The general principles followed in the critical editions of classical texts, Greek or Latin or Sanskrit, can be applied to a critical edition of the Mahābhārata only with great limitations and modifications. It is simply impossible to trace a genealogical tree of all the Mss of the Ādiparvan, and only in some cases are we

Having admitted the force of these criticisms V.S. Sukthankar pleaded that the C.E. of the *Mahābhārata* should be evaluated, not by the standards used for a classical text, but by a standard of its own. "The Mahābhārata problem is a problem *sui generis*", he often repeated,[47] and he appealed for "prolonged and considerable discussion and exchange of ideas and opinions" before "the principles of textual reconstruction could be finally considered as settled". This emphasis on the uniqueness of the *Mahābhārata* textual tradition and the inadequacy of traditional techniques of textual criticism to deal with the problem is of special relevance to the historian. He cannot, in the light of this warning, treat the *Mahābhārata* as a source whose textual tradition can be traced, with a high degree of probability, to an original text to which an author, date and locality might be assigned. Instead he has to be prepared to deal with a text of which there is not a single line which is free from variations, or even complete omission, in a larger or smaller number of manuscripts. This variation extends to all other units of the text in some degree or other: *adhyāyas*, sub-*parvans*, *parvans*.

The text of the *Mahābhārata* as it appears in the C.E. cannot be regarded as a version known in any part of India at any time in the past. To accept it as such would be to ignore what has been shown about the "regionalism" of every version of the *Mahābhārata* for which there is evidence. If this regional variation is eliminated (or is only conceded to a limited degree) so that only the parts of the text which are shared by all versions (or those versions regarded as "purer") remain, then the resulting text is a reconstruction that is not genuinely historical at all. It is, instead, an edition based on the "common denominators" (which are not necessarily all of the oldest common denominators) of all versions, but it cannot be shown to have been a stage in the historical development of any one of them.

Before historians make use of any edition of the *Mahābhārata* they must inquire into the critical apparatus on which it is based. They should be aware of the kinds of manuscripts used and whether these can be tentatively assigned to any particular branch of the manuscript tradition. They should not disregard features of the edition which appear to be characteristic of only one of the tradition's branches, dismissing them too

able to state how Mss are related to one another. On the whole we have to be satisfied with a classification of the Mss according to the script, and the provinces to which they belong. And we have more often to refer to classes of Mss than to individual Mss.

[47] See "Epic Studies I. Some Aspects of the Mahābhārata Canon", *JBBRAS*, n.s. vol. 4 (1928), 156; "Epic Studies III. Dr. Ruben on the Critical Edition of the Mahābhārata", *ABORI*, vol. 11 (1930), 262; *Ādiparvan*, p. lxxxvi.

readily as "later" interpolations. Even if a convincing case cannot be made out for accepting such features as being part of the earliest phases of the development of the *Mahābhārata*, it should be borne in mind that they may be part of a pattern of development peculiar to that branch but nonetheless of ancient origin.

Much more research needs to be done before the discussion of the manuscript tradition can be said to have been thoroughgoing. There is a need to investigate versions of the *Mahābhārata* in scripts other than those used to date. Where only a small number of manuscripts have been used in the C.E. to represent a version (e.g., Nepālī, Maithilī, Śāradā), there need to be further searches made of manuscripts even if these are found to be of a date later than the ones so far used. The depth and variety of the regional character of the *Mahābhārata* should be surveyed. The fact that such demands can now be made is not a criticism of the C.E.. It is an indication of the progress that its completion marks.

THE *MAHĀBHĀRATA*: STYLISTIC STUDY, COMPUTER ANALYSIS, AND CONCORDANCE

DANIEL H.H. INGALLS AND DANIEL H.H. INGALLS, JR.*

Preface

Much of the following material is taken from papers read before annual sessions of the American Oriental Society in 1974, 1976, and 1980. Section 4 is unchanged from the form in which Daniel Ingalls, Jr., read it in 1980 both before the AOS and before a panel of computer programmers at the Palo Alto Research Center of Xerox Corporation. Two reasons persuade me to consign this material to print now instead of waiting, as I first intended, until the research is complete. The first: we now have working models of the primary tools which I propose to use in dealing with the subject. Second, the conclusions which I hope to achieve lie, even with good luck, three or four years in the future. It may be well for others to know of these tools and of our aims so that if accident or bad luck should overtake us, some other scholar may some day without us duplicate the one and achieve the other.

1. *On the genesis of Sanskrit oral-epic style*

1.1. *Meter*

About ninety-five percent of the *Mahābhārata* is composed in *śloka* meter. The Indian method of describing the regular or *pathyā* variety of this meter is to require a specific quantitative pattern for the cadence of each eight-syllable line (*pāda*) and to prohibit certain combinations in the openings of the lines. The scheme may be represented diagrammatically as in Inset A.

A. Metrical scheme of the epic śloka*:*

line *a*:	x	x_1	x_1	x_1	u	–	–	ū
b:	x	x_2	x_2	x_2	u	–	u	ū
c:	x	x_1	x_1	x_1	u	–	–	ū
d:	x	x_2	x_2	x_2	u	–	u	ū

* Sections 1, 2, 3, and 5 are by Daniel H.H. Ingalls; section 4 is by Daniel H.H. Ingalls, Jr.

On the final syllable of each line line there was a pause, which prolonged the syllable even if it was short by nature. Actually, in the majority of instances it is truly long; but the statistics of this *syllaba anceps* (syllable of ambiguous length, represented in the inset by ū) will not concern me here.

In the inset, u represents a short syllable,—a long syllable, and x a syllable that may be either long or short so long as certain combinations of contiguous syllables are avoided. The x's that I have marked with subscript 1 may never form with each other a tribrach (u u u) or an anapest (u u –). The x's that I have marked with a subscript 2, in addition to these prohibitions, may never form an amphimacer (– u –). Actually one can find other combinations that are avoided in *Mahābhārata ślokas*, combinations that are not mentioned by Piṅgala and the other metricians, but I do not plan to discuss them here.

What I have said is enough to describe rougly the longs and shorts of the regular *śloka*. The metricians go on to describe *ślokas* that are irregular by their departing from the regular cadence of the *ac* (first and third) lines. These irregularities bear the following names:

B. Irregular cadences of ac:

bha-vipulā:	– u u ū
ra-vipulā:	– u – u
na-vipulā:	u u u ū
ta-vipulā:	– – u ū

Now at first sight this metrical scheme seems to be a loose-fitting garment. That is because we have not considered the matter of word break; and on that subject the Indian metricians are no help. Superficially it looks as though, while certain long words might fit into only a certain part of the line, short words at least could be fitted in pretty much anywhere.

It is obvious, of course, that if you have two warriors fighting and you want to call them *mahābalau*, "men of great strength", you will do well to put that word at the end of line *b* and *d*. In fact, the only other possible position would be at the beginning of *a* or *c*. It cannot fit in the cadence of *ac* and the amphimacer prohibition (the *ra-pratiṣedha*) rules it out of the opening of *bd*. In actual fact, as every Sanskritist is aware, the *Mahābhārata* regularly puts it at the end of *b* or *d*. If the poet wants to say the same thing in one of the other lines, he will use a synonym or equivalent of different metrical shape. In the cadence of *ac* he might use *mahātmānau*.

But let us consider some short words. Let us take the spondee (– –).

Spondaic words are fairly common in Sanskrit. More than half the two-syllabled feminines of the –ā declension are spondaic in the singular nominative, accusative, vocative, and in the dual and plural nominative and accusative. Several of these cases are spondaic in the –ī declension also. More than half the two-syllabled masculines and neuters of the commonest declension, in –a, are spondaic in the singular nominative and accusative when these forms are followed by a consonant or fall at the end of a line. Such nouns are always spondaic in the singular ablative and locative and in the dual and plural nominative and accusative. The *aniṭ* continuatives ("gerunds") in *ktvā* are all spondaic; so also several common third singular presents and third singulars of other tenses.

C. Common types of spondaic words:

kanyā	*devī*	*devaḥ* + X	*śrutvā*	*āste*
kanyām	*devīm*	*devam* + X	*viddhvā*	*brūte*
kanye	*devyau*	*devāt*	*uktvā*	*āsīt*
kanyāḥ	*devyaḥ* + X	*deve*		
		devau		
		devāḥ		
		devān		

Let us see where such words can be fitted into the *śloka*. We might begin by considering a half-*śloka* to contain fourteen dissyllabic slots, as indicated in Inset D.

D. The fourteen metrical slots for dissyllables:

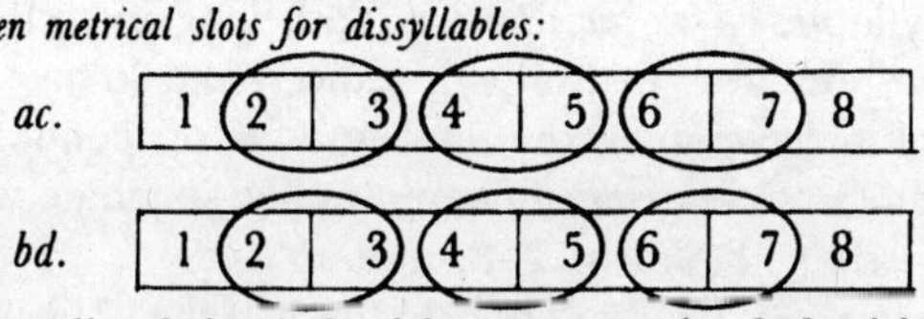

Here I have outlined slot 1–2 with a square, slot 2–3 with a circle, and so on. We can then take various runs of *śloka*s and see how many of these slots are filled by spondaic units and how many are filled by spondaic words. The number of words, of course, will be smaller, as one can see from Inset E, where I show a line from the *Bhagavadgītā*: *viṣīdantam idaṃ vākyam*.

E. Discrepancy of spondaic units and spondaic words:

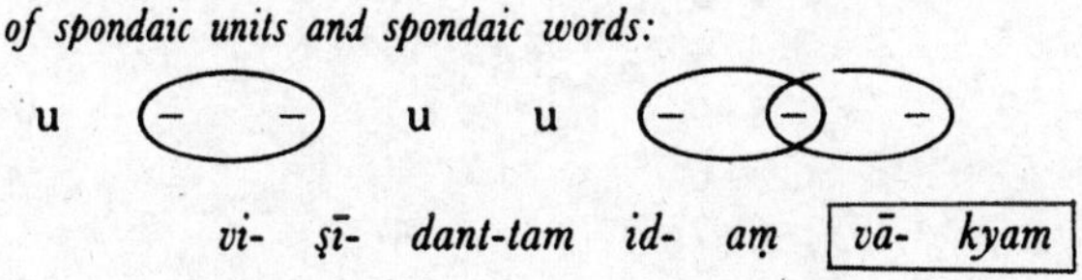

Here you have three spondaic units (enclosed by circles) but only one spondaic word (enclosed by a square).

Inset F gives statistics for a run of twenty-five *ślokas* from a battle scene in the *Mahābhārata* (7.13.19–43).

F. Numbers of spondaic units and spondaic words per slot:

	Slot	*Number of spondaic units*	*Number of spondaic words*
ac:	1–2	16	5
	2–3	12	2
	3–4	24	1
	4–5	3	0
	5–6	0	0
	6–7	43	0
	7–8	46	23
bd:	1–2	15	7
	2–3	18	2
	3–4	21	3
	4–5	0	0
	5–6	0	0
	6–7	0	0
	7–8	0	0
Total		198	43

The first two syllables of an *ac* line are both long in sixteen instances, syllables 2–3 are both long in twelve instances, and so on reading down column one. Column two gives the total number of spondaic words, slot by slot, that occur in the passage. There are five spondaic words that fill slot *ac* 1–2, two that fill slot *ac* 2–3, and so on.

Inset G gives statistics from another battle passage of twenty-five *ślokas* (6.44.1–25) where the incidence of compounds is higher and the total number of spondaic words therefore less.

G. Table similar to the preceding, for MBh. 6.44.1–25:

ac:	1–2	10	8
	2–3	20	3
	3–4	17	0
	4–5	1	0
	5–6	1	0
	6–7	50	1
	7–8	50	14

bd:	1–2	18	2
	2–3	16	0
	3–4	12	0
	Others	0	0
Total		195	28

In both tables you will immediately be struck by the discrepancies between columns one and two. Thus, in Inset F, slot *ac* 6–7 forms a spondaic unit in forty-three instances (in fact, in all the regular *śloka*s of the passage), but in no instance is this slot filled by a spondaic word. Slot *ac* 3–4 shows twenty-four spondaic units but only one spondaic word. On the other hand, in slot *ac* 7–8 there is harmony between the two columns. In both columns this slot shows the highest figure. Why?

Let us go back to our basic metrical scheme and fill in as many long syllables as the rules will permit.

H. Maximization of spondaic units:

ac: – – – – u – – –
bd: – – – – u – u –

I have not found a *śloka* where all four lines fit this pattern. The following, though, exhibits the pattern in both lines *b* and *c* (*MBh.* 7.13.41):

a. . . . .
b. *HaiḍimbĀlambuṣāv ubhau*
c. *cakrāte 'tyadbhutam yuddham*
d. . . . .

Haiḍimba and Alambuṣa were giants and perhaps the meter has been slowed up to produce the effect of these two massive creatures in slow-motion warfare. But turn your eyes back to the diagram of Inset H. It would seem at first that spondaic words might begin on *ac* 1, 2, 3, 6, 7 and *bd* 1, 2, and 3. But that is because we have not yet considered the word breaks.

1.2. *Word breaks*

The problem of word breaks is the most complicated problem in Sanskrit metrics. In this summary I shall overlook word breaks within a compound.

In the *Mahābhārata śloka* a line (*pāda*) normally has from one to three word breaks. Where there are two breaks, the two may be of equal strength and complementary, as is usually the case with the *ac* breaks after syllables 3 and 6; or one break may be subordinate to the other, as the rare break after the first syllable, which is always subordinate. There are lines over which one may argue as to whether a given break is subordinate or not. Accordingly, the safest statistics are those which count all breaks, even breaks before enclitics. I think, though, that the major breaks have a stronger influence than the others on the polarization and freezing of word-types.

Inset I gives the breaks in the passage that was measured metrically in Inset F above.

I. Word breaks in MBh. *7.13.19–43, listed by syllabic position, in order of frequency:*

Position	*Total number of breaks*	*Major breaks*
*bd*4	23	23
*ac*3	23	17
*ac*6	23	15
*ac*4	21	19
*bd*2	15	9
*bd*3	12	11
*bd*5	11	9
*ac*2	11	3
all others	31	14
Total	170	120

Thus there occur in the *śloka*s of this passage twenty-three word breaks, all of them major, after syllable *bd*4; twenty-three breaks, seventeen of them major, after syllable *ac*3; and so on.

Inset J marks the common positions of word breaks on our metrical chart of the maximally spondaic line (see Inset H above):

J. – – , – • –. u – • – –
– – , – , –. u , – u –

A period is here used to designate the four commonest positions of word break, a comma to designate four less common positions. Word breaks in other positions are rare.

It now becomes clear why spondaic words do not occur in slot *ac* 6–7. For such a word to occur, there, one would have to have word breaks after *ac*5 and *ac*7. The break after *ac*5 is rare (only 7 instances in the exemplar passage), while a break after *ac*7 is almost non-existent; it occurs once in the passage in question, before the enclitic *ca*. It will also be clear why spondaic words seldom begin on syllable 2: the break after syllable 1 is too rare. The most natural positions for spondaic word turns out to be *ac* 1–2, *bd* 1–2, and especially *ac* 7–8, for wherever one has the very common break after *ac*6, a spondaic word must occur in *ac* 7–8.

1.3. *Polarization and Freezing*

Other passages in non-battle scenes will furnish somewhat different statistics. The Nala story shows a certain fondness for spondaic words in *ac* 3–4. It begins with one, as most Sanskritists know. But even the Nala story shows only five such spondees to thirty-five in the polarized positions in the first twenty-five *ślokas*.

Word-types, it turns out may be more than polarized; they may be completely frozen. A tribrach, for example, can fit into only one slot in a regular *śloka* verse, namely *bd* 3–4–5, as in

> *droṇaḥ pañcāla-rājānaṃ viddhvā daśabhir āśugaiḥ,*
>
> Droṇa, having pierced the Pañcāla king with ten swift arrows,

Had the poet been unable to save that slot, he would have had to use the *na-vipulā* or, more likely, he would have made Droṇa shoot five or seven arrows instead of ten.

What I have described so far is no more than what many Sanskritists might come close to guessing by instinct. But in order to advance in a theory it is necessary to begin measuring instead of relying on instinct. Incidentally, we can often use the new Pratīka index to the *Mahābhārata* to do our measuring for us. On the subject of spondees, for example, you can there find that the line "*tac chrutvā vacanaṃ tasya*", with the *aniṭ* continuative in slot *ac* 2–3, occurs only five times in the critical text of the *Mahābhārata* whereas the line "*tasya tad vacanaṃ śrutvā*", with the continuative polarized to the end, occurs forty-five times.

Now the case of the continuatives will show that not only do individual words belong to metrical types, in a highly inflected language like Sanskrit, whole morphological categories belong to specific metrical types.

I shall give a sample of the polarization and freezing of morphological types. I take the sample from a listing of all forms of the perfect tense in a run of 500 *ślokas* of battle description in Book 6. Battle descriptions are always rich in perfect forms, but I realize that the run should be longer to arrive at fully reliable results.

One result that I believe has not been noticed before emerges with great clarity. The epic poets disliked metrical ambiguity. Theoretically, for example, a form like *jaghnatus* might appear as a dactyl when followed by a vowel, or as an amphimacer when followed by a consonant or by line boundary. In actual fact this type of perfect appears almost always as an amphimacer. Similarly, forms of the type *jaghnus* appear regularly as spondees rather than as trochees. Exceptions in the run that I tested come to less than five percent.

I furnish below a few laws of usage and position of these perfects.

A. contract perfects, third person plural active always carry verbal prefix or *na*.

A1. Where this combination forms a bacchius (u – –) it always comes first in the *pāda*:

vineduḥ param āturāḥ
vinedur bhinnamarmāṇo
vineduḥ puruṣarṣabhāḥ
nipetur vimalā śaktyo
nipetuś ca gatāsavaḥ
samīyus te didṛkṣayā
na śekus calitum kecit

A2. Where the combination forms a molossus (– – –) it comes either first or last:

sampetur bhujagopamāḥ
vidarśayantaḥ sampetuḥ

B. Strong perfects if amphibrachic (u – u) normally come first:

babhūva rathanirghoṣas
babhūva ghoṣaḥ
nanāda sumahānādam
uvāca rājā durdharṣam
uvāca vācā durdharṣam
jagāma pāṇḍuputrāṇām

B1. Exception one: amphibrachic perfects may begin on syllable 2 if a monosyllabic pronoun object precedes:

tam uvāca mahāprājño
tam uvāca tataḥ

B2. Exception 2: amphibrachic perfects may begin on syllable 5 if they are followed by the particles *ha* or *vai*:

pṛṣṭhato 'nujagāma ha
āhave 'bhijagāma vai

C. Periphrastic perfects are invariably polarized: 85% come first, 15% come last.

D. Perfects third person plural middle which contain three short syllables must begin on the third syllable, or an irregular cadence must be used:

punar jahṛṣire mudā
śirāṃsy ādadire vīrāḥ
evaṃ yuyudhire tatra

1.4. *Formulas*

The basic criterion for the orality of poetry in the works of Milman Parry, Albert Lord, and their followers is the formula. And yet I have postponed mention of formulas to this point because I wanted first to make clear the phenomena of polarization and freezing. The Sanskrit oral epic, I think, cannot be meaningfully analysed without an understanding of those phenomena. Without them the formulas would be entirely different from what they are.

A formula is a framework for expressing any general incident or description that is likely to be needed by the oral performer. One or more words of the formula will remain the same in many occurrences and will always occupy the same metrical slot. In the remainder of the span covered by the formula the syntax will usually remain the same even if the words furnishing the syntax exhibit variation. One or more words of the formula must be varied whenever the reciter needs to express a particular rather than a general fact, and the formula is so built that it can easily be adapted to these particular cases without slowing up the performer in his recitation. For the oral performer, as is abundantly clear from living examples of the profession, improvises as he recites; he does not memorize a text. What he memorizes are the incidents of his tale, the names and epithets of his characters, and the formulas needed for his narration and description. No two recitations of an epic tale by an oral performer are identical. Each performance is a new creation.

A *Mahābhārata* formula for the onset of battle is:

tataḥ pravavṛte yuddhaṃ tumulaṃ lomaharṣaṇam

Then began a battle, noisy and hair-raising.

Notice the frozen verb-type, with three short syllables beginning in slot *ac*3, the one slot where this succession can begin in a regular line, and the polarized spondee *yuddhaṃ*. The reciter may alter the opening adverb to the pronoun *tayoḥ* or *teṣām* "of them", dual or plural as the particular case may demand. Line *b* can be varied by synonyms, as *ghorarūpam bhayāvaham*, or it can give needed particular information: "of the Kurus", "of the Kurus with the sons of Pāṇḍu", or of some individual warrior.

Thus:

tataḥ pravavṛte yuddhaṃ tumulaṃ lomaharṣaṇam
teṣām pravavṛte yuddhaṃ tumulaṃ lomaharṣaṇam
tataḥ pravavṛte yuddhaṃ ghorarūpam bhayāvaham
tataḥ pravavṛte yuddhaṃ kauravāṇām bhayāvaham
tataḥ pravavṛte yuddhaṃ tava teṣāṃ ca bhārata
tataḥ pravavṛte yuddham tatra tatra mahātmanām
tataḥ samabhavad yuddhaṃ tumulaṃ lomaharṣaṇam
tayoḥ samabhavad yuddhaṃ tumulaṃ lomaharṣaṇam
teṣām samabhavad yuddhaṃ tumulaṃ lomaharṣaṇam
tayoḥ samabhavad yuddhaṃ vṛtra-vāsavayor iva

The short verb *āsīt* may be substituted in slot *ac* 3–4. An adjective must then be added to fill up the line:

tatrāsīt sumahad yuddhaṃ tava teṣām ca saṃkulam
tadāsīt sumahad yuddhaṃ kurūṇāṃ pāṇḍavaiḥ saha
tadāsīt tumulaṃ yuddhaṃ bhagadattasya, māriṣa

I find one instance where the verb is pulled pack to the beginning of the line, thus emphasizing that the battle at long last *began*. As three short syllables cannot occur at the beginning of the line, the perfect *pravavṛte* is changed to the imperfect *prāvartata*:

prāvartata tato yuddhaṃ tumulaṃ lomaharṣaṇam

Most formulas in the *Mahābhārata* occur in at least two forms, one to fit *a* and *c* lines with their cadence of u – – – and an alternate to fit the *b* and *d* lines with their cadence of u – u –. I might point out that the development of alternate formulas to fit different exigencies of form is characteristic of formulaic structure in most languages. That is why our old poem of *Beowulf* has so many expressions for king and warrior and ship and sea. A different expression is needed for each alliterative series, for old Germanic poetry was based on a pattern of alliteration. The old English reciters placed the need of form even above the need of sense. King Hrothgar varies from being king of the North-Danes to being king of the South-Danes or West-Danes as the alliteration of the lines shifts from n to s to w. The Sanskrit reciters on their part were not above changing a number, whether of arrows shot or of warriors slain in order to fit a cadence.

I furnish below a collection of instances, as complete as I have been able to make it, of the *Mahābhārata* formulas for licking the lips or flicking the tongue. The first situation occurs when a warrior is taking aim at his enemy. Often he has just been wounded. Usually he is filled with fury, frowning. The *ac* formulas are often followed by a simile. The *ac* formula 1 and the *bd* formula 1 are built around the word *sṛkkiṇī*, "the two corners of the lips". The first four instances may be translated:

> The hero, licking the corners of his lips like a wolf
> in the flock.
> the hero, licking and licking the corners of his lips,
> his eyes red with anger.
> licking around the corners of his lips, O king,
> breathing hard and with eyes red with anger.
> the hero, licking the corners of his lips like a
> proud tiger.

ac formula 1: *sṛkkiṇī* + *vi-/sam-/le-lihan* + nom./voc.

sṛkkiṇī vilihan vīraḥ / paśumadhye vṛko yathā (6.60.27)
sṛkkiṇī lelihan vīraḥ / krodhasaṃraktalocanaḥ (7.109.7)
sṛkkiṇī saṃlihan rājan / krodharaktekṣaṇaḥ śvasan (9.54.19)
sṛkkiṇī vilihan vīraḥ / śardūla iva darpitaḥ (6.92.21)
sṛkkiṇī lelihānasya / bāṣpam utsṛjato muhuḥ (5.50.29)

ac formula 2: *lelih* (participle) + metaphor / *sainya-*

lelihānaṃ yathā sarpaṃ / garjantaṃ vṛṣabhaṃ yathā (8.57.27)
lelihānāṃ iva vibho / nāgakanyāṃ mahāviṣām (9.9.38)
lelihyamānaṃ sainyeṣu / pravṛddham iva pāvakam (6.98.28)
lelihyamānaṃ sainyaṃ me / haviṣmantam ivānalam (6.46.5)

Conflation of *ac* formulas 1 and 2:

lelihan sṛkkiṇī vīro / mṛgarāḍ iva kānane (6.98.28),

bd formula 1: *sṛkkiṇī* + *parile- / parisam-* + *lihan /* */ sam-/le-* + *lihan* + *muhuḥ*

sa ca krodhasamāviṣṭaḥ / sṛkkiṇī parilelihan (6.80.12)
saṃdaśya daśanair oṣṭhaṃ / sṛkkiṇī parisaṃlihan (6.87.29)
sa gāḍhaviddho vyathitaḥ / sṛkkiṇī parisaṃlihan (6.90.5)
uvāca bhīmaṃ samare / sṛkkiṇī parilelihan (6.104.42)
so'tividdho maheśvāsaḥ / sṛkkiṇī saṃlihan muhuḥ (6.107.11)
so 'tividdho maheśvāsaḥ / sṛkkiṇī parisaṃlihan (6.57.22)
so 'tividdho maheśvāsaḥ / sṛkkiṇī parisaṃlihan (7.137.38)
sa cchinnadhanvā saṃkruddhaḥ / sṛkkiṇī parisaṃlihan (6.114.26)
vāyuputraḥ prahṛṣṭo 'bhūt / sṛkkiṇī parilelihan (7.109.18)
triśikhāṃ bhrūkuṭīṃ kṛtvā / sṛkkiṇī parilelihan (9.13.38)
tataḥ kruddho raṇe pārthaḥ / sṛkkiṇī parisaṃlihan (7.78.26)
etac chrutvā tadvacanaṃ / sṛkkiṇī parisaṃlihan (7.121.30)
smayamāno mahātejāḥ / sṛkkiṇī saṃlihan muhuḥ (12.8.2)

bd formula 2: *lelihāna-* + noun/adverb

bhujagā iva saṃkruddhā / lelihānā vṛsolbanāḥ (6.114.58)
jvalantīm agnivat saṃkhye / lelihānāṃ samantataḥ (5.188.5)
trāsayaṃś cāyam āyāti / lelihāno mahīruhān (1.221.4)
eṣa hi jvalamāno 'gnir / lelihāno mahīruhān (1.224.16)
saptajihvo 'nalaḥ kṣāmo / lelihānopasarpati (1.223.5; irregular)

The paired formulas 1 refer specifically to a warrior's licking his lips and are characteristic of Books 6 and 7. One would of course not expect to find them outside a context of battle, but it is strange and I think significant that they are missing from the battle scenes of Book 8. Formulas 2 refer rather to the flickering motion of the tongue of a snake or of fire, a different context, which may occur outside the battle scenes. The *Mahābhārata* shows instances other than these listed above of intensive (*yaṅvat*) forms of *lih*, which seem to me to be not formulaic, e.g.:

lelihyamānas tṛṣitaḥ / pucchasphoṭanatatparaḥ (3.170.39)
lelihyase grasamānaḥ samantāt (*Triṣṭubh* 6.33.30 = *Gītā* 11.30)

Many formulas permit of poetic expansion or variation. It is here that one may observe the genesis of *kāvya* style. To give a single example, the formula of attack at its simplest is no more than two names and a verb:

duḥśāsanas tu nakulaṃ pratyudyāya mahāratham

Duḥśāsana advanced against Nakula of the great chariot.

This may be expanded by adding an adjective or epithet to either warrior's name, by noting his weapon in the instrumental case, or by adding a simile.

yudhiṣṭhiras tu saṃkruddhaḥ saubalaṃ niśitaiḥ śaraiḥ
vyadārayata saṃgrāme maghavān iva dānavam

Yudhiṣṭhira in fury pierced Saubala with sharp arrows in the battle, as Indra did the demon.

Or, as the performer works himself up to a fine rhetoric:

rākṣasaṃ krūrakarmāṇaṃ krūrakarmā ghaṭotkacaḥ
alambuṣam pratyudiyāt valaṃ śakra ihāhave

Against the cruel demon Alambuṣa, Ghaṭotkaca the cruel advanced in battle as Indra against Vala.

Here we have inversion, the alliterative repetition of *krūra*, irregular cadence, and simile. The narrative has finally become poetically interesting.

Even in its simplest, unadorned form an oral formula may be beautiful. John Finlay in his inspired teaching of Homer to Harvard undergraduates used to say that the formulas of the *Iliad* were like pebbles on the beach. They have been worn down by the thousands of performers who have used them to a perfect smoothness, to the most beautiful possible shape. To show that formula criticism is not without its esthetic rewards I shall give one example from the *Mahābhārata*. It is a formula that makes a contrast between joy and tears and it has almost frozen into a cliché. It occurs first when Yudhiṣṭhira makes the most terrible of his wagers. He stakes his wife Draupadī on the dice:

> Karṇa rejoiced beyond measure together with Duḥśāsana and his brothers.
> But from the eyes of other courtiers fell tears.

In the Sanskrit see how slowly and sadly the last line ends:

> *jaharṣa karṇo 'tibhṛṣam saha duḥśāsanādibhiḥ*
> *itareṣāṃ tu sabhyānāṃ netrebhyaḥ prāpataj jalam* (2.58.42)

When Draupadī in exile remembers the dishonor shown to Yudhiṣṭhira by the Dhārtaraṣṭras, the same formula recurs, with the change of just one word but with the formula split between two lines.

> *itareṣāṃ tu sarveṣāṃ kurūṇāṃ kurunandana*
> *duḥkhenābhiparītānāṃ netrebhyaḥ prāpataj jalam* (3.28.9)

The formula occurs a third time, again with just one word changed, at another tragic moment of the epic. The youthful Abhimanyu, who had learned how to break through the enemy line but had not yet learned the technique of retreat, is cornered by six older warriors and killed after being forced to leap from his chariot:

> *āsīt paramako harṣas tāvakānāṃ viśāṃ pate*
> *itareṣāṃ tu vīrāṇāṃ netrebhyaḥ prāpataj jalam* (7.48.19)

> Great was the joy of your warriors, O lord of the clans,
> but from the eyes of other men fell tears.

The compiling of metrical and formulaic statistics would be a boring task if it were not for the flashes of eternal beauty that burst from time to time from the material one is studying.

1.5. *Clichés*

I find it useful to distinguish clichés from formulas although both are members of the same genus and arise out of metrical building blocks in the same way. A cliché is a formula that is frozen; it exhibits no variations. An example is the half *śloka* that occurs 108 times (I can hear the numerologists panting!) in the *Mahābhārata*:

athāpy udāharantīmaṃ itihāsaṃ purātanam

One may ask how this differs from such a half *śloka* as

tataḥ pravavṛte yuddhaṃ tumulaṃ lomaharṣaṇam

which occurs in frozen form eight times. The answer is that the components of the former half *śloka* are *never* varied; those of the latter sometimes are. It is useful to distinguish the two types because the cliché is not peculiar to oral poetry whereas the formula is. Clichés continue to be used throughout written Sanskrit, just as quotations from the Bible or from Shakespeare continue to be used throughout written English.

2. *Computer Analysis of Test Runs*

2.1. *The Need of Computer Aid*

Even as I was forming the theories of polarization and freezing described in the preceding section I was aware of the paucity of my data. The longest run in which I had counted all perfect tense forms was 500 *śloka*s. I had guessed at laws of the polarization of spondees from even shorter runs. Furthermore, all these runs had been selected from a single type of epic poetry, the battle scenes of *Mahābhārata* Books 6 and 7. How could one obtain a broader base without spending a lifetime to obtain it? Naturally I thought of turning to a computer. Barend A.A. van Nooten in California had made use of a computer to analyse the prose sections of the *Ādiparva*.[1] Then Mary Caroll Smith had used a computer to produce a metrical printout of the *Mahābhārata*'s *triṣṭubh* verses.[2] So when a half-year sabbatical fell to my lot in the spring of 1975 I determined to use my free time experimenting with computer-aided analysis.

As I had had no training in computer science, I enlisted the aid of my son, Daniel H.H. Ingalls, Jr., a computer programmer and inventor, who was then working in the Palo Alto Research Center of Xerox Corporation. Without his help my analysis of the *Mahābhārata* would have come to a halt long ago. Our cooperation has taken place in two

---

[1] "Mahabharata Text Analysis with the Aid of a Digital Computer", University of California, Berkeley, Ph.D. dissertation, 1963.

[2] "The Core of India's Great Epic", Harvard Ph.D. dissertation, 1972.

stages. The first stage, which I shall describe here under Section 2 of the present paper, consisted in my typing out portions of the *Mahābhārata* so that they could be fed into a computer memory and of my son's writing programs by which the computer could elicit data of meter and word break together with a concordance which would designate the metrical position of every word it contained. The second stage, which will be described in Sections 3 and 4, consisted of my son's inventing a recognition program which enables a computer to read directly the Devanāgarī text, thus dispensing with the laborious typing out of the text in transliteration. In the second stage my contribution has been limited to the editing of the computer-printed text.

2.2 *The Trial Runs from Typed Tape*

In the spring of 1975 I rented a Telex machine by which transcriptions of *Mahābhārata* text could be typed onto eight-hole Ascii tape. I did this typing in my home in Virginia, sending the completed tapes by mail weekly to my son three thousand miles away in California, where he fed them into a Xerox computer. In order to fit the *Mahābhārata* text to the limitations of the Telex machine, I had to devise a transliteration that made use of no signs other than those of the English alphabet, the one-digit numerals, the period and the plus sign. Inset K exhibits *Mahābhārata* 7.36.5–7 in this transcription.

K. *dron2o draun2ih2 kr2pah2 karn2ah2*
kr2tavarmaa ca saubalah2
br2hadbalo madra.raajo
bhuurir bhuurishravaah2 shalah2

pauravo vr2s2asenash ca
visr2jantah2 shitaan3 sharaan
subhadram2 shara.vars2en2a
mahataa samavaakirat

sam2mohayitvaa tam atha
duryodhanam amocayan
aasyaad graasam iva+aaks2iptam2
mamr2s2e na+arjuna.aatmajah2

It will be seen that I used the period to indicate word boundary in compounds and that I resolved all cases of *ekarūpa-sandhi* between words, using the plus sign to indicate word-seam. As the machine had no diacritical marks in its type, I used numerals in their place. For example, retroflex n was represented by n2, palatal n by n3, gutteral n by n4. Long vowels were indicated by doubling the vowel.

My son wrote a program by which the computer translated my transcription into a second transcription which used a one-to-one representation, that is to say, a single type to represent a single phoneme. This second transcription will look odd to a Sanskritist.

L. *droNo drONiH kRpaH karNaH*
kRtavarmA ca sObalaH
bRhadbalo madra.rAjo
BUrir BUriSravAH SalaH

pOravo vRzasenaS ca
visRjantaH SitAw SarAn
suBadraM Sara.varzeNa
mahatA samavAkirat

saMmohayitvA tam aTa
duryoDanam amocayan
AsyAd grAsam iva +AkziptaM
mamRze na +arjuna.AtmajaH

I next furnished my son with definitions of syllable, line (*pāda*), *śloka*, metrical length, and word, on the basis of which he wrote further programs: a program for giving the metrical length of each syllable and a program for stating the position of all word breaks. He also programmed a translation of our second transcription into the standard transcription used by Sanskritists so that the printout would be easier to use. The result appeared as below.

M.5. *droṇo drauṇiḥ kṛpaḥ karṇaḥ* ----u--- 2 4 6
kṛtavarmā ca saubalaḥ uu--u-u- 4 5
bṛhadbalo madra.rājo u-u--u-- 4 (6)
bhūrir bhūriśravāḥ salaḥ ----u-u- 2 6

6. *pauravo vṛṣasenaś ca* -u-uu--- 3 7
visṛjantaḥ śitāñ śarān uu--u-u- 4 6
subhadraṃ śara.varṣeṇa u--uu--- 3 (5)
mahatā samavākirat uu-uu-u- 3

7. *saṃmohayitvā tam atha* --u--uu- 5 6
duryodhanam amocayan --uuu-u- 4
āsyād grāsam iva +ākṣiptaṃ ---uu--- 2 4
mamṛṣe na +arjuna.ātmajaḥ uu--u-u- 3 (6)

The text here is printed in standard transcription on the left-hand side of the page; the metrical form is given line by line on the right-hand side. The final syllable of each line is designated as long no matter whether it is long or short by nature. Word breaks are indicated by the number of the syllable after which the break occurs. Word break within compound is indicated by a numeral enclosed in brackets.

In this manner we typed and computerized the following material:

Battle scenes	*MBh.* 6.104–112		
	7.35–50	total number of lines:	4,016
Narrative passages	*MBh.* 1.71–80		
	3.50–64	(Nala)	
	5.112–121		4,002
Religious passages	*MBh.* 6.23–40	(*Gītā*)	
	12.203–210		
	12.298–300		
	12.302–304		3,998
Control Runs			
Karna: presumably early	*MBh.* 5.142–144		278
Karna: presumably late	*MBh.* 5.138–141		616
Buddhacarita	All *śloka*s in the poem.		1,184
		Total	14,094

The rationale of the selection is this. I wanted equal numbers of *śloka*s from battle, narrative, and didactic passages to see if there were significant differences of meter and word break among these three types of *Mahābhārata* poetry. Hence the three major runs. Of what I have called the control runs the purpose of the Buddhacarita *śloka*s will be obvious. They are clearly non-oral poetry and should, therefore, show a contrast with such sections of the *Mahābhārata* as are oral. A fault here is that the Buddhacarita run is too short; there are only 296 *śloka*s in the extant portion of that poem. The two Karṇa passages suffer from the same fault, although the results they furnished are interesting. As readers of the *Mahābhārata* will remember, we have in *Mahābhārata* 5.138–144 two conversations with Karṇa that seem to belong to different versions of the epic. In 138–141 Kṛṣṇa attempts to persuade Karṇa to join the Pāṇḍavas. In 142–144 Karṇa's mother, Draupadī, attempts the same purpose. In both conversations Karṇa refuses. Decades ago, when I first read these conversations, I had written in my notebook of the scene with Draupadī:

> This is grand. How much more manly Karṇa is than Hamlet.
> He tells his mother straight out what her crime has been intead of hinting.
> And despite it he is not only polite to her, but even kind. And she blesses him as they part.

On the other hand, I had written of 5.139:

> In terms of the epic narrative and the epic character of Karṇa this passage is ridiculous. Karṇa is supposed not to know of his divine birth (cf. 3.285 and 4.143–144), yet here he knows far more than Kṛṣṇa tells him. He knows of his own death (unknown to him in Book 8) and of events even after that. The picture of Karṇa delighting in listening to Dharmaśāstras is especially out of character and the connection of brahmin reciters with the Mahābhārata is surely later than the oral epic. Karṇa has here become what Bali is in the brahmin-Vaiṣṇava tradition, a wonderfully generous semi-demon *bhakta* of Kṛṣṇa. All these facts are fairly obvious. But I should like to prove linguistically that 5.138–141 are later than 5.142–144.

It was in pursuit of this wish that I included these two brief runs.

2.3 *Metrical Statistics*

Drawing on the computer's memory of the text and meter, my son elicited metrical statistics, of which I give a sample below. The sample furnishes statistics for the b-run, the selections from the battle scenes.

N. METERSTATS 16 -Nov-75 12:08:31

Statistics for b run:

1st 4	a	%	b	%
uuuu	0	0.0	1	0.04
uuu–	1	0.04	0	0.0
uu–u	74	3.68	90	4.48
uu––	179	8.91	191	9.51
u–uu	119	5.92	108	5.37
u–u–	196	9.76	1	0.04
u––u	120	5.97	157	7.81
u–––	159	7.91	184	9.16
–uuu	0	0.0	0	0.0
–uu–	1	0.04	3	0.14
–u–u	185	9.21	261	12.99
–u––	316	15.73	397	19.77
––uu	157	7.81	200	9.96
––u–	188	9.36	0	0.0
–––u	140	6.97	185	9.21
––––	173	8.61	230	11.45

2nd 4	a	%	b	%
uuuu	0	0.0	0	0.0
uuu–	78	3.88	0	0.0

uu–u	0	0.0	0	0.0
uu––	1	0.04	0	0.0
u–uu	0	0.0	0	0.0
u–u–	3	0.14	2006	99.90
u––u	0	0.0	0	0.0
u–––	1775	88.39	0	0.0
–uuu	0	0.0	0	0.0
–uu–	74	3.68	0	0.0
–u–u	0	0.0	0	0.0
–u––	18	0.89	0	0.0
––uu	0	0.0	0	0.0
––u–	0	0.0	2	0.09
–––u	0	0.0	0	0.0
––––	59	2.93	0	0.0

A few words will explain how these statistics are to be read. The designation "1st 4" means "the first four syllables of all the lines in the run". Column *a* gives the number of occurrences of each possible metrical pattern in the first four syllables of the odd *pāda*s (the *ac* lines). The next column to the right gives the percentage which these occurrences bear to the total in each case. Column *b* gives the statistics for the even *pāda*s (the *bd* lines). The lower half of the table gives the statistics for the last four syllables of the lines. For example, if you run down the right hand column you will come to the percentage figure 99.90, that is, practically 100%. This is the double iambic close of the even *pāda*s. For purposes of these tables the computer has regarded the eighth syllable as always long. Accordingly, the patterns with short eighths produce nulls. The question of the final syllable will be handled in a separate study.

Similar statistics were compiled for the story run, the religious run, the two short Karṇa passages, and the Buddhacarita. I shall point out a few items of interest in these statistics.

The double spondee opening is rare in the battle run: 8.61% of *ac* lines, 11.45% of *bd* lines. It becomes more frequent in the story run (11.64% and 12.44%) and distinctly more frequent in the religious run (16.22% and 17.28%) and Buddhacarita run (14.35% and 14.18%). The Karṇa run hypothesized are early agrees fairly well with the story run (12.94% and 10.79%). The Karṇa run hypothesized as late shows an increase (15.03% and 16.99%).

The double trochee opening exhibits an opposite tendency. It is commonest in the battle run: 9.21% of *ac* lines; 12.99% of *bd* lines. In this run it is more frequent than the double spondee. In the story run the double trochee decreases to 7.53% and 10.59%; in the religious run to 7.91% and 9.96%, in the Buddhacarita to 6.92% and 7.09%. In the

Buddhacarita the double trochee is thus less than half as common as the double spondee. The Karṇa passage hypothesized as early shows the highest percentage of double trochees of any run (10.79% and 13.66%). The Karṇa passage hypothesized as late falls between the religious run and the buddhacarita in its percentages (6.53% and 9.57%).

The opening – – u –, which can occur by rule only in an *ac* line (see Section 1.1 above) shows no significant variation of incidence in the main runs but shows a marked decrease in the Buddhacarita (2.19%).

It was the opinion of E.W. Hopkins (*The Great Epic of India* [1901], p. 233) that "there is no "epic usage" in respect to the proportion of *vipulās* to *pathyās*". This may well be true if we take the *vipulās* as a group. But for the runs here tested, at least, the *na-vipulā* (*ac* cadence u u u –) is rarest in the battle run and commonest in the story run and Buddhacarita. The *bha-vipulā* (*ac* cadence – u u –) is rarest in the Buddhacarita and (except for the Karṇa passage hypothesized as early) is commonest in the battle run.

The runs here covered are of less extent than the material metrically analyzed by Hopkins by hand many years ago. They are based on a better text than was available to Hopkins and they present a clearer contrast between battle, story, and religious runs, but they do not add greatly to his conclusions. To do so it will be necessary not only to have data for the whole of the *Mahābhārata* but to contrast specific sections which differ also by other criteria. The statistics of our story run, I now think, would have differed considerably if I had omitted, or substituted something else in place of, the last half of the Nala story. The religious run might have yielded different results if I had distinguished the *Gītā* from the passages in Book 12.

2.4. *Word Break Statistics*

Statistics on the position of word breaks in the lines of our trial runs were compiled in the form given below. Only full word breaks are counted, not breaks within compound. A drawback of these breakstat charts is that they do not distinguish *ac* lines from *bd* lines. On the other hand, the data which they do give are exhibited very conveniently.

O. Break patterns from b run (4016 lines total):

	–	–	–	–	5	5	5	5
	–	–	6	6	–	–	6	6
	–	7	–	7	–	7	–	7
––––	210	21	143	2	251	9	23	0
–––4	559	28	227	1	111	1	12	0

--3-	363	47	339	2	138	4	12	0
--34	117	11	47	0	5	0	2	0
-2--	125	12	181	1	173	2	16	2
-2-4	235	8	80	1	31	4	3	0
-23-	30	7	80	1	21	2	2	0
-234	5	0	5	0	1	0	0	0
1---	8	1	14	0	32	1	3	0
1--4	27	3	22	0	0	0	0	0
1-3-	37	7	51	2	16	2	1	0
1-34	3	0	2	0	1	0	0	0
12--	7	0	6	0	5	0	3	0
12-4	18	0	13	0	0	0	0	0
123-	7	0	7	0	2	0	1	0
1234	1	0	0	0	0	0	0	0

Break totals:

1	303
2	1098
3	1381
4	1584
5	892
6	1307
7	182

The three upper lines refer to syllables 5, 6, and 7 of a line. Thus the left-hand column of these upper lines represents *pāda*s with no break in the second half. The column to the right represents lines where there is only one break in the second half, namely after the seventh syllable. And so on to the extreme right, which represents those freakish lines where there is a word break after every syllable of the second half. Now by looking at the lower portion of the diagram one can correlate the cadences with the openings. At the bottom of the diagram are given the total number of word breaks that occur after each syllable of the line in this battle run. Similar statistics were compiled for the other runs. I give below the comparative figures for the three major runs and the Buddhacarita. The Buddhacarita figures are simulated figures (hence placed within parentheses), being the actual figures multiplied by a factor of 3.38 so as to give results from this run of 1184 lines comparable to those of the 4000 line runs.

P	b	s	r	bc
No. break:	210	208	256	(325)
break after 1:	303	445	451	(416)

after 2:	1098	1392	1369	(1190)
3:	1381	1573	1471	(1470)
4:	1584	1409	1338	(1322)
5:	892	1023	1077	(1011)
6:	1307	1325	1222	(1315)
7:	182	368	317	(341)

There are notable variations in these figures, but I doubt that much significance can be placed on them without combining them with other factors. One may note that in the battle run only 303 out of 4.016 lines show a break after the first syllable and only 1,098 show a break after the second. The corresponding figures for the story and religious runs are 50% higher for the break after first syllable and 30% higher for the break after second. The Buddhacarita run agrees with the s and r runs in frequency of break after first syllable but not in frequency of break after second. The figure most likely to prove significant, I think, is the figure for break after 4. This is commonest in the battle run. If we take the more special case of lines where the sole break comes after 4, the contrast is still stronger: b 559, s 332, r 299, bc (308). These are the evenly broken lines, which I think may prove to be archaic. But the matter is far from proved. The figures for the two Karṇa runs show no significant differences in the position of word breaks so far as I can perceive.

2.5. *Metrical Index*

Three indices were prepared from the computerized material: a metrical index, a concordance, and an index of final words. In the metrical index each instance of each word of the runs was listed and identified by book, *adhyāya*, *śloka*, line, and syllable. These words were then arranged according to metrical type, beginning with words consisting of a single short syllable (e.g., *ca*, *tu*, *hi*) and ending with the various metrical patterns of the longest words. This index formed the primary tool for examining the phenomena of polarization. My hypothesis of the polarization of spondees is clearly borne out. In the indexed lines of the *Mahābhārata* the word *teṣām*, for example, occurs forty-two times. In 82% of the cases it falls in initial or final position. The word *bāṇais* ("with arrows") and its *sandhi* equivalents *bāṇair*, *bāṇaiś*, *bāṇaiḥ* occurs forty-eight times almost exclusively in the battle run. Of the occurrences 92% are polarized, usually at the end. The word *nityam* occurs forty-one times; in 95% of the cases it is polarized. Incidently, I might point out that the word *nityam* is always spondaic, that is, is always followed by a consonant or is in final position. *Niytam* as a trochee does not exist, at least in these runs.

The *aniṭ* continuatives (e.g., *dṛṣṭvā*, *śrutvā*, *hatvā*) prove to be polarized as I had suspected from a much shorter sample (see 1.1 and 1.3 above). The *Mahābhārata* runs furnish 399 examples. A comparison of the ratio of this polarization is highly interesting. In the battle run 83% of *aniṭ* continuatives are polarized, in the story run 68%, in the religious run 62%. The facts, however, are more complicated than I had realized. The very common continuative *uktvā* forms an exception to its morphological category. Out of thirty-five occurrences only ten are polarized; its commonest position is in syllables 3–4. The reason for this anomoly, it seems to me, is that *uktvā* is commonly used in the phrases *evam uktvā* (thirteen times in these runs), *tathety uktvā* (eight times), *ity uktva* (five times), which were treated by the oral poet as single words. In these instances he did not "feel" a continuative as beginning in mid-verse; he felt a four-syllable or three-syllable word as beginning in slot one.

In studying the continuatives of these runs I was surprised to observe the extreme rarity of the *seṭ* formations (e.g. *viditvā*, *arcitvā*, *cintatyitvā*). They occur in only twenty-six instances against 399 instances of the *aniṭ* forms. Again, where many of the *aniṭ* forms figure in common epic formulas (e.g., *viddhvā pancabhir / navabhir / daśabhir āśugaiḥ*) or clichés (e.g., *evam uktvā*), *none* of the *seṭ* forms so far as I can see is so used. One may also note that in several instances the Pāṇinian *seṭ* form is replaced in the *Mahābhārata* by a form in *lyap*, e.g., *gṛhya* for *grhītvā*, *pīḍya* for *pīḍayitvā*. The conclusion seems almost inescapable that the oral epic style developed at a time before *seṭ ktvā* came into use and remained chary of this use down to the time when the *Mahābhārata* was recorded.

I suggested the writing of a program to furnish polarization ratios for each run separately, for it proved a tedious business to compile ratios by hand as I have done for the continuatives. But at just this time my son had made his first breakthrough in the invention of a recognition program (see Section 4), and it seemed more valuable to have him spend his time on that. Ultimately, when we have a complete concordance of the *Mahābhārata*, we will certainly make these comparisons, not only between battle, narrative, and didactic passages but between the individual books and episodes of the poem.

2.6. *The Concordance*

Our concordance lists every occurrence of every word of the runs, identifying each word by book, *adhyāya*, *śloka*, and line. It does not give a figure for the metrical slot because that information appears clearly in the printout: the full line is printed out for the occurrence of each word. The two sample pages which I give below have been subjected to considerable editorial positioning in order to bring inflected forms of the same stem together. Thus, without positioning, the items containing *putram* would precede those containing *putras* and items containing *putre* would precede those containing *putreṇa*. The labor of writing a program to effect such positioning would probably be greater than that of positioning by hand, a task which is facilitated by the use of an electronic beam. One need only point to a line on a television screen and guide it to a new position. We are still undecided whether to print our complete concordance (see Section 3) in this fashion or to leave it in strictly alphabetical order. If we do position by hand, the result in any case will be a compromise. To arrange all instances of all verbal forms under their root would require an immense amount of labor. They will surely be listed in the concordance alphabetically. What I envisage is an appendix volume listing all verbal forms (not all instances) under the respective roots. This would cut the labor by more than half and would not delay the publication of the concordance.

In any event the individual word forms will be arranged in metrical sequence as they are on the sample pages, the occurrences beginning in slot one coming first, those beginning in slot two next, and so on throughout the line. Such an arrangement can easily be programmed and requires no manual positioning.

2.7. *Sample of Concordance of Test Runs*

putra-

putras/ -aś/aḥ/o/a (+ vocalic): see also *ṛsi.putras, kuntī.putras, krātha.putras, droṇa.putras, mādrī.putras, rāja.putras, vaiśya.putras.*

putras tava durādarṣe (6.104.12d)
putras tava viśām pate (6.106.36b, 6.106.44b, 6.107.13b)
putras tu tava taṃ dṛṣṭvā (6.110.20a)
putro duḥśāsanas tava (7.38.26b)
putro bala.ravi.prabhaḥ (5.116.20b)
putro yas tvā + anuvartata (1.80.21a)
putro rājā jayadrathaḥ (7.41.6b)
putraḥ śara.sata.arditaḥ (7.44.30d)
sa putro guṇa.sampanno (1.80.22a)
sa putraḥ putravad yaś ca (1.80.18b)
kasya putras ca śaṃsa me (1.76.12d)
tava putro nyavārayat (6.106.77d)
śaṅkhaḥ putro virāṭasya (5.139.27c)
na sa putraḥ śataṃ mataḥ (1.80.17d)
pāṇḍoḥ putro 'si dharmataḥ (5.138.9b, 5.139.2b, 5.139.4b)

tathā jajvāla putras te (6.112.94c)
pīḍitas ca + eva putras te (6.106.43a)
vijitas tava putro 'pi (6.112.97a)
guru.putrasya putro vai (1.72.9a)
jāto dāna.patiḥ putras (5.117.21a)
yo me dadyād vayaḥ putras (1.78.39c)
pūro tvam me priyo putras (1.79.24a)
vayo dāsyati te putro (1.78.41a)
dvidhā ciccheda te putraḥ (6.112.4c)

putram: see also *kuntī.putram, kula.putram, krātha.putram, guru.putram, droṇa.putram, dharma.putram, mādrī.putram, mādhavī.putram, rāja.putram, sātvatī.putram.*
putram ekam pratardanam (5.115.15d)
putraṃ jyeṣṭhaṃ variṣṭhaṃ ca (1.79.1c)
putraṃ te navabhiḥ śaraiḥ (5.106.37d)
putraṃ dvija gataṃ margam (5.116.12c)
putraṃ śalyasya māninam (7.44.14b)
putraṃ sākṣād bṛhaspateḥ (1.71.17b)
priyaṃ putram apaśyatīm (7.49.8d)
droṇaḥ putram abhāṣata (6.108.3d)
tava putram ayodhayat (6.112.1b)
tava putram ariṃ.dama (7.38.27b)
pūruṃ putram uvāca ha (1.80.8d)
pūruṃ putraṃ kanīyasam (1.80.12b)
yadi putraṃ na paśyāmi (7.50.27.c, 7.50.32e)
jyeṣṭhaṃ putram bṛhaspateḥ (1.71.10d)
tava putraṃ viśāṃ pate (6.112.28b)
uvāca putram āślisya (5.144.23c)
vimukhīkṛtya putraṃ te (6.108.53c)
tava saṃdhārayan putram (6.105.23e)
śaineyo 'pi guroḥ putram (6.112.10a)
māgadhasya punaḥ putram (7.47.1)
kuntyāḥ prathama.jam putram (5.139.21)
bhrātāraṃ pitaraṃ putram (3.62.11e)

putreṇa: see also *drupada.putreṇa, droṇa.putreṇa pāñcāla.putreṇa, saha.putrena*
putreṇa tava dhīmatā (6.106.34b)
tava putreṇa dhīmatā (6.107.33b)

putrāya: see also *drupada.putrāya*

putrasya: see also *guru.putrasya*, *pāṇḍu.putrasya*
śalya.putrasya
putrasya tava paśyataḥ (6.106.5d)
putrasya tava vāhinī (6.107.55b)
putrasya hita-kṛt tava (7.39.22d)
tava putrasya dhanvinaḥ (6.112.90b, 6.112.107b)
tava putrasya pauruṣam (6.112.89b)
tava putrasya māriṣa (7.38.10b)
tava putrasya vāhinīm (6.104.27d)
mama putrasya yat sainyam (7.38.1c)

putre: see also *sūta.putre*
mama putre 'kṣipan śarān (7.50.50d)
priye putre nipātite (7.45.18b)
bhrātuḥ putre mahā.rathe (7.49.3d)

2.8. *Index of Last Words*

It was thought useful to compile an index of the last words of the lines. Where the last word is a compound, it is alphabetized under its final component, which is followed by a comma, which is followed in turn by the prior component. This information can of course be elicited from the concordance, but it proves useful to have the finals brought together because it is in this position that freezing and formulaic structure are most prominent. The sample page will show the frequency of *raṇe* and *mahārathaḥ* in final position; *mahārathaḥ* actually occurs in no other position in the runs.

yoṣitām, gopa- bc0.4.14.d
yauvanam s1.79.9.b
s1.79.16.b
s1.79.26.b
yauvanam, sva- s1.80.10.b
yauvanā, prāpta- s1.77.8.b
yauvanām, prāpta s3.51.7.b
yauvanām, saṃprāpta- s1.71.23.b
yauvane s1.79.2.d
s1.79.24.f
yauvane, 'prāpta- b7.48.32.b
yauvanaiḥ s1.79.6.b
raṃsyate s3.55.13.b
raṃhasaḥ, upama- b7.42.2.d
raṃhobhir, anila- b7.36.21.a
raktam r12.207.16.a
rakṣan bc0.6.3.c
rakṣasām, yakṣa- r6.32.23.b
rakṣiṇī, cāritra- ke5.142.22.d
rakṣitam b7.37.2.d
rakṣitā s3.61.41.d
raṅgam s3.54.8.a
raṅgam, mahā- s.3.54.3.c
rajaḥ r12.207.12.d
r12.207.22.b
rajasam, śānta- r6.28.27.c
rajasas, vi- r12.210.28.c
rajomayam r12.207.14.b
rajjum s3.53.4.c
raṇaḥ b7.38.3.d
raṇam b7.39.8.d
raṇāt b7.43.6.d

raṇāt, mahā-	k15.141.45b
raṇe	b6.104.57.c
	b6.104.58.c
	b6.105.12.d
	b6.107.46.f
	b6.109.39.b
	b6.110.12.b
	b6.110.22.d
	b6.110.35.b
	b6.111.11.b
	b6.111.14.d
	b6.111.34.d
	b6.112.47.d
	b6.112.61.b
	b7.37.3.b
	b7.38.28.d
	b7.39.7.b
	b7.39.21.b
	b7.39.25.b
	b7.40.16.b
	b7.41.3.f
	b7.46.17.d
	b7.46.24.b
	b7.47.22.b
	b7.49.5.b
	b7.50.66.d
	k15.139.33.d
raṇe, mahā-	b6.107.41.b
	b6.109.41.b
	b6.112.43.b
	b6.112.57.d
	b6.112.108.d
	k15.141.33.b
rataḥ	k15.139.7.d
ratam	b7.50.36.b
	s1.75.3.d
ratāḥ	r6.27.25.d
	r6.34.4.d
	r12.299.12.b
ratir, a-	r12.205.23.c
rathaḥ, mahā-	b6.104.6.b
	b6.104.12.d
	b6.104.20.b
	b6.106.4.b
	b6.106.24.b
	b6.107.51.b
	b6.108.2.d
	b6.108.4.b
	b6.108.19.b
	b6.109.14.b
	b6.109.17.d
	b6.109.34.b
	b6.110.22.b
	b6.110.25.b
	b6.110.29.b
	b6.112.4.d
	b6.112.14.b
	b6.112.15.b
	b6.112.46.b
	b6.112.64.d
	b6.112.75.b
	b6.112.77.b
	b6.112.86.b
	b6.112.95.b
	s3.61.41.b
	r6.23.4.d
	r6.23.17.b
	k15.138.23.b
	k15.139.24.b
	k15.139.26.d
	k15.139.27.b
	k15.141.36.b
ratham	b7.42.3.b
	b7.43.7.b
	b7.50.3.b
	k15.138.19.c

2.9. *Sytlistic differences between different Books*

To me the most interesting evidence revealed by our trial run of the *Mahābhārata* is that which concerns the stylistic differences between different books. I shall here describe some differences between the battle passages of Book 6 and 7. The evidence here is strong from our concordance and I have strengthened it further, where I could, from the Pratīka index and from manual collection.

The battle scenes of Books 6 and 7 deal with the same epic characters and the same type of incident. On the whole our two runs from these books show a strong stylistic similarity in meter, polarization, and frequency of formulas and clichés. But there are individual differences between these books that are impossible to explain if they were taken down from the same oral performer or if they were composed by the same author. The battle chapters of Book 6 make heavy use of certain frozen words and formulas that occur very rarely or not at all in Book 7. The opposite also occurs; that is, certain characteristics of Book 7 do not occur in Book 6. I proceed to give some examples.

The word *samare* frozen at the end of an *a* or *c* line occurs twenty-two times in our 2,088 computerized lines of Book 6. It never occurs in the same number of computerized lines of Book 7. I have since found it twice in Book 7 outside the section that was computerized, but it occurs very rarely in that book whereas it is common throughout Book 6. What is more, the Book 6 occurrences are almost all formulaic, as shown in the inset below. The formulas are particularly striking as they form irregular metrical lines, the so-called *na-vipulā* and *bha-vipulā* varieties where a tribrach or dactyl is substituted for the normal bacchius (u – –) of syllables 5–7 of an *ac* line.

Q. *samare* in final position in *pāda*: 22 times in 1,000 AC *pādas* of Book 6.
0 times in 1,000 *padas* of Book 7.
Of the 22 occurrences in Book 6, all the *na-vipulās* are formulaic.

Na-vipulā, formula No. 1. periphrastic perfect + *samare*
preṣayāmāsa samare (6.106.41)
tāḍayāmāsa samare (6.107.7)
tāḍayāmāsa samare (6.109.24)
chādayāmāsa samare (6.110.1)

Na-vipulā, formula No. 2. proper name ± *ca/tu/'pi* + *samare*
sudakṣiṇas tu samare (6.107.19)
prāgjyotiṣam ca samare (6.110.2)
jayatsenas tu samare (6.110.31)
bhīmasenas tu samare (6.111.19)
aśvatthāmā tu samare (6.112.11)

ceḍirājo tu samare (6.112.23)
dhṛṣṭaketuṃ tu samare (6.112.26)
madreśvaraś ca samare (6.112.39)
śikhaṇḍinaṃ ca samare (6.112.77)
duḥśāsanena samare (6.112.92)

Bha-vipulās are mostly formulaic

te vidyamānāḥ samare (6.104.21)
uvāca bhīmaṃ samare (6.104.42)
agacchatas tān samare (6.106.23)
sā vidyamānā samare (6.107.55)
apīḍayetām samare (6.110.8)
pārthaḥ samantāt samare (6.110.24)
na kaścid enaṃ samare (6.112.77)

The rare aorist *ānarchat* occurs fourteen times in our computerized run of Book 6 and once in the story run from Book 3. Eleven of the occurrences are in a formula for arrow shooting. Neither the verb form nor the formula appears in our computerized run from Book 7, and so far as I can see the formula is not used in that book.

R. Arrow attack: *ānarchat*

ac formula No. 1: *śaraiḥ*, etc. + numeral (instr.) + *ānarchat*

bāhlikas tu tato rājan dhṛṣṭaketum amarṣaṇam /
śarair bahubhir ānarchat siṃhanādam athānadat (6.43.36)
śrutakarmā tataḥ kruddhaḥ kāmbojānām mahāratham /
śarair bahubhir ānarchat dārayann iva sarvaśaḥ (6.43.65)
tataḥ śalyo mahārāja svasrīyau rathināṃ varau /
śarair bahubhir ānarchat kṛtapratikṛtaiṣiṇau (6.58.28)
sātyakis tu tatas tūrṇaṃ bhīṣmam āsādya saṃyuge /
śarair bahubhir ānarchat pitaraṃ te janeśvara (6.68.25)
aparājito mahārājan parājiṣṇur mahārathaḥ /
śarair bahubhir ānarchad bhīmasenaṃ mahābalam (6.84.18)
draupadeyā raṇe kruddhā duryodharam avārayan /
ekaikas tribhir ānarchat putraṃ tava viśāṃ pate (6.74.26)
durmarṣaṇaṃ ca rājendra avāntyau ca mahārathau /
ekaikau tribhir ānarchat (6.110.3–4)

viddhvā navabhir ānarchat (6.45.10)
pāñchalyaṃ tribhir ānarchat (6.45.31)

ac formula No. 2 nom./ adv + acc. + *ānarchat*
kirīṭī bhīṣmam ānarchat (6.113.49)

bahudhā bhīṣmam ānarchat (6.113.44)
rāvaṇo rāmam ānarchat (3.269.11)

bd formula ?

gāṅgeyas tu raṇe pārtham ānarchan navabhih śaraiḥ (6.48.41)

Irregular:

tribhis tribhiḥ śarair ghorair bhīmam ānarchur añjasā (6.50.99)
ānarchatuḥ śarair ghorair takṣamāṇau parasparam (6.43.12)

The cliché *apāyāj javanair aśvaiḥ*, "he fled with his swift horses", occurs six times, in Book 6, never in Book 7, once in Book 8. On the other hand, the cliché *anyonyam abhijaghnatuh*, "the two struck at one another", occurs nine times in Book 7, never in Book 6, once in Book 8. Or take the words for elephant. In 4,000 *śloka*s of Books 6 and 7 (2,000 of them indexed by hand) words for elephant occur 316 times. Eleven different words for elephant are used, usually in about the same ratio of frequency in each book. But the word *dantin* ("tusker") is an exception. It occurs ten times in passages scattered through Book 6 and never in the indexed verses of Book 7.

These examples, I trust, will make it seem probable that the battle episodes of Books 6 and 7 were recorded from two different reciters of epic poetry, probably contemporary with one another, both trained in basically the same tradition, but each having his individual style, his own favorite formulas and clichés, just as the modern Serbian reciters each have theirs. If we could go on to show that not only these two sections of the battle narrative go back to separate oral presentations but that the majority of the *Mahābhārata* derives from similar individual recitations, we should have arrived at what seems to me an important historical discovery. We would have arrived in fact at the conclusion that the compilation of the *Mahābhārata* was truly the work of a Vyāsa, an "arranger" or "editor" as that word means. If we could show further that some sections of the *Mahābhārata* are not oral at all, we would be well on the road to describing the growth of the poem into the form in which we now have it.

Having expressed so far-reaching a hope, it becomes me to qualify it with some degree of modesty. There are enough examples of scholars who have ridden a pet theory of the *Mahābhārata* into Cloud Cuckoo Land to serve as warning. Several of the traits which I have mentioned may prove not to be chronologically significant. The double spondee opening, for instance, fits naturally with the serious, reflective context of the *Gītā*, whereas a quicker, lighter metric is demanded by the very context of battle narrative. The most that our technique can hope to distinguish is between oral and non-oral. Surely there existed an oral religious poetry as well as an oral battle poetry. But there are traits of oral poetry that are present in all oral contexts and absent in all literary contexts. To discover these traits and to analyze the *Mahābhārata* in the light of that discovery seems to me a necessary preliminary not only to the historical study of the poem but to its esthetic appreciation.

3. *A Computer Program for Compiling a Concordance*

The programming of a computer to compile a concordance of the *Mahābhārata* is entirely the work of my son. I can claim no credit for it unless it be the good karma of some former life that has born fruit in his help to me in this. Much the most difficult problem—and its solution is also the most valuable part of our project for the future—was the problem of recognition. After typing in transliteration and proofreading 14,000 lines on the Telex machine, I realized that boredom would kill me before I could type out the whole work. Then my son suggested that if a computer could be taught to recognize the *akṣaras*, the work of producing a computer-stored text could be done with no typing at all. He will describe in Section 4 in general terms—the specific software is under patent control by Xerox Corporation—the technique he has invented. As even the general description may be unintelligible to Sanskritists, I shall describe it here in layman's terms. You program the computer to find the first *akṣara* of text on the page, to divide a rectangle enclosing it into approximately 100 squares, then on the basis of white and black in the squares to assign a value to the *akṣara*. We can now reduce errors of recognition to an average of one *akṣara* in twelve *ślokas*. Further refinement would give diminishing gains, for there will always be a residue of error due to broken type or smeared ink. This residue must be edited out by hand and the occasional errors of recognition, as between *p* and retroflex *s* can be edited out at the same time.

In the first stage of the project, then, the machine will memorize the Critical Text of the *Mahābhārata* and will display whatever section of the text that is called for on a video screen in the standard transliteration of the AOS–RAS. It would be possible of course to have it display the text in Devanāgarī and to store its memory in Devanāgarī as well. We have chosen not to do so because it is easier to show word breaks and *sandhi* resolution in transliteration and because a greater number of legible lines can be printed on a single page in transcription. The total concordance will contain over a million lines. In transliteration we hope to get this onto 8,000 pages. In Devanāgarī it would take about 11,000.

The second operation of the project will be to produce a corrected and broken text. The process will be clearer if I explain just what this operation does to the text. It does three things:

1. It corrects all cases of misrecognition.

2. It shows all word breaks. Take the simplest case: *tadeva*. This is printed together in Nāgarī. By pointing an electronic beam at the *e* of *eva* on the screen, we move it one space to the right. The result appears as *tad eva*. Take the case of *tasyeva*. Our electronic beam is connected to a control device called a mouse. By pressing a button on the mouse as we point the beam at the *e* of *tasyeva*, the whole complex is dissolved into *tasya* + *iva*. When we see *kanyeva* on the screen, we press a button on the left side of the mouse. This lengthens the left-hand component so that the result appears as *kanyā* + *iva*. If we see *sarvasyeśvara*, we press the right hand button and so lengthen the right-hand component, giving *sarvasya* + *īśvara*. If the coalesed vowels are both long, press both buttons. Fortunately, no case of vowel or diphthong permits of more than four possible resolutions.

3. Our broken text will show all word breaks in compounds. By the same device that I have described we can resolve the text of *devāsuramahāyuddham* into *deva . asura . mahā . yuddham* using dots instead of periods to show the boundaries of components.

The second-stage operation, after you get used to performing it, goes fairly quickly; I would say normally at about one third the speed at which you would simply read the Sanskrit text. But one must allow extra time for problems, places where the Critical Text is corrupt, as it often is in Book 12, or those rare places where one might actually break a set of syllables in two ways. Allowing for this, I think a single, trained Sanskritist can form a corrected, broken text of the *Mahābhārata* in a little over a year's time.

In the third stage of the project we shall tell the computer to bring out every word in the *Mahābhārata* in an alphabetical list. Under each word will be a cross-reference to every compound in which the word occurs as a non-initial component. There will then follow a printout of every line (*pāda*) in which the word occurs. Identical lines can be abbreviated by giving one printout followed by numerical references. The arrangement of printouts will be by position in the line. Instances where the word in question begins a line will come first, instances where it ends a line last. This will facilitate metrical analysis. Within each positional set, order will be by the alphabetic position of the initial of the next following word in the line. Whether we position the entries manually as suggested in Section 2.6 above is still undecided. If any readers of this article have strong feelings on the subject I would appreciate hearing from them.

4. *Optical Character Recognition of Devanāgarī Text*

4.1. *Hardware Organization*

An optical scanner is connected to a computer in such a way that light and dark areas on a printed page can be transferred to the memory of the computer as a pattern of 0's and 1's. For our application, we use a modified TC200 telecopier to perform the scanning. This scanner provides a resolution of 240 dots per inch. Thus each dot is roughly twice the thickness of a human hair. The scanner is connected to an ALTO minicomputer which provides memory, processing capability, and the ability to display graphical objects (including text) on a TV screen.

4.2. *Particulars of the Text*

Each text to be scanned has its own particular page layout conventions, and these must be taken into consideration prior to the recognition process. Such details include page headings, marginal annotations, footnotes, multiple column layout, chapter breaks, and so forth. In addition there are details which relate to the font set used for setting the type. For instance, most Devanāgarī text makes heavy use of ligatures, combinations of several letters in a single type slug. One has the choice of attempting to separate the components of such compound images or to augment the alphabet to include such polyliteral forms. The present system uses the latter augmentation approach.

4.3. *Locating the Characters*

One primitive operation is used extensively to locate and recognize the characters. It simply returns the number of black dots in any given rectangle of the image. Location of characters proceeds in successive refinement by first locating the horizontal lines of text, then locating the words within a line, and finally the characters within each word.

To find the lines, we first apply whatever rules apply to the layout of text on the page, and then scan down the page counting the number of black dots in each horizontal slice through the image. This results in a profile with large numbers corresponding to the location of each line of text and zeros between the lines. The plot at the left of Figure 1 shows the values of the profile corresponding to the text shown. Once a line has been isolated, we scan a vertical slice rectangle horizontally along the line, resulting in a profile with large numbers at the words, and zeroes between. In this way the individual word segments may be identified.

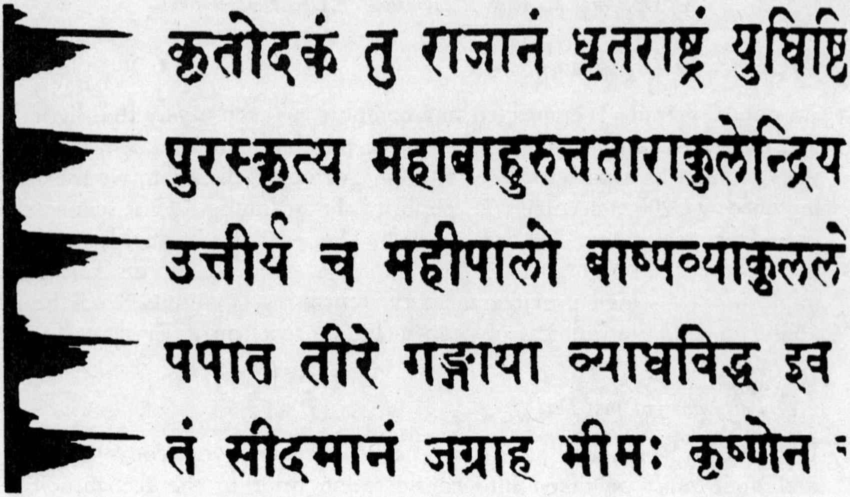

Fig. 1. Showing horizontal profiles used to isolate single lines of the text.

Each segment of Devanāgarī text is printed with consonants descending from a horizontal bar, and vowels are usually indicated either above that bar or below the consonants. Within a word, therefore, another slicing process is used to locate the bar as the horizontal slice of greatest blackness. Finally, the areas above and below the bar can be sliced to locate the consonant and vowel characters themselves. Figure 2 shows the profiles and inferred character locations for the first segment of the text.

Fig. 2. Within a segment, profiles serve to isolate individual characters.

4.4. *Recognizing the Characters*

Recognition of a character depends on having some representation for what that character "should" look like. The technique we use is to store two examples of every character, called the *skin* and the *bones*. The skin has black in *any* place that the character *could* possibly be black. The bones has black only in the places where *every* example of the character *should* have black.

To "learn" a given font with this representation is very simple—one simply identifies several examples of each of the characters by hand. These examples are then superimposed by the computer to obtain skin and bones images of the characters. This process is similar to superimposing several pieces of paper with the examples on them and holding them up to the light to see where the characters overlap. In the computer, the process is done using logical AND and OR functions on the black dots. Figure 4 illustrates the merging process at work on the character *ta*.

To "recognize" an unknown character, it is compared against all the characters learned from the font (actually many can be immediately ruled out by simple checks on size). The comparison consists of counting all the dots which are black in the unknown but not in the skin, and all the dots which are not black in the unknown but are in the bones. A high count indicates a poor match; the lowest count is considered the correct

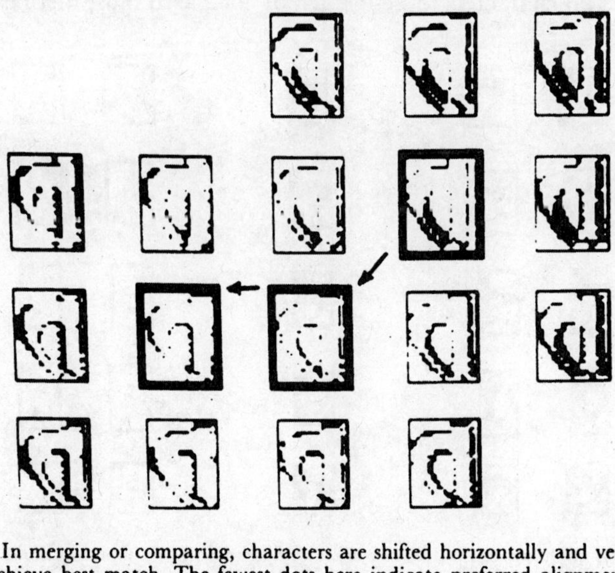

Fig. 3. In merging or comparing, characters are shifted horizontally and vertically to achieve best match. The fewest dots here indicate preferred alignment.

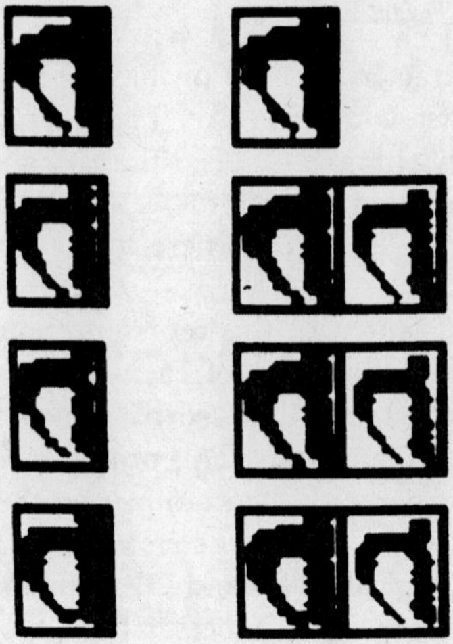

Fig. 4. Each new example (left column) of a known character is merged with the *skin* and *bones* (right columns) during the learning process.

identification. By establishing a threshold, an indication of failure can be given when no score reaches the threshold. Figure 5 illustrates the recognition process at work on an unknown example of *ta*.

Some additional care must be taken, in both learning and recognition, that any two characters to be merged or compared must first be aligned

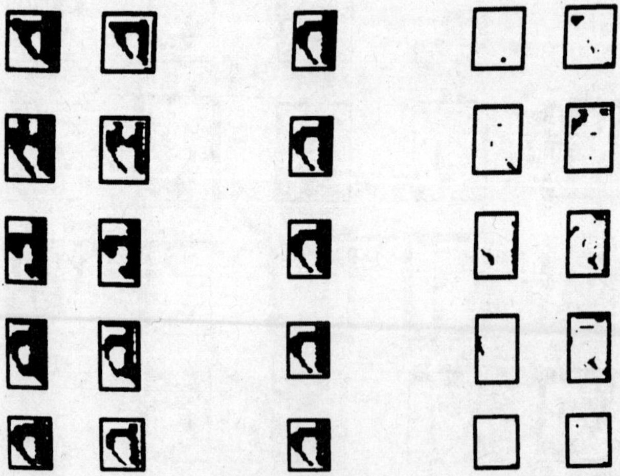

Fig. 5. An unknown character (center) is compared with the skin and bones (left) for similar known characters. The fewest error dots (right) select the preferred match.

as well as possible. The technique we use for alignment is to slide the two around, one step at a time, until they differ in the fewest number of dots (see Fig. 3). This is done simply in the computer by counting the number of dots resulting from an exclusive OR function on the dots of the two characters.

4.5. *Transliteration*

After the characters have been identified, some further work is still required to produce a proper transcription. For one thing, printed Devanāgarī includes many *ligatures*, or compound glyphs, which represent several characters. Then the vowel and consonant areas must be merged in the proper sequence for the syllables being constructed. Use must be made here of the relative location of the glyphs in each area. There are also rules for combining the vowels, as some sounds are represented by several glyphs in combination, Figure 6 shows the transliteration process applied to our sample segment of text.

4.6. *Performance*

The current implementation is a proof of concept written in a very simple manner. It has an accuracy of roughly 99.5%. I feel that it can do

Fig. 6. After individual characters have been recognized, they are merged into the corresponding linear text.

considerably better, but most Devanāgarī type is poorly set, and the figure given is probably realistic. The recognition process runs very slowly, but it could be rewritten to achieve practical speeds on the order of a page per minute.

5. *Present State of the Concordance Project*

In 1980 my son and I applied for a grant to the National Endowment for the Humanities to finance our *Mahābhārata* concordance. The grant was refused. On my inquiring why, I was informed in June 1981 that while the Foreign Literatures Panel had been enthusiastic, the Computer Panel had raised several objections. Among them, they believed on the basis of previous work undertaken with an OCR scanner that the degree of error would be far higher than we stated. They estimated 25 to 40 percent. Furthermore, they wanted the hardware and software being used to be commonly available. Here we found ourselves in a bureaucratic-commercial bind. The modified scanner we were using was not commercially available. Xerox agreed to our publishing the software eventually but only after we had completed the concordance. NEH wanted the material now. In fairness I must state that in all other respects Xerox was extremely liberal. It gave us free computer time, free memory storage, free printouts. As for the modified OCR scanner, we have seen it produce pages that are 99.5% accurate. *Cakṣuṣā vai samrāṭ paśyantam āhur adrākṣīr iti, sa āha adrākṣam iti, tat satyaṃ bhavati, cakṣur vai, samrāṭ, paramaṃ brahma* (*B.A.Up.* 4.1.4).

Finally, last year (1988), on learning of plans at the University of Texas to initiate a program of Sanskrit text concordances, I and my son have given all our materials over to the Center for Asian Studies at that university for use in their program.

KARṆABHĀRA: THE TRIAL OF KARṆA

A one-act play attributed to Bhāsa,
based on episodes from the *Mahābhārata*

Translated by Barbara Stoler Miller

Translator's Note

The *Karṇabhāra* is one of the thirteen plays discovered in 1906 by T. Ganapati Sastri, then curator of manuscripts in the royal library at Travancore. The plays were contained in several palm-leaf manuscripts of Sanskrit *nāṭakas*, written in Malayalam script. Between 1912 and 1918, Sastri published these plays as the works of Bhāsa.[1] Although none of the plays or manuscript colophons referred to the authorship of Bhāsa, the presence in the collection of two plays associated with the name Bhāsa in Sanskrit literary criticism, *Svapnavāsavadatta* and *Pratijñāyaugandharāyaṇa*,[2] encouraged Sastri to argue for the attribution of all thirteen to the author.[3]

That a Bhāsa was a dramatist of some reputation in classical India is attested by the prologue of Kālidāsa's *Mālavikāgnimitra*, where the assistant questions the director about the appropriateness of presenting Kālidāsa's play: "Why ignore works of celebrated poets like Bhāsa, Saumilla, and Kaviputra to bestow honor on a modern writer"?[4] The dramatist named Bhāsa whom Kālidāsa cites may well have authored *Svapnavāsavadatta* and *Pratijñāyaugandharāyaṇa*, as well as the fragmentary *Cārudatta*[5] The date and authorship of the remaining plays seem far more controversial.

The group of nine plays based on epic and puranic episodes fits well within the Kūṭiyaṭṭam tradition of Kerala and it is not unlikely that these

---

[1] All were published in the Trivandrum Sanskrit Series; my comments and translation are based on the more critical edition of the plays entitled *Plays Ascribed to Bhāsa*, by C.R. Devadhar (Poona: Oriental Book Agency, 1962).

[2] See A.D. Pusalker, *Bhāsa–A Study* (Delhi: Munshiram Manoharlal, 1968), chapter 2.

[3] T. Ganapati Sastri, *Bhāsa's Plays: A Critical Study* (Trivandrum: Sridhara Power Press, 1925); cf. A.K. Pisharoty, *Bhāsa's Works* (Trivandrum: N. Kesava Pillai, 1925).

[4] Trans. Edwin Gerow in *Theater of Memory: The Plays of Kālidāsa*, ed. Barbara Stoler Miller (New York: Columbia University Press, 1984), p. 255. Textual comparison of the *Svapnavāsavadatta* and the *Mālavikāgnimitra* shows many similarities of plot and structure.

[5] A good summary of the arguments is given by S.K. De in S.N. Dasgupta and S.K. De, *A History of Sanskrit Literature* (Calcutta: University of Calcutta, 1947), pp. 101–117; see also A.K. Warder, *Indian Kavya Literature*, vol. 2 (Delhi: Motilal Banarsidass, 1974), 262–333.

plays were composed in more recent time and preserved by the Cākyārs, the hereditary actors whose repetoire still includes some of them.[6] The *Mahābhārata* is the source of six of these plays: *Madhyamavyāyoga*, *Dūtavākya*, *Dūtaghaṭotkaca*, *Pañcarātra*, *Ūrubhaṅga*, and *Karṇabhāra*. The plays share a simplicity of language and compressed dramatic structure that mark them stylistically. Although the content and dramatic action of several of the plays do not conform exactly to the genre *vyāyoga*, as delineated in the *Daśarūpaka* by Dhanaṁjaya,[7] they all basically belong to this category. A *vyāyoga* is a one-act dramatization of a heroic conflict in which women play no role (*astrīnimittasaṁgrāma*), the dominant *rasa* is the heroic (*vīrarasa*), and the main characters are renowned men of violent natures (*khyātoddhatanara*). With the exception of *Pañcarātra*, all of the *Mahābhārata* plays are in one act, and the action is concentrated into a brief time of less than a single day. Each dramatizes an incident of personal conflict for the hero, based on epic scenes that are reshaped to emphasize aspects of character and action that are not developed in the *Mahābhārata* itself.

The *Karṇabhāra* is based on episodes related in the first, third, fifth, eighth, and twelfth books of the *Mahābhārata*.[8] The story of Karṇa forms the basis of some of the most poignant epic scenes. Karṇa is the son of the sungod, Sūrya, and the Pāṇḍava queen Kuntī. Kuntī, daughter of King Śūrasena, was raised in childhood by King Kuntibhoja; it was in his house that she served the divine sage Durvāsas with extraordinary hospitality and was rewarded with a *mantra* by which she could invoke any god she named. She used this magic power to invoke the sun while she was still a virgin living in her father's house; the sun embraced her and promised that in bearing his son her virginity would remain pure. The child was born wearing divine solar ornaments: earrings of immortality that made his ears splendid (thus he was called Karṇa) and protective armor. From the sun he also inherited a character of natural generosity that finally cost him his immortality. Afraid to expose her affair with the sun-god, Kuntī placed Karṇa in a box at birth and abandoned him to the river, where he was found by the charioteer Adhiratha, who brought the infant home to his childless wife (I.104; III.287–293). Karṇa, brought up by a humble charioteer, earned royal rank by his skill at

[6] See Kapila Vatsyayan, *Traditional Indian Theatre: Multiple Streams* (Delhi: National Book Trust, 1980), pp. 17–31; also J.L. Masson and D.D. Kosambi, *Avimāraka: Love's Enchanted World* (Delhi: Motilal, 1970), note 20, pp. 21–24.

[7] *DR* 3.60, 61, ed. T. Venkatacharya, *The Daśarūpaka of Dhanaṁjaya* (Madras: Adyar Library, 1969), pp. 161–162.

[8] All references are to the Poona Critical Edition of the *Mahābhārata*; the major episodes involving Karṇa's legend are: I.43, 104, 126; III.284–294; V.143–144; VIII.26, 29, 50–62; XII.2, 3. Subsequent references are cited in the text.

arms, learned from the Pāṇḍavas' teacher Droṇa and from Paraśurāma, Jamadagni's son, who cursed him for pretending to be a brahman (I.122.47; VIII.29). He was made King of Aṅga by his cousin, the Kuru chief Duryodhana, and unknowingly became the sworn rival of his own brother Arjuna (I.126). Only as the war was about to begin did he learn from Kuntī about his true origins. She petitioned him to join his brothers, a plea that was approved by the sun, but he remained loyal to Duryodhana, who had conferred kingship on him. In response to Kuntī's words he promised not to kill any of his brothers but Arjuna (V.143–144). Karṇa's character is throughout the epic challenged by the storm-god Indra, chief of the gods and adversary of the sun-god. Indra's son by Kuntī is Arjuna, the warrior whom Karṇa had to face at the time of his death, when the curse of Paraśurāma rendered his divine weapons useless and the curse of another brahman made the wheel of his chariot sink into the mire of the battlefield (VIII.29; XII.2–3).

These epic incidents are reordered in the play to reveal, through the figure of Karṇa, the heightened mood of heroism (*vīrarasa*), developed through exposition of subordinate moods of fear (*bhayānakarasa*) and compassion (*karuṇarasa*). By transferring to the battlefield the scene of Karṇa's gift of his earrings and armor of immortality, which occurs in the epic at the beginning of the thirteenth year of the Pāṇḍavas' exile (III.284–294), the encounter with Indra intensifies the drama of Karṇa's vision of his own death. In the play, his charioteer Śalya is a foil for Karṇa's dramatic monologue and a sympathetic observer, unlike his haughty role in the epic. At the beginning of the play, Karṇa is overcome by an uncanny fear in the face of battle. Obsessed by what he has learned of his birth from Kuntī (verses 7–8) and by his memory of Paraśurāma's curse (verses 9–10), he finds omens of death in the stumbling of his horses and in the putrid smell of the elephants' ichor, as well as in the dread silence of the war drums and conches. It is at this point in the drama that Karṇa recites a verse (verse 12) that is a variant of Kṛṣṇa's crucial words to Arjuna in the second section of the *Bhagavadgītā* (2.37):

> If you are slain, you win heaven
> if you triumph, you enjoy earth—
> so stand up, son of Kuntī,
> and resolve to fight the war.

Karṇa says to Śalya:

> If a man is slain, he wins heaven,
> if he triumphs, he wins fame—
> both ends are prized in the world,
> so war is not without reward.

The report of the battlefield and Karṇa's depression also recall the opening of the *Gītā*. The vocabulary of duty, action, and sacrifice that is central to the *Gītā* permeates the play and is relevant to understanding Karṇa's response to the realization of his own imminent death. But in a significant variation of the *Gītā* verse, Karṇa sets the contrast not between heaven and earth, but between heaven and heroic fame, which are the rewards of war. This is consonant with Karṇa's character in the epic, where he tells Sūrya that he will win fame as a hero by giving the earrings and armor of his immortality to Indra (III.284.20–35).[9]

The play's exposition of the relationship between sacrifice, mortality, and heroism dramatizes the Indian idea that one must heroically confront death in order to enjoy the freedom that comes by transcending the barrier between mortality and immortality. The immortality conferred by Karṇa's divine paternity is for him less important than his act of heroic sacrifice and generosity, even when he suspects that the demanding brahman has come to deceive him. Karṇa's identity is defined by his earrings and armor, but his nature is determined by his great generosity, which sets up an inevitable conflict between his immortality and ability for self-sacrifice. It is these very ornaments and armor of immortality that are, ironically, his burden—an irony implied in the title of the play, which may also mean "the burden to the ears [of Karṇa]". The mythology of the sun is at the basis of this conflict: in ancient Vedic myth the sun, called Mārtaṇḍa, is the first born of Aditi and is considered the first mortal. There is an intentional parallelism between the sons of Aditi and the sons of Kuntī. Karṇa, being the first born son of Kuntī, must also be the first to die, despite his divine birth. The play thus brings to the fore the epic hero who epitomizes the paradox of Indian epic heroism, which is expressed as extraordinary personal integrity and effort limited by the inevitabilities of destiny, duty, karma, curses, and divine intervention. The magical weapon that Indra grants to Karṇa out of guilt for taking his immortality—a spear that can be used once to kill one of the Pāṇḍavas—is symbolic of the heroic sacrifice. Upon being granted the weapon, Karṇa, mounts his chariot and again hears the sounds of the war conches that his fear had silenced; he directs Śalya to drive him to meet Arjuna.

---

[9] III.284–20–35. Karṇa may be compared here with Achilles, whose sacrifice of long life for the immortality of fame is crucial to the meaning of the *Iliad*. See Seth L. Schein, *The Mortal Hero: An Introduction to Homer's Iliad* (Berkeley, CA: University of California Press, 1984), ch. 3 "War, Death, and Heroism".

CHARACTERS

KARṆA—King of Aṅga, Kuru general.

ŚALYA—The king who is Karṇa's charioteer.

INDRA—Chief of the gods, in disguise as a priest.

SOLDIER/DIVINE MESSENGER.

All the characters speak Sanskrit, with the exception of Indra when he speaks in disguise; then his language is Ardhamāgadhī Prakrit. When he speaks in his own voice, he uses Sanskrit, appropriate to a god.

PROLOGUE

DIRECTOR:

Teeming with women and men,
with demons and gods,
this world and the netherworld reel
at the sight of his man-lion form;
the breast of the demon king
is cut by his axe-blade nails;
he destroys all foes of the gods—
may the glory of Viṣṇu,
Lord of Goddess Śrī, shine for you! (1)

Noblemen and gentlemen, I shall announce... (*Making a round of the stage, listening.*) What's this? I thought I heard a noise as I began to announce the play. Wait, I'll see.

VOICE OFFSTAGE: Report it! Report it to Karṇa, King of Aṅga!

DIRECTOR: Now it is clear.

As the din of battle rises
an agitated messenger
bowing to Karṇa
reports the royal command. (2)

(*He exits and the prologue ends; then a* SOLDIER *enters.*)

SOLDIER: Report it! Report it to Karṇa, Kind of Aṅga! It is time. for battle.

Jubilant lion kings
assembled before Arjuna's flag
with elephants, horses, and chariots
raise the cry of war
and hearing their unbearable roar,
quickly our Kuru king,
intent on battle,
advances under his sèrpent banner. (3)

(*Making a round of the stage, looking.*) Yes! This is the King of Aṅga, armed for battle, coming from his camp with King Śalya. But why does this mighty hero who leads our festivals of war show unprecedented mental anguish?

Dazzling in his fierce light,
first to be counted in battle
and in valor, with sorrow
now the wise hero approaches—
Karṇa shines like the sun,
his natural brilliance
obscured by thick clouds
when the hot season comes. (4)

I'll withdraw. (*He exists; then* KARṆA *enters, as described, with* ŚALYA.)

KARṆA

Kings who became targets in the path
of my arrows have never survived—
I shall repay the Kurus' love
if I see Arjuna at the battlefront. (5)

King Śalya, drive my chariot to where Arjuna is!

ŚALYA: So be it! (*He mimes driving.*)

KARṆA: This is futile!

In great battles
where avenging weapons severed
the limbs of warriors,
horses, elephants, and chariots,
my power was equal
to cruel death—
but this time war strikes
desperate fear in my heart. (6)

What misery!

Long ago I was born of Kuntī,
but I am called the son of Rādhā—
Yudhiṣṭhira and the other Pāṇḍavas
are my younger brothers by blood. (7)

It is time to attack and seize glory,
the day to win great merit is here,
but the magic of my weapons is useless—
and my mother's words inhibit me. (8)

King Śalya, hear the story of how I learned the magic of these weapons.

ŚALYA: I am curious to hear it.

KARṆA: Long ago, I approached Jamadagni's son, the sworn enemy of all warriors . . .

I approached, bowed, waited humbly
near the glory of the Bhṛgu clan,
the stern ascetic
who embodied death for warriors,
his matted hair piled high.
like tawny vines of lightning,
the axe he wielded
circled by flashing light. (9)

Then, blessing me, Jamadagni's son asked me, "Who are you and what is your purpose in coming here"? I said, "Master, I want to learn all the magic of weapons". The sage said, "I give instruction to priests, not to warriors"

ŚALYA: It is true, the sage has an ancient feud with the warrior clans. Then?

KARṆA: Then I said, "I am not a warrior", and I began to take instruction. Some time later, I followed my teacher when he went to gather fruits and roots and fuel and grass and flowers.

When fate made an insect
with thunderbolt jaws bite my thighs,
I calmly endured the pain
from fear of breaking my master's sleep.
Awaking bathed in my blood
he suddenly burst into fiery rage—
he knew who I was and cursed me,
'The weapons will fail at death's time"! (10)

ŚALYA: The story you tell is dreadful.

KARṆA: Let us test my weapons' magic. (*Doing so.*) These weapons seem powerless now. And . . .

These helpless stumbling horses,
their eyes blinded by misery,
and elephants whose ichor smells like weeds
are omens to turn me from battle. (11)

The conches and drums are silent!

ŚALYA: This is dreadful!

KARṆA: King Śalya, stop! There is no need to despair!

If a man is slain, he wins heaven,
if he triumphs, he wins fame—
both ends are prized in the world,
so war is not without reward. (12)

Abandoning any hope for future wars,
my horses will gallop like soaring eagles—
these powerful pure-bred stallions
will save me if I can be saved . . . (13)

Let heaven receive priests and cows! Let heaven receive faithful wives!Let heaven receive warriors who don't retreat in battles! Let heaven receive me now that it is time for me to die! Good, I am calm now.

Breaching the vanguard
of the Pāṇḍava army,
capturing the eldest brother,
whose virtues are famed,
and shooting down Arjuna
with my speeding arrows,
I can easily enter, like a forest
when the lions are slain. (14)

Lord Śalya, let us mount the chariot now!

ŚALYA: So be it! (*They both mime mounting the chariot.*)
KARṆA: King Śalya, drive the chariot to where Arjuna is.
VOICE OFFSTAGE: Hey Karṇa! I beg a great boon!
KARṆA: (*Listening.*) What a strong sound!

This man is not only a high priest,
but a person of enormous power;
hearing his deep resonant voice
my charging horses suddenly stand
like figures painted in picture—
ears erect, glances fixed,
necks turned, faces etched,
and tense limbs taut. (15)

Summon the priest! No, no. I shall summon him myself. Sir, come here! (*Then* INDRA *enters disguised as a priest.*)

INDRA: Clouds, retreat with the sun! (*Approaching* KARṆA.) Hey, Karṇa! I beg a great boon!
KARṆA: I am honored sir!

Today I count myself among men
in the world whose goals are won—
my lotus feet were reddened
by the jewels of great kings' crowns,
by the dust of kingly priest's feet.
Know me as Karṇa, honored sir;
I pay homage to you. (16)

INDRA: (*To himself.*) What should I say? If I say "Long life"! he will have long life. If I do not speak, he will think me a fool. What can I say to avoid either way? Good, I know. (*Aloud.*) Hey, Karna! Like the sun, like the moon, like the Himalayas, like the ocean, may your fame endure!

KARṆA: Master, why won't you greet me with "Long life"! Even so, this is auspicious.

> A man should exert effort to do his duty—
> a king's fortunes flicker like a serpent's tongue,
> but when his mind is bent on guarding his subjects,
> his virtues endure when the body is slain. (17)

Master, what do you want? What shall I give to you?

INDRA: I beg a great boon!

KARṆA: I shall give a great boon. Hear of my wealth!

> I give you a thousand cows with gold-tipped horns!
> Streams of milk pouring like rich nectar
> when the calves have nursed will please you, priest—
> they are young, pure, able to satisfy any demand. (18)

INDRA: A thousand cows? I hardly drink milk! I don't want them, Karṇa! I don't want them!

KARṆA: What do you want, sir? Listen to this!

> I give you thousands of horses!
> Equal to horses of the sun assuring royal fortune,
> pure-bred stallions prized by all kings,
> they race at the wind's speed in battle. (19)

INDRA: Horses? I hardly ride! I don't want them Karṇa! I don't want them!

KARṆA: Why don't you want them, sir? Listen to another boon!

> I give you this great herd of elephants!
> Ichor streams from temples that bees swarm to taste—
> they roar like a mountain range with thunderclouds,
> their nails and tusks of ivory crush the foe in war. (20)

INDRA: Elephants? I hardly ride! I don't want them, Karṇa! I don't want it!

KARṆA: Why don't you want them, sir? Listen to another boon. I shall give you countless gold!

INDRA: I'll take it and go. No, I don't want it, Karṇa! I don't want it!

KARṆA: Then I shall conquer the earth and give it to you!

INDRA: What would I do with the earth?

KARṆA: Then I give you the fruit of the great fire sacrifice!

INDRA: What use is the fruit of the fire sacrifice to me?

KARṆA: Then I give you my head!

INDRA: Enough! Enough!

KARṆA: Don't be afraid! Don't be afraid! Forgive me, sir. Listen to another boon!

> If it would please you, master, with pleasure
> would I give this magic armor with my earrings—
> it was born on my limbs to protect my body,
> making it invulnerable to weapons of gods and demons. (21)

INDRA: (*Joyously.*) Give it! Give it!

KARṆA: (*To himself.*) So this is what he desires! Could this be some trick of Kṛṣṇa's? He is always contriving new deceits. Even so, let it be! It is ignoble to lament so! There is no doubt. (*Aloud.*) Take it!

ŚALYA: Don't give it!

KARṆA: Śalya, don't try to stop me!

> Knowledge declines in passing time,
> well-rooted trees fall down,
> water collected in tanks dries up—
> sacrifice and charity endure. (22)

Take it then! (*Cutting off his armor and earrings, he gives them.*)

INDRA: (*Speaking to himself.*) Now I have them! I have assured the victory of Arjuna that the gods decreed long ago. I shall mount my elephant now and watch the combat between Arjuna and Karṇa. (*He exits.*)

ŚALYA: King of Aṅga, you were cheated!

KARṆA: By whom?

ŚALYA: By Indra!

KARṆA: No, Indra is really cheated by me.

> Though priests offer sacrificial oblations
> and his crown glows as he crushes demon hosts,
> his fingers hard from riding his elephant,
> through me alone can mighty Indra win his goal. (23)

DIVINE MESSENGER: (*Entering in the guise of a priest.*) Karṇa, Indra favors you! He feels remorse for taking your armor, and a weapon named "The Infallible" is granted to you to kill one man among the Pāṇḍavas.

KARṆA: No! I shall not accept repayment for what I have given!

DIVINE MESSENGER: Take it as the request of a priest.

KARṆA: I have never violated the request of a priest. When shall I get it?

DIVINE MESSENGER: When you invoke it, you will get it.

KARṆA: Good, I am grateful. You may return. (*The messenger exits.*) King Śalya, let us mount the chariot! (*They mime mounting the chariot.*) Āh, I hear a sound now. What is it?

> The sound of a conch,
> like the ocean falling into time;
> unless Kṛṣṇa is blowing,
> it must be Arjuna—
> angered in spirit by his elder brother's defeat,
> Arjuna will battle me
> with all his strength. (24)

King Śalya, drive the chariot to where Arjuna is!

EPILOGUE

> May fortune triumph everywhere!
> May misfortune perish!
> May our king with his virtues
> Rule over the earth! (25)

(*The two exit and the play ends.*)

ŪRUBHAṄGA: THE BREAKING OF THE THIGHS

A one-act play attributed to Bhāsa,
based on episodes from the *Mahābhārata*

Translated by Edwin Gerow

(*At the end of the* nāndī, *the* SŪTRADHĀRA *enters*.)

SŪTRADHĀRA: May Lord Kṛṣṇa be the raft that carries you over the flood
Of your enemies—just as Arjuna crossed his flood, the river of war,
Whose sands were arrows and spears, banks were Bhīṣma and Droṇa,
Water Jayadratha, the King of Gāndhāra a whirlpool, Karṇa the waves,
Aśvatthāman a crocodile, Kṛpa the shark, and Duryodhana the torrent! (1)

It's time to greet the ladies and gentlemen of the audience.
Eh!
What noise is this that interrupts my greeting? Aha! I see . . .

OFFSTAGE: We're here! We're here!

SŪTRADHĀRA: Ah! I understand!

PĀRIPĀRŚVIKA: (*Entering*.) Your honour, why do these

Men roam about testing each other's valor
Their bodies marked by tusks of wild elephants?
And limbs scarred by sword and axe? Is it for heaven
That they pour out their bodies' libation on the altar of war? (2)

SŪTRADHĀRA: Well, sir! Don't you know? On the field of Samantapañcaka, Strewn with royal corpses, two sides still face one another: Duryodhana alone on one, for Dhṛtarāṣṭra has lost the eyesight of his hundred sons; the five Pāṇḍavas and Kṛṣṇa on the other, for these alone remain of Yudhiṣṭhira's clan!

The battlefield is heaped with dead horses, elephants, kings and men
Like a wormy manuscript whose characters are corrupt.
And now the battle of Duryodhana and Bhīma will begin:

The few yet alive propose to enter the hero's last
abode. (3)

(*They exit. Thus ends the prologue.*)

(*Enter three soldiers.*)

ALL THREE: Here we are, sirs! Here we are!

FIRST: We have

Reached the battleground! that final royal hermitage
Where life itself is sacrificed, and kings find their peace in heaven!
O solemn place of hate! home of anger; test of strength;
Where heavenly nymphs gather to choose heroic mates! (4)

SECOND: Well spoken!

The earth bears its burden of dead elephants, scattered like rocks;
Carrion vultures perch; war chariots have lost their charioteers.
The lords of earth have found their heaven, their drums are still;
Unflinching, they did their duty: in war, their duty is death! (5)

THIRD: Yes,

The battle-sacrifice proceeds—arrows strewn instead of *darbha*-grass—
An elephant's raised trunk for its sacrificial post: his stricken hulk the altar;
The altar fire is hate; the Vedic chant, a lion's roar!
O'er all, wide canopies of flags; below, the victim: man! (6)

FIRST: And friends, see this:

Birds, their beaks wet with flesh,
Pluck jewels from two heroes' corpses
Where they fell in the quick fight,
Slain by each other's arrows. (7)

SECOND: An elephant in full battle dress falls to an iron arrow's chance,
His chest shattered: one king's armory of arrows and bows is lost! (8)

THIRD: And this, friends:

> A charioteer lies lifeless from a single lucky arrow;
> On his brow a crown of flowers fallen from the banner staff.
> And happy jackals drag him from the chariot's step
> Like maids-of-honor welcoming the son-in-law. (9)

ALL: How terrifying is Samantapañcaka! Its furrows flow with the blood of horses, men and elephants who fell where they were slain! The earth is heaped high with abandoned shields and breastplates, umbrellas and whisks, iron and wooden arrows, swords, javelins and headless torsos! And littered everywhere with pikes, darts, axes, daggers and stakes, pestles and hammers, shafts, bars, hooks and grim maces!

FIRST: Here now

> Flow streams of blood, oozing from the hulks of elephants;
> Horses pull chariots whose drivers fell and no king commands;
> The headless corpses twitch from the habit of life;
> And, heeding no goad, wild elephants run amok. (10)

SECOND: Look, friends, at these

> Vultures wheeling in the sky, ruddy eyes bulging like buds
> Of the arrack tree: beaks as sharp as the demon king's
> Hooked elephant goads! Their wide-stretched wings speckled
> With bits of flesh resemble palm-leaf fans inlaid with coral! (11)

THIRD:
> The daystar's blazing rays reveal fields strewn
> With horses and elephants, kings and soldiers;
> And scattered shining ornaments: sword, shield and axe,
> Have made the earth a sky of fallen stars! (12)

FIRST: Even in disaster, the beauty of the kṣatriya does not abandon them. I see

> Their fearless, upturned faces, like a silent lotus-lake
> Made to bloom by the sun of valor shining in the sky of war!
> For stalks, I see swords bearing buds of diadems; for filaments,
> Frowns; for petals, lips; for bees, those sightless eyes! (13)

SECOND: When such as these are overwhelmed by Death, what man in peril may ever trust his own powers?

THIRD: Only Death overwhelms the kṣatriya!

FIRST: Who can doubt it?

SECOND: Not so! Not quite so! Didn't mortal

> Arjuna also dispatch many haughty kings to beckoning Death
> In the heat of battle, with arrows left from his war with Śiva?
> When he but touched his bowstring, black with Khāṇḍava forest smoke
> The Nivātakavacas offered up their vital breaths;
> the Saṁśaptakas were routed;
> and the plaints of heaven were stilled! (14)

ALL: Ai! A crash! Is it

> The thundering clouds? Or bolts of lightning shattering the peaks?
> Do quakes rend the earth with incessant echoing fury?
> Or is the sea crashing in caves deep in Mount Mandara?
> The wind-tossed, wave-throbbing sea-surf roaring in shock! (15)

Let's see what it is! (*They move in various directions.*)

FIRST: Ai! The great mace fight begins! In the presence of the manes of the Kuru and the Yadu clans, before Vyāsa and Balarāma, before Kṛṣṇa and Vidura—it is Duryodhana and Bhīma, the middle son of Pāṇḍu, who fight, one angry at the murder of his hundred brothers, the other incensed that Draupadī was dragged away by the hair!

SECOND:

> Great Bhīma's breast—broad as a plate of yellow gold—is split!
> Broken are Duryodhana's broad shoulders, rough as elephant hide!
> From the fearsome blows of their two maces came that awesome sound
> Striking at once on their two wide chests!

THIRD: Now, King Duryodhana,

> Angry eyes aflame, crown shaking on his trembling brow,
> Tenses his body to spring; in his outstretched hand
> The mace glistens, besmeared with enemy blood
> Like Indra's sparkling lightning atop Kailāsa peak. (17)

FIRST: Regard the Pāṇḍava, body wet with blood from the blow:

Shoulders broken; blood gushing from the cut on his brow;
More yet anoints his chest, wet from hammer wounds;
Wounds deep and moist from bloody mace blows:
He glistens like Mount Meru with storm-drenched ruddy cliffs! (18)

SECOND: The fearsome mace he hurls; trembling, he roars;
He meets the quick arm and breaks its blow;
He feints and strikes, strikes and feints;
Duryodhana is smart, but Bhīma strong! (19)

THIRD: Wolf-belly Bhīma

Like Viṣṇu himself, unequalled in war,
Limbs moist with the gore of his head's deep gash,
Sinks to earth, like the golden mountain
Releasing its essence after the storm. (20)

FIRST: Seeing Bhīmasena fall, body slack from these heavy blows

Vyāsa stands amazed, hand on his chin, staring.

SECOND: Yudhiṣṭhira is sad; Vidura's eyes are full of tears.

THIRD: Arjuna reaches for his bow; Kṛṣṇa looks up at the sky.

ALL: But Balarāma brandishes his axe, pleased with his pupil. (21)

FIRST: The great King Duryodhana—

Splendid, proud, politely arrogant,
Crown shimmering with jewels of many hues,
Speaks mockingly to Bhīma— "Be not afraid!
No conquering hero slays such piteous foe"! (22)

SECOND: But Kṛṣṇa, seeing Bhīmasena mocked, slaps his thigh and sends some kind of signal!

THIRD: And Bhīma is revived by the signal!

Frowning, he wipes the sweat from his brow's wound,
And seizes in his menacing arms the heavy, marvellous mace;
His father, Wind, had seen his son's despair, and now restores his strength;
Bhīma rises from the earth, eyes flashing like a lion, and roars! (23)

FIRST: Look! the mace fight begins anew:

> Rubbing both hands in the dirt, Bhīma cleans his arms of blood
> By force of valor, and roars his anger through swollen lips:
> No longer friend to tender duty, heeding naught but Kṛṣṇa's sign,
> Pāṇḍu's son cracks his mace against the thighs of Gāndhārī's son! (24)

ALL: O woe! The Great King falls!

THIRD: Seeing the King of the Kurus fall, his body decorated with drops of blood, Vyāsa leaps up—

> Balarāma hides his face behind a garland of flowers
> Too shocked to gaze upon this outrage to Duryodhana—
> The Pāṇḍavas, bewildered, hurried on by Vyāsa, cast a net of hands
> Under Bhīma, who moves away, clinging to Kṛṣṇa's arm. (25)

FIRST: Eyes wide open now in consternation, Balarāma watches the departure of Bhīma, and begins to approach—

> His eyes are red with rage; in haste, he pushes his garland aside
> With its swarm of stinging bees; the crown on his brow shakes;
> He sinks to earth; drags his dark garment behind—
> Revealing a body pale as the moon in a wrack of cloud. (26)

SECOND: Then let us go, so that we may be near the Great King.

THE OTHER TWO: Yes. A good idea.

(*They all leave. Thus ends the entr'acte.*)

(BALARĀMA *enters.*)

BALARĀMA: Hear, hear! O kings! It is not right that

> He should bring his mace down on the thighs of Duryodhana,
> Crushing with one blow the family's honor and prosperity!
> He disregards my plow, a weapon well-timed to the foe's strength—
> Ignores both me and his own battle-winning treachery! (27)

Duryodhana! Stay with us yet a bit

> While I sink my handy plow in Bhīma's broad chest
> To plough a field-path in the mire of his sweat and blood!
> My plow still soiled with the ruins of Saubha!
> Still directing the course of the Kālindī!
> Its hook sharp as the turrets of the demon king's palace!
> And ever consecrated by offerings of enemies' lives! (28)

VOICE OFFSTAGE: Forgive them! O plow-armed Rāma! Forgive them!

BALARĀMA: Ai! Even in this condition, the suffering Duryodhana follows me!

> This splendid prince, crawling in the dirt, is made to play the child:
> Arms dusty, skin smeared with blood—the sandal paste of war!
> He lies like Vāsuki in the primal sea, exhausted, shedding his skin
> After churning the ambrosia: of no use to god or demon! (29)

(DURYODHANA *enters, both thighs broken.*)

DURYODHANA: It is I

> Dragging my half-exhausted body
> Through the mire, on my two arms;
> My thighs broken by the mace
> Of Bhīma, who breaks the rules of war! (30)

Forgive them! O plow-armed Rāma! Forgive them!

> This forehead of me who fell to earth
> Touches your feet: relent your anger!
> Let the smoke of the funeral fire ascend!
> The Kurus have lost—our hate, our cause consumed! (31)

BALARĀMA: Brave Duryodhana! Stay with us yet awhile!

DURYODHANA: What do you intend to do?

BALARĀMA: Listen:

> I will give you the sons of Pāṇḍu as companions to heaven,
> Along with their elephants and horses and chariots;
> I will sever their shoulders with blows of my club;
> Plough deep their bodies with the edge of my plow! (32)

DURYODHANA: Ah no! No, no!

Bhīma's vow is done; my hundred brothers are dead;
And now I die: what will more war decide! (33)

BALARĀMA: But you were tricked before my very eyes! My anger is aroused!

DURYODHANA: Do you think I was tricked?

BALARĀMA: Who doubts it?

DURYODHANA: Not so, friend! They paid dearly for my life!

If Bhīma, who saved by wit alone his kinsmen from the blazing house of lac—
If Bhīma, by whose strength great rocks were split asunder in Kubera's war—
If Bhīma, who levied the penalty of death on the demon king Hiḍimba—
If this Bhīma, you think, must *trick* me to win: then I cannot be slain! (34)

BALARĀMA: But Bhīmasena, who tricked you in battle, survives!

DURYODHANA: Have I then been tricked by Bhīma?

BALARĀMA: Who else brought you to this state!

DURYODHANA: Listen:

It was Hari himself, alien to deceit, who entered the mace
To win me over to the realm of Death. Beloved Hari—
Who stole the coral tree from Lord Indra, along with his pride;
Who sleeps a thousand years, at will, on the timeless sea. (35)

A CHILD'S VOICE OFFSTAGE: Make way, sirs! Make way!

BALARĀMA: (*Looking.*) Ah! It is Dhṛtarāṣṭra and Gāndhārī who come, with little Durjaya showing them the way. And also the wives of Duryodhana. Dhṛtarāṣṭra's heart grieves, and his pace is unsteady:

The gods, fearing for the safety of their heaven,
Made him sightless with a gift of the hostile dark;
Yet he found eyes among his hundred sons
And grew in pride. His arms shone like golden posts! (36)

(*Enter* DHṚTARĀṢṬRA, GĀNDHĀRĪ, DURJAYA, *and* THE TWO QUEENS.)

DHṚTARĀṢṬRA: Where is my son?

GĀNDHĀRĪ: My boy, where are you!

BOTH QUEENS: Prince, where are you?

DHṚTARĀṢṬRA: O, woe!

> My son, they say, has been slain, tricked by a ruse of war;
> My eyes cannot cry their tears; my blindness is complete. (37)

Gāndhārī! Are you bearing up?

GĀNDHĀRĪ: I live: such is my misfortune!

BOTH QUEENS: O King! O Great King!

DURYODHANA: Alas! Even my wives cry!

> I did not know the true pain
> Of the mace, until now:
> My wives enter the field of battle
> Their hair disheveled. (38)

DHṚTARĀṢṬRA: Gāndhārī, have you seen Duryodhana, our family's pride!

GĀNDHĀRĪ: O King! I do not see him!

DHṚTARĀṢṬRA: Why not! I am indeed blind if I cannot find my son when I have need of him! Death, you are unforgiving—

> Should not Dhṛtarāṣṭra partake just once
> Of a funerary meal offered by his son?
> He who begat one hundred bold and haughty
> Heroes that now lie broken on the earth! (39)

GĀNDHĀRĪ: Duryodhana, my son! Make some response! Console your father distraught at the death of his hundred sons!

BALARĀMA: Ai! Gāndhārī, who once

> Looked indifferently on the faces of her sons and grandsons,
> Is now unsteadied by grief at her last son's loss;
> The mask she wears in solemn vow to look on naught
> But what her husband sees, is damp with tears. (40)

DHṚTARĀṢṬRA: Duryodhana, my son! Great King and Commander of an Imperial Army! Where are you!

DURYODHANA: Today I *am* a Great King!

DHṚTARĀṢṬRA: Come, eldest of the hundred! Give me a response!

DURYODHANA: I have responded; I am ashamed of what has happened.

DHṚTARĀṢṬRA: Come, my son! Welcome me!

DURYODHANA: I am coming, I am coming . . . (*He attempts to rise, but collapses.*) O woe! This is my second wound! O most unfortunate!

> Bhīma deprived me not only of my thighs
> When he seized my hair and struck with his mace:
> He robbed me also of my father's welcome! (41)

GĀNDHĀRĪ: Girl, come here!

BOTH QUEENS: My lady, we are here.

GĀNDHĀRĪ: Go look for your husband!

BOTH QUEENS: We go, both most miserable.

DHṚTARĀṢṬRA: Who tugs at my garment to show me the way?

DURJAYA: It is I, grandpa—Durjaya.

DHṚTARĀṢṬRA: Durjaya! Son of my son! Go seek your father!

DURJAYA: Grandpa, I'm tired!

DHṚTARĀṢṬRA: Go anyway; find rest on your father's lap.

DURJAYA: All right, grandpa, I'll go. (*He approaches* DURYODHANA.) Grandpa! Grandpa! Where are you?

DURYODHANA: Has he too come? My son! Love for him stays close to my heart always and consumes me!

> How can this child, who sleeps on my lap
> And knows no sorrow, now look on me
> And call me "unconquered"? (42)

DURJAYA: The king is here and lies on the ground!

DURYODHANA: Why have you come here, my son?

DURJAYA: You took too long!

DURYODHANA: Affection for him consumes my heart, even in my misery!

DURJAYA: Papa! I want to sit in your lap! (*He climbs* [*onto* DURYODHANA*'s lap.*]

DURYODHANA: [*Restraining him.*] Durjaya! Durjaya, my boy! Be careful!

> This young moon of my heart's joy—
> Who has so often delighted my sight—
> Assumes, in my misfortune, the strange
> Shape of a scorching fire! (43)

DURJAYA: Why won't you let me sit in your lap?

DURYODHANA:

> Sit somewhere else!
> This too familiar place
> Henceforth is not for you! (44)

DURJAYA: Are you going away, O King?

DURYODHANA: Following my hundred brothers!

DURJAYA: Take me too!

DURYODHANA: Go, my boy! Just ask Bhīma!

DURJAYA: King! They're looking for you!

DURYODHANA: Who, my boy?

DURJAYA: Grandma and all the harem ladies.

DURYODHANA: Go, my son! I can't come with you!

DURJAYA: I will take you.

DURYODHANA: You are just a child, my son!

DURJAYA: (*Moving about the stage.*) Ladies! Here is the king!

BOTH QUEENS: Woe! Woe! The Great King!

DHṚTARĀṢṬRA: Where is the king?

GĀNDHĀRĪ: Where is my boy?

DURJAYA: The king is sitting on the ground.

DHṚTARĀṢṬRA: O woe! Is this the king who

> Once was the one overlord of Earth?
> In height as tall as a tower of gold?
> Wretched now, fallen onto Earth
> His size supine like a great door-bolt! (45)

GĀNDHĀRĪ: Duryodhana, my son! You look exhausted!

DURYODHANA: Am I then your son?

DHṚTARĀṢṬRA: Remember who she is, my boy!

GĀNDHĀRĪ: King! I am the mother of many fearless sons!

DURYODHANA: Then I am born again today. Well, father! Why this distress?

DHṚTARĀṢṬRA: Son! Why would I not be distressed!

> Your hundred brothers are dead—
> All heroes sacrificed in the rite of war;
> Now that you the last are slain,
> There are no more. (46) (*He falls.*)

DURYODHANA: Help! He has fallen! Father! Calm my mother!

DHṚTARĀṢṬRA: What can I say to her?

DURYODHANA: That I was slain facing the foe! Father, it would please me if you contained your sorrow:

> The crown I wore did never bow
> But at your feet; I fear not even
> The fires of Hell! The pride that blossomed
> At my birth, goes whole to Heaven! (47)

DHṚTARĀṢṬRA:

> My eyes have been sightless since birth;
> I am grown old; life is indifferent to me;
> Yet this overwhelming grief for my son
> Betrays my composure, defeats me utterly. (48)

BALARĀMA: Sir! Alas!

> I find no words to introduce myself
> To this grieving father, blind from birth! (49)

DURYODHANA: I have something to tell you, mother—

GĀNDHĀRĪ: Speak, son!

DURYODHANA:

> If I have done good works, and honored you,
> May I, in the next birth, be again your son! (50)

GĀNDHĀRĪ: Such is my wish also!

DURYODHANA: Mālavī! Hear this:

My brow is broken from mace blows beating to the time
of war;
On my breast, bloody bruises make better ornaments
than pearls.
Look! These two arms are pretty enough, with wounds
for bangles!
Why then weep? Thy warrior-husband fell handsome
facing the foe! (51)

QUEEN [MĀLAVĪ]: I cry, for I share your sorrow!

DURYODHANA: Pauravī! Hear this:

By many Vedic rites I sacrificed; my family did not
want;
To foes I showed a hundred favors, my friends I never
duped;
The princes of my enemies' hosts repent of all their
wars:
Witness of such dignity, no woman of mine shall
weep! (52)

PAURAVĪ: I do not weep, for I am determined to go along with you.

DURYODHANA: Durjaya! Hear this:

DHṚTARĀṢṬRA: Gāndhārī! What will he say?

GĀNDHĀRĪ: I also wonder . . .

DURYODHANA: You must obey the Pāṇḍavas as though they were myself; heed the instructions of the noble Kuntī; take both Draupadī and Abhimanyu's mother as your own two mothers—for you too

Must not grieve for a father who fell facing his equal!
Duryodhana's heart is inflamed with pride! His glory
lives!
Taking the linen-clad arm of mighty Yudhiṣṭhira,
Offer, with the sons of Pāṇḍu, my funeral libation! (53)

BALARĀMA: What! Has his hate become remorse? Hey! What sound is this

That frightens all the birds in heaven?
Whose bowstring bends on this battlefield
Bereft of drum and armor, guard or charioteer—
Strewn with arrows and shields, umbrellas and
whisks? (54)

A VOICE OFFSTAGE: I enter again the sacrificial battle-ground,
Where once Duryodhana trod—bow drawn—
Full thick with warriors and with tumult;
But empty now, a sacrifice without a priest. (55)

BALARĀMA: Ai! It is our teacher's son, Aśvatthāman, who comes:

Eyes wide and bright as full-blown lotus petals,
Arms long and lambent like posts of radiant gold;
In violent haste, he bends his huge and fiery bow
Like Meru with the bow of Indra on its peak! (56)

(AŚVATTHĀMAN *enters.*)

AŚVATTHĀMAN: (*He repeats verse* [*55*].) O Great Kings! O heroes! Is it true that once you made war here, your swords thrashing like crocodiles in violent whirlpools of battle? Now you look like whimpering dogs, with little life left! Listen to me, Great Kings!

I am not the Kuru Lord, thighs crushed in combat foul!
I am not the charioteer's son, of slack and useless sword!
It is I, the one son of Droṇa, who stand here, impatient,
With sword uplifted, gazing on the field of victory! (57)

Of what use to me is the glory of war without the profit of victory! (*He moves about* [*the stage*].) No, indeed! It was while I was away performing my father's obsequies that the King of the Kurus—the jewel of the dynasty—was tricked! Who would believe it? True,

Bhīṣma's heart was found by Rāma's arrow! and my
  father too—
But Duryodhana?— that peerless warrior whom once
The eager faces of eleven armies circled—arms lifted
  in salute—
And all their armories!—even he surprised by
  Death! (58)

Now where has the son of Gāndhārī gone? (*He moves about, searching.*) Ah! There he is, King of the Kurus, arrived on the further shore of the war, in the midst of a camp littered with the wreckage of chariots, elephants, horses and men—

Here he gleams, limbs wet with the blood
Of many blows; rays of his royal diadem shimmer
Amidst the dishevelled locks: the sun of evening
Touches the stony crest of the sunset mountain. (59)

(*Approaching.*) Hail, King of the Kurus! What is this?

DURYODHANA: The just deserts of a dissatisfied man, O son of my teacher!

AŚVATTHĀMAN: O King of the Kurus! I will restore you to a place of honor!

DURYODHANA: What will you do?

AŚVATTHĀMAN: Listen—

With a wave of my sword I will rid you of Kṛṣṇa,
And all the sons of Pāṇḍu; I will throw them away
Like a manuscript of blotted characters! Proud Kṛṣṇa—
Atop Garuḍa, four arms bearing discus and bow! (60)

DURYODHANA: No! No! Desist, friend—

Gone is this clan of kings, clasped in Earth's embrace!
Gone is Karṇa to heaven; gone Bhīṣma, his body felled!
Gone all my brothers, ever brave facing battle!
And now you see my fate! O friend! Lay down your bow! (61)

AŚVATTHĀMAN: Hey, King of the Kurus—

It seems that Bhīma destroyed not only your thighs
With the blow of his mace—but your pride! (62)

DURYODHANA: No! No! A king who's lost his pride is not a king! It is pride that urges me to desist! Look, son of my teacher—

Little have the sons of Pāṇḍu done to diminish my pride!
It was I who wagered Draupadī be dragged away by her hair!
At my behest was young Abhimanyu slain, in fierce battle!
I tricked the Pāṇḍavas at dice to flee and live with animals! (63)

AŚVATTHĀMAN: I have made my vow:

I swear by your honor, and by mine, and all the heroes,
That tonight in battle I'll burn all the Pāṇḍavas alive! (64)

BALARĀMA: What he says will happen!

AŚVATTHĀMAN: As your weapon is the plow!

DHṚTARĀṢṬRA: The trickery was evident to all!

AŚVATTHĀMAN: Durjaya! Come here!

With no ceremony but a brahmin's words
May you be made king in this kingdom

Won by your father's strength,
Legacy of your father's valor! (65)

DURYODHANA: At last! My heart is given leave! My life departs! Here come my fathers and grandfathers, Saṁtanu and the rest! Karṇa comes, at the head of my hundred brothers! And young Abhimanyu, steadied by Indra's arm, speaks to me from atop Indra's elephant, and he is angry with me! Urvaśī and the Apsarases welcome me! Great oceans form before my eyes! The holy Ganges and the Rivers! Death sends the heroes' chariot for me, drawn by a thousand swans: I come! I come! (*He ascends to heaven.*)

DHṚTARĀṢṬRA: (*Pulling the curtain aside.*)

I go to a forest retreat where hermits prosper.
Worthless is this kingdom, barren without sons!

AŚVATTHĀMAN: I go, arrow in hand, on a night attack!

BALARĀMA: (*Speaking the* bharatavākya.)

May the King protect the Earth, his enemies
appeased! (66)

(*All leave. Thus ends the drama* Ūrubhaṅga.)

The translation is based on the text of C.R. Devadhar, *Plays Ascribed To Bhāsa* (Poona Oriental Series, No. 54; Poona, 1962), as revised, 1965 (Poona Oriental Series, No. 72). I discuss the poetic form of the *Ūrubhaṅga* in an article published in the special volume of the *Journal of the American Oriental Society* honoring Daniel H.H. Ingalls [105.3, pp. 405–12].

Verse 2/3: hundred sons; by poetic license: the text reads *tanayaśata*, "100 offspring". The one daughter, Duḥśalā, is apparently ignored. Or perhaps our translation is what the author intended in the first place! (See below note to Verse 15–16).

Verse 11: arrack; Skt. *madhuka* (Madhuca indica), Anglo-Indian *mahwa*, the flowers of which tree, after fermenting, are a source of the country-liquor arrack. See H. Santapau, *Common Trees* (New Delhi, 1966), pp. 83–86.

Verse 14: Nivātakavacas; a class of Demons associated with Hiraṇyakaśipu. Saṁśaptakas; "les conjurés", a group of conspirators led by Trigarta who had sworn to kill Arjuna.

Verse 15: Mandara; the fabled mountain with which, as their churning stick, the Gods churned the primeval ocean in an orgy of creative energy.

Verse 15/16: middle son of Pāṇḍu; a puzzling reference. Bhīma is usually counted the second of the five Pāṇḍavas, Arjuna being the third, and thus, strictly speaking, the "middle Pāṇḍava". If the reading is correct, we must suspect either a variant genealogy, or accept a broader interpretation of "middle". Indeed, in one sense, 2, 3, and 4 are in the middle of a group of five!

Verse 15/16: hundred brothers; the reference is of course loose: if Dhṛtarāṣṭra had 100 sons, Duryodhana had only 99 brothers. The references to Dhṛtarāṣṭra's "100 offspring" (as 2/3 *supra*) are also loose to the extent that Duḥśalā, the one daughter, and 101st child, is considered. We presume that Duḥśalā survived Duryodhana.

Verse 15/16: by the hair; the culprit was of course Duḥśāsana, not Duryodhana.

Verse 18: Meru; the mountain fabled to anchor the universe; the Ganges falls from heaven on its summit and divides into four streams. It is the abode of Brahma and (as here) is brilliant with minerals and gems.

Verse 19: feints, *cārīṁ gatiṁ pracarati*: the reference is probably to a specific dance step.

Verse 19: Bhīma; the verse—a common conceit—plays on the meaning of *Bhīma*, namely "fearsome"; its first and last words are thus the "same".

Verse 21: Balarāma; Kṛṣṇa's elder brother, who was the teacher of mace-fighting to both Duryodhana and Bhīma. More or less a neutral in the war, he is here depicted as proud of Duryodhana's prowess, and much incensed at Bhīma's failure to fight by the rules (infra).

Verse 24/25: leaps up; Skt. *kham utpatitaḥ*: "jumps up *to the sky*".

Verse 27: treachery; reading *atisaṁdhim*. The saṁdhi might however be resolved: *raṇakrta-matisaṁdhim*, "a decision (relating to) opinions formed in (or about) battle".

Verse 29: Vāsuki; the serpent used by the gods as rope when churning the primeval ocean. The verse also alludes to the serpent's earlier function of supporting the ocean before creation: both functions being fulfilled, the serpent is "useless".

Verse 35: alien to deceit; reading *nirvyājayuddhapriya-*. Devadhar's earlier text is in error here.

Verse 35/36: Dhṛtarāṣṭra, et al.; after his teacher, Balarāma, Duryodhana is visited by his immediate family: father, mother, young son, and his two wives.

Verse 39: funerary meal: the *piṇḍa* offering to the deceased; an important duty of the eldest son. Failure of the *piṇḍa* was thought to guarantee swift passage to hell. Hence the social pressure on the wife to produce a son.

Verse 42/43: misery; lit. "in this condition".

Verse 44/45: hundred brothers; see above, note to 15–16.

Verse 45/46: born again today; he means that he basks in his mother's renewed affection, for she deigns to overlook his defeat.

Verse 50/51: Mālavī; in the *Veṇīsaṁhāra*, Duryodhana's wife's name is Bhānumatī.

Verse 51/52: share your sorrow; *sahadharmacāriṇī*, implying that she is the dutiful wife, sharing her husband's every mood. Pauravī; see preceding note.

Verse 55/56: Aśvatthāman; the son of Droṇa, archery teacher to the warriors of both sides. One of the last three Kauravas to survive the battle, he symbolizes intractable hostility to the Pāṇḍavas. In the *Mahābhārata* version of our story, it is Aśvatthāman who sneaks into the Pāṇḍava camp at night and slays the five young sons of the Pāṇḍavas, bringing their heads to the dying Duryodhana. A brahmin, his life is spared by the judicious Yudhiṣṭhira.

Verse 56: bow of Indra; *Indracāpa*, the rainbow; often compared as here, to a warrior's drawn bow, bedecked with ornament.

Verse 57: charioteer's son; Karṇa, half-brother to the Pāṇḍavas, who, though son of the Sun, was brought up by Sūta, the charioteer of Dhṛtarāṣṭra. The reference is to Karṇa's supposedly invincible javelin, gift of Indra, which nevertheless was insufficient in battle against Arjuna, who killed him.

Verse 60: characters; compare Verse 3.

Verse 63: Abhimanyu; Arjuna's son, who had killed Duryodhana's son Lakṣmaṇa earlier in the battle. On the dragging of Draupadī by the hair, see note to 15/16, above.

Verse 65: brahmin's words; Aśvatthāman of course refers to himself and this verse.

Verse 66. bharatavākya; a benediction; the traditional closing verse of a Sanskrit drama, here incorporated into a larger verse.

EPIC PARTHENOGENESIS

MARY CARROLL SMITH

The *Mahābhārata* recounts several stories of the miraculous birth of great warrior (*kṣatriya*) saviors. The birth of the epic heroes or saviors is frequently accomplished by a single parent. Conception without a conjunction of sexual gametes is called parthenogenesis, and the births resulting from such conception are usually marked by signs and wonders. Female parthenogenesis, in which the absent or shadow male is often a god, is best illustrated in the *Mahābhārata* by the story of Kuntī's magical power. Kuntī was given a spell that would allow her to conceive by simply calling on the god. The birth of the great hero Arjuna Pāṇḍava comes as the result of her calling on Indra, who responds only after a period of intense asceticism on her part (*Mahābhārata* 1.114).[1] Kuntī's parthenogenic privilege seems only to result in the birth of sons destined to be great leaders and heroes. One wonders what would have happened if she called on the goddess.

The focus of the female parthenogenic myths is seldom on the mother, but rather on the semi-divine son who sometimes manages to avoid the birth canal entirely in his earthly appearance. Both Gotama Buddha and Jesus Christ are said to have been born thus.[2] In *Ṛg Veda* 4.18.1-3 Indra actually debates with his mother about his intention to avoid the canal and pass through her side. He desists when she is dying from the trauma. The birth of heroic saviors, whether gods or men, causes the natural world great alterations. Another remarkable pattern of mono-gender conception in the Great Epic is presented in three separate accounts of male parthenogenesis. The births of two military saviors and a Warrior God occur without any human mother at all. The focus in these stories is on male prowess, mental, physical and spiritual.

Male parthenogenic births in the *Mahābhārata* occur without mothers as bearers or holders of the seed. Such births are called *ayonija* or "non-womb birth." *Ayonija* should perhaps be translated as "born without the need of a female source," but even that translation fails to signify the full

---

1 Citations to the *Mahābhārata* are from the critical text edited at Poona, the *Adiparvan*, ed. Vishnu S. Sukthankar (Poona: Bhandarkar Oriental Research Institute, 1933).

2 Aśvaghoṣa, *Buddhacarita*, tr. E.H. Johnston (1936; rpt. Delhi: Motilal Banarsidass, 1972), verses 9–11, p. 3.

deprivation entailed in the parthenogenic births of the epic heroes. "In the medical texts, it is clear that women can procreate unilaterally but men cannot; in the myths, the situation is reversed, and men, but not women, are capable of unilateral procreation (albeit men do it into a 'female' receptacle of some sort—any container at all)."[3] It is true that several "female" jars or containers are mentioned in connection with both Vedic seers and epic heroes, but the literal details of such references seem to belong to later text traditions. The Vedic seers Agastya and Vasiṣṭha are reputed to have male parthenogenic origins, but the *Ṛg Veda* contains only elliptical references to their non-womb births.

The birth of Vasiṣṭha and Agastya (*Ṛg Veda* 7.33.9-13) is recounted by Indra in the context of praising the Vaiṣṭhas for bringing him to their soma pressing and thereby engaging him as the champion for Sudās in the battle with the Ten Kings. The inter-relation of cultic activity, both in the pressing of soma and in the composing of hymns, with the increase of warrior *furor* has yet to be investigated. It is the epic that provides actual mythic narratives which illuminate the inherent political and spiritual claims attendant on miraculous birth:

> First, one must note the primacy of the Vedic ritual as a model for sexual creation . . . what happens next is that when an actual birth model is finally constructed, beginning sketchily in the Upanishads, the model is an almost literal application of the ritual metaphors. . . . A second characteristic of the Vedic world view is implicit in the frequent examples of unilateral or competitive procreation that occur in the texts. There are, of course, many examples of more conventional sexual cooperation as well . . . it is the unexpected metaphor that proves ultimately illuminating for the peculiar Indian viewpoint.[4]

It is the unexpected metaphor of the "un-womb born" as it is developed in the three myths of the *Mahābhārata* that helps to illuminate the ideology behind the myth of parthenogenesis.

Non-womb births characterize Kṛpa (*Mahābhārata* 1.120), Droṇa (*Mahābhārata* 1.121), and Skanda (*Mahābhārata* 3.213-218; 9.43). All three myths are concerned with the conditions surrounding the physical birth of heroes who will possess spiritual endowments that result in superhuman military prowess. Arjuna's birth through Kuntī's ability to evoke Indra provides some sense of the inner connection between his consummate heroic achievements and the spiritual principal embodied in his father, Indra. Indra's Vedic persona is of the quintessential Aryan warrior king.

---

[3] Wendy Doniger O'Flaherty, *Women, Androgynes, and Other Mythical Beasts* (Chicago: University of Chicago Press, 1980), p 50.

[4] Ibid., pp. 31–32.

His son then can be expected to have divine capabilities. Linking of miraculous birth with spiritual and military capability is more remarkable in the myths of Droṇa and Kṛpa since both are recognized as mortals in the epic. The endowment of the God's son, Skanda, with military capability makes the fact of his non-womb birth a causal link in his eventual generalship of the gods. The three stories could never claim to primary influence in the present redaction of the epic, but their contexts provide a unique vantage for the study of the meaning of parthenogenesis mythology.

The birth stories of Kṛpa and Droṇa are found in successive chapters of the *Mahābhārata* Book One, *Ādiparvan* (1.120; 1.121). The basic elements of the two myths seem to suggest that the stories are variants, perhaps of an archetypal male supremacy myth. The fathers of both Kṛpa and Droṇa are Vedic seers whose spiritual practices are related to their expertise in weaponry. Droṇa and Kṛpa both become students of weaponry and then famous teachers of the art of weapon attainment and usage. By considering each myth separately, and then comparing and contrasting them and the Skanda myth, a real pattern emerges of archaic warrior spirituality imaged in the process of male birthing. The underlying pattern tends to go unnoticed because of the dramatic, non-ordinary conditions of male parthenogenesis.

Both human saviors are born through the involuntary emission of their fathers' semen (*retas*). Although the common English translation for *retas* is "seed," the primary understanding of the term in the *Ṛg Veda* is of the flow or discharge of the semen.[5] Citing Grassmann, Wendy O'Flaherty says: "in this sense it [*retas*] has the primary connotation of a process rather than a substance, though it is freely applied to many substances, including the embryo engendered by the seed."[6] The untimely appearance of a radiant female figure occurs in the denouement of the male birthings of Droṇa and Kṛpa. The pattern for the female figure occurs in the Vedic citation on the birth of Vasiṣṭha (7.33.11).

utāsi māitravaruṇo vasiṣṭha /
urvaśyā brahman manaso 'dhi jāta: //
drapsam skannam brahmaṇā dāivyena /
viśve devā: puṣkare tvādadamta //[7]

---

[5] Hermann Grassmann, *Worterbuch zum Rig-Veda* (Wiesbaden: Otto Harrassowitz, 1964), 1181.

[6] Ibid., p. 20.

[7] *Rig-Veda-Samhita*, edited by F. Max Müller, V. III, Mandala, VII (Varanasi: The Chowkhamba Sanskrit Series Office, reprint of the 1892 edition), verse 11. I have split the unlawful *saṁdhi* of *vasisthorvaśya*.

The ellipsis of the verse not withstanding, Vasiṣṭha is said to be the son of Mitra and Varuṇa, born from their thought of Urvaśī. *Drapsam skannam*, the "spilled drop", could certainly be the "unexpected metaphor" that gives rise to the later mythic statements. The placing of the "spilled drop" in the blue lotus flower, *puṣkara*, could also mean in "the bowl of a spoon," which would make more ritual sense if the verse has metonymic meaning. Another verse in the hymn (*Ṛg Veda* 7.33.13) says that Vasiṣṭha was born in a pot (*kumbhe*), together with the seer Agastya, from the seed (*retas*) of the two gods. There is no mention in this verse of Urvaśī, but when the later tradition comes to mythologize the reference in regard to Agastya, she appears.

> Agastya is one of the more famous seers of the *Ṛg Veda*, and like Vasiṣṭha and Viśvāmitra, has a rich post-vedic life. His birth was miraculous. When the Gods Mitra and Varuṇa were sacrificing, they saw the nymph Urvaśī and promptly ejaculated. Their seed fell in a jar, from which Agastya arose; hence his common nickname *kumbhayoni*: he whose womb was a jar.[8]

The Vedic verses give no indication that Urvaśī was seen. Sörensen identifies Agastya as Vasiṣṭha's brother and then gives the citation from the *Bṛhaddevatā*, in proper Victorian Latin, which shows that the tradition interpreted the ellipsis in the statements about Vasiṣṭha's birth as a seeing of Urvaśī by the dual divinities which resulted in the birth of Agastya:

> Natus erat cum fratre Vasishtho semine Mitri et Varuni, quum nympham Vrvaçīm vidissent, amore incensorum in urceum profluente. 5.30ff.[9]

The conflation of the two Vedic verses is elaborated on in that the pouring of the semen into the pitcher (*urceum*) is due to passionate fire of love when Mitra and Varuna see Urvaśī. Verse 11 used the term *manaso*, which is "mind," "in its widest sense as the seat of intellectual operation and of emotions."[10] I have followed Geldner in translating the term as "thought" because of the relation of such activity with Kuntī's ability to think of the god and become fertile. Grassmann's reading of the citation is of "der Geist personificirt."[11] On the other hand his reading of *urvaśyās* is of the substantive meaning "violent desire" or "ardent passion."[12] The

---

[8] *The Mahābhārata The Book of the Forest*, vol. 2, tr. and ed. by J.A.B. van Buitenen (Chicago: University of Chicago Press, 1975), p. 187.

[9] S. Sörensen, *An Index to the Names in the Mahābhārata* (Delhi: Motilal Banarsidass, reprint of the 1904 edition), p. 16.

[10] Arthur A. Macdonell, *A Practical Sanskrit Dictionary* (1924; rpt. Oxford: University Press, 1974), p. 216.

[11] Grassmann, pp. 994–96

[12] Ibid., p. 266.

depiction of Urvaśī as the goddess personifying passion for the love-sick Purūravas can be found in hymm 95 of the tenth maṇḍala of the *Ṛg Veda*. She appears in the *Mahābhārata* as the wife of Purūravas and as a stimulant to the parthenogenic birth of Ṛṣyaśṛṅga.

The parthenogenesis that produces Kṛpa and Droṇa is also set in motion by a divine female. The miraculous potency of Kṛpa's father, Śaradvat Gautama, has a more detailed narrative build-up than is the case for Droṇa's father. The narrative prelude highlights the military associations of Kṛpa's birth. Gautama, who is called Śaradvat because he was born with arrows, excels in the study of weaponry and invites the attention of Indra, king of the gods. Indra's position of supreme godly strength can be challenged by the build-up of a seer's ascetic practices, which result in *tapas*, heat or spiritual energy. Gautama's energy also threatens Indra because it is coupled with extreme skill in archery *dhanurvedaparatva*. The text specifically says that Gautama practiced austerities to acquire all weapons in just the same way that Brahman scholars practice austerities to obtain the Vedas. While Indra is frequently depicted in the epic as threatened by the increasing spiritual power of seers, the Kṛpa birth myth discloses a reminder of Indra's Vedic position as Divine Warrior. He is threatened by Śaradvat's knowledge of weaponry. One might suppose that Indra's weapon, the *vajra*, is fashioned in intense spiritual heat.[13]

In recalling aspects of Indra's Vedic position, I do not mean to imply that the present epic text has any direct relation to the Vedic period other than in echoes. It is distinctly possible that the stories as now constituted represent a later, and literal, interpretation of complex symbolic materials. Vedic hymns, on the whole, are composed in an elliptical style that demands great ingenuity on the part of the listener to recall the elided reference. The text of the Kṛpa birth myth is written in a simple descriptive style that seems to spell out each detail; it is also written in common *śloka* meter with an abundance of long compounds which suggest composition in the Classical Sanskrit style.[14] Since the celibacy of warriors is not stressed in the later Hindu tradition, the connection between the diminishment of the skill in weaponry and erotic activity should be examined. Indra's ploy with Gautama is to send a celestial woman, possibly a virgin (*devakanyā*), to tempt the seer.[15] The divine female is also called an *apsaras* in her encounter with Gautama. An *apsaras* is a class of female divinity. They reside in the

[13] *Ṛg Veda*, 1.52.7, 8.

[14] Mary Carroll Smith, "The Mahābhārata's Core," *JAOS*, vol. 95, no. 3, (1975), 479ff.

[15] Wendy Doniger O'Flaherty, *Asceticism and Eroticism in the Mythology of Śiva* (London: Oxford University Press, 1973), pp. 42–52. While citing the Ṛśyaśṛṅga story, O'Flaherty refers to the *apsaras* as "the prostitute."

sky. "They are very fond of bathing, can change their shapes and are endowed with superhuman power." They "are usually described as the servants of Indra, who when alarmed by the rigorous austerities of some mighty sage, sends down one of them to disturb his penance, and her mission is generally successful."[16]

"Create an impediment to his austerities," Indra tells the *apsaras*, who is called Jālapadī. The name means literally "web-footed." "No doubt in origin an aquatic bird."[17] The Vedic *apsarā*, Urvaśī "is a water bird, discovered by her husband among other water birds."[18] When Jālapadī goes to the hermitage in the forest she is wearing a single garment. Gautama is described as carrying his bow and arrows. At first sight, he stares; his bow and arrows drop; he shivers. Verse ten says that his wisdom and his austerity enabled him to stand still, but verse eleven records that Gautama's semen had been discharged even though he was not aware of it. Gautama leaves the hermitage and the *apsarā*. His seed then falls into a reed bed (*śarastambe*). Van Buitenen translates 'reed bed" as "reed stalk", but the compound connotes the clump of reeds rather than the single stalk of white grass or reed used to make arrows (*śara*). The distinction is important to the latter discussion (cf. below p. 93) of the symbolic female presence in the containers for the spilled seed. The seed divides into two when it falls into the clump of reed, and thus twins are born to Śaradvat Gautama. One of the twins is a girl, Kṛpī, and she is mentioned in the Droṇa myth because she is found by Droṇa as his wife when he wants "to obtain a son" (*Mahābhārata* 1.121.12).

"One realizes the importance of the concept of twinship on the level of abundance, vitality, and fecundity. By common agreement among a great number of peoples, the birth of twins is the sign and token of all these things."[19] Thus, even enhanced fertility is attributed to the male conceiving in himself alone. The account of the birth of Gautama's children, Kṛpa and Kṛpī, contains no details beyond the statement that they were born from Gautama's seed which had split in two when it fell into the reed bed. The nurture of the children is also unexplained except for the account of their being found by the king's attendant. "Seeing bows and arrows about them, as well as black antelope skins, he judged that they were the children of a brahmin who was also adept at the mysteries of weaponry." The king

---

[16] V.S. Apte, *The Practical Sanskrit Dictionary* (Poona: Prasad Prakashan, 1957), pp. 164–65.
[17] Van Buitenen, *The Mahābhārata The Book of the Beginning*, vol. 1 (Chicago: University of Chicago Press, 1973), note on p. 459.
[18] O'Flaherty, *Women*, p. 181.
[19] Georges Dumézil, *Archaic Roman Religion*, vol. 1 (Chicago: University of Chicago Press, 1970), p. 252.

raises the twins. Gautama identifies the children to the king; he then teaches his son, Kṛpa, "the fourfold art of archery, the many different weapons, and the secret lore in its entirety." The myth ends with the statement that Kṛpa became a great teacher of archery who taught the Dhārtarāṣṭras, the Pāṇḍavas, the Vṛṣṇis, and other nobles. The *Mahābhārata*, as we know it, has several references to Kṛpa's function as archery teacher, but it is Droṇa who is the actual teacher of both the sons of Pāṇḍu and Dhṛtarāṣṭra in the epic stories (*Mahābhārata* 1.122, 123). The lead-in to Kṛpa's birth story indicates that the king entrusted his sons to Kṛpa so that he would teach them (1.119). At the end of the Bhārata war, Kṛpa is appointed the preceptor of Arjuna Pāṇḍava's grandson, Parikṣit (*Mahābhārata* 17.1.13), but, again, there is no story in the present text to illustrate the reference.

The birth of the Kuru archery preceptor, Droṇa, is also accomplished through male parthenogenesis. Like Kṛpa, his birth is linked to weaponry, knowledge of the Vedas, and the appearance of the mysterious female who stimulates his father, Bharadvāja, to ejaculate. The birth story is told succinctly. The *śloka* verse is of the utmost simplicity:

> *maharṣis tu bharādvajo havirdhāne caran purā* /
> *dadarśāpsarasam sākṣād ghṛtācīm āplutām ṛṣiḥ* // 1.121.3

Indra does not figure in the story, and the appearance of the *apsaras*, Ghṛtācī, may be related to Bharadvāja's activity in the *soma* shed; "*havirdhāna*: an area of the sacrificial terrain where the utensils for the Soma Sacrifice were kept."[20] Macdonell gives as Vedic meanings for *havirdhāna*: "n. (receptacle of the offering), the car for conveying the Soma plants to be pressed; light shed for housing the Soma cars," and an Epic meaning, "place of sacrifice."[21] If Bharadvāja is considered more than a custodian of sacrificial equipment and recognized as a practitioner of the *soma* sacrifice, then the second half of the *śloka* may be interpreted as a mystical statement of the *soma* vision.[22] The name of the *apsaras*, Ghṛtācī, has connections to the *soma* sacrifice as commemorated in the *Ṛg Veda*. The sacrificial spoon or ladle for ghee (clarified or melted butter) is called *ghṛtācī*.[23] In the birth story of Droṇa, then, the *apsaras*' name could carry a weightier symbolic meaning than its onomastic derivations.

---

[20] Van Buitenen, vol. 1, 459.

[21] Macdonell, p. 376.

[22] Cf. R. Gordon Wasson, *Soma: Divine Mushroom of Immortality* (New York: Harcourt, Brace & World, Inc., 1968), p. 10.

[23] Macdonell, p. 89. Macdonell puts emphasis on a note that the butter "has cooled"; *ghrta*, he indicates also means "fat (=fertility)." Cf. also Grassman, p. 425, who gives the literal meaning of the compound as "*der Butter zugewandt*."

Bharadvāja sees the *apsaras* "in person," or even "in the flesh." The *apsaras* has bathed (*āplutām*), which van Buitenen glosses as "after the menses." His gloss could be carrying a negative sense, taken from Western Biblical tradition, of a female's mandatory purification before contact with the male. "When a woman has a discharge, her discharge being blood from her body, she shall remain in her impurity seven days; whoever touches her shall be unclean until evening."[24] The law of uncleanness, "You shall put the Israelites on guard against their uncleanness, lest they die through their uncleanness by defiling My Tabernacle which is among you," (15.31) applies equally to men who "have an emission of semen." In my opinion, however, the bathing has a positive element of divine fecundity, archetypal in the Jungian sense, which may be carried along unwittingly in the myth of male parthenogenesis. While the divine female is specifically associated with the water in the Droṇa myth, in the Kṛpa myth the association with water is found only indirectly in Jālapadī's name. The water reference recalls ancient Goddess traditions:

> The mystery of life lies in water, in oceans, deep seas, lakes or rivers. Gods are born from water. Dionysus comes from water, as do the Bird Goddess, Athena, or Aphrodite. . . . To the poets and philosophers of ancient Greece water was the primordial element, able to produce life, stimulate its growth and nurture it with damp warmth. This concept of the genesis of the universe from an elemental aqua-substance surely extends back in time to the Neolithic-Chalcolithic era.[25]

The Vedic substratum of the epic myths also contains abundant references to life emerging from water. "Though goddesses are not important to the Ṛg Veda, women are—important as things to be possessed, like cattle. Fluids of all kinds are in many ways 'female;' they are the materials of regeneration, the moist, Dionysian element, whether they flow in the veins of men or of women."[26] There is little doubt that in the larger Indic mythic context, rivers and other bodies of water retain the female or goddess archetype. In the present text, however, the goddess has no specific function except as stimulant to Bharadvāja's creativity when her garment blows away in the wind.

The sight or vision of the goddess is enough to arouse the great seer. The semen pours out and the future hero is born in the *soma* vat (*droṇa*), where

[24] *The Torah* (Philadelphia: The Jewish Publication Society of America, 1962), *Leviticus*, 15.19.

[25] Marija Gimbutas, *The Gods and Goddesses of Old Europe* (London: Thames and Hudson, 1974), p. 95.

[26] O'Flaherty, *Women*, pp. 32–33.

his father had placed the seed:

> The male substance, semen, is ritually combined with the female creative fluid, milk, not in an explicit description of the birth process (which is never directly discussed in the Ṛg Veda) but in the metaphor of the Soma ritual. . . . Seed is equated not only with milk but with Soma; and this Soma in later ritual is replaced by ghee, butter, which is churned out of milk just as, in the Ṛg Veda, the Soma juices are often said to be churned or milked from the ocean . . . that is, from the Soma vats metaphorically regarded as an ocean.[27]

The Droṇa birth myth contains a wealth of interpretive possibilities compressed, Vedic style, into three *ślokas*. The whole *soma* setting for the miraculous birth of the Great Warrior needs investigation once the epic texts reveal the means of relating Vedic and Epic traditions in such ways that caste separations can be surmounted. The nurture of Droṇa is limited to his learning the Vedas with all their branches including weaponry, and to his instruction by the illustrious Agniveśya in the *āgneya* weapon. "The word *agniveśya* means 'related to (or born from) the fire hall', appropriate enough for Droṇa himself."[28]

Thus, the parthenogenic birth of Droṇa, like Kṛpa's, is directly related to the possession of the secret lore of weaponry. The birth of the War God Skanda is the third case of male parthenogenesis in the epic. Two versions of Skanda's birth occur: one in Book Three, and the other in Book Nine. Van Buitenen gives the following summary in the introduction to his translation in Book Three:

> The most striking aspect of Kumāra's myth [from the point of view of his sonhood he is Kumāra, the "Boychild;" as son of Rudra he seems to be Skanda, the "Hopper;" as son of the Pleids (*kṛttikāḥ*) he is Kārttikeya;] is the devious way in which he is born. The most persistent trait is that he is, the son of Fire, and if fatherhood is claimed for Rudra-Śiva it is conceded this God had assumed the guise of Fire. While his father is fairly well established, he has a surfeit of mothers. The first "real" mother is Svāhā, the personification of a sacrificial call, *svāhā!*, cried at certain oblations. This word, though an interjection, can be interpreted as a feminine noun, and its exclusive association with the sacrificial fire apparently encouraged the idea of a romance between Svāhā and Fire. . . . Fire falls in love with the chaste wives of the Seven Seers, and the lovesick Svāhā assumes the shape of six of these wives—Arundhatī excepted—to coax out Fire's semen. She collects the spilling and takes it to the mountain Śveta in the shape of a Garuḍa bird; from the six portions of semen Kumāra takes shape, in effect without benefit of

---

[27] Ibid., p. 24.

[28] Van Buitenen, vol. 1, 459. On 121.5 "The lordly Agniveśya, etc.: the authenticity of this line is rather doubtful; it seems to be inspired by 1.122.20, where Droṇa declares that his teacher was Agniveśya."

mother, and thus joins latterly the procession of great men who have assuredly fathers but hardly a mother [E.g., Droṇa, born from a trough; Kṛpa, from a reed stalk; Agastya, from a jar.][29]

For some reason, van Buitenen overlooked the account of Skanda's birth in Book Nine (9.43). He says, "Obviously there were more stories: the motherhood of the Ganges, in which, according to parallel accounts of the myth, Śiva poured his seed, is not recorded in the *Mahābhārata*; nor is the reed bed that elsewhere figures in his conception-and-birth."[30] The myth, as it is related in Book Nine, contains the Gaṅgā episode as well as a version of Skanda's relation to the Kṛtittikās who first see him "in a reed bed" (*śarastambe*). While the story in Book Nine lacks the romance of the stories in Book Three, the male parthenogenic elements are highlighted and a deeper symbolic relation of the birth of the War God to the genesis of the warriors Droṇa and Kṛpa is made more accessible for analysis.

The story of Kumāra/Skanda's birth is the prelude to the story of his investiture as general of the army of the Gods which vanquished the Daityas. The narration of the investiture begins with the statement that Māheśvra's *tejas*, energy/seed fell into a blazing fire which was not able to burn it:

Tejo māheśvaram skannam agnāu prapatitam purā /
tat sarvabhakṣo bhagavān nāśakad dagdhum akṣayam // 6

tenāsīdati tejasvī dīptimān havyavavāhanaḥ /
na cāiva dhārayāmāsa garbham tejomayam tadā // 7
sa gaṅgām abhisaṁgamya niyogād brahmaṇaḥ prabhu: /
garbham āhitavān divyam bhāskaropamatejasam // 8
atha gaṅgāpi tam garbham asahanti vidhāraṇe /
utsasarja girāu ramye himavatyamarārcite // 9
sa tatra vavṛdhe lokānāvṛtya jvalanātmaja: /
dadṛśur jvalanākāram tam garbham atha kṛttikā: // 10
śarastambe mahātmānamanalatmajam īśvaram /
mamāyam iti tā: sarvā: putrārthinyo 'bhicakramu: //

(*Śalya Parvan* 9.43)

The critical edition uses the word *tejas* instead of *retas*, which does occur in two manuscripts as the introductory word of verse six. However, there are no variants for the use of *tejas* in verses seven and eight. "The Purāṇas use *tejas*, fiery energy, as a euphemism for semen."[31]

---

[29] Van Buitenen, vol. 2, 205–206.
[30] Ibid., p. 206.
[31] O'Flaherty, *Women*, p. 55.

In verse six the *tejas* is described as *skannam*, "leaping" or "spurting." The same word is used of the "drop" from Mitra and Varuṇa in *Ṛg Veda* 7.33.11. Several epic texts show a reading of *skandam*. In the Skanda birth story of Book Nine, there is no indication of the cause of the flow of Siva's energy, and the absence of an *apsaras* is noteworthy. The Fire cannot contain the force within himself and throws it into the river, Gaṅgā. She cannot contain such energy either and throws it onto the mountain Himavat (verse nine). The text says that *jvalanātmajah*, the son of the Fire, or perhaps "the one who is self-begotten in the Fire," grew there. The word *garbha* is used in each of the verses from seven through ten to describe the entity that Agni and Gaṅgā could not sustain. The same word is used for the glowing entity that the Kṛittikās see on the mountain. In verse eleven it is clear that it is a male child in the reed bed. Although the usual meaning of *garbha* is womb, in the Skanda story of Book Nine it has the multiple meanings of foetus, embryo, and new-born child. The six Kṛittikā goddesses "who desire a son" cry out, "He's mine," and then vie to nurse the child. Several reactions to the new-born are recorded. The fact that the text says that there is a mental vying among Śiva, Pārvatī, Gaṅgā, and Agni as to whom the child will honor first, indicates the presence of Pārvatī, although she has not appeared previously in this version of the myth.

As in Buddha's birth story, and some of the Christian Apocıypha, the birth of Skanda causes natural wonders to appear in the world. Himavat is transformed into gold and the whole Earth appears beautiful as it holds the Child on her lap, so to speak. Among the divine attendants at his birth: "The *Vedas* assuming a fourfold form, approached the child with joined hands. The Science of arms, with its four divisions, and all the weapons, as also all kinds of arrows, came to him."[32] This reference creates the essential link to the Droṇa and Kṛpa myths. Not only is Skanda the War God, but like Droṇa and Kṛpa he has immediate access from birth to the arts of weaponry.

The three male parthenogenic myths bring together an interlocking pattern involving: (1) ascetic austerity which creates and intensifies energy (*tejas*) or heat (*tapas*); (2) the sexual and creative potency of that hot energy in itself; and (3) the extraordinary prowess in military exploits that the harnessing of that energy can produce. The birth of the War God from the ascetically controlled energy of Śiva which dropped into the Fire gives the motif of Fire meeting Fire. ("We only live, only suspire / Consumed by

---

[32] The *Mahābhārata* tr. under the name of Pratap Chandra Roy, vol. vi. (Calcutta: Datta Bose & Co., 1926), section XLIV, 394.

either fire or fire.")[33] Confrontations between fire and fire become a source of elaborate play in Sanskrit *kāvya*. The adjective *dvijanman* "twice born" is used of Agni in the *Ṛg Veda*. Agni, like Skanda is a "child of double birth."[34] Agni and Skanda are both credited with two birth places. It is said that Agni is first born in the fire sticks and then born in the consecration. Skanda's birth story uses the "twice-born" motif in several variations which may be the result of the coalescence of multiple mythic versions on the birth of the War God.

The first instance of a "twice-born" situation is the Fire (Śiva) to Fire (Agni) transmutation. The second instance is Fire (Agni) to Water (Gaṅgā). "The image of fire placed in water is used throughout Indian mythology to express the control of indestructible excess energy. Although in Western thought water brought to fire usually results in the extinction of fire, in India the fire almost always emerges intact from the combination, merely controlled or transformed. . . ."[35] The Skanda birth story has a third transformation when the embryo moves from the Gaṅgā to the mountain Himavat. In this episode the coming of the child to the mountain causes it to be transformed into gold, and "it is for this reason that mountains are producers of gold." It is certainly within the realm of possibility that the myth combines elements related to the fire used in the melting of metals, in the forging of weapons, and in the spiritual build up of *tejas* or the more familiar *tapas* needed for the "knowing" of the secret lore in any field.

Mircea Eliade asserts that shamanic seers, warriors, and smiths form an interrelated group because each possesses magico-religious accomplishments in respect to fire:

> From the viewpoint of the history of religion, these different accomplishments show that the human condition has been abolished and that the shaman, the smith or the warrior participate, each on his own plane, in a higher condition. For this higher condition can be that of a God, that of spirit, or that of an animal. The respective initiations, though following different paths, pursue the same end—to make the novice die to the human condition and to resuscitate him to a new, a transhuman existence. Naturally, in military initiations the initiatory death is less clearly seen than in shamanic initiations, since the warrior's principal ordeal consists precisely in vanquishing his adversary. But he emerges from the ordeal victorious only by becoming heated and attaining to the berserker fury—symptoms that express

[33] T.S. Eliot, "Four Quartets, Little Gidding," *The Complete Poems and Plays* (New York: Harcourt, Brace and Company, 1952), p. 144.

[34] Grassmann, p. 651. *Ṛg Veda* 1.60.1; 1.140.2; 1.149.4, 5.

[35] O'Flaherty, *Asceticism*, 286–87.

> death to the human conditions. He who obtains magical heat vividly demonstrates that he belongs to a superhuman world.[36]

While Eliade argues that the shaman, smith, and warrior's use of fire causes a participation in a "higher condition" according to a hierarchy ("each on his own plane"), he nonetheless asserts a unified goal for all three. In India, the "knowing" is the highest aspiration. "Knowing" is at once physical, mental, and spiritual attainment in the present life. The single goal of the shaman, the warrior, and the smith is "transhuman" existence from which rebirth results during the initiatory process. The burden of the doctrine of rebirth to the later Hindu tradition should be studied in the context of the warrior cult. Since the "warrior's principal ordeal consists precisely in vanquishing the adversary," it follows that the rebirth signified is accomplished in this life. Thus the connection between the Vedic Aryans concept of themselves as "twice born" and the male parthenogenesis myths is not too difficult to discover once the male bonding of warriorhood is called to mind.

Birth without the aid of a mother is a commonplace in male initiation rites. Initiations at puberty, as well as the initiations for entrance into a secret society, and the initiation requisite for obtaining a higher religious status seem to share "a sort of structural common denominator."[37] The male dominance of religion in India is rooted in the assumptions of secret lore known only to the males. The exclusion of women from the rites of initiation goes without saying. Male birthing can be seen as the ultimate statement of total power in the universe. The psychological factors that demand such a mythic statement are entwined in the spiritual and political values of the male bands. The fact that in the days of Indo-European expansion, the captured females were a primary source of booty cannot be over-looked when examining the negligible role of women in Indic religions. The absence of the mother in the male parthenogenesis myths is an exaggerated statement of a view of women as hindrances to spiritual attainment and as totally dispensable even in the area of mothering.

> *The Mahābhārata*, with all its interest in paternity, is largely indifferent to motherhood. Rare are the passages where the mother reveals herself as the loving nurse or makes any demands on her sons. After having made herself useful as a wife by becoming a mother, the woman seems to recede from view.[38]

---

[36] Mircea Eliade, *Rites and Symbols of Initiation* (New York: Harper Torchbooks, 1958), 86–87.
[37] Ibid., p. 3.
[38] Van Buitenen, vol. 2, 206.

Great Warriors like Droṇa and Kṛpa have absolutely no trace of contact with the feminine either in their birth or in their nurture. It should be small wonder that they would be celebrated as possessors of invincible weaponry that fueled the ferocity of ancient heroes.

> The behaviour of the Indo-European warrior bands offers certain points of resemblance to the secret fraternities of primitive societies. In both alike, the members of the group terrorize women and non-initiates and in some sort exercise a "right of rapine," a custom which, in diluted form, is still found in the popular traditions of Europe and the Caucasus.[39]

Mircea Eliade has shown the strong bonds that exist among shamans, smiths, and warriors because of their concerns with techniques and mystiques of fire. "The Sanskrit term *tapas* finally developed the sense of ascetic effort in general, but its original meaning was extreme heat."[40] The heat of *tapas* is at once both internal and external, spiritual and physical. It is built up by restraint (*yoga*, discipline) which in turn releases extraordinary power:

> This sacred power, which causes both the shaman's heat and the heating of the warrior, can be transformed, differentiated, given various colorings, by subsequent efforts. The Indian word *Kratu*, which had begun by denoting the "energy peculiar to the ardent force and ardor, courage, love of combat," and by extension power and majesty in general, finally came to mean the "force of the pious man, which enable him to follow the prescriptions of *ṛta* and to attain happiness."[41]

Eliade's sense that what was originally warrior-centered effort "finally came to mean 'the force of the pious man'" may be close to the historical and political reality of the loss of spiritual ascendancy by the warriors of ancient India. The *Mahābhārata*, however, affords countless examples that may help to reconstruct the warrior basis of a great portion of the Indian spiritual systems.

Asceticism is the key to the procurement of invincible weapons in several myths of the epic other than the male parthenogenesis stories. Arjuna Pāṇḍava's yogic concentration gives him access to Śiva and the ultimate weapon, *Pāśupata*, which had been used to slay the Daityas (*Mahābhārata* 7.57.19). Arjuna's early visit to the realm of his father, Indra, in order to obtain weapons is so elaborate in its classical Sanskrit style that it is only by oblique references that we find Arjuna's capability to "see the Gods" is caused by his austerities (*tapasā*: 3.37.28). Arjuna's birth is a celebrated example of female parthenogenesis. Under a curse that prevents him on

---

[39] Eliade, p. 83.
[40] Ibid., p. 86.
[41] Ibid.

pain of death from lying with a woman, the king practices austerities to obtain a son through his wife's power to conceive by thinking of a god. Pāṇḍu requires Kuntī to think on Indra, and in preparation she joins him in the practice of austerities. After she keeps a year-long vow and undertakes "awesome austerities," Indra responds that he will give Pāṇḍu a son who will destroy all his enemies. At the birth of Arjuna the sky opens, a voice promises that he will obtain all celestial weapons, and then a pageant of cosmic wonders takes place. The presence of an actual mother who finds favor with the god through austerities and thus produces a world savior has many elements that contrast with the male parthenogenesis myths. In the male myths, the presence of the female is a hindrance to austerities and the birth of the savior takes place without human contact.

Non-womb birth may be the ultimate statement of male exclusivity and total supremacy. Psychoanalytic criticism points out that the substitute birth place such as a jar, trough, or water pot are actually female symbols. The birthplace of Kṛpa in the reed bed is the most difficult to associate with the cluster of goddess symbols. While it is true that reeds grow in a marshy place, and that water may be the primal symbol of the goddess,[42] it would seem that the reed bed as the actual source of arrows was used with intentional symbolic content for a warrior myth. The warrior connection underlying the parthenogenic births of saviors or seers with human mothers should also be considered. The human mother may be a goddess symbol but the political intention of the myth often reduces her to the role of "container."

The relationship of parthenogenesis to the birth of heroes or saviors is attested in many ancient cultures. The birth of Jesus Christ is accomplished without the conjunction of sexual gametes (*Luke* 1.30-38). Gotama Buddha's birth story, as told by Aśvaghosa, has several parthenogenic elements. "Buddhas naturally being born in a supernatural way . . . the Buddha was born free from the ordinary defilements of birth."[43] The later Mahāyāna tradition seems to have expanded the parthenogenic details.[44] The real or shadow presence of a father figure is almost always given concrete mention in the female parthenogenesis myths while the mother is often dispensable in the "non-womb" births. So distorted does the mythic intent become as myth-makers try to envision the vast alterations in the universe that a great man's birth causes, that the mothers often undertake

---

[42] Gimbutas, p. 112ff.

[43] Aśvaghoṣa, p. 3, note on verses 10 and 11.

[44] *The Sacred Books of the East*, vol. XLIX tr. E.B. Cowell (Oxford: Clarendon Press, 1894), 4–6, verses, 15–34.

unbearable suffering without comment. Indra is said to have been in his mother's womb a thousand months and many autumns (4.18.4). The Chinese sage Lao Tzu was conceived "some sixty two years before when his mother had admired a falling star, and after so many years in the womb, he was able to speak as soon as he was born."[45] The parthenogenic power of Zeus is seen as an alternative to the female entirely:

> Zeus to Dionysius:
> Enter now life's secret portal, motherless mystery;
> Lo, I break mine own body for thy sake....
> Come enter this, my male womb.[46]

While miraculous birth without the aid of a mother occurs in the complicated Greek myths concerning the birth of Athena from Zeus, the fact that Zeus swallowed his wife, Metis, who was about give birth to Athena, creates a case of male parthenogenesis dependent on the female for uterine gestation. "A myth in which Zeus swalowed a wife enabled the Athena myth to be rationalized, to the extent that she could be provided with a mother. (In the earlier stage the male seed sufficed for procreation....)"[47] What is meant by an "earlier stage" to the Hesiod commentator is the birth myth of a Hittite weather god, Kumarbi. Like Kuntī's son Karṇa, Athena is also traditionally said to have been born fully armed.[48] The male parthenogenic myths of the *Mahābhārata* provide what may be a missing hermeneutic key not only to the accounts of parthenogeneic birth in the Taoist, Buddhist, Hindu, and Christian religions, but to the stories of ancient Greece and Rome as well. Saviors are not dependent on maternal sources for their potency. They are born with predestination to power.

The underlying unity of parthenogenic myths is not easy to see even in the epic itself. If the text in Book Three or Puranic versions of Skanda's birth are used as the basis for interpretive analysis, there is almost no mention of military concerns. Without the warrior purpose, surely rooted in ancient cultic practices, the myths degenerate into literary pieces, often with a type of sporting anti-female emphasis. One reason for this may be that ancient cultic

---

[45] Holmes Welch, *Taoism* (Boston: Beacon Press, 1966), p. 1.

[46] Jane Ellen Harrison, *Epilogomena to the Study of Greek Religion* (Cambridge, England: The University Press), p. 33.

[47] *Hesiod, Theogony*, ed. M.L. West (Oxford: The Clarendon Press, 1966), p. 401. Cf. verses 886–990; 924–26. Notes, pp. 401–13. See also text ed. and tr. by Hugh G. Evelyn-White (Cambridge, Massachusetts: Harvard University Press, 1954), pp. 143–45.

[48] West, p. 412, commentary on line 924. "Although the following lines emphasize Athena's warlike temperament, it is not explicitly said that she was born fully armed. Stesichorus is said to have been the first to record this detail."

symbols and metaphors come to be taken in a literal sense in later or non-cultic settings:

> A myth may degenerate into an epic legend, a ballad or a romance, or survive only in the attenuated form of 'superstitions,' customs, nostalgias, and so on; for all this, it loses neither its essence nor its significance. . . . But the patterns that have come down from the distant past never disappear; they do not lose the possibility of being brought back to life.[49]

The three tales of male parthenogenesis help to bring some of the ancient Aryan *kṣatriya* spirituality back into view. The purpose of reconstructing the warrior codes is to examine the ancient texts for sources of the distinctive world view that the Aryans brought to India. Such a reconstruction will also help to show the reasons for a residue of a warrior out-look in the Indian religious tradition. As the Brahmanic tradition grew intellectually, religiously and even politically dominant, warrior cult declined; the vitality of the old warrior tales waned. Brahmanization of the epic may be one source of the loss of the warrior connection to spiritual prowess, but the epic, as presently constituted, retains strong evidence of archaic warrior motifs which go back to the Vedic *soma* cult and the era of Aryan expansion in North India.

---

[49] Mircea Eliade, *Patterns in Comparative Religion* (New York: New American Library, 1958), 431–32.

TWO KṚṢṆAS, THREE KṚṢṆAS, FOUR KṚṢṆAS, MORE KṚṢṆAS: DARK INTERACTIONS IN THE *MAHĀBHĀRATA*

ALF HILTEBEITEL

In a recent essay on Arjuna and Kṛṣṇa as the "two Kṛṣṇas on one chariot",[1] I endeavored to update a discussion begun in my book *The Ritual of Battle*[2] on the subject of interactions between the different figures in the *Mahābhārata* who are given the name or epithet Kṛṣṇa/Kṛṣṇā, "black". The essay suggests that it is in particular in his destructive collaboration with Kṛṣṇa on the war chariot that Arjuna is identified as a second Kṛṣṇa, and that further, in carrying out his destructive role, he evokes affinities with the Śiva of the *pralaya*. It is important now to look back at the total configuration of heroes and heroines who bear this same name.

For one thing, as already noted in the same article, they have consistent theological affinites with the most august deities of the *bhakti* universe:[3] Kṛṣṇa with Viṣṇu, Arjuna with Śiva, Draupadī with the Goddess, and—as Bruce Sullivan has observed—Vyāsa (Kṛsna Dvaipāyana, the "Island-Born Kṛṣṇa") with Brahmā.[4] We will not enter here into the problems attendent upon this interpretation of the role of Vyāsa, whom the epic in some possibly late passages identifies as a "portion of Nārāyaṇa" (i.e., Viṣṇu), other than to point out that Brahmā is himself a "portion of Nārāyaṇa", born from the lotus that emerges from Viṣṇu's navel.[5] For Vyāsa, as a "portion of Nārāyaṇa", to fulfill the Brahmā-like role of "grandfather" (*pitāmaha*) of the main epic

---

[1] See Alf Hiltebeitel, "The Two Kṛṣṇas on One Chariot: Upaniṣadic Imagery and Epic Mythology", *History of Religions*, 24 (1984), pp. 1–26.

[2] *The Ritual of Battle: Krishna in the Mahābhārata* (Ithaca: Cornell University Press, 1976), pp. 60–76.

[3] See Madeleine Biardeau, *Études de mythologie hindoue*, Vol. I, *Cosmogonies purāṇiques* (Paris: École Française d'Extrême Orient, 1981), passim.

[4] See Hiltebeitel, "Two Kṛṣṇas on One Chariot", pp. 5–6, 23–26; on Vyāsa and Brahmā, see Bruce Sullivan, "The Seer of the Fifth *Veda*: Kṛṣṇa Dvaipāyana in the *Mahābhārata*", Ph.D. diss., University of Chicago, 1984, especially pp. 160–229.

[5] Sullivan and I seem to have each arrived at this point independently; see his "Seer of the Fifth *Veda*", p. 229.

heroes and progenitor of the forces that usher in the "dark" *kali* age is not incongruous, especially when one examines how he works these things out in collaboration with the other "dark" figures: not only Kṛṣṇa, Draupadī, and Arjuna, but his mother Kālī [another word for "Black"]-Satyavatī.

Our main interest in this essay will be in the symbolic lexicon of dark interactions between these figures. In weaving their story around them, the epic poets occasionally make it clear that the names themselves may be employed as means to indicate especially significant rapports. It is, however, a guarded symbolism, subtly nuanced, and never over-used. Indeed, as is most evident in the evocations of Arjuna and Kṛṣṇa as the "two Kṛṣṇas on one chariot", one has the impression that it is reserved to highlight specific images, themes, and scenes. The intent becomes clearest in passages where the poets refer to two or all three of the Kṛṣṇas at once, juxtaposing the names against each other or combining them together to heighten the dramatic and symbolic impact. Leaving aside Arjuna and Kṛṣṇa as the "two Kṛṣṇas", a theme which we have treated elsewhere as extensively as possible,[6] let us look at some of the passages of this type. The discussion will follow the interplay of Kṛṣṇas in terms of the remaining possibilities of their interaction: first Draupadī and Kṛṣṇa, and then the three together. Examples of the remaining lexical pairings of Arjuna solely with Draupadī, or of any of the others with Vyāsa, were not found[7]—a fact of possible significance since it may be proposed that, as is the case with Arjuna, all of the others are called Kṛṣṇa (or Kṛṣṇā) primarily in terms of their relation to Kṛṣṇa.

1. *Draupadī and Kṛṣṇa*

Throughout the epic, there seem to be two main contexts in which Draupadī and Kṛṣṇa are doubly referred to as Kṛṣṇa/Kṛṣṇā. One is in connection with a theological conundrum. The other has a specific focus in the narrative.

The first concerns the ironies and theological puzzles involved in the "love" triangle between Kṛṣṇa, Arjuna, and Draupadī. As was pointed

[6] See in addition to my "Two Kṛṣṇas" article my "Brothers, Friends, and Charioteers: Parallel Episodes in the Irish and Indian Epics", in Edgar Polomé, ed., "Homage to Georges Dumézil", *Journal of Indo-European Studies*, Monograph 3 (1982), pp. 85–111.

[7] The determination of these patterns has been arrived at simply by checking all references to Draupadī as Kṛṣṇā and to the other figures as Kṛṣṇas in Soren Sorensen, *An Index to the Names in the Mahābhārata* (Delhi: Motilal Banarsidass, 1963).

out in *The Ritual of Battle*, the marriage of Arjuna and Draupadī "brings up a problem of myth and epic: if Viṣṇu's consort is Śrī-Lakṣmī, what is Kṛṣṇa's relationship with Draupadī, Śrī incarnate",[8] once she is married to Arjuna and his brothers? The complexity of this question is enriched now by our recognition of Arjuna's affinities not only with Indra but with Śiva.[9] It would seem that insofar as Kṛṣṇa and Vyāsa are implicated in arranging Draupadī's marriage to Arjuna, they do so not only with an eye to arranging a "royal" marriage between the incarnations of Śrī and Indra,[10] but with the aim of carrying forward the destructive implications of a union between the dark and fiery (fire-born) Draupadī as a form of the Goddess, and the yogic and ascetic prowess of Arjuna as a multiform of Śiva.

With these "background" themes in mind, let us first note that it is certainly the problematic of the "love" triangle that is evoked when Satyabhāmā, "Kṛṣṇa's chief wife, circumambulated Kṛṣṇā" (*tam kṛṣṇāṃ kṛṣṇamahiṣī cakārābhipradakṣiṇam*; 3.224.16ab[11]) to thank Draupadī for answering how she keeps five men in tow: "Tell me, O Pāñcālī, about your glorious knowledge of female sexuality by which, O Kṛṣṇā, Kṛṣna may always do as I wish" (*mama ācakṣva pāñcāli yaśasyam bhagavedanam / yena kṛṣṇe bhavennityam mama kṛṣṇo vaśānugaḥ*; 3.222.7). And it is the same undercurrent of triangular affections that lies behind the curious scene where Draupadī flashes anger at Kṛṣṇa for telling Yudhiṣṭhira that Arjuna has one faulty mark on his body—his cheek bones are a little too high—that leads him to perpetual hardship (*duḥkha*) and constant travels on the roads: "But Kṛṣṇā Draupadī looked askance at Kṛṣṇa, angrily (*kṛṣṇā tu draupadī kṛṣṇam tiryaksāsūyamaikṣata*). And the slayer of Keśi [Kṛṣṇa] approved her show of affection (*praṇayam*)" (14.89.10). These passages thus concentrate their references to Kṛṣṇa and Kṛṣṇā-Draupadī in order to heighten the theological and mythological ambiguities implied in their separate terrestrial ties of love and marriage.[12]

The second context, which presupposes the destructive themes implicit

---

[8] See Hiltebeitel, *Ritual of Battle*, p. 83.

[9] See Hiltebeitel, "Śiva, the Goddess, and the Disguises of the Pāṇḍavas and Draupadī", *History of Religions*, 20 (1980), pp. 153–168; idem, "Two Kṛṣṇas on One Chariot", pp. 5–6, 19–26.

[10] See Hiltebeitel, *Ritual of Battle*, pp. 79–85.

[11] All *Mahābhārata* references are to the Poona Critical Edition (CE).

[12] Cf. 4.8.17—Draupadī introduces herself to Sudeṣṇā, queen of Matsya, at the beginning of her period of disguise: "I have pleased Satyabhāmā the beloved chief wife of Kṛṣṇa, and Kṛṣṇā, wife of the Pāṇḍavas, the unique beauty of the Kurus" (*ārādhyaṃ satyabhāmāṃ kṛṣṇasya mahiṣīm priyām / kṛṣṇāṃ ca bhāryāṃ pāṇḍūnāṃ kurūṇāmekasundarīm*).

in the first, takes us to the heart of the epic narrative. Let us recall[13] a passage which perhaps more than any other demonstrates that the coincidence of names is of dramatic significance. Just before Kṛṣṇa sets off on his pre-war embassy to the Kuru court, a speech by Draupadī concludes the Pāṇdavas' vascillating deliberations over how Kṛṣṇa should represent them. Challenging Kṛṣṇa to vent his wrath on the Kauravas, Draupadī grasps her "deep blue/black mass of hair" (*sunīlam . . . keśapakṣam*) with her left hand: "And the lotus-eyed one of elephant gait, having approached the lotus-eyed one, her eyes filled with tears, Kṛṣṇā to Kṛṣṇa said: . . . 'unless I see Duḥśāsana's dark arm [*bhujaṃ śyāmam*] cut off and covered with dust, what peace will there be in my heart'"? (5.80.33–39). The Sanskrit of the central descriptive verse is clearly composed to confront the two figures in terms of their lotus-eyes (*padmākṣi, puṇḍarīkākṣa*) and dark names: *padmākṣi puṇḍarīkākṣam upetya gajagāminī / aśrupūrṇekṣanā kṛṣṇā kṛṣṇam vacanamabravīt* (35). Moreover, their confrontation is framed by references to Draupadī's "dark" hair and the "dark" arm of Duḥśāsana. This is of course an allusion to the dragging of Draupadī's hair by Duḥśāsana in the Kaurava *sabhā*, and a further look at additional descriptions of that scene will show that the passage just cited is not unique in employing such a lexicon. For instance, when Kṛṣṇa's embassy to the Kuru court has ended with the recognition that war is inevitable, Kṛṣṇa meets, before returning to the Pāṇḍavas, with the Pāṇḍavas' mother Kuntī. The latter, amongst her messages to her sons and daughter-in-law, tells Kṛṣṇa (her nephew): "O Mādhava, say to that auspicious and glorious Kṛṣṇā, O Kṛṣṇa" (*brūyā mādhava kalyāṇīṃ kṛṣṇām kṛṣṇa yaśasvinīm*) that she (Kuntī) is rankled not so much at the loss of the kingdom or the defeat at dice as the recollection of "that great dark woman" (*bṛhatī śyāmā*) weeping and insulted in the *sabhā* (5.135.11 and 17a). Most importantly, the key scene in the *Sabhāparvan* also employs the same thematic lexicon: "Then he [Duḥśāsana] said to her, having violently seized Kṛṣṇā by her black (*kṛṣṇa*) hair: 'Cry out for protection of Kṛṣṇa and Jiṣṇu, to Hari and Nara. I will still pull you'" (2.26.26).[14]

One notes how the poets repeatedly reinforce the links between the identical names by associating them with other "black" referents:

---

[13] See Hiltebeitel, "Draupadī's Hair", in Madeleine Biardeau, ed., *Autour de la déesse hindoue*, in *Puruṣārtha*, 5 (1981), p. 199.

[14] *tato 'bravīttāṃ prasabhaṃ nigṛhya*
keśaṣu kṛṣṇeṣu tadā kṛṣṇām
kṛṣṇaṃ ca jiṣṇuṃ ca hariṃ naraṃ ca
trāṇāya vikrośa nayāmi hi tvam (2.60.26)

Draupadī's hair, her dark complexion, Duḥśāsana's arm. Furthermore, without calling him Kṛṣṇa, the last two passages also evoke Arjuna. Just after she has told Kṛṣṇa what to say to Draupadī, Kuntī tells Kṛṣṇa to urge Arjuna to "follow the path of Draupadī" (*draupadyāḥ padavīṃ cara*; 5.135.19).[15] And Duḥśāsana taunts Draupadī to call not only on Kṛṣṇa or Hari, but Jiṣṇu or Nara, the latter being names primarily associated with Arjuna.[16]

Furthermore, Duḥśāsana's taunt at the hair-pulling is nearly identical with one of the two main early "interpolated" verses that describe Draupadī's prayer to Kṛṣṇa to rescue her at the time of her disrobing.[17] There, just as Duḥśāsana begins to try to undress her, "Yajñasenī [Draupadī] cried out to Kṛṣṇa, Viṣṇu, Hari and Nara for protection [*kṛṣṇaṃ ca viṣṇum ca hariṃ naraṃ ca / trāṇāya vikrośati*]. Then Dharma, concealed, the magnamimous, having a multitude of garments, covered her" (2.544*, notes). One will note the nearly exact correspondences between Duḥśāsana's provocation, which the Critical Edition includes, and Draupadī's actual plea, which it omits. The only variation is in the second name, where Jiṣṇu contrasts with Viṣṇu. But a fair sample of manuscripts have Jiṣṇu instead of Viṣṇu in the disrobing speech as well.[18] Jiṣṇu would certainly be the *lectio difficilior*, so it is quite likely that these two verses were once fundamentally identical and meant to be connected. Both are also in the *triṣṭubh* meter, which may indicate textual antiquity.[19] Such considerations raise questions, of course, about the excision of one such verse from the Critical Edition and the selection of the other. One could argue that Duḥśāsana's provocative words make most sense as an anticipation of an actual "original" plea by Draupadī for help rather than as a coincidence, or an isolated verse seized upon at some later stage of the text's development as the prototype for an interpolation. In any case, the close verbal correspondence between the one verse at the hair-pulling and the other at the disrobing provides an epic foreshadowing of the persistent doubling of themes noticed in Bhaṭṭa Nārāyaṇa's *Veṇī-saṃhāra*: the *keśāmbarakārṣaṇa*, "the pulling of the hair and the garments".[20]

---

[15] See other citations in Hiltebeitel, "Draupadī's Hair", pp. 200–201.

[16] On Jiṣṇu as also an epithet for Śiva, see Hiltebeitel, "Two Kṛṣṇas on One Chariot", p. 19.

[17] See Hiltebeitel, "Draupadī's Garments", *Indo-Iranian Journal*, 22 (1980), pp. 98–101.

[18] See the CE notes to this passage.

[19] See Mary Carroll Smith, "The Core of India's Great Epic", Ph.D. diss., Harvard University, 1973, passim.

[20] See Hiltebeitel, "Draupadī's Hair", p. 183.

2. *Kṛṣṇa, Arjuna, and Draupadī*

There are many scenes where the interplay of Kṛṣṇa, Arjuna, and Draupadī is pivotal: Draupadī's *svayaṃvara*; Kṛṣṇa's absence from the dice match; his promise to Draupadī in the forest that she will once again be the queen of kings; and more generally their mutually supportive roles. The three also combine with the fourth Kṛṣṇa Vyāsa to convince Yudhiṣṭhira to abandon his guilt-ridden determination to renouce his hard-won kingship after the war and to undergo his coronation. But there are only a few instances where the epic poets play upon this interplay in terms of their "dark" names. These instances are nonetheless instructive.

Curiously, the two most concentrated passages, the only ones using the term *kṛṣṇa* to refer to all three figures in brief connected passages, occur in exchanges between Kṛpa and Duryodhana. If this is more than a coincidence, I have no explanation for it.

First, in the *Virāṭaparvan*, Kṛpa addresses Duryodhana and the Kauravas while their cattle raid has been arrested by the eunuch Bṛhannaḍā, whom the Kauravas correctly suspect to be Arjuna: "On reflection, an encounter with Pārtha [Arjuna] is not to our advantage. Singly he rescued the Kurus, singly he sated Agni, singly he bore five years of *brahmacarya*, singly, having lifted up Subhadrā, he challenged Kṛṣṇa to a chariot duel. In this very forest Kṛṣṇa [Arjuna] won back the abducted Kṛṣṇā [Daupadī]" (*ekaḥ subhadrāmāropya dvairathe kṛṣṇamāhvayat / asminneva vane kṛṣṇo hṛtāṃ kṛṣṇāmavājayat*; 4.44.5–6). The emphasis throughout the passage is on Arjuna's autonomous prowess. But this alleged independence is set off in contrast with the concluding words which emphasize Arjuna's consolidarity with the other two Kṛṣṇas, Kṛṣṇa and Draupadī. He is credited with playing the major role in rescuing Draupadī from Jayadratha. And according to Kṛpa, he fought off Kṛṣṇa after abducting the latter's sister Subhadrā. Most ironically, however, unless there is an unknown variant, this latter point of Kṛpa's is untrue. It was Kṛṣṇa's brother Balarāma who wanted to fight Arjuna for abducting Subhadrā, and it was Kṛṣṇa who dissuaded him. The passage thus jars its audience, if it recalls that episode, into appreciating that Arjuna's consolidarity with the other two Kṛṣṇas is deeper than even Kṛpa describes. Indeed, it is possible that the alleged "two chariot" (*dvairatha*) duel which Kṛpa recalls is actually an evocation and inticipation of the "single chariot" (*ekaratha*) which Arjuna and Kṛṣṇa will ride together in battle, the symbol of their perfect complementarity.

The centrality of Subhadrā to this triad is still more evident in the second of the two exchanges. This time, following upon the death of

Karṇa, it is Duryodhana who speaks, answering Kṛpa's counsel to make peace with the Pāṇḍavas before all is lost. How will Yudhiṣṭhira believe him after the deception of the dice match? asks Duryodhana (9.4.7). And so he continues, in a speech that is for him unusually self-searching and self-condemning:

> 8. "So also was Kṛṣṇa Hṛṣīkeśa deceived by me when he was serving as a messenger, delighting in the welfare of the Pārthas. That act was opposed [by Kṛpa and others]. How will he consider my word, O brahman?
>
> 9. "Surely in as much as Kṛṣṇā [Draupadī] wept, having arrived in the middle of the *sabhā*, Kṛṣṇa will not forget that, nor the taking of the kingdom.
>
> 10. "Both having a single life-breath, the two Kṛṣṇas [Kṛṣṇa and Arjuna] are firmly united with one-another. What was once formerly heard, that I now see, O revered one.
>
> 11. "Keśava [Kṛṣṇa] sleeps sorrowfully, having heard that his sister's son [Subhadrā's son Abhimanyu] is slain. We have committed an offense [*agas*] against him. How would he pardon me?
>
> 12. "Since the destruction of Abhimanyu Arjuna obtains no refuge; implored, how will he make an effort for my welfare?
>
> [13–15. Duryodhana calls to mind Bhīma's "terrible vow" to kill him and the animosity of Nakula and Sahadeva and Draupadī's brothers, and continues:]
>
> 16. "Then too Kṛṣṇā [Draupadī], wearing a single cloth and in her period, was tormented by Duḥśāsana in the middle of the *sabhā* while the whole world was looking.
>
> 17. "The Pāṇḍavas now remember her, thus undressed and distressed. Those foe-scorchers are unable to turn back from battle.
>
> 18. "And when Kṛṣṇā Draupadī, the suffering Kṛṣṇā, performs fierce *tapas* for the sake of my destruction [*yadā ca draupadī kṛṣṇā madvināśāya duḥkhitā ugram tepe tapaḥ kṛṣṇā*] and the success of her husbands' aims, she always lies down on the ground [*sthaṇḍile*] so long as the hostilities continue.
>
> 19. "Vāsudeva's [Kṛṣṇa's] uterine sister [Subhadrā], having cast off honor and pride [*nikṣipya manaṃ darpam ca*], having assumed the role of Kṛṣṇā's servant, always acts in obedience to her [*kṛṣṇāyāḥ preṣyavad-bhūtvā śuśrūṣāṃ kurute sadā*]

20. "Thus all is ablaze[21] and can never be extinguished/cooled [*iti, sarvaṃ samunnaddham na nirvāti kathaṃcana*]. On account of the death of Abhimanyu, how can he [Yudhiṣṭhira?] be reconciled with me"? (9.4.8–20).

It is clear that the poets have given considerable weight to the orchestration of the names Kṛṣṇa/Kṛṣṇā. The central two verses (9 and 10) supply three successive lines with the names Kṛṣṇā/Kṛṣṇa/Kṛṣṇau (the dual) as the focal end of the first *pāda*. And then, after describing the individual reactions of the male heroes, Duryodhana thinks of Draupadī by repeatedly referring to her by the name Kṛṣṇā, including the double reference in verse 18. But it is not just a matter of poetic device to bring these names together. The passage shows that the interplay of the three Kṛṣṇas is concerned with, and evocative of, certain specific epic themes. In fact, the passage singles out three such themes, ones which we find persistently in other instances where the three Kṛṣṇas are involved. First is Draupadī's humiliation in the *sabhā* (see verses 9 and 16–17), the "pulling of the hair and the garments". Second is the death of Karṇa, the occasion of the speech itself, and more specifically the focus of Duryodhana's most haunted remark in verse 10: now that Karṇa has been slain, he sees what he had formerly only heard, that Karṇa would not be able to withstand the two Kṛṣṇas united on one chariot.

The third theme, however, involves the three not in pairs but as a triad. It is the death of Arjuna's son and Kṛṣṇa's newphew Abhimanyu (see verses 11–12), and the subordination of Subhadrā—Arjuna's wife and Kṛṣṇa's sister—to Draupadī. It is, of course, this same theme which Kṛpa mentions in the *Virāṭaparvan* passage cited earler when he warns Duryodhana against fighting Arjuna-Bṛhannaḍā: "Singly, having lifted up Subhadrā he challenged Kṛṣṇa to a chariot duel . . ." (4.44.5). It thus deserves some further consideration.

As Duryodhana says, Subhadrā "always acts in obedience" to Draupadī. Her subordination, however, does not begin with the death of her son, as Duryodhana's speech might suggest. It begins when she returns with Arjuna to Hāstinapura after her marriage by abduction. There, encountering her co-wife Draupadī for the first time, Subhadrā follows Arjuna's urgent bidding and changes from wearing red silk "into the dress/disguise of a cowmaid" (*gopālikāvapuḥ*; 1.213.17). As argued elsewhere, this *gopa* "disguise" is reminiscent of her brother Kṛṣṇa, who also—in full

---

[21] See the commentary of Arjunamiśra, glossing *samunnaddham*, "bound up", "swollen", "raised up", by *dīptam*, "ablaze". I follow here the late nineteenth-century Roy and Dutt translations of the *Mahābhārata*.

awareness of the epic poets—takes on his famous cowherd "disguise" as a child and youth.[22] Abhimanyu, Subhadrā and Arjuna's son, then carries forward some of these associations. He is repeatedly described in terms evocative of his maternal uncle: lotus eyes, having all of Kṛṣṇa's virtues and more, Kṛṣṇa's favorite newphew, he even bears a *cakra* (actually a chariot wheel) as his final weapon before dying.[23] But most important, he is an additional Kṛṣṇa, "black" like his father and uncle, his "face dark as the blue lotus" (*indīvaraśyāmam . . . mukham* 7.55.3), and sometimes called Kārṣṇi, "son of Kṛṣṇa" (i.e., Arjuna) to evoke these associations. Most significantly, this name for Abhimanyu is used almost exclusively in the war books, specifically in the scenes building up to his death. Moreover, the name sometimes evokes his connection with the "two Kṛṣṇas" most clearly. For instance: "Whatever weapon he received from Vāsudeva and Arjuna, that Kārṣṇi displayed no differently from the two Kṛṣṇas" (*adarśayata tat kārṣṇi kṛṣṇābhyām aviśeṣayan*; 7.37.15).

During the life of Abhimanyu, his mother Subhadrā's subordination to Draupadī is that of the junior wife to the senior wife, and perhaps of the cowherd theme to the kṣatriya theme. But with Abhimanyu's death, the subordination has much "darker" implications. As her name, which means "very blessed" or "very auspicious", indicates, Subhadrā is Arjuna's auspicious wife, the bearer of his and his dynasty's "fame" (*yaśas*) through the line of succession that extends, miraculously (or, in other words, thanks to Kṛṣṇa), through Abhimanyu to Parikṣit.[24] For her to serve Draupadī while the latter undertakes her destructive war-long *tapas*, as Duryodhana describes, thus indicates the subordination of the auspicious side of the Goddess to the side devoted to destruction, impurity (sleeping on the ground), and death. Moreover, as Duryodhana says, it is all three Kṛṣṇas who are so dedicated, and whose "dark" natures are thus united in this common purpose: "all is ablaze, and can never be extinguished".

---

[22] See above all Madeleine Biardeau, "Études de mythologie hindoue (V) Part II, Bhakti et avatāra", section 2. "L'avatāra, modèle divin du roi", *Bulletin de l'École Française d'Extrême Orient*, 45 (1978), pp. 204–237; cf. also Hiltebeitel, "The Burning of the Forest Myth", in Bardwell L. Smith, ed., *Hinduism: New Essays in the History of Religions* (Leiden: E.J. Brill, 1976), p. 217; idem, "Epic Kṛṣṇa at Mathurā", in Doris Srinivasan, ed., *Mathurā: A Cultural Heritage* (New Delhi: Manohar and American Institute of Indian Studies, 1988), 93–102.

[23] See Hiltebeitel, *Ritual of Battle*, pp. 336–353.

[24] See Hiltebeitel, "Burning of the Forest", p. 217.

THE ORIGINAL DAKṢA SAGA

KLAUS KLOSTERMAIER

The story of Dakṣa's confrontation with Śiva is one of the best known and most widely studied myths in Indian literature. It will be found in nearly every summary of Indian mythology, old or new. Each such summary would also comment on the many and wide variations found in a great number of sources. Thus Wendy D.O'Flaherty in *Hindu Myths* (Baltimore: Penguin, 1975) offers her readers two versions: one from the *Mahābhārata* and one from the *Varāha Purāṇa*. In her evaluation and interpretation she follows D.C. Sircar, who in his renowned work on the *Śākta Pīṭhas*[1] provided in an appendix under the title "Evolution of the Dakṣayajña Story", a selection of texts, leading from *Ṛgveda* 10, 91 (Prajāpati's incest with his daughter) through *Śatapatha Brāhmaṇa* I, 7, 4 (a commentary on this), *Aitareya Brāhmaṇa* 3, 33 (Rudra's piercing of the sacrifice), *Gopatha Brāhmaṇa* 2, 1 (Prajāpati's refusal to sacrifice to Rudra) to the rendition of the full-fledged myth in *Mahābhārata* 12, 283, 17–33, *Bhāgavata-Purāṇa* 4, 5, 14–21, *Kūrma-Purāṇa* 1, 15, 60–64, to the account in *Devībhāgavata-Purāṇa* VII, 30, which connects the origin of the Śakti Pīthas with the Dakṣa story. Sircar states his opinion that the latter development represents an addition to the original story which was made by Śāktas at a relatively late time.

What was the original story? Following the suggestion as regards its evolutions made by Sircar, we would have to assume that at its core it describes the conflict between Vedic sacrificial religion and Rudra-Śiva religion which in the epic-puranic phase was reconceived into a conflict between Vaiṣṇavism and Śaivism.[2]

My own attempts to harmonize the various accounts and to find the original story have led me to the assumption that the core of it consists of the record of the Śaivite conquest of Kanakhala, a *tīrtha* close to today's Hardwār, which was of great importance to Śaivites, Vaiṣṇavas and Śāktas alike, and was linked to an important Vedic settlement associated

---

[1] First published in the *Journal of the Royal Asiatic Society of Bengal*, vol. XIV, no. 1 (1948), 1–108 (reprint).

[2] O'Flaherty, p. 118.

with a famous patriarch Dakṣa. Added to this story were other features designed to connect it with Vedic times as well as with later developments. As a story of the occupation of a holy place of importance it provided legitimacy to the Śaiva sect of the Pāśupatas and in connection with it to the legitimacy of other Śaiva and Śākta sanctuaries in a predominantly non-Śaivite society.

All accounts of the Dakṣa story which provide a geographic location of the event place it at Gaṅgādvāra, the point where the Ganges, India's most sacred river since time immemorial, breaks through the mountains. It is identified with Māyāpura and Haridvāra/Haradvāra of later texts. The place names of the *tīrtha*s along the first few miles of the Ganges after it has emerged from the mountains reveal the competition between different major sects: from Brahmakuṇḍa (today called *Hari kī paiḍī*) one reaches Viṣṇughāt, then one proceeds to Māyādevī, Narāyaṇī Śilā, Nīladhāra, Bilvakeśvara before coming to Kanakhala, where one finds Dakṣeśvara Mahādeva, Satīkuṇḍa, Bhīmagoda and Vīrabhadreśvara.[3]

Of all these places Kanakhala was considered the most important *tīrtha*. As a *Mahābhārata* text has it: The Gaṅgā is the great *tīrtha* of *Kaliyuga*, the holiest of all rivers, and it is especially holy at Kanakhala and at Prayāga.[4] Several of the epic and puranic accounts of Dakṣa's sacrifice explicitly mention Kanakhala as the venue.[5]

Without connection to the Dakṣa story Kanakhala is several times mentioned in the *Mahābhārata* as a *tīrtha* equal to Prayāga[6] and a *tīrtha* where one can gain merit equal to an *aśvamedha* by bathing after having fasted for three nights.[7] It is prominently mentioned in the *Tīrtha-yātrā* section and its holiness is pointed out to Yudhiṣṭhira in connection with

---

[3] See information in *Kalyāṇa: Tīrthāṅka*, vol. 31, no. 1 (1957), 62ff.
[4] On the Ganges as *tīrtha*, see P.V. Kane, *History of Dharmaśāstra*, vol. IV, 585ff.
[5] *Śiva-Purāṇa-Rudrasaṁhitā Satīkhaṇḍa* 27; *Linga-Purāṇa* 100.
[6] *Mahābhārata Vanaparvan*, 82, 26:

tataḥ kanakhale *snātvā trirātropoṣito naraḥ* /
aśvamedham avāpnoti svargalokam ca gacchati //

[7] App.I, 13:

kurukṣetrasamā gaṅgā yatratatrāvagāhitā /
viśeṣo vai kanakhale *prayāge paramam mahat* //

Anuśāsanaparvan 26, 12:

gaṅgādvāre kuśāvarte bilvake nemiparvate /
tathā kanakhale *snātvā dhūtapāpmā divam vrajet* //

Sanatkumāra's penance.[8] The forceful occupation of such an eminent place, vied for by all and sundry, must have made a great impression. Evidently Śaivas were late-comers in the plains and not normally associated with respectable places of worship. Apparently they were as keen as the rest of the population to have access to the Ganges at a favored spot so as to be able to perform meritorious ablutions. Also in more recent times, as our records document, Śaiva ascetics fought for such priviliges as to who was to enter the Ganges at the most auspicious times of the Kumbha-melā. A battle fought in 1760 A.D. proved so decisive that for many decades to come Vaiṣṇavas were not allowed access at certain occasions.[9] Even now the rivalry between Śaivas and Vaiṣṇavas is noticeable at the time of the Kumbha-melās—a rivalry focusing on precisely the same issue.

Geography has always played a great role in Hinduism: specific places, with specific acts of penance or worship performed at them, were identified as "holy places" early on.[10] Māhātmyas of important *tīrtha*s are prominent parts of the Purāṇas, besides the *Sthalapurāṇas*, which provide the holy history of such places. These texts provide at the same time the legitimation of occupation of certain favored spots by specific sects. They are parallels to the *landnama* sagas of Northern Europe or the Biblical legitimization of the occupation of Palestine and the holy places of the Canaanaeans by the tribes of Israel. As a foundational story the successful Pāśupata dislocation of the previous occupants of Kanakhala and the subsequent permanent arrangement with them provided the legitimation of Śaivism, which the Veda did not provide. It is explicitly

---

[8] 88, 18:

bibheda tarasā gaṅgā gaṅgādvāre yudhiṣṭhire /
puṇyam tat khyāyate rājan brahmārṣigaṇasevitam //
sanatkumāra kauravya puṇyam kanakhalam *tathā* /

135, 5a:

ete kanakhalā *rājarṣīṇām dayitā nagāḥ*

[9] G.S. Ghurye, *Indian Sadhus* (Bombay: 1964), p. 112: "Śaiva Samnāysis and Vaiṣṇava Bairāgis fought a great battle at Hardwar in 1760 to decide the dispute about precedence at that place. According to an account recorded by Wilson the total number of dead in that action was 18,000. . . . The 1760 battle of Hardwar completely decided the issue in favor of the Śaiva Samnāysis. Since that year till the time Hardwar territory went under British control the Vaiṣṇavas Bairāgis could not visit that place on special religious occasions".

[10] Cf. the *Tīrthayātrā* section in the *Mahābhārata Vanaparvan* and the *Tīrthaprakāśa* of Vīramitrodaya.

stated that this was Śiva's first exploit, and it is the first in the cycle of major Śiva myths.

The incident is relegated to an earlier *manvantara*[11]—apparently in order to strengthen the case: the more remote the "foundational event", the less it would be apt to be challenged. Whatever the time may have been, it seems to have been a real, i.e., historical, event taking place at a time when Vaiṣṇavism had been accepted as orthodox by the representatives of Vedic religion. Vaiṣṇava gentleness and civility stood in contrast to Śaiva primitivism and savagery. Viṣṇu as Upendra had been accepted into Ṛgvedic sacrificial religion and already in the Brāhmaṇas Viṣṇu is considered as identical with the sacrifice, asked to make good its defects. All the Dakṣa story versions make it clear that Śiva Paśupati, who destroys Dakṣa's sacrifice, is not identical with the Vedic Rudras. Nevertheless, while his major body of followers must have been in the mountains, he possessed sympathizers in the plains too. Dadhīca, one of the guests at the sacrifice, is quoted in virtually all versions as pleading for the invitation of Śiva and the allocation of a part of the sacrifice to him.

The objective both of the historical conquest and of the story reporting it is twofold. The Pāśupatas wanted to become part of the sacrificial community. They wished to share the prestige and recognition associated with the allotment of a portion of the sacrifice, being the equal of the *devas* invited to it, like Indra, Viṣṇu and the *ṛṣis*. They also wanted to get the better of the Vaiṣṇavas, who had apparently succeeded in establishing themselves as the predominant religion in the upper Ganges valley.

Thus, while first seemingly bent at completely wiping out traditional Vedism with its gods (some of the versions make it a point to detail the disrespect shown by Vīrabhadra's army towards the Vedic gods and Vedic institutions), they relent and acquiesce to Dakṣa's plea (supported by Viṣṇu) to restore the sacrifice and its tradition. There are unavoidable changes, though Dakṣa's head can no longer be retrieved and the damage done to the gods can only be partially repaired. Pāśupata Śaivas were obviously prepared to become part of the tradition which they had set out to overthrow.

In turn, Vaiṣṇavas had to accept the legitimacy of Śaivism (even the equality of Viṣṇu and Śiva, who are now co-creators of the world); they

[11] While several previous rebirths of Dakṣa are mentioned in some accounts most seem to agree in placing the story of Śiva's destruction of Dakṣa's sacrifice in the Vaivasvata *manvantara*.

must surrender one of their holiest places and acknowledge the supremacy of Śiva in it.

If such a comparatively minor event connected with a no longer very prominent place seems too small an occasion for the emergence of the vast Dakṣa saga, which occupies a large place, e.g. in the *Śiva-Purāṇa*, we have only to think of the *Nibelungen Saga* and the places connected with it: villages and small towns which are unlikely to evoke any heroic sentiments in today's visitor.

That the Dakṣa saga—once established as a major part of Śiva tradition—had its applications quite apart from legitimating the Pāśupata occupation of the Kanakhala *tīrtha* is evident from its Tamil versions.[12] In these Śiva plays a dominant role from the very beginning, whereas Viṣṇu is relegated to a very subordinate position. Brahmā is prepared to offer Śiva a share in the Vedic sacrifice, which he claims "by Vedic injunction". In the Tamil version Dakṣa is throughout a devotee of Śiva—his conflict with Śiva is due to a temporary clouding of his mind. In the Tamil country there was no need for the legitimation of Śaivism. The story, of course, was part of traditional lore, but its significance changed drastically.

Since it is by origin a North Indian saga, Sanskrit sources will be, generally speaking, closer to it in spirit and articulation. The following reconstruction will be based exclusively on epic and puranic material and will be biased towards those accounts which put Kanakhala into the center of their narration. If that seems to be circular arguing, it should be kept in mind that the idea of the Dakṣa story concerning the Pāśupata Śaiva conquest of Kanakhala emerged, of course, only from a reading and reflecting upon these materials.

Reconstruction of the Story

The following reconstruction is based on the accounts given in the following texts: the *Mahābhārata*, *Śāntiparvan*, Ch. 284;[13] *Rāmāyaṇa*, *Bālakāṇḍa*, Ch. 65, 9–12; *Śiva-Purāṇa*, which has two versions of it: *Rudra-saṁhitā Satīkhaṇḍa*, Chs. 12–42 and *Vayavīyasaṁhitā*, Chs. 18–33;

---

[12] D.D. Shulman, *Tamil Temple Myths* (Princeton: 1980), pp. 337ff.: "Nowhere is the distance between the Tamil myths and their Sanskrit counterparts more evident than in the different versions of the myth of Dakṣa's sacrifice. . . ."

[13] *Śāntiparvan*, Ch. 284 (Vulgate; the Critical Edition [hereafter CE] has relegated parts of it to the Appendices).

Vāyu-Purāṇa, Ch. 30; *Liṅga-Purāṇa*, Ch. 100; *Skanda-Purāṇa, Maheśakhaṇḍa Kedārakāṇḍa*, Ch. 2; *Brahma-Purāṇa*, Ch. 39; *Kūrma-Purāṇa*, Pt. I, Ch. 15; *Matsya-Purāṇa*, Ch. 5; *Bhāgavata-Purāṇa*, Pt. IV, Chs. 1–7; and *Harivaṁśa, Bhaviṣyaparvan*, Ch. 32. It is noteworthy that the story is reported in Śaivite as well as Vaiṣṇava and Śākta Purāṇas (cf. *Devībhāgavatam*, Pt. VII, Ch. 38). Apparently it recalled a historical event of some magnitude which could not be passed over with silence by any sect. Quite clearly too, it was an event which established the indubitable dominance of Śaivas in a particular place which was of interest to all. Śaivites, of course, fully exploit the story to demonstrate the superiority of Śiva over Viṣṇu. Vaiṣṇavas, in most of their versions, while unable to turn their defeat into victory (which the *Harivaṁśa* attempts to do), suggest that it was ultimately Viṣṇu's punishment of Dakṣa, who had not recognized the oneness of Śiva and Viṣṇu.

The report of the crucial event is prefaced in most narrations by background information on Dakṣa. Dakṣa and his clan seem to have been quite prominent apart from the incident described as "Dakṣa's sacrifice". This, in a sense, was the reason why it was so important to get hold of his settlement, Kanakhala, in order to legitimate Śaivism as an equal to Vaiṣṇavism. There is a Dakṣa story in the context of traditions on the patriarchs, the "mind-born sons of Brahmā", whose genealogies formed an early part of puranic traditions. Thus the *Viṣṇu-Purāṇa*, by fairly common agreement one of the oldest in its present form, devotes only a few lines to the Śiva-Dakṣa incident after extensively reporting on Dakṣa's progeny, his sixty daughters and their families. The *Bhāgavatam*, one of the latest and perhaps the best organized of the purāṇas, in which the Dakṣa story fills a whole section and is treated like an epic in itself, devotes hundreds of *śloka*s to describing Dakṣa's career through several incarnations in successive *manvantaras*. By contrast the *Vāyu-Purāṇa*, perhaps the oldest of all the extant Purāṇas, briefly summarizes the story of Dakṣa's sacrifice by Śiva". The *Śiva-Purāṇa*, which has two lengthy different versions of the Dakṣa story, while paralleling the *Bhāgavatam* in its prolixity as regards the pre-history of the Śiva-Dakṣa enmity, connects Dakṣa's importance from the very beginning with Śiva and Śivā.

Parallel to the treatment of the story of Dakṣa before the crucial incident we find the Satī story enhanced or compressed according to need. All sources report Satī's marriage to Śiva—some make it a point to provide also Satī with a "pre-history", others combine it with an apparently independent tradition explaining the origin of Śakti-pīṭhas in order to provide legitimation for them (see Sircar, App. VI).

It is worth noting—in general, before entering into detail—that there must have been a common literary source for the accounts in the *Vāyu-*

Purāṇa, *Mahābhārata*, *Śiva-Purāṇa-Vāyavīyasaṁhitā*, *Kūrma-Purāṇa*, *Brahma-Purāṇa*, which have some crucial *śloka*s in common and agree on most features, whereas considerable divergence as regards detail and no literary dependence either on each other or on a common source characterizes the other sources utilized.

A. *The Story of the* prajāpati *Dakṣa*

Dakṣa must have been a famous and respected personality before the destruction of his sacrifice; that precisely was the reason why his misfortune aroused such an interest. The Śaivite occupation of Kanakhala brought the Dakṣa story to its end; it did not diminish his fame.

The *Śiva-Purāna-Vāyavīyasaṁhitā* narration, which exhibits great hostility towards Dakṣa from the very beginning, traces the various rebirths of Dakṣa in successive *manvantara*s and places even the beginning of his enmity towards Śiva in one of the previous births (18, 4–62). The *Bhāgavatam* describes Dakṣa in a very favorable light. Dakṣa was one of the mindborn sons of Brahmā. From Svayambhū Manu he receives his third daughter, Prasūti, as wife. Together they have sixteen daughters. Of these, thirteen are given in marriage to Dharma, one to Agni, one to Pitṛs and one to Bhava (IV, 1:11–47). In several accounts he is described as "fond of his daughters" and so there is the puzzling question why, out of dislike for his son-in-law Bhava, he slighted his daughter Satī (*Bh.P*, IV, 2, 1).

The *Śiva-Purāṇa-Rudrasaṁhitā Satīkhaṇḍa* has the most tantastic version (Ch. 12, 18ff). Śivā, appearing to Dakṣa after long and arduous *tapas*, grants the boon to Dakṣa that she would (for the first time) incarnate as his daughter and become Śiva's wife. Then and there she admonishes him: "If in the future you were to be less respectful to me I will cast off my body . . ." (v. 33).

In a later chapter we are told that Dakṣa is advised by Brahmā, his father, to marry Vīriṇī (Ch. 13, 6). With her he procreates 5,000 sons, called the Haryāśvas, who go west "to the holy lake Nārāyaṇa where there is the confluence of the celestial Sindhu and the ocean" (Ibid.). Later he procreates 1,000 sons from Pañcajana. They, the Sabalāśvas, also go west. Dakṣa then curses Nārada, the purported instigator of these migrations. It is difficult to say what these stories mean. Perhaps they are memories of parts of the Dakṣa clan moving westwards into the Sindh.

The narration then leads back to the introduction: after sixty daughters have been born to Dakṣa from Vīriṇī, Satī is born. Dakṣa then sings a long hymn in praise of the Goddess (Ch. 14, 28ff).

B. *The Story of Dakṣa's Sacrifice*

The reports about the sacrifice which became the occasion for Śiva's wrathful intervention are again widely divergent. According to *Śiva-Purāṇa-Vāyavīyasaṁhitā*, Dakṣa performed in his various incarnations a series of sacrifices (Chs. 18–19). At the first, in a previous *manvantara*, he insults his daughter Satī, who abandons her body. So does Dakṣa. Reborn in Cakṣuṣa *manvantara* as the son of Pracetas, he is again reported as having offered a great sacrifice (18, 51ff). Finally, in the Vaivaśvata *manvantara*, he prepares the fateful horse-sacrifice: *gaṅgādvāre śubhe deśe*... (19, 5). The *Śiva-Purāṇa-Rudrasaṁhitā* reports but a single sacrifice offered at Kanakhala (Ch. 37). The *Mahābhārata* begins its narration of the Dakṣa episode (*Śānti-parvan*, App. I, no. 28) with Janamejaya's question how the *aśvamedha* of Prajāpati Dakṣa, son of Pracetas, was destroyed, and Vaiśampāyana's report about it, as having taken place "where the Ganges issues out of the mountains".[14]

The *Bhāgavatam* assigns the relevant detail of the Dakṣa-Śiva confrontation to two different sacrifices: the first, a sacrifice arranged by the Prajāpatis for Śrī Hari (lasting 1,000 years) attended by Dakṣa becomes the occasion for Dakṣa's enmity with Śiva, which is sustained for a long time (IV, 2, 4ff). It is at a second sacrifice, the Bṛhaspati-Śava of Dakṣa, that Satī gets insulted, whose suicide then is the reason for Śiva's wrathful intervention (Ibid., Ch. 3).

The *Skanda-Purāṇa* knows of only one sacrifice, a *mahāyajña* at Kanakhala, which becomes the occasion of Dakṣa's being angry with Śiva and Śiva's avenging Satī's death (I, 1, 1, 2). The *Kūrma-Purāṇa* too reports only one sacrifice, set in Gaṅgādvāra (I, 15); so does the *Brahma-Purāna* (39, 21). The *Harivaṁśa* has a widely diverging version (Ch. 32). It tells us that Dakṣa Pracetas began an *aśvamedha* and that Rudra, together with Nandī, appears to avenge the sin of animal killing. The *Liṅga-Purāṇa* locates the sacrifice at Kanakhala, near Gaṅgādvāra.[15] The *Vāyu-Purāṇa* mentions the curious detail that the gods participated at Daksa's sacrifice in Gaṅgādvāra with Śiva's permission (Ch. 30, 80ff).

---

[14] V. 6; this text uses the same expression as *Śi. Pu. Vayavīyasaṁhitā*:

purā himavataḥ pṛṣṭe dakṣo vai yajñam āharat |
gaṅgādvare śubhe deśe ṛṣisiddhaniṣevite ||

[15] Ch. 100, 7:

yajñavatas tathā tasya gaṅgādvāra-samīpataḥ |
taddeśe caiva vikhyātam . . . kanakhalam dvijāḥ ||

C. *The Cause of Dakṣa's Enmity with Śiva*

This issue is for most of the accounts the most crucial one and also the point where the widest divergences and contradictions emerge between the different accounts. In any case, it is a complicated story which has much to do with traditional proprieties broken, with disputed claims within the sphere of Vedic sacrifice and with possible rival loyalties between Vaiṣṇavaṣ and Śaivas.

The *Mahābhārata* account depicts a Dadhīci, who is angry that Śiva had not been invited and who foresees disaster.[16] He pleads with Dakṣa to invite Śiva. Without visible connection to that account we learn thereafter that Umā inquires from her husband what *vrata*s to choose to make sure that one half or one third of the sacrifice would be his.[17] There is no confrontation between Daksa and Śiva.

The *Bhāgavata-Purāṇa*, on the other hand, fully accounts for the hostility between Śiva and Dakṣa (IV, 2): at the great (first) sacrifice arranged by the *prajāpati*s, prepared for Hari, and lasting a thousand years, Śiva (like Brahmā, Dakṣa's father) does not rise to pay respect to Dakṣa. Dakṣa utters then and there a lengthy curse (vv. 9–16). He mentions that Śiva is his son-in-law and that he had been unwilling to give his daughter to him, having been persuaded to do so by Brahmā. The curse culminates in Śiva's exclusion from a share of the sacrifice.[18] It is Nandī, Śiva's companion, who in turn curses Dakṣa and all brahmans (vv. 21–26). Bhṛgu, as spokesman of the brahmans, utters a counter-curse of Nandī and all followers of Bhava, who henceforth would be considered heretics:[19]

> Those who observe *Bhava-vrata*s and those who follow them shall be heretics acting contracy to scripture. Only those who have abandoned purity, are stupid, wear matted locks, ashes and bones, and will receive Śiva-dīkṣā, which is connected with wine. Denouncing the Vedas, which lay down the rules of behavior, and the brahmans, you have embraced the position of heretics. The path of the Vedas is the only eternal one; it has been followed

---

[16] *Śāntiparvan* App. I, no. 28, line 24: *na ayam yajño na vā dharmā yatra rudro na ijyate.*

[17] The CE separates the two accounts and leaves only the conversation between Umā and Śiva in the text; Ch. 274.

[18] V. 18:

ayaṁ tu devayajana indropendrādibhir bhavaḥ /
saha bhāgam na labhatām devair devaganādhamaḥ //

[19] Ibid. vv. 28–32: Bhṛgu accuses:

bhavavratadharā ye ca ye ca tān samanuvratāḥ /
pākhaṇḍinas te bhabantu sacchāstraparipanthinaḥ /

by the ancients and has the authority of Janārdana [Viṣṇu]. By condemning the Vedas, the supreme, flawless, eternal path of the virtuous, you go the path of the heretics with the lord of ghosts as deity.

For a long period this smoldering enmity between Śiva and Dakṣa—and we can infer between Śaivites and brahmans—continues without any further incidents. Dakṣa rises to a high position: Brahmā appoints him "the chief of all lords of created beings" (Ch. 3). When he prepares for the "ultimate sacrifice", Satī is not able to persuade Śiva to join her in attending the sacrifice (Ch. 4). She is slighted by her father (although welcomed by mother and sisters). She speaks out strongly against her father, curses her own birth from him,[20] and eventually kills herself "as a mark of displeasure against Dakṣa" (w. 24–27). Satī's attendants who try to kill Dakṣa are beaten back by Bhṛgu's creatures. Then only we hear about Śiva's rage and subsequent action against Dakṣa (Ch. 5).

What is remarkable in this account is that a daughter considers her bond with her husband stronger than with her natural father: while Vedic religion sanctified the natural ties, sectarianism considers them inferior to the bond that unites fellow-believers.

The *Śiva-Purāṇa-Rudrasaṁhitā* adds a further complication (Ch. 17f.). It first reports that Dakṣa "joyfully gave his daughter Satī to Śiva" (18, 33). Then it mentions how Brahmā angered Śiva and Śiva cursed Brahmā (Ch. 19). Dakṣa (and later Viṣṇu) tries to mediate. Without any obvious connection a later chapter (Ch. 26) tells about the fury of Dakṣa when Śiva, at his sacrifice at Prayāga, fails to bow down to him. Dakṣa calls Śiva names—"shameless frequenter of cremation grounds"—and expels Śiva from the sacrifice.[21] Bhṛgu and others join Dakṣa in cursing Śiva. Nandī countercurses Bhṛgu and the brahmans (v. 19f.). He accuses the brahmans of being "egotistic . . . engaged in discussing Vedas but ignorant of Vedic principles." he foretells them that they would be "beggars, officiating at the sacrifices of Śūdras, perpetually poor."[22]

Curiously enough, the next chapter reports how Viṣṇu, invited by Śiva, presides at Dakṣa's sacrifice at Kanakhala. Dakṣa does not invite

---

[20] Ibid., vv. 11–23:

na etena dehena hare kṛtāgaso dehodbhavena . . . kujanmanā
vrīḍā mamābhūt kujanaprasangatas taj janma dhig yo mahatām avadyakṛt (22)

[21] Ibid., v. 18:

śmasānavāsī kulajanmahīnaḥ

[22] Vv. 30–42. This is materially identical with *Bh.Pu.* IV, 2, 21–26. There is, however, no literary dependence.

Śiva, because he is a kapālin, nor Satī, his daughter, because she is a kapālin's wife (Ch. 27). He defiantly praises Viṣṇu "the prime cause of all deities" and denounces Śiva.[23] Contrary to what we learned above he now says that he had reluctantly given his daughter to Śiva, persuaded by Brahmā. Śiva is not a man of nobility, "he has neither father or mother, he is the lord of goblins, ghosts and spirits and is incorrigible. He is a haughty self-conceited fool, unworthy of this sacred rite" (vv. 42ff.).

Satī, though uninvited and informed by Śiva about the enmity between himself and Dakṣa, decides to attend together with "60,000 attendants, favorites of Śiva, who sang songs of praise of Śiva and who jumped in their joy with hearts of childish innocence" (Chs. 28, 43). Satī does not get attention from Dakṣa or the gods and she gets furious at Viṣṇu, Brahmā and Indra (Ch. 29).

In her presence Dakṣa again denounces Śiva: "Your husband Śiva is known to the wise as inauspicious. He is not of a noble lineage. He is the king of goblins, ghosts and spirits. He is excluded from Vedic rites... Induced by Brahmā I gave you in marriage to the wicked, haughty Śiva who does not know customs" (v. 31ff.). Interestingly, in this version Satī is offered a portion of the sacrifice, which she refuses by saying: "He who reproaches Śiva, and he who hears such reproaches, both of them go to hell and stay there as long as the moon and sun exist".[24]

Satī heaps abuses on her own father: "You are wicked, you are evil-minded . . ." and then burns herself in her own yogic fire (Ch. 30). Many of her attendants also kill themselves, others mutilate themselves, the rest attack Dakṣa. A "celestial voice" reminds Dakṣa of his mistakes and admonishes Viṣṇu and Brahmā to leave the sacrifice (Ch. 31).

The same *purāṇa* in the *Vāyavīyasaṁhitā* locates the source of the enmity between Śiva and Dakṣa in an encounter in a previous *manvantara* (Ch. 18, 4ff.). Dakṣa, visiting Śiva and Satī, did not receive preferential treatment from them and is offended. He, in turn, does not invite them to his *yajña*. Satī attends nevertheless and questions Dakṣa about it. Dakṣa insults her: "The younger daughters are better than you . . . their husbands are superior to your husband . . . he is stiff-souled and he is antagonistic to me" (vv. 10ff.).

---

[23] V. 37:

mūlam viṣṇur devatānām yatra dharmaḥ sanātanaḥ /
samānīto mayā samyak kimūnam yajñakarmaṇi //

[24] Ibid., v. 38:

yo nindati mahādevam nindyamānam śruṇoti vā /
tāvubhau narakam yātau yāvad candradivākarau //

Satī is infuriated and replies that she will not suffer Dakṣa to insult her husband, who is Lord of the World. "Know that your family is defiled and ruined" (vv. 40ff.). Satī then abandons her body and goes to Himavān. Śiva curses the assembly and prophesies about Dakṣa's future. Dakṣa too abandons his body (vv. 50ff.).

The curse, however, is transmitted to his birth as son of Pracetas (vv. 54ff.). Therefore, the report about the wrecking of Dakṣa's sacrifice by Śiva is not preceded by any other explanation of Śiva's anger. Dadhīca enters into a heated exchange with Dakṣa concerning the recipients of his sacrifice, but there is no direct offence to Śiva or Satī contained in Dakṣa's answer. The *Liṅga-Purāṇa* too, without telling the reason for Śiva's anger, introduces the catastrophe by a description of the portents that accompanied the sacrifice (Ch. 100, 8f.).

The *Skanda-Purāṇa* follows the *Śivapurāṇa-Rudrasaṁhitā* in most details (I, 1, 1, 2f.). Dakṣa curses Śiva for not standing up to honor him and refuses to invite him to his sacrifice at Kanakhala. Dadhīci's intervention is fruitless (Ch. 2, 10ff.). Satī, after discussing the situation with Śiva, enters the fire, after which Śiva—through Vīrabhadra—wrecks Dakṣa's sacrifice (Ch. 5).

The *Vāyu-Purāṇa* knows of no previous conflict between Śiva and Dakṣa. Dadhīca pleads for inviting Śiva, which Dakṣa refuses to do (Ch. 30, 80ff.). Dadhīca, after prophesying disaster, leaves. In reply to Umā's question why he is not attending the sacrifice, Śiva says: "This is the contrivance of all the gods, that in all sacrifices no portion should be assigned to me. According to an arrangement formerly devised, the gods allow me no participation".[25] Śiva in this version directs his anger not so much against Dakṣa in punishment for a personal offence but against the arrangement of the gods, the Vedic sacrificial order.

Kūrma-Purāṇa and *Brahma-Purāṇa* similarly do not find it necessary to construe a personal conflict between Dakṣa and Śiva previous to the sacrifice but report—what seemed to be Vedic practice—that no portion of the sacrifice and no official prayer was dedicated to Śiva.[26] It is at

---

[25] Ibid., vv. 112ff.

surair eva mahābhāge sarvam anuṣṭitam /
yajñeṣṇu mama sarveṣu na bhāga upakalpitaḥ //
pūrvopāyopapannena mārgeṇa varavārṇini /
na me sūrāḥ prayacchanti bhāgam yajñasya dhīmataḥ //

[26] *Kūrma-Purāṇa* I, 15, 112f. *Brahma-Purāṇa* Ch. 39, 39:

na me surāḥ prayacchanti bhāgam yajñasya dharmataḥ.

Devī's request that he forcibly intervenes so as to obtain a share and receive official acknowledgement (vv. 50ff.).

D. *The Dadhīci-Dakṣa Dialogue*

The one element which shows most agreement in all the puranic accounts of the Dakṣa episode is the dialogue between Dadhīci and Dakṣa. Identical verses are found in several accounts. It can be assumed that it formed an original and important part of the original Dakṣa saga. It seems to identify the core of the conflict.

Dadhīci apparently was a person of stature; thus he was among the officially invited guests at the great sacrifice. According to the *Mahābhārata* it was he who noticed first the absence of Śiva (*Śāntiparvan*, App. I, No. 28, 1.23). "Foreseeing in a yogic vision the coming disaster", he pleads with Dakṣa to invite Śiva, even at that late time, since he is the "Protector of all creatures, the Creator of the universe, the Lord of all, the Puissant Master, the taker of sacrificial offerings". He urges: "He will soon come . . . you shall see him" (11. 37–39).

Apparently Dadhīci, as Yogī, belonged also to the (extra-Vedic) Pāśupata sect, which was not related to any of the Vedic Rudra cults. Dakṣa retorts (and the phrase is literally repeated in several other accounts in various *purāṇas*): "I know the eleven Rudras, I do not know this Maheśvara".[27] Then he professes his Vedic-Vaiṣṇava faith, which in all probability cost him his life: "Here in this vessel of gold, intended for the Lord of all sacrifices, is the sacrificial offering sanctified by mantras according to the ordinances. I intend to make this offering to Viṣṇu, who is beyond compare. He is puissant and the Maker of all; unto Him should sacrifice be performed".[28]

The *Mahābhārata* account breaks the dialogue off here and shifts the scene to the Himālayas, where Umā confers with Śiva about a plan of action to obtain part of the sacrifice. The *Śiva-Purāṇa-Vāyavīyasaṁhitā*, which has much the same account,[29] even literally repeating the same words (as also the *Vāyu-Purāṇa*) makes Dadhīci reply to Dakṣa's confession of faith: "O Dakṣa, since Rudra, the Lord of the chief of Gods is not

---

[27] Ibid., 11. 40f:

santi no bahavo rudrāḥ śūlahastāḥ kapardinaḥ /
ekādaśasthānagatā nāhaṁ vedmi maheśvaram //

[28] Ibid., 11, 45–48:

etan makheśāya suvarṇapātre haviḥ samastam vidhimantrapūtam / etc.

[29] Ch. 19, 9f. There are slight differences in wording (v. 19).

propitiated, your sacrifice will not be efficacious" (v. 20). With that he leaves the assembly.

In the *Rudrasaṁhitā* account of the same *purāṇa*, Dadhīci is already introduced as a devotee of Śiva, who is worried by Śiva's absence and insists: "The sacrifice cannot be perfect without Śiva"! (Ch. 27, 24ff.) After listening to the reply by Dakṣa, which not only includes the praise of Viṣṇu as "prime cause of all deities" but also abuse heaped on Śiva (vv. 42ff.), he leaves with his colleagues, only to be cursed as "slow-witted and senseless . . . rogues indulging in false deliberations and discussions . . . out of the Vedic circle. . . ."[30]

The *Skanda-Purāṇa* account is much the same as that of the *Mahābhārata* (I, 1, 1, 2f.). In the *Brahmā-Purāṇa* version Dakṣa categorically states in reply to Dadhīci's entreaties: *dadāmi bhāgam na tu śaṅkarāya* (Ch. 39, 33). The *Kūrma-Purāṇa* equally makes Dakṣa state that he does not know any Rudras besides the eleven Vedic ones and that Hari is *īśvara* and *jagatsṛṣṭā* (I, 15, 12f).

Interestingly, the Dadhīca-Dakṣa dialogue is completely absent from the long *Bhāgavata-Purāṇa* account, the *Liṅga-Purāṇa* and the *Harivaṁśa* versions. This may partly have to do with another source which these versions used and partly with the lack of importance attributed to the presence of an adherent of Śiva-Paśupati at Dakṣa's Vedic-Vaiṣṇava sacrifice in Kanakhala.

The dialogue seems, however, to pinpoint the root cause for the incident: a first, peaceful attempt to accommodate Pāśupata-Śaivism within the Vedic context, which had already accommodated Viṣṇu, had failed. The religious sensibilities of the followers of Maheśvara were deeply hurt and thus violence broke out. While some accounts claim that Śiva had a right to receive a share in the sacrifice, most point out, correctly, that Śiva had been denied a share by an ancient convention. Apparently he would have accepted such a state of affairs, but for Satī, his consort, who felt slighted and who did not want her husband to be inferior to others.

E. *The Vīrabhadra Phenomenon*

Vīrabhadra plaques, popular even today in the countryside of Mahārāṣṭra, display the goat-headed Dakṣa at the feet of Śiva Bhairava. The

---

[30] V. 53:

vinaṣṭacitta mandāśca mithyāvādaratāḥ khalāḥ /
vedabāhyā durācāras tyājyājyās te mekhakarmaṇi //

association must be old and must have been made in connection with our Dakṣa episode. If we could find a large amount of even verbal agreement in the Dadhīci-Dakṣa dialogue, we find an even larger amount of disparity in the treatment of the Vīrabhadra phenomenon.

The *Mahābhārata* account is comparatively restrained (CE, XII, 274, 29ff.). It simply reports that the anger of Śiva takes shape in Vīrabhadra, who is joined by Mahākālī, the embodiment of Umā's anger. The *Vāyu-Purāṇa*, also restrained, reports Śiva creating Vīrabhadra from his mouth (Ch. 30, 122ff.). Vīrabhadra then created from his pores a large number of frightening helpers.

The *Śiva-Purāṇa-Rudrasaṁhitā* devotes an entire chapter (Ch. 32) to the description of the birth of Vīrabhadra and another one (Ch. 33) to the account of his march towards Kanakhala, in the company of a large host of frightful beings.

Similarly extensive is the account given in the same *purāṇa*'s *Vāyavīya-saṁhitā*: urged by the goddess, Śiva creates Vīrabhadra, with the intention to destroy Dakṣa's sacrifice (Ch. 19, 24ff.). Vīrabhadra creates from his anger Bhadrā, the representative of the goddess (v. 35). He is described as being fond of cremation grounds. From his body he creates a large number of *gaṇas*.

The *Bhāgavata-Purāṇa* adds a novel feature: the enraged Śiva pulls a lock from his matted hair, dashes it to the ground and thus creates Vīrabhadra (IV, 5, 3). He is described as "touching the sky, having a thousand arms, three eyes, fierce teeth, matted hair, wearing a garland of skulls, with all kinds of weapons" (vv. 4ff.). Arriving from the north he proceeds to "dispose of Dakṣa and his sacrifice".

The *Skanda-Purāṇa* has much the same account as the *Mahābhārata* (I, 1, 1, 2f.). However, here Śiva creates Vīrabhadra only after Satī has entered the fire. In the *Kūrma-Purāṇa* it is the Devī who requests Śiva to create Vīrabhadra (I, 15, 30ff.); similarly in the *Brahmā-Purāṇa* (Ch. 39, 51ff.), where Vīrabhadra id described as accompanied by Bhadrakālī. The *Liṅga-Purāṇa* describes Bhadra "who was like a black fire" only briefly before reporting about his activities (Ch. 100, 11ff.).

F. *The Destruction of the Sacrifice*

We are now at the climax of the Dakṣa episode. The forcible interruption of Dakṣa sacrifice, the assault of the followers of Paśupati Śiva at the Dakṣa settlement in Kanakhala must have shaken the witnesses deeply so that neither friends nor foes could forget it. The Śaivites remembered it as their triumph over Vaiṣṇava brahmans; the Vaiṣṇavas as a sad event in their glorious history. The *Mahābhārata* describes the catastrophe quite briefly (CE, XII, 274, 34ff.): it mentions explicitly the large amount of food and drink stored by Dakṣa and consumed by the Rudras and the fact that they burn the sacrifice, although it was protected by the *devas* (v. 40).

No mention is made of Dakṣa being beheaded. Dakṣa, bewildered, inquires who this Vīrabhadra was and he is instructed that "it is preferable to incur the wrath of that foremost of gods than to obtain boons from any other deity" (Sp. App. I, 28, 1.122). Dakṣa understands, bows down to Maheśvara and begins a hymn: "I throw myself at the feet of the effulgent Iśāna . . ." (1. 124ff.). Maheśvara finally appears from within the sacrificial pit and grants it to the dazed Dakṣa that the scattered sacrifice may be of use to him.

Quite clearly this account stresses the superseding of the Vedic dispensation by the Śaivite one. Śiva, pleased by Dakṣa's conversion, promises him not only his companionship but also the fruit of a thousand horse-sacrifices and a thousand *vājapeyas*. It is Śiva now who reconfirms Dakṣa's eminence as patriarch (CE, XII, 274, 55ff.). The *Śiva-Purāṇa-Vāyavīyasaṁhitā* amplifies the description of the episode by going into a great deal of detail emphasizing the humiliation of the Vedic gods who were defenceless against Śiva (*Vāyavīyasaṁhitā*, Ch. 20f.). Vīrabhadra's gang begins by beating up the gods, including Indra (20, 37). Bhadra strikes Pāvaka, Yama, the Rudras, Varuṇa, Vāyu, Nirṛti. "He attacked the gods and the sages antagonistic to Śiva" (21, 12ff.). Special mention is made of Sarasvatī having the tip of her nose cut off, Bhāga having his eyes plucked out, and Pūṣan having his teeth knocked out (21, 15). Bhadra stamps the moon with his toe (21, 21). He eventually cuts off Dakṣa's head and hands it to Bhadrakālī, who plays with it! (v. 23) The sacrifice itself is hit and smashed (v. 33), the *bhūtas* and *vetālas* molest the women present (vv. 25ff.). The sacrifice in the shape of the deer is decapitated (v. 33). This last act infuriates Viṣṇu, who begins fighting Bhadra. A terrible battle ensues between Viṣṇu and Bhadra, in which the latter proves stronger (*VS*, Ch. 22, vv. 18ff.). Eventually the struggle ends with an intercession by Brahmā (Ch. 23). The few surviving gods (Viṣṇu among them) eulogize Śiva; they repent and express their fear of him (vv. 8–11).

Śiva's reaction is—well—predictable: he laughs. "It is only to bless you that the punishment has been meted out to you by the merciful Lord" (v. 15). Eventually Viṣṇu utters a hymn in praise of Śiva (vv. 27–30). The account in *Rudrasaṁhitā* is almost identical (*RS*, Chs. 37–42).

The anti-Vaiṣṇava bias is overwhelmingly clear. The *Rudrasaṁhitā* adds a chapter entitled "Viṣṇu's folly" (Ch. 38). Viṣṇu had been cursed by the Śaivite Dadhīca and fights (unsuccessfully) with him (Ch. 39).

The *Śiva-Purāṇa*, a Pāśupata scripture, rubs it in: the Vedic gods are powerless; they have been made ridiculous by the injuries inflicted on them by the servants of Śiva; Viṣṇu is second-class; he too depends on Śiva's benevolence. The *Skanda-Purāṇa* has much the same story, but narrated with more restraint and less offensively (I, 1, 1, 5).

Violent anti-brahmanism also seems to guide the author of the account in the *Linga-Purāṇa* (Ch. 100, 11ff.): with glee it reports Bhadra's uprooting of the sacrificial posts and throwing them, together with the *hotṛ* and the *prastotṛ* into the Gaṅgā (vv. 13ff.). It also mentions the uprooting of Bhāga's eyes, the knocking out of Pūṣan's teeth (vv. 16ff.). Here Indra's head is cut off (v. 18), Agni's hands are severed (v. 19), his tongue is torn out (v. 19), he is kicked on the head (v. 19). Yama's staff is cut (v. 20), thousands of *deva*s and *ṛṣi*s are killed (v. 22). In his fight with Viṣṇu, whose discus seems to have lost all its power, Rudra cuts off Visnu's head too (v. 30), as well as the heads of the sacrifice and of Dakṣa (v. 32f.). It requires Brahmā's intervention, who otherwise plays the role of a *deus otiosus*, to restore the heads to Indra, Viṣṇu and Dakṣa (vv. 40ff.).

Among the Śaivite *purānas* the *Vāyu* shows greatest moderation (Ch. 30): it describes the wrecking of the sacrifice but lets Dakṣa, unharmed, take refuge to Śiva: "for the anger of Rudra is better than the blessing of the other gods" (vv. 186ff). Śiva appears from within the ruined sacrifice and promises to let Dakṣa have the merit accruing from his sacrifice.

The *Brahma-Purāṇa* has an almost identical account (Ch. 39).

The Vaiṣṇava *purāṇas* have a most delicate matter before them: they probably could not gloss over the incident and could not make the loss of Kanakhala appear as a gain for Vaiṣṇavism. So the *Bhāgavatam* reports how the Rudras desecrate (!) the sacrifice (IV, 5, 15ff.), how they punish Bhṛgu, Bhāga and Pūṣan for offences against Śiva (vv. 17ff.) (never mentioned before), and how they ritually killed Dakṣa: "Vīrabhadra severed the head of Dakṣa from his body . . . treating the sacrificer as an animal to be sacrificed. . . . He threw Dakṣa's head as an offering into the sacrificial fire, called Dakṣināgni" (vv. 24ff.). Brahmā, together with the other gods, intercedes with Śiva, who, it emerges, is after all an aspect of Viṣṇu, a truth which Dakṣa had not realized (vv. 33ff.).

The *Kūrma-Purāṇa* makes Vīrabhadra realize that Viṣṇu, whom he is about to strike, is the creator of the world (I, 15, 12): instead of hurting Viṣṇu he proclaims the identity of Śiva and Viṣṇu: *yo viṣṇuḥ sa svayam rudro yo rudraḥ sa janārdanaḥ* . . . (v. 89). The world, it states, has been created by Rudra-Nārāyaṇa . . . (v. 90).

A similar compromise is also reached in the *Harivaṁśa* account, which gives Viṣṇu the upper hand (*Bhaviṣyaparva* 32). When Rudra's entourage begins to destroy Dakṣa's sacrifice, Brahmā reports to Viṣṇu, who, enraged, tries to shoot Śiva (v. 20). Not succeeding, he strikes him with his (blue) hand at the throat—which explains why he is called *nīlakaṇṭha* (v. 40). Viṣṇu finally recognizes that Śiva is *sarva-bhūta-āgama-ācārya* (v. 49) as well as *karmaṇām kartā ca vikartā ca . . . sarvabhūteṣu uttama* (v. 51). Viṣṇu asks Śiva for forgiveness and announces that henceforth any slight to Śiva would make an offering to Viṣṇu unacceptable (vv. 54ff). Apparently the "Śaivite revolution" meant much more to the Śaivites than to the Vaiṣṇavas. For the Vaiṣṇavas it was a loss of a cherished *tīrtha* and it implied an arrangement with the Śaivites, who continued to be looked down upon as rather uncouth. For the Śaivites it meant the end of the Vedic-brahmanic supremacy, which had been under Vaiṣṇava protection. It meant equality with the Vaiṣṇavas and social respectability with the possession of a universally acknowledged holy place on the Gaṅgā.

G. *The Aftermath*

In each and every account a reconciliation takes place between Dakṣa and Śiva. The *Mahābhārata* declares Śiva satisfied with Dakṣa's long hymn to Śiva, the All-God, the giver and taker of everything, and Dakṣa can now hold his elevated position on account of Śiva grace. Śiva also mentions that he has "extracted from Vedas, Sāṁkhya and Yoga the Pāśupata religion, which is unparalleled, open to all, leading to emancipation, shrouded in mystery" (XII, App. I, 28, 1). Finally, promises of blessings are attached for those who recite Dakṣa's hymn. In line with its more dramatic style the *Śiva-Purāṇa-Vayavīyasaṁhitā* has a more detailed and more colorful story of the aftermath (Ch. 23, 87ff.). Viṣṇu himself is made to pray to Śiva, who then revives the gods (v. 37). "Lord Brahmā made the face of Dakṣa look like the face of an old goat as a befitting punishment for his sins" (vv. 39 41). The revived Dakṣa, in the course of his prayer to Śiva, calls him "the Lord of Viṣṇu". Dakṣa's prayer is followed by a whole chapter providing the rules governing Pāśupatavrata (Ch. 34). In the *Rudrasaṁhitā* account Śiva, after being eulogized by the devas in Kailāsa, ordains:

"Let the head of Dakṣa be that of a goat, let the god Bhāga receive his share in the sacrifice in conjunction with the sun . . . Bhṛgu shall be goat-bearded . . . " (Ch. 42, 7f.).

Dakṣa, revived with a goat's head, praises Śiva: "Today I have realized the truth. . . . Thou art above all. Thou art served by Viṣṇu, Brahmā and others" (vv. 32ff.). Viṣṇu is made to apologize to Śiva. Nothing remains of the belief in Viṣṇu "the prime cause of all deities".

The *Skanda-Purāṇa* has essentially the same story (Ch. I, 1, 1, 5).

The *Liṅga-Purāṇa* makes Brahmā intervene with Śiva who then restores their heads to Indra and Viṣṇu and the tip of her nose to Sarasvatī (100, 40ff.). Quite clearly, the authority of Vedic and Vaiṣṇava religion now rests with Śiva. "He sportively made another face similar to the head of Dakṣa, whose face had been destroyed" (v. 46). Gaining consciousness, Dakṣa eulogizes Śiva, who makes him the lord of the *gaṇas* (v. 47f.). The *Brahma-Purāṇa*, which does not know of any cutting off of heads, makes Dakṣa implore Śiva that his sacrifice be not in vain and ends with the *Śivasahasranāma* spoken by Dakṣa (39, 60ff.).

The *Vāyu-Purāṇa* also ends with Dakṣa's conversion to Śiva and his plea (answered by Śiva) that the sacrifice be not in vain (30, 189ff.).

The *Bhāgavatam* has a more complicated task to perform (IV, 6, 33ff.). To begin with, the gods under Brahmā's leadership, approach Śiva in Kailāsa after Dakṣa's death. Their eulogy contains a new Śiva-creed: Śiva is Brahmā (v. 42). Śiva becomes vedāntized (v. 43); from now on by right a share of each sacrifice is his (v. 45). Śiva is pleased with that and is now in a forgiving mood: "I never recollect the misdemeanor of fools dominated by the Lord's Māyā. . . . Let Dakṣa have the head of a goat!" (Ch. 7, 2). The limbs lost by the gods and rishis are restored, but a certain amount of exchange takes place (Ch. 3ff.).

Now, finally, Śiva is invited to the sacrifice "Dakṣa, free from malice, felt inclined to offer praise to Śiva . . . but could not do so on account of affection and grief as he recollected his deceased daughter" (vv. 3–5). Dakṣa acknowledges that Śiva did him a favor by punishing him: Śiva,he now understands, is an aspect of Viṣṇu, as is Brahmā (vv. 9ff.). Now Viṣṇu appears in person and is praised by Dakṣa and all those assembled (vv. 17ff.). Dakṣa and the other priests deplore their foolishness to consider their Vedic sacrifice to be above the Lord. Dakṣa appears to remain a Vaiṣṇava: he worships Viṣṇu and offers his share to Śiva too (vv. 48ff.). Eventually Satī too is reborn in Menā, the spouse of Himavān (vv. 58ff.).

For the writer of the *Bhāgavata* the change brought about by the Dakṣa episode was only local and marginal. The *Harivaṁśa* seems to agree.[31]

Conclusion

Assuming, as we did, that the Dakṣa episode refers to a real event in the history of Indian religions, i.e., the Śaiva conquest of the important *tīrtha*

---

[31] *Bhaviṣyaparva* 32. Dakṣa gets the full benefit of his sacrifice which benefits all beings, due to Viṣṇu's dispensation!

of Kanakhala associated with the Patriarch Dakṣa, we can also assume that there were a number of witnesses who disagreed among themselves both with regard to events witnessed and to the possible interpretation of these events.

The basic events included a solemn major sacrifice to which all the important personalities of the area were invited: the setting was vedic-brahmanical, Dakṣa expressing a definite bias towards Viṣṇu, which was widely but not universally shared. A participant, who perhaps as a yogi had links with Śaivite groups, suggests a more ecumenical representation, including also Pāśupatas, who appear to have dominated some mountain regions. Dakṣa, not heeding this piece of advice, courts the enmity of the Śaivas. He has to learn the hard way that Vaiṣṇavism is not all-powerful and so he accepts "a new head". From the standpoint of the Śaivites this was a complete victory of Śaivism over Vaiṣṇavism, from the standpoint of the Vaiṣṇavas, this was an unpleasant incident which necessitated certain concessions to be made in the directions of Śaivism, but it did not fundamentally alter their belief.

The Śāktas, who must have been associated with the Pāśupatas in the high mountains around the Ganges, linked with the basic story, which may indeed have included the protest self-immolation of Dakṣa's daughter, who had become a follower of Śiva, possibly the wife of the Pāśupata chief, their entire foundation story. The Śaivite versions leave little doubt that Śaivites fully exploited this event both to claim a rightful share in what Vedic sacrifices there were still performed and to legitimize their occupation of the Kanakhala *tīrtha*, considered to be as holy as Prayāga.

Postscript

After this article was set I came across a recent essay by Bandana Chatterji, "The Story of Dakṣa-Yajna-Nāśa: A Critical Study", in *Journal of the Ganganatha Jha Kendriya Sanskrita Vidyapeetha*, vol. 36, nos. 1–4 (Jan.–Dec. 1980), 87–101, which in addition to the epic and puranic materials makes use of some later poetic materials as well.

According to P.N. Chopra, ed., in *Religions and Communities of India* (Vision Books: New Delhi 1982), p. 181, "the Bhullar clan of the Sikh Jats claims to have originated when Śiva, enraged at Dakṣa's refusal to invite Pārvatī to his sacrifice, pulled out a hair from his matted locks (*jaṭa*) and dashed it on the ground".

THE *SAUPTIKA* EPISODE IN THE STRUCTURE OF THE *MAHĀBHĀRATA*

RUTH KATZ

Introduction

This paper will suggest that the *Sauptika* episode of the *Mahābhārata* epic, that is, the events detailed in the epic's tenth book, the *Sauptikaparvan* (Book of the Night Attack), encapsulates the central meaning and message of the epic as a whole for a particular poet, or group of poets, who took control of the epic story at a certain stage in its development. The paper opens with a recounting of the *Sauptika* events; its second section shows how these events mark the culmination of two particular threads of the epic narrative. The third section of the paper discusses the disengagement of various levels of the epic plot from one another in the *Sauptikaparvan.* The fourth section speculates upon the party or parties who may have been responsible for the role of the *Sauptika* episode in the extant epic.

I. *The* Sauptika *Events*

The central story of the *Mahābhārata* is the epic tale of a great war on the battlefield of Kurukṣetra between the basically righteous Pāṇḍavas (five brothers: Yudhiṣṭhira, Bhīma, Arjuna, and the twins) and their allies, and the basically evil Kauravas (one hundred brothers, cousins of the Pāṇḍavas, led by Duryodhana) and their allies. Books I–V of the epic recount the events leading up to the war, centering upon the Pāṇḍavas' loss of their kingdom to the Kauravas. The battle books, VI–IX, named after the four Kaurava allies whom Duryodhana appoints successively as his generals, describe the war itself, detailing its vagaries, and telling of how the Pāṇḍavas eventually triumphed, but not without recourse to deceit. After this painfully earned Pāṇḍava victory, the events of the *Sauptika* episode come as a rude shock. They are as follows:

At the end of Book IX of the epic, Duryodhana, dying of wounds sustained late in the war, hastily appoints his follower Aśvatthāman to leadership of the completely broken Kaurava army, as its fifth general

(IX.64.38).[1] Aśvatthāman has been craving revenge ever since his father, Droṇa, weapons teacher of both Pāṇḍavas and Kauravas but fighting for the Kauravas in the war as their second general, was killed unfairly by the Pāṇḍava army in battle. The *Sauptika* episode revolves around Aśvatthāman's deeds as general, and the Pāṇḍavas' reaction to them.

For openers, Aśvatthāman leads the only other surviving Kaurava allies, Kṛpa and Kṛtavarman, on a highly illegal night raid against the sleeping Pāṇḍava camp, in which all surviving Pāñcālas and other Pāṇḍava partisans are killed (X.8). Aśvatthāman obtains the strength to accomplish this feat by dedicating himself to the god Śiva (X.7.50ff.). The five Pāṇḍava brothers themselves escape the slaughter only because their ally and advisor Kṛṣṇa, himself the god Viṣṇu incarnate, has gotten them out of the camp;[2] Kṛṣṇa and his compatriot Sātyaki likewise survive, bringing the Pāṇḍava survivors to a total of seven (I.1.158, X.9.47–48). After the raid, Aśvatthāman and his two aides manage to inform Duryodhana of their success, bringing him a certain satisfaction before he expires (X.9.46ff.).

Among those slain in the Pāṇḍava camp are the five Draupadeyas, sons of the five Pāṇḍavas by their common wife, Draupadī (X.8.50ff.). It is Draupadī who, hearing of the slaughter, first demands that the eldest Pāṇḍava, Yudhiṣṭhira, seek revenge (X.11.14ff.). (He, true to his relatively passive character, has done nothing up to this point but lament). Draupadī threatens to undertake a *prāya* vow (that is, to fast) until revenge is obtained. Aśvatthāman must be slain, and a gem which he has worn on his head from birth (a gem with which he was born) be brought to her if she is to go on living. She reminds the second Pāṇḍava, Bhīma, of his former heroic feats, and he sets out after Aśvatthāman. Some time later, Kṛṣṇa, Yudhiṣṭhira, and the third Pāṇḍava, Arjuna, mounted together on Kṛṣṇa's chariot, follow and catch up with Bhīma. They observe as Bhīma discovers Aśvatthāman, seated by the Ganges river with a group of seers (X.13.12ff.). At the sight of Bhīma and the others, Aśvatthāman calls into being in a reed, *apāṇḍavāya* ("for the annihilation of the Pāṇḍavas"), the great *brahmaśiras* ("head of Brahmā")

---

[1] All references are to the *Mahābhārata* in its Critical Edition, 19 vols. plus 6 vols. of indices, ed. Vishnu S. Sukthankar, S.K. Belvalkar, P.L. Vaidya, et al. (Poona: Bhandarkar Oriental Research Institute, 1933–72).

[2] This he has done simply by telling them, at IX.61.35, that they must spend the night out of the camp *maṅgalārthāya* ("for the sake of good fortune").

weapon, which he learned to use from his father (X.13.17ff.).[3] Arjuna, incited by Kṛṣṇa, calls upon his own *brahmaśiras* weapon, also obtained from Droṇa (I.123.74ff.), to neutralize Aśvatthāman's weapon (X.14.1ff.).[4]

At this point, the seers Nārada and Vyāsa hurry to the scene to pacify Aśvatthāman and Arjuna (X.14.11f.).[5] Upon seeing these two great figures, Arjuna calls back his weapon (X.15.1ff.). The narrator, Vaiśampāyana, states here that none but Arjuna could have accomplished such a feat, not even the gods, including their king, Indra; a great hero, Arjuna was able to recall the *brahmaśiras* weapon by virtue of his adherence to his vows, obedience to his teachers, and especially his *brahmacarya* (chastity). Aśvatthāman is, however, incapable of recalling his *brahmaśiras* weapon. He admits that it was sinful to unloose the weapon, but says he did so in fear of Bhīma, who had killed Duryodhana wrongly (X.15.13ff.). Vyāsa now demands that Aśvatthāman withdraw the weapon, telling him that if he wants his life to be spared, he must also relinquish the gem on his head (X.15.25ff.). The latter Aśvatthāman agrees to do, but he still cannot stop the weapon; the best he can do is to divert it by sending it into the wombs of the Pāṇḍava women, killing the Pāṇḍava heirs rather than the Pāṇḍavas themselves. Kṛṣṇa, however, promises by his power a revival of the as yet unborn son of Arjuna's dead son, Abhimanyu, who will be Arjuna's grandson, Parikṣit, to be the one remaining heir of the Pāṇḍava line (X.16.1ff.). Meanwhile, Kṛṣṇa condemns the child-slayer, Aśvatthāman, to three thousand years of wandering (X.16.10ff.). Kṛṣṇa's actual revival of the murdered fetus is described in *Mahābhārata* XIV.65ff.

II. *Story Threads Culminating in the* Sauptika *Episode*

A. *The Story of the Pāñcāla Line*

As I have indicated in the preceding summary of the *Sauptika* events, all the Pāñcāla allies of the Pāṇḍavas who survived the war die as victims of

---

[3] That the weapon used by Aśvatthāman is indeed the *brahmaśiras* is not actually stated until Vyāsa's speech of X.15.19ff. The way has been prepared, however, by the story of Aśvatthāman's acquisition of this weapon in X.12.4ff.

[4] Again, the weapon's name is not stated until X.15.19ff., but that it is the *brahmaśiras* is implied clearly in the statement that Arjuna learned it from Droṇa (X.14.2). Alternatively, Arjuna learned the *brahmaśiras* weapon from Śiva; see III.41.7ff. and VII.57.79, where the weapon is called the *pāśupata* (see below, n. 21). The *Sauptika* episode does not, however, mention this fact.

[5] Vyāsa's appearance is redundant, as he was already on the scene as of X.13.13.

Aśvatthāman's night raid. To elaborate, these figures include the extremely important Pāñcāla warriors Dhṛṣṭadyumna (X.8.12ff.) and Śikhaṇḍin (X.8.60); and one must also list with them the five Draupadeyas, sons of the Pāñcāla princess, Draupadī, since their metronymic appellation regularly classifies them with their maternal lineage. In fact, all named victims of the night raid are Pāñcālas.[6]

The importance of the Pāñcāla people for the *Mahābhārata* as a whole cannot be overestimated: it is so great that a number of *Mahābhārata* scholars of the past have suggested that the Pāñcālas, not the Pāṇḍavas, were the heroes of the earlier tales upon which the extant epic is based; these tales described a conflict between the Kurus (Kauravas) and Pāñcālas, and it is the place of the Pāñcālas which the Pāṇḍavas, pushing the Pāñcālas into the background, took over.[7] This suggestion appears to have much merit, insofar as one finds a continuous parallelism in the epic between Pāñcāla themes and the dominant Pāṇḍava story, for example, in the peculiar double leadership of the Pāṇḍava army by Dhṛṣṭadyumna *and* Arjuna (V.154.12f.). One can see, furthermore, in two cases, how Pāñcāla themes mold the alliances and paired combats of the Kurukṣetra war: although it is not stated explicitly, scrutiny reveals that the elders Bhīṣma and Droṇa, the first two Kaurava generals, fight on the Kaurava side not because they are really against the Pāṇḍavas but because they are sworn enemies of two Pāñcāla figures, Śikhaṇḍin and Drupada (later his son, Dhṛṣṭadyumna).[8] In fact, the role of the

---

[6] Besides the individually named victims, certain groups mentioned in X.8, Prabhadrakas, Somakas, and Sṛñjayas, appear also to be Pāñcālas: see their entries in Søren Sørensen, *An Index to the Names in the Mahābhārata* (1904; rpt. Delhi: Motilal Banarsidass, 1978).

[7] In this regard, a most useful, though brief, article is B.C. Mazumdar's comment on *Mahābhārata* I.94 (Critical Edition I.89) in the *Journal of the Royal Asiatic Society of Great Britain and Ireland* (1906), pp. 225–26. Mazumdar finds in this chapter remnants of an independent Kuru-Pāñcāla struggle, to which the Pāṇḍava story, he feels, has been grafted "for conferring dignity upon the heroes of the new story . . ." (p. 225). The many arguments in favor of an original Kuru-Pāñcāla conflict are summarized by N.N. Bhattacharya in his paper entitled "The Kurukṣetra War and the Pāṇḍavas", in *The Bhārata War and Purāṇic Genealogies*, ed. D.C. Sircar (Calcutta: University of Calcutta, 1969), p. 37. Of great importance is the fact that the Pāṇḍavas are not known to the pre-epic Vedic literature while the Pāñcālas are.

[8] On the Śikhaṇḍin-Bhīṣma enmity, see V. 170ff. On Bhīṣma as Śikhaṇḍin's "share" in battle, V.56.12, etc. On the Drupada-Droṇa antagonism, see I.122, etc. Once, after being defeated by Droṇa (with Pāṇḍava help, for this was prior to the Pāṇḍava-Pāñcāla alliance!), Drupada had performed a sacrifice to beget a son who would be able to defeat Droṇa; as a result, Dhṛṣṭadyuma was born, from the sacrificial fire, as Droṇa's antagonist. (Note that Draupadī took birth incidentallv at the same time, from the sacrificial altar. The basic story of the birth of Dhṛṣṭadyuma and Draupadī is told in I.155.)

Pāñcālas as embodied in the figure of Draupadī is absolutely central to the *Mahābhārata* as a whole. Draupadī incarnates Śrī (Prosperity) (I.61.95, etc.), and an insult to her punctuates the Pāṇḍavas' loss of their kingdom; to regain the kingdom is to avenge Draupadī/Śrī. As the joint Pāṇḍava marriage to Draupadī and the concomitant alliance best illustrate, a conscious attempt is evidently being made throughout the epic to link the fates of the Pāṇḍavas and Pāñcālas, or to replace the central Pāñcāla role with that of the Pāṇḍava brothers.[9] One might even suggest that the epic makes the Pāṇḍavas five in number so as to link them with the Pāñcāla people, the first element of whose name is *pañc-*, "five".[10]

In the *Sauptika* episode, for Aśvatthāman to avenge the death of his father, Droṇa, means first and foremost to kill Dhṛṣṭadyumna and the other Pāñcālas, against whom he has inherited Droṇa's enmity; that he does so is perfectly understandable as part of the chain of revenge which

---

[9] Note the recurrent phrase "Pāṇḍavas and Pāñcālas" ("pāṇḍupāñcāla . . .") and the frequent appearance of the Pāñcāla pair Yudhāmanyu and Uttamaujas (also killed eventually in the night raid) as the protectors of the wheels of Arjuna's chariot (VI.16.19, etc.). With regard to the Pāñcāla generalship of the Pāṇḍava army, note that XIV.59.9ff. specifies that Śikhaṇḍin was the first general, Dhṛṣṭadyumna the second. Arjuna protected Śikhaṇḍin, it is stated (XIV.59.9), Bhīma protected Dhṛṣṭadyumna (XIV.59.15). Contrast V.149.18ff., in which Arjuna nominates Dhṛṣṭadyumna for general, while Bhīma favors Śikhaṇḍin (Dhṛṣṭadyumna being chosen ultimately).

[10] The number of Pāṇḍavas gives the impression of being an artificial construct, particularly because the two younger brothers, the twins, are separated from the older ones by having a separate mother. In a sense, the three oldest Pāṇḍavas constitute a political grouping which is complete in itself, each making a characteristic contribution to the whole, while the twins look as though they have been added as an afterthought, their characteristics being less clearly and consistently defined than those of their older brothers. If, then, the fivefold grouping is very likely artificial and intentional, what is its basis? Several explanations may be and have been offered: five is a number of totality (possibly with a directional significance); there are many Indo-European parallels and parallels within the *Mahābhārata* itself, etc. What I am mentioning here is merely one additional aspect of a complex issue.

It has been suggested by scholars that the historical name "Pāñcāla" was derived from the fact that the nation was constituted of five tribes, joining together to form it; see Hemchandra Raychaudhuri, *Political History of Ancient India*, 3rd ed. (Calcutta: University of Calcutta, 1932), p. 47. (The fivefold count of these Indo-European tribes would probably have been ideological, rather than real). That the Pāṇḍavas were counted as five by analogy with the Pāñcālas was suggested as early as the nineteenth century by Christian Lassen, seconded by Joseph Dahlmann; see Dahlmann, *Genesis des Mahābhārata* (Berlin: Felix L. Dames, 1899), pp. 224ff.

In conclusion of this note, it is necessary to point out that Georges Dumézil, following Stig Wikander, would not agree that the twins are an afterthought added to bring the Pāṇḍava count to five; see Dumézil's *Mythe et épopée*, I (Paris: Gallimard, 1968), pp. 53ff., for another analysis of the Pāṇḍava family structure (but one which does not attempt to explain why the Pāṇḍava count is precisely five).

constitutes the epic story line. What is shocking about the night raid, however, is its finality: the Pāñcālas can never again avenge themselves; they have been wiped out completely.

This result of the night raid means a major twist in the epic plot as a whole: Draupadī's family has been killed off, and she herself leaves no offspring. If the entire Kurukṣetra war can be described as the Pāṇḍavas' successful revenge for an insult to Draupadī, or, more broadly, as their fight to establish their kingship with Śrī incarnate as their queen, what possibly can be the meaning of a fruitless Pāṇḍava-Draupadī marriage?

It may be argued that many an epic hero leaves no offspring; yet the absolute importance of children for the Pāṇḍava family permeates the *Sauptika* episode. What one may suggest, rather, is that someone is getting rid of the Pāñcālas to make way for another Pāṇḍava heir. Through Book IX the epic is the story of a Pāñcāla war and victory, with a superimposed Pāṇḍava plot. Book X tells of the twilight of the Pāñcālas, but does not provide a Pāṇḍava parallel. Instead, the Pāṇḍavas survive the termination of the Pāñcāla line, and are forced to stand on their own.

B. *The Establishment of the Lineage of Janamejaya*

The offspring left to the Pāṇḍava lineage at the end of the *Sauptika* episode is, as detailed above, Parikṣit. Just like the thread of Pāñcāla events running through the *Mahābhārata*, the events having to do with the ancestry of Parikṣit may be traced through the first nine books of the epic; only in this case they constitute a sub-plot, which does not surface until Book X, when it takes over where the Pāñcāla plot leaves off. The major episodes of this sub-plot are Arjuna's stealing of Kṛṣṇa's sister Subhadrā as his fourth, but for this plot most important, wife (I.211ff.), and the birth of Abhimanyu to Arjuna and Subhadrā; Arjuna's teaching of the Matsya princess Uttarā, and the marriage of Uttarā (first offered to Arjuna) to Abhimanyu (IV.66.27ff.); and the death of Abhimanyu in battle, killed by Kaurava treachery (VII.32ff.), leaving Uttarā a pregnant widow. Note that all of the epic's glorification of Abhimanyu as a great hero reflects favorably upon Parikṣit's line, as does, for that matter, all glorification of the Pāṇḍavas, especially Arjuna.

In the thread of the *Mahābhārata* plot comprising Parikṣit's genealogy, two peoples besides the Pāṇḍavas are particularly important: the Vṛṣṇis (Kṛṣṇa's people) and the Matsyas. (The Vṛṣṇis are doubly important to Parikṣit: first, his grandmother was a Vṛṣṇi; second, when Aśvatthāman killed him, a Vṛṣṇi, Kṛṣṇa—his maternal uncle—revived him). Any information about these two peoples in the first nine books of the epic may be construed as having been included to prepare the way for Parikṣit's birth: for example, the fact that the last year of the Pāṇḍavas' exile from their kingdom was spent in the kingdom of the Matsyas (which is, therefore, the scene of Book IV of the epic).[11] Similarly, any praise of Kṛṣṇa in the epic is indirect praise of Parikṣit's lineage.

Consideration of the frame of the *Mahābhārata* makes it easy to see who was responsible for fostering its Parikṣit-oriented sub-plot. One of the epic's two accounts of its own composition states that it was first recited by the brahman Vaiśampāyana to a King Janamejaya. This Janamejaya was, in fact, the son of Parikṣit, and the recitation took place at a snake sacrifice held by him to avenge the death of his father by snake bite (I.36ff.). Evidently, poets catering to the whim of this king (whatever his historical name may really have been)[12] saw fit to commandeer the Pāñcāla cycle of heroic tales for the glorification of the king's ancestors, known to the epic as the Pāṇḍavas. Eventually, in the *Sauptika* episode, the poets killed off the Pāñcālas to make way for the king's father, the so-called Parikṣit, and the king himself.

III. *How the Levels of Discourse of the* Mahābhārata *Narrative Disengage Themselves in the* Sauptika *Episode*

Careful reading of the *Mahābhārata*, with special attention to its unevennesses and inconsistencies and their causes, suggested to me, as I worked on my doctoral dissertation on the hero Arjuna, that the story line of the epic might be analyzed into three "levels" of discourse.[13] The levels could be identified, I discovered, in terms of their respective emphases: heroic, human, and Hindu. In a brilliant feat of combination and permutation, the *Mahābhārata* plot creates itself through fluctuation between the levels.

---

[11] Note too that Uttara, the Matsya prince who plays an important role in *Mahābhārata* IV, is the first major casualty of the Kurukṣetra war (VI.45.38–39). Peculiarly, some lists of victims of the night raid include the Matsyas along with the Pāñcālas (X.8.15, etc.).

[12] As the name "Janamejaya" is applied to a number of different figures in the *Mahābhārata* and elsewhere, including some from much earlier generations (I.89.44, 47, I.90.11, etc.; see also II.8.21), and so might have been borrowed as prestigious, it cannot be assumed to have been the real name of a historical personage who was Arjuna's great-grandson. Nonetheless, this Janamejaya seems to represent a king or group of kings who flourished historically, most likely Hindu conquerors of the autochthonous inhabitants of northern India (this being the probable meaning of Janamejaya's snake sacrifice and conquest of Takṣaśilā [I.3.18] in the epic).

[13] I studied the Bombay and Poona (Critical) Editions, but what I say in this section could apply to any edition of the epic.

One may, for example, note this fluctuation in the battle books of the epic as follows:

At Level I (the heroic level), the books describe typically Indo-European heroic warfare, very similar in cause, character, and results to the wars described in the *Iliad*, the *Táin Bó Cuailnge*, or any one of a number of other Indo-European works of heroic literature, but, of course, couched in the language of India: *dharma* ("law" or "right") as well as kingdom is at stake, although it is destined to win out in the end ("yato dharmas tato jayaḥ" ["where right is, there is victory"] [V.141.33, VI.2.14, etc., etc.]); the war as a whole is conducted as a sacrifice to preserve world order; it is, too, a reflection of the age-old battle between the Indo-European (Vedic) gods, headed by Indra, and the demons. This heroic level comprises the Pāṇḍava tale built on a Pāñcāla base, as described above.

Level II (the human level) of the battle books focuses upon the human problems emerging in the course of the heroic struggle, as epitomized in the ambiguity of the moral issues set forth: who is right and who is wrong? Issues crystallizing at this level include the following: the complexity of the original dispute (particularly insofar as genealogical irregularities confuse claims to the throne); the necessity of fighting against relatives, and the participation of the elders and teachers of the family on the supposedly evil (Kaurava) side; and the victory of the supposedly good warriors (the Pāṇḍavas) by means of a series of heinous deceits. All heroic epics have a certain human dimension: the epic hero, being, almost by definition, semi-divine, has a human as well as a godlike side, which always emerges at some point in the epic action. One must, however, admit that the human side of the *Mahābhārata* characters is particularly well defined. Surely no other epic has its most powerful hero sitting down in moral despair and refusing to fight, as Arjuna does at the start of the Kurukṣetra war in the episode of the *Bhagavadgītā* (*Mahābhārata* VI.23ff.).[14] Karṇa, the tragic hero of the *Mahābhārata*, summarizes the moral ambiguity of the battle books, and the epic as a whole, in the following pathetic words:

. . . dharmapradhānān abhipāti dharma
ity abruvan dharmavidaḥ sadaiva /
mamāpi nimno 'dya na pāti bhaktān
manye na nityaṃ paripāti dharmaḥ //

---

[14] Achilles' refusal to fight in the *Iliad*, while structurally similar, is not inspired by the same motive. Provoked by anger, Achilles' refusal more closely parallels that of Karṇa in *Mahābhārata* V.61.12f., etc., than that of Arjuna.

> The knowers of *dharma* have always said: "*Dharma* protects those devoted to *dharma*". Since my [chariot wheel] sank today, it does not protect its devotees. I think *dharma* does not always protect!" (VIII.66.43)[15]

It is, perhaps, the *Mahābhārata*'s concern for the human condition which leads it to reach for a higher plane at which ambiguities are transcended and the clear right and wrong of the heroic level restored.

At Level III (the Hindu level), one finds a fully developed Hindu response to the issues raised at Level II. The Pāṇḍavas are right, the epic asserts at Level III, simply because they are devotees of God (the Hindu god Kṛṣṇa, far more important at this level than the Vedic gods), whom the Kauravas, by contrast, have rejected;[16] this is the message, for example, of the *Bhagavadgītā*'s *bhaktimārga* (path of devotion). Even seemingly deceitful actions are good when Kṛṣṇa advocates them; variants of the statement "Where Kṛṣṇa is, there is *dharma*; where *dharma* is, there is victory" (XI.62.34, etc.; compare VI.41.55, etc.) replace, at this level, the heroic level's simpler—but discredited—insistence that *dharma* and victory go hand in hand irrespective of Kṛṣṇa.[17] In the battle books the devotional emphasis appears in intermittent references to the fact that Arjuna and Kṛṣṇa, merely special friends or warrior and charioteer at the heroic and human levels, are really Nara and Nārāyaṇa, the archetypal devotee and his God. Recurrently, then, at the very moment when the Pāṇḍavas' victory is most in doubt from the

---

[15] Dharmic confusion is so omnipresent in the *Mahābhārata* that it misled the nineteenth-century German scholars Adolf Holtzmann elder and younger into inventing a theory which stated that the Kauravas were the heroes of an original version of the epic, the Pāṇḍavas its villains; see Holtzmann, elder, *Indische Sagen* (Stuttgart: Adolph Krabbe, 1854, 1, viiif., etc.).

[16] The major locus of Kaurava rejection of Kṛṣṇa is the period of peace missions before the war. When Kṛṣṇa comes as ambassador to the Kauravas, Duryodhana wishes to imprison him (V.86.13f.; and see also V.128.4ff.); nor does he relent even when Kṛṣṇa grants him a divine vision (V.129.4ff.). If Duryodhana occasionally seems to be starting to understand who Kṛṣṇa really is (VI.64.11), he studiously ignores such an insight for the duration of the war. He does, however, acknowledge Kṛṣṇa shortly before his death (IX.64.28f.).

[17] For the view that Kṛṣṇa is a late addition to the phrase "yato dharmas tato jayaḥ", see Georg von Simson, "Die Einschaltung der *Bhagavadgītā* im *Bhīṣmaparvan* des *Mahābhārata*", *Indo-Iranian Journal*, 11 (1968–69), 166 and 174. Sylvain Lévi, however, seems to hold the opposite view: "yataḥ kṛṣṇas tato jayaḥ" and "yato dharmas tataḥ kṛṣṇaḥ" (and combinations of these) are the primary phrases; "yato dharmas tato jayaḥ" is a derivative (see his article "*Tato Jayam Udirayet*", trans. L.G. Khare, *Annals of the Bhandarkar Institute*. 1 [1918–19], 15).

human perspective, the battle books remind their audience that the power of God and devotion is actually invincible.

In the battle books, the three levels of discourse are intertwined so neatly that it is difficult to envision one or another standing alone. Not so in Book X of the *Mahābhārata*, however; and it is this fact which makes the *Sauptikaparvan* so worthy of attention. For it is in Book X that the intertwined levels of the epic story disengage themselves from one another: the heroic/human plot is killed off with the Pāñcālas, and the Hindu devotional level takes over in the person of the child Parikṣit, dependent upon Kṛṣṇa for his very life.[18] Before speculating on the meaning of this transition, I will devote the remainder of this section to suggesting some of the ways in which the devotional emphasis of the *Sauptika* episode transforms materials from the battle books.

First, one may point to the expanding time frame of the mythic imagery invoked by the *Sauptika* episode as compared to the battle books. Behind and around the Kurukṣetra war lurks the myth of the *kaliyuga* (dark age), the present, degenerate age of world history, as is apparent from the epic's concern with the dharmic decline associated with the conflict. The epic states clearly that the Kurukṣetra war marked the onset of the *kaliyuga* in the present *yuga* cycle.[19] But degeneration of *dharma*, moral ambiguity, is only a Level II (human) problem for the *Mahābhārata*; it is meaningless at Level III. Appropriately, then, the *Sauptika* episode expands beyond the human-oriented, morally determined *yuga* cycle to the tremendously longer cycle of days and nights of the god Brahmā, what might be called divine, or eschatological, time. The myth behind the *Sauptika* episode is the myth of *pralaya*, periodic

---

[18] Parikṣit's dependence upon Kṛṣṇa is evident in the passage which describes the scene at the time of his revival (XIV.69.1ff.). This passage may be contrasted with parallel ones describing the births of other heroes, for example, that which treats of the birth of Bharata, ancestor of the Pāṇḍavas and Kauravas (I.68.1ff.) or that which treats of the birth of the Draupadeyas (I.213.71ff.). For example, it is Kṛṣṇa who names Parikṣit (XIV.69.9f.), while the other heroes tend to be named by sages. With regard to Pāñcāla dissociation from the devotional level of epic narrative in the *Sauptika* episode, it is worth noting that even the earlier books of the epic do not view the Pāñcālas as particularly talented spiritually; see VII.165.41ff. for an illustration of this point.

[19] See I.2.9, III.148.37, IX.59.21; cf. V.72.18, V.140.7ff., VI.62.39, XII.326.82ff. Note that the Purāṇas postdate the *Mahābhārata* chronology slightly, stating that the *kaliyuga* began with the death of Kṛṣṇa. One may conjecture that the *Mahābhārata* is placing greater emphasis than the Purāṇas on the explicit connection between the events of the war and the dharmic decline which is the *kaliyuga*. Many aspects of the *Mahābhārata* story seem to have been shaped consciously with the Kurukṣetra war-*kaliyuga* connection in mind: to give just two examples, the obvious failure of *dharma* during the dice game in which the Pāṇḍavas first lose their kingdom to the Kauravas, and the breakdown of family unity in the struggle.

violent destruction of the universe after a day of Brahmā; the *kaliyuga* is dwarfed by comparison.[20]

One indication that the myth behind the *Sauptika* episode is the myth of *pralaya* is the key part played in the story by the god Śiva, working through Aśvatthāman. Here Aśvatthāman imitates the role of Śiva as World Destroyer at the time of *pralaya*, developed in classical Hindu mythology. Regarding the eschatological role of the *brahmaśiras* weapon, with which Aśvatthāman attempts to complete his work of destruction, it is necessary only to point out that the epic sometimes views the *brahmaśiras* as identical with the *pāśupata* weapon (although the *Sauptika* episode itself does not mention this identification).[21] The name of the *pāśupata* weapon indicates its close connection with Śiva, who himself is Paśupati (Lord of Animals), and the weapon is stated in III.41.8 and elsewhere to be the destroyer at the end of an age.[22] Kṛṣṇa, stopping the

---

[20] The chronology works nicely: the war followed by the night raid parallels the *yuga* cycle followed by *pralaya*. It is necessary to note here that Madeleine Biardeau, whose work on the *Mahābhārata* I greatly admire (see, especially, her "Études de mythologie hindoue", I-V, *Bulletin de l'École Française d'Extrême-Orient*, 54 [1968], 19–45; 55 [1969], 59–105; 58 [1971], 17–89; 63 [1976], 111–263; 65 [1978], 87–238) (partially reprinted with modifications as *Études de mythologie hindoue*, Tome 1: *Cosmogonies puraṇiques*, Publications de l'École Française d'Extrême-Orient, vol. 128 [Paris: École Française d'Extrême-Orient, 1981]), would probably not agree with my distinction between the *kaliyuga*-inspired and the *pralaya*-inspired sections of the epic. She regards both the war and the *Sauptika* episode as based on the image of *pralaya*, and to her the night raid is essentially a "reprise" and clarification of the war; see "Études", IV, pp. 208ff. She does, however, have many interesting ideas regarding the details of the *pralaya* imagery in the *Sauptika* episode: Bhīma as the wind of *pralaya*; Uttarā's womb as the water, etc. ("Études", IV, pp. 210ff.). Similarly, Dumézil seems to view the whole *Mahābhārata* war as a reflection of the Indo-European eschatological conflict, although, in fact, the *Sauptika* material figures most prominently in his discussion of the matter; see *Mythe et épopée*, I, pp. 218ff. Only Alf Hiltebeitel seems to concentrate on the *Sauptika* events (plus the antecedent story of Abhimanyu's death) as particularly eschatological; see his *The Ritual of Battle: Krishna in the Mahābhārata* (Ithaca, NY: Cornell University Press, 1976), pp. 312ff.

It is quite true that imagery of *pralaya* abounds in the battle books, for example, when the battlefield is described as paralleling the chaos of the time of universal destruction (VII.100.5, etc., etc.) or when certain warriors are compared to the forces of nature which destroy the world at the end of a cosmic age. I find it most helpful, however, to view the eschatological imagery of the battle scenes as primarily formulaic. (Hiltebeitel [p. 312] seems to be of the same opinion). The battles are described as resembling *pralaya* in intensity, but this says nothing about the time frame of the epic, which places the war at the onset of the *kaliyuga*, not at the moment of universal destruction. Nor does *pralaya* imagery seem to me to mold the events of the war or the characters involved in it, as *kaliyuga* imagery does, until the *Sauptika* episode.

[21] See III.41.7f. for the identification of *brahmaśiras* and *pāśupata*.

[22] On the other hand, the ultimate nature of the *pāśupata* weapon is not always stressed. It is sometimes grouped on lists with other weapons, and both Droṇa and the Kauravas are said, in such cases, to possess it (VII.163.28, VIII.43.21).

brahmaśiras weapon, functions in his classic Viṣṇu role of Preserver.[23]

In part, the *Sauptika* episode employs the concepts and imagery of the battle books: humanity and Hinduism superimposed upon a heroic conflict. Aśvatthāman justifies his night raid on the basis of previously committed Pāṇḍava misdeeds, and sees it as an act of pragmatic policy (X.1.33f.).[24] In words fraught with emotion, he bemoans Duryodhana's fate (X.4.27) and pledges revenge. Kṛpa disputes the morality of Aśvatthāman's plan, yet agrees to help, predicting an Indra-like performance on Aśvatthāman's part (X.2, 4, 5). The raid is conducted like a sacrificial act, having much in common with the heroic Khāṇḍava burning episode of *Mahābhārata* I.214–25,[25] but it is, like the war as a whole, a sacrifice of human beings. That only a few survivors remain afterwards is very much a *kaliyuga* situation: when Yudhiṣṭhira laments, "jīyamānā jayanty anye jayamānā vayaṃ jitāḥ" ("The others who were being conquered conquer; we, who were conquering, have been conquered") (X.10.10), the ambiguity of the outcome is stressed. Later, when Aśvatthāman throws the *brahmaśiras* weapon, he does so out of a sense of *āpad* (emergency) (X.13.17). The humanity of his reaction is, however, quickly resolved into the divine madness of Śiva at the time of world destruction.

As discussed above, Arjuna is portrayed in the battle books as Kṛṣṇa's devotee *par excellence*. It has also been pointed out that at the Hindu level of discourse in the epic the Kauravas are seen as evil specifically because they reject Kṛṣṇa. The *Sauptika* episode emphasizes this same anti-Kṛṣṇa bias in Aśvatthāman and contrasts Arjuna's attachment to Kṛṣṇa with Aśvatthāman's rejection of him. In this regard, one especially interesting story is told for the first time in *Sauptikaparvan* 12 (Aśvatthāman's relations with Kṛṣṇa not being of particular concern to the earlier books of the epic): Aśvatthāman, wandering the world, had once arrived in

---

[23] Compare the depiction of *pralaya* in *Bhagavadgītā* XI = VI.33. The parallelism between this chapter and the *Sauptika* episode is underscored by the mention in each of the key role of *kāla* (Time or Fate) in world destruction; see VI.33.32, etc., juxtaposed with X.8.65, etc., recounting the appearance of the violent figure of *kālarātri* (Night of Fate) on the scene of the night raid (compare also X.7.62f.). Striking, however, is the fact that in *Bhagavadgītā* XI, Kṛṣṇa himself is Destroyer as well as Preserver, while in the *Sauptika* episode the roles of Destroyer and Preserver are divided between Śiva and Kṛṣṇa (with *kālarātri* as yet a third figure). On *Bhagavadgītā* XI's connection with *pralaya*, see Biardeau, "Études", III, p. 53, IV, p. 116, and V, p. 139.

[24] He copies the conduct of an owl whom he sees killing sleeping crows. This story sounds very much like the sort of parable one might find in a work of *arthaśāstra* (political science).

[25] Outstandingly, the setting of fires and the slaying of those fleeing at the gate (X.8.10ff.), as well as the panic of the victims.

Kṛṣṇa's city of Dvārakā and asked Kṛṣṇa for his discus in exchange for the *brahmaśiras* weapon. When Kṛṣṇa had offered the discus to him, however, he had been unable to lift it. He had then admitted that had he obtained the discus, he would have used it to fight against Kṛṣṇa. Here Arjuna and several Vṛṣṇis are contrasted with the extremely evil Aśvatthāman: these had never made such a request of Kṛṣṇa (X.12.25ff.). In X.12.27, Kṛṣṇa calls Arjuna: "yasmāt priyataro nāsti mamānyaḥ puruṣo bhuvi / nādeyaṃ yasya me kiṃcid api dārāḥ sutās tathā ("He than whom no other person on earth is dearer to me, to whom I would give anything, even my wives and sons").

The contrast between the behavior of Aśvatthāman, who was told even by his father that he would be unrighteous (X.12.9), and Arjuna is also implicit elsewhere in the *Sauptika* episode. Both Arjuna and Aśvatthāman were warned against careless use of the *brahmaśiras* weapon when they were, at separate times, given this weapon by Droṇa (Aśvatthāman against Droṇa's better judgment).[26] The *Sauptikaparvan* states that Arjuna set his *brahmaśiras* weapon in motion "pūrvam ācāryaputrāya tato 'nantaram ātmane / bhrātṛbhyaś caiva sarvebhyaḥ svastīty uktvā . . . // devatābhyo namas kṛtya gurubhyaś caiva sarvaśaḥ / . . . . " ("having spoken a blessing for the son of the preceptor, then at once for himself and also for all his brothers, having honored the deities and also all the teachers. . . .") (X.14.5–6). That Arjuna's goodness is dependent upon Kṛṣṇa is clear from the fact that his good action was prompted by this mentor. For Arjuna, the *brahmaśiras* weapon is devotional in character (marking a development over his other weapons, outstandingly the bow Gāṇḍīva), and he has the devotional power to control it. It is not surprising, then, that Arjuna is able to withdraw the *brahmaśiras* weapon while Aśvatthāman cannot, although a brahmanical weapon (for such its name and source show it to be) should by right be handled better by a brahman than a warrior, especially when that brahman is the weapons teacher's own son. Aśvatthāman fails in his handling of the *brahmaśiras* because he is not a devotee of Kṛṣṇa.

But the Aśvatthāman of the *Sauptika* episode is more than just a human rejector of Kṛṣṇa devotion; he seems, rather, to become an arch-rival god. In this episode, then, Viṣṇu-Śiva opposition completely replaces the heroic and human oppositions of the battle books, defining the

---

[26] At I.123.75ff., Droṇa warns Arjuna not to use the *brahmaśiras* weapon on humans; it could burn the world. Śiva warns Arjuna regarding the *brahmaśiras/pāśupata* at III.41.15: he must not use it without due consideration. At III.163.49–50, Śiva tells Arjuna not to use the *pāśupata* against humans; it must only be used against other weapons. Regarding Droṇa's hesitation and warning to Aśvatthāman, see X.12.6ff.

devotional opposition of the Hindu level of the epic far more sharply than it was defined before.[27]

The metamorphosis of the Aśvatthāman of the battle books into what may best be characterized as an incarnation—or representation—of Śiva is a major accomplishment of the *Sauptika* episode. This transformation provides an example of how each level of discourse in the *Mahābhārata* chooses appropriate materials from other levels to remodel according to its own needs. For equation with Śiva, a more appropriate character from the earlier books of the epic could not have been chosen. Having all the external heroic traits of beauty and auspicious markings (IX.5.7ff.), and known as a hero,[28] Aśvatthāman has nevertheless been a peculiar

---

[27] Before the *Sauptika* episode, Viṣṇu-Śiva opposition in the epic is not clear-cut. Śiva, opposing Kṛṣṇa, is sometimes said to be aligned with destructive forces having some Kaurava or anti-Pāṇḍava affiliation: Jarāsaṃdha, for example (II.13.63, II.17.19, II.20.8), and Jayadratha (III.256.25ff.). Elsewhere, Śiśupāla, Kṛṣṇa's enemy, is said to have been born three-eyed (II.40.1), a Śaivic trait. The births of the Kauravas themselves are sometimes said to have taken place only after the propitiation of Śiva (I.103.9 and III.240.6) (this proves little, however, because propitiation of Śiva is a common action for one desiring progeny throughout the epic, and elsewhere the Kauravas are said to have been born through a boon from Vyāsa [I.107.7ff.]). On the other hand, the magic charm which made possible the engendering of the Pāṇḍavas was a gift to Kuntī from Durvāsas (I.104.4ff.), who is a portion of Śiva (XIII.145.35 and I, Appendix I, No. 118, lines 73f., and later texts; Durvāsas is also given as a name of Śiva in XII.12.61). Śiva is also involved in the various stories which explain how the multiple marriage of Draupadī took place (I.157.189). In many other ways as well, the Pāṇḍavas are associated with Śiva: note especially the Arjuna-Śiva initiatory encounter of Book III (similar in some ways to Aśvatthāman's initial encounter with Śiva in the *Sauptika* episode), in which Arjuna wins weapons from Śiva. During this meeting, Śiva gives Arjuna a vision of himself. Here and elsewhere, Arjuna wins the *pāśupata* weapon (meanwhile, Aśvatthāman has the *nārāyaṇa* weapon, which can be countered only by passive resistance [VII.170.15ff.]). In the battle books, Arjuna is sometimes compared to Śiva; as I have stated in n. 20 above, however, I feel that such formulaic comparisons do not indicate anything regarding mythic affiliation. Far more striking is the fact that Śiva is said to precede Arjuna on the battlefield (VII.173.9f., XII.330.69f.). After the war is over, the Pāṇḍavas propitiate Śiva to get the gold required for their horse sacrifice (XIV.64.1ff.).

The confusion in alignments seems to have a double cause. At the heroic level there is, of course, no Viṣṇu-Śiva opposition, and thus no reason not to permit the Pāṇḍavas to fraternize with Śiva where appropriate. At the devotional level, the epic has been interpolated by both Viṣṇu devotees and Śiva devotees, each group trying to allow its favorite deity to absorb the deeds of his opponent. One thus finds Nārāyaṇa praising Śiva at VII.172.63ff., Kṛṣṇa calling Śiva a *vibhūti* (manifestation) of Viṣṇu (VI.32.33), etc. Even in the *Sauptika* episode there are hints of such admixture, for example, a suggestion, in X.6.17, etc., that Kṛṣṇa somehow stands behind Śiva. Yet a single devotional group which had control over part of the epic could mold it at will, and this seems to have occurred in the case of the *Sauptika* episode as a whole. Śiva reveals himself as a force opposing Kṛṣṇa and the Pāṇḍavas here, as he tells Aśvatthāman that he has until now protected the Pāñcālas for Kṛṣṇa's sake, but that their time is now past.

[28] Even in the words of Arjuna; see VII.167.25ff.

figure, a fighting brahman like his father (IV.46.8f., etc.). In childhood, he distinguished himself among Droṇa's students "rahasyeṣu sarveṣu" ("in all mysteries") (I.123.41). Not only was Aśvatthāman born to enmity against the Pāñcālas; he must also have been resentful of Arjuna from his earliest days, knowing that his father preferred Arjuna to him (I.125.7, etc.). The fire of this enmity would have been fanned by the Pāṇḍava-Pāñcāla alliance, culminating in the unrighteous slaying of Droṇa. A natural by-product of Aśvatthāman's enmity against Arjuna was, of course, opposition to Kṛṣṇa. Just as the imagery of the *kaliyuga* expands into imagery of *pralaya*, so Aśvatthāman's human resentments, combined with his special powers, expand into divine destructiveness in the *Sauptika* episode. Reflecting Aśvatthāman's fully developed role in the epic, the list of partial incarnations of *Mahābhārata* I.61 describes him as "mahādevāntakābhyāṃ ca kāmāt krodhāc ca . . . ekatvam upapannānāṃ jajñe" ("born of the Great God [Śiva], Death, Anger, and Desire combined") (I.61.66).[29]

Aśvatthāman is enabled to act effectively in the night raid by virtue of his devotion to Śiva: he gains power by offering himself as a sacrifice to Śiva, and afterwards his behavior is wildly Śiva-like. The Pāṇḍava camp at the time of the night raid is reminiscent of the cremation grounds frequented by Śiva; the fire set there by the night raiders resembles that with which Śiva burns the world at the time of *pralaya*. The gem on Aśvatthāman's head is like Śiva's third eye.[30] The wandering to which he is condemned ultimately is Śaivic behavior.

Underlining the identification of Aśvatthāman with Śiva, the last two chapters of the *Sauptikaparvan* consist of stories of Śiva, told by Kṛṣṇa to Yudhiṣṭhira in connection with Kṛṣṇa's explanation of how Aśvatthāman was able to succeed in the night raid. One story, a version of the well-known tale of "Dakṣa's sacrifice"[31] (although Dakṣa is not mentioned in it by name) (X.18), has imagery which is connected intimately with that of the night raid, imagery of *pralaya*. Here Śiva is portrayed as a malcontent who feels himself slighted by the other gods; this is a sentiment which closely parallels Aśvatthāman's bitter feeling towards the Pāṇḍavas, as depicted throughout the *Sauptika* episode.

In the ultimate conflict of the *Sauptika* episode, Aśvatthāman as Śiva

---

[29] The same chapter identifies Kṛpa as an incarnation of the Rudras (v. 71), gods closely related to Śiva.

[30] Śiva's third eye is, in fact, mentioned in the *Sauptika* episode (X.7.8).

[31] Found in the *Mahābhārata* at VII.173.29, 41ff., XII.274, etc., as well as in the Purāṇas.

threatens to destroy the universe, represented by the Pāṇḍava family. At this moment of extreme crisis, Kṛṣṇa, aided by his devotee Arjuna, must intervene. Together, Kṛṣṇa and Arjuna manage to preserve world order; or, to be more specific, they manage to rescue that very small remnant which is necessary to recreate the world after its cyclic destruction.[32] That remnant is Parikṣit.[33] The pralayic imagery of rebirth from a remnant is probably based on the imagery of the funerary sacrifice, in which a body is burned and the ashes quickened with water so that rebirth (or, in the case of *pralaya*, a new creation of the universe) may occur.[34] In the *Sauptika* episode, however, the sacrifice turns out to be God's, and its successful outcome is seen to depend upon God's ability to reverse the natural processes of life and death; the message being that of the epic at its Hindu level: that devotion must inform sacrifice.

IV. *Who Composed the* Sauptikaparvan?

Evidently, the composers of the *Sauptikaparvan* were committed devotees of Viṣṇu, who, as outlined above, substituted a devotional version of the epic conflict for a heroic/human one. Equally evident is the fact that the devotees who were responsible for this work were poets in the court of the king known to the epic as Janamejaya; for, as indicated in Section IIB of this paper, a major emphasis of the episode is to establish consciously and deliberately the position of Janamejaya's father, Parikṣit.

For these poets striving to please their king, the *Sauptika* episode encapsulated the central meaning of the *Mahābhārata*, which was a political meaning: the riddles which led to the Kurukṣetra war had been solved perfectly; that is, the succession conflict was over permanently, a single descendant of the entire Kuru line having been provided, and the oppositions of the war dissolved once and for all. "As truth and *dharma* are constantly established in me, let this dead child, the son of Abhimanyu, live" ("yathā satyaṃ ca dharmaś ca mayi nityaṃ pratiṣṭhitau / tathā mṛtaḥ śiśur ayaṃ jīvatām abhimanyujaḥ") (XIV.68.22), said Kṛṣṇa as he revived Parikṣit. The royal claim of Janamejaya, Parikṣit's son, was established absolutely, on the basis of a devotional

---

32 See Biardeau, "Études", IV, p. 127.

33 Biardeau, "Études", V, p. 162. The idea of a child as remnant is found more than once in the *Mahābhārata*: compare the cases of Parāśara (I.167.13ff.) and Aurva (I.169.20ff.).

34 Biardeau, "Études", III, p. 31, n. 1, pp. 75ff., IV, p. 190. Indeed, the main description of *pralaya* in the *Mahābhārata* (III.186.56ff.) follows this pattern.

relationship with Kṛṣṇa (to whom Janamejaya traced his ancestry), who saved world order by saving Parikṣit.[35]

At this point, I ask for my readers' indulgence as I turn to speculation and present the following hypothesis: that the poets responsible for the extant *Sauptika* episode were adherents, or forerunners, of that sect of Viṣṇu devotees known as Pāñcarātrins,[36] who molded the *Sauptika* tale to illustrate their own doctrine symbolically. According to this hypothesis, the night raid, followed by the *brahmaśiras* portion of the episode, would represent the "night" (*rātra*) referred to in the compound "Pañcarātra". This symbolism would correspond well to what Walter G. Neevel, Jr. cites convincingly as an early interpretation of this term (possibly representing its "original" meaning): that "Pañcarātra" refers to the "night of the five", the "five" being the earthly elements, which disappear at the time of *mokṣa* (individual salvation) or *pralaya*.[37] In the night raid of the *Sauptika* episode, the five who are destroyed are the five shadowy Draupadeyas, or, alternatively, the Pāñc-ālas.[38] The point is that even as the worldly elements are destroyed, the power of devotion prevails.

---

[35] Note the words of Janamejaya's ministers to him in praise of Parikṣit: "govindasya prīyaś cāsīt pitā te janamejaya" ("Janamejaya, your father was dear to Govinda [Kṛṣṇa]") (I.45.12).

[36] On the Pāñcarātrins, see, for example: F. Otto Schrader, *Introduction to the Pāñcarātra and the Ahirbudhnya Saṃhitā* (Madras: Adyar Library, 1916); Jan Gonda, *Viṣṇuism and Śivaism: A Comparison* (London: Athlone Press—University of London, 1970); Suvira Jaiswal, *The Origin and Development of Vaiṣṇavism* (*Vaiṣṇavism from 200 B.C. to A.D. 500*) (Delhi: Munshiram Manoharlal, 1967); Mitsunori Matsubara, "The Early Pāñcarātra with Special Reference to the Ahirbudhnya Saṃhitā", diss., Harvard, 1972; and Sushil Kumar De, "Sects and Sectarian Worship in the Mahābhārata", *Our Heritage*, 1 (1953), 1–29.

[37] Neevel, *Yāmuna's Vedānta and Pāñcarātra: Integrating the Classical and the Popular*, Harvard Dissertations in Religion, 10 (Missoula, Mont.: Scholars Press, 1977), pp. 8ff. The emphasis on the night of the raid as "*kālarātri*" (see n. 23 above) goes well with this interpretation. Compare the statement of *Bhagavadgītā* II.69 = VI.24.69:

yā niśā sarvabhūtānāṃ tasyāṃ jāgarti saṃyamī /
yasyāṃ jāgrati bhūtāni sā niśā paśyato muneḥ //

> In what is night for all creatures, one who is restrained is awake. When creatures are awake, that is night for a seeing sage.

For a discussion of some other suggestions as to the origin of the name "Pāñcarātra" in both Hindu texts and modern scholarship, see Jaiswal, pp. 41ff. See also two important articles: J.A.B. van Buitenen, "The Name 'Pañcarātra'", *History of Religions*, 1 (1961–62), 291–99, and V. Raghavan, "The Name Pāñcarātra: With an Analysis of the Sanatkumāra-Saṃhitā in Manuscript", *Journal of the American Oriental Society*, 85 (1965), 73–79.

[38] It is worth noting here that the *pāñcarātraṃ* sacrifice of *Śatapatha Brāhmaṇa* XIII.6.1.1, etc., often cited in discussions of the etymology of "Pāñcarātra", is likewise a human sacrifice.

It is probable that a cycle of Pāñcāla tales which provided the core of the *Mahābhārata* included a story of a night raid.[39] Perhaps some Pāñcarātrins picked up this tale as an illustration of their doctrine, identifying the archenemy of the Pāñcālas, Aśvatthāman, with Śiva; if so, they could have been attracted to it particularly because the name Pāñcāla fits so beautifully into their "five" symbolism. Between Pāñcālas and Pāñcarātrins the five Pāṇḍavas mediate perfectly; so perfectly that it is impossible to determine whether their fivefold count is influenced by the one group or the other, both, or neither.[40]

It is tempting to speculate that Janamejaya and his court poets were themselves Pāñcarātrins. Is Parikṣit's revival, perhaps, the reflection of a Pāñcarātra initiation?[41] It is more likely, however, that the family and court of Janamejaya participated in a pre-Pāñcarātra form of Vaiṣṇavism, and that Pāñcarātra material entered the epic only later, adhering to devotional material already there. It is, of course, possible that the imagery of the *Sauptika* episode influenced Pāñcarātra thought and language, rather than the reverse.

What is absolutely certain, however, is that at some point in time the Pāñcarātrins did take control of the epic text; we know this from their interpolation into it of the clearly Pāñcarātra *Nārāyaṇīya* episode (XII.321ff.).[42] It is reasonable, therefore, to hypothesize some Pāñcarātra influence upon the *Sauptika* episode, whether sooner or later. Strikingly,

---

[39] Compare the night raid on the Thracians of *Iliad* X.469ff. Most likely, the tale of the night raid against the Pāñcālas was the final tale of the original cycle of Pāñcāla stories, just as it is the final Pāñcāla tale in the extant epic. Most epic cycles end with the deaths of their heroes; the *Mahābhārata* itself ends in this way, with the Pāṇḍavas' journey to heaven. The night raid story would have been the equivalent in the Pāñcāla cycle.

[40] In support of the Pāṇḍava-Pāñcarātra connection envisioned here, it is noteworthy that the Pāṇḍavas are sometimes compared with the five elements: V.63.2, XII.53.18

[41] On Pāñcarātra initiation, see Schrader, pp. 121f. and Jaiswal, pp. 140ff. Note that Kṛṣṇa is known elsewhere as a reviver or rescuer of children; see *Harivaṃśa* LXXIX.10ff. and CIff., where Arjuna is brought into the story (compare *Bhāgavata Purāṇa* X.89.22f.). Others, however, also revive children in the epic; see XII.29.141ff., XII.149.106ff. More broadly, of course, Parikṣit's death and revival provide an example of the hero's threatened childhood.

The name "Pāṇḍavas" means "Whites". To some, this name has seemed to identify the Pāṇḍavas as an organization, not a family. Gerrit Jan Held, in his *The Mahābhārata: An Ethnological Study* (London: Kegan Paul, 1935), pp. 297ff., identifies the Pāṇḍavas as a phratry specializing in initiation, named for a color. In fact, the color white is often associated with initiation; see Mircea Eliade, *Rites and Symbols of Initiation: The Mysteries of Birth and Rebirth*, trans. Willard R. Trask (New York: Harper Colophon, 1975), pp. 37, 44.

[42] Besides mentioning the Pāñcarātra school by name, this episode refers to the Pāñcarātra *vyūha* (translated by Gonda [p. 50] as approximately "arrangement") doctrine, whereby Viṣṇu is said to emanate through four or five successive *vyūhas*, named after the various Vṛṣṇi warriors.

the very sages who dominate the *Nārāyaṇīya*, Nārada and Vyāsa, play major roles in the *Sauptika* episode as well.[43]

Conclusion

I have shown in this paper how the *Sauptika* episode of the *Mahābhārata* modified the meaning of the epic by depicting the epic characters as participants at the eschatological turning point in cosmic history. I have shown how the episode completes certain threads and levels of the epic narrative, and suggested that some episodes of earlier books were included or stressed primarily to pave the way for the *Sauptika* events. Devotional redactors were responsible for this reshaping of the epic, and I have made a suggestion as to who they may have been.

To conclude this discussion, I would like to point out that the Pāñcarātrins are certainly not the only identifiable reshapers of the *Mahābhārata* text. The sort of analysis offered in this paper might usefully be applied to other sections of the epic besides the *Sauptika* episode, representing the concerns of other groups. To my mind, one other example is outstanding and particularly deserves mention here. We know that, like the Pāñcarātrins, the Bhārgava brahmans also commandeered the epic at a certain point in its history, adding to it many of their stories, most obviously that of Rāma Jāmadagnya.[44] Moreover, even the most cursory reading of the *Anuśāsanaparvan* (Book of Instruction, Book XIII of the epic) shows it to be the work of brahmans who cavalierly advise their audience that the highest religious act is to give brah-

[43] It is noteworthy that the *Nārāyaṇīya* contains a story of a fight between Rudra (Śiva) and Nara and Nārāyaṇa, at Dakṣa's sacrifice, which greatly resembles the confrontation between Aśvatthāman and Arjuna and Kṛṣṇa of the *Sauptika* episode; see XII.330.42ff. With regard to the difference between the depiction of *pralaya* in the *Sauptika* episode and *Bhagavadgītā* XI (discussed in n. 23, above), might one suggest that perhaps the *Sauptika* reflects the Pāñcarātra understanding of *pralaya* (popular and mythic), while *Bhagavadgītā* XI reflects the Bhāgavata understanding? More generally, with regard to the connection between the *Mahābhārata* and Pāñcarātra doctrine, one may refer to the play by the early Sanskrit playwright Bhāsa entitled *Pañcarātram*. The subject of this play is the imposition of a five-day deadline by the Kauravas late in the Pāṇḍavas' exile; if the Pāṇḍavas can be located during this time, they will be given back their kingdom. (The ending is a happy one). As far as I have been able to determine, this plot has no basis in the epic itself (certainly not in the critical text); nor can a good explanation of the title be found. Might a connection with Pāñcarātra philosophy be suggested here?

[44] See Vishnu Sitaram Sukthankar, "The Bhrgus and the Bharata: A Text-Historical Study", in his *Critical Studies in the Mahābhārata*, Vol. I of *Sukthankar Memorial Edition*, ed. P.K. Gode (Bombay: Karnatak Publishing House, 1944), pp. 278–337, and Robert P. Goldman, *Gods, Priests, and Warriors: The Bhṛgus of the Mahābhārata* (New York: Columbia University Press, 1977).

mans gifts of food, cows, and money. I suggest that one may look for the clearest brahmanical contribution to the central narrative of the *Mahābhārata* in Book XVIII, the *Svargārohaṇaparvan* (Book of the Ascent to Heaven), where the already somewhat brahmanical Yudhiṣṭhira becomes the embodiment of philosophical Hinduism, as the ambiguities of the Kurukṣetra war dissolve into illusion for him. Here is a different version of Level III (the Hindu level) of epic discourse: Yudhiṣṭhira becomes for the *jñānamārga* (path of knowledge) what Arjuna already is for the *bhaktimārga*. The material building up to this late plot twist can be traced through the earlier books of the epic, just as I have traced the material preparatory to the *Sauptika* episode. The importance of the narrative thread culminating in the *Svargārohaṇa* episode is such that Yudhiṣṭhira has often been considered the most important Pāṇḍava, and philosophical peace the epic's message.

Perhaps the most fascinating aspect of such endeavors to trace the reshaping of the *Mahābhārata* by various vested interest groups is that they point to the richness and malleability of the original Indo-European story. Because no final editor saw fit to reduce the vast size of the epic text, and because all layers which found their way into it were permitted to remain intact, the *Mahābhārata* strikingly reveals the process of symbolic growth in epic literature, building upon its Indo-European base.

INDIA'S FIFTH VEDA: THE *MAHĀBHĀRATA'S* PRESENTATION OF ITSELF*

JAMES L. FITZGERALD

One of the most famous and delightful images connected with the *Mahābhārata* is that of the god Gaṇeśa serving as the stenographer for this, the world's largest "epic". The seer Vyāsa has just informed the god Brahmā that he has composed a great poem comprising all valuable knowledge and surpassing all previous expressions of important knowledge. When Vyāsa wonders how he would teach this work to his students, Brahmā suggests the god Gaṇeśa become Vyāsa's scribe :

> Brahmā said, "Call Gaṇeśa in your mind to write this inspired poetic work down", and then he went back home. Satyavatī's son Vyāsa then summoned Heramba to mind, and Gaṇeśa, the lord over obstacles who satisfies the needs that worry his devotees, came where Vedavyāsa was as soon as he was called to mind. Vyāsa received him with great honor and he sat down. Vyāsa then said to him, "Gaṇesá, you must be the scribe for this *Bhārata* as I compose it in my head and speak it forth". The lord over obstacles replied, "If my pen does not stop for an instant as I write, I shall be the scribe". Vyāsa replied to the god, "But never write without having comprehended". "OṂ", said Gaṇeśa and he became the scribe.
>
> Then, with great enthusiasm, the hermit Dvaipāyana secretly composed a difficult knotting of verses, within which, in accord with his stipulation, he recited this here *Bhārata*. There are 8,800 such verses: I, Ugraśravas, your bard, understand them and Vyāsa's son Śuka does too, Dhṛtarāṣṭra's aide Saṃjaya may or may not understand them. Even now that heap of verses remains knotted extremely tightly and cannot be undone, because the meanings in them are so obscure. While the omniscient Gaṇeśa sat pondering these, Vyāsa composed a great many other verses.[1]

---

[1] V.S. Sukthankar, S.K. Belvalkar, and P.L. Vaidya, eds., *The Mahābhārata, for the First Time Critically Edited* (Poona: Bhandarkar Oriental Research Institute, 1933–66), apparatus to line 36 of passage 1 of Appendix I of the *Ādiparvan*, vol. 1, 884–5.

Gaṇeśa is a wonderfully whimsical figure to many Westerners, but the vision of the chubby boy with the elephant's head sitting amid stacks of palm leaves at Vyāsa's feet in the latter's remote forest retreat, breathlessly running his pen over leaf after leaf, must have charmed Indian audiences through the ages as well. But I suspect Gaṇeśa's critical assistance to the composition and transmission of Vyāsa's *Great Bhārata* has been more than a charming story to readers of the text through the ages. Gaṇeśa's presence at the beginning of the *Mahābhārata* tradition reassures anyone undertaking the reading of Vyāsa's poem that the *Great Bhārata* has his divine approval and is thus beneficial to human beings. And his homely warmth and friendly generosity—he is the divine "conqueror of obstacles" (*vighnajit, vighneśa*) millions upon millions have called upon at the beginning of undertakings of diverse kinds and confidently turned to in distress (*bhaktacintitapūraka*)—hearten and encourage the reader, as they promise Gaṇeśa's company and all necessary help. Such blessings are certainly welcome to anyone who would read on through that awesome and daunting work. The text of the Sanskrit *Great Bhārata* that was received by Indian tradition contains an overwhelming 100,000 *śloka* couplets (which comes to about eight times the length of the *Iliad* and the *Odyssey* combined), and the narrative of war which makes up the central continuity of the text is a profoundly horrifying account of social fission, treachery, grotesque violence, and quasi-parricide that has troubled many Indian people through the past 1500 years.

Though this passage has a bearing on my argument, I mention it more as an invocation of Gaṇeśa at the beginning of this small contribution to the understanding of the *Mahābhārata*. The argument I present here is an interpretation of the beginning of a *Mahābhārata*, an interpretation undertaken and presented because it represents an important key to the apprehension of that *Mahābhārata's* general nature, as it was designed by its authors and intended to be appropriated by its audiences. The *Mahābhārata* has played a major role in educating Indian peoples, in structuring and informing their imagination and sensibilities in fundamental ways for the past 1500 years or more, alongside the Tripiṭaka of the Buddhists and the *Rāmāyaṇa* and several smaller *corpora* of sacred texts. The *Mahābhārata* gave them grand heroes and villains, thrilling stories, and profound crises; it schooled them in cosmology, philosophy, theology, and ethics, and through it all it legitimized and inculcated ethical and political patterns fundamentally important to "Hindu" civilization, patterns which had been cogently criticized and strongly challenged from within and without Aryan Brahmanism. Joseph Dahlmann alone among major scholars of the *Mahābhārata* understood and tried to explain it as such a dynamic spiritual and cultural reality.[2] He saw the *Mahābhārata* as "die Erzieherin des Volkes zu höheren religiösen und sittlichen Ideen, Lehrerin des Volkes" (the tutor of the people for higher religious and moral ideas, the schoolmarm of the people).[3] But Dahlmann's basically sound apprehension of the *Mahābhārata* was too strikingly alien to the predilections of late nineteenth-century Sanskrit philology; and parts of his argument were not sound, so his understanding of the *Mahābhārata* was buried in a heap of criticism and remains largely unknown today.[4] But Dahlmann was right in seeing the *Mahābhārata* as the educator of the Indian people, and my modest exegetical effort here is part of a program to interpret the *Mahābhārata* which derives fundamental inspiration from Dahlmann's general understanding of it. The kinds of claims the *Mahābhārata* makes for itself and the way in which it presents itself demonstrate manifestly that it sought self-consciously to be the educator of India. Gajānana's help will be most welcome in this effort from now until the *Mahābhārata* is understood.

I say this, though one of the first obstacles to be faced is to state as clearly as possible what I mean here by "*Mahābhārata*", and as a result of my doing that Gaṇeśa becomes invisible. The effort to establish a critical edition of the Sanskrit text of the *Mahābhārata* (carried out at the Bhandarkar Institute in Poona between 1919 and 1970) revealed that a single Sanskrit version of the "*Mahābhārata*", fixed in writing, was at the base of the entire manuscript tradition of the Sanskrit *Mahābhārata*, and it revealed that this lovely Gaṇeśa episode was not present in that version. The collation of Sanskrit manuscripts (which were gathered from every part of the Indian subcontinent) carried out for the critical edition disclosed a great amount of variation in the readings of individual lines, passages contained or omitted, and in the ordering of passages (sometimes even of longer passages, or whole sections of the text), as well as in the overall size of the

---

[2] Dahlmann's two main works on the *MBh* are: *Das Mahābhārata als Epos und Rechtsbuch* (Berlin: F.L. Dames, 1895) and *Genesis des Mahābhārata* (Berlin: F.L. Dames, 1899). Vittore Pisani ("The Rise of the Mahābhārata", in *A Volume of Eastern and Indian Studies Presented to F.W. Thomas*, ed. by S.M. Katre and P.K. Gode [Bombay: Karnatak Publishing House, 1939], 59–62) and Sylvain Lévi ("Tato Jayam Udīrayet", in *Commemorative Essays Presented to Sir Ramkrishna Gopal Bhandarkar* [Poona: Bhandarkar Oriental Research Institute, 1917]) also made significant contributions to this understanding of the *MBh*.

[3] *Genesis des Mahābhārata*, p. 142.

[4] Dahlmann was also stubbornly wrongheaded on a number of significant issues which are not relevant to what I consider his main point to have been. Dahlmann's writings have never been made available in English, and I intend to publish a review of his contributions to the study of the *MBh*. For a brief review of his theses in the context of turn of the century scholarship on the *MBh* see my "The *Mokṣa* Anthology of the *Great Bhārata*: An Initial Survey of Structural Issues, Themes, and Rhetorical Strategies", unpublished Ph.D. diss., University of Chicago, 1980, pp. 36–46.

different, orthographically distinct versions. But at the same time there emerged an overwhelming unity amidst all of these versions, and geographic patterns of agreement and disagreement in readings and in passages included or not included, which point conclusively to a single written "text" of a *Mahābhārata* at some point in the ancestry of these manuscripts.[5] This old Sanskrit *Mahābhārata* is the "*Mahābhārata*" this paper is concerned with, though there is no hope of ever seeing the original text of this version of it. For though it is clear that all Sanskrit manuscripts of the *Mahābhārata* basically derive from this single text, the complexity of this text's transmission is such that many of the disagreements among the witnesses cannot be resolved cleanly through the standard principles of textual criticism.[6] The critical edition of Poona is the closest approximation to the archetype behind the manuscript tradition we will ever get,[7] and, practically speaking, it is this version of the *Mahābhārata* that, generally, I intend by "*Mahābhārata*" (*Great Bhārata* sometimes, for effect, and *MBh* sometimes, for economy).

It is not possible to say exactly what this text, the archetype of all the Sanskrit manuscripts, was in relation to its antecedents, nor to say how it has interacted with other parts of the tradition of *Mahābhārata* in the time after its creation. In its largest sense, "the *Mahābhārata*" is a wide and varied tradition which has existed in ancient and "medieval" India in several forms (oral, written, dramatic, danced, in puppet performances) in many languages and in numerous versions, and it is entirely uncharted as such a super-textual tradition. It is conceivable that this tradition is best imagined as a generative matrix of themes, fixed in part, but very fluid and

[5] See Sukthankar's "Prolegomena" to the critical edition, Sukthankar et al., *The Mahābhārata*, vol. 1, xxxiv, liv–v, lxxxviii–xci. The amount of unity, both petty and general, that exists among the *MBh* manuscripts, particularly between geographically remote traditions which often have discrepant traditions intervening between them such as Kashmir and Kerala, can be explained only on the assumption of a fixed text antecedent to those manuscripts, an archetype. For the variations which exist can be explained as later, particular innovations resulting from various dynamic factors in the tradition, while the unity cannot be explained, generally, as parallel independent invention.

[6] Sukthankar, "Prolegomena", pp. lxxvi–xcii.

[7] Obviously Sukthankar's attempt to recover the archetype contains a large amount of reconstruction by conjecture or speculation, and plainly there is room for honest doubt whether the manuscript tradition is clear enough to allow for sound conjecture. My own sense now is that there seem to be clear enough indications in the tradition to tempt a bold or courageous scholar to make the try. Having gone as far as he had by the early thirties, Sukthankar did not find the situation so hopeless as to dissuade him from finishing what he had so energetically started, and he did not make that assessment recklessly. It is worth noting here too that Franklin Edgerton strongly endorsed the attempt to reconstruct, and argued that the situation was not as difficult as he and Sukthankar sometimes made it out to be (Franklin Edgerton, in his introduction to his edition of the *Sabhāparvan*, *The Mahābhārata*, Vol. 2, xxxvi–xxxvii).

dynamic, and that the Sanskrit version, which became the archetype, is but one specific realization of this ideal tradition of "*Mahābhārata*", alongside the thousands upon thousands of other realizations of it (including all actual oral recitations and dramatic performances). It is also quite conceivable that such a tradition as this changed, perhaps in fundamental ways, with the emergence of a written tradition of a Sanskrit *Mahābhārata*. The prestige of Sanskrit in "medieval" India, and the relative stability of its being written down may have made this version of the *MBh* the single most determinative factor in the general *MBh* tradition. On the other hand, it may be that the creation of this Sanskrit text, or of similar texts directly antecedent to it, constituted the very creation of the tradition of "*Great*" *Bhārata* from some prior tradition or traditions. Recent investigations by P.A. Grintser make it seem highly probable that the Sanskrit text of the *MBh* was extracted from an improvisational oral tradition that functioned in terms of compositional formulas and themes rather than a fixed text.[8] I suspect further, in some agreement with Dahlmann's general view of the genesis of this *MBh*,[9] that this abstracted text was, as imagined most simply, an elaborate fabrication (basically simultaneous with the invention of the *Bhagavadgītā*, which is the center and heart of our text) in which old epic narrative materials of a "*Bhārata*" cycle were adapted to, and re-imagined in synthesis with, materials that existed in a distinct tradition of religious didacticism to create the "*Great*" *Bhārata* of Vyāsa. I suspect that this *Great Bhārata* was subjected to deliberate extension or "updating" at least once after the original creation of the text, for there are certain parts of it (for example, the *Dānadharmaparvan*) which, while not deviating significantly form the basic thrust of the text as read without them, do not seem to have the same general measure of inter-dependent continuity with other parts of the text that is found in the rest of the text. Neither the creation of this text nor the effort to promulgate it could have been casual, and I suspect both were undertaken by some royal house for important symbolic or propagandistic purposes. The likely date for this was somewhere in the long period between 100 B.C. and 350 A.D.[10]

---

[8] See Wendy O'Flaherty's article reviewing publications on the *MBh* in *Religious Studies Review*, 4, 1 (Jan. 1978), 19–28 and J.W. de Jong's "Recent Russian Publications on the Indian Epic" in the *Adyar Library Bulletin*, 39 (1975), 1–42 for accounts of the theses of P.A. Grintser's *Drevneindiiskii Epos*: *Genezis i Tipologiya* (Moscow: 1974).

[9] See Dahlmann, *Genesis des Mahābhārata*, pp. 129–130, 135, 162ff., and 172–174.

[10] Various pieces of literary evidence indicate that many themes and stories that we find in our Sanskrit text of the *MBh* existed in Indian culture between 300 B.C. and 100 A.D., but there is no definite evidence of our *MBh* before 532 A.D. Georg Bühler (George Bühler

Whether this text of the *MBh* is only one realization of an old and prolific matrix of themes, or is a representative of the first "*Great*" *Bhārata* and father of all "*Mahābhāratas*", it is not *the Mahābhārata*, the "*real*" *Mahābhārata*, nor even the "best" *Mahābhārata*. But in either case, it is probably the most important *Mahābhārata* in the history of Indian culture, that is, the most influential, determinative version of it, the one through which one gains the most knowledge about the whole of the *MBh* tradition. It was written and thus highly fixed and stable relative to the vast majority of other realizations of the text; it was plausibly a complete and full rendition of the ideal *Mahābhārata*; it was successfully propagated over the whole of the subcontinent; and it was in Sanskrit, the language commonly favored in numerous ways as the normative linguistic realization of any truly valuable knowledge. Thus this version of the *Mahābhārata* was uniquely charged to function as the measure of *Mahābhārata* in India, and it probably did, though "measure" does not imply the western concepts of "canon" or "text" in any narrow way.

The Gaṇeśa passage occurs only in the North Central version of the text (that consituted, basically, by the Devanāgarī script), is not present in the important manuscript traditions of Kashmir, Bengal, or Kerala.[11] It was deliberately invented and inserted into the text sometime after a written

---

and J. Kirste, "Indian Studies No. II: Contributions to the History of the Mahābhārata", *Sitzungsberichte der philosophischen-historischen Classe der kaiserlichen Akademie der Wissenschaften*, 127 [Vienna: 1892], *Abhandlung* 12, pp. 25–26) showed that the full *MBh*, including its *Harivaṃśa* appendix, certainly existed by 532 A.D. and that the *MBh* was definitely perceived by Indian kings as a normative sacred text by 450 A.D. Bühler made the not implausible inference that the text existed at least as a normative sacred text by 300 A.D. (It should be borne in mind that the Gupta dynasty, which eventually united most of Northern India, came to power about 330 A.D.) E.W. Hopkins' examination of the text's knowledge of different, dated aspects of Indian economic realia led him to the conclusion that the bulk of the *MBh* text existed by 200 A.D. (though these arguments do not bear upon the question whether all of this textual material had been synthesized into the *MBh* by then or not) (*Great Epic of India* [New York: Scribner & Sons, 1901], pp. 387–89). The city of Rome is named in our version of the second major book of the *MBh*, a fact which prompted its editor Franklin Edgerton to conclude that "our text cannot have been composed at any time before this city name came to the ears of the Indians. This means surely not before the first century B.C., and very likely not until a century or two later" (in his introduction to vol. 2 of Sukthankar et al., *The Mahābhārata*, xxviii).

[11] The passage is found only in manuscripts written in Devanāgarī script: D2–12, Dnl–3, (three manuscripts of the text also containing Nīlakaṇṭha's commentary) and Drl–4 (four manuscripts of the text containing the commentary of Ratnagarbha), and in two manuscripts written in Devanāgarī script classified by Sukthankar as part of the Kashmiri-Devanāgarī tradition, K4 and K6, which, along with K3 and K5 of that tradition, generally exhibit "contamination" from the North Central tradition. This Gaṇeśa passage is found in K4 on a separate folio, a "correction sheet" (*śodhapattra*). See Sukthankar's "Prolegomena" to the critical edition, Sukthankar et al., *The Mahābhārata*, vol. 1, li.

Sanskrit version of the *MBh* was fixed and promulgated. This passage was inserted into the passage mentioned above which describes an explicit blessing of Vyāsa's composition given by the great god Brahmā, the "guru of the worlds" (*lokaguru*). It acknowledges and sanctions a written version of the *MBh*–a highly remarkable development in itself for a text "sacred" to brahmans. It also acknowledges and explains the numerous difficult verses found in the written Sanskrit tradition. And it provides a touch of humane levity that counterbalances the majesty and solemnity of Vyāsa's somewhat embarrassed presentation of his *Great Bhārata* to the god Brahmā and the latter's grandiloquent endorsement of it (see below). This small addition to the text was an ingenious and persuasive way to bring the manuscript tradition of a profoundly disturbing text under the benevolent aegis of the god Gaṇeśa, and if it had occurred to the redactors or promulgators of the fixed, written Sanskrit *MBh*, the text may have had a somewhat different, less clouded history.[12]

This passage presents a deliberately developed conception of the fixed, written text of the *MBh* as a distinct cultural entity. It makes certain important claims about the *MBh* as a whole, as a unitary composition, and it implicitly relates the *MBh* to other texts or textual corpora of ancient India. The specific claims of this passage, however, are not what concern me here. Brahmā's blessing Vyāsa's composition is more directly germane to my themes. Brahmā happened to visit Vyāsa while the latter was wondering how he would teach his work to his students. After he had made his guest comfortable, Vyāsa told him that he had composed an artfully sophisticated, inspired work, a poem (*kāvya*), which contained within it knowledge of the secret essence of the Vedas, of events past, present and future, of the units of time, of the movements of celestial bodies, of the rules for religious actions, and of much more. He concluded this recital by asking Brahmā to excuse the fact that the poem presented all this knowledge that was normally Brahmā's role to promulgate. Not only was Brahmā not offended by Vyāsa's emulation of him, he praised Vyāsa as more excellent than Vasiṣṭha, the dean of the "college" of ancient Vedic seers, and he praised Vyāsa's work in the highest terms, likening it and its functioning to his own creative promulgation of knowledge.

---

[12] The *MBh* has long been regarded as an inauspicious text in spite of the text's own internal attempt to neutralize its presentation of evil and grotesque violence through the instructional *śānti* which is constituted by the twelfth and thirteenth major books of the *MBh*, the *Śāntiparvan* and the *Anuśāsanaparvan* (see note 28 below). Typically the *MBh* "proper" (as distinct from certain segments of it, most notably the *Bhagavadgītā*) is not read or recited in their homes by pious Hindu people.

> Had you not made the world blaze up with the fire of knowledge, it would have become darkness—mute, blind, deaf, insane. For the world which is blind and wrapped round by darkness because of its own actions, you have created a merry riot for the eyes of its mind with your paint-sticks of knowledge. You have driven off people's darkness with the sun of your *Bhārata*, with its short and long accounts focused on *dharma*, *artha*, *kāma*, and *mokṣa*. You have awakened the minds of people, who are sensitive to the moon like red lotuses, with the full moon of *purāṇa* shining forth with the light of *śruti*. Rightly have you fully illumined the entire inner chamber of the world with the torch of *itihāsa* that dispels the fog of muddleheadedness.[13]

The critical editorial process disclosed that this passage too was absent from the promulgated fixed text of the *Great Bhārata*, though present in a wider range of manuscript traditions than the Gaṇeśa passage inserted into it in the Devanāgarī tradition.[14]

Like the Gaṇeśa passage, this blessing was inserted into the already existing text of the *Great Bhārata* for some purpose. It too intends the text as a whole and makes important claims about it, but the purposes behind this episode are more complicated than those of the Gaṇeśa passage, and they are not immediately apparent. This passage offers an unambiguous and strong characterization of the *MBh* as a comprehensive source of all important knowledge, and Brahmā's blessing of it provides Vyāsa's work with one of the most convincing endorsements of the great importance and truthfulness of its contents imaginable. Brahmā had come to be widely recognized as the major source within the samsaric system of the world for knowledge important within that world. In the general *Weltanschauung* which evidently prevailed between approximately 300 B.C. and 300 A.D. in those cultural milieu where the brahman elite was an important social and cultural fact, Brahmā had come to be regarded as the maker of the world, grandfather (*pitāmaha*) of all its inhabitants, and the formulator of or inspiration for valuable knowledge in the world.[15] Recurrent in literary allusions to Brahmā are the themes of his active concern for the well-being of the creatures descendent from him and an association with important knowledge. Sarasvatī, the goddess of wisdom, is his daughter in the *MBh*,

---

[13] Sukthankar et al., *The Mahābhārata*, lines 37–46 of passage 1 of Appendix I of the *Ādiparvan*, vol. 1, 885.

[14] The passage is found in the North Central, Devanāgarī, tradition and in all Southern manuscript traditions (those of Kerala, Andhra, and Tamil Nad). It is absent from the Northeastern tradition (Bengal and Nepal) and from the Northwestern, except for the borderline manuscripts K4.6. As with the Gaṇeśa passage, this passage is physically interpolated into K4 on a "correction sheet".

[15] See Jan Gonda, *Die Religionen Indiens*, 2 vols. (Stuttgart: W. Kohlhammer, 1960–63), 1:263–264. See too E.W. Hopkins, *Epic Mythology* (Strassburg: K. Trubner, 1915).

and in later mythology also becomes his consort. For brahmans, Brahmā's four mouths were the points from which the four Vedas were first uttered in the world and the ultimate source from which brahmans themselves were created. For Buddhists, it was Brahmā's advocacy, on behalf of his offspring, that finally convinced the Buddha to preach his insight to suffering sentient beings (an insight, of course, which could not have come from Brahmā, who as progenitor of and lord over *saṃsāra* could not be the source of knowledge which is based in something other than *saṃsāra*). Several Buddhist accounts of the Buddha's life record this impulse from Brahmā to promulgate the Buddhist *dharma*[16] and the *Rāmāyaṇa*, our text of which also originated in this general period, and which, like the *MBh* and the *buddhavacana*, came to have a far-reaching and profound role in the shaping of the sensibilities of the peoples of India, was inspired directly by Brahmā.[17] So the figure of Brahmā constitutes a powerfully authoritative presence guaranteeing the transcendent value of Vyāsa's great *Bhārata*. But, when read in the context into which it was inserted, Brahmā's blessing seems incongruous, superfluous. The text of the Sanskrit *MBh* which existed before this passage was inserted into the manuscripts of the central traditions had already made similar claims for the text—had established it as a work reliably teaching the kinds of knowledge most important for human beings on the basis of a theme of inspiration and authority that had an integrity and power which had once seemed sufficient by itself. I shall offer a suggestion concerning the motivation for the invention and insertion of the Brahmā blessing at the end of this paper. What is most important now is the original theme grounding the *MBh* as an authoritative corpus of knowledge.

Those responsible for the *Great Bhārata* that was fixed in writing and promulgated between 100 B.C. and 350 A.D. designed this text as a grand work of instruction for kings, dealing with critical issues concerning the proper action of kings in the samsaric system of the world, and they grounded the authority of their text in the archaic theme of the Vedic poetic composition proclaimed by a preternaturally insightful and expressive seer, an *ṛṣi*. They presented their *Great Bhārata* as a new Veda come forth from the mind of the seer Kṛṣṇa Dvaipāyana Vyāsa, the Veda of Kṛṣṇa (Kārṣṇa Veda), the fifth Veda, thus calling upon the great evocative power of the most hallowed of holy things in the world of brahmanic Indians.

---

[16] See Edward J. Thomas, *The Life of Buddha as Legend and History*, third ed. revised (1949; London: Routledge and Kegan Paul, 1975), pp. 81–86.

[17] See S.K. Mudholkar, *Vālmīkirāmāyaṇam*, 7 vols. (Bombay: "Gujarati" Printing Press, n.d.), 1:1:22ff.

"The Veda", the (corpus of) "Knowledge", had been, and was then, an ever available, multiform religious phenomenon which members of brahmanic Indian society experienced, conceived of, and used in various ways. The Veda was a sacred acoustic substance, a long concatenation of uttered syllables which a person heard in special, ritualized contexts, laboriously learned over a period of years, and produced ritually through the action of one's own chest, throat, nose, and mouth. Part of the Veda was an effective instrument for producing and controlling things and events in the world (*mantra*). Other parts of the Veda were collections of authoritative (cognitively infallible) texts (Brāhmaṇas, Āraṇyakas, Upaniṣads) which made available to Aryan people different kinds of important knowledge (injunctions for the sacrificial ritual [*vidhis*] and specifications of the critically important homological equivalences [*upaniṣats*] between the infrahuman microcosm [*ādhyātmika* reality], the universal macrocosm [*ādhibhautika* reality], and the system of sacrificial ritual [*ādhiyājñika* reality]; by knowing which equivalences a person might attain beatitude, power, and or, immortality, depending upon their desire). This learning had its ultimate source in the eternal potent reality which was understood as the ground of all being (*brahman*), and the acoustic form of this knowledge, the known Veda, was a direct manifestation among humans of that reality. As a source of cognitive knowledge, the semantically meaningful form of the Veda (the non-*mantra* part) provided knowledge or instruction of the most important kind for human welfare in this world and the world beyond death. The redactors of the *Great Bhārata* sought to invest their text with as much of the power and authority of this ancient, primordial, but palpably living "Body of Learning" as it would carry. They claimed that it had come to exist among human beings as a result of the same kind of preternatural insight and expressive genius by which the Aryan people came to possess the Veda and that it too was a source for the most important knowledge, that required to make the world a place that facilitated all aspects of the welfare of all creatures. They did not quite make the explicit claim that the *Great Bhārata* was a direct manifestation of *brahman*, but they did claim that the simple acoustic realization of parts of their text was efficacious in producing some aspects of human welfare, as were the *mantras* of the Veda. And the awesome size, grandeur, and complexity of the *Great Bhārata* they created do arouse some of the same feelings of transcendence that the size, claimed comprehensiveness, and apparent agelessness of the Veda do. As a written text and as a *new* "Veda", it was obvious that the *Great Bhārata* was a Veda only metaphorically. The *Great Bhārata* was a very different sort of text from the Veda in many more ways than the two were substantively similar. But the *Great Bhārata* was intended to function in Indian culture in the same imposing and authoritative way the ancient Vedas had, and the formulators of this *Great Bhārata* developed their metaphor with some care.

The Vedic idea of the *ṛṣi* was essentially that of someone "who sees the secret matters of the gods with an inner eye" and gives what he sees powerful expression.[18] The redactors of the *MBh* presented Vyāsa as having such preternatural abilities and as having composed the *MBh* as a preternaturally insightful and instructive account of the epoch-making, trans-human events which constituted and surrounded the Bhārata war. Though not himself an *ṛṣi* who composed any of the hymns of the *Ṛg Veda*, Vyāsa was a "seer of the *brahman*" (i.e., a *brahmarṣi*, a "seer of the Veda", a brahman seer in contrast to a *rājarṣi*, a seer who was a king), the son of the important Vedic seer Parāśara, who was himself the son of Vasiṣṭha, the pre-eminent Vedic seer. Vyasa is characterized in the text as possessing visionary intellect,[19] as a learned seer of the *brahman*,[20] who knows the high and the low, an inspired poet dedicated to truth,[21] and as possessed of boundless intellect, or thought.[22] Three times in its introductory passages the *MBh* is referred to simply as "what was thought" (*matam*) by Vyāsa,[23] and at one point it is described as "the narrative which sprang from the ocean of the great seer's mind" (*MBh* 1.53.33c-34b), suggesting inexhaustible and protean powers of mind. Before composing the *Great Bhārata* Vyāsa had divided (*vivyāsa*) the previously unitary Veda into four parts, four Vedas, as a favor to the Veda and

---

[18] "Seher heisst im Veda, wer die geheimnisvollen göttlichen Dinge mit dem inneren Auge erschaut:" K.F. Geldner, *Der Rig-Veda aus dem Sanskrit ins Deutsche übersetzt*, 3 vols. (Cambridge, MA: Harvard University Press, 1951), 1:2:n.2; cited by Jan Gonda, *The Vision of the Vedic Poets* (The Hague: Mouton & Co., 1963), p. 40. Further from Gonda: "A ṛṣi obviously is the functionary who enters into contact with divinity . . . he has an insight in the nature of the gods' greatness . . . he associates with gods . . . he may address them . . . extol them . . . honour or praise them . . . and invoke their aid and favour . . . " (p. 40). ". . . according to the ancients the title *ṛṣiḥ* is to be explained in connection with this functionary's faculty of "seeing" . . . . The *ṛṣiḥ* is the man who uttered the sacral word . . . .The ṛṣis are, in the Indian traditional view, said to have visualized the mystic form of *vāc-* which according to the Indian conception is a more sacred idea than our "speech", carrying with it a far deeper significance. *Vāc-* is not only eternal or imperishable but also subtle and incomprehensible by ordinary sense-organs . . . *vāk* in its ultimate shape is identical with brahman, and . . . the great ancient ṛṣis were born with such a spiritual power and faculty of vision as to possess omniscience and that through them the sacred texts were revealed to man". (p. 42)

[19] *dhīmān*, *MBh* 1.1.55c.

[20] *vidvān brahmarṣiḥ*, *MBh* 1.1.53ab; see too *MBh* 1.54.1c.

[21] *parāvarajño brahmarṣiḥ kaviḥ satyavrataḥ* . . . *MBh* 1.54.5cd.

[22] *amitabuddhi*, *MBh* 1.56.21d.

[23] *MBh* 1.1.23c; 55.2c; 56.12c; see too *MBh* 1.53.35cd.

brahmans, because he observed that the abilities of mortals had decreased with each passing *yuga* (*MBh* 1.57.69).

The *Great Bhārata* presents itself as based in Vyāsa's preternatural sight and insight into divine events and realities. Either with his physical eyes or with the inner eye of the seer, Vyāsa was a witness to all the events narrated in the *MBh* from his vantage point as an important participant in them. The text depicts the first public presentation of his composition as being called forth by a king asking for what Vyāsa had seen:

> The deeds of the Kurus and Pāṇḍavas—your honor saw them with his own eyes! Tell them to me, brahman. How did the split between those men whose actions were always effortless come about? And how did that great war that finished off so many happen? You are thoroughly conversant with it all, blessed one, so tell me everything about this of my ancestors. (*MBh* 1.54.18–20)

With these words Janamejaya Bharata, the paramount king of the world, asked Vyāsa to tell him about the awesome events involving his Bhārata ancestors. Vyāsa had recently arrived to attend a great sacrifice King Janamejaya was holding, and he was the pre-eminent guest there among many brahmans and others. Janamejaya was the great grandson of the Bhārata Pāṇḍava hero Arjuna, and the dynast of the Bharatas a number of years after the Bhārata war had occurred and all its protagonists had departed the terrestrial scene.

Janamejaya's request occasioned the first public recital of Vyāsa's "*Great*" *Bhārata* composition, and the characterization of the text as a "Veda" is the most prominent feature of the statements the text makes about itself in this introductory passage. Vyāsa responded to Janamejaya's request by commanding his pupil Vaiśampāyana to tell the king everything he had heard about the deeds of the Kurus and Pāṇḍavas from Vyāsa. Vaiśampāyana proceeded to introduce Vyāsa's massive account in 100,000 *śloka* couplets as being much more than a chronicle of the deeds of Janamejaya's ancestors. Vyāsa's text, he said, was equal to the Veda in its purifying sacramental power, was itself a Veda, the Kārṣṇa Veda. He elaborated some on the sacramental powers of Vyāsa's text. It could remove even the most serious evil *karman* attached to a person, elevate a person's position in the samsaric system of the world, bring about the birth of a son, bring victory, and so on. And it could do all this through the mere hearing of the text or causing others to hear it (*MBh* 1.56.18–20). Furthermore, he announced that the text was a comprehensive source of instruction (*śāstra*) for all the behavior and knowledge important to human beings. He told Janamejaya that Vyāsa's work contained exhaustive teachings on profit in material affairs (*artha*), on the law of the cosmos which regulates movement and action in the world (*dharma*), and on the knowledge of ultimate things (*buddhi parinaiṣṭhikī*, that is, knowledge concerning trans-samsaric reality, i.e., ultimate being and the *mokṣa* [escape] from *saṃsāra* into that being). It is a complete set of teachings on these subjects and on *kāma* (love and sex) too. Vaiśampāyana concluded his introduction of the text to Janamejaya with this statement: "Kṛṣṇa Dvaipāyana the sage worked assiduously for three years and composed this supreme *Great Bhārata* account. What is here on *dharma*, *artha*, *kāma*, and *mokṣa* exists elsewhere, but what is not in here does not exist anywhere" (*MBh* 1.56.33).

After this brief but exalted introduction to Vyāsa's *Great Bhārata*, Vaiśampāyana began his narrative with a long account of the human and trans-human background of the Bhārata lineage and the Bhārata war that further develops the text's claim of being a Veda spoken forth by an *ṛṣi*. His account began with one of the most important actors in the events described in the *MBh*, Vyāsa, and presented, among others, the facts that he was the son of the *ṛṣi* Parāśara, that he performed the *ṛṣi's* activity of dividing the Veda, and that he taught the Vedas to his pupils, the *Great Bhārata* being the fifth (*MBh* 1.57.1–75). The account then listed the births of the other principal figures of the Bhārata narrative, dwelling at some length on the supreme God Viṣṇu–Nārāyaṇa's taking birth of human parents (*MBh* 1.57.83–87). Vaiśampāyana went on to explain the human and trans-human, divine, background of the Bhārata war. He set forth here two themes as constituting the background of the Bhārata war. First he invoked the history of the brahman Rāma Jāmadagnya's killing of the entire kṣatriya male stratum of society twenty-one times in the past (with new kṣatriyas arising when strict brahmans impregnated the kṣatriya widows). In the wake of the golden age following the last such occurrence of Rāma's slaughter of kṣatriyas, a host of demons incarnated themselves on earth among kṣatriyas and various animals after their most recent defeat at the hands of the gods. This latter event is Vaiśampāyana's second theme and the immediate setting of the Bhārata conflict. The demons living on the earth heavily oppressed the earth and its inhabitants, to the point that the earth entreated the grandfather of the world, Brahmā, for help. Brahmā commanded all the denizens of heaven to have portions of themselves born on earth to combat the demons. Led by Indra, who enlisted Viṣṇu-Nārāyaṇa in the enterprise, the gods and other denizens of heaven took birth on the earth. Vaiśampāyana then listed the principal incarnations of demons and gods and took up the human ancestry of Bharatas (*MBh* 1.58–61), arriving eventually at the Bhārata narrative. Vyāsa's *Great Bhārata* is indeed a chronicle of the deeds of Janamejaya's ancestors, but Vyāsa was able to see that those men and their deeds had a trans-human significance, to see that the Bhārata war was much more than a grand melée of kings and armies. His account of those gods and their struggle with the anti-gods, and of God and his actions and revelations in the course of this crisis of the entire world system, is the most important text to be presented to human beings since the *ṛṣis* proclaimed the Vedas among them—is itself a Veda in its import and value.

Vyāsa's *Great Bhārata*, understood as a quasi-Vedic text, was received enthusiastically by a most important group of people after Vaiśampāyana's recitation of it to Janamejaya (according to the "greater" *Great Bhārata* we have). The *Great Bhārata* presented to us is not simply Vaiśampāyana's recitation of Vyāsa's insightful and instructive account of the Bharatas to Janamejaya. We, and every other audience of this version of the *MBh*, are witness to a *rehearsal* of Vaiśampāyana's recitation to Janamejaya, a recounting to an enthusiastic brahman audience. This skillful framing of the text fills an important place in the Veda metaphor and enlists a very important authoritative voice for the startling teachings of the *Great Bhārata*. The text explains that Vaiśampāyana's original recitation was witnessed and picked up by *sūtas* (wandering bards, storytellers). Our text is the rehearsal of Vaiśampāyana's recitation by one such *sūta* witness, Ugraśravas, to a community of ascetic and ritualistic brahmans living in a retreat in the Naimiṣa forest under the leadership of Śaunaka. These brahman "seers" had heard of Vyāsa's *Great Bhārata*, and when Ugraśravas offered to entertain them with stories they immediately and eagerly requested Vyāsa's wondrous "Vedic" text:

> We want to hear that *saṃhitā*[24] of the prodigious Vyāsa which is equal to the four Vedas, which deals with *dharma*, strikes off evil, and removes fear; that primordial account uttered forth by the supreme seer Dvaipāyana, which was received with high honor by the gods and brahmic seers when they heard it; that edifying brahmic utterance[25]—reinforced by diverse teachings, furnished with refinements, and containing matters presented in books of the history of the Bharatas; the most excellent of tales, delightful in word and marvelous in its parts, which contains subtle matters with subtle resolutions and is adorned with matters from the Vedas, which the seer Vaiśampāyana correctly and satisfyingly proclaimed during Janamejaya's sacrificial session at Dvaipāyana's command. (*MBh* 1.1.19, 15–18)

This request occurs at the very beginning of our text. That is, the framers of our written *Great Bhārata* present the text *first of all* as respected by a community

[24] "*saṃhitā*" can refer to anything "put together, compiled", but refers to the four *saṃhitās* of the Vedas in a primary way.

[25] "Brahmic utterance", *brāhmī*; literally "of the *brahman*, of the Veda".

of brahmans as a quasi-Vedic text well uttered by a prodigious *ṛṣi*. These men know nothing whatsoever about military affairs, yet they eagerly request to hear Vyāsa's account of the war between the Pāṇḍavas and the Kauravas.[26] This enthusiasm for the text by Śaunaka's company is not only a rhetorically important endorsement of the text, legitimizing and recommending it as reliable teaching, it implies a necessary feature of the text's being a Veda. The most important distinctive characteristic of the brahman caste as the learned elite of ancient India was their possession and maintenance of that "brahmic" acoustic substance which is the Veda. Accordingly, a text which is a Veda must be endorsed, possessed, supported, and maintained by brahmans as part of its constitution as a Veda. Soon the text twice makes the point explicitly that Vyāsa's *Bhārata* is supported, that is, learned and recited, by brahmans (*MBh* 1.1.25, 49–51).

As Vaiśampāyana had done in recommending the text to King Janamejaya, Ugraśravas praised the *MBh* for its quasi-Vedic sacramental power, but more forcefully and at greater length: "For the man who grasps the immeasurable *Bhārata*, as it is recited, come forth from the space between Dvaipāyana's lips, holy and purifying, evil-removing and blessed, what need is there for ablutions with the waters of Puṣkara?" (*MBh* 1.2.242; 18.5.54) After a number of statements such as this one praising the sacramental value of the text, Ugraśravas recommended the regular recitation of the first chapter of the *MBh*, the *Anukramaṇīparvan* (as an epitome of the entire text fully as efficacious as the complete text), at the ritual recitations brahmans perform at the morning and evening twilights of every day (*saṃdhyājapa*). But for Ugraśravas the heart of the Vedic metaphor lay in the *MBh's* being a sufficient guide to proper human thought and behavior on *all topics of significance*. That is, it was a text which in some essential way corresponded to, and made available to the human mind, the ultimate pattern of the cosmos, and thus the proper place of human beings in that pattern and human possibilities within that pattern. Ugraśravas claimed that Vyasa's text, as the product of preternatural insight, did just this. Early in his recommendation of Vyāsa's text to the

---

[26] In what is otherwise a puzzling passage, the framers of our *MBh* cleverly portray a great discrepancy in the initial interests in the text held by Śaunaka and his company on the one hand and by Janamejaya and men of arms like him on the other. The redactors presented the Naimiṣa brahmans as being completely ignorant of the make-up of a kṣatriya "army" or "division", an *akṣauhiṇī*. When Ugraśravas mentioned in passing the eighteen *akṣauhiṇīs* that met to fight the Bhārata war, the brahmans interrupted him and demanded to know what an *akṣauhiṇī* was, and Ugraśravas itemized its composition for them. An audience more alien to heroic epic could hardly be imagined. *MBh* 1.2.13–23.

Naimiṣa brahmans Ugraśravas concluded a brief account of cosmogenesis with the appearance of the eponymous ancestors of the lineages relevant to the Bhārata narrative and with a statement concerning Vyāsa's work:

> The great-souled Daśajyotis had ten thousand sons, Śatajyotis had ten times as many sons as that, and Sahasrajyotis had ten times more than that again. Many lineages arose from these—this line of the Kurus, those of the Yadus, Bharata, Yayāti, Ikṣvāku, and those of all the kings who were *ṛṣis*—and created things were sent forth in extensive waves. [And there arose] all the specific situations of created things and the threefold secret, which is connected to the Vedas, and the explanation of it—*dharma*, *artha*, and *kāma*. The seer Vyāsa saw the teachings on *dharma*, *kāma*, and *artha*, diverse other teachings, and the rule which had arisen for the maintenance of the world. (*MBh* 1.1.43–47)

The *Great Bhārata* was not the mere chronicle of his ancestors' heroic deeds that King Janamejaya had requested from Vyāsa. To be sure, it was a historic account of the Bharatas and the Bhārata war between the Kauravas and the Pāṇḍavas, but it was a historic account containing "elaborations" (*vyākhyās*). The *Great Bhārata* was an *itihāsa savaiyākhya*, a chronicle of events which examined and explained those events in accompanying or interposed or appended elaborations (*MBh* 1.1.48a). Vyāsa's "great" Bhārata tale contained and presented to King Janamejaya, to all kings and kṣatriyas, and to all else who heard it, the insights of a seer into the fundamental principles by which the world works. It was fundamentally a *śāstra*, a text which teaches on the basis of the Bhārata chronicle.

The enthusiasm for Kṛṣṇa's Veda on the part of these forest-dwelling, ritualistic brahmins had another important rhetorical function. As they heard Ugraśravas' rehearsal of Vaiśampāyana's recitation of Vyāsa's didactic history to the interested Bhārata dynast Janamejaya, Śaunaka and his company became viewers of Janamejaya's reception of the text and its teachings. That is, as the written text presents itself to all its audiences through the ages, the royal audience which was the primary audience of the text, itself became part of the greater text which is attended to by the brahmans, who, as audience for Ugraśravas' rehearsal, themselves became part of the greater text presented to Indian audiences and, eventually, to us. Janamejaya and every subsequent king who might be identified with him have had to answer to the enthusiasm of Śaunaka and his followers and all subsequent people who might identify with them or be persuaded by their view.

So did the creators of the Sanskrit *MBh* give power to the voice of their new text. As extravagant as their claims might appear, the new *Great Bhārata* which they presented in this way is a text commensurate to them. They made the *Great Bhārata* an extravagant text. It teaches such important ideas with such force and at such length that it makes full and convincing use of the power and authority of the Vedic transcendence claimed for it. Both dramatically and didactically their text presents a contentious new ethic set within a new understanding of the cosmos, an understanding which is in turn rooted in a new vision of the ultimate reality as the personal deity Lord Viṣṇu-Nārāyaṇa. Its central narrative is the rescue-action Lord Viṣṇu, incarnate as Kṛṣṇa, and the subordinate gods carried out in the face of the threat to the world posed by the anti-gods—everything taking place on earth in the guise of events involving the Bharatas and their kingdom and their allies. They carefully constructed the central part of this narrative around the figure of the divine incarnation Kṛṣṇa—around his herding of events to the virtual annihilation of the kṣatriya *varṇa* and his revelations of himself as God Viṣṇu-Nārāyaṇa. And they framed this central narrative between two passages that raise powerfully the major practical issue of the new ethic—whether the people involved should participate in or withdraw from the war and its consequences (a partly hyperbolic representation of all human action). Each time the issue resolved in favor of dharmic participation in the war (that is, in proper social, political, economic, and ritual action).[27] As a moral counterweight (*śānti*) to the grotesque war, the creators of the text depicted the new king Yudhiṣṭhira receiving *extensive* instructions on numerous aspects of kingship and society and philosophy, theology, and ethics, instructions which are offered basically by Kṛṣṇa as a textual resource for people in the new age.[28] And stories, lectures, sermons, and debates occur throughout the text, developing themes on a number of ethical and cosmological topics. Janamejaya did indeed receive a Veda from Vaiśampāyana, a great body of important knowledge which supports royal action after the example of Lord Viṣṇu and provides a basic textual resource both for a king's enlightenment and his enlightenment of his subjects. The conception and execution of this *Great Bhārata* was a truly creative appropriation of the most potent brahmanic theme of authoritative knowledge. It produced a text which in the nature and scope of its teaching

---

[27] For a statement of the "messages" actually taught by the *MBh* see my paper, "The Great Epic of India as Religious Rhetoric: A Fresh Look at the *Mahābhārata*", *Journal of the American Academy of Religion* 51.4 (Dec. 1983): 611–630.

[28] I discuss the brahmanic theme of *śānti* and its function in the integration of the large didactic anthologies of the twelfth and thirteenth books of the *MBh* with the rest of the text in a paper currently in progress, "*Śānti*, the *Śānti Parvan*, and the Rhetoric of *Śānti* in the *Great Bhārata* of Vyāsa". For a more complete discussion of these didactic anthologies of the *MBh*, and for a thorough discussion of the *Mokṣadharmaparvan* in particular, see also my dissertation, "The *Mokṣa* Anthology of the *Great Bhārata*" (see above, n. 4).

and in the power of its central rhetorical presentation—the account of an epoch-making, family-splitting, kṣatriya-annihilating war—strongly rivalled the pre-eminent and relatively new textual corpus of the day, the record of the Buddha's words, with its central rhetorical presentation—the biography of the *bodhisattva* and Gautama the Buddha. And though inspiration afterward continuously found voices in India, from Vālmīki's *Rāmāyaṇa* to the hymns of the Ālvārs, to the *Jñāneśvarī*, the *vacanas* of the Vīraśaivas, and the verses of Kabir, and beyond, to people like Ramakrishna and Śri Aurobindo, India's fifth Veda was its last and perhaps its greatest Veda.

While basically ignoring the metaphor of the *MBh's* being a Veda, important elements of the brahman tradition in succeeding centuries accepted the essence of this metaphoric claim and regarded Vyāsa's *Great Bhārata* as an authoritative source of important knowledge. The brilliantly magisterial Mīmāṃsaka Kumārila Bhaṭṭa of the seventh or eighth century discussed the *MBh* and the *Rāmāyaṇa* and other *smṛtis* in terms of the categories with which the Mīmāṃsā analyzed all texts. The tradition of Pūrva, or Karma, Mīmāṃsā was concerned to derive (*mīmāṃsā*) directives for action (*dharma*) from whatever authoritative sources were available to human beings. While the Veda (*śruti*) was the infallible source for the knowledge of *dharma*, tradition (*smṛti*) was also authoritative, when it did not contradict the Veda, and the *MBh* was a principal *smṛti*. Kumārila characterized the *MBh* and similar types of works (such as the Purāṇas) as having as their ultimate purpose the enjoining of the accomplishments of the four human ends, the *puruṣārthas* (*dharma*, *artha*, *kāma*, and *mokṣa*). These works are made up of (1) injunctive sentences (*vidhis*), which are found chiefly in the *Śāntiparvan* and *Anuśāsanaparvan* (the two long books containing the instruction of the new king Yudhiṣṭhira at the beginning of the new era over which he will preside), and (2) narrative episodes which praise the injunctions, make them more attractive for people to perform (*arthavādas*, any kind of utterance which enhances the injunctive power of a *vidhi*). The epic narrative and heroic stories attached to it are authoritative because they enhance the injunctions contained in the text. Some of the parts of these texts are composed as genuine poetry and often function as *arthavādas* merely by pleasing the hearer, while descriptions of battle are useful to kings in that they rouse the brave and cowardly alike to do battle. And, as their function is rhetorical, such passages have no strict requirement to be truthful.[29]

---

[29] Kumārila, *Tantravārttika* on 1.2.7; see too on 1.3.2 and 1.3.7. Kumārila's understanding of the *MBh* was first discussed by Georg Bühler in Bühler and Kirste, "Indian Studies No. II"

In light of such an understanding of it, the *MBh* exerted great influence on the tradition of Dharmaśāstra. It was often quoted in commentaries written on such texts as the *Mānavadharmaśāstra* (the *Laws of Manu*) and the *Yājñavalkyasmṛti*, and didactic portions of it were transferred wholesale into the *dharmanibandhas* written after the twelfth century A.D., such as Lakṣmīdhara's *Kṛtyakalpataru*. The great Vedāntācāryas Śaṅkara, Rāmānuja, and Madhva took the didactic authority of the *MBh* for granted. Generally, when he quoted it in the course of arguments, Śaṅkara would simply refer to the *MBh* with a confident "*smṛteḥ*", "from authoritative tradition". As the final redactors of our Sanskrit *MBh* evidently were, Rāmānuja was a Vaiṣṇava and the *MBh* was particularly authoritative for him. At one point in the course of an argument Rāmānuja matter-of-factly stated that Vyāsa had expounded the Pāñcarātra doctrine (the particular Vaiṣṇava theological tradition to which Rāmānuja belonged[30]) at great length in the *Mokṣadharmaparvan* of the *MBh*. He went on to cite a long passage taken from several places within the *Mokṣadharma* to the effect that a body of doctrine had been extracted from the epic narrative of the Bharatas—the Pāñcarātra doctrine which was a great Upaniṣad consistent with the Vedas.[31] Madhva was also a Vaiṣṇava, and with him there is a real twist. His *opera* include not only the standard commentaries of the other Vedāntācāryas (on the Brahmasūtra, important Upaniṣads, and the most important didactic passage of the *MBh*, the *Bhagavadgītā*), but a commentary on the entire *MBh*, the *Mahābhāratatātparyanirṇaya*.[32] Madhva's sense of the *MBh's* instructional value was explicitly based on the *narrative* of the *MBh* as much as on the overtly didactic portions. According to Suzanne Siauve, Madhva was concerned "to establish relations between the figures of the epics and *purāṇas* by way of the theory of incarnations, showing in them the law of *karman*-retribution for acts—at work".[33] (Madhva viewed himself as the third incarnation of the wind-god Vāyu after Hanuman of the *Rāmāyaṇa* and Bhīmasena of the *MBh*.)

While brahman intellectuals did not require the Veda metaphor to be persuaded that the *MBh* was an important authoritative text, it seems likely that this deliberately archaic theme was a potent theme of authority

---

[30] See J.A.B. van Buitenen, ed. and trans., *Yāmuna's Āgamaprāmāṇyam* (Madras: Rāmānuja Research Society, 1971), introduction.

[31] *Śrībhāṣya of Rāmānuja*, ed. R.D. Karmaker, 3 vols. (Poona: University of Poona, 1962, 1964), on 2.2.42.

[32] See Suzanne Siauve, *La doctrine de Madhva* (Pondichery: Institut Française d'Indologie, 1968).

[33] Ibid., p. 6, n. 2

for the kings who were the first audience in the imagination of the text. Vyāsa's "Vedic" instruction of Janamejaya on his proper action in the world, and the brahman community's monitoring of that instruction represented the ancient Indian complementarity between *brahman* and *kṣatra*–transcendent wisdom and governmental power. But what of the Brahmā episode, which was one of our beginnings? It does not seem to recommend the text either to the brahmans or the kṣatriyas. Why was it invented, inserted into some version of the text, and then widely accepted in the manuscript tradition? What did this blessing of the text add to its authority or power? Does it coordinate with the Veda metaphor in any subordinate or complementary way? As I noted above, the passage seems superfluous. It merely reproduces the same sort of claims for the scope and value of the knowledge taught in the *MBh* that the text has already made for itself in its introductions, through the Veda metaphor. Although the long list by which the comprehensiveness of the *MBh* is indicated in this passage differs from the earlier introductions in style and detail, the only new substantive element is the approval of the text by the god Brahmā.

Vyāsa's excusing himself before Brahmā suggests that we have here two not unrelated but different, and potentially competing, rhetorics of inspiration and authority. With that possibility in mind, I propose that this episode was composed and welcomed into many of the regional traditions of the written Sanskrit *MBh* because it incorporated an important new audience into the imagination of the text, an audience the text actually acquired sometime after its creation and promulgation. I am referring to the most extensive, and in some ways most important audience the text came to have—the audience which watched both the *brahmarṣis* and King Janamejaya, an audience excluded, in large part, from the real Veda, and to whom the Vedic metaphor probably meant little or nothing; that is, the majority of Indian people, and eventually western scholars and the western public.[34] The Brahmā passage provides an important supplemental recommendation of the text to this vast audience new to the imagination of the *MBh* and, indeed, of all brahmandom. The passage also justifies that audience as an audience of the new Vedic text. Because much of this

[34] Referring to a description of the *MBh*'s being read in a temple given by the seventh century A.D. author Bāṇa in his *Kādambarī*, Georg Bühler remarks, "Public and private recitations of the Epics and of the Purāṇas are common enough also in modern India, and they are always instituted for one and the same purpose, viz. the edification and religious instruction of temple-worshippers or of the domestic circle. Mostly the Sanscrit texts are not only read, but also explained in the verancular for the benefit of the women and of the males of the classes unacquainted with the idiom of the Brahmanical schools." ("Indian Studies No. II": 24).

audience (śūdras and lower peoples) was prohibited from even hearing the Veda, not to speak of their ever appropriating and using it, the expansion of the audience challenged the Veda metaphor. The tradition developed two parallel remedies to resove this dilemma. On the one hand the metaphor of the *MBh* as the "fifth Veda" was quite plausibly extended; having been simply the fifth Veda, the *MBh* came to be the Veda of women and śūdras (*strīśūdraveda*).[35] On the other hand, the author of the Brahmā episode left the Veda metaphor behind, resorting instead to the *universal* benevolence of grandfather Brahmā and his general responsibility for knowledge within the samsaric system of the world. This passage incorporates the actual mass audience of the text into the text's imagination by adding Brahmā's praise of the text as a universal, creative promulgation of knowledge onto the Veda metaphor. Like the light of the sun, the *MBh* shines for the welfare of everyone. Brahmā's blessing of the text justifies the appropriation of the "Vedic" text by all the different strata of Indian society, transforming the *Great Bhārata* from an imitation of the exclusive and esoteric Body of Knowledge of the ancient brahmans into an imitation of the universal wisdom of the *buddhavacana*–a not unlikely fate for a fifth Veda, a Kārṣṇa Veda.

---

[35] See Adolf Holtzmann, *Zur Geschichte und Kritik des Mahābhārata* (Kiel: C.F. Haesler, 1892), p. 178. See too the injunction to teach which Vyāsa gives his students at *MBh* 12.314.45cd: śrāvayec caturo varṇān kṛtvā brāhmānam agrataḥ // 45 // and Bühler's report of how Kumārila construes this *vidhi* ("Indian Studies No. II": 10).

ŚĀNTARASA IN THE *MAHĀBHĀRATA*

GARY A. TUBB

The study of the *Mahābhārata* by those viewing it from outside the Indian tradition has always been marked by controversies concerning the extent to which the work can be said to possess any unity, and by disagreements about the nature of any unifying principles that may be discerned. In continuing these discussions, we might do well to pause long enough for a more careful look at what thoughtful experts within that tradition have had to say on such matters, especially in view of the widespread suspicion that the meanings Indians have found, or have hoped to find, in the *Mahābhārata* have contributed at times to the contents of the work as we now have it.

Indian tradition has ascribed to the *Mahābhārata* at least a superficial unity by claiming that the work was designed by a single author of great wisdom, the sage Kṛṣṇa Dvaipāyana, known also as Vyāsa. Any attempt to go further and to claim for that author a unifying vision with demonstrable effects, must face at the outset a considerable difficulty in identifying the level or levels on which those effects are to be found. Are we to view the *Mahābhārata* as a work of philosophy, of history, of mythology, of religion, or of poetry? Most Indian readers of the *Mahābhārata*, as indeed most of its readers throughout the world, have agreed that more than one of these designations are to be applied simultaneously, although different readers may disagree on the list of available categories.

In this paper I propose to examine the view of the *Mahābhārata* put forward in the most influential Indian work on the literary aspects of unity, the *Dhvanyāloka* of Ānandavardhana, written in Kashmir in the second half of the ninth century. While the *Mahābhārata* as a work of literature can be analyzed in terms of other traditional approaches as well,[1] Ānandavardhana's comments are of particular interest for two reasons. One is that the *Mahābhārata*, somewhat surprisingly, served as his chief example of a work that fulfills in its entirety the demanding requirements of poetic unity. The other is that in his explanation of this success Ānandavardhana brought

[1] Analyses of the *Mahābhārata* based on several traditional systems of literary theory may be found in J.P. Sinha, *The Mahābhārata: A Literary Study* (New Delhi: Meherchand Lacchmandas, 1977).

together several of the designations I have just mentioned, while describing aspects of the *Mahābhārata* that, he believed, are inseparably intertwined in the achievement of its purpose.

The categories applied by Ānandavardhana and his colleagues in their discussions of Sanskrit compositions differ from those used in many other traditions. Within the Sanskrit tradition the didactic value of a work has not usually been of fundamental importance in classification; while theorists have argued over the ultimate end of various sorts of compositions, it was taken for granted that any work of value, whatever the principal aim of its author, will necessarily provide instruction in at least one of the four major goals of human life (*puruṣārtha*). What furnishes the basis for distinction is the way in which a work provides such edification.

On this basis a classification that has been widely accepted for many centuries, and that found its classical expression around the time of Ānandavardhana, divides works into three categories. A *śāstra*, or prescriptive work, is of interest because of the authority of its pronouncements; in such a work the word itself is of primary importance. In an *ākhyāna*, or story, what holds our interest is the plot being presented; in such a work it is therefore the sense rather than the word that is predominant. Finally, in a *kāvya*, or work of belles lettres, the predominance lies not in the words alone, nor in their ultimate meaning, but in the special operation (*vyāpāra*) through which the words are linked to our apprehension of that meaning; in such a work what holds our attention is the beauty of the poetic act of expression.[2]

These basic distinctions were put more interestingly in the analogies made famous in the great commentary on Ānandavardhana's work, the *Locana* of Abhinavagupta, written around 1000 A.D. Scripture, Abhinavagupta said, teaches after the fashion of a master, by giving direct commands. The story literature edifies us more gently, after the fashion of a helpful friend, by presenting interesting examples of what fruits befell the actions of others in the past. And poetry instructs us in the most effective way, after the fashion of a beloved woman, by so delighting us that we are scarcely aware of an underlying purpose.[3]

---

[2] Bhaṭṭa Nāyaka's verses outlining these categories are preserved by Abhinavagupta, *Loc.* on *Dhv.* 1.5 (p. 87):

> *śabdaprādhānyam āśritya tatra śāstram pṛthag viduḥ |*
> *arthatattvena yuktaṃ tu vadanty ākhyānam etayoḥ |*
> *dvayor guṇatve vyāpāraprādhānye kāvyadhīr bhavet.*

[3] In the *Locana* Abhinavagupta uses these analogies three times: on 1.1 (pp. 40–41, *anyathā prabhusaṃmitebhyaḥ* . . .), on 3.10–14 (p. 336, *iha prabhusaṃmitebhyaḥ* . . .), and on 3.30 (p. 399, *etac ca prabhusaṃmitebhyaḥ* . . .).

The express purpose of Ānandavardhana in writing his *Dhvanyāloka* was to explain the most important operation through which the third category of composition provides its delight. His treatise propounded the theory of *dhvani*, or poetic suggestion, and, most importantly, explained that by means of this *dhvani* the reader is granted the experience of *rasa*, a phenomenon that had long been spoken of in Sanskrit literary theory, but the nature of whose evocation in poetic works had not yet been described.[4]

The notion of *rasa*, literally the "flavor" of a work, had first come into prominence in the tradition of dramaturgy. In the theory set down centuries before Ānandavardhana in the *Nāṭyaśāstra* of Bharata, the eight varieties of "flavor" correspond to eight stable emotions (*sthāyibhāva*) made known in a play through the presentation of their objects (the persons or things toward which a character represented on stage is supposed to feel the emotion—e.g., a woman with whom he is in love), their stimulants (e.g., the fragrance of flowers or the presence of a full moon), and their effects in the character who feels the emotion (in the form of physical manifestations such as sweating, and accompanying feelings such as agitation). In the *Nāṭyaśastra* the precise connection between the *sthāyibhāva* and the *rasa* was left rather mysterious, and a long history of speculation, now preserved largely in the works of Abhinavagupta, had addressed the problem. The early results of this speculation, far from resolving the ultimate question of the nature of *rasa* itself, did not even manage to settle the preliminary problems concerning the *sthāyibhāva*, such as whether the emotion supposed to exist in the actor is an imitation of the emotion belonging to the person portrayed, or whether it is through inference that the audience comes to know of the emotion in the actor.

It fell to Ānandavardhana's theory of suggestion to give a more satisfactory answer to these problems. Each of the earlier speculations had failed in its own way to account for the status of the savoring of the "flavor" as a purely esthetic experience, distinct from the emotions of practical life. In the real world the effect of imitation, for example, is more often ludicrous than profound, and the effect of inferring another's emotion, like the effects of any of the other everyday acts of knowledge, leaves us indifferent or concerned, as the circumstances warrant, but seldom evokes an esthetic response. The theory that the work of art artistically *suggests* the existence of the stable emotion provided, for the first time, a mechanism for

[4] For the most helpful introduction to *dhvani*, *rasa*, and related notions, see Daniel H.H. Ingalls, *An Anthology of Sanskrit Court Poetry: Vidyākara's "Subhāṣitaratnakośa,"* Harvard Oriental Series 44 (Cambridge, MA: Harvard University Press, 1965), General Introduction, Part One: "Sanskrit Poetry and Sanskrit Poetics."

explaining the special quality of the savoring of *rasa* as an experience different from those of everyday life.

The nature of *rasa* itself was later explained more fully by Abhinavagupta, who developed a detailed psychological theory that drew heavily on the contributions made in the intervening years by the brilliant theorist Bhaṭṭa Nāyaka. Abhinavagupta explained that the effect of suggesting the stable emotion, rather than presenting it baldly as an imitation or logically implying it, is to remove it from the restrictions of personal interest and the limitations of time and place, and so to universalize it and make possible an identification with it on the part of sensitive readers or spectators. Such persons, by virtue of impressions of past experiences of the same stable emotion stored in the heart, are then able, as in no other way, to savor the essence of emotion without the entanglements of individual limitations. The resulting experience, because of this special freedom, is essentially blissful, even when the corresponding personal emotion—grief, for example, or disgust—is unpleasant when experienced in everyday life.[5]

Ānandavardhana concentrated on the elucidation of the suggestive function that makes the experience of esthetic flavor possible. What helped to make his theory plausible was that in presenting it Ānandavardhana repeatedly appealed to the observable features of successful poetry that distinguish the operation of *dhvani* from more mundane functions, pointing out, for example, that to blatantly name the emotions to be suggested may preclude the evocation of the flavor.

It was in connection with this appeal to the data found in the great poems of the past that Ānandavardhana made his first reference to the *Mahābhārata*. Near the beginning of his work he proposed to reveal the precise nature of the suggestive function "so as to provide a foundation for the delight in the minds of sensitive readers who have been aware all along of its operation in works such as the *Rāmāyaṇa* and the *Mahābhārata*."[6]

Here the mention of the *Rāmāyaṇa* is natural enough, as it was traditionally considered the first *kāvya*. The reasons for including the *Mahābhārata*, however, are less obvious. In the traditional view of history

---

[5] For accounts of Abhinavagupta's theory and his description of earlier speculation, see Raniero Gnoli, *The Aesthetic Experience According to Abhinavagupta*, 2nd ed., Chowkhamba Sanskrit Studies 62 (Varanasi: Chowkhamba Sanskrit Series Office, 1968 [1st ed.: Rome, 1956]; and J.L. Masson and M.V. Patwardhan, *Aesthetic Rapture: The Rasādhyāya of the Nāṭyaśāstra*, 2 vols., Deccan College Building Centenary and Silver Jubilee Series 69 (Pune: Deccan College Postgraduate and Research Institute, 1970).

[6] *Dhv.*, end of *vṛtti* on 1.1 (p. 38): [*tasya dhvaneḥ svarūpam*] *rāmāyaṇamahābhārataprabhṛtini lakṣye sarvatra prasiddhavyavahāraṃ lakṣayatāṃ sahṛdayānām ānando manasi labhatāṃ pratiṣṭhām iti prakāśyate.*

the *Mahābhārata* did succeed the *Rāmāyaṇa*, having been composed by Vyāsa in the present Kali Age, whereas the author of the *Rāmāyaṇa*, Vālmīki, lived in the previous Dvāpara Age. But it was usually included in the second category of composition, that of the *ākhyāna*, rather than in the category of *kāvya;* in its broader form that second category contains, along with works of fiction, works of mythology and legendary history (*itihāsa*), and of these the *Mahābhārata* is traditionally the foremost example.[7] Even so, any suspicion that the *Mahābhārata* is mentioned here merely out of piety, or perhaps out of regard for the excellence of individual verses contained in it, is dispelled in the final chapter of the *Dhvanyāloka*, when Ānandavardhana finally turns to an exposition of the unity that each of these two great epics possesses as a complete work.

In this section as well, Ānandavardhana's opening remarks on these works might surprise some readers of the *Mahābhārata*, for here his original purpose in mentioning the epics is to explain how it happens that even the repeated occurrence of similar scenes in these works never strikes one as tedious. This is so, he says, because when a poet is attentive to *rasa* and its related phenomena, and to the things in a poem that serve to suggest them, "then his entire poem becomes fresh. And this is how in works such as the *Rāmāyaṇa* and the *Mahābhārata* the battles and so on, even though described again and again, appear ever new."[8]

Ānandavardhana then describes what gives these works their unity—the employment of a single predominant *rasa*, to which all the other *rasas* are subordinated. And again his remarks may provoke some surprise, for in each of these works what he identifies as principal is not the heroic flavor (*vīrarasa*) that one might expect to find predominating in an epic poem, but another flavor altogether.

> Furthermore, when in a complete work one presents a single flavor as predominant, it fosters freshness of meaning and abundance of beauty. If you ask for examples, we point to the *Rāmāyaṇa* or the *Mahābhārata*. For in the *Rāmāyaṇa* the First Poet [Vālmīki] has set forth *karuṇa* [the compassionate flavor] as the *rasa* by making such statements as "Grief was made into verse,"

[7] Only very late in the tradition, and with conscious awareness of Ānandavardhana's views, is the place of the *Mahābhārata* within the genres of Sanskrit *kāvya* specified. Thus, in the fourteenth century Viśvanātha, discussing the genre of the ornate court epic, the *mahākāvya* (great *kāvya*), remarks that in the *mahākāvya*s from the age of the ancient seers the sections are called "stories" rather than "cantos" (*SD* 6.325cd: *asminn ārṣe punaḥ sargā bhavanty ākhyānasaṃjñakāḥ*), and in his own commentary on this statement he names the *Mahābhārata* as an example of such a poem (*asmin mahākāvye; yathā–mahābhāratam*).

[8] *Dhv.*, *vṛtti* on 4.5 (p. 529): *rasabhāvatadābhāsārūpe hi vyaṅgye tadvyañjakeṣu ca yathānirdiṣṭeṣu varṇapadavākyaracanāprabandheṣv avahitamanasaḥ kaveḥ sarvam apūrvaṃ kāvyam sampadyate. tathā ca rāmāyaṇamahābhāratādiṣu saṅgrāmādayaḥ punaḥ punar abhihitā api navanavāḥ prakāśante.*

> and he has carried it through by composing his work so as to extend to the final separation [of Rāma] from Sītā.
>
> Likewise in the *Mahābhārata*, which has the beauty of a *kāvya* while being in the form of a *śāstra*, the great sage [Vyāsa] has demonstrated that the creation of dispassion is the principal purport of his work, by composing a conclusion that produces a despondent feeling in response to the sorry end of the Vṛṣṇis and the Pāṇḍavas, and in doing so he has suggested that what he intended as the principal subject of his poem is the peaceful flavor [*śāntarasa*] and the human aim characterized by liberation [*mokṣa*].[9]

Before continuing with the rest of Ānandavardhana's remarks on the *Mahābhārata*, several theoretical problems raised by his approach must be examined.

To begin with, there is the general question of whether the *Mahābhārata*, with its huge collection of such diverse material, is capable of sustaining the difficult task of evoking *rasa*, for this is said to be so delicate a business that any significant imbalance or impropriety can be fatal. Yet Ānandavardhana repeatedly insists on reminding us that the epics are models of success in this regard.

On scrutinizing the list given in the *Dhvanyāloka* of prescriptions for the arrangement of a complete work conducive to *rasa*–the requirement, for example, that any elements of the story not suitable to the appropriate flavor must be abandoned[10]—we may wonder how fully the *Mahābhārata* meets the prescription. But Ānandavardhana introduces the list with the assertion that it is quite well known that the sort of suggestion needed to evoke *rasa* in an entire composition "shines forth in such works as the *Rāmāyaṇa* and the *Mahābhārata*," and that the list is intended "to make clear how that shining forth is accomplished."[11]

This list is followed by another list outlining the things that hinder the evocation of *rasa*, and here we may wonder especially whether the *Mahābhārata* really avoids such faults as "the extensive description of some other matter, even if it is connected,"[12] but Ānandavardhana ends this list

---

[9] *Dhv.*, *vṛtti* on 4.5 (pp. 529–530): *prabandhe cāṅgī rasa eka evopanibadhyamāno 'rthaviśeṣalābhaṃ chāyātiśayaṃ ca puṣṇāti. kasminn iveti cet–yathā rāmāyaṇe yathā vā mahābhārate. rāmāyaṇe hi karuṇo rasaḥ svayam ādikāvinā sūtritaḥ "śokaḥ ślokatvam āgataḥ" ity evaṃvādinā. nirvyūḍhaś ca sa eva sītātyantaviyogaparyantam eva svaprabandham uparacayatā. mahābhārate 'pi śāstrarūpam* [read (with Krishnamoorthy) *śāstrarūpe*] *kāvyacchāyānvayini vṛṣṇipāṇḍavavirasāvasānavaimanasyadāyinīṃ samāptim upanibadhnatā mahāmuninā vairāgyajananatātparyaṃ prādhānyena svaprabandhasya darśayatā mokṣalakṣaṇaḥ puruṣārthaḥ śānto rasaś ca mukhyatayā vivakṣāviṣayatvena sūcitaḥ.*

[10] *Dhv.* 3.11ab (p. 329): *itivṛttavaśāyātaṃ tyaktvānanuguṇāṃ sthitim.*

[11] *Dhv.*, intro. to 3.10 (pp. 328–329): *idānīm alakṣyakramavyaṅgyo dhvaniḥ prabandhātmā rāmāyaṇamahābhāratādau prakāśamānaḥ prasiddha eva. tasya tu yathā prakāśanaṃ tat pratipādyate.*

[12] *Dhv.* 3.18cd (p. 361): *vistareṇānvitasyāpi vastuno 'nyasya varṇanam.*

with the remark, "And the principles we have presented contain nothing not found in the policies of the most celebrated master poets, led by Vālmīki and Vyāsa."[13]

Beyond these general problems, there are theoretical problems connected specifically with *śāntarasa* (the flavor of peace). This *rasa* was not included among the original eight in the *Nāṭyaśāstra* and has always been a source of controversy. The stable emotion associated with it, often called *śama* (tranquility), is that of the person who has passed beyond the ordinary desires and fears of life, and because of its dependence on this peculiar and rare psychological state, the very possibility of *śāntarasa* has frequently been questioned. For reasons of space I cannot rehearse here the details of that controversy, and a bare outline will have to suffice.[14]

If this *sthāyibhāva*, tranquility, is interpreted strictly as a state in which all desires have been gotten rid of, then a few would deny its existence absolutely, refusing to believe that complete liberation is possible for any human. Many more would accept its occurrence in the real world but question its possibility in literature on the grounds of its rarity in the outside world: no member of the audience at a play is capable of identifying with the suggested stable emotion without having experienced that psychological state in the past, and no audience is likely to include many of those liberated masters who have experienced true tranquility. And even if those who are capable of savoring the *rasa* should come to see a play in which the flavor of peace is predominant, it may be impossible to represent on stage such an unworldly state: if we do take *śama* to mean absolute tranquility, then no gestures or actions can adequately convey it, and if the actor is

---

[13] *Dhv.*, verse before 3.20 (p. 365):

vālmīkivyāsamukhyāś ca ye prakhyātāḥ kavīśvarāḥ |
tadabhiprāyabāhyo 'yaṃ nāsmābhir darśito nayaḥ ||

[14] For the details, see Shashthi Prasad Bhattacharya, *Śānta Rasa and Its Scope in Literature*, Calcutta Sanskrit College Research Series 110, Studies No. 73 (Calcutta: Sanskrit College, 1976); Sushil Kumar De, "The Śānta Rasa in the Nāṭya-Śāstra and the Daśa-Rūpaka," in *Some Problems of Sanskrit Poetics* (Calcutta: Firma K.L. Mukhopadhyay, 1959), pp. 139–143 [reprinted from *Siddha-bhāratī*, Hoshiarpur 1950]; J.L. Masson and M.V. Patwardhan, *Śāntarasa and Abhinavagupta's Philosophy of Aesthetics*, Bhandarkar Oriental Series 9 (Pune: Bhandarkar Oriental Research Institute, 1969); Edwin Gerow and Ashok Aklujkar, "On Śānta Rasa in Sanskrit Poetics," *Journal of the American Oriental Society* 92 (1972), 80–87 (a review article examining Masson and Patwardhan's *Śāntarasa*); V. Raghavan, *The Number of Rasa-s*, 2nd ed., Adyar Library Series 23 (Adyar, Madras: The Adyar Library and Research Centre, 1967) [1st ed. 1940]; and K.C. Pandey, "Dhanañjaya and Abhinavagupta on Śāntarasa," *Proceedings of the All India Oriental Conference* 12 (1944), 326–330.

presented as completely devoid of activity, it will make for an exceedingly dull play.[15]

These objections were countered in detail by Abhinavagupta.[16] He speaks of the stable emotion in terms of the knowledge of reality, thus avoiding an insistence on the final state of absolute liberation, and on the problems of identifying with the *sthāyibhāva* and of representing it on stage, he remarks:

> But while it is true that in its ultimate state it cannot be acted out because of the absence of [detectable] effects, presentation on stage is just as impossible in the case of such [stable emotions] as love and grief when they have reached their highest pitch. And identification with it is clearly possible on the part of those who possess the stored impressions that are the seeds of that sort of knowledge or reality.[17]

In referring to the highest pitch of love and grief, which are the stable emotions corresponding to the erotic and compassionate flavors, Abhinavagupta presumably has in mind the prohibition against explicitly presenting sexual intercouse or death on stage.[18]

Ānandavardhana himself was not troubled by the rarity of this stable emotion in the real world: "If it does not fall within the range of experience of all people, this fact is not enough in itself to allow one to deny that particular psychological state in noble individuals who are unlike other people."[19] And, at least where his analysis of the *Mahābhārata* is concerned, the problems of representation are not as serious as in a play. As Dhanika put it shortly before the time of Abhinavagupta, "Although *śāntarasa* is not brought into plays because it cannot be acted out, there is nothing to prevent its occurrence in poems, since all things, including those that are

---

[15] The objections to the possibility of *śāntarasa* are enumerated by Dhanika (*DRAva.* on 4.35, pp. 202–203: *iha śāntarasaṃ prati vādināṃ anekavidhā vipratipattayaḥ* . . .), and again by Abhinavagupta in several portions of the *śānta* section of the *Abh.*

[16] His fullest discussion of the topic is in the section on *śāntarasa* in the *ABh.* (Kangle, pp. 316ff.; *GOS*, pp. 333ff.). The Sanskrit text of this section is also available in emended form in Raghavan, *The Number of Rasa-s*, pp. 104–117, which is reproduced, together with a complete English translation, in Masson and Patwardhan, *Śāntarasa*, pp. 113–143.

[17] *ABh.* (Kangle, p. 338; *GOS*, p. 340): *yadā tu paryantabhūmikālālabhe 'nubhāvabhāvaḥ tadāsyāprayojyatvam, ratiśokādau api paryantadaśāyām aprayogasyaiva yuktatvāt. hṛdayasaṃvādo 'pi tathāvidhatattvajñānabījasaṃskārabhāvitānām bhavaty eva.*

[18] This is the interpretation suggested by Masson and Patwardhan (*Śāntarasa*, p. 100); their view is attacked by Gerow and Aklujkar (see note 56 below).

[19] *Dhv.*, *vṛtti* on 3.26 (p. 393): *yadi nāma sarvajanānubhavagocaratā tasya nāsti naitāvatāsāv alokasāmānyamahānubhāvacittavṛttiviśeṣaḥ pratikṣeptum śakyaḥ.*

subtle or in the past, can be presented through their ability to be described in words."[20]

Once the possibility of suggesting *śāntarasa* in a poem is granted, a further theoretical problem arises: can *śāntarasa* also be the predominant flavor (*aṅgī rasa*) in the work, as Ānandavardhana explicitly claims is so in the *Mahābhārata*? The *Dhvanyāloka* insists on the treatment of one flavor as predominant in any larger work that aspires to excellence,[21] and on this level the difficulties of representation that separate the plays from the non-dramatic poems become even more serious. Beginning with the *Dhvanyāloka*, most of the treatises that concern themselves with the topic of the predominant flavor in plays discuss a single play, the *Nāgānanda*, in which *śāntarasa* might be considered dominant, and, as we shall see, they end up deciding that there the *aṅgī rasa* is actually the flavor of heroism rather than that of peace. But from Ānandavardhana's time most of those who accept the existence of *śantarasa* concede that it can be dominant in a non-dramatic poem. Viśvanātha, for example, stipulates that the predominant *rasa* in a major play must be either *śṛṅgāra* (the erotic flavor) or *vīra* (the heroic flavor),[22] but when he later discusses the major genre of non-dramatic poetry he adds *śāntarasa* to the list of possibilities.[23] It therefore seems that the status of *śāntarasa* as the predominant flavor in the *Mahābhārata* is at least theoretically possible.

If Ānandavardhana's theory is supportable on the level of practical criticism as well, it should be possible to trace the outlines of the ways in which the *sthāyibhāva* corresponding to the peaceful flavor is suggested in the poem.

As I have mentioned, the prescise identification of the stable emotion associated with *śāntarasa* cannot proceed on the basis of such exalted authority as is possible in discussing the other flavors, since the old *Nāṭyaśāstra* did not originally recognize the flavor of peace as a *rasa*. The widespread designation of the *sthāyibhāva* as *śama* (tranquility) is based on an interpolated passage in the *Nāṭyaśāstra* that deals specifically with *śāntarasa*. Many theorists preferred to draw their conclusions from what

---

[20] *DRAva.*, intro. to 4.45cd (p. 223): *nanu ca śāntarasasyānabhineyatvād yady api nāṭye 'nupraveśo nāsti tathāpi sūkṣmātītādivastūnāṃ sarveṣām api śabdapratipādyatayā vidyamānatvāt kāvyaviṣayatvaṃ na nivāryate.*

[21] *Dhv.* 3.21 (p. 378):

prasiddhe 'pi prabandhānāṃ nānārasanibandhane |
eko raso 'ṅgīkartavyas teṣām utkarṣam icchatā ||

[22] *SD* 6.10ab (in defining the *nāṭaka*, p. 258): *eka eva bhaved aṅgī śṛṅgāro vīra eva vā.*

[23] *SD* 6.317ab (in defining the *mahākāvya*, p. 353): *śṛṅgāravīraśāntānām eko 'ṅgī rasa iṣyate.*

they recognized to be the older portion of the work, and to rely on implications found in Bharata's list of the other eight *sthāyibhāva*s and in the immediately following list of the more numerous *vyabhicāribhāva*s, the temporary feelings that accompany the basic emotions. One way of getting around the mention of only eight basic emotions was to borrow, as the *sthāyibhāva* connected with *śāntarasa*, the first of these accompanying feelings listed by Bharata, called *nirveda*, and so have it do double duty. Abhinavagupta, in reviewing the various attempts to extract a *sthāyibhāva* for the flavor of peace from Bharata's text, explains that this interpretation was thought to account both for Bharata's omission of *nirveda* in the list of *sthāyibhāva*s and for his starting the subsequent list of *vyabhicāribhāva*s with so inauspicious an item, which the sage would presumably not have done without some special purpose.[24]

In this view, which seems to agree well with Ānandavardhana's own conception of the *sthāyibhāva* connected with *śāntarasa*, there are thus two kinds of *nirveda*. In reference to a *vyabhicāribhāva*, the term means a feeling of discouragement or temporary disgust; this feeling may accompany many of the stable emotions. In reference to a stable emotion, *nirveda* means a more fundamental disillusionment, a psychological state of disregard directed against the entire phenomenal world rather than merely a response to an individual source of pain. While both forms of *nirveda* share an origin in suffering, they differ in the ways in which all *vyabhicāribhāva*s differ from *sthāyibhāva*s. The *vyabhicāribhāva* is occasional and temporary, while the *sthāyibhāva* is more lasting: to use Abhinavagupta's example, on hearing that someone is suffering from exhaustion (i.e., from the *vyabhicāribhāva* called *glāna*), the natural reaction is to ask why, but on hearing that Rāma is a man of heroism (i.e., that he possesses the *sthāyibhāva* called *utsāha*), no one asks for a reason.[25] And the practical effects of the *vyabhicāribhāva* are correspondingly fleeting, while the *sthāyibhāva* can have lasting results: the temporary despondency does not move beyond a state of pain, while the more fundamental version culminates in freedom.

Ānandavardhana, in his own treatment of the *sthāyibhāva* associated with the flavor of peace, emphasized this characteristic of having already passed beyond pain. If Abhinavagupta and I have read him correctly,[26] he

---

[24] *Abh.* (Kangle: on 6.17, p. 112; *GOS*: on 6.18, pp. 269–270): *tattvajñānajo nirvedo 'sya sthāyī, etadartham evobhayadharmopajīvitvakhyāpanāyāmaṅgalabhūto 'py asau pūrvaṃ nirdiṣṭo, sthāyiṣu ca saṃkhyā noktety apare.*

[25] *ABh.* (Kangle, p. 168; *GOS*, p. 284): *glāno 'yam ity ukte kuta iti hetupraśnenāsthāyitāsya sūcyate. na tu rāma utsāhaśaktimān ity atra hetupraśnam āhuḥ.*

[26] In defining the *rasa* as a "fostering" (*paripoṣa*) of the emotion of happiness, Ānandavardhana does not explicitly say that the happiness is the *sthāyibhāva*, but this is the natural way of interpreting his remarks in the context, and Abhinavagupta makes this interpretation explicit (*Loc.* on 3.26, p. 390): . . . *tad eva sukhaṃ tasya sthāyibhūtasya yaḥ paripoṣo rasyamānatākṛtas tad eva lakṣaṇaṃ yasya sa śānto rasaḥ.*

defined the *sthāyibhāva* as "the happiness produced by the extinction of craving," a phrase he borrowed from a verse in the *Mahābhārata*, which he quotes in the same passage: "The happiness of pleasures in this world and the great happiness in heaven cannot match the sixteenth part of the happiness produced by the extinction of craving."[27]

It is this transcendental happiness that, in theory, we should find suggested throughout the *Mahābhārata* as the prevailing psychological state of the protagonist in the poem. The focus of the *Mahābhārata* story is on the five Pāṇḍavas, and to most readers of the poem it will seem obvious that among them it is the eldest, Yudhiṣṭhira, who functions as the hero in the poem. Within the Sanskrit tradition the awareness of the central role of Yudhiṣṭhira is so strong that even when another of the Pāṇḍavas has been made the focus of a later work of poetry, commentators are likely to persist in viewing Yudhiṣṭhira as the real protagonist in those poems. This is done, for example, by Citrabhānu in his commentary on the *Kirātārjunīya* of Bhāravi, an ornate epic dealing with the deeds of Arjuna. In discussing the underlying predominance of Yudhiṣṭhira in the poem, Citrabhānu explains, with reference to the *Mahābhārata*, that "even though 'Bhārata' is the name of all the Bhāratas, nevertheless it is the deeds of Yudhiṣṭhira that are presented there as the principal topic. Just as he alone was predominant in (the depiction in the *Mahābhārata* of the Pāṇḍavas') ascent into heaven, just so should it be here (in this poem) as well."[28] Citrabhānu goes on to cite a verse from the *Mahābhārata* that has often been quoted in this connection:

> Yudhiṣṭhira is the great tree composed of dharma,
> Arjuna is its trunk, and Bhīmasena its branches,
> The two sons of Mādrī are its rich blossoms and fruit,
> and its root is Kṛṣṇa, Brahma, and the brahman.[29]

We come now to the central problem in Ānandavardhana's analysis of the *Mahābhārata*: in the career of Yudhiṣṭhira as it is presented in the poem,

---

[27] *Dhv.*, *vṛtti* on 3.26 (p. 390): *śāntas ca tṛṣṇākṣayasukhasya yaḥ paripoṣas tallakṣaṇo rasaḥ pratīyata eva. tathā hi–*

> *yac ca kāmasukhaṃ loke yac ca divyaṃ mahat sukham |*
> *tṛṣṇākṣayasukhasyaite nārhataḥ ṣoḍaśīṃ kalām ||*

[The verse appears in *Mahābhārata* 12.168.36, 12.171.51, 12.268.6, and elsewhere.]

[28] Commentary on *Kir.* 1.1 (p. 4): *bhāratam ity eva kṛtsnasya bhāratasya saṃjñā. tathāpi yudhiṣṭhiracaritam eva tatra prādhānyena pratipādyate. svargārohaṇe tasyaiva śeṣitvam iti tadvad atrāpi syāt.*

[29] *MBh.* 1.1.66, repeated at 5.29.46:

> *yudhiṣṭhiro dharmamayo mahādrumaḥ*
> *skandho 'rjuno bhīmaseno 'sya śākhāḥ |*
> *mādrīsutau puṣpaphale samṛddhe*
> *mūlaṃ kṛṣṇo brahma ca brāhmaṇāś ca ||*

the blissful freedom from desire that Ānandavardhana considers the *sthāyibhāva* of the peaceful flavor is by no means conspicuous. It is true that towards the end of the poem, in the events culminating in the ascent to heaven that Citrabhānu mentions, Yudhiṣṭhira is finally prompted by weariness and disappointment to leave the world behind him. But if, as Anandavardhana expressly maintains, the flavor of peace is supposed to be the *aṅgī rasa* in the *Mahābhārata*, then it ought to be predominant throughout the work and not merely come into prominence at the end.

Ānandavardhana describes this requirement in commenting on the conditions under which the predominance of the *aṅgī rasa* is not impaired by the evocation of other *rasa*s within the same work: "If in larger works a certain flavor is taken up first, and then becomes lasting by being brought in again and again, then, since that flavor pervades the entire composition, its predominance is not destroyed by the coexistence with it of other flavors that appear at intervals."[30] He tells us further that "when in a work a certain *rasa*—the flavor of love, for example—is suggested as predominant, then no other flavor, whether compatible or incompatible, it to be brought to full development."[31]

In the *Mahābhārata* the more obvious candidate for the status of the *rasa* that fulfills these requirements is the flavor of heroism, *vīrarasa*. Ānandavardhana himself discusses the possibility of confusing *śāntarasa* and *vīrarasa*, and provides the criterion for distinguishing one from the other, in a part of his argument for the existence of the flavor of peace: "Nor is it proper to include it within the flavor of heroism, for the occurrence of that (heroic flavor) is determined on the basis of its being composed of pride, while the existence of this (flavor of peace) depends upon its consisting entirely of the cessation of ego."[32] In speaking of the two *rasa*s here, Ānandavardhana is actually referring to the corresponding *sthāyibhāva*s, a loose but common practice. The pride or self-conception that he mentions constitutes, as the commentator Abhinavagupta makes explicit,[33] the very life of the stable emotion associated with the flavor of heroism, the *sthāyibhāva* called *utsāha*, exertion. The notion is that those who undertake energetic activity do so in order to fulfill the obligations of a noble self-image.

---

[30] *Dhv.* on 3.22 (pp. 378–379): *prabandeṣu prathamataraṃ prastutaḥ san punaḥ punar anusandhīyamānatvena sthāyī yo rasas tasya sakalabandhavyāpino rasāntarair antarālavartibhiḥ samāveśo yaḥ sa nāṅgitām upahanti.*

[31] *Dhv.* on 3.24 (p. 382): *aṅgini rasāntare śṛṅgārādau prabandhavyaṅgye saty avirodhī virodhī vā rasaḥ paripoṣaṃ na netavyaḥ.*

[32] *Dhv.* on 3.26 (p. 393): *na ca vīre tasyāntarbhāvaḥ kartuṃ yuktaḥ. tasyābhimānamayatvena vyavasthāpanāt. asya cāhaṅkāraprasamaikarūpatayā sthiteḥ.*

[33] *Loc.* on *Dhv.* 3.26 (p. 393): *abhimānamayatveneti–utsāho hy aham evamvidha ity evaṃprāṇa ity arthaḥ.*

This conception of *vīrarasa* is open to the objection that energetic undertakings are possible without dependence upon self-conscious pride. For example, the deeds of the Buddha, as depicted in a poem like the *Buddhacarita*, can reasonably be called heroic, and yet they proceed from an inherent compassion rather than from any element of ego. From early times the Sanskrit tradition enumerated several special types of *vīra* in recognition of the variations in motive that underlie them. For the Buddha's type of heroism the name is *dayāvīra*, the heroism of compassion; for Yudhiṣṭhira it is *dharmavīra*, the heroism of righteousness. For both types the question arose, based on the objection I have mentioned, of whether they should be considered *vīrarasa* proper or a form of *śāntarasa*.

For Ānandavardhana the decision in any given instance follows from the distinction quoted above. "Particular psychological states such as *dayāvīra*," he continues, again using the name of the *rasa* to refer to the *sthāyibhāva*, "are varieties of *śāntarasa* if they are devoid of ego in any form, but otherwise they are varieties of *vīra*."[34] To apply this to the case at hand: what distinguishes Yudhiṣṭhira from the Buddha is that Yudhiṣṭhira consciously identifies with righteousness—he thinks of himself as the Dharmarāja—and he strives to live up to that identity, with all the desires and attachments that such an endeavor involves. The Buddha, in contrast, has passed beyond desire and attachment, having attained the "extinction of craving" that Ānandavardhana mentions as a prerequisite in the *sthāyibhāva* associated with the flavor of peace.

While Ānandavardhana himself does not give specific examples of the practical application of this distinction, the example of the Buddha and Yudhiṣṭhira that I have used appears after Ānandavardhana in the *Avaloka* of Dhanika, where Dhanika discusses the question of whether the Buddha, Yudhiṣṭhira, and Jīmūtavāhana (the hero of the *Nāgānanda*) are to be connected with *śāntarasa* or with *vīrarasa*. He focuses on the *Nāgānanda*, pointing out the description of Jīmūtavāhana's love for Malayāvatī and his winning of sovereignty at the end of work, and concludes:

> Although the Buddha and Jīmūtavāhana do not differ in being compassionate, there is a distinction in whether or not their compassion is accompanied by desire. Hence Jīmūtavāhana and the others like him are heroes of the firm type (appropriate to *vīrarasa*, rather than of the peaceful type appropriate to *śāntarasa*).[35]

---

[34] *Dhv.* on 3.26 (p. 394): *dayāvīrādīnāṃ ca cittavṛttiviśeṣāṇāṃ sarvākāram ahaṅkārarahitatvena śāntarasaprabhedatvam, itarathā tu vīraprabhedatvam.*

[35] *DRAva.* on 4.4cd–5ab (p. 79): *buddhajīmūtavāhanayos tu kāruṇikatvāviśeṣe 'pi sakāmaniṣkāmakaruṇādibhedād bhedaḥ. ato jīmūtavāhanāder dhīrodāttatvam iti.*

The elements of desire, attachment, exertion and striving that characterize heroism are all bound up together in opposition to peacefulness, as Abhinavagupta brings out when he explains that "passion and anger, having attachment to objects as their very life, are altogether incompatible with the peaceful, which is by nature totally devoid of striving, since it has as its essence disillusionment with all the objects of transmigratory existence, arising from the knowledge of reality."[36] This does not mean, however, that any trace of these heroic elements will preclude the possibility of *śāntarasa*; as Abhinavagupta says in discussing the appearance of *utsāha* in connection with the peaceful mood, "No state is entirely void of exertion, for without will and effort one would be a stone."[37] What is important is the relative prominence given to these elements. Thus Dhanika, in another of his discussions of Jīmūtavāhana, emphasizes the pervasive presence of the love for Malayāvatī and the preeminent position of the winning of sovereignty: "But the contention of some, that tranquility is the *sthāyibhāva* in the *Nāgānanda*, is contradicted by his love for Malayāvatī, which extends throughout the work, and by his gaining the status of Emperor of the Vidyādharas as the fruit attained at the very end."[38]

These principles clearly rule against the choice of tranquility as the stable emotion of Yudhiṣṭhira, even if we concentrate solely on the final episode of the ascent to heaven. What Yudhiṣṭhira seeks and finds is not the liberated state of one who has passed beyond attachment, but rather the engaging world of a warrior's paradise. And to the end his actions could not be further from fulfillment of the most consistently mentioned aspect of freedom from attachment, indifference to friend or foe. In the literature on *śāntarasa* this requirement is repeated from the time of the interpolated verses in the *Nāṭyaśāstra*, which define the flavor of peace as that "in which there is no pleasure, no pain, no hatred, and no envy, but equanimity toward all creatures,"[39] to the time of the last major literary critic, Jagannātha Paṇḍitarāja, who begins his list of the manifestations of tranquility with "the lack of attraction towards objects, and indifference to

[36] *Loc.*, end of comm. on *Dhv.* 3.23 (p. 381): *śāntasyāpi tattvajñānasamutthitasamastasaṃsāraviṣayanirvedaprāṇatvena sarvato nirīhasvabhāvasya viṣayāsaktijīvitābhyāṃ ratikrodhābhyāṃ virodha eva.*

[37] *ABh.*, *śānta* section (Kangle, p. 334; *GOS*, p. 338): *na tūtsāhaśūnyā kācid apy avasthā, icchāprayatnavyatirekeṇa pāṣāṇatāpatteḥ.*

[38] *DRAva.* on 4.35 (p. 203): *yat tu kaiścin nāgānandādau śamasya sthāyitvam upavarṇitam, tan malayāvatyanurageṇāprabandhapravṛttena, ante vidyādharacakravartitvaprāpteś ca phalatvena viruddham.*

[39] *NS.*, *śama* section (Kangle, p. 315; *GOS*, p. 315):

na yatra duḥkhaṃ na sukhaṃ na dveṣo nāpi matsaraḥ |
samaḥ sarveṣu bhūteṣu sa śāntaḥ prathito rasaḥ ||

enemies and friends."[40] Yudhiṣṭhira's differing reactions to Duryodhana and to his own family in the final scenes are too obvious to require comment.

Still less can the descriptions of tranquility as a stable emotion be applied to Yudhiṣṭhira's wife and brothers, who fall behind him one by one, to the announcing of their particular excesses of attachment and egoism.

Thus it appears that here we cannot apply the standard canons of *rasa* theory by looking for the required *sthāyibhāva* in the hero of the work. Indeed, there is ample evidence to show that, whatever the overall *rasa* in the *Mahābhārata* may be, the careers of Yudhiṣṭhira and Arjuna have been drawn on by the Sanskrit poets for works intended to evoke the heroic flavor rather than the flavor of peace. Ānandavardhana tells us that in the *Rāmāyaṇa* and other such works that serve as the source of traditional plots, the *rasas* connected with the characters are fixed, and must not be tampered with.[41] But he also teaches that one must abandon anything in the original story that is contrary to the appropriate flavor,[42] and remarks that he himself had to make certain changes when he took up the story of Arjuna in his own *mahākāvya*, the *Arjunacarita*.[43]

In this connection the later critic Kuntaka accepts Ānandavardhana's explanation of *śāntarasa* as the predominant flavor in the *Mahābhārata*, only to applaud a switch to *vīrarasa* when treating the story of Yudhiṣṭhira. In a long passage on changing the flavor of a story taken from an old original, Kuntaka cites as an example the play *Veṇīsaṃhāra*, explaining that the author had wisely scrapped the gloomy emphasis on the vanities of this world that is found in the *Mahābhārata*, replacing it with the heroic flavor more appropriate to the tale of the Pāṇḍavas, so that the play, ending with Yudhiṣṭhira victorious on a battlefield strewn with the bodies of his slaughtered enemies,

> ... imparts delight to cultured readers, since they see that [the Pāṇḍavas], even though they have suffered such great misfortunes, still conquered their

---

[40] *RG*, definition of *śāntarasa* (p. 168): *viṣayārucisatrumitrādyaudāsīnyaceṣṭāhāhāninasāgradṛṣṭyādayo 'nubhāvāḥ.*

[41] *Dhv.* on 3.10 (p. 335): *kiṃca–*

> "*santi siddharasaprakhyā ye ca rāmāyaṇādayaḥ |*
> *kathāśrayā na tair yojyā svecchā rasavirodhinī ||*" etc.

[42] *Dhv.* 3.11 (*p.* 329):

> *itivṛttavaśāyātaṃ tyaktvānanuguṇāṃ sthitim |*
> *utprekṣyāpy antarābhiṣṭarasocitakathonnayaḥ ||*

and *vṛtti* on this (pp. 335–336).

[43] *Dhv.* on 3.11 (p. 336): *yathā ca madīya evārjunacarite mahākāvye.*

> enemies through their own prowess, fortified by their allies, and enjoy this royal glory, so that [the readers themselves] are endowed with broad powers of exertion and remain undaunted even in misfortunes.[44]

Of course, the *Mahābhārata* extends beyond the victory of Yudhiṣṭhira to include the many sad events that follow, and the lesson that Ānandavardhana draws from it, as we saw in the opening section of his analysis of the *Mahābhārata* quoted above, is quite a different one. His reference there to a "conclusion that produces a despondent feeling in response to the sorry end of the Vṛṣṇis and the Pāṇḍavas" is an indication in itself that the disillusionment required as the stable emotion associated with the flavor of peace is not to be found in the Pāṇḍavas themselves, since the response he mentions must necessarily be subsequent to their end—and must in fact be sought, if we take his words literally, outside the poem, as a response to its conclusion. Ānandavardhana strengthens his statement of this moral, and of its predominance in the poem, in the continuation of his analysis:

> This has already been partially revealed by other commentators. It has also been declared by the Protector of the World [i.e., the sage Vyāsa] himself, who, imparting the light of immaculate knowledge out of his desire to save a world drowning in great delusion, has many times said such things as this: "There is no doubt that the more the insubstantial workings of this world (are seen to) turn out badly, the more a feeling of dispassion is produced" [*MBh.* 12.168.4]. And from this the purport of the *Mahābhārata* appears quite clearly indeed: it is *śāntarasa* among all the *rasa*s, and the aim of man characterized by liberation among all the aims of man, that through the subordination of all the others is the principal subject matter.
>
> We have already described the manner in which the predominance and subordination of the flavors operates. It is no contradiction that a subordinate flavor or a subordinate human aim may appear beautiful through its own (assumed) predominance, independent of the ultimate inner reality, just as the body [which is in reality subordinate to the soul] may be considered beautiful through its own [apparent] predominance, independent of the ultimate inner reality.[45]

---

[44] *VJ*, *vṛtti* on 4.17 (p. 276): . . . *abhijātānām āhlādam āvahati. te hi tathāvidhavyasanakṣetrībhūtair api punaḥ svapakṣopabṛṃhitaparākramaparājitaparipanthibhir bhujyata eṣā rājyaśrīr iti akhidyamānā vipatsv api vipulotsāhabhājo bhavanti*. The discussion of the *Veṇīsaṃhāra* begins on p. 275 in the Sanskrit text; Krishnamoorthy provides his own translation of the whole passage on p. 569.

[45] *Dhv.* on 4.5 (pp. 530–531): *etac cāṃśena vivṛtam evānyair vyākhyāvidhāyibhiḥ. svayam eva caitad udgīrṇam tenodīrṇamahāmohamagnam ujjihīrṣatā lokam ativimalajñānalokadāyinā lokanāthena–*

> *yathā yathā viparyeti lokatantram asāravat |*
> *tathā tathā virāgo 'tra jāyate nātra saṃśayaḥ ||*

ityādi bahuśaḥ kathayatā. tataś ca śānto raso rasāntarair mokṣalakṣaṇaḥ puruṣārthaḥ puruṣārthāntarais tadupasarjanatvenānugamyamāno 'ṅgitvena vivakṣāviṣaya iti mahābhāratatātparyaṃ suvyaktam

The last statement is apparently made in recognition of the fact that on a superficial level the heroic flavor, rather than the flavor of peace, seems predominant in the poem. But Ānandavardhana also takes the trouble to remind us that he has already described the ways in which a *rasa* is made predominant in a work, and we should expect, if *śāntarasa* is predominant in the *Mahābhārata*, that it will be evoked through the process to which Ānandavardhana devotes so much attention, a process that involves the suggestion, not of the *rasa* directly, but of the corresponding stable emotion, by means of presenting that emotion's *vibhāva*s (the object toward which the emotion is felt, and the things that serve to provoke or stimulate it), its *anubhāva*s (the effects of the stable emotion in the person who experiences it), and its *vyabhicāribhāva*s (the temporary feelings that accompany it).

Since the primary goal in a poem is the evocation of *rasa*, and the *sthāyibhāva* is only a means toward that goal, there is a natural tendency to speak of the resulting *rasa* in discussing a poem, rather than of the intervening stable emotion; we have already seen how frequently Ānandavardhana speaks of the *rasa*s when his remarks actually apply only to the *sthāyibhāva*s instead. And even the *rasasūtra* itself, the classical explanation of the evocation of *rasa* given in the *Nāṭyáśāstra*, does not mention the *sthāyibhāva*, but says only that the origination of *rasa* is due to the combination of the *vibhāva*s, the *anubhāva*s, and the *vyabhicāribhāva*s. As Abhinavagupta explains, however, this failure to mention the stable emotion in the *rasasūtra* is due to the importance of maintaining an awareness of the difference between the stable emotion and the corresponding flavor:

> Thus a cognition of the stable emotion arrived at through inference is not the *rasa*. This is precisely why there is no mention of the *sthāyibhāva* in the *sūtra*, [because not only would such a mention not be helpful] but, to the contrary, it would actually be an obstacle. It is merely because of correspondence that the *sthāyibhāva* is said to become the *rasa*, and this correspondence is due to the fact that those things that were known as causes, etc., in relation to the stable emotion have now become the *vibhāva*s, etc., by virtue of their aiding in the relishing [of the flavor].[46]

These causes—in particular the *anubhāva*s and *vyabhicāribhāva*s mentioned

---

evāvabhāsate. aṅgāṅgibhāvaś ca yathā rasānām tathā pratipāditam eva. paramārthikāntas tattvānapekṣayā śarīrasyevāṅgabhūtasya rasasya puruṣārthasya ca svaprādhānyena cārutvam apy aviruddham.

[46] *ABh.* on the *rasasūtra* (Kangle, p. 174; *GOS*; p. 285): *tena sthāyipratītir anumitirūpā prāptā na rasaḥ. ata eva sūtre sthāyigrahaṇaṃ na kṛtam. tat pratyuta śalyabhūtaṃ syāt. kevalam aucityād evam ucyate sthāyī rasībhūta iti. aucityaṃ tu tatsthāyigatatvena kāraṇāditayā prasiddhānām adhunā carvaṇopayogitayā vibhāvāditvālambanāt.* In translating *aucitya* as "correspondence" I follow Gnoli (pp. 80–81).

in the *rasasūtra*–presuppose the presentation of the character in whom they reside.

In technical terms the problem that confronts us here is one of finding the *āśraya* of the stable emotion, i.e., its locus or substrate, the character in whom the *sthāyibhāva* resides and through whose reactions and accompanying experiences the stable emotion is made known. The question of the presence of the *āśraya* of the stable emotion, like the question of whether *śantarasa* is possible, takes a somewhat different form when one turns from the world of drama for which the theory of *rasa* was originally worked out, to the sphere of non-dramatic poetry.

In drama the explicit presentation of the *āśraya* is usually inevitable, since a play cannot be performed without characters. Abhinavagupta goes so far as to say that the *sthāyibhāva* of the principle character *is* the drama, explaining, in his opening remarks on the *Nāṭyaśāstra*'s enumeration of the *rasa*s, that

> ... drama is a meaning to be unwaveringly determined [by the spectators] with one-pointed minds, being made present through the power of the acting of the actor, and that is to be suggested through one of the particular types of poetic composition such as the *nāṭaka* [a genre of plays]. And although it consists of an infinite number of *vibhāva*s and so on, nevertheless, since all insentient things find their culmination in consciousness, and it in a sentient subject, and all such subjects in a predominant subject, that [meaning that constitues drama] is (in the end) a particular stable psychological state belonging to a particular subject, who is called the protagonist.[47]

He goes on to explain how that emotion, through a process of being universalized, is transformed into an experience of *rasa* on the part of the spectator.

In a non-dramatic poem the poet is free to leave much more to the imagination of the reader. Once again it is Abhinavagupta who gives the most provocative explanation of the process involved, in discussing the differences between plays and poems in presenting the elements connected with the evocation of *rasa*:

> The most intense form of the savoring of *rasa* occurs when [the *vibhāva*s, the *anubhāva*s, and the *vyabhicāribhāva*s] are of equal prominence. Actually this happens only in a play. As Vāmana [the author of an early work on poetics] says, "Among compositions the play is best, because, like a cloth of many

[47] *Abh.* (Kangle: on 6.15, p. 105; *GOS*: on 6.16, p. 268): *tatra nāṭyaṃ nāma naṭagatābhinayaprabhavasākṣātkārāyamānaikaghanamanasaniścalādhyavaseyaḥ samastanāṭakādyanyatamakāvyaviśeṣāc ca dyotanīyo 'rthaḥ. sa ca yady apy anantavibhāvādyātmā tathāpi sarveṣāṃ jaḍānāṃ saṃvidi tasyāś ca bhoktari bhoktṛvargasya ca pradhāne bhoktari paryavasānān nāyakābhidhānabhoktṛviśeṣasthāyicittavṛttiviśeṣaḥ.*

> colors, it possesses variety through the completeness of its particulars." However, [the savoring of *rasa* is possible] in a longer work [of non-dramatic poetry] due to the arranging of such things as the appropriateness of language, dress, and style. [And it is even possible] in an isolated stanza, through dependence on [a presumed longer work of poetry]. And thus in this [single stanza] expert readers, by inventing a suitable context, generate a considerable foundation [for the stanza, by deciding] that in this instance such and such a person is speaking on such and such an occasion. In this way, for those who, by virtue of such reasons as their practice in poetry and their former good deeds, are expert readers, the meanings of such compositions burst forth quite clearly, as if they were directly perceived, even when the unfolding of the *vibhāva*s and so on is limited. This is why for them poetry by itself can be a source of delight and edification, even without the drama.[48]

These remarks on the stanza are in line with the general tendency within the tradition to view every piece of poetry smaller than the *mahākāvya* as a fragment of a hypothetical larger work, and with the standard practice in the treatises and commentaries of supplying the details of the elements connected with *rasa*, even if these are no more specific than "a certain woman speaking to her friend about some lover." The problem in the *Mahābhārata*, however, is of a different order, for here there can be no larger poem, and the *rasa* that we are concerned with is the predominant flavor in a complete work.

Somewhat surprisingly, the problem of a missing *āśraya* is not uncommon even in plays, despite the boasts of Abhinavagupta concerning the completeness of detail in the drama. The problem occurs most often in connection with *hāsyarasa*, the comic flavor, for which the corresponding *sthāyibhāva* is *hāsa*, the emotion of laughter or amusement. When one character laughs at another, there is no problem: the one who laughs is the *āśraya*, or subject, of the emotion, and the butt of his laughter is the *ālambana* or object (literally, the "prop" or "support"). And when a character—usually the jester—laughs at himself, he is simultaneously the *āśraya* and the *ālambana*. But when a character who is obviously intended to be amusing appears without being amused himself and without the presence of an onlooker to laugh at him, as happens in many soliloquies and comic interludes, then we have only an *ālambana*, and in the absence of an *āśraya*

---

[48] *ABh.* near the end of the comm. on the *rasasūtra* (Kangle, p. 183; *GOS*, p. 288; beyond the portion included in Gnoli): *kiṃtu samaprādhānya eva rasāsvādasyotkarṣaḥ. vastutas tu daśarūpaka eva. yad āha vāmanaḥ "saṃdarbheṣu daśarūpakaṃ śreyaḥ. tad dhi citraṃ citrapaṭavad viśeṣasākalyāt" iti. tadrūpasamarpaṇāya tu prabandhe bhāṣāveṣapravṛttyaucityādikalpanāt. tadupajīvanena muktake. tathā ca tatra sahṛdayāḥ pūrvāparam ucitam parikalpya īdṛg atra vaktāsminn avasare ityādi bahutaraṃ pīṭhabandharūpaṃ vidadhate. tena ye kāvyābhyāsaprāktanapuṇyādihetubalād iti sahṛdayās teṣāṃ parimitavibhāvādyunmīlane 'pi parisphuṭa eva sākṣātkārakalpaḥ kāvyārthaḥ sphurati. ata eva teṣāṃ kāvyam eva prītivyutpattikṛd anapekṣitanāṭyam api.*

the *anubhāva*s and *vyabhicāribhāva*s cannot possibly by represented. Theoretically such a situation cannot evoke an experience of *rasa* in the spectators, since there is no substratum for the *sthāyibhāva* upon which the phenomenon of *rasa* is said to be based. Yet the commentators do not hesitate to speak of *hāsyarasa* in such instances.

The critical tradition seems to have been very slow in recognizing this theoretical problem, unless we believe that it is referred to in the *Nāṭyaśāstra*'s division of *hāsa* into two types, that which is "situated in oneself" (*ātmastha*), and that which is "situated in another" (*parastha*), together with its explanation that the former is "when one laughs oneself" and the latter "when one makes another laugh."[49] The writers within the tradition, however, do not interpret this distinction as referring to the lack of an *āśraya*. The primitive explanation is that *rasa* is *ātmastha* when one laughs at oneself, and *parastha* when one is laughed at by another person who is also on stage (the stock example of the latter being the queen's laughter at the court jester). Abhinavagupta rejects this interpretation on the grounds that it involves a difference in the location of the cause of laughter rather than of the laughter itself, as he claims the actual wording in the *Nāṭyaśāstra* should require. He offers instead the perceptive explanation that laughter is uniquely contagious, and that in the *parastha* form of *hāsa* one causes another to laugh merely by one's own laughter rather than by presenting an amusing appearance or action, adding that this may happen either when the second person laughs without even knowing why the first person laughed, or when the second person has also seen the cause of the amusement but is too serious to laugh until someone else laughs first.[50] In both interpretations the *āśraya* of the amusement is presented in the work.

As in many instances of phenomena that are not noticed in the ground-breaking theoretical treatises and that require independent attentiveness to the poetry itself, the first clear treatment of the problem of the lack of an explicit *āśraya* that I have seen is in the *Sāhityadarpaṇa* of Viśvanātha, who makes no mention of the distinction of *ātmastha* and

---

[49] *NS* in *hāsya* section (Kangle: prose after 6.48, p. 267; *GOS*: 6.56, p. 314): *dvividhaś cāyam ātmasthaḥ parasthaś ca. yadā svayaṃ hasati tadātmasthaḥ. yadā tu paraṃ hāsayati tadā parasthaḥ.*

[50] The primitive interpretation is presented in *DRAva.* on 4.76 (p. 246), and is the version used by Regnaud (*La Rhétorique sanskrite* [Paris: Ernest Leroux, 1884], p. 307). Abhinavagupta's explanation is in *ABh.* on 6.56 (Kangle, pp. 270–271; cf. *GOS* pp. 314–315), and is repeated by Hemacandra in the *Viveka* on *KAnu.* 2.11 (p. 114). Both interpretations are combined in the anonymous *ṭippaṇa* given in Appendix I of Parikh and Kulkarni's edition of the *KAnu.* (p. 578, comm. on p. 114 line 5).

parastha, but who says:

> If in some instances the one to whom the amusement belongs is not directly presented, he is nevertheless implied by the *vibhāvas* and so on. Therefore, the spectators can identify with [the *sthāyibhāva*] through the universality of the *vibhāvas*, etc., and they experience this comic flavor. One should understand that this applies to other flavors as well.[51]

A second solution is offered by the later critic Jagannātha Paṇḍitarāja, who takes up the problem not under the heading of amusement, but of the stable emotion of loathing, which is similar in that we may be given a description of a loathsome object without the presentation of the person who is disgusted by it. Jagannātha mentions Viśvanātha's answer to the problem, and then suggests an alternative:

> One might make the objection that, whereas in [the stable emotions of] love, anger, exertion, fear, grief, astonishment, and dispassion, examples of which were given earlier, one perceives both the object [*ālambana*] and the locus [*āśraya*], it is not so in amusement and in loathing, for there we may perceive the object alone. [And this is improper,] because since the reader is the locus of the savoring of the *rasa* it is not possible for him to be the locus of the everyday emotions of amusement or loathing. If [this objection is made, we reply]—True, [but this is not improper,] because there one is to assume by implication some observer as its locus. Even if he is not assumed, however, [there is still no problem,] because there is nothing to prevent the experience of *rasa* in the reader, just as [in the case of a man's experiencing *rasa*] due to a verse describing the woman with whom he himself is in love.[52]

On this passage the modern commentator Madhusūdan Shāstrī remarks that the observer who is implied is in fact the speaker of the verse in question, and that while Jagannātha seems to regard the reader as the locus of loathing, but the speaker as the locus of amusement, he himself sees no

---

[51] *SD* 3.220–221 (p. 176): *atra ca—*

> *yasya hāsaḥ sa cet kvāpi sākṣān naiva nibadhyate |*
> *tathāpy eṣa vibhāvādisāmarthyād upalabhyate ||*
> *abhedena vibhāvādisādhāraṇyāt pratīyate |*
> *samājikais tato hāsyaraso 'yam anubhūyate ||*

evam anyeṣv api raseṣu boddhavyam.

[52] *RG*, first *ānana*, under *bībhatsarasa* (vol. 1, p. 198): *nanu ratikrodhotsāhabhayaśokavismayanirvedeṣu prāgudāhṛteṣu yathālambanāśrayayoḥ saṃpratyayaḥ, na tathā hāse jugupsāyāṃ ca. tatrālambanasyaiva pratīteḥ. padyaśrotuś ca rasāsvādādhikaraṇatvena laukikahāsajugupsāśrayatvānupapatter iti cet. satyam. tadāśrayasya draṣṭṛpuruṣaviśeṣasya tatrākṣepyatvāt. tadanākṣepe tu śrotuḥ svīyakāntāvarṇanapadyād iva rasodbodhe bādhakābhāvat.*

difficulty in taking the speaker to be the *āśraya* in both instances.[53]

For the *Mahābhārata* it might be possible to impart continuity to the *sthāyibhāva* in question by viewing it as residing in the poem's author, the sage Vyāsa. We have seen that in his analysis of the *Mahābhārata* Ānandavardhana places great emphasis on the persistent vision that Vyāsa seeks to communicate. And in his role as a character within the poem, as opposed to his function as author, Vyāsa maintains the same attitude; one could find no better example of the outlook of disillusionment with the world than the verse from the *Mahābhārata* that Ānandavardhana quotes earlier in the *Dhvanyāloka*, recording the ominous words addressed by Vyāsa to his mother after the death of Pāṇḍu:

> The times have passed beyond happiness,
> and bring down horrors hard upon us.
> With each new morrow another day worse,
> the youthfulness of Earth has gone.[54]

In reality, however, remarks such as those of Madhusūdan Shāstrī have in view the isolated stanza, for which the speaker is not the author of the verse, but the character who would speak the verse if it appeared within its larger context.

It would be equally implausible to maintain that our *āśraya* is to be found in a character such as Janamejaya, to whom the whole *Mahābhārata* story is told within the poem. Although his reactions to what he hears are reported here and there, and in fact become increasingly important toward the end of the poem, he is surely too much in the background to perform this role. It also seems likely that if Ānandavardhana had intended his analysis of the poem to require any such devious mechanism he would have said so.

It might be argued that ultimately there is little practical difference between Viśvanātha's view that an *āśraya* must be assumed as implied, and Jagannātha's view that the reader himself may fulfill that function. But the latter view involves a serious danger, as Jagannātha himself recognizes, in that it is difficult to explain how the esthetic distance that is inherent in the phenomenon of *rasa* can be achieved if the reader who experiences the flavor also experiences the concrete emotion to which it corresponds. The central requirement in the evocation of *rasa*, at least in Abhinavagupta's

---

[53] *Madhusūdanī* on *RG* (vol. 1, p. 199): *jugupsāyāṃ tu tādṛśavākyaprayoktaivāśrayaḥ samākṣipyate ālambanānurodhād iti. hāsyasamānā sthitir na. mama tu mataṃ hāsye 'pi tādṛśavākyaprayoktā evāśrayo bhavatu kāpi kṣatir nāsti.*

[54] *MBh.* 1.19.6 (cited in *Dhv.* on 3.16, p. 350):

> *atikrāntasukhāh kālāḥ pratyupasthitadāruṇāh |*
> *śvaḥ śvaḥ pāpīyadivasā pṛthivī gatayauvanā ||*

explanation of the phenomenon, is that of generalization or universalization (*sādhāraṇīkaraṇa*): before the *sthāyibhāva* can give rise to the experience of *rasa*, it must be cognized as belonging neither wholly to another, nor wholly to oneself. If the reader himself is the *āśraya*, the first condition is easily attained, but the second may be impossible, and this is why Viśvanātha refers to the generalization of the *bhāva* as following from the assumption of some *āśraya*.

The theoretical problem we are dealing with is a product of the massive confusion between *sthāyibhāva* and *rasa* that has been a prominent feature of discussions of *rasa* from the *Nāṭyaśāstra* onward. I have mentioned several times Ānandavardhana's laxity in this regard, and he himself seems to have had to correct this same mistake in the very *kārikā* of the *Dhvanyāloka* that proclaims the central importance of *rasa* in poetry.[55] And the problem continues in astonishing proportions throughout the works of modern scholarship in the West as well.[56] The problem is particularly acute in dealing with Ānandavardhana's view of *śāntarasa*. He wrote in the period before the detailed theories of Bhaṭṭa Nāyaka and Abhinavagupta on the relation between *bhāva* and *rasa* had been developed, and has little to say on the matter, so that we cannot really be sure how he conceived of the difference between the two. As Gerow and Aklujkar point out, it is Abhinavagupta's theory, not Ānandavardhana's, in which "the notion of generalization and the attendant radical distinction between *bhāva* and *rasa*" become so important.[57] And the peculiar nature of *śāntarasa* brings

---

[55] *Dhv.* 1.5 (pp. 84–85) is intended to declare that the suggestion of *rasa* as the soul of poetry: *kāvyasyātmā sa evārthas tathā cādikaveḥ purā / krauñcadvandvaviyogotthaḥ śokaḥ ślokatvam āgataḥ*, "That very meaning is the soul of poetry, and so it was that in ancient times the grief of the First Poet, produced by the separation of the pair of herons (of whom one had been killed by a hunter), was transformed into poetry." But, as Abhinavagupta argues in his *Loc.* on this section, what Vālmīki actually felt was not grief (for that belonged to the bird), but rather the corresponding flavor of compassion. It was for this reason, Abhinavagupta claims, that in his *vṛtti* on this verse Ānandavardhana added the explanation that grief is the stable emotion associated with the compassionate flavor (p. 89: *śoko hi karuṇasthāyibhāvaḥ*).

[56] Gerow and Aklujkar ("On Śānta Rasa in Sanskrit Poetics," p. 84) rightly complain of the frequency with which Masson and Patwardhan ignore the distinction between *rasa* and *bhāva* in their book *Śāntarasa*. Yet in their attempted correction of the passage in which they claim this problem is most blatant (p. 85 and fn. 13, referring to Masson and Patwardhan's p. 100 and fn. 2), Gerow and Aklujkar introduce precisely this mistake where Masson and Patwardhan had gotten it right. In this passage Abhinavagupta is explicitly and clearly speaking of the depiction of *nirveda* as a *sthāyibhāva* rather than of the *śāntarasa* itself (as parallel passages in the *DRAva.* and elsewhere make even clearer), and the context has been one of discussing different degrees of intensity of the emotion of a represented character, rather than of the esthetic response of the spectators. Furthermore, the *anubhāvas* are always the "indicatory or suggestive signs" of the *sthāyibhāva*, not of the *rasa*, and for that matter there is never any question of the "depiction of any *rasa*"—it is only the *sthāyibhāva* that is depicted through suggestion, and the *rasa* is an esthetic response to this depiction.

[57] "On Śānta Rasa in Sanskrit Poetics," p. 82.

added difficulties; as the same scholars suggest, the "renunciation of emotional attachment" that is associated with this flavor alone threatens to obliterate the possibility of moving from the "concrete emotion" that is the *sthāyibhāva* to the esthetic experience that is the *rasa*.[58]

A recognition of differences in the degree of distinction between *bhāva* and *rasa* among the particular types of *rasa* is present early on within the Sanskrit tradition, and may go back to the *Nāṭyaśāstra* itself. In commenting on the definitions of the individual flavors in the *Nāṭyaśāstra*, Abhinavagupta points out a curious inconsistency: the erotic flavor (which corresponds to the stable emotion of passion) and the compassionate flavor (which corresponds to the emotion of grief) are said to "arise from" (*-prabhava*) their corresponding stable emotions, while all the other flavors are said to be "of the nature of" (*-ātmaka*) the corresponding emotions. As in the discussions in later treatises of the problem of the lack of an *āśraya*, it is in connection with the comic flavor that Abhinavagupta explains this inconsistency:

> In using the expression "of the nature of," what he is saying is this. When [the stable emotion of] passion brings about the awareness called savoring [i.e., the experience of *rasa*], it does not bring it about in the form of passion itself, because the primary *vibhāvas* [the causes of passion, e.g., the woman with whom a character is in love] are not universal. In the case of amusement, however, the flavor is of the same nature as the amusement itself, through the universality of the *vibhāvas*, since such things as the mixing up of clothing can be causes of amusement in the spectators in the ordinary way, so that [the flavor] is tasted in an act of savoring that is referred to as a tasting having the nature of amusement. In contrast, passion and grief, since they consist of constant pleasure and pain [respectively], have corresponding flavors that differ from them in nature, and they arise from causes that are restricted in their application to particular persons, since they are by nature not universal; therefore the sage has used the expression "arising from" in connection with these two alone. But in connection with the others he has used the phrase "of the nature of," since for them the *vibhāva* is capable of being universal, in that, for everyone, policy and training are causes of exertion, one who acts unjustly causes anger, a battle causes fear, such things as a skeleton cause loathing, and a novelty causes astonishment, so that for these the *vibhāvas* are universal.[59]

---

[58] Ibid.

[59] *Abh.* on *hāsyarasa* (Kangle, p. 268, on prose after 6.48; *GOS*, p. 313 on 6.56): *ātmaśabdenedam āha—ratir āsvadanākhyāṃ pratītiṃ vidadhānā na tāṃ ratirūpām eva vidhatte, pramukhe vibhāvādau asādhāraṇyat. hāse tu ya āsvādaḥ so 'pi vikṛtaveśādināṃ samājikān prati lokavṛttena hāsahetuteti vibhāvasādhāraṇyadvārena tadekasvabhāva eveti hāsātmakarasanākhyacarvaṇā-carvaṇīyatāsya. ratiśokayor eva paramatajjātīyasaṃvidāsvādau* [read (with *GOS*) *ratiśokāv eva param atajjātīya-*] *dhārārūḍhasukhaduḥkharūpatvena niḥsādhāraṇātmīyatvaniyamagrahagṛhitahetubalād evotpadyete yataḥ, ato 'nayor muninā prabhavagrahaṇaṃ kṛtam. anyeṣu tu vibhāve sādhāraṇyasaṃbhāv-anāt tadātmakagrahaṇam, nayavinayāder anyayakāriṇah saṃgrāmasya kaṅkalāder apūrvavastunaś ca sarvān prati utsāhakrodhabhayajugupsāvismayahetutvena sādhāraṇavibhāvatvāt.*

The underlying idea here is simply that when a character is presented as being in love with a particular woman, we can identify with the general state of being in love, but we do not fall in love with that same woman, nor would it be proper for us to do so. Similarly, the grief of a character is due to his loss of a person with whom he is personally involved, and with whom we are not, so that rather than feeling grief we taste the flavor of compassion. All the other flavors, although they still differ from the corresponding *sthāyibhāvas* in being esthetic experiences rather than everyday emotions, do not differ from them in the impossibility of our being provoked to the same emotions by the same objects: while a proper reader will not fall in love with Rāma's wife, we can all be angered by the actions of any unjust man or amused by those of any clown.

In the passage just quoted, Abhinavagupta does not mention *śāntarasa*, because it is not included in the *Nāṭyaśāstra*'s list. Later he applies the same reasoning to that flavor as well, but takes care to insist on the difference between *rasa* and *bhāva*:

> The use of *śama* and *śānta* as synonyms is explained by (what I said about) *hāsa* and *hāsya*. Yet even between *śama* and *śānta* the difference is easily arrived at, because the first is accomplished (i.e., is represented as already existing in a character), while the second is yet to be accomplished (i.e., is to be evoked in the audience); the first is ordinary (i.e., an experience possible only in everyday life), while the second is extraordinary (i.e., possible only in the world of esthetic experience); the first is particular, while the second is universal.[60]

In Ānandavardhana's analysis of the *Mahābhārata*, however, what is presented as "yet to be accomplished" in the reader is the emotion of disillusionment with the world, as the continuation of his remarks makes even clearer:

> [Here one may make the following objection.] Everything contained in the *Mahābhārata* is given in its list of contents, and this does not appear there; on the contrary, it is explicitly made known in that list that the *Mahabharata* is the source of knowledge on all the aims of human life, and that it contains all the *rasas* within it.
>
> On this we say [the following]. True, it is not explicitly set forth by the list that in the *Mahābhārata* it is the flavor of peace that is predominant, and that among all the aims of human life it is liberation that is foremost.
>
> But it is conveyed through suggestion in this statement: "And here the eternal Lord Vāsudeva is praised" [*MBh.* 1.1.193ab]. For through this

[60] *ABh.* in the *śāntarasa* section (Kangle, p. 321; *GOS*, p. 336): *śamaśāntayoḥ paryāyatvaṃ tu hāsahāsyābhyām vyākhyātam. siddhasādhyatayā laukikalaukikatvena sādhāraṇāsādhāraṇatayā ca vailakṣaṇyaṃ śamaśāntayor api sulabham eva.* In translating "*sādhāraṇāsādhāraṇatayā*" I have followed logic rather than parallelism.

> statement is meant to be conveyed, by means of suggestion, the idea that here in the *Mahābhārata* all the deeds of the Pāṇḍavas that are praised come to a painful end and are by nature a manifestation of nescience, whereas the Lord Vāsudeva who is praised here is by nature absolutely real. Therefore, it is only to that Blessed Lord that you should be devoted; do not be enamoured of empty glories or wholeheartedly attach yourselves solely to any one of those [worldly accomplishments] such as policy, training, or prowess. So also the statements in subsequent passages are seen quite clearly to be expressing that very idea, "Behold the insubstantiality of this world," and [in doing so] are aided by the power of suggestiveness. The verses that follow immediately, "For He is the Real" [*MBh*. 1.1.193cd], etc., are observed to reveal as their inner meaning the same sort of notion.[61]

Thus, the suggested moral is that the best that worldly civilization has to offer is ultimately futile, and this is suggested by setting the early glories and the distressing end of the Pāṇḍavas against the unchanging background of God. At this point it is important not to misinterpret the role of God in Ānandavardhana's interpretation of the *Mahābhārata*. In a poem in which theistic devotion to a personal God is prominent, the tendency of the Sanskrit critics is to explain elements connected with *śāntarasa* as secondary to an emphasis on devotion, which falls within the category of the flavor of love rather than the flavor of peace.[62] And when the deeds of a personal God are viewed as foremost in a poem, the tendency is to identify the predominant flavor in terms of those deeds, with results that often differ from the conclusion that those deeds would lead to if they were actions of

---

[61] *Dhv*. on 4.5 (pp. 531–532): *nanu mahābhārate yāvanvivakṣāviṣayaḥ so 'nukramaṇyāṃ sarva evānukrānto na caitat tatra dṛśyate, pratyuta sarvapuruṣārthaprabodhahetutvaṃ sarvarasagarbhatvaṃ ca mahābhāratasya tasminn uddeśe svaśabdaniveditatvena pratīyate. atrocyate—satyaṃ śāntasyaiva rasasyāṅgitvaṃ mahābhārate mokṣasya ca sarvapuruṣārthebhyaḥ prādhānyam ity etan na svaśabdābhidheyatvenānukramaṇyā darśitaṃ, darśitaṃ tu vyaṅgyatvena—"bhagavān vāsudevaś ca kīrtyate 'tra sanātanaḥ" ity asmin vākye. anena hy ayam artho vyaṅgyatvena vivakṣito yad atra mahābhārate pāṇḍavādicaritaṃ yat kīrtyate tat sarvam avasānavirasam avidyāprapañcarūpaṃ ca, paramārthasatyasvarūpas tu bhagavān vāsudevo 'tra kīrtyate. tasmāt tasminn eva parameśvare bhagavati bhavata bhāvitacetaso, ma bhūta vibhūtiṣu niḥsārāsu rāgiṇo guṇeṣu vā nayavinayaparākramādiṣv amīṣu kevaleṣu keṣucit sarvātmanā pratiniviṣṭadhiyaḥ. tathā cāgre—paśyata niḥsāratāṃ saṃsārasyety amum evārthaṃ dyotayan sphuṭam evāvabhāsate vyañjakaśaktyanugṛhītaś ca śabdaḥ. evaṃvidham evārthaṃ garbhīkṛtaṃ saṃdarśayanto 'nantaraślokā lakṣyante—"sa hi satyam" ityādayaḥ.*

[62] Jagannātha, for example, remarks as follows in explaining why a particular verse that evokes the *sthāyibhāva* connected with the flavor of peace actually serves to support a different flavor (*RG*, *śāntarasa* section, pp. 176): *atrāpi yady api viṣayagaṇālambanaḥ surasrotasvinītaṭādyuddīpito nayananimīlanādibhir anubhāvitaḥ sthāyī nirvedaḥ pratīyate, tathāpi bhagavadvāsudevālambanāyāṃ kaviratau guṇībhuta iti na śāntarasadhvanivyapadeśahetuḥ*, "Here although there is the cognition of the stable emotion of *nirveda* having the objects of the senses as its objects, such things as the holy Ganges as its stimulants, and such things as the closing of the eyes as its results, nevertheless it is subordinated to the poet's emotion of love, which has Lord Vāsudeva as its object, and therefore this does not furnish grounds for speaking of the suggestion of the flavor of peace."

human heroes.[63] Here, however, Ānandavardhana removes both these possibilities by making it clear in his further remarks that Vāsudeva is important in the *Mahābhārata* not primarily because of his appearance in the form of the individual incarnation known as Kṛṣṇa, whom one may worship, but because he is the impersonal, absolute Brahma, the reality behind this vain world, to be reached through the cultivation of dispassion:

> And that same master poet, Kṛṣṇa Dvaipāyana [i.e., Vyāsa], has made this deep and beautiful meaning completely clear by using the depiction of the genealogy of Hari [the *Harivaṃśa*] as his conclusion at the end of the *Mahābhārata*. And by virtue of this meaning, which impels one toward an abundance of devotion for that other reality that transcends transmigratory existence, all the activities of transmigratory life appear in their entirety as simply a *prima facie* view. And the depiction of the abundant greatness of deities and sacred bathing places and austerities and so on is due to their being means to the attainment of that same Supreme Brahma, and the depiction of particular gods and others is due solely to their being manifestations of the powers of that Brahma. And the depiction of the deeds of the Pāṇḍavas and the others—since its purport is the production of dispassion, and since dispassion is the root of liberation, and since liberation is the means of attaining the Lord—is, indirectly, simply a means to the attainment of Supreme Brahma, which is set forth as the principal topic in such passages as the Gītā.
>
> Furthermore, the one referred to in being denoted by such names as "Vāsudeva" is the Supreme Brahma—the abode of unlimited power, which has become well known by those names in other passages such as the Gītā, and whose entire nature was taken on in the incarnation at Mathurā—rather

[63] So, for example, Kālidāsa's *Kumārasambhava* is said by some Sanskrit critics to have the flavor of compassionate heroism as its predominant *rasa*, although the erotic flavor is the more obvious choice. Aruṇagirinātha presents this view in his commentary on *Kum.* 1.52 (vol. 1, p. 95; the verse is number 1.53 in Mallinātha's commentary): *itaḥprabhṛti svecchāparigṛhītodāttāvasthāsya devasya lokānugrahahetāv itivṛtta ādhikārikatayā varṇyamāne dayāvīro raso 'ṅgī; tad anyeṣām aṅgatvam*, "What constitutes the principal plot is the description from this point on of the deeds of Śiva, performed for the benefit of the world when he had voluntarily assumed the state of a self-controlled and exalted hero, and in that plot the predominant flavor is that of compassionate heroism; therefore, the other flavors are subordinate." In further remarks on this near the end of his commentary (on *Kum.* 8.90, vol. 3, pp. 325–326), Aruṇagirinātha explains that the lovemaking of Śiva and Pārvatī depicted in the poem is really just an act, and that Śiva can not actually be subject to passion; that this doctrine will remove the locus of what had seemed to be a prominent flavor in the *Kumārasambhava* does not bother him at all: *nanu rāgitvasyāparamārthabuddhau kathaṃ śṛṅgāraḥ prāṇiti. mā prāṇitu. camatkāraś ca prākpratipāditena jagadrakṣaṇodyamātmanā vīreṇaivāṅginā rasena siddhaḥ. camatkāre ca siddhe kiṃ śṛṅgāranibandhena.* "'But, (you may object,) if the notion that Siva is under the influence of passion does not reflect reality, then how can the erotic flavor be able to breathe?' Then let it not be able to breathe. The charm (in the poem) is already established through the predominant flavor, which is the previously presented heroic flavor, having as its essence as undertaking made for the protection of the world."

than merely a portion of it that took birth at Mathurā [i.e., Kṛṣṇa], because [the names are] qualified by the word "eternal," and because we see that in the *Rāmāyaṇa* and elsewhere this name is applied to other foms of the Lord. And this meaning [of the name] has been ascertained by the grammarians themselves.[64]

It seems clear from all this that what Ānandavardhana considers the primary end of the *Mahābhārata* is a state of mind in the reader evoked by the suggestiveness of the contents of the poem, but not an esthetic response corresponding to the emotions of the characters within the poem through the standard form of correspondence that is involved in the basic theory of the suggestion of *rasa*. This raises the possibility that what Ānandavardhana has in mind here is not the primary form of the evocation of *rasa*, which depends upon the presentation of a *sthāyibhāva* as occurring in the principal character and which is thought to evoke the experience of *rasa* in the reader without any noticeable lag in time after that presentation, but rather the second important form of the suggestion of elements of *rasa*, which is said to be based on the content of the poem and to produce its effect with a discernible sequence of time—i.e., to depend upon some process of deliberation on the part of the reader.

This second form of suggestion, that of "suggestion based on the power of the meaning, with a discernible sequence" (*arthaśaktimūla-saṃlakṣyakrama-dhvani*), is also called suggestion through "aftertone" (*anuraṇana*), because it does not accomplish its effect until the reader has taken the time to ponder the implications of the statement in question. Ānandavardhana expressly distinguishes it from the primary form of the suggestion of *rasa* "in which there is the cognition of the *rasa* and so on by means of the *vibhāvas*, *anubhāvas*, and *vyabhicāribhāvas*, made known directly through the words [of the text]."[65] As we have seen, the *anubhāvas* and *vyabhicāribhāvas* cannot be

---

[64] *Dhv.* on 4.5 (pp. 532–533): *ayaṃ ca nigūḍharamaṇīyo 'rtho mahābhāratāvasāne harivaṃśa-varṇanena samāptiṃ vidadhatā tenaiva kavivedhasā kṛṣṇadvaipāyanena samyak sphuṭīkṛtaḥ. anena cārthena saṃsārātīte tattvāntare bhaktyatiśayaṃ pravartayatā sakala eva sāṃsāriko vyavahāraḥ pūrvapakṣīkṛto nyakṣeṇa prakāśate. devatātīrthatapaḥprabhṛtīnāṃ ca prabhāvātiśayavarṇanaṃ tasyaiva parabrahmaṇaḥ. prāptyupāyatvena tadvibhūtitvenaiva devatāviśeṣāṇām anyeṣām ca. pāṇḍavādicaritavarṇanasyāpi vairāgyajananatātparyād vairāgyasya ca mokṣamūlatvān mokṣasya ca bhagavatprāptyupāyatvena mukhyatayā gītādiṣu pradarśitatvāt parabrahmaprāptyupāyatvam eva. paraṃparayā* [read *paraṃparayā* with the preceding sentence, as is done by Masson and Patwardhan (*Śantarasa*, p. 108 n. 1)] *vāsudevādisaṃjñābhidheyatvena cāparimitaśaktyāspadaṃ param brahma gītādipradeśāntareṣu tadabhidhānatvena labdhaprasiddhi māthuraprādurbhāvānu-kṛtasakalasvarūpaṃ vivakṣitaṃ na tu mathuraprādurbhāvāṃśa eva, sanātanaśabdaviśeṣitatvāt. rāmāyaṇādiṣu cānayā saṃjñayā bhagavanmūrtyantare vyavahāradarśanāt. nirṇītaś cāyam arthaḥ śabdatattvavidbhir eva.*

[65] *Dhv.*, *vṛtti* on 2.22 (p. 248): *yatra sākṣāc chabdaniveditebhyo vibhāvānubhāvavyabhicāri-bhāvebhyo rasādināṃ pratītiḥ.*

made known within the poem without an *āśraya* of the *sthāyibhāva* to whom they can belong. Ānandavardhana also speaks of the occurrence of this "aftertone" variety of suggestion in a *prabandha*, i.e., a larger work, and gives as his example a passage in the *Mahābhārata*, in which the remarks of a vulture and a jackal, spoken at the cemetery following the death of a brahman boy, serve to suggest, on the simplest level, the selfish interests of the two animals.[66] As Abhinavagupta explains, these two suggestions culminate in the suggestion of the flavor of peace.[67] While some later treatments of this example seem to interpret the word "*prabandha*" as referring simply to an extended statement rather than to an entire composition,[68] the suggestions involved are consistent with Ānandavardhana's analysis of the *Mahābhārata* as an entire work. At any rate, Ānandavardhana's analysis of the poem ends by following the comments quoted above with a repetition of his view of the overall purport of the poem:

> Therefore, the statement cited from the list of contents, by revealing the impermanence of everything other than the Lord, has firmly established that what is intended in the *Mahābhārata* is, from the didactic point of view, solely the highest human aim characterized by liberation, and, from the poetic point of view, the flavor of peace, characterized by the fostering of the happiness produced by the extinction of craving, as the predominant *rasa*.
> And because this meaning is absolutely essential, it is made known through suggestion, not through explicit denotation. And it is quite well known in sophisticated and learned circles that one's ultimate intention is revealed through suggestion, rather than through direct and explicit statement.[69]

In closing his analysis of the *Mahābhārata* with this description of the flavor of peace as "characterized by the fostering of the happiness produced by the extinction of craving," Ānandavardhana is repeating verbatim the definition of *śāntarasa* that he offered earlier in his argument

---

[66] *Dhv.*, *vṛtti* on 3.15 (pp. 345–346): *asya vivakṣitānyaparavācyasya dhvaner anuraṇanarūpavyaṅgyo 'pi yaḥ prabheda udāhṛto dviprakārah. so 'pi prabandheṣu keṣucid dyotate . . . yathā ca gṛdhragomayusaṃvādādau mahābhārate.* In commenting on this, Abhinavagupta (*Loc.*, p. 345) quotes four verses, *MBh.* 12.149.8, 9, 15, and 60.

[67] *Loc.* on 2.22 (p. 345): *sa cābhiprāyo vyaktaḥ śāntarasa eva pariniṣṭhitatāṃ prāptaḥ.*

[68] Cf. *KPra.* under 4.42cd (*sūtra* 60), which cites the same verses mentioned by Abhinavagupta (see note 65) as examples 93–96 (pp. 166–168), and glosses "*prabandha*" with "*vacana.*"

[69] *Dhv.* on 4.5 (p. 533): *tad evam anukramaṇīnirdiṣṭena vākyena bhagavadvyatirekiṇaḥ sarvasyānyasyānityatāṃ prakāśayatā mokṣalakṣaṇa evaikaḥ paraḥ puruṣārthaḥ śāstranaye, kāvyanaye ca tṛṣṇākṣayasukhaparipoṣalakṣaṇaḥ śānto raso mahābhāratasyāṅgitvena vivakṣita iti supratipāditam. atyantasārabhūtatvāc cāyam artho vyaṅgyatvenaiva darśito na tu vācyatvena. sārabhūto hy arthaḥ svaśabdānabhidheyatvena prakāśitaḥ sutarām eva śobhām āvahati. prasiddhiś ceyam asty eva vidagdhavidvatpariṣatsu yad abhimatataraṃ vastu vyaṅgyatvena prakāśyate na sākṣācchabdavācyatvena.*

for the existence of that *rasa*. When viewed together with the analysis that precedes it, this description brings into focus one last time the theoretical problem that has concerned us. The "happiness produced by the extinction of craving" (*tṛṣṇākṣayasukha*) to which Ānandavardhana refers must exist outside the work, since the desires of the Pāṇḍavas pursue them to the very end, and the Lord whose importance Ānandavardhana emphasizes has no desires to be extinguished. Gerow and Aklujkar recognized that this dispassion is to be found in the reader when they wrote that Ānandavardhana uses the term *śāntarasa* to refer to "an intense experience (not a hardened attitude like that of a true *saṃnyāsin*) of detachment that comes from reading or witnessing a work of art depicting ruin, impermanence, the transitory character of worldly existence, and the futility of ambition," yet they also maintained that Ānandavardhana "accepts, purely and simply, *śānta* as one of the many *rasas*—as the ninth o*rasa* among the already accepted *rasas*—with its proper *sthāyi-bhāva* (*tṛṣṇā-kṣaya-sukha*) and its epic (*Mahābhārata*) if not dramatic (*Nāgānanda*) exemplification."[70] What makes the exemplification of *śāntarasa* in the *Mahābhārata* less than simple is the difficulty of determining how Ānandavardhana viewed the difference between the *sthāyibhāva* and the *rasa*.

Since Ānandavardhana never discusses this problem in detail, the most that can be said with confidence is that the experience of detachment described by Gerow and Aklujkar is in fact the goal of the poem in Ānandavardhana's interpretation. As their reference to the difference between the experience of the reader and the attitude of a true ascetic implies, the explanation of the status of this experience as *rasa* rather than as an ordinary emotion is surely to be sought in the simple fact that this form of detachment, however intensely it may be felt, is still a response to a work of art rather than a product of direct confrontation with one's personal situation in the real world.

In the end the theoretical difficulties involved are subordinate to Ānandavardhana's insistence at the conclusion of his analysis that the evocation of this experience is the essential core of the poem, and that it is carried out not directly, but in a subtle and suggestive manner. The result of this insistence is to assure us that we must not expect to find a neat and clear pattern of manipulation of the elements associated with *rasa*, but rather must be attentive to the cumulative effect of less obvious processes. We are thus nudged away from the realm of the problems that

---

[70] "On Śānta Rasa in Sanskrit Poetics," p. 83.

Abhinavagupta and others struggled with later. Abhinavagupta himself seems to have been aware of this, since his commentary on Ānandavardhana's analysis of the *Mahābhārata* is surprisingly meager, ignoring questions that provoke him to lengthy discussions elsewhere, and yet in other works he fervently echoes Ānandavardhana's conclusions.[71]

Once Ānandavardhana's interpretation of the poem is accepted, it solves more problems than it raises. In terms of the questions with which this paper began, two areas of problems are of particular importance.

The first is that of the didactic role of a poem. The emphasis on esthetic distance that appears throughout the theories of Abhinavagupta and others brings with it a host of difficulties, for it is difficult to explain how so pure and disinterested an experience as the *rasa* they describe can contribute to the practical fulfillment of the aims of human life, and it is especially difficult to see how particular aims can be associated with particular flavors, given the tendency of the theory to imply the generic unity of all *rasa* experiences. We should know a great deal more about these problems if we still had Ānandavardhana's treatise entitled *Tattvāloka*, for the work seems to have dealt with the connections between *śāstra* and *kāvya*.[72] And where *śāntarasa* in particular is concerned, together with its role in the attainment of liberation, we must also mourn the loss of the *Kāvyakautuka* of Bhaṭṭa Tauta and the commentary on it by his pupil Abhinavagupta.[73] Yet even without the assistance that such works might have provided, the connection that Ānandavardhana makes between the didactic and the poetic purposes of the *Mahābhārata* follows easily enough from his description of the attitude evoked in the reader, and the ways in which he says that evocation is accomplished are clearly applicable to both purposes.

The second area of problems is that surrounding the question of the poetic unity of the *Mahābhārata*. Here Ānandavardhana's interpretation of the deeper intent of the poem provides an impressive foundation—and perhaps the only possible foundation—for a serious claim that the apparently disparate elements of the poem work together toward a single goal. On one level his interpretation may seem too easy: to say that the unifying purpose of the *Mahābhārata* is to produce a cumulative effect of disillusionment provides the perverse possibility of justifying every tedious

---

[71] See Raghavan, *The Number of Rasa-s*, p. 35 n. 2(1).

[72] See Masson and Patwardhan, *Śāntarasa*, p. 33, p. 54 n. 7, and p. 112 n. 2.

[73] That the work addressed such problems is clear from Abhinavagupta's brief reference to it (*Loc.* on 3.26, p. 394): *mokṣaphalatvena cāyaṃ paramapuruṣārthaniṣṭhatvāt sarvarasebhyaḥ pradhānatamah. sa cāyam asmadupādhyāyabhaṭṭatautena kāvyakautuke, asmābhiś ca tadvivaraṇe bahutarakṛtanirṇayapūrvapakṣasiddhānta ity alaṃ bahunā.*

accretion in the poem on the grounds of its own contribution to the frustration of the reader. On a more serious level Ānandavardhana's view of the inner meaning of the poem recognizes an essential concern that is genuinely present in the *Mahābhārata*, a central focus that can legitimately be recognized both in the thoughts of the poem's characters and in the shaping of the work through the centuries.

The extent to which that focus is still recognized within the tradition is eloquently exposed in the comments of modern Indian scholars who discuss the theme of disillusionment in the *Mahābhārata*.[74] And for an answer to the objection that the same focus could be found in any other major work within the Hindu tradition that deals with philosophical and religious questions, one need look no further than Ānandavardhana's own analysis of the other great Hindu epic composed in Sanskrit, the *Rāmāyaṇa*. But that is another story.

Abbreviations

ABh. *Abhinavabhāratī* of Abhinavagupta, a commentary on the *Nāṭyaśāstra* of Bharata. Except where noted, I have used the Sanskrit text as emended in R.P. Kangle, *Ras-bhāv-vicār: bharatmunīṃcyā "nāṭyaśāstrā" tīl adhyāy 6 va 7 yāṃce "abhinavabhāratī" ṭīkesaha saṭīp marāṭhī bhāṣāntar*, Bhāṣāntarmālā 22 (Bombay: Mahārāṣṭra Rājya Sāhitya-Saṃskṛti Maṇḍal, 1973) [abbr. Kangle]. For comparison I have also noted the location of each passage in Volume I of M.R. Kavi's edition of the *Nāṭyaśāstra* with the commentary of Abhinavagupta, Gaekwad's Oriental Series 36 (Baroda: Central Library, 1926) [abbr. *GOS*].

Dhv. *Dhvanyāloka* of Ānandavardhana, with the *Locana* commentary of Abhinavagupta and the *Bālapriyā* commentary of Rāmasāraka, ed. Pt. Pattābhirāma Śāstrī, Kashi Sanskrit Series 135 (Benares: Chowkhamba Sanskrit Series Office, 1940). Where noted, readings have been taken from the edition of K. Krishnamoorthy (Dharwar: Karnatak University, 1974).

DR *Daśarūpaka* of Dhanaṃjaya, with the commentary *Avaloka* by Dhanika and the sub-commentary *Laghuṭīkā* by Bhaṭṭanṛsiṃha, ed. T. Venkatacharya, Adyar Library Series 97 (Adyar, Madras: The Adyar Library and Research Centre, 1969).

---

[74] See especially Raghavan, *The Number of Rasa-s*, pp. 32–36; Sinha, *Mahābhārata*, chapter 5: "The *Śānta* as the *Kāvyārtha* of the *Mahābhārata*," pp. 71–84; and Bhattacharya, *Śāntarasa and Its Scope*, chapter 12: "Śānta rasa in the great epics and in allied literature," pp. 164–183.

DRAva. *Avaloka* of Dhanika, a commentary on the *Daśarūpaka* of Dhanamjaya. See *DR.*

GOS See *ABh.*

Kangle See *ABh.*

KAnu. *Kāvyānuśāsana* with *Alaṃkāracūḍāmaṇī* and *Viveka* of Hemacandra, ed. with two anon. *ṭippanas* by Rasiklal C. Parikh and V.M. Kulkarni, 2nd rev. ed. (Bombay: Sri Mahavira Jaina Vidyalaya, 1964).

Kir. *Kirātārjunīya* of Bhāravi, with the *Śabdārthadīpikā* commentary of Citrabhānu, ed. T. Ganapati Sastri, Trivandrum Sanskrit Series 63 (Trivandrum: Government Press, 1918).

KPra. *Kāvyaprakāśa* of Mammaṭa with the *Bālabodhinī* of Vāmanācharya Rāmabhaṭṭa Jhalakīkar, ed. R.D. Karmarkar, 17th ed. (Pune: Bhandarkar Oriental Research Institute, 1965).

Kum. *Kumārasambhava* of Kālidāsa with the *Prakāśikā* of Aruṇagirinātha and the *vivaraṇa* of Nārāyaṇapaṇḍita, ed. T. Ganapati Sastri, 3 vols., Trivandrum Sanskrit Series 27, 32, 36 (Trivandrum: Government Press, 1913–14).

Loc. *Locana* of Abhinavagupta, a commentary on the *Dhvanyāloka* of Ānandavardhana. See *Dhv.*

MBh. *Mahābhārata*, critically edited by V.S. Sukthankar et al., 18 vols. (Pune: Bhandarkar Oriental Research Institue, 1933–66).

NS *Nāṭyaśāstra* of Bharata. See *ABh.*

RG *Rasagaṅgādhara* of Jagannātha, with the *Marmaprakāśa* commentary of Nāgeśa Bhaṭṭa, ed. Madhusudan Shastri, 3 vols. (Varanasi: Banaras Hindu University, 1964–73).

SD *Sāhityadarpaṇa* of Viśvanātha, ed. Pt. Rāmacharaṇa Tarkavāgīśa Bhaṭṭachārya and Pt. Durgāprasāda Dviveda (Bombay: Nirnaya-Sagara Press, 1902).

VJ *Vakroktijīvita* of Kuntaka, ed. and trans. K. Krishnamoorthy (Dharwad: Karnatak University, 1977).

THE EPIC'S TWO GRANDFATHERS, BHĪṢMA AND VYĀSA

BRUCE M. SULLIVAN

Two characters in the story of the *Mahābhārata*, the brahmin Vyāsa and the *kṣatriya* Bhīṣma, are often called *pitāmaha* (grandfather). They are the patriarchs of the epic's central family, the Bhāratas. Consideration of these two grandfather figures together will shed light on both. After describing how the epic depicts Vyāsa and Bhīṣma, I shall state my views on the meaning of each character and suggest how to fit them into the interpretation of the text as a whole.

In the *Mahābhārata* (*MBh*), Vyāsa is a great brahmin whose connection to the royal family of *kṣatriyas*, the Bhāratas, is through his mother Satyavatī. She describes in these words to Bhīṣma how she had given birth to the sage Vyāsa.[1]

> My father, who was yoked to the *dharma*, had a ferry, and one day when I was in my youth I went on it, O *dharma*-spirited sir. Then that greatest of the supporters of *dharma*, the great seer Parāśara the wise, came to the ferry because he wanted to cross the Yamunā River. While we were crossing over the Yamunā, that greatest of ascetics approached me and, possessed by love, coaxingly said to me many sweet things. Fearful of both his curse and of my father, but promised desirable boons, I was unable to reject him, O Bhārata. After covering the area with darkness, with his virility he overcame me, a young maiden, and did with me as he desired right in the boat, O Bhārata. Formerly I had a strong, repellent odor of fish; the ascetic took it away and gave me this pleasant fragrance. Then the ascetic said to me that upon delivering my child on an island in the river, "you will still be a virgin". Thus, the great yogi and seer Pārāśarya, the son I had as a virgin, was born at that time, the one who is known as Dvaipāyana—the blessed lord and seer who, by the power of his asceticism, divided the *Vedas*

This essay is a somewhat altered form of a paper presented at the 14th Annual Conference on South Asia in November, 1985, in Madison, Wisconsin. I would like to thank especially Alf Hiltebeitel for comments helpful to me in preparing this paper. For more detailed treatment, see my book *Kṛṣṇa Dvaipāyana Vyāsa and the Mahābhārata: A New Interpretation* (Leiden: E.J. Brill, 1990).

[1] *MBh.* I.99.6–15.; all citations of passages are to the critical edition edited by V.S. Sukthankar, *The Mahābhārata*, 19 vols. (Poona: Bhandarkar Oriental Research Institute, 1933–59). See also the capsule descriptions of Vyāsa's career at I.54.2–6. and I.57.55–75., and the many references to Vyāsa in I.1. and I.2.

> into four, and hence became in the world "Vyāsa", and because of his darkness, Kṛṣṇa. He is a speaker of the truth, an ascetic devoted to tranquility, all of whose sins are burned away.

Thus, Vyāsa was born out of wedlock, the son of a great brahmin ascetic by a woman whose social class is much less clear.

Vyāsa's mother Satyavatī later met Śaṃtanu, king of the Bhāratas, who was also struck by her beauty and wanted to marry her. Śaṃtanu, however, already had a son—by Gangā the river goddess in human form[2]—and Satyavatī's family feared that, as he was the elder son, he and his descendants would inherit the kingdom leaving nothing for her and her descendants. To aid his father in wooing Satyavatī, the prince vowed that not only would he never rule, but also that he would never marry or have offspring, and because of this awe-inspiring vow he was known ever after as "Bhīṣma".[3] Bhīṣma's vow eliminated all misgivings, and Satyavatī married King Śaṃtanu, in time bearing two sons, two princes for the kingdom (I.95.).

At this point in the epic, the structure of the Bhārata family has a remarkable symmetry: the king and queen, their two royal sons, and the two extramarital sons, one on either side of the family. The king's extramarital son Bhīṣma, born of Gangā, is paralleled by the queen's extramarital son Vyāsa, born in the Yamunā River (he was conceived in mid-river, born on an island in that river, and born of a woman who was herself Yamunā-born).[4] The Gangā and Yamunā Rivers, the dominant geographical features of north-central India, frame the Bhārata kingdom, one on either side, much as these two river-born sons frame the royal family.

The brahmin Vyāsa and the *kṣatriya* Bhīṣma are complementary figures who in certain respects are mirror-images of each other. Both remained unmarried and became the Bhārata family's elders, vigilant guardians of their family's fortunes. Bhīṣma, though childless, sought to perpetuate the Bhārata lineage by carrying off from their *svayaṃvara* and

---

[2] This is the result of an intricate series of events, including Brahmā cursing a king in heaven to be reborn on earth while at the same time the celestial brahmin Vasiṣṭha was cursing the Vasus, eight demigods, to be born on earth as well. The goddess Gangā agreed to be the wife of the king and the mother of the Vasus in their earthly incarnations. Śaṃtanu and Gangā had sons, and as each was born it was thrown in the river by Gangā, until the eighth son was born; it was allowed to live. Thus, the agreement reached in heaven was fulfilled, and king Śaṃtanu had a son by Gangā who was Dyaus the Vasu incarnate; he was called Devavrata Gāngeya, and was later to be known as Bhīṣma. Most of I.91–99. concerns Bhīṣma; see I.91–93. for his birth.

[3] I.94.50–94.; "*bhīṣma*" means terrible.

[4] For details on Vyāsa's mother, see I.57.36–55.

bringing to court two *kṣatriya* women to become brides (I.96.). However, both young princes of the dynasty died suddenly, one in combat and the other from illness or dissipation, leaving the family childless and the kingdom without an heir to the throne. A family member was needed to produce offspring with the young widows, but because the *kṣatriya* Bhīṣma had vowed celibacy, the deceased prince's other brother, the brahmin Vyāsa, was summoned to substitute for Bhīṣma in this role.[5] Upon the birth of two princes, Vyāsa left the court to return only occasionally (I.100.), while Bhīṣma remained to raise the boys as *kṣatriyas*, substituting for Vyāsa in the role of parent. These princes, Dhṛtarāṣṭra and Pāṇḍu, call both Vyāsa and Bhīṣma "father",[6] and their sons, the Kauravas and Pāṇḍavas, call both "grandfather".[7] Although Bhīṣma is in fact the biological grandfather of no one, family members call him *pitāmaha* out of respect.[8] Despite Bhīsma's refusal to procreate, he is very much a family man, a celibate ascetic *kṣatriya* in a social setting, while Vyāsa, though a father, is no family man at all—he is a brahmin ascetic of a more solitary inclination. These two Bhārata family patriarchs form a complementary pair, and may be seen as embodying two different approaches to the problem of the incompatibility of asceticism and family life. They also represent the ideal of an alliance between brahmins and *kṣatriyas* which the *MBh* so often advocates, but which was shattered so dramatically by fratricidal competition for the throne. In that struggle, Bhīṣma died while Vyāsa survived.

To set the interpretation of Vyāsa and Bhīṣma within the context of the *MBh* as a whole, one must consider that the epic depicts its main characters as incarnations of gods or demons. Some are sons of gods (such as Bhīma, son of Vāyu), and some are said to be a portion (*aṃśa*) of a god on earth (such as Kṛṣṇa Vāsudeva, who is Nārāyaṇa Viṣṇu's *aṃśa*).[9] In general, each of the main characters is depicted as sharing

---

[5] Though they are related only by the marriage of one's father to the other's mother, and not at all genetically, both are regarded as the brother of the deceased; see I.99.25–38.

[6] Compare VI.16.7. and VI.17.7.

[7] On Bhīṣma, see V.23.8.; VI.14.3.; XII.38.6.; and XIII.152–54. On Vyāsa, see I.54.2.; I.144.5.; I.157.16.; XII.33.2–3 and 12.

[8] Typically in India, all the brothers of the grandfather would be called *pitāmaha*; for details and documentation see I. Karve, "Kinship Terminology and the Family Organization as found in the Critical Edition of the Mahābhārata," *Bulletin of the Deccan College Research Institute*, 5 (1944): 61–148.

[9] Arjuna Pāṇḍava is such an important and multivalent character that he has three divine identities: he is Indra's son, Nārāyaṇa's companion Nara, and, according to Vyāsa (I.189.), he and the other Pāṇḍavas are all incarnations of former Indras.

with some particular deity many of the same attributes and epithets, so that the epic character at times symbolically represents that deity and evokes in the audience memories of the god's nature, mythic deeds, etc. The war between the Bhārata cousins is seen as another battle in the eternal struggle between the gods and demons, this time fought on earth.[10] The many accounts in literature of the battles between the gods and demons have a fairly consistent pattern, and the myth—which has been called the central myth of Indian civilization[11]—may be summarized as follows. The gods and demons, descended from a common progenitor, Prajāpati Brahmā, once were contending for sovereignty. The demons began to defeat the gods due to receiving a boon from their *pitāmaha* Prajāpati Brahmā; because they had pleased him either with their sacrifice or their asceticism they won a boon such as invincibility to the gods in battle. Then the gods go to Prajāpati Brahmā (who is also their *pitāmaha*) asking for his aid in the battle and he tells them how to defeat the demons. It seems that there is almost always a defect in the boon Brahmā has given the demons, a loophole of which the gods can take advantage once Brahmā gives them the knowledge, and in this way the gods triumph. This is the well established pattern of the myth about the gods and demons and their progenitor Brahmā which is the basic, underlying myth of the MBh.

The Pāṇḍavas are the sons of the gods and their allies are portions of the gods on earth, while their cousins the Kauravas are incarnate demons.[12] Although this is clearly specified, the epic does not explicitly name any character as the incarnation or portion or son of Brahmā. To complete the pattern of the myth, however, there should be present in the story a *pitāmaha* of these incarnate gods and demons, and to some extent he should be reenacting the role of the divine *pitāmaha* Brahmā. In my view, Vyāsa represents Grandfather Brahmā much more effectively and often than does Bhīṣma.

Looking first at the epic's explicit citations of a divine identity for Bhīṣma, one sees that he is depicted as an incarnation of Dyaus, or Dyaus Pitṛ, the Sky Father of the *Ṛg Veda*.[13] Certainly this is a deity who has

---

[10] As in III.92.; VI.20.5.; XII.34.13–21.; and in the descriptions of the conflict as a "sacrifice of battle' (e.g., V.139.) taking place on the altar of Brahmā (III.81.177–78. and III.129.22.).

[11] Jan Gonda, *Aspects of Early Viṣṇuism* (Utrecht: Oosthoek, 1954).

[12] Lists of epic characters and their divine identities occur in several places in the *MBh*, including I.61.; XI.8.; XV.39.; and XVIII.5. On the divine plan to oppose the demons through incarnation on earth, see especially I.58.25.–I.59.6.

[13] In addition to the previously cited I.91.–93., see I.61.68–70.; XV.39.15.; and XVIII.5.9.

appropriately fatherly attributes to be the divine alter ego of Bhīṣma. Beyond this, however, the connection between Bhīṣma and Dyaus is tenuous and not particularly meaningful. There is little mythology about Dyaus the Vasu with which the character of Bhīṣma might interact, and the fact that this motif remains undeveloped in the text indicates that the epic poets were uninterested in it. The identification of Bhīṣma with this superseded, retired god Dyaus Pitṛ seems to be an afterthought, as if Bhīṣma were thought to need a divine figure with which to be associated because each of the other important epic characters already was associated with a *deva* or *asura*.

The case of Vyāsa is much more complex. The MBh omits him from the incarnation lists in which the divine identities of various epic characters are revealed. However, there are two references to Vyāsa as an incarnation of Nārāyaṇa Viṣṇu, both found in the *Nārāyaṇīya* section of the *Śānti Parvan*.[14] Because these two references are not supported by similar statements elsewhere in the MBh, and because they are found in a section of the text which is widely regarded as among the most recently interpolated parts of the *MBh*,[15] consideration of these two references will be postponed until other material has been presented.

Rather than emphasizing the two references which associate Vyāsa with Nārāyaṇa, I see many ways in which Vyāsa evokes the memory of Brahmā, and would suggest that Vyāsa often represents Brahmā in the *MBh*. Correspondences between these two figures are too numerous to discuss in detail here,[16] but examples of the major points may be adduced. In comparing Vyāsa and Brahmā, one may well begin with the fact that both are depicted as brahmins who epitomize the this-world

---

[14] The first reference is a one verse statement (XII.334.9.) which I translate as follows: "Know that Kṛṣṇa Dvaipāyana Vyāsa is Nārāyaṇa the Lord, for who other than the Lord could be the author of the *Mahābhārata*, O tiger among men, and who other than the Lord could enunciate truly the manifold *dharmas*?" A few chapters later (XII.337.), Vyāsa describes himself as "born a portion of Nārāyaṇa" and as Nārāyaṇa's son, born to divide the *Veda* and to participate in the Bhārata war. These are the only two such references in the critical edition, though three manuscripts have inserted the lines of XII.334.9. into the epic's first book as well; see Appendix I, Nos. 2 and 3 of the *Ādi Parvan* volume.

[15] Anne-Marie Esnoul dates the *Nārāyaṇīya* in the third century A.D., describing it as among the most recent sections of the *MBh*, certainly composed after the *Bhagavad-Gītā*, and as contemporaneous with the *Harivaṃśa*; see her *Nārāyaṇīya Parvan du Mahābhārata* (Paris: UNESCO, 1979), p. 3. Much earlier, E.W. Hopkins had commented on this passage that "by the end of the pseudo-epic, even Vyāsa Kṛṣṇa was . . . an emanation of Nārāyaṇa. . . . But this is the last word of the Bhāgavatas and not early epic." See his *Epic Mythology* (Strassburg: Trübner, 1915), p. 216.

[16] See Chapter 4 of my book, mentioned above, for citations.

values of ritual activity and *dharma*, as opposed to the other-worldly values of *saṃnyāsa* and *mokṣa*. Brahmā is depicted in the epic as the presiding deity of the religious path of *pravṛtti*, which is characterized by the performance of Vedic sacrificial rites and the other injunctions of *dharma* and leads to the temporary respite of heaven. This is explicitly contrasted with the path of *nivṛtti*, presided over by Nārāyaṇa, which is characterized by the abandonment of ritual activity for asceticism and leads to *mokṣa*, permanent release from transmigration.[17] Like Brahmā, Vyāsa is strongly identified with *pravṛtti* values and *dharma* rather than *nivṛtti* values and *mokṣa*. The *MBh* depicts Vyāsa not as a *saṃnyāsin* striving for *mokṣa* but as an ascetic of the forest-dwelling *vanaprastha* type; he lives at an *āśrama* and serves as *guru* and priest for the dynastic family.[18] Another significant point in the comparison of Brahmā and Vyāsa is the striking similarity in the relationship each has to the *Veda*. In the *MBh*, Brahmā is said to have created the *Veda* just before creating the world with its gods, demons, and men.[19] He is depicted in the text and iconographically as having four heads, one facing in each direction, each mouth busy chanting *Veda*.[20] Vyāsa performs among mankind a role remarkably similar to that performed by Brahmā in mythology. The title "Vyāsa" was given to Kṛṣṇa Dvaipāyana for his act of dividing the unitary *Veda* into four texts.[21] He took this seemingly revolutionary step to make the *Veda* easier for mortals to learn and retain in the difficult era of Kaliyuga. Thus, just prior to the beginning of Kaliyuga, Vyāsa disseminated among mankind the *Veda* as he had arranged it in four texts, which is an epic parallel with the myth of Brahmā, at the beginning of time, creating the *Veda* in four streams, one from each of his four mouths. With regard to the *Veda*, Vyāsa seems to be replicating the mythology of Brahmā. Certainly Vyāsa and Brahmā are unique in having such a relationship to the *Veda*.

Particularly convincing of the correspondence between Vyāsa and Brahmā is the fact that each is the grandfather of a family which splits into two factions that fight for sovereignty, and that they have structurally similar relationships to their belligerent offspring. The pattern of Brahmā's actions with regard to the gods and demons is replicated in

---

[17] As revealed by Vyāsa in a pair of sermons, XII.327. and XII.336.

[18] Although his *āśrama* is often mentioned, no location is ever specified in the *MBh*. Vyāsa is the *brahman* (or *brahmā*) priest at the Rājasūya ritual (Book II.) and is the chief priest at the Aśvamedha (XIV.).

[19] As in XII.181.1–5. and XII.327.30–32.

[20] III.192.12.; III.275.17.; XII.330.56.; XII.335.18–25.

[21] I.1.52.; I.54.3–5.; I.57.72–74.; I.99.14.; etc.

that of Vyāsa's actions regarding the Pāṇḍavas (who are incarnate gods) and the Kauravas (who are incarnate demons). At first, Vyāsa's actions have the effect of aiding the demonic Kauravas to gain ascendancy—he helps to bring the Kauravas into the world,[22] and the Rājasūya he supervises results in the exile of the Pāṇḍavas[23]—which necessitates his intervention to assist the Pāṇḍavas in overcoming them. The advice and guidance Vyāsa gives the Pāṇḍavas parallels the knowledge Brahmā gives the gods, and has the same effect: the Pāṇḍavas win. In its salient features, Vyāsa's career in the *MBh* reveals close correspondences with the mythology and character of Brahmā.

Comparison of Brahmā and Bhīṣma, however, is much less rewarding. Bhīsma is not a brahmin, has no priestly functions, and seems closer to being a *saṃnyāsin* than does Vyāsa—Bhīṣma delivers the long discourse on *mokṣa* that ends the *Śānti Parvan*, and is a celibate ascetic. Moreover, Bhīṣma does not share the relationship to the *Veda* which is unique to Brahmā and Vyāsa; though his lectures on *dharma* are extensive, they have very little indeed to do with the *Veda*, and he has no role in the creation and dissemination of the *Vedas*. Finally, though Bhīṣma is respectfully called *pitāmaha* by all the Bhāratas, he fights on the side of the demonic Kauravas and dies doing so, which does not correspond at all to the role of Brahmā in mythology. Vyāsa's non-combatant neutrality toward his contentious descendants, and his survival of the conflict, accord with the role one would expect of the *pitāmaha*.

One final parallel between Vyāsa and Brahmā is noteworthy, and may provide the key to understanding why we now find references to Vyāsa as a portion of Nārāyaṇa in two chapters of the *Śānti Parvan*. Over the course of the several centuries during which the *MBh* was composed, the status and the worship of Brahmā apparently declined.[24] By the time the composition of the epic was being completed, Brahmā was conceived by Vaiṣṇavas as functioning at the behest of Nārāyaṇa Viṣṇu, and was pictured as seated on a lotus that emerged from the navel of the recumbent Viṣṇu; Brahmā had become a mere appendage or portion of

---

[22] He gave Gāndhārī a boon that she would have 100 sons, and when the time came for the monstrous birth, he prevented her attempted abortion and acted as midwife at the birth (I.107.). Vyāsa's creation of the demonic horde of Kauravas parallels Brahmā's creation of the *asuras*.

[23] Vyāsa was the priest supervising this rite; he chose the other priests involved, and functioned as the *brahman* whose responsibility it was to oversee the actions of all of them; see II.30.33–35.

[24] The argument is presented convincingly by Greg Bailey in his "Notes on the Worship of Brahmā in Ancient India", *Annali del Instituto Orientale di Napoli* 29 (1979): 149–70. See also his *Mythology of Brahmā* (Delhi: Oxford University Press, 1983).

Nārāyaṇa Viṣṇu. In a similar fashion and for much the same reason, Vyāsa apparently also came to be seen as a portion of Nārāyaṇa, and the idea was recorded in the *Nārāyaṇīya* section of the *Śānti Parvan.*

Depicting Vyāsa as the Bhārata *pitāmaha*, the epic poets evoked in their audience recognition of meaningful correspondences with the divine *pitāmaha* Brahmā. The *MBh*, presenting itself as the "fifth *Veda*,"[25] was created by *pitāmaha* Vyāsa as the quintessence and completion of the four *Vedas* created by *pitāmaha* Brahmā. In many subtly suggestive expressions, the *MBh* reveals continuities between Vyāsa and Brahmā.

---

[25] As in I.57.74. and XII.327.18.; see also I.1.19.

ARJUNA'S COMBAT WITH THE *KIRĀTA*: *RASA* AND *BHAKTI* IN BHĀRAVI'S *KIRĀTĀRJUNĪYA*

INDIRA V. PETERSON

I. *Introduction: Rasa and Bhakti in the Kirātārjunīya*

The narrative of the Pāṇḍava hero Arjuna's penance and his combat with the god Śiva in the guise of a *kirāta* (wild mountain man, hunter) is a well-known episode in the Forest Book of the epic *Mahābhārata*.[1] During the forest exile of the Pāṇḍavas, at the behest of the seer Vyāsa, Yudhiṣṭhira sends Arjuna to the Himalayas, where he practices severe asceticism (*tapas*, penance) in order to propritiate the gods and win from them divine weapons which will destroy the enemies of the Pāṇḍavas in battle. Desiring to test the hero's courage, Śiva disguises himself as a wild hunter and picks a quarrel with Arjuna over a boar. Arjuna proves his mettle as a warrior in the single combat that ensues. Pleased, Śiva reveals his identity; Arjuna bows to Śiva and begs forgiveness for his impertinence in fighting with God; Śiva praises the hero and gives him the divine weapon (*astra*) called Pāśupata or Brahmaśiras. These are the main events of the *kirāta* story as told in the *Mahābhārata*.[2] In this essay I shall examine the treatment of heroism and divine grace, the principal themes of the *Mahābhārata kirāta* episode, by Bhāravi (*circa* 6th c. A.D.), in his Sanskrit *mahākāvya* (court epic) *Kirātārjunīya* (*Arjuna's Combat with the*

---

[1] *Mahābhārata*. Book III. *Āraṇyakaparvan* (*The Book of the Forest*). Kairātaparvan (31), 13 through 42 in the Critical Edition. The numbering is somewhat different in other editions. My references to the *Kairātaparvan* in this essay are from: *The Mahābhārata*. Critically Edited by V.S. Sukthankar. Volume 3. *Āraṇyakaparvan* (part I). Poona: Bhandarkar Oriental Research Institute. For a translation of this episode in the version of the Critical Edition, see J.A.B. van Buitenen, *The Mahābhārata*. Volume 2, (Chicago: The University of Chicago Press, 1975). "The Mountain Man", pp. 244–305.

[2] The narrative of the central event begins with *adhyāya* 28, in which is related the beginning of a long argument among the Pāṇḍavas. Madeleine Biardeau rightly sees the episode as being closely connected with earlier events, and with Arjuna's journey to Indra's heaven in the *Indralokābhigamanaparvan*, which immediately follows the *Kairātaparvan*, as being significant to our understanding of the *kirāta* episode in the context of the *Mahābhārata*. See: Madeleine Biardeau, "Études de mythologie hindoue <henceforth referred to as EMH> (V) Part II. Bhakti et avatāra", *Bulletin de l'école française d'Extreme Orient* 65 (1978): 146–64 (this section is significantly entitled "Arjuna dans le ciel d'Indra"). However, the importance of these connections is minimal in detached versions of the story, such as the *Kirātārjunīya* of Bhāravi, which is the subject of this essay.

Kirāta), the earliest and most celebrated literary adaptation of the epic tale.[3] Bhāravi's long poem is known as one of the earliest and best examples of the *mahākāvya* or court epic genre; it is usually evaluated according to the aesthetic standards of *kāvya*, Sanskrit classical or "court" poetry.[4] At the same time, the theme of the *kirāta* story, as well as the time and place in which Bhāravi lived,[5] demand a serious consideration of the religious dimensions of the poem. I therefore approach Bhāravi's epic from the twin perspectives of *kāvya* poetics and devotional religion, of *rasa* and *bhakti*.

Bhāravi's Kirātārjunīya and the Poetics of Rasa

Though the theory of *rasa* (aesthetic experience conceived as mood, flavor) was not expressly formulated for the analysis of *mahākāvya*, it is one of the few tools available for determining the aesthetic aims and

---

[3] *The Kirātārjunīya* of Bhāravi. With the commentary (Ghaṇṭāpatha) of Mallinātha. Edited by Pandit Durgaprasad and Kasinath Pandurang Parab. 9th edition. (Bombay: Nirnaya-Sagar, 1922).

[4] For a discussion of the characteristics of *kāvya* poetry, see Daniel H.H. Ingalls, *An Anthology of Sanskrit Court Poetry: Vidyākara's Subhāṣitaratnakoṣa*. Harvard Oriental Series Vol. 44, (Cambridge, Ma.: Harvard University Press, 1965). Introduction, pp. 2–29; and Louis Renou, "Sur la structure du *kāvya*" *Journal Asiatique*, volume 247 (1959: 1–113). *Mahākāvya* or *sargabandha* is the long stanzaic epic genre in *kāvya* poetry. The classical form, style and themes of the *mahākāvya* distinguish it from the older Sankrit epics, the *Rāmāyaṇa* and the *Mahābhārata*. In this essay I refer to the *mahākāvya* genre by the term "court epic"; the *mahākāvya* has also been called "literary" or "classical" epic, to distinguish it from older epic. Bhāravi's *Kirātārjunīya* is known in the Indian tradition as one of the five great epics. For a study of the *Kirātārjunīya* as an exemplary *mahākāvya*, see my 1976 Ph.D. thesis (unpublished), under the name Shetterly: Indira V. Shetterly, "Recurrence and Structure in Sanskrit Literary Epic: A Study of Bhāravi's *Kirātārjunīya*", Harvard University Ph.D. Thesis, Department of Sanskrit and Indian Studies, 1976. Other studies concerned with the *mahākāvya* genre are: Gary Alan Tubb, "The *Kumārasaṃbhava* in the Light of Indian Theories of the *Mahākāvya*", unpublished Ph.D. thesis, Harvard University, Department of Sanskrit and Indian Studies, 1979; and David Smith, *Ratnākara's Haravijaya: An Introduction to the Sanskrit Court Epic*. (Delhi: Oxford University Press, 1985).

[5] The *Kirātārjunīya* is the only poem known to have been composed by Bhāravi, about whose life we know very little, except that he seems to have lived in the Deccan/Karnataka area of South India some time before 634 A.D., at which date he is praised as a master-poet in an important Chalukya inscription at Aihole. Information given by the 7th century poetician Daṇḍin, who lived at the South Indian Pallava court at Kāñcī, suggests that Bhāravi was connected with the Chalukya court, but was known to the Ganga and Pallava courts as well. On these and other matter concerning Bhāravi's date, see the discussion in A.K. Warder, *Indian Kāvya Literature*, Volume 3 (Delhi: Motilal Banarsidass, 1977), pp. 198–200.

effects of the court epic as an extended poetic composition.[6] There is general agreement among the theorists that one should speak of the overall effect of a court epic in terms of mood.[7] The later critics expect the court epic to include all the canonical moods (held to be nine in number), but to have *one* of these as the dominant or principal (*aṅgī*, *pradhāna*) *rasa*.[8] In accordance with the general view of the primacy and universality of particular moods, the 14th century poetician Viśvanātha spitulates that a *mahākāvya* should have one of the three *rasas* *śṛṅgāra* (the erotic), *vīra* (the heroic), and *śānta* (the calm or tranquil) as the dominant.[9]

The criticism of the *Kirātārjunīya* from the point of view of *rasa* is a relatively straightforward task. The direct experience of the poem leads the reader to conclude that, among the canonical *rasas*, *vīra* (the heroic), with its basis in the stable emotion (*sthāyibhāva*, "constant" emotion) *utsāha* (energy, action), is the principal *rasa* of the *Kirātārjunīya*. The poem is certainly dominated by the tireless and heroic effort of Arjuna to achieve of his martial goal of obtaining weapons from the gods. Other features of the poem point in the same direction. Bhāravi chose for his poem an explicitly martial theme from the older war epic, and one that fitted in well with the essentially heroic associations of many of the topics prescribed for treatment in court epic, such as "councils of war or political affairs, spies (or embassies), military campaigns, battles, and the victory of the hero".[10] Our impressionistic judgment is affirmed by the critical tradition: we are fortunate in having a late but excellent commentary on the first three cantos of the epic, in which the commentator, Citrabhānu, identifies the *kārya* (the ultimate goal or aim of the action) of the *Kirātārjunīya* as a heroic aim, and the principal mood of the

---

[6] It is clear from the *Nāṭyaśāstra*, the early canonical work on *rasa* poetics, and from the history of dramatic criticism, that the theory of *rasa* was formulated with respect to the drama. The poetics of *alaṃkāra* (figures of speech) is best suited to the stanza or quatrain, which is the standard unit of *kāvya* verse. The critics did not develop a comparable poetic appropriate to the court epic as an extended composition, and seem to apply a combination of *rasa* and *alaṃkāra* poetics to this genre. For a lucid and perceptive analysis of the history and implications of the application of *rasa* poetics to the *mahākāvya*, see Tubb, 1979.

[7] Seen in the reference to *rasa* (mood) as on of the important requirements of a *mahākāvya*, in the best known early definitions of the genre. Daṇḍin, *Kāvyādarśa*, I.18: "*rasabhāvanirantaram*" ("pervaded by *rasa* <mood> and *bhāva* <the emotional basis of mood>").

[8] On the doctrine of the principal or *aṅgī rasa*, see Tubb, 1979, pp. 189–192.

[9] Viśvanātha, *Sāhityadarpaṇa*, 6.317.

[10] "mantradūtaprayāṇājināyakābhyudayair api". Daṇḍin, *Kāvyādarśa*, I.17.

poem as *vīra*, the heroic.[11] Citrabhānu's commentary is one of the few works in which the plot of a *mahākāvya* is analyzed in detail in terms of the components and stages of the plot (*arthaprakṛti* and *avasthā*), as well as the principal junctures (*sandhi*), as these are defined in the canonical literature with regard to the development of *rasa* in dramatic works.[12] My own concern in the present essay is to determine and describe in a more general way the particular strategies which Bhāravi employs to suggest, nourish, and sustain the heroic mood (*vīra rasa*) as the dominant *rasa* in his epic, and especially in its climactic scenes.

Bhakti in the Kirātārjunīya

The role of devotional religion in the *Kirātārjunīya* is a matter of some complexity. That the poem has an important religious dimension has always been acknowledged. In the *Mahābhārata* itself the *kirāta*-Arjuna encounter is presented as having both heroic and devotional implications. Even if, along with the Editors of the Critical Edition of the older epic, we reject as problematic the incidents of Arjuna's ritual worship of Śiva and the long hymn of praise (*stotra*) with which he addresses the god upon discovering his identity, we cannot dismiss the overtly devotional focus of the climax of the tale.[13] In the epic episode, after giving Arjuna divine "vision" (<*divyaṃ*> *cakṣus*) with which to behold him, Śiva reveals his divine persona to the hero, who worships him in wonder;[14] the scene constitutes what Alf Hiltebeitel has aptly called a "*bhakti* tableau",[15]

---

[11] *Kirātārjunīya* (I–III) with the commentary of Citrabhānu. Edited by T. Ganapathi Sastri. Trivandrum Sanskrit Series 63, 1918.

[12] See Gary Tubb's discussion of the question of the analysis of the plots of court epics according to the schemes devised for the dramatic genre, and the significance of such a critical approach for the study of Kālidāsa's *mahākāvya Kumārasaṃbhava*: Tubb, 1979, Chapters I and V. For a contemporary scholar's analysis of Bhāravi's poem according to the *saṃdhi-avasthā* schemes, see Warder, 1977, Chapter XXVII.

[13] Madeleine Biardeau considers these "devotional" passages essential to the meaning of the *kirāta* episode in the *Mahābhārata*, and condemns the decision of the Editors of the Critical Edition: EMH (V), 1978, p. 157, n.1. Biardeau's excellent study of the religious meaning of the *kirāta* episode has been followed by a complementary study of this episode in: Jacques Scheuer, *Śiva dans le Mahābhārata* (Paris: Presses universitaires de France, 1982).

[14] This feature occurs in the context of the *Bhagavad Gītā* as well, where Krishna gives Arjuna the *cakṣu* with which to see his Universal Form (XI. 8). Bhāravi omits this detail in his version of the *kirāta* narrative.

[15] "Rather than being a patchwork of myths, legends, and historical reminiscences overlaid with *bhakti*, what the narrative builds up to and works around are a series of what I would call "*bhakti* tableaux", scenes which present images that hold themselves before the hearer's mind". And "the epic language of images is not, however, simply visual (or visional). It is also highly intellectual". Alf Hiltebeitel, "The Two Kṛṣṇas on One Chariot: Upaniṣadic Imagery and Epic Mythology", *History of Religions*, Volume 24, Number 1, (August 1984, 1–26), p. 2.

analogous to the more familiar scene in the *Bhagavad Gītā*, of the theophany of Krishna which Arjuna receives along with the god's counsel on the battlefield in Book VI of the *Mahābhārata*.[16] The powerful appeal of the tableau of Śiva's self-revelation of Arjuna in this episode to the imagination of South Indian monarchs and sculptors in the period immediately following Bhāravi's composition of the *Kirātārjunīya* is evident in the monumental 6th century Pallava rock-cut sculpture known as "Arjuna's Penance" at Mahabalipuram.[17] It was also in the 6th–7th centures that the *kirāta* tale became standardized as an illustration of one of Śiva's "forms or personae of grace" (*anugrahamūrti*) in the ecstatic devotional hymns of the Nāyaṉārs Appar and Ñāṉacampantar, the saint-leaders of the Tamil Śaivite devotional (*bhakti*) movement.[18] In a recent study of the *kirāta* episode in South Indian art M.S. Nagaraja Rao has shown that, from the 7th century onwards, the Karnataka region of South India, in or near which Bhāravi is said to have flourished, abounds in temple sculpture and long devotional poems in Kannada dealing with the *kirāta*-Arjuna theme.[19] It is clear then, that, rooted as it is in the classicist tradition of *kāvya* poetry and criticism, Bhāravi's poem is equally deeply embedded in the atmosphere, milieu and lore of early Śaiva *bhakti* cults and Śaivite religion in general in the Kannada, Telugu and Tamil-speaking areas of South India. Yet the fact remains that the *Kirātārjunīya* is celebrated as a great court epic, not as a poem in the *bhakti* (devotional) genre, and it is difficult to precisely characterize the role of *bhakti* in this work.[20] Moreover, since we know

---

[16] *The Bhagavad Gītā*, Chapter XI.

[17] "Arjuna's Penance" is a well known rock-cut sculpture in the Mahabalipuram complex in South India, said to have been sculpted during the reign of the Pallava king Mahendravarman (600–640 A.D.). Among the central images in this sculpture are the figure of an ascetic performing penance, standing on one leg, a monumental divine figure bearing a weapon, in front of whom stands a man in reverent attitude, and a group of ascetics in front of a shrine with an image of a deity within. T.N. Ramachandran has argued the case for viewing this sculpture as a depiction of events in the *kirāta*-Arjuna story, and not a representation of the "descent of the Ganges" myth, as some would have it. T.N. Ramachandran, "The *Kirātārjunīyam* or "Arjuna's penance" in Indian Art", *Journal of the Indian Society of Oriental Art* (volume XVIII, 1950–51, pp. 1–111). See especially pp. 58–89.

[18] E.g., Appar (Tirunāvukkaraçar), *Tēvāram* IV.73.3, and Ñāṉacampantar, *Tēvāram* I.75.3, in the South India Saiva Siddhanta Works Edition. Translated in Indira V. Peterson, *Poems to Śiva: The Hymns of the Tamil Saints* (Princeton: Princeton University Press, 1989).

[19] M.S. Nagaraja Rao, *Kirātārjunīyam in Indian Art* (*With Special Reference to Karnataka*) (Delhi: Agam Kala Prakashan, 1979).

[20] Although it might be argued with some justification that the dividing line between "*bhakti*" and "non-*bhakti*" works can often be unclear, the classics of the court epic genre are treated as *kāvya* poems, rather than as works with a primarily "religious" intent.

very little about Bhāravi's life, we can only speculate about the role that the burgeoning Śaivite *bhakti* cults and sects might have played in the personal religion of the poet and that of his royal patron, and the extent to which these factors might have influenced Bhāravi in his approach to the theme of the *Kirātāruniya*, the only work he is known to have authored.[21] Under these circumstances, how are we to "read" the *bhakti* tableau at the end of the poem? How does Bhāravi relate the interests of the heroic *rasa* to the proper presentation of a scene of devotion and grace? How does he let the *bhakti* tableau emerge without overshadowing the *vīra rasa*? To find an answer to this question, we must turn to the poem itself, considering it in relation to its older epic source, as well as to its many counterparts in South Indian religious art and letters.

II. *Rasa in the Kirātārjunīya: Structural Considerations*

In the traditional poetics of *rasa*, the aesthetic experience is seen as arising from the poet's skilful manipulation of the various objective and psychological elements of the poem.

The basis of *rasa* <mood> is the presentation in a play or a poem of factors connected with the presence of emotions <*bhāva*> in the characters portrayed in the work.[22] In lay terms, the portrayal of selected emotional states, in conjunction with the incidents and components of the plot, poetic conventions, characterization, description, language, imagery, and other factors, leads to the experience of a dominant flavor or mood in the poem. In long compositions such as the drama and the court epic, the plot is the basic frame or structure around which the development of *rasa* takes place; and, as Gary Tubb points out, the *kārya*, the goal or aim towards which the principal action of the work is directed", may be regarded as the central element in the analysis of plot . . ." for, in practical terms, this goal is "the overall meaning that connects the different parts of a complete work".[23] Arjuna's attempt to propitiate the gods is motivated by his desire—on behalf of his family—to obtain celestial weapons with which to destroy their unscrupulous enemies in

---

[21] It is probably safe to assume that Bhāravi was himself a Śaivite, although, as will be shown below, several Jaina authors have treated the *kirāta* theme in their retellings of the *Mahābhārata*.

[22] Further, "When a properly qualified spectator or reader perceives the existence of a *sthāyibhāva* <stable emotion, the basis of the principal *rasa*> through the observation of the associated *vibhāvas* <causes of emotion>, the resulting experience is spoken of as a savoring (*āsvāda*) of the corresponding *rasa*". Tubb, 1979, pp. 187–8. material in < > mine. See Tubb, Chapter VI, for a discussion of the arrangement of *rasas* in a *mahākāvya*.

[23] *Ibid.*, p. 142 and 150.

battle. The development of the principal mood in the poem, as well as the hero's climactic encounter with Śiva, should be seen in the context of this heroic purpose towards which the major action of the poem is directed.

In his treatment of the plot of the *kirāta* tale, Bhāravi is clearly influenced by the traditional conception of a *mahākāvya* as a literary work which should teach as well as delight, and do both on a grand, "epic" scale. The early poetician Bhāmaha, for instance, describes the court epic as a genre which is "about great things" (*mahatām*), and "great, that is, grand and inclusive", (*mahat*), in its scope:[24] specifically, a *kāvya* epic must have a great, elevated theme; it must include all the canonical *rasas*; it must refer to the four aims (*puruṣārtha*) of man's life; and it must be replete with as many as possible of the rhetorical and descriptive topics established by poetic usage and prescription as appropriate for a *kāvya* epic.[25] The content and style of the *mahākāvya* together contribute to its aesthetic and didactic aims. In the following outline of the narrative of the *Kirātārjunīya*, I have tried to show how Bhāravi relates the principal generic requirements of the *mahākāvya* with the development of the principal mood in the poem.

An Outline of the Narrative of the Kirātārjunīya

Canto; type of kāvya topic	*Content; Aim of life (puruṣārtha) presented*	*Rasa*
I–III rhetorical (speech)	Argument among the Pāṇḍavas regarding their course of action. Vyāsa sends Arjuna to the Himalayas to win divine weapons. *Aim: Artha* (*nīti*, politics) / *Dharma* (The Law, Right conduct)	*vīra*; (the heroic) contrasted with *śānta* (the calm)
IV–VI descriptive (in rhetorical frame)	Arjuna and his *yakṣa* companion enjoy the beauty of autumn and the Himalaya; Arjuna's penance (*tapas*). *Aim: Dharma.*	*śānta*; enhanced by *vīra*; *sṛṅgāra* (the erotic) is foreshadowed.
VII–IX descriptive	The erotic revels of the nymphs sent by Indra to tempt Arjuna.	*śṛṅgāra*; foil for

[24] Bhāmaha, *Kāvyalaṃkāra*, I.19: "(Sargabandho mahākāvyam) mahatāṃ ca mahac ca yat".
[25] See, for instance, the definition of Daṇḍin, *Kāvyādarśa* I.14–22. Translations of this and other definitions can be found in Tubb, 1979, Chapter III.

interlude; (No basis in the *Mahābhārata*)	*Aim: Kāma* (worldly pleasure, sexual activity).	śānta and *vīra.*
X descriptive	The nymphs fail in their attempt to seduce Arjuna. *Aim: Dharma.*	*śṛṅgāra*; explicitly pitted against *śānta* and *vīra.*
XI rhetorical	Indra questions Arjuna's integrity and offers him *mokṣa* (ultimate release); the hero rejects the offer, and stands by his duty as a warrior (*kṣatriya*) *Aims: Dharma* and *Mokṣa* (liberation)	*śānta* and *vīra*
XII descriptive	Arjuna resumes his awesome penance; wants to propitiate Śiva.	*śānta* and *vīra* perfectly balanced.
	Śiva sets out to test Arjuna. *Aim: Dharma.*	
XIII-XIV descriptive and rhetorical	Arjuna shoots the boar, which is a demon in disguise; argument with Śiva's messenger, who claims the boar. Arjuna resists the offer of wealth. Battle. *Aims: Artha* (wealth), and *Dharma*	*vīra.*
XV–XVII mainly descriptive	Arjuna fights with Śiva disguised as a *kirāta*. The hero is progressively stripped of his arms. *Aim: Dharma.*	*vīra*, colored by *bhakti.*
XVIII mainly descriptive	Climax of combat: In the midst of a wrestling bout, Śiva reveals himself. Arjuna praises him, asks for forgiveness and the gift of weapons. He receives arms from Śiva and the gods, then returns to his brothers, confident of Pāṇḍava victory. *Aim: Dharma.*	*vīra* (and *bhakti*).

Comparing the *Mahābhārata* narrative with that of the *Kirātārjunīya*, we may conclude that, on the whole, the classical poet keeps to the "situations" presented in the original, amplifying their meaning, and adding descriptive material which will help him achieve the range required of a *kāvya* epic. Yet inclusivity is not all; my brief outline of the development of the *vīra rasa* in the poem shows that the poet has successfully put his material to use in the service of the principal mood.

Bhāravi invokes heroic action as the central theme of his poem in the argument among the Pāṇḍavas regarding their course of action against the enemy, in the opening scene of the epic. In these three cantos the Pāṇḍava goal is defined, and the strategy (*upāya*) for the accomplishment of this goal is outlined: the Pāṇḍavas must restore their lost honor; they must obtain the means with which to defeat their enemies in war; Arjuna will perform penance in the Himalayas, in order to propitiate the gods and win the boon of celestial weapons. Arjuna's penance, his "undertaking", is the main theme of the middle portion of the epic; it is described in different ways, and at various degrees of intensity, throughout this section (especially in Cantos VI, X, and XII).[26] The mood suggested here is *śānta*, the calm, which is ordinarily the antithesis of the heroic mood. However, as I shall show below, Bhāravi uses *śānta* as a foil to *vīra* with twofold effect, to sustain and nourish the heroic, as well as to provide a contrast to it. In the same section, in his arguments with Indra, his nymphs, and Śiva's messenger, all of whom question the integrity of his endeavor, Arjuna chooses *dharma* as the aim of life most appropriate for him in his station and stage of life, rejecting the other three aims (*kāma*, *artha* and *mokṣa*), as distractions from his duty as a warrior, though they are worthy goals in themselves.[27] Arjuna's defence of a hero's *dharma* in the context of the scheme of the "four aims of life" highlights the moral basis of the heroic mood. We are thus prepared for the full flowering of the heroic mood in the scenes of conflict (Arjuna's conflict with the demonic boar, his quarrel with Śiva's messenger), combat (the battle with Śiva's army, and the combat with Śiva himself), and success (in achieving his goal) in the last six cantos of the poem. In Arjuna's perseverant courage and activity in the face of every kind of challenge, we must discern *utsāha* (energy, relentless effort toward a goal), the *sthāyibhava* or emotional constant which is canonically defined as the basis of the heroic *rasa*. In what follows I will provide a summary analysis of heroic themes in the first part of the poem (Cantos I–XI), leading to a detailed discussion of the rhetorical strategies Bhāravi uses to suggest the heroic mood in the combat scenes. I close with a consideration of the essential question of *bhakti* in relation to *rasa* in the climax of the poem.

---

[26] I have discussed in detail the development of meaning through repeated description in the context of Arjuna's penance in the *Kirātārjunīya* in Shetterly, 1976, Chapter III, pp. 281–299.

[27] The tradition does not see the four aims of life (*dharma*, *artha*, *kāma* and *mokṣa*) as incompatible with each other, but as complementary ends, to be pursued at the proper time and stage of one's life. It is also understood that the other three aims should be tempered and governed by *dharma*.

III *Prelude to combat: The Warrior as Yogi (Kirātārjunīya VI–XI)*

Among the great *mahākāvya* poets, Bhāravi is distinguished for the lofty intellectualism and depth of meaning of his poetry.[28] This description applies not only to individual verses in the *Kirātārjunīya*, but to the tone of the poem as a whole. In the first section of the epic, Bhāravi focuses on two themes: the warrior ideal of courage and heroic effort involved in Arjuna's endeavor, and the apparent incompatibility of Arjuna's nonviolent ascetic practice with his militaristic goal. The heroic emphasis of the former, which forms the topic of argument among the characters (the Pāṇḍava brothers and their wife Draupadī in cantos I–III; Indra and Arjuna in Canto XI), is explicit. As the underlying theme of the entire middle section of the poem, the latter deserves comment.

At the beginning of the epic, Draupadī and Bhīma try to persuade the gentle Yudhiṣṭhira that, since their unscrupulous enemy is flourishing, the time has come for him to take action against him. As befits the topic, and as is typical of the *kāvya* style, these fiery speeches are delivered in the form of elegant general statements, in which the qualifications and conduct of a hero are defined. Bhīma and Draupadī repeatedly invoke the ideals of *pauruṣa* (manliness), *vikrama* (heroic deeds), *tejas* (heroic splendor), and pride or honor (*abhimāna, māna*).[29] The power of Arjuna's response to Indra in Canto XI derives largely from the many resonances it has in theme, language and imagery with the earlier debate.[30]

In the middle segment of the poem, Bhāravi's primary concern is to sustain the heroic mood in the context of Arjuna's penance, which is essentially a topic conducive to *śānta*, the "calm" mood, the antithesis of the energetic flavor of *vīra*. Here the poet structures his rhetoric of the heroic mood around the incongruous image of Arjuna as the warrior-ascetic. At the end of the third Canto, Arjuna proceeds to the Indrakīla peak[31] on the Himalayas, dressed according to the seer Vyāsa's command; he is fully armed, and outfitted with a warrior's attributes, but also wears the bark garment, antelope-skin and sacred thread of the *yogī*

---

[28] According to a popular verse, the distinctive excellence of Bhāravi's poetry is "*arthagauravam*" (depth of meaning).

[29] See Shetterly, 1976, Chapter II, for a discussion of these speeches.

[30] *Ibid.*, pp. 168–174, and 215–222, for an analysis of the poet's use of the technique (unusual for *mahākāvya* upto Bhāravi) of focusing on a specific concept (here, *puruṣa*), over several verses in a sequence, with many verbal echoes, as a rhetorical strategy in Arjuna's speech (*Kirātārjunīya* XI.37–79).

[31] The *Mahābhārata* does not identify the Himalayan peak by this name, which means "Indra's post or pillar". The difference between the location of Indrakīla in Bhāravi and later poets is noted below.

or ascetic who has undertaken a vow (*vrata*). Arjuna's appearance is puzzling and disturbing to the foresters and ascetics who dwell in the Himalayas; they suspect him of performing penance with some evil purpose in mind, like the many demons who have wrested boons from the gods by the power of their ascetisicsm, which threatens the gods. As Arjuna's ascetic practices grow in severity, the heat generated by them threatens to consume the universe.[32] Bhāravi makes full use of the dramatic possibilities of these circumstances.

Indra, his nymphs, and Śiva's messenger, who seek to thwart the hero's purpose by shaking his resolution, suggest that the two sorts of power Arjuna combines in his Arjuna's warrior-ascetic persona are inherently antithetical. Indra, who approaches Arjuna disguised as a brahmin ascetic, poses the problem thus in his address to Arjuna:

XI.15. Why are you clad in armor,
like a warrior ready for battle?
Ascetics wear only deerskin and bark.

16. And if you are truly detached,
and seek liberation,
why this fierce bow, these two mighty quivers,
on the body of a man
who would harm no living creature?

17. If you are indeed a renouncer,
this sword of yours, as fearsome to mortals
as Death's own arm,
does not convince me
of your peaceful thoughts.

18. Surely you seek to vanquish your foes!
Where is a symbol of anger, and where are men of peace?
Where is a weapon, and where are renouncers?

The message is clear: men undertake the peaceful vows of asceticism striving for final release, not for worldly and violent ends such as victory over enemies; Arjuna's incongruous appearance reflects the incongruity of his means with his ends. In the arguments of Indra and the hero's other interlocutors, which seem to express the Buddhist criticism of the brahmanical practice of *tapas* (asceticism) as a means to achieving worldly goals,[33] the peaceful way of life is presented as an alternative to

---

[32] The result of the enormous quantity of heat-energy-power (*tapas*) stored up through ascetic discipline; the standard effect of extreme *tapas*.

[33] See Shetterly, 1979, Chapter III, pp. 305–341.

the violent *dharma* of the warrior, and *śānta* offers a powerful contrast to the heroic mood.

However, by the end of the segment Bhāravi has established that, far from being incompatible with Arjuna's heroic goal, his asceticism is an essential component of his nature and endeavor as a warrior. The *vīra rasa* comes into its own in Arjuna's spirited defence of his *dharma* as a warrior (*kṣātra-dharma*). The hero explains that his ascetic vow is a temporary one with a limited purpose; not for him is the *dharma* of a renouncer, leading to final release, however covetable that end may be. As a *kṣatriya* (warrior) who has set out to restore the honor of his king and family, Arjuna must fulfil his duty by winning weapons from the gods. Even *mokṣa* (ultimate release), which is the ultimate goal towards which man must strive, becomes a distracting temptation which, if attained before the proper time, i.e., before one has duly discharged one's duties (*dharma*), will render one's life a failure. Therefore, Arjuna rejects even the offer of liberation which the god Indra, who is also the hero's divine father, offers him.[34]

Whatever the nature of his immediate activity, the hero cannot swerve from his innate (*sahaja*) *dharma* or *sva-dharma* (*own-dharma*), which is that of a warrior: "Men of self-respect stand by their own-dharma, and do not transgress it"[35] The arms which Arjuna bears throughout his ordeal are outward symbols and reminders of his sacred duty as a warrior; this is implied in the ease with which Arjuna balances seemingly incompatible attributes and aims in his person and activity. In his descriptions of Arjuna's penance the poet portrays the hero as successfully combining the physical and spiritual attributes of a warrior and an ascetic: the bow and arrow and the peaceful mien of the hermit, *jaya* (military victory) and peace (*śama*; this is the stable emotion of the calm mood); the active power and splendor of a warrior (*vīrya*, *ojas*, *jayalakṣmī*), and the spiritual power of the ascetic (*tejas*, *tapolakṣmī*) (e.g., VI.22 and VI.32).[36] The theme is sustained through the later cantos, for at the end of poem, the

---

[34] Arjuna, *Kirātārjunīya* XI. 76. "Moreover, how can I take up renunciation / before its due time, / when such a course would violate *dharma*? / The ancients teach us / to take the stages of life in order, / and not violate their sequence".

[35] "svadharmam anurundhante . . . mānaśālinaḥ". (XI.78).

[36] VI.22. "At once he bore twofold splendor, / one inborn, the other learned, / a warrior's superior power, / and supreme tranquility". "*sahajetarau jayaśamau* dadhatī bibharāmbabhūva yugapan mahasī". Compare: "dhāmnā *tapovīryamayena* yuktam" ("yoked with twofold splendor, / from the white heat of *tapas*, and intense war might . . ." (XVII.48); also XII.27.

jubilant Arjuna is described as representing the perfect synthesis of *tapas* and war might:

XVIII.47. The gods loudly sang the praise
of him who had gained his place above the worlds,
like the sun,
with his own fiery splendor,
and the incandescence of *tapas* (heat/penance). . . .

In sum, through his depiction of Arjuna's penance and of the hero's defence of his warrior-*dharma*, Bhāravi shows that Arjuna's ascetic discipline is only a prelude to his final combat with Śiva, which, as the most appropriate arena for the expression of his *sva-dharma*, is itself the highest *yoga* for him. As for the penance, it is a spiritual discipline necessary for preparing him for his encounter with God, which in turn initiates him into his role in the righteous war against his enemies on "Kurukṣetra, the field of Dharma".[37] These ideas have obvious resonances with the *Bhagavad Gītā*, where Krishna reveals himself as God to Arjuna in the major theophany of the *Mahābhārata*, and teaches him the *yoga* of war as the highest *dharma* of the warrior. Since the ultimate purpose of Arjuna's penance is to obtain divine weapons with which to destroy his enemies in the Bhārata war, Bhāravi's reflections on war as *yoga* clearly apply to Arjuna's engagement in the great war as well as to his heroic-devotional encounter with Śiva in the immediate context.[38] These considerations bring us to the final combat scenes, in which the heroic flavor and implications of Arjuna's penance are fully developed.

IV *Heroic Action in Bhāravi's Epic: Kirātārjunīya XIV–XVIII*

Bhāravi and the epic tradition of combat description

Though in its capacity as a book of Dharma the *Mahābhārata* is a repository of heterogeneous material dealing with a wide range of topics, in its essential form it is "Jaya" (Victory), the story of the war between

[37] *Bhagavad Gītā* I.1, "dharmakṣetre kurukṣetre. . .".

[38] In the combat scenes, Bhāravi often refers to Arjuna as "*muni*" (ascetic, sage). In XVII.48, he describes the hero's combat with Śiva as a variety of ascetic discipline: "The self-controlled ascetic (Arjuna), / whose endeavor was about to bear its auspicious fruit, / underwent, in the form of Śiva's arrows, / austerities (*tepe*) akin to incantation and fasting, / as he stood maintaining his *ascetic vow of heroism* (*vīravratam*) / there in the *holy hermitage of battle* (*puṇyaraṇāśramasthaḥ*).

the Kuru princes.[39] Four of its eighteen Books are devoted to detailed description of the Bhārata war, with large segments devoted to the description of large-scale clashes as well as single combat between individual heroes. The *Mahābhārata* offers a wealth of material for the study of battle description as an epic genre, and, along with the *Rāmāyaṇa*, it is the primary source from which the later *kāvya* epic poets draw the inspiration for their own descriptions. Combat description in the *Mahābhārata* ranges from the depiction of massive battles, as well as single combat between individual heroes. The great, bloody clashes (*tumula-yuddha*) involve footsoldiers and warriors fighting from elephants, horses and chariots, using bows, arrows, spears and other weapons.[40] When the scene narrows down to the description of single combat, besides the equipment of the average warrior, the principal heroes have recourse to celestial weapons (*divyāstra*) given by the gods; such as the Brahmaśiras which Arjuna wins from Śiva. In the *Rāmāyaṇa*, which makes far greater use of the fantastic than the *Mahābhārata*, Rāma and the Rākṣasas fight with supernatural weapons which are capable of creating magical effects and transformations. Battle description in both epics is characterized by frequent reference to certain cosmic phenomena (the sun and the moon) grand images from nature and the animal kingdom (mountains, lions) and figures in mythology (Indra and Vṛtra). Warriors are compared to the sun and moon at the end of a cosmic cycle, or to Añtaka, the god of Death.[41] Especially in the generic battle-scenes of the *Mahābhārata*, there is an inclination toward the macabre. The celebrated grisly images in the brief battle-description in Kālidāsa's court epic *Raghuvaṃśa* (Canto VII), such as the headless torso of the warrior dancing in the battlefield, vultures and jackals wrenching limbs and flesh off corpses, and the heads of kings rolling on the battlefield like clusters of

---

[39] See Sylvain Levi, "Tato jayam Udīrayet", trans. L.G. Khare, *Annals of the Bhandarkar Oriental Research Institute* 1 (1918–19): 13–20; and Irawati Karve, *Yugānta; The End of an Epoch* (Poona: Desmukh Prakashan, 1969)

[40] For details about the art of war and other military matters in the *Mahābhārata*, consult E. Washburn Hopkins, "The Social and Military Position of the Ruling Caste in Ancient India as Represented by the Sanskrit Epic", *Journal of the American Oriental Society* (volume 13: 181–329).

[41] E.g., *Mahābhārata*, Gorakhpur: Gita Press Edition. *Droṇaparvan* 101. Krishna and Arjuna are compared to twin suns released from the mouth of Rāhu (the demon of eclipse), (5), two suns at the time of dissolution (7), thirsty elephants (19), shining suns (22), blazing with splendor like Indra and Agni (Fire, 24), mountains (25), the sun and the moon (27), tigers (30), and so on.

lotuses, are in reality refinements on specific images found in the spectacular combat scenes in the *Mahābhārata*.[42]

In the *Mahābhārata* the *kirāta* episode is not used as the occasion for a full-scale battle-description involving the repertoire described above. It is a unique vignette. At the beginning of the combat, Arjuna and Śiva (disguised as a *kirāta*) engage in a fierce exchange of arrows, but the *kirāta* progressively strips Arjuna of his weapons—bow, arrows, sword—and armor, and forces the hero to fight with uprooted trees and rocks, then with his fists, and finally, to engage in a wrestling bout.[43] Bhāravi expands the simpler combat of the *Mahābhārata* episode into a full-fledged battle between Arjuna and *kirāta*-Śiva with all his troops, along the lines of the war-scenes in the older epic. In cantos XIV–XV Arjuna faces not *kirāta*-Śiva alone, but his entire army of *gaṇa*s[44] led by Śiva's son Skanda, general of the army of the gods. In Canto XVI Śiva and Arjuna discharge magical missiles at each other, creating supernatural effects: the serpents materialized by Arjuna's serpent missile are vanquished by the Garuḍa-birds, sworn enemies of snakes, which are created by the magical formula of Śiva's Gāruḍāstra, while the terrible fire produced by Arjuna's Āgneyāstra is quenched by torrential rain issuing from Śiva's Vāruṇāstra. It is only in Canto XVII that Bhāravi returns to the narrative according to the older epic, describing the progression from combat with bow and arrows to the fistfight between the opponents. The wrestling bout, Śiva's revelation of his true identity, Arjuna's prayer and hymn of praise, the arrival of celestial beings and the *lokapāla* (world-guardian) gods, the gift (from Śiva) of the Raudra (*Pāśupata*) shaft, which is the embodiment of the science of weapons, and other weapons (from the *lokapāla*s), and Arjuna's return to his brothers in the forest— all these incidents are compressed into the XVIIIth canto.

---

[42] Compare the following: Kālidāsa, *Raghuvaṃśa* VII.7 and *Mahābhārata*, *Droṇaparvan* 97.7 (heads like lotuses); *Raghu*. VII.49 and *Droṇa*.97.14 (carrion birds); *Raghu*. VII.37 and *Droṇa*. 97.19 (the clash of matched warriors), and *Raghu*. VII.51 and *Droṇa* 97.12 (the trunk of a warrior dances on the battlefield). Note that all the parallels occur in a single *Mahābhārata* passage. The numbering is according to the Gita Press edition.

[43] Biardeau notes that, in resorting to treetrunks and rocks, Arjuna appears to be using the techniques his strong-man brother Bhīma employs in combat with *Rākṣasa* demons. EMH (V), 1978, p. 156, n.(1). I would add that treetrunks and rock serve as weapons for the monkeys in their battle with the Rākṣasas in the *Rāmāyaṇa*. In both cases the combat "regresses" to increasingly "primitive" levels; stripped of his weapons, Arjuna must prove his heroism at the primal level. See below for a discussion of the symbolism of the hero's weapons.

[44] The *gaṇas*, Śiva's goblin hosts, are transformed into a great army of mountain hunters who accompany Śiva as the *kirāta* chief.

Considered from the point of *mahākāvya* poetics, Bhāravi's treatment of the combat scenes appears to be yet another instance of the court epic poet trying to expand the descriptive and topical scope of his poem. In effect, in the *kirāta*-Arjuna combat, Bhāravi provides a combat sequence which is longer and more complete in every respect than those which appear in earlier *mahākāvyas*.[45] However, as before, it is far more illuminating and productive to study what Bhāravi does with the subject matter he chooses to include, than to simply note what he includes. Bhāravi's description of the combat is at once replete with concrete physical detail and abstract to the extreme. Not only the human participants in the battle, but also inanimate objects such as Arjuna's weapons function as the emotional and psychological bases of the heroic mood, or otherwise contribute to the atmosphere of the heroic. The conventional cosmic imagery of epic battle-description acquires deeper significance in the contest between the god and the hero. And, finally, the very modes and terms in which the combat is depicted serve to illuminate the complex relationship between the Great God and the divine hero.

Arms and the Man: A Warrior's Identity

The imagery associated with arms in the combat scenes in the *Kirātārjunīya* suggests that Bhāravi intends the symbolism of arms and the hero in this sequence to provide a poetic solution to the riddle posed by the image of the warrior-ascetic earlier in the poem. In the battle episodes, Arjuna relates to his weapons as a man would to his close and trusted friends. When they are not thus humanized, the weapons are portrayed as the abstract qualities which constitute a warrior's heroism, the very qualities which formed the themes of the debate among the Pāṇḍava brothers and between Arjuna and Indra. Bhāravi makes

---

[45] The life of the Buddha and the union of Śiva and Pārvatī, the principal themes of the *Buddhacarita* and the *Kumārasaṃbhava*, made extended combat scenes irrelevant in these epics of Aśvaghoṣa (*circa* first century) and Kālidāsa (fourth century A.D.). It is, on the other hand, remarkable that Kālidāsa's *Raghuvaṃśa*, an epic with overtly martial and heroic themes, contains only two relatively short, sustained descriptions of combat, and one stylized description of a campaign of conquest. The great battle between Rāma and Rāvaṇa, which is so spectacularly depicted in the *Rāmāyaṇa*, is treated in a brief and subdued description in Kālidāsa (XII.84–100)); the focus of the description of Raghu's campaign, in Canto IV, is on cultural geography and the mood of victory; the only full-fledged battle description occurs in a minor episode, and concerns Aja's clash with the disappointed suitors of Indumatī (VII.37–63). As I noted above, this is a powerful passage which includes the entire battle repertoire of the *Mahābhārata*, with specific parallels in *Droṇaparvan* 97.

particularly striking and sustained use of these metaphorical strategies at critical points in the development of the action.

A fine example of the process of the humanization of the hero's weapons occurs at a crucial moment in the plot, the moment when Arjuna's *tapas* is interrupted by the demon Mūka, who attacks the hero in the guise of a wild boar (Canto XII). Arjuna is unaware that Śiva, disguised as a hunter, has arrived on the mountain in order to shoot at the boar at the same time as Arjuna, leading upto the quarrel over the arrow, and the subsequent combat in which the god will test and reveal the hero's prowess. When Arjuna sees the boar charging at him, he agonizes over his course of action (Canto XIII). It does not befit him, as an ascetic observing a vow (*vrata*), to kill any living being. Yet the seer Vyāsa himself has commanded him not to yield to anyone who might confront him in a hostile manner. Considering the maintenance of his vow in strict accordance with the seer's command to be his foremost responsibility, Arjuna decides to resist the boar's attack. Then he reaches for his bow, which responds to him in the manner of a trustworthy friend:

XIII.14. When he had thus thought over (his course of action),
he took up that foremost symbol of manhood called "a bow":
Stringing it, he fitted it with a straight arrow,
which was like an honest counsellor
who knows the enemy's might,
and helps (his king) to act against him.[46]

15. Drawn taut by Dhanañjaya (Arjuna) with determination
in spite of his physical exhaustion,
the great strung bow bent readily,
though it was so firm as to be unbreakable,
just as a noble friend,
never-failing in his steadfastness, readily responds
when a man who has lost his wealth
appeals to him for aid.[47]

When, having killed the boar, Arjuna runs towards the animal to recover his arrow, he treats it with love and gratitude; the arrow, for its part,

---

[46] (He took up the) "foremost symbol of manhood": "prathamaṃ pauruṣa-cihnam".

[47] The double meaning in this verse is built around such words as *sthira-* (firm, steadfast), *guṇavat* (with a bowstring / endowed with virtue). The effect of such punning verses is discussed below.

behaves as a modest and sensitive friend would:

XIII.32. Then Pārtha ran towards the boar,
wishing to recover that arrow
which had exhibited its prowess,
even though he had a great store of arrows—
for one who has accomplished his task
is dearer to a grateful man
than one who merely holds out
the promise of future of deeds.

33. Like a favor done to a villain,
that arrow did not find a foothold
in the (carcass of) the beast,
but vanished into it;
Having shown its prowess,
it nobly faced downward (as if weighed down),
as though such a display of valor
were an embarrassment. . . .

34. And it bore its lustre
as through this were its peerless glory.
As Arjuna stood there,
thoughtfully drawing the arrow out,
was he enquiring aloud of its welfare,
or clasping it in the warm embrace of his eyes?

The symbolism of arms as friends is the framework of Bhāravi's description of another crucial point in the action, the moment during the *kirāta*-Arjuna combat when Arjuna discovers to his amazement that the *inexhaustible* quivers given to him by the god Agni[48] are, for the first time, empty of arrows. The imagery of this long sequence of verses (XVII.36–47) unfolds as follows: Arjuna dips his hand into the quiver (36); though the quiver is empty, "like a friend suddenly gone bankrupt", the hand continues to search (37); the finger gropes frantically (38); Arjuna is compared to the world at the time of dissolution (39); ignoring his own misfortune, Arjuna grieves over the emptiness of his quivers, as a good man would when his benefactors are in distress (40); At a loss for a remedy, his hand parts from the quiver with reluctance, like "a nobleman from his friends . . ." (41); and the quivers appreciate being placed on Arjuna's back because, "when one has failed one's master in

---

[48] These are the inexhaustible quivers which Agni, the Fire-god, gave Arjuna, at the burning of Khāṇḍava forest (*Mahābhārata*, Book I).

his hour of need, to remain in front of him is impudence". The personification of the quivers is doubly effective because of the remarkably slow pace of the description. In this sustained descriptive segment which is stylistically unique even in the tradition of court poetry (in which detailed and leisurely description is the norm), Bhāravi more than describes an event; he paints a portrait of a *human relationship*, with all its psychological nuances.

The consistent personification of arms as a hero's friends is only one of the many threads which link such verses as the above to one another; martial prowess or valor (*pauruṣa*), virtue (*guṇa*), steadfastness, trustworthiness (*sthiratva*), nobility, greatness (*gurutva*), all of which are the qualities of the ideal warrior, are invoked in varied clusters in each verse. The verbal resonances are multiple and complex: for instance, in XIII.32, a specific act of courage is attributed to Arjuna's arrow, which is said to have "exhibited its prowess" (*sphuṭapauruṣaṃ śaram*), while in XIII.14, the bow is called the foremost symbol of manliness (*pauruṣa*). Both references recall the didactic verses on *pauruṣa* (heroism) and *puruṣa* ("a real man") in the speeches of the Pāṇḍavas (Cantos II–III) and of Arjuna (Canto XI). The verses gain in depth and scope through the double-entendre which Bhāravi intends with respect to most of the above concepts and words. *Guṇa* is not only "virtue" but also "a bowstring"; *guru*: "strong, mighty, noble", also "heavy"; and *sthira* is "firm, hard", as well as "steadfast, stable". The same words can thus simultaneously apply to a hero's weapons, to his noble friends, and to the hero himself: verbal identification effects a metonymical relationship between arms and the man. Furthermore, the symbolism gains in power and authenticity because, as with his other devices, the poet makes sustained use of such punning words in identical or related contexts, as exemplified in the following verse from a different scene in the battle cantos:

XIV.28. Some (of Śiva's troops)
stood leaning on their strung bows
as they would on worthy friends
who are noble and steadfast
because of their birth in the best of families,
(in the case of the bows, "from the best cane" <*vaṃśa*>),
and whose strength is tried and true
from long acquaintance.

Here, as in the verses on Arjuna's arms, the words *guru*, *sthira* and *guṇa* apply to both bows and friends.[49]

---

[49] See also XVII.29 (*ṛjutāguṇa*) and XIII.33 (*gurutvāt*).

In the *Kirātārjunīya*, the likening of weapons to a warrior's attributes is as frequent as the conception of arms as friends, as can be seen in the following examples, also drawn from turning points in the combat: The first verse rounds off a long sequence of connected verses which depict the first impression Śiva's troops get of Arjuna; the second marks the point in the combat where Arjuna, having lost his bow and arrow, reaches for his sword.

XIV.37. (Śiva's troops beheld Arjuna)
leaning on his bow, his means
for overcoming hostile forces,
as if on his inflexible courage,
adhering to his true nature (courtesy),
and yet invincible, like the ocean
unmoving without a breath of wind.[50]

XVII.55. Then he grasped as his last resort
a man's ultimate means for achieving his goals,
that which is invincible by enemies,
that treasure-house of war-might,
the mighty sword,
as though it were his pride embodied.[51]

In other verses, Arjuna's arrows are compared to political strategies (*upāya*; XIV.52), or to his heroic energy (*utsāha*; XIV.57), while the weapons of his opponents in battle are likened to the fruit of action (*kriyāphala*) nullified by time and fate (*kāla*, *kṛtānta*; XIV.51 and XVI.29). When Arjuna discharges the serpent-missile at Śiva, he wards it off with his Garuḍa missile, just as a king counters the divisive tactics of his enemy with *naya* (political strategy; XVI.42). In canto XVII, Śiva's attempts to parry Arjuna's arrows are compared, in technical terms, to the tactics of a general in battle.[52]

As embodiments of heroic qualities, a warrior's weapons symbolize his identity. This is why Arjuna cannot abandon his weapons even during his penance; having undertaken penance in order to destroy his enemies, in accordance with his *dharma* as a warrior, he must continue to bear the symbols of his identity as a warrior, preserving his heroic persona even in the context of asceticism. The enigma of the warrior-ascetic is solved in the multiple identifications in the combat cantos.

---

[50] "As if on his inflexible courage": "dhairya iva anapāyini".
[51] "As though it were his pride embodied": "sākṣād ahaṃkāram iva".
[52] XVII.27.

The imagery of arms in the combat scenes in the *Kirātārjunīya* covers the entire domain of conflict, kingship, and heroic conduct. In these contexts the description of heroic action turns into a philosophical contemplation and a psychological exploration of the nature of heroism itself. When the hero's arms are humanized, the focus is on the emotional bases of the heroic; when weapons are likened to combat tactics and aspects of heroic action, the focus is on the metaphysical implications of the action. In the latter case in particular, the description becomes reflexive; action is compared to the thoughts and feelings which motivate it, that is, action is, in a sense, compared to itself. A sustained abstraction and intellectualization of action is the hallmark of Bhāravi's battle description; in sheer scope and consistency, there is nothing comparable in *kāvya* battle description before him. It is perhaps this quality that made F.W. Thomas remark that, in Bhāravi we have" . . . a hard-thinking poet, in whom we feel at work a certain intension of will".[53] Whether this is indeed the essence of Bhāravi's style is hard to tell, since we do not have any other works by him. But this much we can say with certainty: the poet's unique descriptive style is well suited to his heroic and philosophical theme, and makes the *Kirātārjunīya* a genuine study in the heroic mood.

Cosmic Imagery in the Battle Scenes in the Kirātārjunīya

It is not surprising that the Sanskrit poets speak of war, and the general devastation brought about by war, in terms of cosmic dissolution. As I noted earlier, reference to the cosmic gods of the Hindu triad (Śiva, Viṣṇu and Brahmā), and images connected with cosmic dissolution and recreation (*pralaya*) are common in battle descriptions in the *Mahābhārata*. Madeleine Biardeau and Alf Hiltebeitel have shown that the imagery of *pralaya* (the dissolution at the end of a cycle of cosmic time) has a special significance in the case of the Bhārata war, which not only *resembles* the end of a Yuga, (a cosmic Age), but marks the actual end of one: "the *Mahābhārata*, which tells about the end of the yuga previous to our and involves an *avatāra* <Krishna>, incorporates a variety of rich and perhaps very ancient, eschatological symbolism".[54] Hiltebeitel

[53] F.W. Thomas. Review of Carl Cappeller's German translation of the *Kirātārjunīya* (Harvard Oriental Series 15,1912). In *Journal of the Royal Asiatic Society* (1917: 869–77), p. 870.

[54] Alf Hiltebeitel, *The Ritual of Battle: Krishna in the Mahābhārata* (Ithaca: Cornell University Press, 1976), p. 299. Hiltebeitel discusses this eschatological symbolism with reference to Madeleine Biardeau's work, in Chapter 12 of *The Ritual of Battle*. On p. 310,

has also shown that, in especially "charged" situations in the *Mahābhārata*, such as the death of Karṇa,[55] or the chief episode in the Sauptika Parvan where the warrior Aśvatthāman, possessed by Śiva, raids the sleeping camp of the Pāṇḍavas, rendering death and destruction on a mass scale,[56] the cosmic imagery functions as a coherent symbol system, referring to "background myths", such as the destruction of the three cosmic "cities" of the demons (*tripura*) by Śiva.[57] In such scenes, the comparison of warriors with Śiva, or with Antaka (or Yama, god of Death) has precise cosmic and mythic nuances. In the *Kirātārjunīya*, Bhāravi makes sparing use of cosmic imagery in the conventional manner,[58] but the evocation, in specific mythological and imagistic detail, of Śiva as Destroyer, or Viṣṇu in one of his cosmic incarnations, is reserved for significant moments in the psychological development of the plot, and is presented with a controlled elegance.

When Śiva, disguised as a *kirāta*, arrives on the scene of the boar's attack on Arjuna, this is how he sees the hero, who is poised to shoot an arrow at the beast:

XIII.17. Śiva beheld him with wonder,
as he stood with bow drawn taut
in a full circle,
as if he were Śiva himself,
terrifying his enemies
as he stood poised
to destroy the three cities.

Here Śiva sees Arjuna as imbued with his own qualities as the destroyer, epitomized in the image of himself as the Destroyer of the three cosmic cities or citadels of the demons, in the most celebrated myth of cosmic destruction involving Śiva. Several levels of meaning are suggested. In his aspect as the warrior who destroys his enemies, Arjuna is identified with Śiva, the divine Destroyer. In the specific context of the *kirāta* tale,

---

Hiltebeitel notes that, of the three types of cosmic dissolution (on different scales of cosmic time) which the Puranas describe, the *Mahābhārata* imagery is concerned with the *naimittikapralaya* or "the occasional reabsorption", related to the *yuga* cycle. For specific references and further discussion, see Hiltebeitel, 1984 ("The Two Kṛṣṇas on One Chariot. . ."), especially p. 7. on p. 310.

[55] Hiltebeitel, 184, "The Two Kṛṣṇas. . ."

[56] Hiltebeitel, 1976, Chapter 12.

[57] Ibid. Chapters 6 and 12. For the myth of the Destruction of the three cities, see Wendy D. O'Flaherty, *Hindu Myths* (Penguin, 1975), pp. 125–137.

[58] E.g., In XIV.50, Arjuna is compared to "the end of the *kalpa*" (the time of dissolution itself).

the very purpose of the hero's encounter with *kirāta*-Śiva is the ultimate destruction of his enemies in the Bhārata war. Through this encounter, Arjuna is to receive the boon of the Pāśupata, Raudra (or Brahmaśiras) weapon, which is, as its names indicate, the embodiment of the destructive aspect of Śiva himself, as well as a representation of the cosmic role of Brahmā in conjunction with Śiva as depicted in the myth of the three cities.[59] In his persona as Nara, the human counterpart of Viṣṇu-Nārāyaṇa, Arjuna himself forms the third member of the triad of gods who participate in the cosmic process. Several pointed references are made, both in the *Mahābhārata* episode and in the *Kirātārjunīya*, to Arjuna's identity as Nara of the Nara-Nārāyaṇa pair, which, embodied in the partnership of Krishna and Arjuna, directs and effects the action of the *Mahābhārata* war.[60] Thus, in this image of the Great God seeing "himself" in the warrior, Bhāravi brings together several strands of the meaning of the *kirāta* story: the cosmic implications of Arjuna's endeavor, the terrible destruction to come, and the complex relationship between Śiva and the hero.

Yet other themes are brought into play in a sequence of images in which Arjuna is portrayed as he appears to Śiva's troops when they come upon him standing over the carcass of the giant boar which he has slain with his arrow.

(The *gaṇas* saw Arjuna)
XIV.38. Endowed with the splendor
of the god of Death,
because he had slain the boar
which lay at his feet,
Like Paśupati, Lord of the Beasts,
standing over the victim (*paśu*)
placed before him
by priests who have invited him
to the sacrifice, . . .

40. Broad-necked,
with the shoulders of a mighty bull
and a chest massive as a stone wall,

---

[59] *Raudra*: "the terrific", connected with Śiva as Rudra; *Pāśupata*: "related to Śiva as Paśupati, Lord of Beasts (and god who dismembers the sacrificial victim <paśu>?)"; *Brahmaśiras*: "The Head of Brahmā". In the triple ciy myth, Brahmā is Śiva's charioteer. On the significance of Brahmā's role, see Hiltebeitel, 1984, pp. 15–26.

[60] *Mahābhārata* III.37.29, II.41.1, 2, 3. *Kirātārjunīya* VI.19, XII.33 and 35, and XIV.41. See discussion below.

Looking like the Great Cosmic Boar
about to lift up overburdened Earth
out of the great ocean, . . .

41. Dark as an emerald, with a noble figure,
surpassing all creatures in splendor,
Like the Primal Person
manifest in human form
like the sun mirrored in water. . . .

In XIV.38, a concrete object in the scene, the carcass of the demonic boar, becomes the pivotal point of the cosmic imagery, allowing the stereotyped likening of the warrior to the god of Death to unfold into a foreshadowing of Arjuna's role as agent of destruction in the Bhārata war. The comparison with Paśupati, Śiva as Lord of the Beasts, suggests the terrible Pāśupata weapon, the multiform of Rudra-Paśupati, which is Arjuna's goal: In the *Mahābhārata kirāta* narrative, Arjuna begs Śiva to give him ". . . that divine weapon, the dreadful Pāśupata weapon, my lord, which is called Brahmā's Head, gruesome, of terrible power, which at the horrible end of the eon will destroy the entire world. With it I may burn down in battle the Dānavas and the Rākṣasas, the evil spirits and Piśācas, Gandharvas, and Snakes".[61] Arjuna himself, standing over the slain boar with drawn bow, is Rudra-Paśupati standing over the animal victim at the sacrifice, suggesting that the war itself is a great sacrifice, a ritual for the performance of which the war-hero has been consecrated and readied.[62] I have by no means exhausted the meaning of this vivid and complex image, but have noted only those suggestions which seem relevant here.

A similar process is at work in XIV.40, where Arjuna is compared to the Mahāvarāha, Viṣṇu in his incarnation as the Great Boar, rescuing the Earth from the flooded ocean, in which she has been hidden by the demon who has stolen her.[63] The actual presence of the demonic boar,

---

[61] J.A.B. van Buitenen, 1975, p. 302.

[62] On the identity of Arjuna, Paśupati, and the sacrificial victim in the *Mahābhārata kirāta* episode, see Biardeau, EMH(V), 1978, pp. 150–151. On Arjuna's encounter with Śiva as *dīkṣā* (consecration for sacrifice) for *ātma-yajña* (sacrifice of oneself as the victim), see Ibid., 149, and 155 ff. Alf Hiltebeitel sheds further light on the implications of Arjuna's identification with Śiva through his encounter with Śiva in the *Mahābhārata*, in: "Śiva, the Goddess, and the Disguises of the Pāṇḍavas and Draupadī", *History of Religions*, Volume 20.1 and 2 (1980:147–174).

[63] On the myth of Viṣṇu's incarnation as the Cosmic Boar, see O'Flaherty, 1975, pp. 184–197. On the symbolism of the boar as the Yajñavarāha (The Boar as the Vedic Sacrifice), see Biardeau, EMH (V), p. 151.

the anti-hero, no doubt suggested to the poet its converse, the Cosmic Boar as the redeemer of Dharma at the end of the eon. The description of the Earth as "overburdened" refers to the oppression of the earth by evil beings such as the demon Mūka. Arjuna's act of slaying the boar is thus established as a prelude to his great heroic acts in the Bhārata war, as an incarnation who rids the earth of evil oppressors and restores *Dharma*.

The suggestion of Arjuna's identity as an incarnation is fleshed out in the last verse, where he is directly described as "the Primal Person manifest in human form". This could refer only to Arjuna's being Nara, the human counterpart of the Primal Person, Puruṣa, who is also Nārāyaṇa.[64] Both in the *Mahābhārata* and in the *Kirātārjunīya*, Śiva explains the appropriateness of Arjuna's deeds in this episode by revealing that Arjuna is Nara, the primal hermit-warrior who, along with Nārāyaṇa, performed penance for thousands of years in the Badarī hermitage prior to taking up arms in order to save the oppressed earth from the forces of evil.[65]

The effect of such images as the ones discussed above is to reveal the hero's divine aspect, and the cosmic significance of his actions. The exaltation of the hero is one of the strategies whereby the heroic mood is developed in a *kāvya* work; the exaltation of Arjuna is certainly beneficial to the realization of the *vīra rasa* in the final segment of Bhāravi's poem, but its effect on the final scene of revelation can be understood only by studying the specific details and nuances of the poet's portrayal of the hero's encounter with the god.

V *Points of View: Ignorance and Knowledge in the Kirātārjunīya*

Some of the details in which Bhāravi's account of the *kirāta*-Arjuna encounter diverges from the *Mahābhārata* seem to be motivated by considerations of purity of mood and the interests of *kāvya* conventions. I believe this to be the case with the absence of the Goddess Umā (Pārvatī) from the final segment of Bhāravi's poem. In the *Mahābhārata*, the Goddess, also dressed as a huntress (*kirātī*), accompanies *kirāta*-Śiva to the scene of the combat, and participates in the divine revelation which Arjuna experiences; as we shall see below, Umā has an even more important role in some folk versions of the tale. Madeleine Biardeau

---

[64] On Nara-Nārāyana in the *Mahābhārata*, see Ibid., p. 161; Scheuer, 1982, pp. 240–44; and Hiltebeitel, 1984, p. 6.

[65] *Kirātārjunīya* XII.35. "This man (Arjuna-Nara) and Acyuta (Krishna) have come down to earth at the behest of lotus-born Brahmā, and live among men in order to protect the world from being destroyed by demons (*asuras*)".

suggests that the hunter-garb of the Goddess in the *Mahābhārata* episode indicates that she is appearing in her persona as the war-goddess, Durgā.[66] Why did Bhāravi omit the lady from his account? It seems to me that he might have considered the presence of women—even though the woman be the Goddess herself—to be an intrusion of the erotic on the heroic *rasa* at an inappropriate part of the tale. My conclusion is supported by two related facts: Pārvatī and Śiva appear in full glory as the divine couple in the poet's description of the Himalaya in Canto V; and Bhāravi's decision to provide the *kirāta* with an army of *gaṇa*s disguised as hunters, instead of the horde of *kirāta* women who accompany him in the older epic, must have been based on similar considerations. There are a number of points in which Bhāravi's inventions and general approach to the final combat serve to highlight the unique nature and circumstances of the *kirāta*-Arjuna combat.

An overview of the battle scenes leading upto the final combat in Bhāravi's poem reveals that, even though the poet seeks to establish Arjuna as the ideal warrior-hero, and his encounter with Śiva as the perfect situation for the manifestation of the heroic mood, the structure and tone of these scenes introduce other feeling-complexes into the action. For one thing, Bhāravi emphasizes the unreality of the combat in a far more pronounced fashion then the older epic. We have seen that the large-scale battles and the combat with supernatural weapons in the *Kirātārjunīya* have no counterparts in the *Mahābhārata* episode. Apart from using these additions as occasions to compose fine descriptive verses on spectacular topics, Bhāravi puts them to good use in underlining the superhuman and illusory quality of the combat. We are struck by the absence of the carnage which characterized the real-life battles of the *Mahābhārata*. What might be called the main attributes of human, down-to-earth battle are relegated to the position of becoming the subject of a wistful, hortatory speech made by the general of Śiva's army, when the troops flee in the face of Arjuna's valor. As if to stress the hypothetical character of the scenes portrayed in this canto, the speech is couched in verses of the *citra-kavya* type, in which the reader's attention is focused on verbal and visual riddles, puzzles and patterns, and nuances of meaning are of incidental interest.[67] The only person to mention and describe a bloody battle is Arjuna, but his speech turns out to be a parody of epic battle description, for he wonders *why* physical injury and bloodshed of the sort one would expect are not occurring in a battle of this mag-

---

[66] Biardeau, EMH (V), 1978, p. 159.

[67] See, for example, *Kirātārjunīya* XV.10, 12, 14.

nitude![68] Finally, the extravagantly beautiful images in the fight with supernatural weapons—of skies crimsoned by the fire born from Arjuna's missile, and covered by golden-winged Garuḍa birds created by Śiva's *astra*—also serve to highlight the unreal, illusotry nature of the battle. The wonderful (*adbhuta*) *rasa* created in these passages, a *rasa* which enhances and nourishes the development of other *rasas*, both here and elsewhere in the *Kirātārjunīya*,[69] is also clearly an important component of scenes and situations of divine revelation, such as the one with which this epic ends. Here, perhaps, is one of Bhāravi's bridges between the heroic and the devotional points of view. Throughout the action, Arjuna plunges into combat with a vigor, sincerity and manly courage (*vīrya*) which make the "hair stand on end" for the many human and celestial spectators, even for "sages who know the true nature of things" (and, therefore, must know that Śiva intends only to test the hero, not harm him).[70] Arjuna's heroism is in no way called into question by the understanding that this is not really a fight between equals, nor a fight unto death. Bhāravi makes it clear that the combat is simultaneously a *genuine* test of Arjuna's valor, *and* an instances of *līlā*, divine sport, on Śiva's part; he ensures this double vision for his reader by strictly and carefully controlling the perspectives from which both actors and audience view the events of the combat. In Bhāravi as well as in the epic episode, the power of Śiva's revelation depends on the delicate balance of ignorance and knowledge on the part of Arjuna, Śiva, and the audience.

In the *Mahābhārata*, right from the beginning of the episode we know—through the seer Vyāsa's speech to Yudhisṭhira—that Arjuna will receive celestial weapons from Śiva, Indra and the other *lokapāla* gods. By contrast, Bhāravi keeps Śiva's role concealed both from Arjuna and the reader till the end of the XIth canto, where, after Arjuna has ably responded to the god's challenge, Indra commands Arjuna to perform penance in order to propitiate Śiva. In the *Mahābhārata*, when the Himalayan ascetics, disturbed by the great heat generated by Arjuna's intense asceticism, approach Śiva for help, the god merely assures them that he knows Arjuna's purpose, and will help him accomplish it. In the XIIth canto of the *Kirātārjunīya*, Bhāravi uses the same context to reveal the divine plan in its entirety to the reader: Śiva gives the sages a

---

[68] *Kirātārjunīya* XVI. 1–16.

[69] For instance, *adbhuta* enhances *śānta* and *vīra* in Cantos VI and XII, and *śṛṅgāra* in Canto V.

[70] Śiva has invited the Himalayan sages to witness Arjuna's heroic deeds. These ascetics are rather like sage-narrators of the *Mahābhārata*, whose thirst for heroic tales seems to be boundless.

detailed account of Arjuna's divine identity as the warrior-ascetic Nara, and foretells the precise manner in which he, Śiva, will test the hero's courage, using the boar as a pretext.[71] He ends his speech by inviting the sages to come and watch Arjuna's heroism manifest itself in combat with the god in disguise. The seers, the gods, and the reader become knowing witnesses to the events which follow, culminating in the boon of the knowledge of the Pāśupata and other weapons.

In the older epic, the hero fights with sincerity because he does not know that he is fighting with God; it is precisely this sincerity which pleases Śiva, and compels him to reveal his identity. The *Mahābhārata* is well aware of the importance of Arjuna's ignorance; but Bhāravi goes to great lengths to preserve it till the very end of the combat, reshaping even minor details to suit his purpose. For instance, Bhāravi changes the content of a brief sequence in the *Mahābhārata*, in which Arjuna wonders whether his opponent might be Rudra; in Bhāravi's version, the hero does suspect that his opponent is a superhuman entity, but no mention is made of Rudra.[72] Bhāravi's careful use of epithets for Śiva during the combat sequences is equally illuminating, for here his purpose is to pit Arjuna's ignorance against his own, and the reader's, knowledge of Śiva's identity. While the *Mahābhārata* text refers to the god both by the standard names and epithets of Śiva (e.g., Mahādēva, III.40., v.49), and by reference to his identity as a *kirāta* (verses 45, 47), Bhāravi refers to Śiva exclusively in his divine persona, as "the Lord" (Īśvara, XVII.22), Śaṃbhu (XVII.27, 51), Śiva (XVIII.3), Smarāri (XVII.30), and so on. From the XVth canto onwards, there are only three verses where Śiva is called "the *kirāta*". Significantly, these are the only three verses in which we see *kirāta*-Śiva *through Arjuna's eyes*: XVI.1 and 18 mark the beginning and the end of Arjuna's speculation about the unreal nature of his combat with the *kirāta*. In XVII.25 the hero views with misgiving the "*kirāta* chieftain" advancing towards him, "twanging his bow to the left and right, as a mahout who has lost control over a wild elephant would view the beast as it advances, flapping his ears in alternation". We are to understand that, to the hero, his opponent is never anything other than an arrogant mountain man, albeit one with superhuman powers, while, to us, the knowing witnesses, the "*kirāta*" is always Śiva, the Lord.

---

[71] *Kirātārjunīya* XII.33–39.

[72] *Mahābhārata* III.40.28–31. *Kirātārjunīya* XVI.19–25. Arjuna ends his speculation with a reference to Śiva as "this savage, battle-crazed fellow"!

What of the perspective of Śiva, who is the director of the drama, as well as one of its principal actors? As if Śiva's omniscient speech in the XIIth canto were not enough, at every stage in the combat, Bhāravi makes us privy to Śiva's intentions and his reactions to Arjuna's deeds. In this he departs quite radically from the *Mahābhārata* account of the combat, which we see primarily from the point of view of the bewildered Arjuna. In these contexts, Śiva is portrayed quite unambiguously as the gracious God of the *bhakti* tradition. We should recall that Śiva's plan is to demonstrate to the world Arjuna's "unparalleled, innate (physical) strength" (XII.39 "sattvavihitam atulam bhujayor balam"). In accordance with this intention, throughout the combat Śiva takes measures to protect the hero from genuine physical injury, as in XIV.48:

> Wishing to show that his opponent's valor
> was quite invincible,
> Śiva shot a harmless arrow
> at the mighty warrior
> who stood parrying hundreds of arrows. . . .

At the end of the XVth canto we are reminded that Arjuna's valor is both genuine and a function of Śiva's grace:

> XV.53. As they watched the valiant deeds
> of splendid prince Arjuna,
> which were thus displayed by Śiva
> even sages who know the true nature of things
> were thrilled, and felt the hair on their limbs
> stand up on end.

Śiva himself receives the fiercest of Arjuna's assaults with supreme indulgence, love, and delight. Two verses in Canto XVII reveal Śiva's feelings at the height of the combat:

> XVII.13. The Lord of the *gaṇas*
> experienced great delight
> at his extreme heroism,
> just as the Himalaya mountain
> welcomes the unbearably powerful thrusts
> of Indra's elephant
> when it rams its tusks against its slopes.

> XVII.14 Then he endured defeat for a long time,
> though he is himself
> the origin of all origins;

it was as though he wished to extend to the hero,
in the form of mighty deeds,
an arm fit for bearing all his burdens.

The above verses are followed by Śiva's reflections on the absolute inner necessity of a hero to prove himself in combat; the vignette ends with the god's resolve to further engage Arjuna in furious battle, in which neither opponent would have a clear advantage—all in the cause of Arjuna's glory, which is here likened to the white crescent moon on Śiva's own head.

XVII.18. Wishing to create, among the hero's enemies,
a reputation for him
white as the streak of moon on his own head,
Śaṃbhu proceeded to engage
in a systematic pattern of combat,
in which each experienced
victory and defeat by turns.

In the next stage of the combat, Arjuna unwittingly experience the effect of Śiva's love.

XVII.33. The hermit found Śiva's arrows delightful,
like the kind counsel of good friends,
for they were sent with his welfare in mind,
and did not wound him
in any critical spot.

At the end of this canto Arjuna has been stripped of all his weapons, including his bow, and has resorted to rocks and treetrunks in his efforts to ward off his opponent. The loss of weapons implies the ultimate crisis of identity for the hero. Finally, in despair, he strikes at Śiva's chest, which is like "a golden rock", with his bare fists. The final verse in the canto likens Śiva's reaction to an indulgent father's response to the childish anger of an only son:

XVII.64. As a father indulges even rude acts
on the part of his dear son,
an only child who has climbed up on his lap,
so Smara's enemy endured
even the impertinence of the Pāṇḍava,
who had come to him seeking a warrior's prowess,
a means to fame and royal glory
beyond the reach of his foes.

This verse reminds us of the imagery of early (5th–6th centuries A.D.) Tamil Śaivite *bhakti* hymns, in which the saints call out to Śiva as the loving father who forgives their transgressions.[73] In the context of the *Mahābhārata* narrative, there is also an implied contrast between the paternal pride Indra feels in Arjuna's valor when he passes Indra's test with flying colors (*Kirātārjunīya*, cantos VI and XI), and Śiva's fatherly pride. Indra is, after all, Arjuna's natural father, and though he is himself a god, his feeling for the hero is of a mundane order. Śiva, on the other hand, is the *bhakti* God who loves his devotee like a son.

In Bhāravi's poem, as in the *Mahābhārata*, the climax of Arjuna's heroic activity prompts, and coincides with, the complete revelation of Śiva's love for Arjuna as his devotee. The moment is captured in three verses early in the XVIIIth canto.

XVIII.12. When the Conqueror of the Three Cities
took a flying leap into the sky,
Arjuna of the monkey-banner
swiftly leaped up after him,
depressing the earth with his feet,
and seized the god's feet in mid-air.

XVIII.13. Astonished by that deed,
the Highest person, Ender of all deeds,
at once gathered into his arms the peerless hero,
who was about to throw him on the ground,
and pressed him to his chest
in a tight embrace.

XVIII.14. Not with his penance was the Lord as pleased
as with his boundless courage.
How much more valuable is inborn courage
to a good man
than a host of learned virtues!

The significance of Arjuna's gesture in the first verse is obvious: by grasping the Lord's feet (*caraṇagrahaṇa*), Arjuna unwittingly assumes the position of the devotee or suppliant who has taken refuge (*śaraṇāgata*,) in the Lord. In the theology of *bhakti* devotion, God, by definition, bestows his grace upon any devotee who seeks him as his sole refuge.[74] In

---

[73] E.g., *Tirumuṟai* XI (South Indian Saiva Siddhanta Works Publishing Society Edition), *Aṟputat Tiruvantāti*, 70; and Appar, *Tēvāram*, IV.15.11.

[74] Krishna teaches Arjuna the doctrine of refuge in the *Bhagavad Gītā*. See especially *Gītā* XVIII.62–66.

Arjuna's case it is clear that the gesture of taking refuge, though unconscious, is a genuine one, since it is the culmination of a steadfast vow of *yoga* and penance directed towards Śiva, as well as of resolute action according to his own *dharma* (*sva-dharma*), both of which are pleasing to God. Here is a *bhakti* tableau which causes the Lord himself to react with wonder (*vismaya*); the impact of Arjuna's act is captured in verse 13, which begins with the word "*vismita*", and is marked by a sudden change of meter.[75] In verse 14, it is revealed that Arjuna's heroism in combat is the direct cause of the Lord's pleasure, confirming the equation of battle with *dharma* and *yoga* for a *kṣatriya*. It is only with this fact firmly in mind that we are allowed to witness the moment in which Śiva reveals his true identity to Arjuna, who immediately bows to him in worship. At the same time, the hero sees himself fully restored to his former glory, with all his weapons intact, affirming the fact that his *innate* heroic splendor has never been in serious danger of being diminished; it is his turn to display wonder (*vismaya*).[76]

In the presence of the celestial beings (including the *lokapāla* gods) who have arrived on the scene, Arjuna sings a rich hymn of praise (*stotra*), in which he describes Śiva as the supreme Deity (XVIII.21–41). He ends the *stotra* with two verses expressing his own concerns and wishes. The first of these is a plea for forgiveness:

XVIII.42. O Lord of all Knowledge,
Please forgive this misdeed
which I have committed in ignorance!
For you are the sole refuge,
even for wicked men
who seek shelter with you,
having opposed you when they were deluded.[77]

In the next verse, Arjuna asks for the means for victory in battle, the ultimate goal (*kārya*) of his penance. Śiva and the World-guardians grant him the Pāśupata and other weapons. Towering over the world, ablaze with the double splendor of asceticism and war-might, and commanded

[75] The verse begins thus: "*vismitaḥ* sapadi tena karmaṇā. . . ." The use of a single meter as the carrying meter in a canto is the standard practice in *mahākāvya*. Kālidāsa, Bhāravi, and poets after them do have one or more cantos in which they use a variety of meters, as does Bhāravi in the final canto of his epic, immediately following the scene of Śiva's revelation. However, it is unusual for a poet to sustain a meter for thirteen verses, and then suddenly change to a plethora of meters, as Bhāravi does here.

[76] *Vismaya* is the *sthāyibhava* (stable emotion) of the marvelous (*adbhuta*) *rasa*.

[77] "upāyayau *vismayam*", XVIII.16.

by Śiva to go and conquer his enemies, Arjuna returns to his family in the forest (XVIII.47 and 48).

VI *Climax: The Moment of Revelation in the Kirātārjunīya and other Versions of the Kirāta Tale*

The precise nuances of the *rasa-bhakti* configuration in the *Kirātārjunīya* are thrown into relief when we compare Bhāravi's treatment of the moment of Śiva's revelation with other accounts of this situation in the *kirāta* tale. In the *Mahābhārata* text according to the Critical Edition, when Arjuna is forced to engage in the wrestling bout with Śiva, he rapidly loses strength. The Lord crushes and mangles his body, till the hero is rendered unconscious, and his body looks like a ball of flesh (*piṇḍa*).

> The Great God got a good grip on Arjuna and assaulted him mightily and furiously, *stunning him out of his wits*. And so, Phalguna, *looking like a ball of flesh* with his limbs mangled by the God of Gods, O Bhārata, *lost control of his body*. Subdued by the great-spirited God, his breathing stopped and *he fell down unconscious*. And Bhava was pleased.
>
> The Blessed Lord said:
>
> *Bhoḥ*, *bhoḥ*, Phalguna, *I am pleased with your gallantry and endurance*. There is no baron <*kṣatriya*> like you! *Your splendor and mine, and our might, have been matched* (*samam*) *today*, prince sans blame. I am pleased with you, strong-armed bull among men, set eyes on me! I shall give you eyesight, wide-eyed hero![78]

In the above account, as in Bhāravi's, Śiva responds specifically to Arjuna's *heroism*, rather than to any devotional acts, including his penance itself. In the *Mahābhārata* he explicitly identifies the source of his pleasure as Arjuna's "gallantry and endurance" (*vīryeṇānena dhṛtyā ca*), and declares that Arjuna is the ideal warrior-hero, a prince whose heroism in the *kirāta* combat has rendered him equal to Śiva himself in splendor and might (*tejas* and *vīryam*). By undergoing the test of heroism, by persevering in the face of the loss of all his own weapons, Arjuna has become qualified to receive Śiva's mighty weapon of destruction. In spirit, Bhāravi's interpretation is very close to the older epic on these points. Why, then, does he change the details of the specific act which triggers Śiva's revelation? It seems to me that the *kāvya* poet's interpretation of the event is different from the *Mahābhārata*'s in a subtle, but

---

[78] J.A.B. van Buitenen, 1975, P. 301. Biardeau, 1978, and Scheuer, 1982, see the reduction of Arjuna to a *piṇḍa* (embryo)-like state as an integral part of the initiatory and sacrificial symbolism of this episode in the *Mahābhārata*. Scheuer, pp. 232–7, and Biardeau, p. 150–1.

significant way. The *Mahābhārata* hero is reduced almost to a ball of flesh, stunned out of his wits, deprived of bodily control and consciousness; in short, he is *subdued*, if not soundly *defeated*, in combat by *kirāta*-Śiva. Bhāravi's Arjuna, on the other hand, is not only fully conscious at this critical moment, but also tireless, uninjured and vigorous; he has *all but* gained the upper hand in the battle, for, having seized his opponent by the feet, he is about to dash him to the ground. In terms of combat, the near-devotional gesture of foot-grasping actually signifies a *potential* victory for the hero; it is only after this moment that Śiva reveals himself, and Arjuna is allowed to assume a thoroughly devotional attitude. As the archetype of the invincible hero, Arjuna is not allowed to be defeated, even though his opponent is Śiva himself.

The text of the Critical Edition is not entirely representative of the treatment of the critical moment in the *Kirāta* episode in the *Mahābhārata* tradition, for the editors have rejected some explicitly devotional material found in several important groups of *Mahābhārata* manuscripts.[79] At the point in the narrative, at which Arjuna becomes unconscious, these manuscripts contain a passage describing Arjuna worshipping Śiva. In these versions, the hero lies unconscious for a short while (*muhūrtaṁ*), then, regaining consciousness, quickly makes a *sthaṇḍila*, an altar of earth, at which he offers ritual worship to Śiva.[80] When in the course of his worship the hero places a garland of flowers on the *sthaṇḍila*, he finds that the flowers are miraculously transferred to the *kirāta*'s head, revealing that the *kirāta* is none other than the Great God himself.

Whatever be the truth concerning the textual authenticity of the above-described sequence, it is clear that to include it would mean altering the flavor of the passage considerably. In this case, an act of conventional and ritual devotion is interposed between the warrior's heroism in combat with the god, and the god's revelation of his identity; Śiva's response is not as immediately related to Arjuna's "gallantry and endurance" as in the Critical Edition or the *Kirātārjunīya*. This version of the sequence appears to be an effort to make Arjuna's deeds more compatible with the behavior of the ideal *bhakta* (devotee), and to subsume the climax of the episode under a type of plot common in the later accounts of divine revelation in the lives of *bhakti* saints, particularly

---

[79] These include manuscripts from the North-western, Central and Southern recensions of the *Mahābhārata*. See Critical Edition, critical apparatus under III.40.51.

[80] In early texts, a *sthaṇḍila* is supposed to signify an altar made of earth. The later tradition assumes that Arjuna worshipped a *linga*. See below.

as found in the South Indian tradition.[81] The result, however, is not particularly convincing, since the purpose of the *kirāta* episode is to test Arjuna's commitment to his heroic cause and way of life, whereas even the most dramatic of the tests of saints such as the sixty-three Nāyaṉārs of the Tamil tradition, are intended to test their fanatic devotion to Śiva, especially as revealed in their commitment to the ritual worship of Śiva or his devotees. This is vividly illustrated in the case of the hunter-saint Kaṇṇappar, who plucked out his own eyes and offered them to the image of Śiva when the latter made his eyes bleed in order to test the saint's devotion. Few of the *bhakti* saints direct their acts *against* Śiva, even unwittingly, as Arjuna does, and all their actions are motivated by a complete, exclusive, almost fanatical devotional love for Śiva.[82] And yet, while Arjuna does not fall under the category of the *bhakti* saint, neither is he typical of the antinomian *bhakta*,[83] the reformed sinner of his own description: "the wicked man" who, "having opposed Śiva when he was deluded" (*mohād virodhya*; in *Kirātārjunīya* XVIII.42, quoted above), ultimately turns to him for refuge. Far from being the product of arrogance or mundane delusion, his temporary clash with Śiva is a positive instance of divine *līlā*, desired and brought about by the Lord himself. The *kirāta* story is far more powerful as a tale of heroism, *līlā* and grace, without the intrusion of ritual devotion at the climactic moment. The folk versions of the *kirāta* story endorse this judgment, demonstrating that the heroic elements of the narrative, which are so prominent in Bhāravi's version, are indeed the very soul of this tale.

The Kirāta Tale in South Indian Art and Literature

In an essay published in the *Journal of the Indian Society for Oriental Art*, T.N. Ramachandran suggested that Bhāravi's poetic description of the *kirāta*-Arjuna episode was the inspiration for the many sculptural depic-

---

[81] Such as the lives of the sixty-three Śaivite Nāyaṉārs, retold in the Tamil *Periya Purāṇam* of Cēkkiḻār (12th century).

[82] For a summary of the story of Kaṇṇappar and other Nāyaṉārs, see Yogi Suddhananda Bharati, *The Grand Epic of Śaivism* (Madras: The South India Saiva Siddhanta Works, 1970). I have discussed the significance of some of these revelatory scenes in my *Poems to Śiva*. Among the Tamil Śaivite narratives, the *kirāta* story is closest to the "conversion" of Cuntaramūrtti, who quarreled with Śiva, who tested him in the guise of an old man, and ultimately revealed himself.

[83] Such as the many demons of later Hindu devotional literature, who are redeemed by taking refuge in the Lord, even if it be for the wrong reasons. See the discussion in Wendy D. O'Flaherty, *The Origins of Evil in Hindu Mythology* (Chicago: University of Chicago Press, 1976), Chapters 4 and 5.

tions of this episode in South Indian art from the 6th century onward.[84] While it is likely that individual sculptures like the famed Arjuna's penance were directly inspired by the *Kirātārjunīya* narrative, Bhāravi's version of the tale appears to have had very little impact on the majority of sculptural representations. Nagaraja Rao has shown that many of Ramachandran's examples from the Andhra and Tamil countries appear to follow the *Mahābhārata* version of the story.[85] Even more surprising is Rao's finding that, at least in the Karnataka and Andhra areas, the sculptors diverge significantly from both Bhāravi and the *Mahābhārata* in their depiction of the narrative, especially in their portrayal of the scenes surrounding Śiva's revelation. According to Nagaraja Rao, they are based on a local, folk version of the *kirāta* tale which must have had strong currency in the Karnataka area for several centuries after Bhāravi.[86] The salient points of this version are as follows:

> Parvati, having heard that Arjuna was invincible because of an auspicious mark on his back, expressed a desire to see this mark of Arjuna. This could be done only when he was defeated and turned his back. This was impossible, as Arjuna was invincible. So Śiva thought of a plan. . . ."

Disguised as a *kirāta*, Śiva goes to Indrakīla mountain,[87] where Arjuna is performing penance; he also sends the demon Mūka to the mountain, instructing him to attack Arjuna. The *kirāta* and the hero quarrel over the boar, and begin to fight.

> During this fight, Śiva purposely *fell in such a way that Arjuna came over him*, and Pārvatī, standing behind Arjuna, could see the back of Arjuna, with broad shoulders and auspicious mark. *She then indicated to Śiva that she has seen the back and auspicious mark by raising her right hand. Thereupon Śiva revealed his true form and Arjuna begged his pardon for his ignorance and the consequent fight.* Śiva bestowed the boon of *Pāśupata* and Pārvatī, the *añjalikāstra*.[88]

According to Nagaraja Rao, a number of narrative sculptures of the story depict the following sequence of frames for the concluding events of the tale: Arjuna sits on top of Śiva at the end of the wrestling match,

---

[84] Ramachandran, 1950–51.

[85] Though the influence of Bhāravi may be detected in a few details, the emphasis is on the *Mahābhārata* version. See Nagaraja Rao, 1979, Chapter V, and plates.

[86] Ibid., Chapter V, p. 85. Consult plates and discussion concerning sculptures in the Kedāreśvara (Haḷebid), Mallikārjuna (Basarāḷu), Sirivāla Īśvara, Kaḍūr, and the Pāpanātha and Virūpākṣa (Paṭṭaḍakkal) temples in Karnataka.

[87] Nagaraja Rao, Chapter II, notes the identification of particular hills in Karnataka and Andhra Pradesh as Indrakīla. Bhāravi might have combined a local Indrakīla tradition with the Himalayan location of Arjuna's penance in the *Mahābhārata*.

[88] Ibid., p. 18.

while Pārvatī, dressed as a *kirātī*, peers at his back. Both Śiva and Pārvatī appear in the final scene, and Pārvatī is often depicted as holding an *astra*. As Rao points out, these scenes are perfectly in accordance with the folk version of the tale, while there is nothing in the *Mahābhārata* or the *Kirātārjunīya* versions to support them.[89]

The element of *līlā*, or play, is prominent in this version of the tale, and the playful relationship between Pārvatī and Sīva motivates the action here, as it does in many stories in the Puranas. However, the revelation of Arjuna's heroism clearly stands out as the central theme and goal of the narrative. After all, it is because the invincible hero will never turn his back to anyone, that Śiva has been forced to stage the fight. As the gracious *bhakti* god and goddess, Śiva and Pārvatī take equal delight in the revelation and vindication of the hero's reputation, even *if it means letting him gain the upper hand in the fight*. And here we have the fundamental difference in the climax of the tale as told in the several versions we have looked at so far. In the *Mahābhārata* version, Arjuna seems to have lost the fight when Śiva reveals himself. It is not clear which way the combat would have gone in Bhāravi's version, had Śiva not revealed himself. But here, in the folk version, Arjuna has all but overcome *kirāta*-Śiva at the moment of revelation. Arjuna is portrayed as the victor in his wrestling match with Śiva in some of the Kannada literary versions of the tale as well. In his Kannada epic *Vikramārjunavijaya* (10th c.A.D.), Pampa actually depicts Arjuna as throwing Śiva down, and attempting to throttle him, till he catches sight of Śiva's third eye, and realizes his error.[90] Nagaraja Rao suggests that there is no reason to attribute Śiva's defeat to Pampa's Jaina sectarian prejudice against the Hindu gods, since it is most likely that Pampa was simply recording a version of the *kirāta* episode which was popular in his time, and which is also reflected in the sculpture of the period.[91]

Finally, we find in the Karnataka area several literary works in Kannada dealing with the *kirāta* theme, some of which are *bhakti* poems, literary works whose primary intention is the celebration and expression of devotional religion, while the others are epics or poems with a *bhakti* tone and secretarian point of view. The most important examples of the *bhakti* tone and sectarian point of view. The most important examples of the *bhakti* genre are: the *Kirāta-līlā* portion of the *Śivatattvacintāmaṇi* of Lakkaṇṇa Daṇḍeśa (a 15th century poem) and of the *Channabasavapurāṇa*

---

[89] Besides his analysis of individual sculptures, see the Epilogue, p. 90.
[90] Ibid., p. 6.
[91] Ibid., pp. 89–90.

of the Vīraśaiva poet Virūpākṣa Paṇḍita (1585 A.D.); and the *Śabaraśaṅkaravilāsa* of another Vīraśaiva, Shaḍaksharadeva (17th century), whose work is devoted exclusively to the *kirāta* story. All these works closely follow the version of the story as found in the manuscripts of the Southern Recension of the *Mahābhārata*, adding a few details, such as the identification of the location of Arjuna's penance as Indrakīla, and the gift of a weapon (here called *añjanāstra*) from Pārvatī. In all three works, at the end of the wrestling scene, Arjuna loses strength, blood oozes from his mouth; he decides that he must have committed some sort of error in his daily worship of Śiva (the term used for "error" or "offense" is *śivāparādha*, a technical term in the South Indian Śaivite sects, signifying an offense of commission or omission, especially in ritual conduct, against Śiva). Then, as in the *Mahābhārata*, he quickly fashions a *sthaṇḍila*—according to these texts, a *liṅga* image made of earth[92]—and offers worship to it. As in the epic narrative, the flowers he offers to the *liṅga* are miraculously transferred to the *kirāta*'s head, whereupon Arjuna recognizes Śiva; when Arjuna has asked for forgiveness and praised Śiva, Śiva and Pārvatī grant him weapons.[93]

Conclusion: Rasa and Bhakti in Balance

When we recall that the Deccan/Maharashtra/Karnataka area is the region where Bhāravi must have flourished, it seems all the more remarkable that so many variants or interpretations of the *kirāta*-Arjuna story have persisted in the native land of the celebrated *kāvya* poet. The fact that Bhāravi's poem became known as a masterpiece does not seem to have induced Karnataka poets and sculptors to accept his "Kirātārjunīya" as authoritative. The Kannada poets who interpret the climactic scene according to their conception of the story as a narrative of "devotion rewarded" obviously belong to the tradition of poets who must have reworked this episode, to suit the devotional atmosphere of their times, in the Southern manuscripts of the *Mahābhārata*. At the other extreme are the local artists, who stress the heroic role of Arjuna to such an extent that he is allowed a hero's victory before he becomes the privileged recipient of Śiva's grace. Bhāravi seems to stand midway between these two groups, allowing neither combatant to achieve a decisive victory before the moment of truth.

In the final analysis, Bhāravi's approach to the climax of the *kirāta*-Arjuna combat satisfies the demands of both *rasa* and *bhakti*. In the

---

92 The *liṅga* is depicted in some sculptural representations.
93 Nagaraja Rao, Chapter I, pp. 7–13.

Kirātārjunīya rasa and *bhakti* are in a symbiotic relationship. Each needs the other for its fullest manifestation, and neither prevails at the cost of the other. As the quintessential hero and springboard for the suggestion of the *vīra rasa*, Arjuna cannot lose the fight, even in a battle which has been "staged" by God, lest the *rasa* experience be disturbed. The hero must win Śiva's grace only in the heroic idiom, by a sustained exhibition of valor. As the Great God who in effect accomplishes the hero's purpose for him, Śiva too must remain exalted, his glory undiminished even by a pretended "defeat". Seen in this light, Bhāravi's climactic scene emerges as being no less a *bhakti* tableau than the scene of Śiva's revelation in other versions of the tale. In spirit Bhāravi's vision of *bhakti* is closer, on the one hand to the *Bhagavad Gītā*, and on the other, to the folk tradition of the relationship between heroes and gods, than to traditions of "devotional" literature, for he chooses to portray the *bhakti* God as one who looks for integrity of character rather than an attitude of abject submission in his devotee. So Arjuna must grasp the Lord's feet, as a *bhakta* would, but he must be completely ignorant of the devotional implication of his gesture. Śiva, on the other hand, can and does immediately respond to this gesture in both its heroic and devotional meanings. The heroic-devotional tableau of Arjuna grasping Śiva's feet in mid-air is an apt metaphor for Bhāravi's approach to *rasa* and *bhakti* in his poem: in this visual pun the poet achieves a creative suspension of the two themes.

THE JAINA *MAHĀBHĀRATA*

B.N. SUMITRA BAI AND ROBERT J. ZYDENBOS

Jaina Mahābhāratas in Sanskrit, Prakrit and Apabhramsa
(B.N. Sumitra Bai)

1. *Early Forms*

Popular legends of ancient heroic figures like Kṛṣṇa and the Pāṇḍava-s have entered into all the three major religious-literary traditions of ancient India.[1] Thus we have Buddhist, Jaina and the widely known Brahminical versions of these legends.

The Buddhist interest in these stories seems limited to a few anecdotes which we come across in Jātaka tales,[2] and their chief aim is to preach some moral or the other. Originally, the Jainas too seem to have had a similar attitude. Their earliest existing literature, viz. the Ardhamāgadhī canon, contains stray episodes from the Kṛṣṇa–Pāṇḍava cycle of stories. Here they are centred around Ariṣṭaneminātha, the twenty-second Tīrthaṅkara. The whole of the Yādava clan and the Pāṇḍava-s are depicted here as his followers. Though we have here the earliest form of the Jaina Mahābhārata, the purpose of these stories is to illustrate some aspects of the Jaina theories of karma and metempsychosis.[3]

The Brahminical works, on the other hand, laid great stress on the stories about the Pāṇḍava-s, exploiting their narrative contents to achieve sectarian influence over the masses. Thus Vyāsa's *Mahābhārata*, its supplement the *Harivaṃśa* and other Vaiṣṇava *purāṇa-s* relied upon the popularity of the stories of Kṛṣṇa's childhood and the Pāṇḍava stories as bits of living folklore to gain immense popularity among the masses for centuries together.[4] This popularity reached its peak in the Middle Ages.[5]

---

[1] Bhandarkar 1927 and 1965, Ray Chaudhuri 1936, Barnett 1977 discuss the development of Kṛṣṇa tales into sectarian literature.

[2] Chatterjee 1940:37–40.

[3] Upadhye 1943, Introduction.

[4] Farquhar 1967:144–45 and Hazra n.d.: 109–14.

[5] Vaidya 1924:197–98.

2. *Later Jaina Harivaṃśa Literature*

It was also during the Middle Ages that Jainism reached its heyday. Especially in the southern and western parts of India long-standing patronage from various royal dynasties made it possible for Jaina authors and artists to produce great cultural achievements.[6] In this period many Jaina authors, through their religious zeal and artistic genius, enriched their literatures. The popularity of the Brahminical *Mahābhārata* and *Harivaṃśa* may have made these authors feel the need to provide the Jaina layfolk with their own versions, for we see a large number of Jaina works with Mahābhārata themes emerge from the Middle Ages onwards. These are the works which are usually referred to as "Jaina Bhārata-s" or "Jaina Harivaṃśa-s", and they show an original way of narrating the Kṛṣṇa–Pāṇḍava stories in relation to the biography of the Tīrthaṅkara Ariṣṭanemi. All the popular figures of these stories are made to fit the Jaina mythological molds of the *śalākāpuruṣa-s*, of whom Kṛṣṇa is the ninth *vāsudeva*, Balarāma the ninth *baladeva* and Jarāsandha the ninth *prativāsudeva*.[7] Along with these biographies, stories of Vasudeva, Kaṃsa, Pradyumna and others are narrated incidentally. All these characters are described as belonging to the different offshoots of one principal lineage called Harivaṃśa, named after the Vidyādhara prince Hari.[8] The Yaduvaṃśa is a major branch of this Harivaṃśa, and the stories of the Pāṇḍava-s are introduced here as they are related to this vaṃśa. Such works are called Nemināthacarita-s if they deal only with Nemịnātha's story and Harivaṃśapurāṇa-s if they describe the biographies of other *śalākāpuruṣa-s* as well. Whether they are *purāṇa-s* or *carita-s*, they are harmonious literary works, usually composed by single authors, unlike the Brahminical *purāṇa-s*. They show all the conventional features of ornate *mahākāvya-s*.

3. *The Development of Jaina Harivaṃśa Literature*

As mentioned above, the Ardhamāgadhī canon contains a good deal of this kind of narrative material, characterized by the typical didactic and

---

[6] Saletore 1938 discusses in detail the position of Jainism in India during the Middle Ages.

[7] Jaina mythology is mainly concerned with the biographies of sixty-three great men or *śalākāpuruṣa-s*. They are the 24 Tīrthaṅkara-s, the 12 *cakravartin-s*, the 9 *vāsudeva-s*, the 9 *baladeva-s* and the 9 *prativāsudeva-s*.

[8] In the Brahminical version the Yaduvaṃśa is called Harivaṃśa because Hari-Viṣṇu-Kṛṣṇa took birth in that lineage. It has in fact been a tradition in India to name a lineage after a person of historic achievements. It is strange that the Jaina authors name the lineage after someone of whom nothing is known but his name, whereas all the prominent characters like Nemi, Kṛṣṇa, Vasudeva, Baladeva etc. are just the descendents of this "Hari".

edifying outlook of the Jainas. The narrative portions dealing with Nemi and Kṛṣṇa must have led the way to the later *purāṇa* works.

(A) The *Samavāyāṅga* gives a list of fifty-four *śalākāpuruṣa-s* in which the names of Ariṣṭanemi, Kṛṣṇa and Balarāma can be found.[9] Of course Jarāsandha's name is not found here as the work does not take into account the nine *pratiśatru-s*.

(B) The *Kalpasūtra* gives the lives of four Tīrthaṅkara-s in a shortened form. Here we get a glimpse of Nemi's life: his birth, parents, renunciation, *tapas*, *nirvāṇa*, the number of his disciples etc. are mentioned here.[10]

(C) In the *Uttarādhyayanasūtra* the section titled *Rahaṇemijjam* narrates the events leading up to Nemi's renunciation (especially his compassion with the victims for the wedding feast). Rājīmati's devotion to Nemi and her retirement from worldly life also form part of the subject matter of this section. The relationship between Nemi and the Yādava-s is clearly stated in this story.[11]

(D) The *Nāyādhammakahāo*[12] relates the episode of Draupadī's previous life. Nāgaśrī offered poisoned food to a Jaina monk and thereby caused his death; as a consequence, she was born as a sickly poor woman named Sukumārikā who, not being sufficiently liked by any suitor, becomes a nun. The sight of a harlot kindles passion in her, and she develops a craving for amorous satisfaction in the next life. First she becomes a harlot of gods, then she is born as Draupadī and is married to the five Pāṇḍava-s. Padmanābha of Amarakanka robs her, instigated by Nārada, but Kṛṣṇa defeats him and returns her to the Pāṇḍava-s. After listening to the accounts of their previous lives from Ariṣṭanemi, the five Pāṇḍava-s became monks and after severe penance attained liberation. Here the relationship between Kṛṣṇa, Nemi and the Pāṇḍava-s is stated. Here we can also see an effort on the part of the Jaina authors to make the Draupadī story acceptable to their layfolk.

(E) In the *Antagaḍadasāo*[13] we find information about the destruction of Dvārakā and about the Yādava clan. On being asked by Kṛṣṇa, Nemi foretells that Dvārakā will be burnt to ashes by the anger of Dvīpāyana and that wine will be the cause of it. He also reveals that Kṛṣṇa, when he is lying in the forest after escaping from the city, will be killed by his brother Jaratkumāra. Immediately after his death Kṛṣṇa will be born in

---

[9] *Samavāyāṅgasūtra*, sutra 246–272 and 132.

[10] *Kalpasūtra* pp. 276–9.

[11] *Uttarādhyayanasūtra*, *upadeśa* XXII.

[12] *Nāyādhammakahāo*, ch. 16.

[13] *Antagaḍadasāo and Anuttarovavaiyadasāo*, ed. M.C. Modi, 1932. Law 1949:36–49; Upadhye *op. cit.* pp. 21–2.

the third hell. This story brings some mythological concepts of the Jainas to light. Being a *vāsudeva*, Kṛṣṇa is bound to his karma: he cannot escape from his fate by renouncing the world. He is also told that through loss of karma he will become the twelfth Tīrthaṅkara in the next *utsarpiṇī* era.

We find another story related to Kṛṣṇa in this text,[14] viz. the story of Gajasukumāra. Prior to Kṛṣṇa's birth, Devakī had given birth to six male children; through the divine grace of Harinaigameśi, they were transferred to the womb of Sulasā. When they had grown up they entered the order of ascetics. When Kṛṣṇa visited Devakī after six months and she was suffering because none of her sons was with her, Kṛṣṇa propitiated the same god, by whose grace Devakī gave birth to a son named Gajasukumāra. The story further tells us how this youth exhibited great heroism and forbearance in penance.

In other chapters[15] the canon mentions many personalities of the Vṛṣṇi race, such as Andhaka Vṛṣṇi, Kuntī, Mādrī, Pradyumna, Sāmba, Aniruddha a.o. From these references we may conclude that by the time these *āgama-s* were compiled (c. 5th cent. A.D.) all the major elements of the Kṛṣṇa story and some aspects of the Pāṇḍava tales had entered into the corpus of Jaina narrative literature. No doubt Kṛṣṇa Vāsudeva stands out as a prominent figure in all these stories; but nowhere do we find the sort of deification which we find in Vyāsa's *Mahābhārata* and *Harivaṃśa*.

These stray episodes form more or less essential parts of later literary works in both the Digambara and Śvetāmbara traditions.

4. *Literary Works with the Harivaṃśa Theme*

It is believed that Bhadrabāhu wrote a work titled *Vasudevacarita*, but no such work has come down to us. The earliest work that gives us a comprehensive notion of what the Jaina Harivaṃśa is is the Prakrit prose work *Vasudevahiṇḍi* of Saṅghadāsa–Dharmadāsa (c. 6th cent. A.D.), but this work, as the title already indicates, deals mainly with Vasudeva, and the biography of Neminātha comes only in second place.[16]

Vimalasūri, the author of the first Jaina Rāmāyaṇa, is referred to by some as the author of the first Jaina Harivaṃśa as well, but this is a doubtful matter, and no such work of his is available now.[17]

---

[14] Law, *op. cit.* pp. 49–50.
[15] *Ibid. p.* 51.
[16] J.C. Jain 1961:44.
[17] Premi 1956:113–4; Upadhye 1969:105 n.4; Chaudhuri 1973:39.

Svayambhu, the author of the *Paumacariu*, has written a work known as the *Riṭṭhanemicariu* between A.D. 756 and 783 in Apabhramsa. This work gives a complete biography of Ariṣṭanemi, but it was later developed into a Harivaṃśapurāṇa by Yaśaḥkīrti.[18]

The first independent work that presents a complete version of the Jaina Mahābhārata/Harivaṃśa is the *Harivaṃśapurāṇa* of Jinasena (of the Punnāṭa Saṅgha), in Sanskrit.[19] It is an enormous work of 12,000 *śloka-s* divided into 66 cantos. Both in the eminence of its subject matter and the majesty of its form this purāṇa was intended as a formidable alternative to the Brahminical Mahābhārata-Harivaṃśa pair, and thus it set a model for later authors. Hence it may be not improper if we take this work as representative of the essential Jaina Mahābhārata.

The gist of the main story of Jinasena's work is as follows:[20] In the Yaduvaṃśa were born two brothers, Andhaka Vṛṣṇi and Bhojaka Vṛṣṇi. Andhaka Vṛṣṇi, who ruled over Śauripura had ten sons, of whom Samudravijaya was the eldest and Vasudeva the youngest. Kuntī and Mādrī were their sisters. Bhojaka Vṛṣṇi had three sons, viz. Ugrasena, Mahāsena and Devasena. Vasudeva's love for adventure made him leave home on some pretext. He wandered through many countries performing many heroic deeds and married a number of *vidyādhara* damsels. On the occasion of Rohiṇī's *svayaṃvara*, he met his brother Samudravijaya on the battlefield. Two reunited brothers happily returned to Śauripura. Vasudeva had a son with Rohiṇī, who was named Rāma and became the ninth *baladeva* of that period.

At Śauripura, Vasudeva taught the sciences of arms to many princes, among whom Kaṃsa was one. Actually, Kaṃsa was a son of Ugrasena who was forsaken as soon as he was born, hence he was brought up elsewhere. On one occasion Jarāsandha, the sovereign of the Māgadha-s, made the announcement that whoever would conquer his enemy Siṃharatha would have his daughter as well as a desired part of the kingdom. Vasudeva guided Kaṃsa to achieve this end. Before giving his daughter in marriage, Jarāsandha found out the truth about Kaṃsa's early life. Kaṃsa was filled with hatred towards his father and overthrew him with Jarāṣandha's help. To show his gratitude to his teacher, Kaṃsa offered his sister Devakī (Devasena's daughter) to Vasudeva. Later Kaṃsa came to know, through the sage Atimuktaka, that Devakī's son would turn into an enemy and cause his death. He kept Devakī in his palace and planned

---

[18] Premi 1956:383.
[19] Sumitra Bai unpubl.:147–493.
[20] Pannalal Jain 1978, cantos 16–64.

to kill all of her sons as soon as they were born. Devakī, in the course of time, gave birth to twins three times consecutively. Each time, god Harinaigameśi replaced them with still-born twins, thus restoring all the six sons of Devakī, who later became monks. With the fourth delivery Devakī gave birth to a brilliant-looking son, Kṛṣṇa, who had all the auspicious marks of a great man. Vasudeva and Baladeva took the boy to the house of Nanda, brought back Nanda's newly born daughter and kept her in Kṛṣṇa's place. Kaṃsa was relieved to find a baby girl instead of a boy, but he damaged her nose, lest any mighty man would marry her in future.

Kṛṣṇa grew up in Nanda's village and performed a number of special feats, exhibiting his superhuman powers. Kaṃsa heard about this, suspected that he was his secret enemy and tried several methods to kill him, but failed. Finally he invited both Rāma and Kṛṣṇa to Mathura on the pretext of a duel with two mighty wrestlers: in that fight Kṛṣṇa killed Cāṇūra and Rāma killed Muṣṭika. Kaṃsa then rushed towards Kṛṣṇa to kill him, but was instead killed by him.

Jarāsandha was very upset by the murder of his son-in-law and came with a mighty army to attack the Yādava-s. The Yādava-s, however, knew that bloodshed now would be untimely and unnecessary, so they secretly fled from the city of Mathurā and went to the western coast. With the help of gods they founded the city of Dvārāvatī and there they dwelt peacefully. There king Samudravijaya and queen Śivādevī had a son named Ariṣṭanemi, who was to become the twenty-second Jina.

Once the Pāṇḍava-s, who were Kṛṣṇa's relatives on his mother's side, came to Dvārāvatī as refugees. They had a long quarrel with their cousins the Kuru-s, who had cheated them at a game of dice and exiled them. On their way the Pāṇḍava-s had experienced many adventurous situations, of which Arjuna's winning of Draupadī in the *svayaṃvara* was one. Kṛṣṇa welcomed them and granted them the favour of allowing them to reside in his city. By that time Kṛṣṇa had married eight princesses, of whom Rukmiṇī had given birth to a son called Pradyumna, who turned out to be a great hero.

Jarāsandha heard of the Yādava-s' well-being at Dvārakā, and in order to punish them for their earlier crimes he declared a war against them. All kshatriyas were divided into two groups. The Kuru-s sided with Jarāsandha while the Pāṇḍava-s fought for the Yādava-s. The great battle took place at Kurukṣetra. In that battle Kṛṣṇa killed his *pratiśatru* Jarāsandha and established himself as the ninth *nārāyaṇa* of that period. Then he conquered in all directions and became the *cakravartin* of half of Bhārata.

Once Draupadī was abducted by a king named Padmanābha of

Amarakanka. Kṛṣṇa went there along with the Pāṇḍava-s, defeated that enemy and brought back Draupadī. On the way home Kṛṣṇa was highly enraged by a practical joke played on him by Bhīma; he reprimanded the Pāṇḍava-s for their act and ordered them to leave his kingdom immediately. Accordingly the Pāṇḍava-s left Dvārakā, went southwards where they founded another city, and resided there.

Once the Yādava-s wanted to know who was the mightiest among them. Kṛṣṇa challenged Nemi's power but found himself a weakling, who could not move a single finger of Nemi.

Kṛṣṇa and the other Yādava-s had gone to Mount Raivataka for recreation; there Nemi was chided by the wives of Kṛṣṇa. He became so enraged that he performed many superhuman feats, and the Yādava-s were stunned by his power. Kṛṣṇa thought that the usually dispassionate Nemi had now turned passionate, so he arranged Nemi's marriage with princess Rājīmati. One day, when he was out in his chariot enjoying the beauty of the forest while the wedding preparations were going on, he saw a number of animals bound together in one place: they were trembling with fear and screaming helplessly for their freedom. He asked his charioteer the reason why they were there, and thus he came to know that they were meant for a feast of kshatriyas who had come for his wedding. Feeling pity for the poor animals, he immediately ordered their release, and he felt disgust with the kshatriyas' craving for worldly pleasures. He understood that such a life would lead to nothing but self-destruction and decided to follow the path of renunciation. He entered the order of ascetics and performed tapas. After severe penance on Mount Ūrjayanta he attained omniscience and then travelled to many places, teaching the right path of dharma to the masses.

When he came to Dvārāvatī, the Yādava-s too sought his instruction. After a detailed exposition of dharma, many of them heard their previous lives from him and became ascetics. Then Baladeva questioned Ariṣṭanemi about the time and manner of the destruction of the city of Dvārakā and who would be the cause of Kṛṣṇa's death. Nemi replied that after twelve years Dvārakā would be burnt to ashes due to the anger of Dvīpāyana, and that wine would be the cause; Kṛṣṇa, while lying in the forest of Kusamba, would be killed by an arrow shot by his brother Jaratkumāra.

Depressed by this prophecy, Jaratkumāra left the city and went to the forest. Dvīpāyana too renounced the world and went to perform tapas, resolving not to return until the fateful period would be over. Kṛṣṇa banned all drinking and preparation of arrack in his kingdom: the people took out all their stocks of wine and poured them into a stonepit outside the city. Delusion filled Dvīpāyana's mind; he returned to Dvārakā that very twelfth year and stood outside the city performing penance.

Some Yādava princes, who had gone for an outing, felt thirsty, found the wine in the stonepit, thought it was water and drank it. Intoxicated, they wandered around, saw Dvīpāyana, remembered that he would be the cause of their destruction and stoned him to death. With his last breath the sage uttered a curse that would destroy the Yādava-s and their city. Kṛṣṇa and Balarāma pleaded with him in vain. He died, was reborn as a fire-god and began burning the city. Kṛṣṇa and Balarāma could not succeed in saving the people.

Having lost everything except their lives, the two brothers, now destitute, went southwards in the hope of joining their relatives the Pāṇḍava-s. When they reached Kusamba forest, Kṛṣṇa felt immensely thirsty and Balarāma went in search of water for his brother while Kṛṣṇa was lying under a tree. Jaratkumāra came there hunting, saw at a distance something lying under a tree, and thinking that it was a spotted deer he shot an arrow which pierced Kṛṣṇa's foot. Kṛṣṇa understood that it was Jaratkumāra who had shot the arrow and that his time had come, and he sent Jaratkumāra off to the Pāṇḍava-s to convey the news to them. Balarāma returned with the water, and deluded by grief he wanted to believe that his brother was still alive, hence he took Kṛṣṇa's body on his shoulder and wandered thus for six months. The Pāṇḍava-s came to console Balarāma but could not persuade him to part with the dead body of Kṛṣṇa; finally he was brought to his senses by a god, whereupon he became a monk and performed tapas.

Then the Pāṇḍava-s went to offer their respect to Nemi. He told them about their previous lives, they gave up worldly life and after severe penance they attained *mokṣa*. Neminātha too attained *mokṣa* after severe penance on Mount Ūrjayanta.

This is the framework on which different authors have based their works. Though in essence it is always the same, smaller differences may appear due to differences of sect, *saṅgha*, or oral tradition. The differences in the writings may be found in the order of events, in the stories relating the previous lives of different characters, et cetera. Furthermore these authors took the liberty to enlarge or alter, or blend in parts of earlier works.

5. *Differences Between the Jaina and Brahminical Versions*

Three main themes, viz. the biography of Neminātha, the life of Kṛṣṇa and the story of the Pāṇḍava-s, are fused together in the Jaina version. Nemi's biography more or less occupies the middle position, and before and after his story the stories of prominent persons of the Harivaṃśa are narrated. Here the stories of the Pāṇḍava-s are brought in. In Jinasena's work we see that by the time of Nemi's birth, Kṛṣṇa and Balarāma are already established heroes among the Yādava-s. Ample space is given to Vasudeva's adventures and to the stories of Kṛṣṇa's childhood. It is only after Nemi's birth that the great battle at Kurukṣetra takes place, where with Nemi's moral support Kṛṣṇa is established as a suzerain.[21]

The court episode where Nemi is depicted as a powerful man helps to establish his physical superiority over the Yādava-s, especially over Kṛṣṇa.[22] The story of his renunciation demonstrates his spiritual sublimity.[23] Among the Yādava-s, those who follow in Nemi's footsteps attain redemption, whereas those who do not are destroyed.[24]

(A) The Jaina way of presenting Kṛṣṇa's character demands our attention. Though he is recognized as a great hero and has been given the position and dignity of a *śalākāpuruṣa*, the stories about his previous lives try to show him as a crude and lowly type of human being, who through his own righteous deeds attains the blessed state of a *nārāyaṇa*. He enjoys immense power and all the pleasures that accompany such a status. He is a mighty hero, an affectionate husband, a lovable father, a bounteous and kind relative; yet his life is not what Jaina authors project as a model, for such a life leads to karma and bondage.[25]

(B) The Pāṇḍava-s in these Jaina versions are not the glamorous and domineering characters that we find in the Brahminical versions. The central battle, which in Vyāsa's work symbolizes the eternal struggle between good and evil, has been turned into a conventional fight between a *nārāyaṇa* and his enemy, a *pratinārāyaṇa*. This shift enhances the position of Jarāsandha, who is not so prominent in the Brahminical versions, but drives the Pāṇḍava-s into a completely insignificant position. Their relation to Kṛṣṇa is more or less like that of feudatories to their overlord.[26]

(C) The stories of Vasudeva and Balarāma's affection for Kṛṣṇa are peculiar to the Jaina Harivaṃśa-s. Vasudeva, who in the Brahminical versions is an insignificant character, becomes a romantic hero, in the imitation of Naravāhanadatta of the *Bṛhatkathā*.[27] The Jaina versions become more attractive on account of these stories. Baladeva's story lays more emphasis and depth to that character and brings more emotionality into the Kṛṣṇa story.[28]

---

[21] Jinasena cantos 50–54.
[22] Jinasena canto 55:1–12 and 59–67.
[23] Jinasena canto 55:72–127.
[24] Jinasena cantos 61–65.
[25] Jinasena canto 33:96–140.
[26] Jinasena canto 54:4–74.
[27] J.C. Jain 1977:1–155.
[28] Jinasena canto 63.

(D) The most important difference between the Jaina and Brahminical versions is the difference between the two world-views. The chief aim of the Brahminical works is to instruct the people in achieving the four goals in life (*dharma*, *artha*, *kāma* and *mokṣa*). All these four need to be achieved within the lifespan of a human being. Kṛṣṇa, through his mundane form, demonstrates this achievement in these works, and hence his lifestyle is honoured, eulogized and upheld as a model. The Jainas, on the other hand, uphold *mokṣa* as the only goal in life, and this can be achieved only through renouncing the world, as is demonstrated by Nemi's life. His life thus stands for the *nivṛttimārga*, whereas Kṛṣṇa's stands for the *pravṛttimārga*. Nemīnātha had the ideal opportunity to lead a princely life, but he renounces life in the prime of his youth. To him the cry of a few bound animals sounds like the cry of all the souls that are bound in *saṃsāra*, and just as he sets those animals free, he leads other souls to liberation. In serving this greater cause his determination and perseverance elevate him to the position of a leader of people, but the Yādava-s (who are affected neither by his way of life nor by his achievements) end their lives in misery, as symbolized by the tragedy that befalls Dvārakā and Kṛṣṇa. This opposition between the *pravṛtti* and *nivṛtti* ways of life forms the core of the Jaina versions.[29]

6. *Antiquity of the Jaina Version*

Scholars differ on the question of the antiquity of the Jaina version. Alsdorf thinks that the original Jaina reception of the Kṛṣṇa–Mahābhārata saga has not come from the literary sources of the Brahminical version.[30] According to him a really original Jaina version existed independently of the Brahminical one. P.C. Divanji, who considers the Jaina version as old as Vyāsa's work, says that "the charge that the Jainas have made out their puranic works from the Bhāgavata sources on twisting facts so as to suit their purpose must be dismissed as unfounded".[31] The fact that the Jainas had their own versions of the Mahābhārata since very early times cannot be denied. But we should not forget the typical attitude that Jaina authors have shown time and again: they brought into their own religion whatever they found attractive in other religious systems.[32]

---

[29] Sumitra Bai unpubl.: 124–39; Divanji 1917–42:107–25.
[30] L. Alsdorf as quoted in Upadhye 1943:86.
[31] Divanji 1917–42:120.
[32] Bruhn 1961:9–10.

Some mediæval poets, like Svayambhu and Dhavala,[33] who wrote mainly for laymen, openly express their gratitude to Vyāsa's work. The works of Sanskrit poets like Jinasena and Śubhacandra,[34] who wrote for pundits, show a remarkable influence of both the Brahminical *Mahābhārata* and the *Harivaṃśa*. Two instances from Jinasena's work seem to presuppose the Brahminical version:

(a) When describing Draupadī's *svayaṃvara*, Jinasena writes: "When Arjuna won the stake, Draupadī put the garland around his neck. Because of the blowing wind that garland blew over the other Pāṇḍava-s too. Then a convictionless fellow cried aloud that Draupadī married all the five brothers. But actually she was the dutiful wife of Arjuna: toward the two elder brothers she behaved with respect as she would have done with her father-in-law. She treated the two younger brothers as her brothers-in-law. Men may share their wealth, but not their wives. This is true of even baser men; how can the noble behave otherwise"?[35]

The Śvetāmbara tradition accepts that Draupadī had five husbands, but the Digambara writers either say nothing about this or will try to modify it, as Jinasena has done.

(b) Similarly, Baladeva's question about the destruction of Dvārāvatī and Kṛṣṇa's death seem too artificial to be original. Questions like "after what time will this city of Dvārāvatī be destroyed? Will it sink into the ocean by itself, or will there be some cause for its destruction"?, "Who will cause Kṛṣṇa's death at the end of his life"?, et cetera[36] can be asked only with a foreknowledge of events. As soon as we read this passage we are reminded of another version, where the city sinks into the ocean.

(C) In the story of Kaṃsa, at the time of Kṛṣṇa's birth, in the episode with Kīcaka Muni and other such passages we can easily recognize efforts at what we may call "Jainifying" non-Jaina elements of the narrative. Ghatge's opinion that these traits of the Jaina version may be "rather due to the criticism of the Mahābhārata itself and not due to anything more original",[37] still seems reasonable.

Some efforts have been made to establish Ariṣṭanemi as a historical person,[38] but nothing substantial has come out of this.

---

[33] (i) *Indena samappiu vayaranu rasu bharaheṃ vaseṃ vittharanu* (*Riṭṭhaṇemicariu* of Svayambhu); (ii) *Hari paṇḍavāṇa kahā caumuha vasehiṃ bhasiyaṃ jamha | taha virayami loyapiyā jeṇa ṇa ṅāsei damsaṇam pauram ||* (*Harivaṃśapurāṇa* of Dhavala)—quoted in Premi 1942:172 and 392.

[34] Doshi 1961:9–10.

[35] Jinasena 45:135–160.

[36] *Ibid.*

[37] Ghatge 1950:43.

[38] Radhakrishnan 1923:287; Sastri 1961:3; Zimmer 1961:225; K.C. Jain 1974:8.

7. *A Survey of Jaina Harivaṃśa Literature*[39]

(A) *Sanskrit works*

Apart from Jinasena's work many others with the title *Harivaṃśapurāṇa* have come down to us, written by Sakalakīrti (A.D. 1464), Śrutakīrti (1496), Dharmakīrti, Raviṣeṇa, Śrībhūṣaṇa, another Śrutakīrti, Jayasāgara and another Sakalakīrti.

Works dealing primarily with Nemi's biography have been written by Sūrācārya (1053) and Udayaprabhasūri (13th century), titled *Nemināthacarita*. Kīrtirāja's work of the same title (1438) as well as the *Nemināthacaritra* of Guṇavijaya (1611) and many more bearing the same title are available now.

Among the works that narrate Nemi's biography in the larger context of the sixty-three *śalākāpuruṣa-s*, the *Mahāpurāṇa* of Jinasena–Guṇabhadra and the *Triṣaṣṭiśalākāpuruṣacaritra* of Hemacandra are prominent. Malliṣeṇa (1047), Candramuni, Vimalasūri and Vajrasena have written works titled *Mahāpurāṇa*.

Brahmanemidatta's *Neminathapurāṇa*, Vāgbhaṭa's *Neminirvāṇakāvya* and Hemacandrasūri's *Nemidvisandhānakāvya* are of the *mahākāvya* type.

Works dealing with the Pāṇḍava story titled *Pāṇḍavacarita* have been written by Vijayagaṇi, Devaprabhasūri, Śubhavardhana, Hemacandra, Śrībhūṣaṇa a.o. Śubhacandra's *Pāṇḍavapurāṇa* (1550) paved the way for similar such works by Vādirāja and Vādicandra. Jayacandra wrote a work titled *Pāṇḍavacaritoddhāra*.

(B) *Prakrit Works*

In Prakrit, Śīlāṅka's *Cauppannamahāpurisacaria* is a prominent work, written in 869. Maladhāri Hemacandra has written a work titled *Nemiṇāhacariya*. Also Udayaprabhasūri's *Neminirvāṇakāvya* is remarkable.

(C) *Apabhramsa Works*

After Svayambhu's *Riṭṭhaṇemicariu* or *Harivaṃśapurāṇa*, a large number of works of the same type have been written in Apabhramsa. The works of Dhavala (10th–11th century) and Yaśaḥkīrti's work are of significance.

Haribhadrasūri wrote his *Nemiṇāhacariu* in 1159. Puṣpadanta's work *Tisaṭṭimahāpurisaguṇālaṅkāru* is famous as a Apabhramsa Mahāpūraṇa (959–965).

---

[39] This survey is based on the information found in H.D. Velankar's *Jinaratnakośa*, vol. 1, Poona 1940.

The biography of Pradyumna, which is an interesting part of the Jaina Harivaṃśa, has inspired a large number of poets. Works with the title *Pradyumnacarita* have been written in Sanskrit, Prakrit and Apabhramsa; *Pradyumnacarita-s* have been written by Raviṣiddha, Bhogakīti, Rollaṇa, Vādicandra, Somasena, Sakalakīrti, Ratnacandra, Śubhacandra, Mallibhūṣaṇa, Mahāsenācārya, Somakīrti, Jineśvarasūri, Ravisāgara, Raighupaṇḍita, Yaśodhara, Samayasundara a.o. The *Kṛṣṇacarita* of Devendrasūri deals with Kṛṣṇa's life.

From this survey it is amply clear that the Harivaṃśa theme gained popularity during and after the mediæval period; in fact, according to one assessment, the works with the story of Neminātha exceed in number those devoted to other Tīrthaṅkara-s.

Some Notes on the Jaina Mahābhārata in Kannada

(Robert J. Zydenbos)

The oldest specimens of literary Kannada are found in inscriptions, beginning with the Halmidi inscription (± 450 C.E.); but by the year 850 C.E. the Rashtrakuta king Nṛpatuṅga writes his *Kavirājamārga*, a work on Kannada poetics which provides us with many valuable quotations from older authors whose works are no longer available, and with this we suddenly find ourselves in a highly sophisticated literary landscape.

In this period, though the religious composition of the population of the region is quite varied, we see that Jainism is firmly established as the foremost *Hochreligion*.[40] Royal patronage gives ample possibilities for Jaina culture to express itself in architecture, of which still much exists, and in literature: as far as we can see, Kannada literature was a purely Jaina affair at the time, with other religious groups, beginning with the Vīraśaiva-s, taking up Kannada literature as a serious vehicle for their thoughts only in the twelfth century.

Nṛpatuṅga's work gives Kannada the distinction of being the living language with the second oldest literature in India, second only to Tamil. Unlike Tamil, Kannada has undergone Sanskritic influence to a much greater extent, in its phonetic system and its vocabulary, and we see this stronger mingling of cultures also in the influence which Sanskrit literature had on that of Kannada. We see this influence already at the very

[40] A nice study of the period in which Jainism flourished in Karnataka, 500-1200 C.E., is Singh 1975.

beginning of Kannada literary history in the Jaina *purāṇa-s*, all of which show, to some degree, a dependence on Sanskrit models. The relationship between Sanskrit and Kannada throughout practically the whole of the literary history of the Kannada-speaking region (which for the sake of convenience I will refer to as "Karnataka", though the present-day state of this name is smaller than that linguistic region once was) can be compared with the relationship between Latin and the Germanic languages of northern Europe from the middle ages to the 19th century; and just as much of the best writing in later Latin was done in northern Europe, Sanskrit language and literature were highly cultivated in Karnataka–the names of Kālidāsa and Sāyaṇa immediately come to mind here. But however much Sanskritic learning was appreciated, the Indo-European language with its literature remained alien in their pure forms. Jainism had its origin in northeastern India and was first communicated through a form of Prakrit, hence the Jainas of Karnataka too held certain ancient Prakrit texts in high esteem, but the independent creation of new works in Prakrit was practically non-existent.[41] Apabhramsa was not at all used in southern India. Dravidian culture expressed itself, of course, mainly in Dravidian languages.

The first complete literary work in Kannada is by Pampa (941 C.E.), who was a Jaina, and though his *Vikramārjunavijayam* (also known as the "Pampabhārata") is a complete Mahābhārata in Kannada, it does not follow the pattern of the Jaina Mahābhārata-s that were already in existence in Sanskrit and Prakrit at the time, but that of the work ascribed to Vyāsa. In the poem, which is a *campū* (a composition in which verse and prose passages alternate), Pampa identifies his patron, King Arikēsari, with Arjuna, and the obvious reason why he chose to follow the Vyāsa version, apart from his literary appreciation of that work, would be that his patron was not a Jaina but a Hindu.

Yet being a Jaina, there are things in his treatment of the Mahābhārata story which upset modern Hindu authors. R.S. Mugaḷi seems unable to appreciate Pampa's portrayal of Kṛṣṇa, whose "personality as a hero on the side of the good and as a crafty fellow is shown more than his nature as the Supreme Being".[42] B.M. Śrīkaṇṭhayya goes still further and says, referring to Pampa's Hindu ancestry, that when it came to the depicting of Kṛṣṇa and the Bhagavadgītā episode, "a struggle arose between his

---

[41] Sastry 1976:898.
[42] Mugaḷi 1971:176.

Jaina faith and the Vedic *saṃskāra*[43] of his ancestors, innerly Pampa's mind was torn, and an impediment arose which must be said to have decreased his poetic vision and enthusiastic tone to some extent".[44] This sounds rather exaggerated to me, and also to G.S. Śivarudrappa, who in his article on Pampa's treatment of the Bhagavadgītā[45] argues that it is not necessarily a sign of disrespect that the Gītā has been reduced to a single stanza of four lines preceded and followed by only a few lines of prose. It must indeed go against the grain of a poet with a strong tendency towards realism to have a lengthy religious discourse take place in the middle of a battlefield, just when the battle is about to commence; and in spite of the sharp reduction in space, Śivarudrappa writes, nothing that is essential in the message of the Bhagavadgītā has been left out.[46] The Pampabhārata remains a literary masterpiece, and still today Kannada authors look upon Pampa as the model poet who demonstrated the literary potential of the Kannada language.

Much the same can be said about the *Sāhasabhīmavijayam* of Ranna (993 C.E.), which is also known under the name *Gadāyuddha*. Here too we have a Jaina poet who follows the general pattern of the Mahābhārata of Vyāsa and who identifies his patron, King Satyāśraya, with one of the heroes of the story, this time Bhīma, who becomes the main character.[47] Ranna does not mention Pampa or other earlier Kannada authors in his work, though we may assume that he was to some extent influenced by them when he wrote it, just as he shows the influence of the Sanskrit works *Ūrubhaṅga* by Bhāsa and *Veṇisaṃhāra* by Bhaṭṭanārāyaṇa; he does mention Vyāsa, Vālmīki, Kālidāsa and Bāṇa.[48] He too is considered one of the classical Kannada poets of what is thought of as the golden age of Kannada literature, but G.H. Nayak points out that as Ranna was living in what is called the *vīrayuga* or "heroic age" and wrote in the style of that age, there are passages in the work which may repel today's reader because of the pompousness, anger, gruesomeness, violence, and coarseness of language of the protagonist.[49]

---

[43] A *saṃskāra* is usually understood as a trace of a person's karma, which influences one's individual behaviour; here Śrīkaṇṭhayya sees it as something quasi-genetic, as though religion is inherited or bound to race and an individual is unable to develop his own beliefs and sentiments. This mentality is quite common among conservative Hindus.

[44] Thus Śrīkaṇṭhayya on pp. 518–19 in vol. 2 of the University of Mysore's *Kannaḍa kaipiḍi*, quoted by Śivarudrappa 1972:19 n. 3.

[45] "Pampanalli Bhagavadgīte", Śivarudrappa 1972:18–29.

[46] *Ibid.*, p. 27.

[47] G.H. Nayak 1976:642.

[48] *Ibid.*, p. 620.

[49] *Ibid.*, pp. 642–43.

After Ranna we come to the Kannada renderings of the Mahābhārata which we can call specifically Jaina in composition. Just as is the case with the works in Sanskrit, Prakrit and Apabhramsa, the narrative acquires its typical Jaina colouring by being interwoven with the story of the Tīrthaṅkara Ariṣṭanēmi / Nēminātha. The Jaina tradition of south India is that of the Digambara-s, and the story of Nēminātha as we found it in the Kannada *purāṇa-s* generally follows the pattern set in Jinasena's *Harivaṃśapurāṇa* and the *Mahāpurāṇa* of the other Jinasena and Guṇabhadra, rather than the Śvētāmbara pattern which we see in the works of Śīlāṅka, Haribhadra and, most importantly, Hemacandra. It may be noted that the difference between the two traditions is in any case very small, the main events of the story being the same and differences occurring primarily in the stories of Nēminātha's previous births.[50]

The Nēmināthapurāṇa-s are basically like other Jaina *purāṇa-s* insofar as their composition is concerned, and their authors devote much space to the *pañcakalyāṇa* or five especially auspicious occasions in the life of the Tīrthaṅkara, viz. the descent into the womb, birth, renunciation of worldly life, the attaining of omniscience and liberation. On all these five occasions the gods come to adore the Tīrthaṅkara, and they offer the authors scope for praise of the Tīrthaṅkara and for elaborate descriptive passages in which they can display their poetic abilities to the full. Two things set the Nēmināthapurāṇa-s apart from other Jaina *purāṇa-s*: (a) The connection of the story of Nēminātha with that of the two *vaṃsá-s* in the Mahābhārata; this makes them more attractive for the readers/listeners and also "gives them more importance and scope".[51] (b) The events which make Nēminātha decide to renounce the world are particular for his story and are given great importance in the *purāṇa-s*.[52] Later we also come across works which have the separation of princess Rājīmati from her fiancé Nēminātha on account of his renunciation as their theme,[53] just as also other characters from the Jaina Harivaṃsápurāṇa start leading lives of their own in other works, such as Kṛṣṇa, Pradyumna and Vasudeva.[54] The story of Kṛṣṇa begins with his birth and is usually spun out elaborately; the story of Pradyumna is usually mixed in with it.[55]

---

[50] Sastry 1973:10–18.
[51] *Ibid.*, p. 18.
[52] *Ibid.*, pp. 18–19.
[53] *Ibid.*, p. 19.
[54] Nagarajaiah and Kulkarni 1981:14–15.
[55] *Ibid.*

The first Kannada Harivaṃśapurāṇa was written by Guṇavarma (the first known author of that name in Kannada) in ± 900 C.E., but is now known to us only through fragments which have been quoted in later works. He must have been considered an influential writer, for his *Harivaṃśapurāṇa* is mentioned by Pārśvapaṇḍita in his *Pārśvanāthapurāṇa* (1222)[56] and his other known work is quoted by Abhinava Vādividyānanda as late as 1533.[57]

With Guṇavarma's writings being lost, the first available work in Kannada containing the Nēminātha–Pāṇḍava story is the *Triṣaṣṭiśalākāpuruṣacarita* (978) of Cāvuṇḍarāya (also written 'Cāmuṇḍarāya'), more popularly known under the name *Cāvuṇḍarāyapurāṇa*. This is the first and only Jaina *mahāpurāṇa*, dealing just as its Sanskrit and Prakrit counterparts with the lives of the 63 *śalākāpuruṣa-s*,[58] and a particular feature of the work is that it is written practically entirely in prose instead of being a *campū* like the other Jaina *purāṇa-s*. Cāvuṇḍarāya was a remarkably many-sided person, a military commander for the kings of the Ganga dynasty and a student of Jaina philosophy, for whom his teacher Nēmicandra wrote the *Gommaṭasāra*, a work on Jaina thought of major importance ("Gommaṭa' was Cāvuṇḍarāya's nickname, and Cāvuṇḍarāya wrote a Kannada commentary on the work). If this were not enough to earn him everlasting fame, he also ordered the sculpting of the famous statue of Bāhubali, who in Jaina mythology is the first *siddha* or liberated one of our era, on the top of the larger hill at Shravanabelagola; to this day the statue is known as the *Gommaṭēśvara* or "lord of Gommata". Though the *Cāvuṇḍarāyapurāṇa* is historically important because of the influence which it had on later works, it is itself not considered a literarily great piece of writing; it is perhaps what one could expect from a person whose interests are more philosophical and religious than æsthetic. The author mentions that in writing the work he relied heavily on a work which he calls *Vāgarthasaṃgraha* by one Kaviparamēṣṭhi or Kaviparamēśvara: this person must be Kūcibhaṭṭāraka or Śrīnandi, both of whom wrote Sanskrit *mahāpurāṇa-s* that are no longer available.[59]

---

[56] H.M. Nayak 1976:360.

[57] Narasimhacharya 1972:26.

[58] The various classes of *śalākāpuruṣa-s* are listed above, n. 7. A *śalākā*, according to Monier–Williams' Sanskrit dictionary, is a small stick or rod, or a piece of bamboo borne as a kind of credential by mendicants, but I fail to see how this is relevant in the case of emperors etc. It seems not unreasonable to see in the word *śalākā* a re-Sanskritization of *ślāghā*, "praise" or "commendation", which through a possible Prakrit form such as **silāhā* entered Tamil as *calākai* (*Tamil Lexicon*, vol. III. Univ. of Madras, 1982 , p. 1329) and may have done something similar in other languages as well.

[59] Prasad 1976:519–20.

The *Vāgarthasaṃgraha* was a *gadyakathe*, a prose work, which Jinasena and Guṇabhadra refashioned in Sanskrit verse and Cāvuṇḍarāya later rendered in Kannada prose. Because some smaller subsidiary episodes in the *Cāvuṇḍarāyapurāṇa* are not found in the *Mahāpurāṇa* of Jinasena and Guṇabhadra, T.V. Venkatachala Sastry remarks that it is not a pure derivative of the Sanskrit work, and D.L. Narasimhachar suspected that these Cāvuṇḍarāya-episodes were borrowed from the older and now lost prose work.[60] Similarly verses from Jaṭāsiṃhanandyācārya and Kaviparamēśvara were borrowed into this work, and Cāvuṇḍarāya quite soberly and honestly says so.[61]

Cāvuṇḍarāya's work is very summary, dealing with much narrative material in a relatively short work; also much that it is not absolutely essential in Jinasena and Guṇabhadra's *Mahāpurāṇa* is simply left out. With Karṇapārya (± 1160) we find the first full-size Nēmināthapurāṇa in Kannada, of which three more would follow. The expert on Kannada Nēmināthapurāṇa-s and the Jaina Mahābhārata-s is indisputably Professor Venkatachala Sastry, whose dissertation "A Comparative Study of Kannada Nēminātha Purāṇa-s"[62] runs into 548 pages. He also has a monograph on Jaina Bhārata-s and Bhāgavata-s to his credit.[63] In his dissertation he gives the following list of works in Sanskrit and Prakrit relating to our topic, which may be of interest to the reader: there are 13 Nēmināthapurāṇa-s and–caritra-s in Sanskrit, 5 in Prakrit; 11 Sanskrit Harivaṃśapurāṇa-s, 3 in Prakrit; 9 Triṣaṣṭiśalākāpuruṣacaritra-s in Sanskrit, and 3 in Prakrit.[64] Nagarajaiah and R.V. Kulkarni, on the other hand, give lists of 11 Nēmināthapurāṇa-s in Prakrit, 11 Harivaṃśapurāṇa-s in Sanskrit and 22 Sanskrit Nēmināthapurāṇa-s.[65]

Karṇapārya was not a great poet, but rather a pundit who admired Pampa and Ranna and tried to rival them by a display of learning. In writing this first Kannada *Nēmināthapurāṇa* he drew from Sanskrit and Prakrit sources, mainly Guṇabhadra, and his learnedness also showed in his too frequent use of Sanskrit expressions, which at times are quite lengthy and make his language pedantic.[66] Also he could not impose any limitations upon himself, like Cāvuṇḍarāya could.[67]

---

[60] Sastry 1973:195.
[61] *Ibid.*, p. 527.
[62] Sastry 1973.
[63] Sastry 1980.
[64] Sastry 1973:27–45.
[65] Nagarajaiah and Kulkarni 1981:20–22.
[66] Sujata 1977:436.
[67] Sastry 1973:532, 542.

But in spite of his shortcomings, Karṇapārya started something new in Kannada, and the first consequence occurred in his own time, when Nēmicandra (not to be confused with his namesake, who was Cāvuṇḍarāya's guru) produced his *Nēmināthapurāṇa*. Nēmicandra was a very different personality: he was a gifted poet who felt that he was not bound to tradition if he did not like parts of it, and he simply dropped many episodes which are found in the works of his predecessors for apparently no other reason than that they did not appeal to him.[68] R.S. Mugaḷi, who is concerned about Kṛṣṇa, writes: "Though he may have seen Sanskrit and Prakrit models, it seems that he has mainly followed the *Cāvuṇḍarāyapurāṇa*. He has shown an independent spirit in dropping some of the details, changing some, and giving prominence to the story of Kṛṣṇa. The obscurity of the story of the previous births and the missionary tastelessness are not found in this part".[69] Nēmicandra earned the title *caturbhāṣācakravarti* for his mastery of Kannada, Sanskrit, Prakrit and perhaps Apabhramsa as the fourth language, and in the two works which he wrote we read sprinklings of Sanskrit and Prakrit verses, which he may have composed himself.[70] From the point of view of characterization, descriptive ingenuity and style in general, Nēmicandra's work is considered the best of the Kannada Nēmināthapurāṇa-s[71]—despite its being incomplete, for which reason it is commonly called the *Ardhanēmipurāṇa*. The work ends with the slaying of Kaṃsa by Kṛṣṇa. At times Nēmicandra tends to overreach himself in wordplay and fantasy, but he remains suggestive.[72]

Not long after Karṇapārya and Nēmicandra comes Bandhuvarma (±1190), who wrote his *Harivaṃśābhyudaya*, the first Kannada Harivaṃśapurāṇa which has come down to us complete. Qua personality Bandhuvarma is more like Karṇapārya, but he keeps himself in check: his language is not so highly Sanskritized as that of his predecessor. Numerous technical terms from music and dance appear in the work; he elaborated much that is short with Karṇapārya, but his characters remain suggestive.[73] Another noteworthy feature of the work is the appearance of satire of Hinduism, which is no doubt the reason why he was praised by his notorious contemporary Brahmaśiva.[74]

---

[68] *Ibid.*, p. 535, 543.
[69] Mugaḷi 1971:177.
[70] Sastry 1977:979–80.
[71] Sastry 1973:543.
[72] Sastry 1977:1025.
[73] Śāntā 1977:1066, 1072, 1080.
[74] *Ibid.*, p. 1066. For an introduction to the historically highly interesting satirist Brahmaśiva, see Zydenbos 1986.

Bandhuvarma in turn became a model to be emulated by a few later and less prominent authors. Mahābala wrote a *Nēminăthapurāṇa* (1254) displaying his wide reading; in certain episodes he clearly let himself be guided by the corresponding episodes in Ranna and Karṇapārya.[75] Around 1485[76] or 1550[77] Sāḷva, who also wrote two works on poetics, wrote his *Nēmīśvaracarite*, which is a complete Jaina Mahābhārata and hence also known as the *Sāḷvabhārata*, in sixteen books. In roughly the same period (±1500) Maṅgarasa, the third and best known poet of that name, who also wrote other religious works and a remarkable cookbook, wrote his *Nēmijinēśasaṅgati* in 5138 *sāngatya* verses.[78] Based on Maṅgarasa's work is the *Jinabhārata* of Brahmanāṅka (±1800), in which the author also praises divinities like Sarasvati, Jvālāmālini, Padmāvatī and Brahmadēva,[79] thus reflecting the tantric religious elements which by that time had entered southern Jainism.

Finally, this survey of the Jaina Mahābhārata in Kannada would be incomplete without mentioning a book by L.R. Heggaḍe, published in 1974.[80] This "*dhārmika bṛhadgrantha*" gives a modern Kannada prose version of the Jaina Mahābhārata as found in the older works of Nēmicandra and Karṇapārya, but more material has been drawn from supplementary stories in the Sanskrit work by Kīcaka; also other Sanskrit works, the *Pāṇḍavacaritra* of Devaprabhasūri and the *Pāṇḍavapurāṇa* of Śubhacandra, "were a bit useful. But Draupadī's being married to five husbands has entered into them".[81] The inspiration for writing the book apparently arose out of the author's anger at seeing that "the great scholar Winternitz, who wrote a history of Sanskrit literature in English [*sic*]" wrote that the Jaina authors had in some cases "completely changed and spoilt [some of the stories in the epic] . . . in order to give them a Jainistic appearance".[82]

What strikes one immediately about the book is that besides a photograph of the author, a picture of—not surprisingly—an image of Nēmināṭha and pictures of three Digambara monks, there are photographs of 34 people from across Karnataka by whom or in whose name financial

---

[75] Sannaiah 1977a:xxviii. Excerpts from the works, showing the parallels, are given *ibid.*, pp. xxix–xxx.
[76] Nagarajaiah and Kulkarni 1981:19.
[77] Narasimhacharya 1974:194.
[78] Narasimhacharya 1973:132.
[79] Narasimhacharya 1974:147.
[80] Heggaḍe 1974.
[81] *Ibid.*, p. xii.
[82] Quoted without reference in Heggaḍe 1974:xi.

contributions towards the publication of the book were made. The inclusion of such portraits is in itself not unusual in modern Jaina books (the traditional act of *śāstradāna* or the spreading of edifying literature is still considered very meritorious in the Jaina community), and on p. vi we find a list of 20 people who pledged to donate 25 copies to others; but that such a large number has come forward in this case demonstrates that the Jaina Mahābhārata still has a function in Jaina society today. From Heggaḍe's remark, quoted above, and remarks of a similar nature in the *māleya mātu* or introduction to the series in which the book appeared by the editor, we see that for the Jainas their Mahābhārata is an instrument, to put it in pithy German terms, of their *Selbstdarstellung* and *Selbstbehauptung*. Through their opposition in the case of certain issues in the Mahābhārata (such as their aversion to Draupadī's polyandry and their favouring of the *nivṛttimārga* rather than the *pravṛttimārga*, as we have seen above) the Jainas, using the same mythological narrative material, show that they have a Weltanschauung which differs in some ways from that of the predominantly Hindu society in which they live. And not only that: by collectively bringing out such a book, they publicly assert their distinctiveness and refuse to accept certain values that are expressed in the Hindu version. It is no doubt for this function that the Jaina community, as one of the prefaces in the book has it, is indebted to the author.[83]

Bibliography

PRIMARY LITERATURE

Antagaḍadasāo and Anuttarovaiyadasāo. Ed. M.C. Modi, 1932.

Jinasena: *Harivaṃśapurāṇa*. 2nd ed., ed. Pannalal Jain. Varánasi: Bharatiya Jñanapitha, 1978.

Kalpasūtra, tr. H. Jacobi in Jaina Sūtras vol. 1. Sacred Books of the East Series vol. XXII (Oxford; repr. Delhi).

Karṇapārya: *Nēminātha purāṇam*. Ed. H.P. Nagarajaiah and R.V. Kulkarni. 2 vols. Bangalore: Kannada Sahitya Parishat, 1981 (in Kannada).

Mahābala kavi: *Nēminātha purāṇam*. Ed. B.S. Sannaiah. Mysore: Inst. of Kannada Studies, Univ. of Mysore, 1977 (in Kannada).

SECONDARY LITERATURE

Barnett, L.D. (1977): *Hindu Gods and Heroes*. Delhi.

Bhandarkar, R.G. (1927): *Collected Works, vol. 3*. Poona: Bhandarkar Oriental Research Institute.

——(1965): *Vaishnavism, Saivism and Minor Religious Systems*. Varanasi.

[83] *Ibid.*, p. x.

Bruhn, Klaus (1961): *Introduction to Cauppannamāhapurisacariya of Silanka*, ed. A.M. Bhojak. Ahmedabad: Prakrit Text Series.

Chatterjee, S.K. (1940): "Itihasa, Purana and Jataka", in *Woolner Commemoration Volume, vol. VIII*. No place given.

Chaudhuri, B.C. (1973): *Jaina sāhitya kā bṛhad itihāsa, pt.* 4. Varanasi (in Hindi).

Divanji, P.C. (1917–42): "Origin of Bhagavata and Jaina Religions". *Silver Jubilee Volume, B.O.R.I.*, pp. 107–25.

Doshi, J.C. (1961): *Introduction to Pandava Purana of Shubhacandra*. Jivaraja Jaina Granthamala. Sholapur: Jaina Samskrti Samraksaka Sangha.

Farquhar, J.N. (1967): *An Outline of the Religious Literature of India*.

Ghatge, A.M. (1950): *Introduction to Kahāṇayatigam*. Kolhapur: Bharat Bookstall.

Hazra, R.C. (n.d.): *Studies in the Upapuranas, vol. 1*. Calcutta.

Heggaḍe, L.R. (1974): *Jaina Mahābharāta*. Gudibande (Kolar Dist.): Vivēkōdaya Granthamāle (in Kannada).

Jain, J.C. (1961): *Prākṛta Sāhitya kā itihāsa*. Varanasi: Chowkhamba Vidya Bhavana (in Hindi).

——(1977): *The Vasudevahindi–an Authentic Jain Version of Brhatkatha*. Ahmedabad.

Jain, K.C. (1974): *Lord Mahāvīra and His Times*. Delhi / Patna / Varanasi: Motilal Banarsidass.

Law, B.C. (1949): *Some Jaina Canonical Sutras*. Bombay: B.B.R.A.S.

Mugaḷi, R.S. (1971): *Kannaḍa sāhitya caritre*. 5th ed. Mysore: Uṣā Sāhityəmāle (in Kannada).

Nagarajaiah, H.P. and R.V. Kulkarni: "Prastāvane", in Karnaparya, pp. 1–43.

Narasimhacharya, R. (1972): *Karṇāṭaka kavicarite, vol. 1*. 2nd ed. Bangalore: Kannada Sahiya Parishat (in Kannada).

——(1973): *Karṇāṭaka kavicarite, vol. 2*. 2nd ed. Bangalore: Kannada Sahitya Parishat (in Kannada).

——(1974): *Karṇāṭaka kavicarite, vol. 3*. 2nd ed. Bangalore: Kannada Sahitya Parishat (in Kannada).

Nayak, G.H. (1976): "Sāhasabhīmavijaya", in Nayak and Sastry 1976, pp. 620–51 (in Kannada).

Nayak, H.M. (1976): "Guṇavarma", in Nayak and Sastry 1976, pp. 359–365 (in Kannada).

Nayak, H.M. and T.V. Venkatachala Sastry (eds.): *Kannaḍa Adhyayana Saṃstheya Kannaḍa Sāhitya Caritre*, vols. 3 (1976) and 4 (1977; pt. 1 containing pp. 1–864, pt. 2 containing pp. 865–1832; in Kannada).

Prabhu Shankar (1976): "Vikramārjuna Vijaya", in Nayak and Sastry 1976, pp. 447–72 (in Kannada).

Prasād, K.G. Nārāyaṇa (1976): "Cāmuṇḍarāya purāṇa", in Nayak and Sastry 1976, pp. 517–28 (in Kannada).

Premi, Nathurām (1942): *Jaina sāhitya aura itihāsa*. Bombay (in Hindi).

——(1956): *Jaina sāhitya aura itihāsa*. 2nd ed. Bombay (in Hindi).

Radhakrishnan, S. (1923): *Indian Philosophy*, vol. 1. London.

Ray Chaudhuri, H.C. (1936): *Material for the Study of Early History of the Vaisnava Sect*. 2nd ed. Calcutta.

Saletore, B.A. (1938): *Mediæval Jainism*. Bombay.

Sannaiah, B.S. (1977a): "Pīṭhike [Introduction]", in Mahābala (in Kannada).

——(1977b): "Mahābala", in Nayak and Sastry 1977, pp. 1619–33.

Śāntā, C.N. (1977): "Bandhuvarma—itivṛtti, Harivaṃśābhyudaya", in Nayak and Sastry 1977, pp. 1053–82 (in Kannada).

Śāstrī, Kailāsacandra (1961): *Jaina Dharma*. Jivaraja Jaina Granthamala. Sholapur: Jaina Samskriti Samraksaka Sangha (in Kannada).

Sastry, T.V. Venkatachala (1973): *Kannaḍa Nēminātha purāṇagaḷa taulanika adhyayana*. Mysore: Inst. of Kannada Studies, Univ. of Mysore (in Kannada).

——(1976): "Vaiśiṣṭya, sādhane [viz. of Kannada literature between 850–1150 C.E.]", in Nayak and Sastry 1976, pp. 897–907 (in Kannada).

——(1977): "Nēminātha purāṇa [of Nēmicandra]", in Nayak and Sastry 1977, pp. 1003–31 (in Kannada).

——(1980): *Jaina Bhāgavata Bhāratagaḷu*. Mysore: Ta. Vem. Smaraka Granthamale (in Kannada).

——(1981): *Mūru samīkṣegaḷu*. Mysore: Uṣā Sāhityamāle (in Kannada).

Singh, R.B.P. (1975): *Jainism in Early Medieval Karnataka*. Delhi / Varanasi / Patna: Motilal Banarsidass.

Śivarudrappa, G.S. (1972): *Pariśīlana*. 2nd ed. Mysore: Uṣā Sāhityamāḷe (in Kannada)

Sujātā, H.S. (1977): "Nēminātha purāṇa [of Karṇapārya]", in Nayak and Sastry 1977, pp. 417–37 (in Kannada).

Sumitra Bai, B.N. (unpubl.): *Jinasena's Harivaṃśa Purāṇa–a study*. Unpublished Ph.D. dissertation, Dept. of Jainology, Univ. of Mysore.

Upadhye, A.N. (ed.) (1943): *Bṛhatkathākośa*. Bombay: Bharatiya Vidya Bhavan.

——(ed.) (1969): *Kuvalayamala of Udyotasuri*. Kolhapur.

Vaidya, C.V. (1921–26): *History of Mediæval Hindu India*, vols. I, II, III. Poona.

Velankar, H.D. (1940): *Jinaratnakośa*, vol. 1. Poona.

Zimmer, H. (1961): *The Philosophies of India*. 7th ed. New York.

Zydenbos, R.J. (1986): "Jainism Endangered: the view of the medieval Kannada poet Brahmaśiva", in H. van Skyhawk (ed.), "*Minorities*" *on Themselves* (= *South Asian Digest of Regional Writing*, SADRW, Heidelberg) vol. 11 (1985). Stuttgart: Fr. Steiner, 1986, pp. 174–86.

RITUAL AND PERFORMANCE IN THE PĀṆḌAVALĪLĀ OF GARHWAL

WILLIAM S. SAX

The Mahābhārata in Performance

> . . . instead of continuing to rely upon texts considered definitive and sacred, it is essential to put an end to the subjugation of the theater to the text, and to recover the notion of a kind of unique language half-way between gesture and thought". (Artaud 1958: 89)

When nights grow long and cold and winter snow begins to fall in the Himalayas, drums echo through the mountains of Uttarākhaṇḍ. Wrapped in homespun blankets or huddled around fires for warmth, peasants assemble at their village squares for a nightlong entertainment. They come to learn of the deeds of ancient kings and usurpers, to see the battles of gods and demons enacted upon the rough stage, and to dance away the bitter cold along with their friends and relatives. They come to see the Pāṇḍavalīlā, a local drama in which the Mahābhārata is 'danced' or 'played'[1] by amateur performers for an audience of fellow villagers and guests.[2] In this essay I hope to show that in Uttarākhaṇḍ, the "subjugation" of theater to text of which Artaud complained cannot exist, since the Mahābhārata is thought of as a kind of performance, and not as a book. Here is an example of a text that is emobodied in people and their memories—as Pāṇḍavalīlā, the 'play' of the five Pandava brothers. Whether or not this embodied text can be understood as "sacred", is a question to which I shall return at the end of the essay.

Uttarākhaṇḍ is the locally preferred local name for the high-altitude regions of Garhwal in the central Himalayas in the north Indian state of

---

[1] Throughout this essay, I use single quotation marks (") for direct translations of native terms, and double quotation marks (" ") for extrinsic terms that do not have precise translation equivalents.

[2] I would like to thank the Fulbright-Hays Commission and the National Science Foundation for generously funding my doctoral research in 1983–1986, when I attended several Pāṇḍavalīlā in Uttarākhaṇḍ. I would also like to thank my friends at the South Asia Graduate Seminar at The University of Chicago for their insightful criticisms of an earlier draft of this essay, and the Ira Kukin program at the Harvard Academy for International and Area Studies, under whose aegis I have written this essay.

Uttar Pradesh.[3] It is bordered by Tibet on the north, Kumaon to the east, the lower-altitude districts of Garhwal on the south, and the state of Himachal Pradesh to the west. Throughout this predominantly Hindu region, the "most extensive body of folklore is that based on the *Mahābhārata* tales" (Chandola 1977:18). As an oral, performative tradition, Pāṇḍavalīlā resembles the kind of genre from which many scholars believe the Mahābhārata developed. Goldman for instance hypothesizes that the epics were

> delivered and consumed orally in the discrete performance units over a period of time as is indicated in the Rāmāyaṇa. My suspicion is that when one conceived of a text like the Mahābhārata as a whole, if ever one did, it was not so much as a book but as a whole body of literature from which specific characters, incidents, or scenes could be adduced from memory to illuminate questions in social life, etc. (1986:19–20)

Change the tense from past to present, and one has a serviceable description of the Pāṇḍavalīlā of Uttarākhaṇḍ. It illuminates social issues, and informs local culture more, perhaps, than any other text.[4] The Mahābhārata is constantly cited to explain almost everything, from the nature of polyandry to the origin of warts.

The concept of *līlā* is an important one in South Asia, but difficult to translate. Although it bears some superficial resemblance to Christian "miracle plays", *līlā* is at the same time a "theological", "mythical", and "performative" concept that has no apparent analogue in the Judaeo–Christian–Islamic traditions. Theologically, it relates to an old problem: if the Supreme Being is self-fulfilled and desireless, what could possibly motivate him to create the world? Badarayana wrote in his *Brahma-Sūtra* (II.1.33) that creation is a "mere sport" (*līlā kaivalyam*) to Brahma, the Creator. This 'sport' or 'amusement' is what is called *līlā*, a kind of cosmic game in which the Supreme Being indulges, with no desire for the fruits it may bring. It is this desirelessness that prompted J.A.B. van Buitenen to suggest that *līlā* is the opposite of *karman*, since "in creating, sustaining, and resorbing the world God has no cause to effectuate and no end to achieve" (1956:192 n. 83). *Līlā* also refers to Krishna's mischievous antics as a child in Braj, and to his amorous dalliances with

---

[3] The wider region within which Uttarākhaṇḍ is situated is usually called "Garhwal", though the checkered administrative history of the area makes this a somewhat ambiguous term (see Berreman 1972:11–14). My informants generally preferred the name Uttarākhaṇḍ, said to be employed by the Skanda Purāṇa to designate this region.

[4] Ethnographers have for the most part remained silent about Pāṇḍavalīlā and the peculiar prominence of the Mahābhārata in the Central Himalayas (though see Chandola 1977:18–21, and Nautiyal 1981:127–46).

the Gopis, both of which have been represented countless times in the artistic traditions of South Asia.

Finally, *līlā*s are enactments of events in the lives of incarnate gods such as Rama and Krishna, folk dramas characterized "by a heightened use of many media of communication and a charged and expectant mass participation" (Tambiah 1985:126–7) in which the gods themselves become present on the stage. As such, *līlā*s have been important performance genres for centuries. By far the best-known such traditions are Kṛṣṇalīlā and Rāmlilā, which have recently been the subject of much scholarly research and writing (e.g. Hein 1972 and 1987, Hess 1986, Kinsley 1979, Lutgendorf in press, Sax 1990, and Schechner and Hess 1977). By contrast, little has been written about Pāṇḍavalīlā in Hindi, and almost nothing in English. However, like Kṛṣṇalīlā and Rāmlīlā, Pāṇḍavalīlā represents a kind of folk theatre in which "ritual" and "performance" are inextricably intertwined.

There are many forms of Pāṇḍavalīlā, or *pāṇḍav nṛtya* (the Pandavas' 'dance') as it is sometimes called. It usually occurs during 'the dark months' (*andhere gā maiṇā*) of *mārgaśīrṣa* and *pauṣa*, roughly mid-November to mid-January, a time associated with animal sacrifice, exorcism, and the worship of Shiva and his fierce henchmen. However this is not an absolute rule, and one-day *līlā*s during the hot season are not uncommon. People tend to relate occasions of performance to the movements of the stars, saying that *līlā*s are sponsored by that person or village whose astrological sign corresponds to the initial date of the performance. *Līlā*s may last for three days, or for a single afternoon. The first performance I saw was in remote Sutol village, a two-day walk from the nearest road. It lasted nine days, and occurred three years after the previous one in that village. The second *līlā* I saw, in Bhatgwali village, lasted thirteen days and was occurring after thirty-five years.

Longer performances are often called by the name of the chief episode enacted in them: there are for instance the *cakravyūha* or 'Circular Array' which enacts the capture and death of Arjuna's son Abhimanyu; the *kamalavyūha* or 'Lotus Array', about which I have no information other than its title; the *śami* tree *līlā* whose culminating episode is the uprooting and establishing of the tree which protected the Pandavas' weapons while they were in exile; and the *gaiṇḍā* or 'Rhinoceros', the culminating episode of which is the hunting of a rhinoceros so that its hide may be obtained for use in the mortuary rites of the Pandavas' father, King Pandu. Different areas tend to specialize in one or another such *līlā*, but despite variations, all Pāṇḍavalīlās have this in common, that they are recitative, musical, and dramatic 'showings' or 'dancings' of the Mahābhārata.

Each village has its own traditions of dance and recitation. In Sutol, group dances alternated with discrete *līlās*. Most of the dances were very rustic: milking cows, cutting grass, pounding grain, and so forth. There were two bards, who cooperated in recounting the Mahābhārata. In Bhatgwali by contrast, dancing and recitation were both competitive: pairs of male dancers who had come from the surrounding villages were called, one pair at a time, to dance the battle between Arjuna and his son Nagarjuna. This dance was performed over and over every night until everyone had received an opportunity to compete. Bards also challenged one another to recall details of the Mahābhārata story, and if the bard so challenged failed to remember, he was considered defeated. Alternatively, one bard could put down (*dabā denā*) another by interrupting his recitation with a correction.

Two performances in Bhatgwali were of special interest: the Rhinoceros and the *śami* tree *līlās*. The Rhinoceros is always performed in the middle Chandpur region near Bhatgwali, in brief half-day *līlās* as well as the one and two-week performances that are themselves called *gaiṇḍā*. Though immensely popular in Chandpur Pāṇḍavalīlās, the story of the hunting of the rhinoceros is, to the best of my knowledge, unknown in the Pune edition of the epic. In this *līlā*, a pumpkin is decorated to look like a mustaschioed rhinoceros (few of these mountain peasants have ever seen a rhinoceros, so the representation is a bit odd), and stood on four legs made of cut bamboo, in a corner of the dancing square. This corner represents the serpent underworld (*nāgīlok*) where it lives. Bhima and Arjuna go searching for the rhinoceros, accompanied by a comic figure called the *naṭ* or (using the English word) *joker*, whose cowardly reluctance to stalk the rhinoceros contrasts with the Pandavas' own warrior-like courage and determination. After several false starts, the Pandavas bribe their companion with golden ornaments, and finally the three of them confront the rhinoceros, which Bhima kills with his club. In the more elaborate version performed in Bhatgwali the entire army of the Pandavas went in procession to a spring-fed pond, confronting and destroying en route several demons fashioned from pumpkins. The slaying of the rhinoceros was followed by the mortuary rituals of King Pandu, performed by a local Brahman priest. That afternoon in the main dancing square, a live goat representing the rhinoceros was beheaded, and later cooked and distributed as the powerful *prasād* or 'edible grace' of the Pāṇḍavalīlā.

Another popular *līlā* is that of the *śami* tree, the story of which corresponds for the most part to written versions of the Mahābhārata. It is said that when the Pandavas left for their exile, they were required under the terms of their agreement with the Kauravas to leave their weapons behind. They sought a place to hide them in Vishnu's heaven, in the mortal realm, and at Krishna's fortress-city of Dwaraka, but no one was able or willing to keep them. Finally the *śami* tree, which was growing in a cremation ground, split open its own stomach and hid the weapons inside. But it named a condition, saying "I will protect your weapons, but later you must protect me". The Pandavas left their weapons in the tree and proceeded into exile. Hence when the *śami* tree is carried to the Pandavas' dancing square and joyfully erected, participants say they are fulfilling the agreement made between the original tree and their ancestors, the Pandavas. In the *śami* tree *līlā*, a pine tree with no blemish is selected and carefully uprooted, enlivened through the *prāṇa-pratiṣṭhā* (literally 'establishment of breath') rite, delimbed by Bhima with his club, and carried to the dancing ground where it is proudly erected. Bards sing to it, weapons from the previous *līlā* are placed at its base, and on the final day of the *līlā*, both weapons and tree are 'buried' at a nearby water source. It needles are distributed amongst all villagers as the true *prasād* of the Pāṇḍavalīlā.

Perhaps the most humorous *līlā* I saw depicted the Pandavas' exile: when they reach the court of King Virata incognito and apply for work, they are given job interviews by his secretary. "What work can you do"? the secretary asks Arjuna. "Well", replies the latter, "I can teach singing and dancing." "Singing and dancing", replies the secretary. "Hmmm. Things are pretty tough these days. Tell you what: don't call us, we'll call you." Seeing the gods of the universe thus treated like ordinary hillbillies, the audience in Sutol responded with howls of laughter.

Every day in Sutol at about three p.m., two members of the *dās* caste would play their drums, summoning villagers to the dancing square, variously called the *pāṇḍav cauk, maṇdaṇ*, or *dyokhāḷ*.[5] The reciter of the Mahabharata, called a *paṃwāḷ*, would welcome the guests and then introduce the major characters of the drama—the five Pandava brothers, their wife Draupadi, mother Kunti, and so forth—one at a time. After each introduction, always chanted in a particular style (called *paṃwāṇī*), the bard would tell the drummer to 'call so-and-so present', then play the character's distinctive drum ryhthm (*bol*) while reciting a powerful invocation.[6] The player dancing the part of the character thus sum-

[5] The character ! represents the inter-dental lateral of spoken Garhwali, not normally represented in transliterations of Hindi and related languages.

[6] *birad*, possibly from Sanskrit *vṛddhi*, 'growth'.

moned would evince characteristic signs of possession: rolling of eyes, initial stiffness of limbs followed by uncontrollable trembling and rapid, deep breathing. These symptoms would become more intense as the invocation reached its climax, upon which the player, now fully "possessed" by the character, burst into the square and began dancing. In this way, the Pandavas and their entourage were summoned and caused to dance singly, then collectively. Along with certain other rituals discussed below, this constituted the afternoon's performance, which lasted about two hours. Afterward, villagers and their guests returned to their homes, rested and ate, then about eleven p.m. the drums sounded again. The afternoon sequence was repeated, and for the remainder of the night, from perhaps two until seven a.m., group dancing by the Pandavas and their 'army' alternated with discrete *līlās*, episodes or vignettes selected from the Mahābhārata and often dramatized in a humorous manner.

In Sutol village there were only two bards, but in Bhatgwali there were many of them engaged in competition. In one recorded example, a bard was challenged by another to answer a specific question, and this was his cue to take over the recitation:

Come forth, my son!
into the assembly of Dharamaraj awhile;
and sing the Pandavas' praises;
come into the assembly of Dharmanandana Yudhisthira!
Such is the *dharma* of those who live on.
Man dies, but the Pandavas' tale remains;
the bird flies, but the summit remains.
Blessed, oh blessed is a human birth;
and blessed, oh blessed, is a vision of the Lord!
Unions are at pilgrims' places, Badari and Kedar;
unions are in festivals, in this moonlit silver square.
And how many reunions in the parents' loving lap!
Yayati, Puru, Ikshvaku, Mirag,[7] Muchkunda, Pratipa,
Mahabhish, the woman named Ganga . . . .
Oh my bumblebee messenger,
How many kings from diverse countries have come today!
How did Mother Ganga become the queen of King Shantanu?

---

[7] This name does not seem to belong in the list. My recording is less than clear at this point.

How did King Shantanu receive the boon
that his woman would be named 'Ganga'?[8]

The bard who was challenged answered in the polite language characteristic of these exchanges.

Thank you, O Vyas, for the wisdom that
has emanated from your mouth!
In the mortal realm of diverse creatures this conference of gods,
this conference of men, has been established.
What a happy day it is, there are cheers in the assembly
of Dharmanand, praise, praise to the Pandavas!
Blessed be the lineage of Vyases, who have learned the entire Veda
and put it in their hearts;
the four Vedas that Brahma spoke with his four mouths.
You spoke the Vedas with four mouths,
you told the fundamental truth.
You examined the matter to its very root,
and told us the fifty-six lineages.

He next began to tell the story of Shantanu, and also of Parasara. Note how the audience is drawn into the performance, being explicitly likened, sometimes to an assembly of men, sometimes of kings, and sometimes of gods. Before completing Shantanu's story the bard quoted above addressed his audience:

Oh brothers, are you listening?
It is such a long, long story,

---

[8] *merā beṭā, hājurī ai jāṇo!*
dharmarāj kī patī vṛttikā sabhā mā o
ke ghaḍī beṭā, pāṇḍvoṃ kī stutī
dharmanandana yudhiṣthir kī sabhā mā hājurī hvai jāṇ!
raiyāṃ bacyūṃgo dharam yan huṇ.
manakhī mar jāṇ, paṃvāra rai jānā
pañchī uḍ jānī, ḍhayā rai jānā
dhanya ho dhanya ho, manuṣya deī
dhanya ho dhanya ho, haridarśana!
kit bheṭ huṇī badarī kedār mā
kit bheṭ huṇī tīrathoṃ bartoṃ mā
cholā cāndī cauk māṃ, mā bāpoṃ ke god māṃ

yayātī, pūrū, ikśākū, mirag, muckunda, pratīp mahābīs,
gañgānām strī. . .

myār bhañvar āj āyāṃ hvala deś deśom gā nareśa tuma
ek gañgā nām strī gañgā māī kan rājā śañtanu kī rānī hvae?
rājā śañtanu ne kahāṃ pāe varadān?
ki terī strī gañgā nām hvale?

and the frost has reached our knees,
on this star-filled night, in this assembly of men,
even the Pandavas who won the Mahābhārata are shivering!

As the Pāṇḍavalīlā progresses, it becomes more "polished". Initially, the dancers in Sutol struck me simply as farmers dressed in their workaday rags, inelegantly whirling about the square to the beat of a drum. Even their fellow-villagers showed little interest in the first few days of rehearsal. But after two or three days, dancers' movements became more graceful and coordinated, and they began to wear costumes, long flowing robes that drew my eye into the orbit of their steps. People began to arrive from more and more distant villages for each night's performance, until the crowd had grown into the hundreds. Every day additional characters were summoned, more members added to the Pandavas' army. They began to wear makeup, and then came the crucial day when the last player had been summoned, and the village god distributed weapons to the Pandavas (see below). As time went on, other elements of the performance became more sophisticated as well. At first, entrances had been a bit ragged: sometimes the proper dancer wasn't there, sometimes he or she would not be in the mood to dance. But by the end of the *līlā*, after the drummer summoned some character, just as newcomers in the audience began to look about to see where he or she would come from, the character would 'come over' his or her player, who would suddenly leap into the square and began dancing, to the delight of the crowd.

Inexorably, life in the village came more and more to center around the *līlā*. Days were rather listlessly spent eating, socializing, or surreptitiously sleeping, while each evening's drumbeat signaled that the 'real', focal activity, the Pāṇḍavalīlā, was about to begin. People were disoriented from lack of food and sleep; the normal world was de-emphasized, while in its place the world of the Mahābhārata was constructed anew each night.[9]

Pāṇḍavalīlā is in one sense performed for the sheer fun of it, for 'entertainment' (*manorañjana*). People in Uttarākhaṇḍ call it a *kautīk*, a 'spectacle', and having returned from a Pāṇḍavalīlā one is not asked "Did you enjoy the *līlā*"? or "Was it a good *pūjā*"? but rather, "How was the *kautīk*"? Singing, dancing, recitation of dramatic stories, the presence

---

[9] Cf. Hess (1986), who writes that Rāmlīlā, like the *Rāmacaritamānasa* of Tulasi Das upon which it is based, "forces an experience" of the world as *māyā* and/or *līlā*, through the dissolution of the boundaries it initially sets up between the play and the world, and between actors and spectators.

of the gods, elaborate drumming, visiting with friends and relatives, an engrossing competition—all of these factors combine to make Pāṇḍavalīlā one of the most popular entertainments in Uttarākhaṇḍ. However it is much more than that. After one *līlā* was over, I asked villagers why they had gone to so much trouble and expense to sponsor it. After some group discussion, they gave me a rather formal summary of the purposes behind it, to wit: (1) it is a commendable form of worship of their personal gods (*iṣṭadevatā*), the Pandava brothers; (2) they learn the Mahābhārata story, and also learn about religious and moral matters from performing and observing Pāṇḍavalīlā; (3) it 'closes the circle' of their relations, providing an opportunity to visit with distant relatives whom they rarely have a chance to meet; and (4) they stage the *līlā* out of self-interest (*svārth*), since from doing so they obtain some benefit (*fāyadā*) with regard to the health of their crops, avoidance of disease and calamity, and general well-being. In what follows, I would like to elaborate on this answer, explaining the assumptions and presuppositions that lie behind it, as well as suggesting how we can best understand the juxtaposition in Pāṇḍavalīlā of social event, ritual, and performance, in a mutuality that is though of as uniquely powerful and efficacious.

Interpreting Pāṇḍavalīlā

Pāṇḍavalīlā is a social event involving intra-caste visiting, commensality, and other transactions; within this event is a ritual directed toward specific ends; and at the core of this ritual is the playful *līlā per se*, characterized by the presence of gods upon the stage. Although boundaries between social interaction, worship, and play are fluid and changing, these three kinds of action are nevertheless thought of as distinct, and participants in the *līlā* orient themselves differently with respect to each. In paying especially close attention to local understandings of Pāṇḍavalīlā as ritual, we are enabled to make some inferences about the cosmology that lies behind it. This leads in turn to some ideas about how best to characterize that cosmology, and especially the nature of the "sacred" beings who inhabit it. For all these questions, the advantage of privileging native exegeses is that by doing so we are not limited to our own, extrinsic questions. By paying close attention to what participants say and do, we are also enabled to address those issues that are of greatest importance to them.

It is a point of honour among the Rajputs of Uttarākhaṇḍ (who comprise roughly eighty per cent of the local population) to bear the expenses of Pāṇḍavalīlā, and to feast as many friends and relatives as possible during its course.[10] After the first Pāṇḍavalīlā I witnessed (a simple one-afternoon affair) a local bard announced his plans to sponsor a nine-day 'Rhinoceros *līlā*' the following month. Bystanders expressed doubt that a single man could bear the costs of such a project, and suggested that he open a small teashop during the *līlā* to help cover his expenses. He took great offense at this, and insisted that he alone would bear all expenses. He would die, he said, and become nothing (*śūnya*), but his name would live forever because he had sponsored this Pāṇḍavalīlā singlehandedly.

For the Pāṇḍavalīlā, as for all spectacles in Uttarākhaṇḍ, the participation of all villagers, and hence the unification of the village, is deemed essential. Men working elsewhere return for the festivities, quarrelling factions declare a truce, and every household contributes labor and materials. Among the most important guests are village daughters (*disā-dhiyāṇī*) and their families. Because of virilocality, these women nearly always live elsewhere with their husbands. Thus they are simultaneously treated as non-resident members of the village and as honored guests.[11] When they are invited to their natal villages for such occasions, they must be given at least one item of clothing, as well as some 'dowry' money, before being sent back to their husbands' places. Villagers' maternal and paternal relations are also invited for the *līlā*. This pattern of feasting was very significant in Bhatgwali, where villagers sponsor a performance only once each generation. In 1985 the *līlā* occurred after a thirty-five year hiatus, and lasted thirteen days, during four of which I was the guest of Vishnu Singh. On the first two days Vishnu Singh and his family fed about thirty-five people twice daily, and on the last two days the figure jumped to about one-hundred. Vishnu Singh's case was typical: he calculated that each village household spent seven to eight-hundred rupees on the *līlā*, including supplies for its own members and guests, contributions to the collective stores, clothes and sweets for all the village daughters, and a parting 'mark' or 'gift' (*piṭhāiṃ*) of one rupee to each guest. Eating guests were almost exclusively limited to members of the Negi subcaste, since there would be difficulties if other Rajput castes attended, to say nothing of Brahmans. The local people took pride in their *līlā*, and confidently asserted that no

---

[10] The precise origin of the Rajputs of Uttarākhaṇḍ is a complicated and controversal question. Here it is enough to say that in Uttarākhaṇḍ, 'Rajput' refers to any member of any of the castes of the Kṣatriya *varṇa*.

[11] See Sax 1991 for an extended discussion of the place of the *dhiyāṇī* in Garhwali culture and society.

one could feast their castemates in such quantity, or with such quality foods, as could the Negis.

Local persons cite two precedents for such feasting from the Mahābhārata. It is said that after Bhima killed the demon Bakasur, King Naganjit in whose dominions the demon had been wreaking havoc rewarded him by feeding him *roṇṭ*, *pūḍī*, *pakoḍā*, *khājā*, *dūdh*, *ghī*, and *makkham*.[12] This is virtually a paradigm list of the "food of feasts" (Marriott 1968), properly fed by Raja Naganjit as an inferior to Bhima his divine superior. A second precedent is even more interesting. It is said that once, Duryodhana sent Durvasa and all his disciples to test Mother Kunti's *sat*, her 'goodness' or 'authenticity'. The Pandavas had finished eating when Durvasa and his entourage showed up.[13] What to do? They'd finished and there was nothing left. Krishna saw that there was only one rice grain remaining, instructed Kunti to cook it, and told Durvasa and his disciples to go and bathe in the river while their meal was being prepared. Through Krishna's *māyā*, they all felt as though their bellies were filled at the river and began burping and farting. When they returned to where Kunti had cooked up the single grain into a pot full of rice, they protested that they had no more room in their bellies. Thus Krishna saved Kunti's *sat*, even as he'd previously saved Draupadi's.[14] The point is that to be able to feed others is more than a matter of honour and prestige; it is a reflection of one's *sat*, of the truth of one's being, and thus of one's most fundamental nature. To be unable to feed others is to be profoundly inauthentic, and to lack the resources to do so, humiliating.

On those rare occasions when Brahmans stage a Pāṇḍavalīlā, their transactions are strictly limited. They invite neither friends nor village daughters, and no feasting occurs. A Brahman Pāṇḍavalīlā is, as one of my Rajput friends succintly put it, a 'matter of false impersonation' (*ḍhakosalewālī bāt*), since the *līlā* is thought to be more properly done by Rajputs. When the (mostly young, male) residents of the Brahman village where I normally resided sponsored a Pāṇḍavalīlā, they invited

---

[12] Bread sweetened with jaggery and fried in ghee or oil; plain, deep-fried bread; gram-flour cakes stuffed with vegetables and deep-fried in oil; pounded, dry-fried grains; milk; clarified butter; butter.

[13] In local versions of the Mahābhārata, Kunti accompanied her five sons on their forest exile.

[14] Another version has it that it was Draupadi who was tested: she had a basket from Surya Bhagawan that magically filled with food once each afternoon. The Pandavas had finished their daily meal when Durvasa and his disciples came: Krishna through his *māyā* saved her honor, even has he'd saved it at the *cīr-haraṇ*.

no guests. There was some exchange, but it was all directed inward, to fellow-villagers. In the Brahmans' Pāṇḍavalīlā, preliminary dancing began one evening, and on the next afternoon they 'danced' the Pandavas' weapons at the village goddess' temple, and sought her permission to perform the *līlā*. On the remaining three days, the same sequence was repeated in every courtyard in the village. Each house had prepared a platter with red powder, flowers, yogurt, an orange, and some raw, husked rice grains. A four-legged stool was placed in the middle of the square, and Bhima held his club upright on it. The village goddess's Brahman priest poured yogurt and then water over the club, and marked it with red powder. Then the red powder offered by the household was mixed with that in the platter brought by the Pandavas, and this was used to mark all the weapons and drums. Dancers, priest, and visitors were served tea, then left. The village was divided into three sections, and this kind of worship occurred in each house of a section, successively on the three final days of the Pāṇḍavalīlā. Local people told me that it was done to ensure good crops and weather, and general prosperity. They also stressed the mixing of the red powder from each household, which brought about the union of Brahman and Rajput residents of the village.

No Brahman caste-fellows from outside the village were invited, and to do so would have seemed ludicrous, since the Pāṇḍavalīlā is thought properly to be a Rajput rather than a Brahman tradition. In fact, aside from this single example, all the Pāṇḍavalīlās discussed here occurred in villages whose population was ninety to one-hundred per cent Rajput. When the Rajputs of Bhatgwali processed through the Brahmans' village on their way down to cut the *śami* tree, and later while carrying it back up, they were offered no hospitality whatsoever by their Brahman neighbours, with whom they were otherwise on good terms. The Rajputs were angry about this, and asserted that although it was perhaps true that the Brahmans had no duty to fete them *as* Rajputs, it was certainly the case that as the Pandavas, they were worthy of respect and even worship, and that by failing to provide the minimum of tea and biscuits, the Brahmans were guilty of a significant omission.

In general, then, Pāṇḍavalīlā is sponsored and performed by a community of Rajputs for their caste-fellows. In the process of sponsoring a performance, the village is constituted as a unity. As the men in Bhatgwali told me, Pāṇḍavalīlā 'closes the circle' of relations, so that distant relatives may be briefly united in its context. Large expenditures of wealth and effort to unite a wide-ranging group are characteristic of the maximal strategy predicted for the Kṣatriya *varṇa* by Marriott (1976:125–26), as is the pseudo-aristocratic reluctance of the Bhatgwali

Negis to feast Rajputs of other castes (though they were willing to feed Brahmans). Hence the Pāṇḍavalīlā is bound up with conventional caste identities and their associated transactional strategies. This is hardly surprising, since it is evident that most Hindus think of the content of their everyday social relationships as determined by transactions among persons and other beings. What is significant about the Pāṇḍavalīlā—and for that matter about feasting and public spectacle generally in India—is the reflexive nature of the transactions involved. By uniting, and in that sense defining, the persons and communities considered necessary for their performance, such spectacles create the social conditions of their own existence. Moreover they occur "on stage", as dramatic, foregrounded objects of attention, so that, in principle, both participants and observers are party to the creative processes involved.

Pāṇḍavalīlā is also understood as a ritual. Observers and participants explicitly identify it as a form of worship (*pūjā*) of the Pandavas, their relatives and allies. A successful Pāṇḍavalīlā generates not only group unity, but other fruits as well. In Bhatgwali, I heard a drummer remark "Wherever there is a Pāṇḍavalīlā, good crops and prosperity follow in every house". Recall that commendability of worship of the Pandavas as personal gods (*iṣṭadevatā*), health of crops, avoidance of disease and calamity, and the fastering of general well-being were all given as reasons for sponsoring Pāṇḍavalīlā. What sort of world is it in which the dance of the Pandavas can achieve such positive results? What is the relationship between dramatic performance and ritual, or—which is not quite the same distinction—between *līlā* and *pūjā*? What native term or concept am I glossing as 'ritual', and how is this related to Pāṇḍavalīlā?[15]

Because the efficacy of ritual depends upon ideas about the nature of the universe, cosmology can (to some degree) be inferred from ritual. And since rituals are directed to specific ends, those who perform them are careful to follow their procedures with some exactitude, so that the

---

[15] In addressing these questions, I have been greatly influenced by Stanley Tambiah's "performative approach", in which he boldly assays a "working definition of ritual", to wit: "Ritual is a culturally constructed system of symbolic communication. It is constituted of patterned and ordered sequences of words and acts, often expressed in multiple media, whose content and arrangement are characterized in varying degree by formality (conventionality), stereotypy (rigidity), condensation (fusion), and redundancy (repetition). Ritual action in its constitutive features is performative in these three senses: in the Austinian sense of performative wherein saying something is also doing something as a conventional act; in the quite different sense of a staged performance that uses multiple media by which the participants experience the event intensively; and in the third sense of indexical values—I derive this concept from Peirce— being attached to and inferred by actors during the performance" (1985:119).

desired ends might be obtained. Fail to observe the rules, and you don't get the results. Taken together, these ideas go far toward accounting for the contrast between the serious, rule-bound Pāṇḍavalīlā viewed as a ritual, and the playful, irreverent *līlā*s included within it.

What actions are necessary for a properly-performed Pāṇḍavalīlā, and how do they so effect the world that positive fruits result? Briefly, three sets of actions are important here. The first ensures the relative purity of the environment in which the Pāṇḍavalīlā is to take place. The 'four passes' (to the village) are 'bound' (*caukhāḷā bāndhā jātā hai*) before the *līlā* begins, so that negative and inauspicious begins or forces may not enter. A bamboo workbasket is torn into four pieces, each of which is filled with equal parts of squash, yellow pumpkin, 'seven-grain mixture' (*satanāj*), green and yellow powder, and an uncooked mixture of rice and lentils. Four men then take these basket-shreds (*caṅgtīra*) to the village periphery and fix them to the ground at the four cardinal points with cut lengths of bamboo and split nails fashioned from iron plough heads. These offering-filled baskets placate any malevolent beings who might be tempted to disrupt the *līlā*, and also bar their entry into the village. The 'piercing arrow' ritual (*bhed-bāṇ*) is performed at the beginning and end of each night's performance to chase away disruptive beings and counteract the potentially harmful effect of the wind, which is said to make people unconscious (*behoś*). Arjuna (or, more rarely, another character) takes a lit brazier of incense in his left hand, at the same time grasping grains or a lemon in his right. He approaches the fire which remains burning in one corner of the dancing square throughout the *līlā*, illuminates and honors (*ārati karnā*) it and the other three cardinal directions, and spins rapidly in a circle, with the brazier dramatically shooting off sparks and smoke. He then places the brazier on the ground and spins about again, hurling handfuls of grain into the air. Each time after hurling grain, he pounds the fist in which the remaining grain is clenched into his other, open palm, 'closing' the direction and thus keeping beneficial energies inside the village as well as inauspicious beings out. I was told that a *mantra* accompanied this action, but was unable to learn what it was.

These actions are formal, stereotypical, condensed and redundant—rituals in Tambiah's sense (see note 15). Moreover, since they are performed at temporal junctures (beginnings and endings) they serve to mark off the "ritual phase" of the Pāṇḍavalīlā within its larger, "social" context. This ritual phase is attended by a great deal of seriousness. People are concerned that the proper procedures be followed, in order that the Pāṇḍavalīlā may bring about its desired results. There are yet more procedures to ensure that negative and/or polluting beings do not participate in the *līlā*: for instance singers, dancers, drummers, their drums, and visiting village gods are marked with the five 'purifying' products of the cow (*pañca-gavya*—milk, butter, curd, dung, and urine) as they arrive in the square, and this is thought to drive off any polluting or disruptive substances or beings that may be 'adhering' to them. Theoretically, anyone is allowed to dance in the Pāṇḍavalīlā except for polluting beings such as dogs, untouchables, menstruating or post-partem women and those in contact with them, whose presence might invalidate the performance.

Local gods are perhaps the most effective removers of pollution. In Sutol village, the goddess Uluga Mai, a form of Kali, was especially fastidious about keeping the *līlā*'s environment pure. I recorded one of her outbursts, which went like this:

> There's no sugar for the tea, the rules are not being followed! Pollution (*chuachut*) has fallen in your courtyard. Don't blame me, and don't blame the Pandavas! . . . There's no order in this Pandavas' exercise (*ākhāḍā*). The god of your land (*bhūmī kā mālik*) can see all that you're doing, you'll have to answer to him! I cannot burn the blood of the transgressor. Promise me, promise me—I tell the *dharam* to all. . . . I am not a (blood-) sucking goddess; demand the oath of your old established (village) gods as well! Dance! Play! Perform your *līlā*!

Kali's accusations were borne out the next day when it was discovered that the wife of the man who was dancing the part of Krishna had given birth to a baby, so that all those affected by the consequent birth pollution had to stop dancing. However it was not to this event that Kali's remarks were understood to have referred, but rather to the likely onset of menstruation among some of the female dancers.

Disruptive entities appear even in the most carefully choreographed performances. In Bhatgwali for instance, I was seated precariously on a rooftop watching the *līlā* in which a goat representing the rhinoceros is beheaded. This was followed by the *līlā* in which Arjuna is wounded by his son Nagarjuna.[16] At the climax of this scene several women shrieked and swooned, while below in the dancing square men shouted, collapsed, or began agitatedly dancing. The large crowd surrounding the dancers surged forward, nearly engulfing them, at which point a pumpkin was shattered and its pieces tossed in all directions as a 'small sacrifice' to the malevolent beings (*chaḷ/pret*) hovering about, so that they would not harm Arjuna. This all happened so quickly that I had hardly recovered

---

[16] Nagarjuna of the Pāṇḍavalīlā is similar in many respects to the character Babhruvahana in the Pune edition of the Mahābhārata.

my bearings before it was over. Participants said that the swarming ghosts and demons, attracted by the goat's blood and the passion of the father-son battle, 'seized' members of the audience. However these beings were apparently pacified by the squash offering and subsequent rejuvenation of Arjuna, for when the latter arose, "possessed" persons quickly returned to normal. People sitting near me emphatically pointed out that in the following dance Nagarjuna recognized Arjuna as his father, and the two were reunited as father and son. It is important to note that Arjuna is in many respects the chief protagonist of the Mahābhārata; certainly he is the most heroic character in the Pāṇḍavalīlā. Parricide is almost never represented in Hindu art and literature (Ramanujan 1983), so this scene suggests extreme social and moral disturbance. Evidently most of the villagers knew that it was coming, so that the temporary mass possession was not as "spontaneous" as it initially appeared, however the episode does suggest that disruption of the Pāṇḍavalīlā by malevolent beings is a real and ever-present danger. At the conscious level, ritual actions that protect the environment of the performance are not "symbolic" of an underlying order so much as they are practical expedients in a world inhabited by numerous, potentially disruptive beings and forces.

Not only is Pāṇḍavalīlā itself a ritual, it also includes several rituals. Local Rajputs consider themselves the direct descendants of the Pandavas, and therefore consider it their duty to perform mortuary rites for King Pandu, which they often do by incorporating *śrāddha* rites into the performance. These are performed by Brahmans hired for the purpose, acting as priests for Nakul, regarded as Pandu's only biological son (by Madri). Participants were emphatic that these were 'complete' rituals in every sense. Not only Pandu's *piṇḍa śrāddha*, but also the *aśvamedha yajña* and accompanying *rāj tilak*, the final expiatory *yajña*s, the *prāṇa pratiṣṭhā* of the *śami* tree, and a goat sacrifice in the "orthodox" Garhwali fashion (some of these are described below) were all performed by Brahman priests.

Throughout this article I have called Pāṇḍavalīlā a 'ritual', intending by that term a translation of the local word *devakārya*, the 'work' (*kārya*) of the gods (*deva*). In a broad sense, any act of worship or devotion can be called *devakārya*, though in practice the term is usually applied only to public spectacles involving the physical presence of divine beings. In the Pāṇḍavalīlā, the most notably present gods are the Pandavas, but there are others as well. Some people told me that Pāṇḍavalīlā was the equivalent of worship of the goddess Kali, since Draupadi plays such an important part and is regarded as an incarnation of the goddess Kali. As the local saying goes,

> *āṭho avatār duropati līno*
> *kālī ke kavilās kurukśetra kīno*
>
> Draupadi took eight incarnations;
> the Kali of Kailash did the Kurukshetra (war).[17]

Thus by invoking Draupadi, honoring her and causing her to dance, villagers believe that they are worshipping Kali as in the so-called *caṇḍī pūjā*.[18]

However, by far the most important reason Pāṇḍavalīlā is regarded as a *pūjā* is that in it, the Pandavas are summoned, worshipped, and 'caused to dance'. The initial, purifying rituals are performed for the sole purpose of enabling them to enter safely and without hindrance.[19] Summoned in the manner described at the beginning of this essay, they and their 'army' are honored, and use their brief period of embodiment to engage in the pleasurable activity of dancing, to bless their devotee/descendents with good health and crops, etc., and to provide them with oracular information. In this sense the *pūjā* which is Pāṇḍavalīlā exemplifies pan-Indian patterns: worshippers summon a divine or royal guest, who is fed and/or honored, blesses the worshipper(s), and is dismissed.

It is also thought essential that the Pandavas' weapons, containers of their specific powers, participate in the *līlā*. In all Pāṇḍavalīlā, Arjuna and his son Nagarjuna dance with bows and arrows, Bhima with a club, Nakul with a scythe, Sahadev with a slate, Yudhisthira with a staff, Krishna with a *cakra*, and Draupadi with a dagger (again suggesting her identification with Kali). It should be emphasized that these weapons are indices (in the Peircean sense) of power by virtue of their infusion with it; they are neither icons nor symbols of it. They are intrinsically powerful and dangerous, and a great deal of care is taken to ensure that they are given only to the appropriate persons and in the proper circumstances. Participants stress that only the village deity (*bhūmyāḷ*, literally 'god of the land') can distribute weapons, and that this distribution constitutes his permission to sponsor the *līlā*, a permission which must be obtained before the performance can proceed.

---

[17] This adage confirms Hiltebeitel's deduction that Draupadi, who is explicitly identified with Shri in the printed versions of the epic, has at a "deeper" level more similarities to Kali. Uttarākhaṇḍī experts on the Mahābhārata harbor no doubts that Draupadi is a form of Kali. As Hiltebeitel has suggested, "living traditions of and about the Mahābhārata are often in close touch with traditional epic meanings that have escaped the classically based literary scholars" (1980:152).

[18] Worship according to the *durgā saptaśati* or *devī māhātmya*, the most popular local text for goddess-worship.

[19] Nautiyal (1981:127–130) also mentions the summoning (*āhut*) and dismissal (*vidāī*) of the Pandavas' *ātmas*, either by a *pūjārī* or by the *paṃvāḷ*.

In Bhatgwali for instance, there were a series of "rehearsals" from the sixth solar day, permission was sought from the *bhūmyāḷ* and the passes 'closed' on the ninth, and the weapons were first 'played' only on the fourteenth solar day of the month of *māgh*. When the *śami* tree was being carried up the mountainside to be installed in the Pandavas' courtyard, players were extremely careful that their weapons not touch the ground, lest the power contained in them escape (*śakti cūṭ jānā*). Recall that in this village, the Pāṇḍavalīlā was happening after thirty-five years. The weapons were manipulated in such a way that the continuity of three generations was assured: the youngest generation, referred to as 'little dancers', who were in effect novices or understudies, and had almost no contact with weapons; their fathers, who were the 'big' dancers of the *līlā* and performed with newly-made weapons; and the previous generation of dancers (most of them deceased) virtually represented by the weapons they had used in the previous *līlā*. These older weapons were not employed in the dance, but remained instead on the Pandavas' altar at the northeast corner of the square. On the final day of the *līlā*, they were taken in procession along with the *śami* tree (itself an index of the Pandavas' victory and rule), and 'buried' above the village water source, where their power could be recycled, as it were, into local residents. This manipulation of weapons seemed intended to facilitate an unbroken transmission of royal power (*kṣatra*) within the Pandavas' lineage, thought to include living village Rajputs.

In contrast to other aspects of the performance (e.g. the feasting that surrounds it, the episodic *līlās* per se), these rituals are undertaken with the utmost seriousness, since the ultimate success of the event is dependent upon them. By means of the rituals, the Pandavas can be summoned and their blessings obtained. There is however another important source of power in the Pāṇḍavalīlā: the villagers themselves. Although the designation of positive ritual benefits as 'fruits' is primarily metaphorical, the heat required to ripen them is more literally construed as *tap*, 'ascetic heat' generated by human action. Singers, dancers, and even some village spectators engage in a number of ascetic practices such as going without sleep, restricting the diet, foregoing sexual activity, and so forth. Such actions are generally talked about in terms of devotion (*bhakti*), but devotion often takes ascetic forms in India as elsewhere. Pāṇḍavalīlā performances generally begin around midnight, and last until dawn, for several nights in a row. After the third such 'night of standing',[20] when I went to interview the chief bard Padam Singh, he

[20] *khaḍī rāt* in Hindi; also *syūṃratā* (one's own night?) in Garhwali.

told me he'd been "awake for thirty-one hours, and asleep for one". This was typical of most of the players, who slept very little during the *līlā*. It was considered bad form, whereas to stay awake as long as possible was regarded as a merit-generating practice. Consumption of country liquor notoriously accompanies a great many local spectacles, but is unambiguously proscribed for the Pāṇḍavalīlā. Padam Singh told me that his own rule (*niyam*) was to abstain completely from sex, meat, and any contact with polluting persons for the duration of the Pāṇḍavalīlā. On the night before the *śami* tree *līlā* in Bhatgwali, the chief dancer came to the house where I was staying to inform all the dancers there that until they returned next evening, they were to observe a total fast. Evidently, the actions of humans are believed to have an important effect on the success or failure of a Pāṇḍavalīlā.

Possession and "The Sacred"

In a recent essay, A. K. Ramanujan asserts that there is an important difference between classical and folk aesthetics in India. Distinctions between poet and audience, poet and character, and character and actor are, says Ramanujan, the bases of classical poetics and its theory of emotions, while in folk theater,

> notions of possession are never far from the audience's mind . . . bard and character, bard and audience, bard and actor, actor and character are merged at crucial moments and separated at ordinary times. One goes to the theater/ritual to experience such mergers in different degrees (1986:69–70).

In Pāṇḍavalīlā, the boundary between actor and character is permeable, fluid and shifting. Bards play characters (the chief bard in Sutol also played the part of Arjuna, and recited the story *as* Arjuna to his brothers); characters possess members of the audience; and these onlookers-cum-players proceed to dance the characters' parts. Here Derrett's assertion is literally true: possession is theatre (1979:287). The most dramatic sort of possession in Pāṇḍavalīlā involves local village gods, what one might call "special guest-stars". Just as a village's resident humans, their relatives and friends enjoy coming to see the *līlā*, so resident gods, along with their relatives and followers, enjoy participating in the *līlā* by 'dancing' in the bodies of their human 'beasts' (*pasvā*) or 'abodes' (*dhāmī*). Their presence is auspicious, and they often give oracular information to members of the audience, usually with the *haiṃsaṇ juṇyāḷ* (literally "laughing barley"). In this oracular technique, a god approaches a spectator with a handful of unhusked grain and hurls it at him. The spectator counts the number of grains caught in his upraised hand: an odd number is bad, and an even number is good. Gods may also give verbal oracles to human members of the audience, pledge to eliminate their troubles or fulfill their desires, tell them the cause of some difficulty they are experiencing, and so forth. Sometimes during Pāṇḍavalīlā, new deities manifest themselves by spontaneously 'coming over' a person, causing him or her to begin dancing in the middle of a performance. In the two cases I saw, the possessed person was a woman, and the incident provoked a debate as to whether this 'new *śakti*' should be allowed to dance or not. Onlookers tried to find out the new goddess's name, allowed her to do obeisance to the Pandavas, and dismissed her as quickly as possible.

The typical style of possession of the Pandavas was quite different than that of local deities. At the beginning of every performance in Sutol, the Rajput priest of the local village deity would hurl some barley seeds, along with the appropriate *mantras*, at the Pandava brothers standing shoulder-to-shoulder on the small wooden stage elevated above the dancing square. They would tremble and shake, evincing the characteristic signs of possession, then leap on the the square and begin dancing. But aside from this initial and rather conventional sequence, they did not exhibit the characteristic trembling, wild dancing, rolled-up eyes, changed voice, and so on, of possession. Initially I thought this was evidence that the actors were not "really" possessed, but villagers told me that this was not so. Their possession was certainly authentic, but it was more subtle (*sūkṣma*) than possession by other gods. This is consistent with the Pandavas' benevolent natures, their kingly self-control as opposed to the typically fierce (*ugra*), uncontrolled natures of less refined village deities. Of course the Pandavas are the major characters of the *līlā*, and the positive benefits of a performance are due above all to their auspicious and benevolent presence.

What can we conclude about Pāṇḍavalīlā? It is certainly the case that through rituals and other practices, this form of "folk theatre" seeks to overcome distinctions between actors and the characters they play. If classical Indian aesthetic theory does indeed insist upon the separation of actor and character, where actors only "pretend to be like" the characers they play, then it seems that we are dealing with a very different sort of cultural form in Pāṇḍavalīlā, which seeks through ritual to make the characters literally present and thus achieve, by means of a transference of their inherent energy, a beneficial result (cf. Sax 1990 for a very similar process in Rāmlīlā). All of this relates to a central point regarding the interpretation of Hindu cosmology. If it is true as Tambiah writes that rituals "enact and incarnate cosmological conceptions" (1985:121), then we may infer the folk cosmology of these Uttarākhaṇḍ peasants from their rituals. An examination of the Pāṇḍavalīlā clearly suggests a cosmology in which the boundaries between gods and men are not only fluid, but can even sometimes be overcome. Although it has been claimed (chiefly by Eliade and his followers) that in some or all cultures, people react to a pre-existent and self-contained category called "the sacred" which occasionally "irrupts" into the profane, everyday world, Hindus by contrast often say that the gods they worship, the places to which they perform pilgrimage, the rituals they perform, are 'good' (*bhalā*), 'holy' (*pavitra*), and 'auspicious' (*śubh/maṅgala*), or have 'power' (*prabhāva/śakti*)—all of which I take to be major components of the notion of "the sacred"—only because of human action. Pilgrimage places, for instance, are often said to derive their unique qualities from the ascetic practices of sages in past epochs, and to retain their power through the continuing actions of pilgrims. The creative power of faith (*viśvās*), understood as an active expression rather than a passive attitude, is also important. When rural Hindus attempted to provide me with global exegeses of their religion they almost always included a line of explanation that went something this this: "In the Hindu *dharma*, we worship stones. If one has faith and worships in the proper way, then even a stone becomes God. But without faith, it is only a stone".

The Pāṇḍavalīlā requires a special environment prepared and maintained by humans, and humans are the vehicles in which gods speak and dance. The auspicious power of the performance is to some degree dependent upon the asceticism of humans who participate in it, and the Pandavas themselves could not become present if humans did not possess the appropriate *mantra*s with which to summon them. Now whether the Pāṇḍavalīlā, as it is experienced by peasants in Uttarākhaṇḍ, is to be seen as an "irruption of the sacred" into everyday life, or as a "deliberate human creation", is largely a matter of interpretation, since the question is not relevant to those who sponsor and perform it. But if we wish to understand their categories rather than reify our own, we must attend to their understandings and actions, and in doing so we discover human creativity at the heart of Pāṇḍavalīlā.

Bibliography

Artaud, Antonin. 1958 (1938). *The Theatre and its Double*. New York: Grove Press.

Berreman, Gerald D. 1972. *Hindus of the Himalayas*. Berkeley: University of California Press.

Chandola, Anoop. 1977. *Folk Drumming in the Himalayas: A Linguistic Approach to Music*. New York: AMS Press.

Courtright, Paul B. 1985. On This Holy Day in my Humble Way: Aspects of *Pūjā*. *In* Joanne Punzo Waghorne and Norman Cutler, eds., *Gods of Flesh/Gods of Stone*. pp. 32–50. Chambersburg: Anima.
Derrett, J. Duncan M. 1979. Spirit-Possession and the Gerasene Demoniac. *Man* 14(2): 286–93.
Goldman, Robert P. 1986. *Structure, Substance, and Function in the Great Sanskrit Epics* (*I*). Paper presented at the Festival of India Conference on Indian Literatures, The University of Chicago, April 1986.
Heesterman, J.C. 1962. Vratya and Sacrifice. *Indo-Iranian Journal* 6: 1–37.
—1964. Brahmin, Ritual and Renouncer. *Wiener Zeitschrift für die Künde Süd-und Ostasiens* 8: 1–31.
Hein, Norvin. 1972. *The Miracle Plays of Mathura*. New York and London: Yale University Press.
—1987. Lila. *In* Mircea Eliade, et al, eds., *The Encyclopedia of Religion*, vol. 8, pp. 550–54. New York: Macmillan.
Hess, Linda. 1986. *Staring at Frames Till They Turn Into Loops: An Excursion Through Some Worlds of Tulsidas*. Paper presented at the Festival of India Conference on Indian Literatures, The University of Chicago, April 1986.
Hiltebeitel, Alf. 1976. *The Ritual of Battle: Krishna in the Mahābhārata*. Ithaca and London: Cornell University Press.
—1980. Śiva, the Goddess and the Disguises of the Pāṇḍavas and Draupadī. *History of Religions* 19: 147–74.
Kinsley, David R. 1979. *The Divine Player: A Study of Kṛṣṇa Līlā*. Delhi: Motilal.
Lutgendorf, Phillip. In press. *The Life of a Text: Tulsīdās' Rāmcaritmānas in Performance*. Berkeley: The University of California Press.
Marriott, McKim, 1968. Caste Ranking and Food Transactions, a Matrix Analysis. *In* Milton Singer and Bernard S. Cohn, eds. *Structure and Change in Indian Society*. Chicago, Aldine.
—1976. Hindu Transactions: Diversity Without Dualism. *In* Bruce Kapferer, ed., *Transaction and Meaning*, pp. 109–42. Philadelphia: ISHI.
Nautiyal, Shivanand. 1981. *Gaḍhwāl ke Lokanṛtya Gīt* (Folk Songs and Dances of Gadhwal). Prayag: Hindi Sahitya Sammelan.
Ramanujan, A.K. 1983. The Indian Oedipus. *In* Lowell Edmunds and Alan Dundes, eds., *Oedipus, A Folklore Casebook*, pp. 234–65. New York and London: Garland Publishing.
—1986. Two Realms of Kannada Folklore. *In* Stuart Blackburn and A.K. Ramanujan, eds., *New Essays in the Folklore of India*. Berkeley: University of California Press.
Sax, William S. 1990. The Ramnagar Rāmlīlā: text, pilgrimage, performance. *History of Religions* 29(1).
—1991. *Mountain Goddess: Gender and Politics in a Himalayan Pilgrimage*. New York: Oxford University Press.
Schechner, Richard and Linda Hess. 1977. The Rāmlīlā of Ramnagar. *The Drama Review* 21(3): 51–82.
Singer, Milton. 1955. The Cultural Pattern of Indian Civilization. *Far Eastern Quarterly* 15: 23–36.
Smith, Brian K. 1987. Exorcising the Transcendent: Strategies for Defining Hinduism and Religion. *History of Religions* 27(1): 32–55.
Tambiah, Stanley J. 1985. A Performative Approach to Ritual (the Radcliffe-Brown Lecture for 1979). *In Culture, Thought, and Social Action: An Anthropological Perspective*. Cambridge: Harvard University Press.
Van Buitenen, J.A.B., ed. 1956. *Rāmānuja's Vedārthasaṃgraha*. Pune: Deccan College Monograph Series (#16).

RĀKṢASA BHĪMA: WOLFBELLY AMONG OGRES AND BRAHMANS IN THE SANSKRIT *MAHĀBHĀRATA* AND THE *VEṆĪSAṀHĀRA*[1]

DAVID L. GITOMER

ABSTRACT

Bhīma's killing of Duryodhana ends the great *Mahābhārata* war and intiates the reestablishment of dharma in the reign of his older brother Yudhiṣṭhira. Like many of the Pāṇḍava victories, however, the act itself is essentially one of adharma. Yet the extreme violence, submerged sexual cannibalism, and suggested sacrificial motifs in Bhīma's murder of Duryodhana and especially of his brother Duḥśāsana go beyond mere adharma: they look like the work of a rākṣasa. This observation prompts a reexamination of the preceding Bhīma stories in the main narrative. Not only does Bhīma possess certain physical and behavioral characteristics of these ogres, he actually weds a rākṣasī (Hiḍimbā) and on her fathers a son (Ghaṭotkaca) who figures significantly in the later narrative. Further, a programmatic series of encounters with (and killings of) rākṣasas construct (or reveal) the various aspects of Bhīma's identity, culminating in the persona capable of destroying Duḥśāsana by ripping open his chest and drinking his blood. Most important, these encounters place Bhīma in the center of the opposition between brahmans and rākṣasas, the keepers of the sacrifice and the smashers of the sacrifice. He intervenes as a "good" rākṣasa in scenarios of distress involving these two orders of beings (who are actually mirror images of each other), with the result that rākṣasas and Pāṇḍavas undergo transformations. All these motifs are highlighted in the Sanskrit drama called *Veṇīsaṁhāra* of Bhaṭṭa Nārāyaṇa, which uses Bhīma's bloodthirst to articulate his passionate devotion to Draupadī; the dynamics of this relationship can thus be more easily traced in the epic itself. Since the play also features a number of rākṣasas who seem to be functioning as vidūṣakas (normally the degraded brahman buffoons), we find peculiar confirmation of the brahman-rākṣasa connection as well as new insights into the nature of the comic in the classical drama.

Bhīma, the voracious and often violent Pāṇḍava brother of the *Mahābhārata*, is also aptly known as Vṛkodara, "Wolfbelly." His most significant characterological features, some of which are only suggested in the epic narrative (his passionate devotion to Draupadī chief among them) are explicitly delineated in the Sanskrit drama called the *Veṇīsaṁhāra* of Bhaṭṭa

---

[1] This essay was first delivered as a paper at the Madison South Asia Conference in 1985 and later revised for publication. It began as a condensation of parts of the second and third chapters of my doctoral dissertation. See David L. Gitomer, "The *Veṇīsaṁhāra* of Bhaṭṭa Nārāyaṇa: The great epic as drama" (Ph.D. dissertation, Columbia University, 1987) All translations from the play are mine. I thank Alf Hiltebeitel for his response to the Madison paper. His comments helped especially in modulating and refining the similitude between Bhīma and rākṣasas, in filling out the typology of the brahma-rākṣasa, and in stimulating further insights on Bhīma's role in "the sacrifice of battle." Thanks also to Norman Cutler for his many suggestions on a later draft.

Nārāyaṇa. This play, written around 700 A.D., is one of the very few post-Bhāsa compositions based on the *Mahābhārata* to have secured a prestigious place among Sanskrit dramas. In retelling the epic, the play, like any retelling, is actually interpreting it, but interpreting it within the expectations defined by the genre prescriptions of dramaturgical manuals such as the *Naṭyaśāstra* and other texts descended from it. This interaction between the epic story and the dramatic genre will figure in this discussion, but its theoretical aspects cannot be detailed here.[2] The fulcrum for this essay is an exploration of the range of affinities between Bhīma and the race of cannibalistic ogres called rākṣasas, clearly creatures who haunt the sacrificing, order-maintaining brahmans as their shadows. Yet there is even more to learn from rākṣasas than their role in this crucial psycho-mythic reality: Since the *Veṇīsaṁhāra* contains a number of horrific and horrifically funny rākṣasas—but no vidūṣaka (the brahman buffoon of the Sanskrit drama)—the play presents a wealth of insights into the peculiar nature of the comic in the classical Indian theater.[3]

There are several features originating in the play that seem so powerfully "correct" that they long ago seeped into the *Mahābhārata* most Hindus

---

[2] See Gitomer (1987), Chapter Three.

[3] After this essay achieved roughly its present form, I came across the wonderfully stimulating work of Kuiper (*Varuṇa and Vidūṣaka*) and Shulman (*The King and the Clown in South Indian Myth and Poetry*). Both works contain arguments too complex to be faithfully reproduced here, but mention of some of the main features of each must be given in order to acknowledge those points where the present essay, though different in orientation from either, approaches these other studies. Kuiper researches the Vedic god Varuṇa who, in his role as a sometime-asura, confronts the deva Indra in a verbal contest which replicates an original cosmogonical fight. This dynamic is repeated in the Trigata part of the *pūrvaraṅga*, the preliminary ritual to the drama proper. Kuiper sees the interaction of the nāyaka and the vidūṣaka in the play itself as an echo of this dynamic as well, and thus has traced a strong argument for a Vedic origin of the Sanskrit drama. He does not include the evidence of the *Veṇīsaṁhāra* in his "Dramas without a Vidūṣaka" section, pp. 210ff. Shulman discovers a primary and mutually transforming relationship between a mode of "tragic" limitation within an obsessively ordered "*saṁskāra*" and the mode which breaks free of this limitation through comic critique and "frame-shifting"—that is, clowning, an activity associated with the vision embodied in divine play (Tamil *vilaiyāṭal*, Sanskrit *līlā*). The dynamics of the Sanskrit drama are only used to begin a delineation of the typologies and interactions of the king and the clown, which would seem to be more vividly and radically realized in the Tamil and Telegu materials. While the discussion of these modes and typologies is genuinely revelatory, I feel uncomfortable with Shulman's identification of them with "tragedy" and "comedy." I have explored the possibilities of the use of these terms in the final chapter of my dissertation, and more fully in an unpublished essay, entitled "Karma and the Question of Tragedy." In the end, because of my very strong conviction that the aesthetic agenda of the classical drama tends, quite self-consciously, to naturalize all Vedic, mythic, psycho-spiritual and political themes to its own purposes much more than it "expresses" them, I decided to leave this essay basically unaltered, since it too observes these motifs from the perspective of classical form and aesthetics.

carry around in their heads; in fact, they recur in a number of later vernacular versions.[4] One is the figure of Bhānumatī, the wife of Duryodhana. She does not appear in any accessible Sanskrit recension of the *Mahābhārata* (actually, none of Duryodhana's wives are named); but most Indians (especially South Indians) familiar with the epic, even Sanskritists, when asked the name of Duryodhana's wife, will respond "Bhānumatī."[5] Another striking feature is the vow which forms the substance and the name of the play: In the epic, Bhīma vows to smash Duryodhana's thighs and drink Duḥśāsana's blood (2.63.10–15; 2.68. 27–29),[6] but in the play another element is added: With hands bloody from smashing of Duryodhana's thighs, Bhīma will bind up Draupadī's hair, which has been loosened from the time when she was sexually taunted and humiliated at the royal dicing assembly, the *sabhā* at which Yudhiṣṭhira gambled away the kingdom. And whereas the epic simply lets it be known at a certain point after the war (12.16.25) that Draupadī's hair is once again restored to its condition before the dicing, Bhīma's announcement of his vow at *Veṇīsaṁhāra* 1.21 promises a new, non-epic but epic-resonant motif—the bloody binding of the hair.

> Swinging around my throbbing arms
> I will smash this wrathful mace
> and grind the pair of Sudyodhana's thighs.
> With hands reddened by Kuru blood,
> clotted, sticky and thick, my queen,
> Bhīma will bind up your lovely hair.

This verse, and the enactment of its promise in the sixth act, carries an unavoidable visual reminder of Draupadī's menstrual condition in the epic, despite the play's avoidance, out of propriety, of any direct reference to a current menstrual condition.[7] For Hiltebeitel has shown, following

---

[4] Gitomer (1987), p. 251ff.

[5] Gitomer (1987), pp. 337–8; p. 419, n. 3.

[6] *Mahābhārata*, crit. ed. V.S. Sukthankar, et al. (Poona: Bhandarkar Oriental Research Institute, 1933–66). All citations refer to this edition by book, chapter and verse; translations from Books 1–5 of the *Mahābhārata* are from the translation of J.A.B. van Buitenen (Chicago: University of Chicago Press, 1973–78), except where I have indicated a retranslation in order to highlight the issues under discussion. I have also consistently made certain changes throughout, such as brahman for brahmin, kṣatriya for baron, baronial, etc. Elsewhere brackets will contain a rephrasing, parentheses the original Sanskrit. Translations from books 6–18 of the epic are mine.

[7] In verse 1.11 of the play Draupadī is described as *tathābhūtām*, "thus being," or "thus having become," i.e. "in that condition." Commentator Jagaddhara glosses this expression *ṛtumatīṁ nagnāṁ ca*, "having her period and naked." The more recent and more circumspect Lakṣmaṇasūri explains the term, "degraded because of the inappropriate actions of the dragging of the hair and garment, etc."

Hershman's observations concerning the close symbolic connections between women's head hair and female genitals, how the menstrual flow is represented as a form of purification for certain forms of rape.[8]

That this "menstrual" blood is the blood of sacrifice—at least, as a *literary* association—is made evident in the play; verse 1.25 is a beautiful extended metaphor of the sacrifice of battle, an image imported from the epic:

> We four brothers will officiate
> as priests while Lord Hari oversees
> the performances of the rite:
> Our king is initiated
> in the sacrifice called battle;
> his wife's loosened braid
> shows the purity of her vow.
> We will offer the Kauravas
> as victims; the fruit shall be
> the quelling of the painful insult
> to our beloved Pāñcālī.
> Now the drum of glory beats wildly,
> calling warrior kings to join the slaughter.[9]

After that sacrifice has, for Pāṇḍava purposes at least, been completed, the frightening visage of Bhīma finally appears on the stage in the last act of the

---

[8] Alf Hiltebeitel, "Draupadī's Hair," *Puruṣārtha 5, Autour de la deésse hindoue: études réunies par Madeleine Biardeau* (Paris: Editions de l'école des hautes études en sciences sociales, 1981), pp. 204–205, citing P. Hershman, "Hair, Sex and Dirt," *Man* IX (1974), pp. 274–298.

[9] The original actually has merely *patnī gṛhītavratā* for the fourth line, "[our] wife is one who has undertaken a vow." But the commentators realize the implications. Lakṣmaṇasūri explains that the wife along with the *yajamāna* (the patron of the sacrifice) becomes a beneficiary of the fruit of such a sacrifice because the vow she maintains is part of the consecration. Kale's subcommentary on Jagaddhara states that the vow being spoken of here is Bhīma's—when the Kauravas are destroyed, I will bind the hair. Identifications made in the *Brāhmaṇas* of Viṣṇu with Prajāpati, particularly in his role of sacrificer, are alive in the epic, especially in the *Udyoga Parvan*, where Krishna the ambassador is seen as fanning the flames of the enmity between the two families and in the *Āśvamedhika Parvan*, where Krishna plays a central role in producing the Aśvamedha sacrifice (14.70.21). As part of the peace mission, Krishna offers the kingship to Karṇa who, in his bitterness toward the entire kṣatriya race, predicts a slaughter in the form of a sacrifice; the metaphor is quite specific and extended there (5.139.29–40), and may have been an inspiration for Bhaṭṭa Nārāyaṇa. Compare also *Ūrubhaṅga* 1.6, 1.46, and 1.55. Again, immediately after Duryodhana has been felled by Bhīma's adharmic thigh-smashing, Balarāma turns the metaphor around to praise the Kuru king against Krishna's defense of Bhīma (9.59.25). My notice of the notion is as a metaphor within the economy of meanings shared by the *Mahābhārata* and the *Veṇīsaṁhāra*. The mythic and symbolic importance of the great war as sacrifice has been plumbed by Alf Hiltebeitel in *Ritual of Battle: Krishna in the Mahābhārata* (Ithaca and London: Cornell University Press, 1976).

Veṇīsaṁhāra to fulfill the promise of this verse by lovingly binding Draupadī's hair. By that act he is not only celebrating a sexual revenge; he is also ending, with his bloody hands, a period of impurity after menstruation, and ending her life as a *virahiṇī*, a woman bereft; he is proclaiming her an auspiciously married woman by applying the bloody *sindūra* to her part; he is anointing and reconsecrating a queen with that blood; he is, further, applying an auspicious "sandal paste" of blood to the icon of goddess Śrī, conferrer of kingship, and, finally, he is ornamenting his lover in an erotic ritual.

The artful union of these bloody motifs in the play leads us to a reconsideration of their epic sources. Although there are particularly Indian sexual overtones in the revenge on Duryodhana's thighs—there still exists a taboo against scratching the thighs for Indian men[10]—we are more interested here in the vow pointing toward the murder of Duryodhana's younger brother Duḥśāsana. It was Duḥśāsana who actually dragged Draupadī by her hair and garments while Duryodhana looked on, lewdly stroking his thigh. Bhīma vows he will rip open Duḥśāsana's chest and drink the blood while it still runs warm. Although it has been noticed with greater or lesser explicitness that the slaying of Duryodhana looks like a castration in return for an attempted rape,[11] one wonders why no explanation seems to have been offered about the configuration of Duḥśāsana's gory end.

Images from hymns to Durgā came to mind, and inevitably the story of Narasiṁha and Hiraṇyakaśipu. These may yet suggest further connections, but they seem to have no other apparent resonances with the character of Bhīma as he is developed in the epic. It is likely that if there is a quality of karmic revenge to Duryodhana's death, "the recoiling of the deed upon the doer," as Hiriyanna puts it,[12] then perhaps that same quality exists in the destruction of Duḥśāsana: he who violated Draupadī when she was

---

[10] On the male thigh, see O'Flaherty, *Origins of Evil*, p. 322–324, 334. There are also specific vernacular traditions about Duryodhana's thigh; see Hiltebeitel, "Draupadī's Hair," p. 205. Van Buitenen, vol. 2, p. 817, note to 2.63.10, stresses that the exposure of the thigh is not a bowdlerized version of a more specifically sexual exposure; rather, the invitation to sit on the left thigh is tantamount to claiming Draupadī as his wife. He cites legend and iconography depicting consorts seated on their husbands' left thighs. In the context of the mythological framework in which Śrī (Draupadī) is the conferrer of kingship, this would be a powerful and repugnant overture indeed. Van Buitenen does not draw this implication, nor does he choose to introduce the independently sexual nature (that is, apart from marriage) of the left male thigh.

[11] Hiltebeitel (1981), p. 205; also see Gitomer (1987), pp. 294, 296.

[12] M. Hiriyanna, *Outlines of Indian Philosophy* (London: George Allen & Unwin, Ltd., 1932), p. 96.

menstruating is made to "menstruate" by having a monstrous cavity torn out of his middle. Thus Duḥśāsana is literally unmanned, as will be his older brother Duryodhana when Wolfbelly breaks his thigh. The commission of this pair of acts constitutes *adharma* of the most extreme kind, especially for one like Bhīma who ought to be following the warrior code.

Yet even these mutilations do not seem to be the whole story; there is still the drinking of the blood. We can acknowledge that in a Dumezilian analysis Bhīma gets to be the ferocious side of the warrior as Arjuna is the chivalrous,[13] but Bhīma's actions go beyond mere ferocity. The more familiar one becomes with the epic, the more one sees that this cannabalistic carousing is Bhīma's way, and that, moreover, he always seems to be running afoul of those lascivious, cannibalistic wreckers of the sacrifice, the ogres called rākṣasas; rather, they always seemed to be running afoul of him. On the other hand, we shall show how Bhīma's fighting and killing rākṣasas indicates his likeness to that order of creatures. For the image of the middle Pāṇḍava ripping out the guts of a warrior (Duḥśāsana) and drinking his blood replicates the standard description of the rākṣasa feasting on battle carnage.

It should not be surprising, then, that Bhīma also enters into alliances with the ogres. There are, in particular, two features of the epic which are to a great extent articulated by Wolfbelly's interactions with rākṣasas. The first is the suppressed but genuinely passionate relationship of Bhīma and Draupadī, the relationship Mrs. Karve so convincingly presented as imaginative fantasy in *Yuganta.*[14] The second is an aspect of the overarching metaphor of war as sacrifice, evinced above, and Bhīma's role in that.

Though the *Veṇīsaṁhāra* does persistently fuse the patterns of the heroic, romantic *nāṭaka* with the chaotic and bloody epic narrative, a few words of explanation may be in order to elucidate the relationship between the various modes of presentation. In the Sanskrit belletristic tradition, which includes drama, the primary concern is with beauty and the response to beauty, love, always understood as erotic passion. Though the drama may have its origins in ritual or ritual enactment of myth, the content, style and implicit values of the developed *nāṭaka* are those of the lyric—sensual textures and human emotions. From the standpoint of this literature, then, the continuum from myth to lyric becomes one of increasing individuality, emotionality, and intimacy. In a play like the *Veṇīsaṁhāra* (or even one like the *Śākuntala*), the heroic events of birth, marriage, battle, kingship, and

---

[13] Georges Dumezil, *The Destiny of the Warrior*, trans. Alf Hiltebeitel (Chicago: University of Chicago Press, 1970), pp. 5, 59, 82–93.

[14] Iravati Karve, *Yuganta: the End of an Epoch* (New Delhi: Sangam Books, 1974).

death in battle form its epic- and myth-resonant *structure*, but dramatic genre expectation "fills in" that structure with its own content and style, its own content and style, its own implicit values. There is naturally a more distant, and certainly more complex, relation to myth: whereas the *Mahābhārata* resonates with living myths, the *Veṇīsaṁhāra* resonates with the *Mahābhārata* thematically and aesthetically, evoking the aesthetic universals, the *rasas*, as well as the epic ones.

Thus the more raw sexual motifs of the epic—menstruation and castration—are not obliterated in the *Veṇīsaṁhāra*, but become at once more symbolically and less explicitly suggested, finding a place within the more graceful norms of erotic passion between a man and woman, here between Wolfbelly Bhīma and Draupadī. For despite attempts by Indo-Europeanists such as Dumezil to pair Draupadī (who incarnates Śrī) with Arjuna (who incarnates Indra and is therefore the "type" of the king),[15] it is only Bhīma whose passionate devotion claims her in such a way that in the epic's transformation to drama the couple can become *nāyaka* and *nāyikā*. The great number of episodes in the epic in which Bhīma's special relationship with Draupadī is narrated cannot be detailed here; the abduction by Jayadratha (3.248–263), the killing of Kīcaka in *Virāṭa Parvan* (4.13–23), and the fetching of the *saugandhika* flowers (3.146–153; 3.157–159) are chief among them. What the abduction story achieves, and the killing of Kīcaka in an even more focused manner, is the bringing together in a single cohesive and continuous narrative what in the main narrative is separated by thirteen years in time and at least six *parvans* of text: the sequence of Draupadī's sexual humiliation, her call for revenge (coupled with a reviling of Yudhiṣṭhira's inaction), Bhīma's response in the form of a vow (coupled with a declaration of his willful rebellion against Yudhiṣṭhira's wishes), and his enactment of her revenge in gory mutilation. (And it is important to remember that Draupadī and Bhīma's collaboration against Yudhiṣṭhira constitutes a very real and literal opposition to Dharma—they desire the justice of a revenge that cannot be contained within the notion of dharma.) It is almost as if the authors of this episode were attempting to reintegrate the primary narrative, whose plot had gotten pulled apart by mountains of rich interpolative material, by creating microcosms with the original dynamic intact. Bhaṭṭa Nārāyaṇa, using the *nāṭaka* format, was able to do the same thing with the main narrative itself.

---

[15] Alf Hiltebeitel (1976), p. 169. Hiltebeitel is actually footnoting Georges Dumézil, *Mythe et Epopée*, I, p. 633. See Gitomer (1987), pp. 298–299, for a discussion of the traces of the Draupadī-Arjuna relationship that remain in the epic.

Although the Killing of Kīcaka draws together and recapitulates elements from the primary narrative of the epic, there are new elements as well. The absence of a royal-contest setting and the emphasis on Draupadī's beauty casts the story of humiliation and revenge in a mold more markedly romantic than heroic. The extremes of tenderness and violence on the part of both Draupadī and Bhīma (as opposed to a programmatic polarization) are part of the dynamic of passion and mutual empowerment original to the epic and necessarily retained in this episode and in the *Veṇīsaṁhāra*. Yet there are intermittent motifs in the epic, woven into the Kīcaka story, which suggest a further dynamic in the Draupadī-Bhīma relationship, the kind of romantic love that is seen in the *saugandhika* episode, to be discussed below. Yet in most of the epic this dynamic parallels in an exaggerated fashion the conventional depiction of female and male in Sanskrit dramas: the physical loveliness of Draupadī and the fierce bloodthirstiness of Bhīma. It is in the enactment of this bloodthirst that Wolfbelly shows his rākṣasa nature. In fact, when Draupadī is first pursued by Kīcaka, she prays for protection to the sun, who sends an invisible rākṣasa to guard her (4.14), but that ogre is only partly successful at assisting Draupadī in repulsing Kīcaka's advances while the courtiers and the powerless Pāṇḍavas look on (4.15). She then seeks help from Bhīma, who is shown to be, in contrast, a more effective rākṣasa:

> Holding Kīcaka the powerful Bhīma roared out like a tiger that is hungry for meat and has caught a large deer. He pushed [Kīcaka's] feet, hands, head, and neck all into his trunk . . . When Kīcaka had been rendered one mangled ball of flesh, mighty Bhīmasena showed him to Draupadī. (4.21.58–60)

Yet the killing of Kīcaka is not only significant as an inset of Bhīma's larger drama of adharmic revenge; even if Bhīma did not make and fulfill a vow which entailed tearing open the chest and drinking the blood of a presumably still living warrior (Duḥśāsana), there are a number of other narrative and characterological motifs which reveal affinities to the race of ogres. In epic literature, a sound interpretive principle is that "the details of the hero's death and the fatalities that bring it on are telling strokes in the protrayal of his character."[16] As Victor Turner has written, "Since most epics are replete with combats, battles, wars and assassinations, the killing scene is often an epitome or multi-vocal symbol of the scheme of values underpinning the whole work."[17] A corollary of this principle is that a hero

---

[16] Hiltebeitel (1976), p. 39.

[17] Unpublished article, cited in Alf Hiltebeitel (1976), p. 37.

incorporates an enemy's power by killing him. In the *Mahābhārata* the clearest example of this is the slaying of the courageous and battle-ready Karṇa by the supremely skilled but reluctant-to-fight Arjuna.

Bhīma kills rākṣasas. Although in the list of partial incarnations Duryodhana himself is identified with Kālī, "Discord," the personification of the evil age which will be ushered in as the epic closes, "all his brothers were born among men as creatures of the Rākṣasas, one hundred in all, from Duḥśāsana onward, cruel of deeds." (1.61.80–85) The killings of the various rākṣasas prefigure Bhīma's decisive role in the destruction of the Kauravas headed by Duḥśāsana, and prepare us for the ugly, unchivalric and gory manner of his human killings. It seems as if Bhīma must, through his encounters and killings of rākṣasas during the two forest exiles, incorporate more and more of the nature of rākṣasas, the enemies of dharma, in order to commit the deed he has vowed on Duḥśāsana, an adharmic deed unthinkable for the other Pāṇḍavas—the ripping apart of a fellow kṣatriya while alive, and the drinking of his blood. The litany of "Hiḍimba, Baka and Jaṭāsura" is used by Bhīma to proclaim his capacity for such violence, and by Draupadī to remind him of it. Each of these episodes, however, has an individual character which shows a different aspect of Bhīma's rākṣasa persona, and of the corporate Pāṇḍava ethos as well.

Bhīma's first encounter with rākṣasas is fraught with the greatest consequences for him personally and for later developments in the epic. It occurs soon after the fire in the lacquer house (1.124–138), which itself is precipitated by Bhīma when he learns that Duryodhana has plotted to have Kuntī and the Pāṇḍavas burned alive to remove them from possible succession to the Kuru throne. Bhīma then carries the entire family to safety, and stays awake the whole night while the rest of his family sleeps, lamenting this forced exile. The story that follows gives us a brother and sister rākṣasa pair; the brother, Hiḍimba, would eat Kuntī and her sons, and must be slain by Bhīma. The sister named as his twin—Hiḍimbā—falls in love, or lust, with the beautiful, brawny Bhīma, is wed to him, more by order of Yudhiṣṭhira and Kuntī in response to her plight than because of Bhīma's desires, and bears him a son, Ghaṭotkaca, who later becomes a faithful soldier, a "good rākṣasa," in the Pāṇḍava war with the Kauravas. The story (1.139–143) seems to want to say more about Bhīma than that he is capable of competing with and defeating a rākṣasa on its own terms: on the one hand he does incorporate the rākṣasa's adharmic might by fighting and killing him; on the other hand, he acquiesces to a lusty union with a rākṣasī that is procreative and ultimately of value to the family's efforts to regain the kingdom; Hiḍimbā even expressly claims that she will save the Pāṇḍavas (1.143.5–15), as Draupadī is later said to do (2.64.1–3). The story goes a long way in reconciling the adharmic aspect of rākṣasa Bhīma with his role as a Pāṇḍava brother.

Yet there is another aspect of Bhīma's rākṣasa nature that has wide-reaching effects. Bhīma's entering into rākṣasa-hood is somehow able to transform bad rākṣasas into good rākṣasas. The thoroughgoing good-heartedness of Ghaṭotkaca is our first clue to this transformation. When Hiḍimbā and Ghaṭotkaca take leave of Bhīma, Ghaṭotkaca promises his father that he will come whenever he is needed (1.143.37). During the forest exile, the brothers and Draupadī are journeying to holy sites in the Himalayas in hopes of meeting up with Arjuna. When Draupadī becomes weary, Bhīma merely thinks of Ghaṭotkaca, described as *dharmātmā* ("whose soul is dharma"), and he comes along with his rākṣasa friends to carry Draupadī as well as the Pāṇḍavas themselves while Bhīma guides the way. When Bhīma addresses Ghaṭotkaca he says, "Son of Hiḍimbā, your undefeated mother has become weary (*haiḍimbeya pariśrāntā tava mātāparājitā*)." (3.145.4) Ghaṭotkaca is being told that he has two mothers, his rākṣasa mother Hiḍimbā, and Draupadī, the primary wife of his father.

Bhīma's intervention between brahmans and rākṣasas shows another, more complex face of his capacity to transform rākṣasas. There is a curious connection between brahmans and rākṣasas. They are first of all opposites: brahmans are the keepers of the sacrifice which sustain the world and the dharma of society; rākṣasas destroy the sacrifice, and are especially associated with the carrying off of married women, an act which strikes directly at the Brahmanically-defined social fabric. Brahmans obsessively maintain their purity by ritual cleansing and vegetarianism; rākṣasas are foul-smelling man-eaters. Being opposites, the two orders of beings are brought together by natural enmity in scenarios of distress. Whenever a great sacrifice is performed, one can be sure that a menacing rākṣasa lurks nearby, ready to jump in and wreck its order. When anxiety about the sacrificial order takes the form of a voracious, rapacious creature who cannot tolerate that order and who suddenly appears to destroy it, it seems likely that one function of rākṣasas is to be the dark side of brahmans. Thus, while demons (*asuras*) in general may represent the structural and functional opposite of gods (*devas*),[18] rākṣasas in particular are the opposite of brahmans. The astonishing resemblance between the comic manifestation of the brahman as the vidūṣaka (in the drama) and the rākṣasa confirms the perception of their mirrored twinhood, as does the existence of brahma-rākṣasas such as Jaṭāsura, whose story will be discussed below.

---

[18] Wendy Doniger O'Flaherty, *The Origins of Evil in Hindu Mythology* (Berkeley: University of California Press, 1976), p. 64.

Bhīma, by being like a rākṣasa (and fighting like a rākṣasa) is able to destroy rākṣasas, and is therefore capable of neutralizing the brahman anxieties about rākṣasas, that is, about the chaotic violence involved in the sacrifice. In the *Mahābhārata* narrative, this finds expression in making bad rākṣasas into good rākṣasas. A secondary result, as we shall see in the next story, is somehow to make the Pāṇḍavas into brahmans. Such a transformation makes us suspect that we have a dynamic similar to that found in the stories of violent brahman revenge (Paraśurāma and, to a lesser extent, Aśvatthāman), but from the opposite side: these are kings who would appropriate the entire symbolic apparatus of order—the order-defining (brahman) as well as order-maintaining (kṣatriya) modalities.. The second rākṣasa-killing episode, the killing of Baka (1.145–152), follows immediately upon the first (the killing of Hiḍimba), and is at least in part an ambivalent parable of the king-brahman relationship.

After the Pāṇḍava family has wandered for some time disguised as ascetics, Vyāsa appears to encourage Kuntī and the brothers, disguised as brahmans, to reside with a brahman family in the nearby town of Ekacakra. The brothers go out begging everyday, and give what they receive to Kuntī. Half the entire amount of food is fed to the voracious Bhīma (Vṛkodara, "Wolf Belly"); this same apportioning is specified when Kuntī later gives instuctions to the new bride Draupadī (1.184.6). In a grotesque perversion of kingship, it turns out that the Ekacakra region is held in the grip of a rākṣasa named Baka, who in return for protection demands a wagonload of rice, two buffaloes and a human. The families take turns satisfying Baka's demands; if a family should refuse, Baka eats everyone in it. It is now the turn of the Pāṇḍava's brahman host. In return for the hospitality offered them, Kuntī volunteers Bhīma to take the tribute and destroy Baka. Yudhiṣṭhira berates his mother for sacrificing Bhīma, whom he considers their ultimate weapon (1.150.5–11).

Kuntī replies that it is precisely because Bhīma has proven himself so powerful that she has confidence in him. Further, she identifies the act as precisely manifesting the dharma of kings—protection, first of all to the brahman hosts, but more generally to the entire community which is at the mercy of the terrible Baka. Out of this will accrue the religious merit and worldly fame which will establish Pāṇḍava identity as kings. At this point, exiled and thought to be burned alive through the machinations of Duryodhana, they barely exist. Kuntī's argument, speaks directly to Yudhiṣṭhira's kingly concerns, and convinces him. (1.150.21–25)

Bhīma takes the food to Baka's grove, but when the rākṣasa arrives Bhīma begins eating the food himself, heedless of Baka's rage. Even though Baka smashes a tree on his back, Bhīma waits until he is finished eating the rākṣasa-sized meal to start fighting. After much wrestling and tree-throwing, Bhīma finishes him off.

> When he saw that the rākṣasa was fading, the Wolf-Belly squeezed him to the ground and pounded him with his fists. Then he forcefully pushed his back down with his knee, grabbed his neck with his right hand and his loincloth with the left, and broke in two the frightfully screaming rākṣasa. Blood gushed from the ogre's mouth, as the loathsome Baka was broken by Bhīma. (1.151.21–24)

Bhīma then instructs the frightened members of Baka's household and retinue never to harm the humans of the country again, under penalty of death. They agree; "henceforth the rākṣasas there were friendly whenever they were sighted by the townfolk about the city." (1.152.5) The Pāṇḍavas' host tells the people that it was a powerful brahman (!) who destroyed Baka. All four castes then institute a *brahmamahā*, a festival or feast in honor of brahmans.

Because of the initial frame of the brahman host's hospitality and the endearing protrayal of his family, it does not seem that the intention of the story is to take a jab at brahmans for arrogating to themselves credit for maintaining the good of the people. On the other hand, stories such as this one and Arjuna's triumph at the *svayaṁvara* of Draupadī, in both of which the Pāṇḍavas display their prowess in the disguise of brahmans, may have been included to "balance" the force of the Droṇa-Aśvatthāman narratives, themselves an "historical" surfacing of the Jāmadagnya Bhṛgu materials in which brahmans appear as better warriors than, or even as weapons-gurus of kṣatriyas. Yet as we saw above, Bhīma's role of neutralizing the menace of rākṣasas for brahmans, which even on the literal level is certainly a proper function of kings, becomes possible through his being a rākṣasa. Given the deeper symbolic connection between brahmans and rākṣasas, it is not at all surprising that once he kills the rākṣasa (who here functions as a "bad" kṣatriya), Bhīma, the "good" kṣatriya, also usurps the brahman role as well.

Were it not for the element of a brahman-rākṣasa ambiguity, the final incident in which Bhīma slays an individual rākṣasa, "The Slaying of Jaṭāsura," (3.154) would be "a fairly routine rākṣasa story, which serves to remind us that the forest is not only the tranquil domain of saints but the terrifying haunt of demons."[19] For Jaṭāsura is a brahma-rākṣasa who

---

[19] Van Buitenen, Introduction to *The Book of the Forest*, in Volume 2 of *The Mahābhārata*, p. 201.

wears his hair in an ascetic's matted locks, a class of ogres much better known in the *Rāmāyaṇa*.[20] He resides with the Pāṇḍavas and Draupadī for some time, harboring designs on their weapons. Then he carries off Yudhiṣṭhira, Draupadī and the twins (Arjuna is visiting Indra) while Bhīma is away hunting. Typically, Yudhiṣṭhira lectures the ogre on dharma even as he is being abducted; then makes himself heavy to slow Jaṭāsura's progress until Bhīma arrives. Sahadeva attempts to engage him in combat. When Bhīma shows up, he characterizes the crime as an *abduction of Draupadī* while acknowledging at least the partial authenticity of Jaṭāsura's brahmanhood:

> Why should I have killed you—you were doing us favors, never giving offense, a guest who appeared to be an innocent brahman. Anyone who had killed you, even though knowing you for a rākṣasa, would have gone to hell [for the crime of *brahmahatya*]. (3.154.33–34)

Bhīma then promises to destroy him, reminding him of the deaths of Baka and Hiḍimba. The conventionalized wrestling and throwing of trees and rocks culminates in a scene no less vividly gory for its predictability:

> The strong-armed god-like Bhīma lifted him up high and powerfully crashed him to the ground. The Pāṇḍava fractured all his limbs and with a blow of his elbow snapped the head off the trunk. Jaṭāsura's head, severed by Bhīmasena's force, fell with clamped lips, bulging eyes, and clenched teeth to the ground smeared with blood. (3.154.58–60)

The epic motifs involving brahmans and rākṣasas are found in surprising aesthetic transpositions in the *Veṇīsaṁhāra*. When first we encounter the rākṣasas of the play, they seem to possess the conventionally recognizable marks of their breed; they are scavenging the battlefield for the carrion of the combatants in the great war. Within the aesthetic norms governing the classification of experience in literary works, such a scene ought to be a depiction of *bībhatsa rasa*, the disgusting. Yet it is unquestionably comic, and emerges as a species of *hāsya*; these rākṣasas, and another in the final act

---

[20] The most famous, of course, of the *Rāmāyaṇa* brahma-rākṣasas is Rāvaṇa. At *Rāmāyaṇa* 3.32.12 he is described as *paradārābhimarśanam*, "seizing other men's wives," and in the next verse as *yajñavighnakaram*, "making obstacles to the sacrifice." The same chapter, verse 23, uses the epithet *paulastyakulanandanam*, "delight of the Paulastya clan," which recalls another epic theory about rākṣasas: they are all descended from Pulastya, fourth son of Brahmā. (This is presumably the reason why Pulastya intervenes when Parāśara tries to destroy all ogres at a *rākṣasasattra*, "sacrificial session whose sacrificial victims are rākṣasas.") This means that technically *all* rākṣasas are brahmans, but this fact seems to have only intermittent significance for *Mahābhārata* authors. Commentaries on *Rāmāyaṇa* 1.8.17 make it clear that brahma-rākṣasas are brahmans who have not properly observed the sacrificial ordinances; these creatures themselves seek and enter the *chidras* ("gaps, holes, fissures") in the sacrifice and destroy it—truly, a nightmare of anxiety about the sacrificial procedure.

of the *Veṇīsaṁhāra*, function in a kind of vidūṣaka (buffoon) role in a play where there is no vidūṣaka. Before looking at the tantalizing possibilities in this substitution, we ought to consider a number of motifs found in the Bhīma-rākṣasa encounters in the *Mahābhārata* which are carried over into the play. To see these motifs more distinctly, especially that of the passion of the passion of Bhīma and Draupadī, we will have to look back and forth from play to epic to play.

The Act Three prologue begins as the ogres Lardbouquet (Vasāgandhā, Skt. Vaśagandhā) and her husband Bloodfiend (Luhilappia, Skt. Rudhirapriya) are gorging themselves on the blood, fat and flesh of soldiers killed in the great war. As they name the warriors they are eating, the audience learns how far the battle has progressed. The relationship of Bhīma and his first wife, the rākṣasī Hiḍimbā, is given particular attention. We learn that the son born to her and Bhīma, Ghaṭotkaca, has been killed. In the play (3.3 +), Hiḍimbā is afforded the status of a queen of rākṣasas, a status not known elsewhere; for the rākṣasas at least, she is an intimate of Subhadrā and Draupadī, who share her grief in their own loss of Abhimanyu. In the epic, as we have seen, Ghaṭotkaca promises to come whenever Bhīma wishes, but Hiḍimbā largely disappears after her marriage and world-ranging dalliance with Bhīma. (In the manner of rākṣasas, Ghaṭotkaca is born on the the very day he is conceived, and born as a vigorous child, not a helpless infant.) The play wants to afford a continuing power and status to the rākṣasa consort of Bhīma, and conversely to "royalize" Bhīma's rākṣasa nature.

The rākṣasa of Act Six, called Cārvāka (perhaps in derogation of the materialist philosophic school known by that name) identifies himself as a friend of Duryodhana and pretends to be a brahman in order to deceive the Pāṇḍavas. He convinces Yudhiṣṭhira and Draupadī that Bhīma and possibly Arjuna have been slain by Duryodhana in the final battle of maces, and nearly succeeds in driving them to a desperate suicide on the funeral pyre. The character and the incident are no doubt inspired by *Śānti Parvan* 12.39, where a rākṣasa named Cārvāka, also called a friend of Duryodhana (12.39.22,33), and also disguised as a brahman, deceives the assembly of brahmans gathered to greet the victorious Yudhiṣṭhira as he enters the *sabhā* of the palace at Hastināpura. He curses the Pāṇḍavas and tries to convince the brahmans that Yudhiṣṭhira is a killer of their kinsmen. The brahmans recognize the ruse and burn him on the spot with their *tejas*. It turns out that in a former *yuga* this Cārvāka had practiced *tapas* and pestered Brahmā to grant him a boon of protection. It was predicted, however, that he would become a friend of Duryodhana's and, through insulting brahmans, be burnt by them. Since the Cārvāka incident in the *Mahābhārata* occurs at a point in the story after the close of the *Veṇīsaṁhāra*, the use of Cārvāka in the play, though invented by Bhaṭṭa Nārāyaṇa, is nicely consistent with the ogre's character in the epic. There may have even been a special delight for the audience watching Cārvāka try to get Draupadī and Yudhiṣṭhira to immolate themselves on the funeral pyre, knowing that the rākṣasa himself would end up burnt to ashes.

There are some loose similarities between the Jaṭāsura episode of the epic and Cārvāka's role in the play. Both make victims of Yudhiṣṭhira and Draupadī *together* while Bhīma is away, suggesting the crucial role Bhīma plays in enabling Draupadī (as Śrī) effectively to confer kingship on Yudhiṣṭhira. Both work their deception by using a brahman disguise to gain trust. It is interesting is that both Jaṭāsura and the Cārvāka of the previous *yuga* are actually living as brahmans. We saw above that Jaṭāsura had enough authenticity in his brahman role to make Bhīma angrily declare that anyone who killed him would be guilty of *brahmahatya* and go to hell. The *kṛta yuga* Cārvāka performs mighty austerities. The *Veṇīsaṁhāra* Cārvāka relishes his part, enacting all the stereotypical (but perhaps exaggerated) *noli-me-tangere* obsessions associated with brahmans. Beyond the comic potential of these scenes, they again serve to remind us of the peculiar relationship between brahmans and rākṣasas, a relationship in which Bhīma always seems to be intervening. A minute before the offstage uproar signalling the entrance of a Bhīma so bloody he has to announce "I am no ogre (*nāham rakṣo* 6.37)," the ogre disguised as a brahman suddenly exits. This exit is as mysterious and unmotivated as the sudden appearance of the "foremost brahmans" praising Bhīma in the very last verse of the Jaṭāsura episode (3.154.61).

The tale of the slaying of Jaṭāsura is sandwiched between two versions of a story that not only draws together Bhīma's affinity with the rākṣasas and his devoted service to the beautiful Draupadī, but presents these motifs in a romantic framework with delicate hints of the erotic mood. After the incident recounted above in which Ghaṭotkaca arrives to carry the weary Pāṇḍavas, the brothers and Draupadī sojourn in a holy region of the Himalayas abounding in hermitages and brahmans. Such a place must also abound in all the *vibhāvas* of *śṛṅgāra rasa*—beautiful flowering trees, flocks of cuckoos, tranquil lakes variegated with lotuses and lilies, fragrant breezes. When such a breeze blows in a beautiful, divine flower, Draupadī declares she must have more.

It is the story which unfolds from Draupadī's declaration and challenge ("If you love me, Pārtha, bring me many more!") that, along with the killing of Kīcaka, defines most clearly that relationship of Bhīma and Draupadī. But these dazzlingly gorgeous flowers from the divine realm also impel Bhīma towards an encounter with the most basic, yet least known aspects of his identity, knowledge of which in turn grants him cosmologic vision. For on this journey he meets his brother, another son of the wind god, the great ape Hanumān who served Rāma in the *kṛta yuga*. The episode is, as it were, Bhīma's *Bhagavadgītā*; in their colloquy, Hanumān reveals to Bhīma the cosmological truth of the deterioration of time.[21]

But what needs to be cited here as an important postscript to the account of Bhīma's interaction with rākṣasas in the epic is the problem of the two versions of the story. It turns out that the flower has originated in the garden of Kubera, lord of wealth. In the first version of the story, Bhīma finds the garden guarded by a group of rākṣasas known as Krodhavasas. They try to prevent him from sporting in the pool and stealing the lotuses, but they run off to Kubera when he displays his prowess by killing *paraḥśatam*, "over a hundred of them"— a number perhaps significant for its allusion to the Dhārtarāṣṭras. (3.152.18) The conclusion of this version contains some confusion about rākṣasas which demands that the story be retold and "corrected." Ghaṭotkaca's rākṣasa friends are pressed into service to carry the Pāṇḍavas to Bhīma, while Ghaṭotkaca himself, standing in for Bhīma, carries Draupadī. Coming upon Bhīma, they find him looking like Yama, the god of death wielding his club, standing amidst the slain *yakṣas*—everywhere else in this first version the guardians are referred to as rākṣasas. After admonishing him, Yudhiṣṭhira is confronted by a new appearance of the guardians of the garden, *udyānasya rakṣiṇaḥ*. However, when they recognize the Dharmarāja, the sage Lomaśa, and the other Pāṇḍavas, they do obeisance. Then, we are told, "these stalkers of the night [rākṣasas] were appeased by Yudhiṣṭhira and grew calm, *sāntvita dharmarājena praseduḥ kṣanadacaraḥ*." (3.153.31)

We do have here the expected "good" rākṣasas, led by Bhīma's son and acting on behalf of Bhīma, as well as the (somewhat belated) transformation of the "bad" (i.e. violent, behaving hostilely to humans) rākṣasas. But why are the creatures slain by Bhima identified as rākṣasas rather than yakṣas? Another story is provided: After the slaying of Jaṭāsura, the Pāṇḍavas stay at the hermitage of Arṣṭisena. With no reference to the previous incident, once more Draupadī is enchanted by celestial flowers wafting in on a mountain breeze, and once more she sends Bhīma off to fetch more (3.157). Van Buitenen explains:

> In his first encounter he got embroiled with Rākṣasas; in the present one with Yakṣas, which is indeed more appropriate, for Kubera, whose playgrounds he violates, is the king of the Yakṣas, who are generally portrayed as genial

---

[21] For a somewhat fuller analysis of the striking comparison between this episode and the *Gītā*, see Gitomer (1987), pp. 322ff.

> leprechauns. One has the impression that the present story is a recast of the first one; it corrects the "mistake" of introducing Rākṣasas where Yakṣas ought to roam and play—although Kubera does have genealogical connections with the Rākṣasas. It also provides a rationalizing explanation of Kubera's inexplicable benevolence toward Bhīma, who in fact had been devastating his parks. The narrator of the second version felt that some reason was in order; he provides it with the usual power *ex machina*, a curse: by his killing of Maṇimat [a leader of the rākṣasas who, in this version, guard Kubera's precincts, *along with* the yakṣas] and harassing of the Yakṣas Bhīma unwittingly sets free the God of riches from a curse by Agastya.[22]

While van Buitenen's analysis is true as far as the rākṣasa/yakṣa problem is concerned, it misses the main point: the first version is about Bhīma, the second version is not. It merely uses Bhīma's well-known propensity to kill rākṣasas to get rid of the chief rākṣasa Maṇimat and move on to the explanation of Kubera's curse. In fact, there is a kind of anti-Bhīma frame in this version: Draupadī's desire is to visit the mountain; she does not ask Bhīma to bring her flowers; she uses Arjuna as a foil for Bhīma, and in the end Bhīma is ridiculed by Kubera while Arjuna is praised. By contrast, the first version has been sensitively shaped to highlight and integrate Bhīma's characterological features, his particular relationship to rākṣasas, his devotion to Draupadī, and his whirlwind-like violence as he swings his club, pressaging war. Most important, the first narrator has granted to Bhīma the encounter with Hanumān, his brother and perhaps prototype, who explains to him the mysteries of time and its cosmic cycles.

Though the first version of the fetching of the *saugandhika* flowers can be seen as a romantic episode specifically tailored to Bhīma's character, the epic writers had very good reasons to suppress any tendencies to collapse the complexities of Draupadī's personality into the profile of a conventional heroine. In spite of these reasons—the dangerous implications of an attractive woman in a polyandrous marriage, that woman's burden of carrying the symbolic persona of Śrī, conferrer of kingship, and the wild wrath she must from time to time manifest to protect her integrity and reanimate her husbands—Draupadī does also emerge as a beautiful heroine, a *virahiṇī* recognizable by her hair and costume, who has a special relationship with one man, Bhīma. This image of this epic Draupadī and especially of her relationship with Bhīma must have been powerful enough to allow the playwright to use her and Bhīma as a sort of *nāyaka/nāyikā* pair in the play without too much anxiety about audience acceptance. But even

---

22. Van Buitenen, Introduction to *The Book of the Forest*, pp. 201–202.

more than this, the demands of poets, aestheticians, audience and the Sanskrit dramatic genre itself required the *depiction* of *śṛṅgāra rasa*, which meant the inclusion of an actual love scene.

The play, while it need not account for all the complexities of the epic Draupadī, nonetheless cannot depict an actual love scene between Bhīma and Draupadī. In the play, as in the epic, it is almost as if, out of modesty at the polyandry or a desire to contain its chaotic implications, the audience has entered into the compact Nārada struck with the brothers—that we are not allowed to look on one of them while he is sitting with Draupadī (1.204.28). Yet somehow the playwright must more strongly delineate the faint outlines of the erotic relationship seen in epic Draupadī and Bhīma, precisely because he is writing a classical Sanskrit drama. An analysis of the complementary structure of the first and second acts of the *Veṇīsaṁhāra* shows that Bhaṭṭa Nārāyana has invented a wife, Bhānumatī, for Duryodhana and depicted an inappropriate and ineffective passion between them in order to reflect the passion of Bhīma and Draupadī which may not be shown.[23]

Just as in the second act the playwright uses Bhānumatī and Duryodhana to suggest aspects of Draupadī and Bhīma's relationship, so in the third act the rākṣasa pair Bloodfiend and Lardbouquet, a kind of passionate, though comic, couple, are used to present information and attitudes about Bhīma and his rākṣasī wife Hiḍimbā, who in turn further illumine the passion of Bhīma and Draupadī. This rākṣasa interlude before Act Three actually accomplishes many purposes and has many meanings. The *praveśaka*, like the *viṣkambhaka*, is intended to present to the audience in a condensed fashion parts of the story that have happened or are about to happen. As was mentioned above, when the rākṣasas tell us which generals they are eating, we learn how far the war has progressed. By virtue of the relationship Bloodfiend and Lardbouquet have with Hiḍimbā, the Interlude also serves to keep Bhīma's rākṣasa nature in the foreground. The couple here become part of the class of tamed or friendly rākṣasas, like the companions of Baka, the kingship-usurping ogre slain by Bhīma. Again, by serving Hiḍimbā, they are sympathetic to Bhīma, not to his enemies. Bloodfiend is to attend Bhīma at the killing of Duḥśāsana: by Bloodfiend's drinking Duḥśāsana's blood, the onus of *adharma* will not accrue to Bhīma, though this nicety is not only inconsistent with the epic account, but inconsistent with Bhīma's announcement, elsewhere in the play, that he has actually drunk the blood (e.g. 5.28). In any event, these are clearly

---

[23] Gitomer (1987), pp. 355–380.

Pāṇḍava rākṣasas—they flee as Aśvatthāman storms on stage. That they should do so is comic: rākṣasas can change form at will, and are not ordinarily slayable—except by the likes of Bhīma.

But is the scene supposed to be comic, or disgusting? An ogress gleefully dances while singing of all the body parts she has gathered from the battlefield to feed her husband. She calls for him longingly. He enters wearily, craving warrior's flesh dripping with blood to slake his thirst. The two share a moment of rapturous reunion. Lardbouquet carefully describes her neat and plentiful larder—the mighty warriors of the great Bharata war. Her husband Bloodfiend praises her "good household management." He tells of the arrangements Queen Hiḍimbā has made concerning his assistance in Bhīma's killing of Duḥśāsana. When they see Dhṛṣṭadyumna killing Droṇa offstage, Lardbouquet enthusiastically suggests that they go to drink his blood. Bloodfiend cautions her: "Lardbouquet, don't you know this is the blood of a brahman? It burns the throat when it goes down. So what's the use of it?" (3.3+) Then they beat a hasty retreat as Aśvatthāman enters.

There are clearly a number of parodistic elements here. At the same time the content can be nothing other than *jugupsa*, the *sthāyibhāva* of *bībhatsa*, the aesthetic emotion of disgust. All the *alaṁkāraśāstra* manuals define this *rasa* with the mention of stinking flesh, worms, etc., and this omnipresent example, which could be describing our Bloodfiend and Lardbouquet, from the fifth act of Bhavabhūti's *Mālatimādhava*, in Michael Coulson's delicious translation.[24]

> This starveling ghost, having ripped at the skin and feasted
> On bloated stinking cuts of shoulder, rump and rib,
> Has removed eyes, tendons and guts, and with bared teeth
> Sits quietly picking at the bones of the carcase on his lap.

Quite naturally, the commentators and editors have seen the signs of *bībhatsa*,

OGRESS (LARDBOUQUET)

Bloodfiend! Look what I've brought specially for you. It's a prime cut from the flesh around the heart of some royal sage who was just killed.

---

[24] Bhavabhūti, *Mālatīmādhava*, with the commentary of Jagaddhara, critically edited by R.G. Bhandarkar. 3rd ed., revised V.V. Mirashi. (Poona: Bhandarkar Oriental Research Institute, 1970), 5.16; translated by Michael Coulson. *Mālatī and Mādhava*, in *Three Sanskrit Plays* (Hammondsworth: Penguin, 1981), p. 358. It should be mentioned that another variety of *jugupsa* concerns the aversion, presumably to the same degree of disgust, felt by ascetics at the sight of women. In such a case, breasts and hips take their place alongside rotting flesh and worms as *vibhāvas* for this *rasa*. See *Nāṭyaśāstra* 6.72, 7.25; *Daśarūpaka* 4.74 [Haas trans. 4.80]; *Sāhityadarpaṇa* 3.239–241.

> You can wash it down with warm blood, oily rich with lots of globs of fat! (3.3+)

and solemnly identified the scene as such, without a word about *hāsya*, the comic.

Humor in Sanskrit drama is often a kind of witty irony when it involves the hero, the heroine, and the go-between.[25] The alaṁkārikas consider it an accessory aesthetic mood to the erotic. Yet the definitions of the *bhāva* called *hāsa* and its *rasa*, *hāsya*, which would seem to have been traditionally retained from the *Nāṭyaśāstra* all the way to the *Rasagaṅgādhara*, invariably center around the notion of the *vikṛta*, literally "changed, altered," but a word commonly used in the sense of "strange," and almost as commonly "deformed, disfigured, mutilated"—in short: grotesque. By the time of the *Daśarūpaka*, humor is formulaically characterized as *vikṛtakṛtivāgveśa*, "strange behavior, speech and dress," but the *Nāṭyaśāstra* also mentions *vyaṅga*, "a defective limb," which Abhinavagupta glosses as *vikhuṇādi*, "such as a noseless face."[26]

The *Nāṭyáśāstra* seems to harken to a more archaic understanding of the comic, archaic at least when viewed from the point of view of classical norms. As in other pre-classical theaters, such as that of Greece, what was funny was originally the grotesque, the deformed; only later did the grotesque become symbolic of psychological or spiritual deformity. We will see how the vidūṣaka, the brahman buffoon of the drama appears as a tamed transformation of the threatening rākṣasa—both are creatures who might be seen as shadow aspects of the brahman psyche escaped from the cage of brahmanical order, though to different degrees. But with his exaggerated features standing out like a sore member in the genteel world of the Sanskrit court, and his incessant jokes about eating (which, considering the cultural configuration implied by the verbal root *bhuj*, are perhaps about sex as well) the vidūṣaka also stands as a reminder of this earlier kind of humor described in the *Nāṭyáśāstra*.

The humorous and the disgusting meet in the grotesque, which has been defined as "characterized by distortion or unnatural combinations," and "combining heterogeneous and incongruous details or employing distortion for artistic effect." The textual evidence is that Bhaṭṭa Nārāyaṇa self-consciously produced a text which is really both humorous and disgusting. The first stage direction of Act Three is *tataḥ praviśati vikṛtaveśā*

---

[25] See for example the *Vikramorvaśīya* of Kālidāsa, 2.15–2.15+, Gitomer trans. in *Theater of Memory*, pp. 198–199.

[26] See *Nāṭyaśāstra* 6.47; *Daśarūpaka* 4.76 [Haas trans. 4.82]; *Sāhityadarpaṇa* 3.214; *Rasagaṅgādhara*, Benares Sanskrit Edition, p. 56, Jha, p. 182.

rākṣasī, "an ogress enters, grotesquely attired," and the second stage direction, which follows immediately, is *vikṛtam vihāsya saparitoṣam*, "laughs grotesquely, [and recites] with delight." It is as if, at the very beginning of the scene, the reader (and the spectator) are being signaled, by the very prescriptive terms the *śāstra* uses to define humor, to look for what follows to be funny, even though the content is all disgusting. Just as in the second act of the play, where Duryodhana's inappropriate erotic pursuit of Bhānumatī was awkwardly "misused" to stir up a painful reminder of Draupadī's humiliation, and to look forward to the horrible smashing of Duryodhana's thigh, in this interlude before the third act, the many constraints (or "codes," as some might say) which come together to write this text, forced the author into a novel solution. Though the dramatic problem solved is how to provide a scene of comic relief in a play in which a buffoon would be entirely out of place, Bhaṭṭa Nārāyaṇa's cultural instincts about the use of rākṣasas affords a further insight confirming the brahman-rākṣasa connection.

In his *Rasagaṅgādhara*, Jagannātha Paṇḍitarāja, the last great creative aesthetician, offers an observation which sheds some light on the relationship between the disgusting and the humorous. In discussions and exemplifications of the various *rasa*s, the *ālambanavibhāva* (person who inspires the *sthāyibhāva* underlying the *rasa* to be invoked in the spectator) is specified, as well as the *āśraya* (the receptacle, that is, the spectator). This argument, too convoluted and technical to be detailed here,[27] raises a major problem in the Sanskrit psychology of aesthetics, namely that of how and in whom does the *rasa* occur.[28] Lurking in the discourse is the problem of a specific *sādhāraṇīkaraṇa*, the universalization, of the comic and disgusting emotions, within the larger problem of *sādhāraṇīkaraṇa* of all emotions in aesthetic experience. The issue hinges on a theoretical point—what sort of relationship is posited between *bhāva* (*laukika* or worldly emotions) and *rasa* (aesthetic sentiments). In the context of the present discussion, it seems that a particular likeness is seen between *jugupsa* and *hāsa*, which are similar in that they possess a reactive rather than identifying quality. The response to a person or event as comic has to do with its strangeness. Disgust and

---

[27] Jagannātha, *Rasagaṅgādhara*, with the commentary *Gurumarmaprakāśa* of Nageśa Bhaṭṭa, edited by Gangadhara Sastra (Benares: Benares Sanskrit Series, 1903), p. 74; edited and with commentary Candrika by Badarinath Jha and Madan Mohan Jha; Vols. 1–3 (Varanasi: Chowkhamba Vidyabhavan, 1970), pp. 186–187. See Gitomer (1987), pp. 394–5, for translation; p. 424, n. 60 for text.

[28] A full discussion of this problem is found under Abhinavagupta's commentary on the *rasa sūtra* of the *Nāṭyaśāstra* (6.31 +) in the *Abhinavabhāratī* and is summarized by Mammaṭa in the fourth chapter of *Kāvyaprakāsa*, 4.27, 28ff.

laughter (it may be more useful and accurate to identify the latter as ridicule) both involve an active distancing of oneself form the *ālambana*.

In this regard it is interesting to observe that Indian performers in the various dance-mime traditions always "depict" the disgusting as humorous. The great Odissi dancer Sanjukta Panigrahi, for example, in one portion of her performance, represents in succession the nine *rasas*. Not only is *bībhatsa* alone presented with narrative content (finding a worm in the food), but the performer's shrinking grimaces seem to be meant to evoke laughter on the part of the audience, not revulsion. Since *aucitya*, "aesthetic propriety," is paramount in Sanskrit, the disgusting can be presented in a refined form by making it into the object of laughter, or by describing it in elegant language, such as that of Bhavabhūti in the example cited above. This is the real point of Jagannātha's argument. It does not matter that the connoisseur is not a fit *āśraya* for *laukika* (mundane) *jugupsa*, for it is the *alaukika* (transmundane) *bībhatsa*, (literally) refined by the aesthetic experience and the Sanskrit language itself, that he or she savors: hence the aesthetic delight, comically disgusting, of the Act Three Interlude.

The more genre-specific source for the comedic nature of this interlude must be further examined. The stock comic character in the Sanskrit *nāṭaka* is the vidūṣaka, or buffoon. He is presented as a kind of degraded brahman, unable to speak Sanskrit but ready to pull rank with his prestigious status when it is to his advantage to do so. The *Nāṭyaśāstra* describes his appearance as dwarfish, hunchbacked, baldheaded, red-eyed, and having big teeth—not unlike some descriptions of rākṣasas.[29] Both the buffoon in *Mālavikāgnimitra* (4.17+) and the one in *Vikramorvaśīya* (2.0,5.11+) are said to look like monkeys. Finally, it must be observed that two of the most basic physical characteristics of the vidūṣaka are exaggerations of stereotyped brahman features—obesity from gorging on food served as part of the rituals and baldness due to regular tonsure.

Whether or not one could go so far as to say that the standard vidūṣaka of the drama is a kind of safe, tamed half-rākṣasa (monstrous-looking, but not cannabalistic), half-brahman (obsessed with food, but without wrath), it is clear that the ogres of the *Veṇīsaṁhāra* are functioning as vidūṣakas with brahman overtones. We have seen how the rākṣasas of the Act Three Interlude and Act Six have particular connections to the complex of notions surrounding Bhīma's rākṣasa nature, one of which is an intervention in the brahman-rākṣasa opposition. There are still further ways that the ogres of the play enact "brahman-ness." First, simply by being comical

[29] *Nāṭyaśāstra* 35.9–11, 35.79. See also G.K. Bhat, *The Vidūṣaka*, Ahmedabad: New Order Book Company, 1959).

they are taking the role reserved for brahmans, or the vidūṣaka species of brahman. This results in a double parody on brahmans, since the characterization of the vidūṣaka is a parody to begin with; the usurping of their function by ogres points up their similarity to ogres.

One of these points of similarity is appetite. The typical vidūṣaka is obsessed with food, always looking for an opportunity to eat. He regards food the way his companion, the king, regards passionate lovemaking. Indeed food is the buffoon's passion. Considering that the Sanskrit words for enjoyment of sex and food are the same, as we saw, it is unavoidable that the vidūṣaka's jokes about food are also about the lewd aspects of *rati* which would have no propriety on the Sanskrit stage.

Māṇavaka's "consolation" to King Purūravas in the second act of *Vikramorvaśīya* is an example. The king here is trying to determine whether the viḍūṣaka has kept the secret of his passion for the nymph Urvaśī.

KING: Why are you silent?
BUFFOON: I've been holding my tongue so well I can't even answer you.
KING: Very good. But where should I entertain myself now?
BUFFOON: Let's go to the kitchen!
KING: Why there?
BUFFOON: We'll watch them take what's been brought from the market and make it into all the five kinds of food—the kind you have to chew, the kind you don't have to chew, the kind you can lick, the kind you can suck, and the kind you can slurp. That's the stuff to make you forget your yearning!
KING: You'll be happy in the kitchen, surrounded by what you want. But how am I to enjoy myself when my desire is impossible to attain?[30]

In fact, the Act Three rākṣasa interlude is all about eating as a passion, in this case a shared passion between a couple. It is appropriate that rākṣasas should be presented as ravenous and disgusting, for that is their nature. But that they should also be comic has to do with their functioning as buffoons. Bloodfiend's remark that the blood of a brahman (Droṇa) is unfortunately undrinkable not only prepares the audience for the entrance of Droṇa's son Aśvatthāman, it also serves as a reminder of the brahman-rākṣasa connection/opposition, thereby looking forward to the other comic rākṣasa of the *Veṇīsaṁhāra*, the false brahman Cārvāka who deceives Yudhiṣṭhira and Draupadī in Act Six.

Earlier we noticed Cārvāka's affinities to a Cārvāka in the *Śānti Parvan* (12.39) of *Mahābhārata*, who also attempts to deceive the Pāṇḍavas using

---

[30] 2.2+, Gitomer trans., *Theater of Memory*, p. 191. The five kinds of food are not listed in the original, but have been supplied from Kāṭayavema's commentary.

the guise of a brahman, as well as to Jaṭāsura (cf. 3.154), a rākṣasa living as a brahman who is killed by Bhīma for trying to steal the Pāṇḍava weapons. Dramatically, he parodies an additional cluster of stereotypical brahman traits—the demand for hospitality, obsession with the purity of his person, and, when these are violated or denied, an easily triggered irascibility. Strangely, though such personalities might be easy targets for ridicule, they do not seem to appear as subjects for caricature in dramas. They are, however, frequently depicted in a serious fashion, the most well-known perhaps being the cursing of Śakuntalā by Durvāsas (4.0–4.1+).

Could it be that expression of resentment towards the status-obsessed brahmans, enacting their prestigious identities through demands for reverential hospitality and public displays of purity in food and cleanliness, was off-limits for the classical Sanskrit drama (in a way that it is not in folk theater)? Perhaps the bumbling, endearing vidūṣaka, who parodies only one, safe brahman excess—gluttony—an excess surely resented, but one with less direct harm on others than the taunting hospitality which demeans and even excludes the host, was as far as a Sanskrit, i.e. ultimately brahmanical, form would go in mockery.[31] In any case, Bhaṭṭa Nārāyaṇa is taking a tremendous risk in the character of Cārvāka, not so much because he is depicting an obnoxious brahman sage—after all, we know that he is really an ogre from the moment he appears on the stage—but rather because he seems to work himself into a dilemma of characterization just as the play is about to reach its dénouement. Yudhiṣṭhira, ever respectful towards brahmans, reveals the "weak," hopeless side of his personality in believing the deception that both of his brothers have been killed by Duryodhana. As with the second act, this part of the play has never been well received by the tradition.

Cārvāka disappears after manipulating Yudhiṣṭhira and Draupadī into a pathetic attempt at suicide. Suddenly Bhīma arrives, though no one, not even the audience this time, can recognize him at first. His entire body is drenched in blood, as the stage direction (6.36+) has it, and he is calling for Draupadī: Though he is feared to be Duryodhana, he knows he looks like a rākṣasa himself, or someone from the dead:

I am no ogre,
I am no ghost
but a wrathful warrior
who cooled his body
in the pool of his enemies' blood,

---

[31] Recent typologies of the vidūṣaka, such as Jefferds (1981), p. 67, and Shulman (1985), pp. 155–169, emphasize that he does not enact the potential of his role as critic or alterer of perspectives in any radical way.

and crossed the vast abyss
in the ocean of his vow.
You royal heroes,
the charred remnant
of the battle blaze,
Why do you crouch, quivering in fear,
hiding behind carcasses
of elephants and horses? (37)
Tell me where Pāñcālī is!

With the advent of Bhīma, the dramatic dynamics seem to regain integrity, force and direction. In the first part of the act, the audience was aware of the true identity of the source of danger, the rākṣasa Cārvāka; when Bhīma enters, the audience must believe him to be Duryodhana. Where before we saw a comic rākṣasa pretending to be a brahman, and inspiring the most embarassingly maudlin behavior on the part of two noble characters, now we see a warrior who likes look an ogre or a wraith and is feared to be the wicked villain. Yudhiṣṭhira is in a stupor, and Draupadī is fearfully slinking away from this creature pursuing her toward her funeral pyre. Suddenly Yudhiṣṭhira awakens, regaining his courage along with his consciousness. As Bhīmasena reaches for Draupadī's hair in fulfillment of his vow, Yudhiṣṭhira tries to stop this "Duryodhana" from completing the rape he began at the dicing assembly. The stage direction says he "impulsively throws his arms around Bhīma." (6.37+) In the midst of this fierce embrace, the two brothers joyously recognize each other. Bhīma can now complete his vow, tying up his queen's hair with his bloodied hands. Krishna arrives with Arjuna to resume the preparations for Yudhiṣṭhira's royal consecration. Benedictory verses conclude the play.

It seems that this situation is constructed to allow Yudhiṣṭhira and Draupadī to enact their radical dependence on Bhīmasena. On the verge of restoration through the agency of Bhīma, each is at his and her most characteristically vulnerable, Yudhiṣṭhira abounding in dharma but only intermittently able to assert the strength which betokens the Pāṇḍava right to the throne, Draupadī after so many episodes of being championed and rescued by Bhīma, once again in danger of being violated by Duryodhana. In other words, Yudhiṣṭhira needs Bhīma in order to be king and Draupadī needs Bhīma in order to be queen. Without him they are so vulnerable they can be destroyed by a trickster. This trickster is a rākṣasa and a "brahman," reminding the audience of the situations in which Bhīma has intervened. Moreover, he is an agent of Duryodhana, whose attempts to bring about the downfall of the Pāṇḍavas by trickery have been well-rehearsed throughout the play.

Without Bhīma to uphold it, the Pāṇḍava royal *tejas* has dwindled to near-extinction in death. Not only do the king and queen prepare to cast off their lives, but they see death everywhere; they vie with each other for the privilege of entering the fire first. Into this scene of death, Bhīma arrives, looking like the very picture of death (6.33+):

CHAMBERLAIN

[*Entering in agitated confusion.*]

Save us! Save us, great king! I see the
wicked Kaurava filth, his body and tunic
bathed in blood and his terrifying club
smeared with it, like the god of death
brandishing the staff of time . . . .

Yet it is life that he brings with this blood, reinvigorating the royal pair. It is as if rākṣasa Bhīma has caused the the promise of verse 1.25, "the sacrifice called battle" to be realized, the sacrifice Lord Hari has supervised. *This* sacrifice, however, has not been delimited by procedures expressive of brahman anxieties about the chaotic release of blood; *this* sacrifice will therefore not be compromised to an uncertain conclusion. In the sacrifice of war the rākṣasas are permitted to overrun the sacrificial enclosure, the battlefield, resulting in the complete triumph of both death, for the land and people of Āryavārta have been destroyed, and life, for the Kuru line has been revivified.

First the failed king Yudhiṣṭhira, who has fainted, revives ("Suddenly getting up; resolutely" is the stage direction, 6.35+) and calls for his bow. When no servant appears he resolves to fight barehanded. Draupadī also revives from her swoon, and once Bhīma has been recognized she prepares for her royal reconsecration as Yudhiṣṭhira prepares for his. Bhīma explicitly understands his gory triumph over Duryodhana as the act which reestablishes Yudhiṣṭhira's legitimate kingship:

BHĪMASENA

I tossed his body on the ground
and made mine gleam with his blood like sandal.
The royal splendor now lies in you
along with the earth to its four-oceaned borders.
. . . (39)

[*Yudhiṣṭhira, slowly letting go,*
gazes at Bhīma, wiping away his tears.
Bhīma falls to his feet.]

Victory, noble brother!

This last speech (*jayatvāryaḥ*) is significant; in dramas only a king is properly greeted with the word *jaya* or *jayatu*, and here Bhīma has pronounced it.

The blood-drenched reunion of Bhīma and Draupadī that follows immediately upon Yudhiṣṭhira's recognition of his brother constitutes the conclusion of the drama in terms of the agenda of meanings Bhaṭṭa Nārāyaṇa pursues throughout the play. The vow with its barely disguised significance of menstrual purification through menstrual revenge, a revenge that Bhīma has accomplished for his royal wife, the disinherited personification of Śrī (royal prosperity) who must now act as the violent, gory Kālī through her husband—this vow takes center stage in the action; Bhīma, in fact, declaims once again verse 1.21, cited at the beginning of this essay.

Although all three of the main characters on stage affirm the importance of the vow's completion, it is Bhīma who repeatedly fixes on the blood, reveling in the emblems of his bestial nature. We should remember that Bhīma has appeared so much like a rākṣasa at his entrance shortly before this that he must announce in his first speech: *nāham rakṣo*—"I am no ogre!" Here are Bhīma's speeches from this passage (6.40cd + –6.41 +), which beautifully reveal the integration of its themes:

BHĪMASENA

With this very hand smeared with Suyodhana's blood
I will bind up Pāñcālī's black tresses, pulled apart
by Duḥśāsana.

[*Approaching Draupadī.*]

My queen, daughter of the Pāñcāla king,
your good fortune waxes with the eclipse of
our enemies' clan. Look at me, and cease
this fearful trembling.

Touch this blood, clotted on my hands—
all that remains of the beast Duḥśāsana
who dragged you into the council of kings;
and, beloved, touch this blood as well,
still liquid and smeared on all my body,
of the Kuru king whose thigh my mace crushed
to extinguish the fire of your disgrace. (41)

Selected Bibliography

SANSKRIT TEXTS AND TRANSLATIONS

Abhinavagupta. *Abhinavabhāratī*. Commentary on Bharata's *Nāṭyaśāstra*. Vols. 1–4. Edited by M.R. Kavi. Gaekwads Oriental Series, nos. 36, 68, 124, 145. Baroda, 1934–64. Text with Hindi and Sanskrit commentaries. Edited by A. Madhusudan Shastri, 2 vols. Banaras: Banaras Hindu University, 1971, 1975.

Bhaṭṭa Nārāyaṇa. *Veṇīsaṁhāra: die Ehrenrettung der Königen, ein Drama in 6 Akten von Bhaṭṭa Nārāyaṇa*. Kritisch mit Einleitung und Noten herausgegeben von Julius Grill. Leipzig: Fues Verlag (R. Reisland), 1871. *Veṇīsaṁhāra of Bhaṭṭa Nārāyaṇa*. Edited with the commentary of Jagaddhara, curtailed or enlarged as necessary, various reading, a literal English translation, critical and explanatory notes in English by M.R. Kale. Second ed. Bombay, 1918. Reprint ed, Delhi: Motilal Banarsidass, 1977. *Veṇīsaṁhāra of Bhaṭṭa Nārāyaṇa* with the commentaries of Lakṣmaṇasūri and Jagaddhara. Madras: V. Ramaswamy Sastrulu, 1939. See also translation in Gitomer (1987).

Bhavabhūti. *Mālatīmādhava*, with the commentary of Jagaddhara. Critically edited by R.G. Bhandarkar. 3rd ed., revised V.V. Mirashi. Poona: Bhandarkar Oriental Research Institute, 1970. Translated by Michael Coulson. *Mālatī and Mādhava*. In *Three Sanskrit Plays*. Hammondsworth: Penguin, 1981.

Jagannātha. *Rasagaṅgādhara*, with the commentary *Gurumarmaprakāśa* of Nageśa Bhaṭṭa. Edited by Gangadhara Sastra. Benares: Benares Sanskrit Series, 1903. Edited and with commentary Candrikā by Badarinath Jha and Madan Mohan Jha. Vols. 1–3. Varanasi: Chowkhamba Vidyabhavan, 1970.

Kālidāsa. *Abhijñānaśākuntala*, with the commentary of Rāghavabhaṭṭa. Edited by N.R. Acharya. 12th ed. Bombay: Nirnaya Sagar Press, 1958.

——. *Mālavīkāgnimitra*, with the commentary of Kāṭayavema. Edited by N.R. Acharya. 9th ed. Bombay: Nirnaya Sagar Press, 1950.

——. *Vikramorvaśīya*. Edited by H.D. Velankar. Delhi: Sahitya Akademi, 1961. With the commentaries of Kāṭayavema and Raṅganātha, ed. S.P. Pandit. Bombay Sanskrit Series, no. 16. Bombay: Central Book Depot, 1889. Translations of the three plays in *Theater of Memory: The Plays of Kālidāsa*. Edited by Barbara Stoler Miller. New York: Columbia University Press, 1984.

Mahābhārata: the text as constituted in its critical edition. Edited by V.S. Sukthankar et al. Poona: Bhandarkar Oriental Research Institute, 1933–66. Translated by Kisari Mohan Ganguli and Pratap Chandra Roy (publisher), 1884–1896. Reprinted in 12 vols., New Delhi: Munshiram Manoharlal, 1970. Trans. J.A.B. van Buitenen, vols. 1–3 (comprising parvans 1–5). Chicago: University of Chicago Press, 1973–78.

Rāmāyaṇa of Vālmīki, with three commentaries called *Tilaka*, *Shiromani*, and *Bhoosana*. Edited by Shastri Shrinivasa Katti Mudholkar. Bombay: Gujurati Printing Press, n.d.

SECONDARY SOURCES

Bhat, G.K. *The Vidūṣaka*. Ahmedabad: New Order Book Co., 1959.

Dumézil, Georges. *The Destiny of the Warrior*. Trans. Alf Hiltebeitel. Chicago: University of Chicago Press, 1970.

Gitomer, David. "The *Veṇīsaṁhāra* of Bhatta Narayana: the great epic as drama." Ph.D. dissertation, Columbia University, 1987.

Hiltebeitel, Alf. "Draupadī's Garments." *Indo-Iranian Journal* (1980), 22:97–112.

——. "Draupadī's Hair." Puruṣartha 5, *Autour de la deésse hindoue: études réunies par Madeleine Biardeau*. Paris: Editions de l'école des hautes études en sciences sociales (1981):179–214.

——. *The Ritual of Battle: Krishna in the Mahābhārata*. Ithaca and London: Cornell University Press, 1976.

M. Hiriyanna. *Outlines of Indian Philosophy*. London: George Allen & Unwin, Ltd., 1932.

Hopkins, E.W. *Epic Mythology*. Reprint ed., Delhi: Indological Book House, 1968.

Jefferds, Keith N. "Vidūṣaka versus Fool: A Functional Analysis." *Journal of South Asian Literature 16* (1981), pp. 61–73.

Karve, Iravati. *Yugānta: the End of an Epoch* (New Delhi: Sangam Books, 1974).

Kuiper, F.B.J. *Varuṇa and Vidūṣaka: On the origin of the Sanskrit drama*. Amsterdam: North Holland Publishing Company, 1979.

O'Flaherty, Wendy Doniger. *The Origins of Evil in Hindu Mythology*. Paperback ed. Berkeley: University of California Press, 1980.

Shulman, David Dean. *The King and the Clown in South Indian Myth and Poetry*. Princeton: Princeton University Press, 1985.

SĀVITRĪ: OLD AND NEW

VIDYUT AKLUJKAR

The old myth of Sāvitrī as it appears in the Mahābhārata (Āraṇyakaparvan 277–283; hereafter Mbh.) is cherished by countless generations of Indians. In many ways, this is a unique story, and perhaps that explains the fascination with it to some extent. Yet, as far as I have been able to find out, it has not enjoyed the varied treatment that some other stories from the same epic have in Classical Sanskrit or medieval Indian literature. This paper will examine the reasons behind this curious lack of reinterpretation and will discuss a couple of its modern reinterpretations.

Before proceeding further, let me recount the Mbh. myth in some detail. Aśvapati, the childless king of the Madras, performs penance for eighteen years in the hope of obtaining sons. At last, the goddess Sāvitrī is pleased and offers him a daughter, whom the king names after the goddess. Sāvitrī grows up, unsurpassed in beauty, wisdom and virtue. Awed by her radiance, however, no one comes forward to seek her hand. So the king sends her off to find a match for herself.

Sāvitrī comes back having chosen Satyavat, the son of the blind, dethroned king Dyumatsena, who is residing in a forest with his wife and son. She tells her father of her choice, in the presence of sage Nārada, who then discloses the sole flaw in her choice, namely, that Satyavat is destined to die within a year. The king hesitates, but Sāvitrī is firm in her choice, and finally, with the blessings of Nārada and her parents, she marries Satyavat and goes to live in the forest with her new family. Within a year, Sāvitrī charms everyone by her virtuous behaviour. She, however, carries within her heart the knowledge of the dreadful destiny.

Three days before the fateful day, she observes a vow of standing and fasting. On the last day, with the permission of her parents-in-law, she accompanies Satyavat into the forest where he is going to gather some firewood. Suddenly Satyavat complains of a piercing headache and lies down with his head on her lap. Sāvitrī keeps vigil.

Yama, the king of Death, approaches and starts to take the soul of Satyavat away with him. Sāvitrī follows him. When told to go back, Sāvitrī gently reminds Yama that her place is where her husband is. Yama admires her courage and offers her a boon—anything except the life of Satyavat. She asks for the restoration of sight for her sightless father-in-law, and Yama grants her that. Sāvitrī still follows Yama. Again he tells her to go back, again she refuses, and he offers her one more boon—anything except the life of Satyavat. This time she asks him to restore the lost kingdom to her father-in-law. She is granted this second boon. The same senario repeats itself two more times, and Sāvitrī is granted by the third boon a hundred sons for her own father, and lastly, a hundred sons for herself. She still follows Yama, and when told to go back, answers by praising the virtues of the company of the righteous.

Finally, Yama is thoroughly pleased with her courage and wisdom, and he grants her an *unconditional* boon. At this point Yama has already lost the battle. Sāvitrī simply reminds him of his earlier boon that she would have a hundred sons and asks him how this is possible without her husband. Yama accepts defeat, and retreats, giving her the gift of the life of Satyavat. Satyavat is revived, he returns home with Sāvitrī, is reunited with his joyous father, who has regained his sight. There, at the bidding of the forest sages, Sāvitrī relates the whole story and thus everyone comes to know of the victory of love and wisdom over Death.

Broadly speaking, this is a myth of a mortal's close encounter with Death with the special motif of regaining the life of someone already dead. There are a few parallels to it in Indian as well as in other mythologies. In terms of close encounter with Death, the myth probably belongs to the broad type of myths such as that of Naciketas, where an account is given of the conversation between Death and a mortal. However, the narrower category of comparable myths seems to be of the type in which one of the two lovers dies or is taken to another world, and the survivor tries to win back the life of the lost one. Sister Nivedita (1975) and Anthony Horowitz (1985) have compared it with the story of Alcestis, wife of Admetus, who bargains her life for that of her cursed husband's. Two other myths from Greek mythology come to mind: the myth of Orpheus and Eurydice and the myth of Laodamia and Protesilaus. (Grant and Hazel, 1979). In spite of broad structural similarities, Sāvitrī in the Mbh. is noticeably different from either one of these myths.

Consider the myth of Orpheus. Eurydice's death by snakebite is an accident. It is not in any way pre-destined nor is it anticipated in agony by her lover. Orpheus does not follow his beloved as soon as she is dead, but ceases to sing and play and while hopelessly wandering, by chance enters the underworld. Moved by his sad music Hades grants him a favour, but it is not unconditional. He may take Eurydice back, only if he does not look back before he reaches the upper worlds. Unlike Sāvitrī, at this point, there are two versions of the conclusion. According to the oldest, Orpheus succeeds, but according to Virgil and Ovid (Metamorphoses: Tenth Book) he looks back just as he is about to enter this world and thus through an excess of love, loses Eurydice. There is only sadness of loss and pitiable imploring on the part of Orpheus, and we do not see there anything close to Sāvitrī's determination, fortitude, quiet persistance and wisdom in dialectic.

The other Greek myth, that of Laodamia and Protesilaus is closer in some respects to Sāvitrī, but that too, is not without points of difference. There is an element of pre-destination in this myth, although not quite in the same manner as in Sāvitrī. It is learned from an oracle that the first Greek to tread on the Trojan soil will be the first to die. In a sense, the outcome is pre-destined for a blank slot as it were, and Protesilaus fulfills the destiny by jumping on the Trojan soil before anyone else. Unlike the myth of Orpheus, and like the Sāvitrī myth, the one to die in the myth of Laodamia is the husband and the one to pray to the gods is the faithful wife. However, unlike Sāvitrī who gains back everything that was lost and much more, Laodamia gets her husband back for three hours only, at the end of which period, according to one version of the story, she dies with him and accompanies him back to the underworld.

The Sāvitrī of the epic stands out by contrast. The similarities with the other myths are only superficial, confined to the general outline of the story. The main differences are in characterization and in the import of the myth within each tradition. Unlike the Greek lovers, Sāvitrī knows about the impending death of her chosen mate, but in spite of that, she enters the union. The Indian ideal of marriage finds expression in Sāvitrī's words, "Only once is a daughter given in marriage. Blessed with a long life or not, virtuous or otherwise, once I have chosen a husband, I shall not wed anyone else". (Mbh. 1971, 3.278.25–6) Unlike the lamentations of the Greek lovers, or unlike the *vilāpas* in the Indian tradition, when Satyavat dies, Sāvitrī does not lament. Hers is only a calm, resolute confrontation with Death. She has the strength of character that is a natural outcome of a life of righteous observances, and although she is neither impolite nor aggressive, she never gives up. Like a calculating diplomat, she accepts whatever is offered to her and perseveres in the quest for more. In the end, when she returns, she has her mission fulfilled and has earned a perennial place in the list of great women—the *pativratās*.

By now some of the reasons for the everlasting fascination that the epic Sāvitrī holds should be clear. In the Indian tradition, the essence of the Sāvitrī myth lies in precisely those areas in which it differs from the

Greek myths. In pan-Indian lore and literature Sāvitrī is often used as a standard of comparison for a devoted wife. There is a spill-over of this myth in certain rituals and in everyday language as well. Even today, married women in India observe a vow of fasting and praying for their husband's long life in memory of Sāvitrī. The often uttered blessing for a newly married girl in India is still (*janmasāvitrī bhava*) "May you be like Sāvitrī all your life".

Although Sāvitrī has thus won a perpetual place in the collective memory of the Indian audience, there is a relative lack of reinterpretations of this old myth in Indian literature. This is all the more surprising in view of the fact that myths about the other *pativratās* from the epics seem to have inspired many generations of poets and dramatists to create new bottles in which to pour the old wine. Take the case of Sītā or Ahalyā. We find not only faithful retellings of these myths but numerous reinterpretations both in Sanskrit and in other Indian languages.

It should be noted at this point that there is a distinction between two qualitatively different art-forms. The former is a more or less faithful rendering of the original myth, allowing for a few cosmetic changes in narrative detail, or introduction of a few minor characters or events, without changing the backbone of the original myth. This is mere retelling. We find many examples of this kind in the medieval period of Indian literature i.e. 11th century onwards.

The other, more interesting art-form is reinterpretation or re-creation based on the old myth. In this the author uses the old myth to take off, but it is the new content that he gives to the old myth that elevates it to the level of recreation. This new content may be manifest in the form of a postscript to the old myth or a revelation of an entirely new trait of a major character or it may consist of a completely different interpretation given to the major events or characters of the old myth. Examples abound in the Indian as well as other literary traditions. In the Indian tradition, we have Bhāsa's *Pratimā*, Kālidāsa's *Śakuntala*, Bhavabhūti's *Uttara-rāma-carita*, to name just a few. In the western tradition, the classic examples are Milton's *Paradise Lost*, Joyce's *Ulysses*, etc. Karel Çapek's *Apocryphal Stories* provide instances of re-creative postscripts. To come to contemporary scene, Timothy Findley's *Not Wanted on the Voyage* is an excellent reinterpretation of the Biblical myth of Noah's ark.

As I mentioned before, there are many retellings of the epic Sāvitrī in Sanskrit and in the vernacular languages of India; but surprisingly, there are virtually no re-creations of Sāvitrī, with only two exceptions that I have come across, one in English (by Sri Aurobindo) and the other in

Tamil (by K. Santhanam).[1] The retellings of Sāvitrī in Sanskrit are to be seen in the Matsya-purāṇa, Brahma-vaivarta-purāṇa, Devī-bhāgavata etc., and they can be found in the numerous translations of the Mbh. in the vernacular languages as well. For example, Moropant, (1729–94) a Marāṭhī writer of the 18th century wrote a Sāvitrī-ākhyāna (Godbole, 1854, 379–388) that is essentially the same as the story in the epic. A modern Bengali writer, Toru Dutt (1856–77), has rendered the Sāvitrī myth in her *The Ancient Ballads and Legends of India*. She simply recounts the original with a few peripheral changes in detail. (Dwivedi, 1977).

Speculations as to why the Sāvitrī myth has not inspired more authors would be idle; however, I might offer some suggestions. If one compares Sāvitrī with the other celebrated *pativratās* or devoted wives of the Indian lore, she stands out by herself. Ahalyā, Draupadī, Sītā, Tārā, Mandodarī—these are the commonly cited names of *pativratās* in the Indian tradition. (*ahalyā draupadī sītā tārā mandodarī tathā / pañcakaṁ nā smaren nityam mahāpātaka-nāśanam* / /) Each one of these devoted wives was treated unjustly, knowingly or unknowingly by her husband at some point. With the exception of Draupadī, all the rest appear to be silent sufferers. Sītā accepts the fire ordeal, the abandonment and the final ordeal. Ahalyā is literally petrified by the wrath of her husband, sage Gautama. All these are somewhat passive women, who endure ordeals and yet come out virtuous and devoted towards their husbands. Even though Draupadī is more active than the rest in her stunning questions and her passionate scoldings, she seeks to avenge only through the agency of her husbands. But Sāvitrī has outdone them all. Far from being passive, she takes charge of the situation whenever there is a stumbling block. She is not won by the hero in the *svayaṁvara* contest like Sītā or Draupadī, nor is she simply offered in wedding by her father, but chooses her husband entirely by herself, and stands by her choice even after learning of the fateful flaw in it. Sītā is rescued by her husband, Draupadī is avenged by her husbands. But it is Sāvitrī herself who rescues her husband, and that too, from no ordinary foe, but Death

[1] Here I must mention, if only to set aside, two modern stories which are neither retellings nor recreations. These are Dharmavir Bharati's "Sāvitrī Nambar Do" in Hindi, and Sivasankari's "Pārvai" in Tamil. (The latter was kindly sent to me by Ginette Ishimatsu in an English translation.) Both these stories use the name of the epic heroine for their heroines, and then depict an entirely different life for them, which has no resemblance to the story in the original. They therefore, cannot be considered recreations of the old myth. Rather, they are instances of a favourite literary mode employed by modern Indian authors, namely, of creating utter behavioural contrasts to the old *pativratās* in their modern namesakes.

himself! All this puts her in a class by herself. There is no match for this active *pativratā*, either in her own era or in the later ones. At Satyavat's death, Sāvitrī follows him but her accompaniment of the dead husband is not the passive following (*sahagamana*) of a *satī* that later became the model in life and in literature. Her *saha-gamana* is purposeful, she follows him only to bring him back alive with her. It is interesting to note that the other princess of the Madras from the same epic—Paṅḍu's wife Mādrī, hailing from the same lineage as that of Sāvitrī—has neither the courage nor the wisdom of Sāvitrī. She follows her husband in death by becoming a *satī*. So, all things considered, Sāvitrī exhibits the ideal qualities (as recognized by the Indian literary tradition,) of a hero, not so much of a heroine, and yet the guiding force behind all her activity seems to be her love for her husband. Perhaps it was this apparent anomaly in the old Sāvitrī that stumped the authors and instead of creatively handling the myth from different angles they simply preferred to worship this unusual heroine in their rituals.

The only new creations of the old myth of Sāvitrī known to me are the English epic Sāvitrī by Yogī Śri Aurobindo (1954), and a Tamil short story "Sāvitrī" by a modern writer K. Santhanam (1963). It is the latter that interests me more. The former is a better known re-creation, and has been commented upon by many able critics. For this reason I will be brief in my treatment of it. Out of the Mbh. myth of about 700 verses Aurobindo has created what is perhaps the largest epic in Modern English, of about 24,000 lines and 17 cantos. His Sāvitrī is steeped in Vedic symbolism and Upaniṣadic mysticism. He interprets the old myth as an allegory, where "Satyavān is the symbol of the Soul of Truth that in its descent into the earth atmosphere is caught up by Death and ignorance, while Sāvitrī is the Divine Light that comes down to release the Soul from the grips of death and ignorance and to enact with him the union of the passive truth of being and the active power of grace" (Iyengar, 1975).

Apart from the symbolic interpretation that changes the impact of his new epic, Aurobindo has introduced many significant changes in the story. Aurobindo's Aśvapati (Aswapathy in his spelling) is an active seeker of truth, a yogin, "the leader of the human race on its evolutionary march", whose journey into the occult worlds occupies more than one third of the epic. Aurobindo's Sāvitrī, unlike the Mbh. Sāvitrī, does not return to her father to seek approval of her choice. She meets Satyavān, there is a mutual recognition of love, a romantic exchange of ideals, and a willing consummation of the union before she returns to her father. The opposition to this choice of Sāvitrī comes not so much from the seer-King but from his queen who does not figure in the Mbh. story at all. The *tri-rātra-vrata* of Sāvitrī in the Mbh. expands in Aurobindo's hands into a full-fledged yoga performed by Sāvitrī, the yoga of Self-discovery and the yoga of preparation for the coming struggle. And finally, Sāvitrī's victory over Death is not just an individual gain but the victory of Divine Light over Death and ignorance. The myth ends by being a futuristic, cosmic epic of superhuman grandeur.

The other new re-creation is found in a Tamil short story by K. Santhanam. This is a far cry not only from the Sāvitrī of Aurobindo, but even from the epic Sāvitrī. To me this is an extremely intriguing short story because the author consciously accepts a challenge by shedding most of the fascinating aspects of the old myth and yet succeeds in creating a self-contained, original and chiselled piece of literature which claims inheritance from the old myth. This is a remarkable accomplishment because the author, according to my sources, is not regarded as one of the masters of the short story genre. Although he has published 16 books in Tamil and English, he is better known as the Lt. Governor of Vindhya Pradesh in 1952–56 and as the chairman of the finance commision of India in 1956–57. His books such as *India's Road to Socialism* are more widely read than his short stories. And yet, from this unlikely source comes what I consider a most remarkable recreation based on the myth of Sāvitrī.

If you strip Sāvitrī of her independent choice of mate, the self-confidence in sticking to her decision, the calm fortitude in observances of vows, the strength of character manifest in enduring the agonizing secret in her heart for a whole year, and the towering courage and wisdom in confronting Death, if you strip Sāvitrī of all these aspects, what is then left of the myth? You would be forced to say, nothing much of interest. And yet this is the challenge that Santhanam has taken and created a memorable story out of it.

Santhanam's story is that of a girl called Sāvitrī in contemporary Madras. When she is fifteen, her father consults a distinguished astrologer, who informs him that in Sāvitrī's horoscope, there is a chance of widowhood when she will be twenty-nine. There is also a crisis in the intended bridegroom's horoscope, about the same time,but the boy is attractive in every other respect, and the father is keen on the match, so the astrologer gives a false horoscope for Sāvitrī so as to match the horoscopes and blesses the union. The astrologer consoles the father by saying "For all we know, this girl might have the same good fortune of the Sāvitrī of the purāṇas who won back her husband's life from the hands of the God of Death".

The wedding takes place, Sāvitrī lives a happy life as a wife of a thoroughly westernized doctor for about fourteen years without the knowledge of the impending crisis. Her father has told her to chant daily the thousand names of the Goddess. Her husband, Sunderasan, is a product of modern scientific age and education, who ridicules old rituals and superstition. Under his silent scorn, Sāvitrī gradually gives up the practice of chanting the thousand names of the goddess. The father tells her of the dreadful prophecy only on the death-bed, and then, in a panic, she employs Vedic Brahmins to chant the holy *mantras* in her house, and tries to atone for her former lack of faith. As the fateful day approches, her mother in the agony of anticipation takes seriously ill, Sāvitrī calls her husband to come right away, he drives at the top speed, meets with an accident, almost dies, but recovers in the hospital under Sāvitrī's vigil. Sāvitrī's mother dies on that day. The conclusion of the story is as follows:

Savitrī waited till the year was out before she revealed the secret. Sundaresan's disbelief in astrology was only confirmed by the revelation. There were frequent and excited disputes between them on this subject.

"It is this superstition that killed your mother and nearly killed me too", Sundaresan would declare.

"No. The prediction was true and it was only God's mercy that saved us", said Savitrī with conviction.

After reading Santhanam's Sāvitrī, one realises that even in this age of science and scepticism, the Sāvitrī myth has an appeal that defies the passage of time. Santhanam has taken the task of interpreting the myth of a bygone age, of *satya-yuga* in the context of *kali-yuga* and still has succeeded in retaining an element of drama in it. This he has achieved by focussing on the classic tension between blind faith and open-eyed skepticism.

What he had to lose in the characterization of Sāvitrī he has gained in terms of realism in the story. The characters that are the counterparts of king Aśvapati and sage Nārada of the old myth are extremely realistically portrayed by him. Savitri's father in the short story shares with the old king the same concern about finding a good match for his daughter, but unlike Aśvapati, he has occasion to be critical of his son-in-law's eccentric, untraditional ways. The counterpart of sage Nārada of the old myth, astrologer Rāju Śāstrī can peep into the future and predict crisis just like Nārada; however, unlike the old sage, he also suggests the falsification of the horoscopes to achieve the intended marriage. This is not only realistic in the context of Indian match-making practices, but interestingly, also reminds an Indian reader of the scheming character often attributed to sage Nārada elsewhere in the purāṇas.

The heroine is but a pale shadow of the original; but she is, after all, merely a name-sake of the radiant Sāvitrī. Her destiny resembles the destiny of the old Sāvitrī, but whereas the old Sāvitrī represents steadfast faith in her own conviction, the new Sāvitrī represents the blind, borrowed faith which is never much sure of its shaky foundations. This contrast is brought out very vividly in the account of Sāvitrī's efforts to rectify the slackness of her own righteous observances by employing the vedic Brahmins to chant holy *mantras* in order to ward off the evil. The old Sāvitrī trusts in her own ability and silently performs a *tri-rātra-vrata*, the new Sāvitrī has more faith in the vedic Brahmin's efficacy than in her own. The old Sāvitrī is calm, deep and unwavering even when Satyavat dies, the new Sāvitrī panics under the tension and in a sense contributes to fulfil the density she is trying to avoid. The counterpart of Satyavat in the new story, namely Sundaresan, is Santhanam's original creation, an agnostic and a skeptic who beautifully balances the element of faith in the tension between faith and reason.

Given the context of the scientific, rational age the story unfolds quite naturally, and the conclusion comes almost inevitably. In the case of the old Sāvitrī, there is no doubt about Sāvirī's conquest of Death. However, in the framework of Santhanam's modern story, given the new interpretations of these characters, the classic tension between fate and free-will is never resolved. Instead of the Sāvitrī-Yama dialectic of the old myth, Santhanam's Sāvitrī ends with a new dialectic, the everlasting battle between faith and skepticism. Thus even after giving up most of the elements that made the old Sāvitrī memorable, Santhanam has succeeded in rebuilding the edifice on the foundations of yet another conflict that can be drawn from the old myth, namely, the question of pre-determination and free-will.

These are the new garbs that the old Sāvitrī has donned so far. When compared with the other *pativratās*, one feels that she could don many more.

Bibliography

Bharati, Dharmavir. 1969. *Banda Galī kā Ākharī Makāna*. Lokodaya series, Title no. 286. Bharatiya Janapith Publications.

Dwivedi, A.N. 1977. *Toru Dutt*. New Delhi, Arnold-Heinemann Publishers, Indian Writers Series, Vol. XV.

Dwivedi, A.N. 1977. *Sri Aurobindo—A Study of Selected Poems*. Bareilly, Prakash Book Depot.

Godbole, P.B. 1854, ed. *Navanīta*. Poona, Poona College Printing Press, 1st edition; 18th edition: 1957. ed. A.K. Priyolkar, Bombay, Government Central Press.

Grant, Michael and Hazel, John. 1979. *Gods and Mortals in Classical Mythology: A Dictionary*. New York, Dorsett Press.

Horowitz, Anthony. 1985. *Myths and Mythology* in the Children's Library: Little Simon. Simon and Schuster Inc.

Iyengar, K.R. Srinivasa. 1975. *Dawn to Greater Dawn*: Six Lectures on Sri Aurobindo's Savitri. Simla, Indian Institute of Advanced Study.

Mahābhārata text as constituted in its critical edition, Ed. The Bhandarkar Oriental Research Institute, Poona. 1971.

Matsya-purāṇa. Vidyāsāgara-Bhattācāryā, Jîvānanda. 1876. Calcutta.

Metamorphoses by Ovid. translated by Rolfe Humphries, Bloomington, Indiana University Press, 1955.

Santhanam, K.R. 1963. "Sāvitrī" in *The Plough and the Stars*: Stories from Tamilnad ed. K. Swaminathan, Periaswami Thooran and M.R. Perumal Mudaliar. New York, Asia Publishing House.

Sister Nivedita. *Cradle Tales of Hinduism*. Calcutta, Advaita Ashrama, Third Illustrated Impression, 1975

Sri Aurobindo. 1954. *Sāvitrī*. Sri Aurobindo International University Centre Collection Vol. II. Pondicherry, Sri Aurobindo Ashram.

THE EPIC CONTEXT OF THE *BHAGAVADGĪTĀ*

MADHAV M. DESHPANDE

1. *Introduction*

1.1. In trying to understand the meaning of the *Bhagavadgītā*, the relation between the situational context which forms the frame for the philosophical discussion and the philosophical discussion itself becomes a very important question, and our entire understanding of the text may be colored by how we tend to view this relationship. Is the situational element of the *Bhagavadgītā* subservient to the philosophical element, or is the philosophical element subservient to the situational element? These are not the only two choices, but represent the extremes of a spectrum of possibilities. This general question is very important in trying to understand the true import of the *Bhagavadgītā*. Is it the case that the author of the *Bhagavadgītā* had a preconceived systematic philosophy which he chose to express by using the particular context of the *Mahābhārata* war as a frame? Or is it the case that the story of the *Mahābhārata* was the preeminent concern of the author and that the philosophical doctrines were custom designed to fit the exigencies of the larger plot? We may never fully know the historically justifiable answers to these questions, since we know very little about the author or the authors of the *Bhagavadgītā* in particular, and the *Mahābhārata* in general. While resolving such questions in a totally conclusive fashion may be beyond our means, one can certainly keep in mind these issues in evaluating the contents of the *Bhagavadgītā* and its commentaries such as that of Śaṅkara. If the particular situation of Arjuna and its evolution turns out to be a factor which significantly molds the direction of the philosophical discussion, it may serve as a warning against uncritically accepting the dominant cultural belief in India that Kṛṣṇa used Arjuna's battle situation simply as an occasion to teach his philosophical message to the world, a message which he would have communicated in any case.

1.2. Such an impression is created by the phrase *arjunam nimittīkṛtya* "by using Arjuna as the occasion" used by Śaṅkara in the introduction to his *Gītābhāṣya*. Most traditional commentators believe that the *Bhagavadgītā* intends to convey a systematic doctrine, but may contain occasional deviations from this main doctrinal systematicity. Since the commentators do not agree upon what this main doctrine is, their notions of what the occasional deviations are are also divergent.

However, no commentator in the tradition ever argues that it is the context of Arjuna's situation on the battlefield which is the most powerful factor actually shaping and reshaping the line of Kṛṣṇa's argument. Again looking at the extremes of the spectrum of opinions concerning the *Bhagavadgītā*, the tradition holds that the *Bhagavadgītā* is not only a genuine part of the *Mahābhārata*, but that it is directly a representation of God's words. On the other hand, modern scholarship is willing to consider the whole or parts of the *Bhagavadgītā* as being interpolations. In this paper, I propose to build an argument based on the consistency of the plot of the epic to show which parts of the *Bhagavadgītā* may be most central and therefore original and which in all likelihood may be later additions.

2. *Arjuna's Depression*

2.1. The description of the state of Arjuna's mind in the first chapter of the *Bhagavadgītā* makes it clear that Arjuna's decision not to fight is not a conclusion based on well thought out philosophical or any other reasoning. It was the climax of a total breakdown of self-confidence caused by fear, uncertainty, compassion etc. His initial statement (*Bhagavadgītā* I.29–30) starts out with a description of the shock:

> *dṛṣṭvemaṃ svajanaṃ kṛṣṇa yuyutsuṃ samupasthitam /*
> *sīdanti mama gātrāṇi mukhaṃ ca pariśuṣyati / /*
> *vepthuś ca śarīre me romaharṣaś ca jāyate /*
> *gāṇḍīvaṃ sraṃsate hastāt tvak caiva paridahyate / /*
> *na ca śaknomy avasthātuṃ bhramatīva ca me manaḥ /*
>
> "Kṛṣṇa! having seen these assembled relatives who are eager to fight, my limbs sink and my mouth dries up. My body is trembling and my hair stands on end. My bow slips from hand and my skin is burning. I am not able to stand still. My mind is as if circling around".

2.2 It is only after this initial description of his shock that Arjuna begins to present a series of arguments to justify the conclusion that he has decided not to fight. These arguments seem to place a greater emphasis on external factors such as the impropriety of killing relatives in battle, danger of the mixture of castes etc., while Arjuna projects himself as a compassionate knowledgeable person (*asmābiḥ . . . prapaśyadbhiḥ*, *Bhagavadgītā* I.39) without acknowledging his own fear, uncertainty, confusion and ignorance. Arjuna had fought many battles in the past and this was certainly not his first experience of war. Naturally, Kṛṣṇa admonishes him to abandom this unmanly (*klaibya*) and uncivilized (*anāryajuṣṭa*) behavior which would not lead him to heaven nor fetch him any glory (*Bhagavadgītā* I.2–3). In response to this prodding from Kṛṣṇa,

Arjuna reveals a much greater depth to his emotional problem, his fear of killing his own teachers in the battle, and most importantly his concern that he was not sure whether the Pāṇḍavas would win or lose the war (*yad vā jayema yadi vā no jayeyuḥ*, *Bhagavadgītā* I.6). This last doubt is the most significant factor in Arjuna's reaction. The Pāṇḍavas are outnumbered almost two to one, i.e. eleven Kaurava *akṣauhiṇīs* versus seven Pāṇḍava *akṣauhiṇīs* according to the story of the *Mahābhārata*. Similarly, the moral factor of killing one's teachers and relatives in battle was also very significant. The rest of the *Bhagavadgītā* is a masterly argument built by Kṛṣṇa to refute Arjuna's logic, and to encourage him to fight. During the course of this discourse, Arjuna slowly reveals his lack of full acceptance of Kṛṣṇa's divinity, and a major portion of the *Bhagavadgītā* is spent on convincing Arjuna of Kṛṣṇa's divinity. In the course of revealing his own divinity to Arjuna, Kṛṣṇa shows him his cosmic form in which the great Kaurava heroes were being destroyed. Such a specialized cosmic form again has a very closely contextual significance. Finally, Arjuna is convinced of Kṛṣṇa's divinity and agrees to follow his advice and fight.

2.3 This is briefly the situational frame of the *Bhagavadgītā*. While this frame is widely known, the antecedents of many elements of this frame in the story of the *Mahābhārata* are not so widely known. These antecedents throw a great deal of light on Arjuna's state of mind in the *Bhagavadgītā* and Kṛṣṇa's response to it. It is commonly believed that Arjuna's reaction to the battle scene was an instantaneous response and therefore it shocked Kṛṣṇa all the more. A study of the antecedents in the *Mahābhārata* point to quite a different picture. In fact one may be able to say that it was Kṛṣṇa who was more bent upon going to war against the Kauravas and that he could not let Arjuna resign from carrying out this plan. The *Udyogaparva* and the *Bhīṣmaparva* of the *Mahābhārata* provide ample evidence to create a profile of the pre-war attitudes of the *Mahābhārata* characters. With this evidence, we are better able to understand the *Bhagavadgītā* in its proper epic context.

3. *Acceptance of Kṛṣṇa's Divinity by Other Participants*

3.1. It is clear from the *Mahābhārata* that not all characters were sure of or even aware of Kṛṣṇa's divinity before the war. Even with the various textual accretions, the story retains its integrity to a large extent. To put it simply, if characters like Arjuna had been already fully convinced of Kṛṣṇa's divinity, a large part of the *Bhagavadgītā* as we have it would not make any sense. The evolution of the discourse in the *Bhagavadgītā* shows that Arjuna was aware of Kṛṣṇa's divinity through hearsay, though he had no personal experience.

3.2. In chapter MB 5.7., we are told how both Arjuna and Duryodhana approach Kṛṣṇa to seek his assistance in their war effort. Kṛṣṇa says that all of his army will be on one side and he will be himself on the other side, unarmed and not taking part in the fighting itself (*ayudhyamānaḥ saṅgrāme nyastaśastro' ham ekataḥ*, MB 5.7.17). After being told this, Arjuna chose Kṛṣṇa, while Duryodhana chose Kṛṣṇa's army. After Duryodhana left, Kṛṣṇa turned to Arjuna and asked him: "With what idea did you choose me who will not fight in the battle?" (*ayudhyamānaḥ kāṃ buddhim āsthāya ahaṃ tvayā vṛtaḥ*, MB 5.7.31). Arjuna answered:

bhavān samarthas tān sarvān nihantuṃ nātra saṃśayaḥ /
nihantum aham apy ekaḥ samarthaḥ puruṣottama / /
bhavāṃs tu kīrtimāloke tad yaśas tvāṃ gamiṣyati /
yaśasā cāham apy arthī tasmād asi mayā vṛtaḥ / /

"O Puruṣottama, without doubt you are capable of killing all of them (= Kauravas). I too am capable by myself. However, since you are so famous in the world, you will be successful. I too am desirous of success, and therefore I chose you".
MB 5.7.32–33.

Interestingly, Arjuna does not bring in any notion of or acknowledgement of Kṛṣṇa's divinity in this context. However, Arjuna had heard about Kṛṣṇa's divinity and that was indeed a factor in his choosing Kṛṣṇa over his army. During the period when both sides were exchanging messages, Sañjaya reports Arjuna's words to Duryodhana:

ayudhyamāno manasā pi yasya
jayaṃ kṛṣṇaḥ puruṣasyābhinandet /
dhruvaṃ sarvān so' bhyatīyād amitrān
sendrān devān mānuṣe nāsti cintā / /

"Even though Kṛṣṇa is not fighting, if he even contemplates in his mind the victory of a person, that person will indeed overcome his enemies, even the gods along with Indra. There is no question about human (enemies)." MB 5.47.64.

Sañjaya reports Arjuna's belief that Kṛṣṇa was the powerful Viṣṇu himself (*viṣṇum anantavīryam*, MB 5.47.82), and that gods had asked Kṛṣṇa to rescue them from the demon Naraka (*jānanto' sya prakṛtiṃ keśavasya nyayojayan dasyuvadhāya kṛṣṇam*, MB 5.47.74–76). How did Arjuna know about Kṛṣṇa's divinity? Certainly not through personal experience. It was through indirect reports from Nārada and others.

Looking at the invincible arrangement of the army made by Bhīṣma, Yudhiṣṭhira was terribly worried and depressed. He asked Arjuna how they were going to emerge successful from this battle. Arjuna replied:

evaṃ rājan vijānīhi dhruvo' smākaṃ raṇe jayaḥ /
yathā me nāradaḥ prāha yataḥ kṛṣṇas tato jayaḥ //
anantatejā govindaḥ śatrupūgeṣu nirvyathaḥ /
puruṣaḥ sanātanatamo yataḥ kṛṣṇas tato jayaḥ //
purā hy eṣa harir bhūtvā vaikuṇṭho' kuṇṭhasāyakaḥ /
surāsurān avasphūrjann abravīt ke jayantv iti //
anu kṛṣṇaṃ jayemeti yair uktaṃ tatra tair jitam /
tat-prasādād dhi trailokyaṃ prāptaṃ śakrādibhiḥ suraiḥ //
tasya te na vyathāṃ kāṃcid iha paśyāmi bhārata /
yasya te jayam āśāste viśvabhuk tridaśeśvaraḥ //

"You should know, O King, that our victory in the battle is absolutely certain. As Nārada has told me, where there is Kṛṣṇa, there goes the victory. Infinitely powerful, Govinda is painless (while moving) in the midst of the throngs of enemies. He is the most ancient spiritual being. Where there is Kṛṣṇa, there goes the victory. Previously, indeed the same Kṛṣṇa, having assumed the form of Hari, the being from Vaikuṇṭha with invincible arrows, spoke with a resounding voice to gods and demons, "who should win?" Those who said that they will win by following Kṛṣṇa won in those battles. Only through his grace did Indra and others gain the kingdom of the three worlds. Since that lord of the gods, the ruler of the universe, wishes for your victory, O Bhārata, I do not see any trouble for you". MB 6.21.11–17.

The identity of Kṛṣṇa with Viṣṇu was thus communicated to Arjuna by Nārada, and Arjuna did put a great value on this supposed divinity, though he did not have a personal experience. As is clear from the *Bhagavadgītā*, Kṛṣṇa's divinity was not beyond doubts and questions for Arjuna. Kṛṣṇa had to establish it for Arjuna not only through his discourse, but by granting him a vision of his cosmic divine form, which was normally accessible only to mystics.

3.2. While normal characters like Arjuna did not have any personal knowledge of Kṛṣṇa's divinity, several mystically oriented characters "knew" Kṛṣṇa to be Viṣṇu. Consider the situation of Dhṛtarāṣṭra. Through hearsay, he also seems to have been aware of Kṛṣṇa's divinity, which he uses to convince Duryodhana to make peace with Pāṇḍavas:

tathā viṣṇuḥ keśavo' py apradhṛṣyo
lokatrayasyādhipatir mahātmā /
tiṣṭheta kas tasya martyaḥ purastāt
yaḥ sarvadeveṣu vareṇya īḍyaḥ //

"Similarly, this Keśava, who is Viṣṇu himself, is invincible and a great soul, the overlord of the three worlds. Which mortal would be able to confront him, who is the best and the most praiseworthy among all the gods"? MB 5.22.10.

However, it is clear that Dhṛtarāṣṭra had no personal experience of Kṛṣṇa's divinity. In chapter MB 5.67, Dhṛtarāṣṭra asks Sañjaya:

katham tvam mādhavam vettha sarvalokamaheśvaram /
katham enam na vedāham tan mamācakṣva sañjaya / /

"How come you know Mādhava to be the overlord of the entire universe, and how come I do not know him? O Sañjaya, please explain this to me". MB 5.66.1.

Sañjaya says:

vidyayā tāta jānāmi triyugam madhusūdanam /
kartāram akṛtam devam bhūtānām prabhavāpyayam / /

"Through wisdom, I know Madhusūdana, who has existed through all the three Yugas, to be the uncreated creator, the god who is the source and the final return of all beings". MB 5.67.3.

At this point, Sañjaya then explains in detail the doctrine of Kṛṣṇa's divinity to Dhṛtarāṣṭra. This discussion continues into chapter MB 5.68. In the next chapter, Dhṛtarāṣṭra then tries to convince Duryodhana of Kṛṣṇa's divinity. Thus, it is clear that in the story of the *Mahābhārata*, Kṛṣṇa's divinity is heard about by most of the heroes, but very few if any have had a first hand experience. The Pāṇḍavas are not yet convinced beyond a shadow of doubt, though they would like to believe in it. In the light of such a background in the story, it makes perfect sense why Arjuna could not accept Kṛṣṇa's exotic doctrines and claims immediately.

4. *Doubts about Pāṇḍava Victory*

4.1. In *Bhagavadgītā* (2.6.), Arjuna expresses his doubt about the outcome of the war. He could not be certain whether his side will emerge victorious in the battle. While he was a brave warrior, he could still see that the odds were stacked against the Pāṇḍavas. This realization was shared by other Pāṇḍavas. Interestingly, the three sons of Kuntī shared a very ambivalent attitude, an oscillation between willingness and unwillingness to go to war. While Arjuna is confident of his own prowess, and he boasts about it to scare the Kauravas (MB 5.47.91ff), he still cannot forget that the Pāṇḍavas were outnumbered by their enemies. Such doubts were shared by others. Kṛṣṇa says to the allies of the

Pāṇḍavas at the court of Virāṭ:

tathāpi neme' lpatayā samarthāḥ
teṣāṃ jayāyeti bhaven mataṃ vaḥ //
sametya sarve sahitāḥ suhṛdbhiḥ
teṣāṃ vināśāya yateyur eva //

"Even if you may think that because of numerical inferiority these (Pāṇḍavas) are not capable of gaining a victory over them (=Kauravas), still, joined together with all their friends, they will certainly attempt to destroy them (=the Kauravas)". MB 5.1.22.

In chapter MB 6.21, Yudhiṣṭhira is worried about the Pāṇḍavas' ability to break through the formations arranged by Bhīṣma. On this occasion, Arjuna tries to console Yudhiṣṭhira by referring to Kṛṣṇa's reported divinity. However, it is obvious that such an explanation was not fully convincing even for Arjuna himself.

5. *The Will to Fight*

5.1. The *Mahābhārata* depicts a picture of different individuals with different responses to the idea of war. Among the Pāṇḍavas, clearly the three sons of Kuntī emerge as the soft-hearted warriors, to the great irritation of Draupadī, Nakula and Sahadeva, as well as Kṛṣṇa. After the Kauravas refuse to give even five villages to the Pāṇḍavas, Yudhiṣṭhira realizes that war is the only option. However, even at this point, he would rather avoid war, if peace could be attained in some way or another. Therefore, he sends Kṛṣṇa on a final peace mission. These are Bhīma's words to Kṛṣṇa before his departure:

api duryodhanaṃ kṛṣṇa sarve vayam adhaścarāḥ /
nīcair bhūtvānuyāsyāmo mā sma no bharatā naśan //
apy udāsīnavṛttiḥ syād yathā naḥ kurubhiḥ saha /
vāsudeva tatha kāryaṃ na kurūn anayaḥ spṛśet //
....
aham etad bravīmy evaṃ rājā caiva praśaṃsati /
arjuno naiva yuddhārthī bhūyasī hi dayārjune //

"We may even walk behind Duryodhana, bending low and walking at a lower level, O Kṛṣṇa, but let not our Bharatas be destroyed (in the war). O Vāsudeva, please arrange it in such a way that we will have a peaceful relationship with the Kurus. That way no injustice will fall upon the Kurus . . . I say this and the king also approves of it. Arjuna is indeed not desirous of war. Arjuna has a great deal of compassion". MB 5.72.20–23.

Draupadī recognizes that Bhīma and Arjuna have a weak resolve to go to war. This angers her immensely:

> *yadi bhīmārjunau kṛṣṇa kṛpaṇau sandhikāmukau /*
> *pitā me yotsyate vṛddhaḥ saha putraiḥ mahārathaiḥ / /*
>
> "O Kṛṣṇa, if the wretched Bhīma and Arjuna want to make peace (with the Kauravas), then my old father, along with his mighty warrior sons, will go to war". MB 5.80.37.

Such angry words, coming from Draupadī, who was insulted at the court of Duryodhana, seem to be quite natural. Nakula and Sahadeva have a similar reaction. Their advice to Kṛṣṇa, who is about to leave for his peace mission, is:

> *yadi praśamam iccheyuḥ kuravaḥ saha pāṇḍavaiḥ /*
> *tathāpi yuddhaṃ dāśārha yojayethāḥ sahaiva taiḥ / /*
>
> "Even if the Kurus would want to make peace with the Pāṇḍavas, still, O Kṛṣṇa, you should plan to bring about a war with them". MB 5.79.2.

Sahadeva says:

> *yadi bhīmārjunau kṛṣṇa dharmarājaś ca dhārmikaḥ /*
> *dharmam utsṛjya tenāhaṃ yoddhum icchāmi saṃyuge / /*
>
> "If Bhīma, Arjuna and Dharmarāja are righteous (in thinking about not going to war), then, O Kṛṣṇa, I would like to abandon Dharma and fight in the battle". MB 5.79.4.

Kṛṣṇa is the one character that is consistently advocating war with the Kauravas. Even before leaving on his final peace mission, Kṛṣṇa says that for every possible reason he advocates war with the enemies (*sarvathā yuddham evāham āśaṃsāmi paraiḥ saha*, MB 5.71.34). He promises Draupadī that there will indeed be a war in which she will see the Kaurava women crying after their relatives have been killed. This, Kṛṣṇa says, is destined to happen and it cannot be altered (MB 5.80.44ff).

6. *Moral Dilemmas*

6.1. Arjuna makes a number of moral arguments against fighting the war in the *Bhagavadgītā*. Again it must be said that Arjuna is not unique in making such arguments. The same moral issues faced a number of characters. Arjuna says that he sees evil omens (*nimittāni ca paśyāmi viparītāni keśava*, *Bhagavadgītā* 1.31). Many such descriptions of evil omens before the war are found in the *Mahābhārata*. The most detailed description is perhaps found in chapters MB 6.2 and MB 6.3, where Vyāsa describes numerous evil omens to Dhṛtarāṣṭra. Dhṛtarāṣṭra sends Sañjaya as a messenger to Yudhiṣṭhira (chapter 5.25) and a large part of the message is the description of the evil effects of the war and the resulting sin. Sañjaya, in communicating Dhṛtarāṣṭra's message, says:

yatra bhīṣmaḥ śāntanavo hataḥ syāt
yatra droṇaḥ sahaputro hataḥ syāt //
kṛpaḥ śalyaḥ saumadattir vikarṇo
viviṃśatiḥ karṇaduryodhanau ca /
etān hatvā kīdṛśaṃ tat sukhaṃ syāt
yad vindethās tad anubrūhi pārtha //
labdhvāpīmāṃ pṛthivīṃ sāgarāntām
jarāmṛtyū naiva hi tvaṃ prajahyāḥ /
priyāpriye sukhaduḥkhe ca rājan
naivaṃ vidvān naiva yuddhaṃ kuruṣva //

"(In this war) where Bhīṣma, the son of Śantanu, would be killed, and where Droṇa would be killed along with his son; where Kṛpa, Śalya, Saumadatti, Vikarṇa, Karṇa, Duryodhana and scores (of others would be killed), tell me, O son of Pṛthā, what would be the pleasure that you will earn by killing these? Even after obtaining the kingdom upto the limits of the oceans, you will not be free from old age and death, pleasant and unpleasant things, sorrows and happiness. O king! Knowing thus, you ought not to make war". MB 5.27.24–26.

Kuntī faces the same dilemma, knowing the kind of disaster the war would bring upon everyone:

dhig astv artham yat-kṛte' yam mahān jñātivadhe kṣayaḥ /
vartsyate suhṛdāṃ hy eṣāṃ yuddhe' smin vai parābhavaḥ //
pāṇḍavāś cedipāñcālā yādavāś ca samāgatāḥ /
bhāratair yadi yotsyanti kiṃ nu duḥkham ataḥ param //
paśye doṣam dhruvaṃ yuddhe tathā yuddhe parābhavam /
adhanasya mṛtaṃ śreyo na hi jñātikṣaye jayaḥ //

"Cursed be the riches for which this great destruction of the relatives in the battle will occur. Similarly, there will be the defeat of these good hearted persons in this battle. If the Pāṇḍavas, Cedis, Pāñcālas, and Yādavas come together and fight with the Bhāratas, what greater pain could there be compared to this? I certainly see the fault in the war and I also see the defeat in the war. It is better to die poor than attain victory in the destruction of one's kinsfolk". MB 5.142.11–13.

Similar issues are raised even by Dharmarāja in deciding to take up arms against the Kauravas. The *Udyogaparva* (5.151.19–22) describes the moral dilemma faced by Dharmarāja:

kathaṃ hy avadhyaiḥ saṃgrāmaḥ kāryaḥ saha bhaviṣyati /
kathaṃ hatvā gurūn vṛddhān vijayo no bhaviṣyati //

"How one would have to fight with those who are not to be killed? Having killed the aged elders, how could victory be ours"? MB 5.152.22.

Upon listening to these woes of Yudhiṣṭhira, it is Arjuna who cites Kṛṣṇa's advice to the Pāṇḍavas that they must fight for their just cause (MB 5.151.23–4). Arjuna tells Yudhiṣṭhira that this war, in the opinion of Kṛṣṇa, Kuntī and Vidura, was indeed not *adharma*, and that the Pāṇḍavas could not simply withdraw without giving a fight. Kṛṣṇa himself is present on this occasion and he approves Arjuna's justification with a smile (*tac chrutvā vāsudevo' pi savyasācivacas tadā smayamāno' bravīt pārtham evam etad iti bruvan*, MB 5.151.27). Again Arjuna is not alone in leaving up to Kṛṣṇa the decision between what is *dharma* and *adharma*. After listening to Sañjaya's message that fighting the war may lead to *adharma*, Yudhiṣṭhira replies:

> *yadi hy ahaṃ visṛjan syām agarhyo*
> *yudhyamāno yadi jahyāṃ svadharmam* /
> *mahāyaśāḥ keśavas tad bravītu*
> *vāsudevas tūbhayar arthakāmaḥ* / /
> . . . .
> *īdṛśo' yaṃ keśavas tāta bhūyo*
> *vidmo hy enaṃ karmaṇāṃ niścayajñam* /
> *priyaś ca naḥ sādhutamaś ca kṛṣṇo*
> *nātikrame vacanaṃ keśavasya* / /

"Would I be free from blame if I were to give up? Would I be abandoming my own duty by fighting? Let Kṛṣṇa, of great fame, speak about that. Vāsudeva wishes well for both sides. Sir, such is this Kṛṣṇa. Moreover, we know him as one who can decide between various possible actions. Kṛṣṇa is dear to us and he is most noble. I will not transgress Kṛṣṇa's words". MB 5.28.10,14.

7. *Kṛṣṇa's Special Relationship to Arjuna*

7.1. In the *Bhagavadgītā* (10.37), Kṛṣṇa says that, as God, he represents the best of everything, and that among the Pāṇḍavas, he is Arjuna himself (*pāṇḍavānāṃ dhanaṃjayaḥ*). Kṛṣṇa also says that Arjuna is his friend and is devoted to him (*bhakto' si me sakhā ceti, Bhagavadgītā* 4.3). In the story of the *Mahābhārata*, Kṛṣṇa's relationship with Arjuna is particularly intense. In general, the Pāṇḍavas are Kṛṣṇa's cousins. Kuntī, the mother of the Pāṇḍavas was Kṛṣṇa's father's, i.e. Vasudeva's, sister. Additionally Kṛṣṇa's sister, Subhadrā was married to Arjuna. Kṛṣṇa also had an intense brotherly affection for Draupadī, the wife of the Pāṇḍavas. There were no such links with the Kaurava side. The fact that the Pāṇḍavas are deemed to be followers of the righteous conduct is also a factor. Kṛṣṇa explains to Duryodhana:

yas tān dveṣṭi sa māṃ dveṣṭi
yas tān anu sa mām anu /
aikātmyaṃ māṃ gataṃ viddhi
pāṇḍavair dharmacāribhiḥ //

"He who hates them hates me, and he who is behind them is behind me. Know me to have reached a state of identity with the Pāṇḍavas of righteous conduct". MB 5.89.28.

Arjuna in particular was Kṛṣṇa's most favorite Pāṇḍava and this relationship had been recognized by others as well. Vidura explains to Dhṛtarāṣṭra that Arjuna is as dear to Kṛṣṇa as his own life and that Kṛṣṇa will never abandon him (*atyājyam asya jānāmi prāṇais tulyaṃ dhanaṃjayam*, MB 5.85.12).

8. *Arjuna's Baggage*

8.1. The above discussion makes it clear that Arjuna's reaction to the war as depicted in the *Bhagavadgītā* was neither unusual nor unexpected in the light of the preceding descriptions in the *Mahābhārata*. The Pāṇḍavas were aware of the moral issues involved in killing their own kinsmen, teachers and relatives in the battle. They were also aware of the larger cultural damage which would inevitably result from the war. They were numerically inferior to the Kauravas. Such facts naturally led to doubts in their minds about the moral justification of their venture as well as the prospects of success in the war. Arjuna was aware of Kṛṣṇa's affection and support for him and valued this special relationship. While he had heard about Kṛṣṇa's divinity, and had come to view it as an important asset, he personally had no experience of this aspect of Kṛṣṇa's personality. It is necessary to understand this as an important point in the story of the *Mahābhārata*. Between Arjuna's concern about the possibility of losing the war and the solace he gained in knowing that Kṛṣṇa was on his side, ultimately it is the concern over who may be victorious (*yad vā jayema jadi vā no jayeyuḥ*, *Bhagavadgītā* 2.6) that proves to be more powerful. Arjuna sinks into depression even while Kṛṣṇa is standing next to him. It is obvious that Arjuna's second-hand knowledge about Kṛṣṇa's divinity was not strong enough to help him pull out of this depression. Nor was it strong enough to make him accept Kṛṣṇa's philosophical claims without objections.

9. *Back to the* Bhagavadgītā

9.1. On this background, we can understand why Arjuna could not simply accept Kṛṣṇa's initial admonitions in the *Bhagavadgītā*. It should be noted that most of those initial admonitions are not new but have occurred earlier in the *Mahābhārata*. Kṛṣṇa has already explained the moral issues to the Pāṇḍavas on many previous occasions and there was very little new. Even the doctrine of *karmayoga*, the argument based on the duty of a Kṣatriya, had been made previously (cf. MB, Chapter 5.29). Therefore, Arjuna's reluctance in accepting the same old arguments is quite understandable. The new arguments in the *Bhagavadgītā* begin with Kṛṣṇa gradually introducing supernatural claims about himself and introducing a hierarchy between himself and Arjuna. Such issues are introduced from the beginning of the fourth chapter of the *Bhagavadgītā*.

> *imaṃ vivasvate yogaṃ proktavān aham avyayam /*
> *vivasvān manave prāha manur ikṣvākave' bravīt //*
>
> "I explained this imperishable doctrine of *yoga* to Vivasvat. Vivasvat explained this to Manu, who explained it to Ikṣvāku". *Bhagavadgītā* 4.1.

This is the first time when Kṛṣṇa has directly brought in a notion that he represents the eternal godhood and that he is more than and beyond the limitations of his particular mortal appearance. This was not immediately acceptable to Arjuna, and with an air of disbelief he asks:

> *aparaṃ bhavato janma paraṃ janma vivasvataḥ /*
> *katham etad vijānīyāṃ tvam ādau proktavān iti //*
>
> "Your birth is recent, while the birth of Vivasvat is in the remote past. How can I comprehend that you explained this [doctrinel] first to [him]"? *Bhagavadgītā* 4.4.

This is the beginning of the new element in the *Bhagavadgītā*. Kṛṣṇa has now taken the argument to a new height and the validity of this new argument depends not just upon the value of the ideas, but upon the truth of the personal claims about Kṛṣṇa's divinity. The fourth chapter of the *Bhagavadgītā* introduces Kṛṣṇa's claim to godhood directly, and then this idea is slowly developed in the later chapters. In the eleventh chapter of the *Bhagavadgītā*, we reach the climax of this argument with an opportunity offered to Arjuna to have a direct realization of Kṛṣṇa's divine form. After this vision of Kṛṣṇa's cosmic form, Arjuna needs no more verbal descriptions. Arjuna now personally knows that Kṛṣṇa is God and that his promises about everything now override all other prior ideas about mortality, fear, duty and defeat. After this cosmic vision of Kṛṣṇa, Arjuna's resistance is completely broken and till the very end of the *Bhagavadgītā*, he is only at the receiving end, willing to carry out Kṛṣṇa's advice.

9.2. In order to get Arjuna back on his feet, Kṛṣṇa has to deal with all aspects of Arjuna's psychological breakdown, from his pseudo-wisdom and pretence of self-confidence to fear, uncertainty and ignorance. The shape of Kṛṣṇa's discourse is primarily circumscribed by this task. His exposition of philosophy is not an excercise in pure philosophy. It is applied philosophy, philosophy manipulated and reorganized to suit a special purpose. It is through this manipulation and reorganization of various strands that a new application of old philosophies is gradually developed and perfected. While the individual philosophical ideas in most cases are old, their peculiar redesigning and reorienting is the contribution of the author of the *Bhagavadgītā*, or of Kṛṣṇa himself as the Indian tradition believes.

10. *The Contextualized Cosmic form of Kṛṣṇa*

10.1. Thus the context of the *Bhagavadgīta* shaped its philosophy and therefore is of primary importance. In the cosmic form of Kṛṣṇa, Arjuna sees the Kaurava heroes entering into the mouth and being chewed up and destroyed. Even a traditional commentator like Śaṅkara recognizes that the purpose of this cosmic form being shown to Arjuna is to remove his doubt about his victory once and for all (*athādhunā purā "yad vā jayema yadi vā no jayeyuḥ" ity arjunasya yaḥ saṃśaya āsīt tan-nirṇayāya pāṇḍavajayaṃ aikāntikaṃ darśayāmīti pravṛtto bhagavān / Gītābhāṣya* on *Bhagavadgīta* 11.20). The *Bhagavadgītā* itself makes this situational significance of the cosmic form quite clear. Kṛṣṇa says:

kālo' smi lokakṣayakṛt pravṛddho
lokān samāhartum iha pravṛttaḥ /
ṛte' pi tvāṃ na bhaviṣyanti sarve
ye' vasthitāḥ pratyanīkeṣu yodhāḥ / /
tasmāt tvaṃ uttiṣṭha yaśo labhasva
jitvā śatrūn bhuṅkṣva rājyaṃ samṛddhaṃ /
mayaivaite nihatāḥ pūrvameva
nimittamātraṃ bhava savyasācin / /
droṇaṃ ca bhīṣmaṃ ca jayadrathaṃ ca
karṇaṃ tathānyān api yodhavīrān /
mayā hatāṃs tvaṃ jahi mā vyathiṣṭhā
yudhyasva jetāsi raṇe sapatnān / /

"I am the Time that causes the worlds to perish, matured and here come forth to destroy the worlds; even without you not one of the warriors drawn up in the opposing ranks shall survive. Therefore arise, win glory, defeat

> your foes, enjoy wide sovereignty! I have already slain these men; be no more than a means, O Arjuna. Droṇa and Bhīṣma and Jayadratha and Karṇa and other mighty warriors too are already slain by me and now you may slay them. Tremble not! Fight! You shall conquer your rivals in the battle". *Bhagavadgītā* 11.32–34.

On these verses too, Śaṅkara brings out the situational significance of the particular visions. Kṛṣṇa refers only to those major Kaurava heroes as already being killed who worried Arjuna in one way or another (*yeṣu yeṣu yodheṣv arjunasyāśaṅkā tāṃs tān vyapadiśati bhagavān mayā hatān iti, Gītābhāṣya on* 11.34). Thus, the situational context is a major factor shaping the particular philosophical and theological arguments.

11. *Conclusion*

11.1. In this brief paper, I have tried to show that the *Bhagavadgītā* as it is available to us is deeply embedded in the story of the *Mahābhārata*. It represents a progression of the *Mahābhārata* narrative rather than an intrusion. Does this mean that the *Bhagavadgītā* as we have it is all by one author, or that it belongs, as a whole, to the oldest stratum of the epic? This is a difficult question. To state my conclusions briefly, it seems most likely that there was a version of *Mahābhārata* which did not contain a notion of Kṛṣṇa as a divinity. A version of the *Bhagavadgītā* most probably existed before Kṛṣṇa's divinity developed and was added to the epic. Perhaps the first three chapters of the current *Bhagavadgītā* contain material that goes back to this older core. A reflection of this state of the *Bhagavadgītā* is seen in the *Anugītā*, which purports to summarize the *Bhagavadgītā*, and yet does not contain references to Kṛṣṇa as a divinity. However, once the notion of Kṛṣṇa as a divinity developed in the history of Indian religions, new layers were added to the epic across the board, not just to the *Bhagavadgītā*. Those redactors who added these new layers of Kṛṣṇa religion made use of this new motif in enhancing the story element of the *Mahābhārata*, and the evidence presented in this paper demonstrates that the newly formed version of the *Bhagavadgītā* also shows the use of the motif of Kṛṣṇa as a divinity in its contribution to the story, i.e., this new element has been successfully used as an argument to show why Arjuna must fight the battle. This layer of Kṛṣṇa devotion is added in such a skillful way that Arjuna does not have a first hand experience of Kṛṣṇa's divinity until the eleventh chapter of the *Bhagavadgītā*. Thus, the progression of arguments in the *Bhagavadgītā* as we have it makes eminent sense.

We know that the epic continued to grow past this phase, and newer elements of Kṛṣṇa devotion were added to the epic. A student recently asked me the following question. When Draupadī was being stripped by Duḥśāsana at the court of Duryodhana, she prayed to Kṛṣṇa. Kṛṣṇa then provided a continuous unending sari for her, so that Duḥśāsana finally was exhausted and Draupadī was saved by Kṛṣna from being disgraced. Arjuna was supposedly at the court watching this incident. If he realized at that time that Kṛṣṇa was God, how does he not assume that at the beginning of the *Bhagavadgītā*? The best answer to such a dilemma is provided by the fact that the critical edition of the *Mahābhārata* does not contain this episode, indicating that it must be a later addition to the epic. Thus, it seems likely that elements of Kṛṣṇa religion were added intially in ways which would keep the logical progression of the *Mahābhārata* story unimpaired. However, in later times, this process of adding elements of Kṛṣṇa religion continued past a point of maintaining the integrity of the plot of the *Mahābhārata*.

Bibliography

Bhagavadgītā. Edited and translated by S.K. Belvalkar. *Hindu Viśvavidyālaya Nepāla Rājya Sanskrit Series*, Vol. I. Banaras: Banaras Hindu University, 1959.

Gītābhāṣya by Śaṅkarācārya, with a sub-commentary by Ānandagiri. *Ānandāśrama Sanskrit Series, No. 34*. Second edition. Pune, 1909.

MB, Mahābhārata. The Critical Edition of the *Mahābhārata*. Pune: Bhandarkar Oriental Research Institute, 1933–1959.

THE BATTLE OF KURUKṢETRA IN TOPOLOGICAL TRANSPOSITION

VICTORIA URUBSHUROW AND T.R. SINGH

I. *Introduction*

In 1924 Stanley Rice, in his introduction to *Tales from the Mahābhārata*, observed that

> [the Indian epics] are living and throbbing in the lives of the people of India, even of those illiterate masses that toil in the fields or maintain a drab existence in the ghettos of the towns. To such as these the famous old stories are the music and color of life. They are the perennial fount from which the oft-repeated draughts never quench an insatiable thirst. In the kings' palaces and in the peasants' huts you may still hear the grand legends of the Great War and the pathetic sufferings of Rāma. . . .[1]

This observation is borne out by the example of the Bābā of Sahāvalī, a low-caste agriculturalist *camār*[2], for whom the epics were, indeed, the "music and color of life."

Sahāvalī village is situated about sixty miles east of Kurukṣetra, directly across the Yamunā, and Bābā was acutely aware of living on the soil of

A note on transliterations: Pan-Indian concepts are treated as Sanskrit terms, and transliterated in a standard manner. Regional Hindi terms, including some proper names and places, are rendered according to Library of Congress transliteration tables, except that unpronounced a's are dropped. Major place names are rendered in accord with the spelling of the Survey of India. Special thanks go to Allen W. Thrasher of the Library of Congress for help with the diacritics. The authors take responsibility for any persistent errors or inconsistencies.

[1] Stanley Rice, *Tales from the Mahābhārata* (London: Selwyn & Blount, 1924), p. 9.

[2] Originally "*camār*" referred to a *jāti* of leatherworkers who helped drag away dead cattle, etc. They were among the untouchables of north India. Today they are one of the scheduled castes. For some generations many have worked as field laborers.

> "The great Camār caste is found all over the country except in the south, but in the tract where it is most numerous, between the east Panjāb and Bihār, it is not exclusively a leatherworking caste as its name denotes. It supplies . . . the main body of field labour, and receives its share of the harvest like the other village menials on the establishment."

Jervoise A. Baines, *Ethnography: Castes and Tribes*(Strassburg: Verlag von Karl J. Trübner, 1912), p. 78.

ancient Āryāvarta.[3] He claimed that the whole of western Uttar Pradesh was a sacred place due to its connection with the Mahābhārata war. (p. 114)[4] For Bābā, the sacred space of Kurukṣetra provided grounds for a contemporary concatenation of epic history. From a young age Kanval Dās (later known as "Bābā") took a keen interest in recitation of the Indian epics. His devotional fervor matured about fifteen years ago when he dreamed of a child who manifested the four-armed Viṣṇu. Thereafter, Viṣṇu duly tested the devotee and granted him numerous supernatural weapons. In time, Bābā used those weapons to heal people afflicted with spirit possession.

In 1983 word spread about a vision of Manśā Devī[5] that came to Bābā's daughter, auguring that water from the family tube-well would have curative properties for four months. During the presaged period, in fact, literally thousands of people with various ills descended upon Sahāvalī—especially on Sundays. Many local villagers were dismayed at seeing their fields badly trampled, while others seized the opportunity to do business.

---

[3] The Indian village of Sahāvalī is located in the Muzaffarnagar district of western Uttar Pradesh. It is midway between the Yamunā and Gangā rivers, about sixty miles due east of Kurukṣetra, seventy-five miles northwest of Delhi, and forty miles southeast of Hardwar. This area between the Himālaya and Vindhya mountain ranges is the ancient "land of the Āryas" or Āryāvarta—scene of the Mahābhārata war and other epic events.

[4] All citations from Bābā's biography, media reports, personal interviews, and photos follow the pagination of an unpublished manuscript by T.R. Singh, J.M. Mahar, and Victoria Urubshurow, "Bābā Project: Material Collected during 1983–1984." The mauscript is divided into three parts: (a) Hindi texts and English translations of booklets prepared by Bābā's followers, with local newspapers and magazine accounts; (b) English translation of the Bābā interviews conducted and tape recorded in Sahāvalī in June 1984; and (c) Photos of Bābā and his family prepared by local photographers and sold at the site of the healing. Newspaper and magazine accounts were translated by T.R. Singh and Ganesh Ṣaili (Landour Cantonment, Mussoorie, U.P.). The interviews were conducted by T.R. Singh (with K.S. Chauhan, Caroline Mahar, and V. Urubshurow), and translated by T.R. Singh.

[5] In the biography of Bābā distributed at the *melā*, the name of the goddess is rendered as "Manśā Devī." Her identity is somewhat mysterious or ambiguous. When asked, "Tell us something about 'Manśā,'" Bābā chose to speak of the *Mahābhārata* goddess:

> "'Manśā-jī' [?] is the queen of *nāgas*. She is the daughter of Kaśyapa, Jaratkāru's wife, Āstīka's mother. You might know the story of Vāsuki—the story of the serpent ... churning the ocean. She is the sister of Netiki. This is 'Manśā-jī' [?]. She is the disciple of Śaṅkar Bholānāth."

Yet, Bābā responded "No." to the question, "Is this [i.e. your deity] the Manasā of the *Mahābhārata*?" (p. 102) He further stated, "This is not that 'Manśā' [?]. This [goddess of the *Mahābhārata*] is the queen of serpents. Her husband's name is Jaratkāru." (p. 103) Bābā did not disclose the identity of his own "Manśā Devī."

The snake goddess's story is told in the *Mahābhārata*, I (5) where she is known by the same name as her husband, Jaratkāru. Otherwise, the epic deity's name is spelled variously as Mānasā or Manasā. The *Purāṇic Encyclopedia* describes Mānasā Devī [*sic*] as, "A devī

Small cottage industries sprang up to accommodate the needs of the faithful. The enterprising heaped up for sale old bottles in which Bābā's tube-well water might be stored, and arranged stalls where an official biography and photos of the Viṣṇu *bhakta*, or devotee, were peddled, along with mustard oil, etc. (for treatments prescribed in Bābā's biography). The October 1983 issue of the periodical *Sṛjan* described the incident as follows:

> India is a country of miracles. From days of old until today, numerous miracles have been seen and heard of. Every day some incident takes place that becomes an object of surprise and attraction to one and all. Such an incident of interest today is in a place some four kilometers on Jānsaṭh Road in the village Sahāvalī, near the jungle. A village *bhakta* is distributing water from the tube-well on his field with the belief that it will cure all the ills of the human body. For the last two months, thousands of people from nearby and far-flung areas have been flocking there in tractors, buggies, tongas, and busses to get this miraculous water. (p. 12)

---

born of the mind of Kaśyapa Prajāpati. She is known as Jaratkāru also." (p. 474) It further states:

> "This devī (goddess) is the daughter of Prajāpati Kaśyapa, born from his mind. She got the name Manasādevī [*sic*] (goddess born from mind). Some think that she got the name Manasādevī because she is the deity of mind. There are some who imagine that she got the name Manasādevī because she held Śrī Kṛṣṇa Paramātman (the Supreme Spirit) firmly in her mind."

Vettam Mani, *Purāṇic Encyclopedia* (Koṭṭayam, Kerala: n.p., 1964; reprint ed., Delhi: Motilal Banarsidass, 1984), p. 348.

Along different lines, it is uncertain whether Bābā's "Manśā" bears any relation to Manasā, the snake goddess identified by N.N. Bhattacharyya:

> "All over India and especially in Bengal, Manasā is worshipped as the goddess presiding over snakes. She is sometimes described as Jagad-Gaurī as well as Padmavatī. Her other names are Viṣahari [*sic*] and Bhujaṅgajananī Kamalā. . . . Among the Mals, Mal Paharias, etc., who are generally agricultural peoples having a wide distribution in different parts of the country, such goddesses as Manasā and others are worshipped."

Narendra Nath Bhattacharyya, *The Indian Mother Goddess*, 2d. ed., rev. (New Delhi: Manohar, 1977), pp. 52, 72. As this Manasā Devī is popular especially among agriculturalists, Bābā's status as a *camār* is consistent with the profile of those who worship her.

Yet, according to the research of T.R. Singh "Manśā" or "Manśā Devī" is a regional deity, and a favorite of women and students in Meerut, U.P.. She is believed to be the goddess of wishes, fulfilling the desires of her devotees. Manśā is enshrined in Hardwar where a special tree grows near her shrine. A devotee ties a thread around one of its twigs and opens the knot when his or her wish is fulfilled. Untying the knot involves quite a formality because there are hundreds, even thousands of threads tied to the branches. When a knot is untied the devotee thanks Manśā Devī.

Many journalists and "intellectuals" were piqued by the Bābā spectacle. Attempting to bring village folk into the twentieth century, they mightily tried to expose the healer as a fraud. On November 14, 1983 the local paper *Dainik Dehāt* ran the editorial headline, "This is not elixir! It is death-water!" and proclaimed:

> There is no dearth of blind faith in any corner of India. Sādhus, saints, mullās, and maulavīs use magical amulets, etc. to befool the simple people of this land. This is more so with people living in the rural areas, as the fear of ghosts, demons, etc. is put into their minds and hearts by such frauds to the extent that sometimes they give their lives for no reason. The intellectual of today can raise his voice against these evils because he understands that the "ghosts," etc. are the product of evil frauds, and there is no basis in reality for these things. (p. 43)

In spite of an onslaught of media harangue, not until the presaged term of hydrotherapy expired did the hopeful sick cease to overwhelm Bābā's village. Even then, a handful of the faithful continued to seek treatment.

After the hoopla, in June 1984 during private interviews, Bābā spoke of his vocation and other biographical matters.[6] He drew freely on epic themes, and spontaneously identified himself as a participant in the battle of Kurukṣetra—as it continues in the realm of spirits. According to his own testimony, Bābā healed people with the aid of good spirits of combatants killed in the Mahābhārata war by "destroying the [evil] powers of Kurukṣetra." (p. 85) In explaining the mechanics of his healing practice, Bābā employed a logic of topographic transposition. By virtue of this "topo-logic" the continuity of history from the Mahābhārata wartime until now was preserved on account of its transfer from the earthly realm to the realm of spirits. With topographic tenacity, spirits of combatants killed in the epic war never abandoned their locale, and remained ready to do battle in an invisible realm superimposed onto contemporary Āryāvarta. Moreover, Bābā could insert himself into this persistent gathering of "Kurukṣetra" by using his talents as story-teller, healer, and devotee of Viṣṇu.

---

[6] During the June 1984 interviews Bābā told stories, answered questions, and performed healing rites on a few afflicted persons who were among the handful present. Bābā was seen on a few other occasions by V. Urubshurow (Religious Studies, Catholic University of America), and more often by T.R. Singh (Sociology, B.S.M. College, Roorkie, U.P.) and J. Michael Mahar (Oriental Studies, University of Arizona) who were present during the healing *melā*. With no luck, T.R. Singh sought to contact Bābā in Sahāvalī after June 1984. Some villagers claimed that Bābā had absconded. Others said that he may have been in Delhi; while a caste fellow noted, in secret, that Bābā may have been with his *guru* in Sukartāl.

Bābā was an illiterate peasant—with a lively imagination. Although he was billed as a devotee of Viṣṇu, Bābā's activities were far more eclectic. Elements of three vocations were involved in the realization of his accomplishments: bard, shaman, and *bhakta*.[7] Bābā was neither a full-fledged story-teller nor healer, but to appreciate the dynamic of his devotional life it is useful to recognize the extent to which it embodied bardic and shamanic functions. As bard Bābā envisioned and portrayed epic events. As shaman he diagnosed ills caused by malevolent spirits and harnessed the aid of the beneficent. As *bhakta* he devoted himself to Viṣṇu's cause of promoting *dharma* in the world. Bābā was unusually creative in appropriating the diverse vocational possibilities submerged in his syncretic cultural milieu. The result was an imaginative blend of an ancient Āryan concern with the power of recitation, an indigenous folk involvement with spirits, and a Hindu fascination with the *darśana* of personal divinities.

II. *Bābā as Bard: Reconstitution of Epic History*

Bābā stepped into the stream of an ancient oral Indian tradition and embodied the basic, raw elements of a primitive bard. Though from a young age he recited the epics, Bābā was not an accomplished performer and apparently was not connected with any bardic lineage. Ideally, a bard has command of numerous narrative themes, complex sequences of events, and mnemonic devices suitable to sustain lengthy recitations. Moreover, members of a bardic lineage customarily have inbuilt checks on the range and variation of epic content by which they are "brought back into line ... by the songs and singers of the tradition itself."[8] In contrast, Bābā mainly just alluded to characters and events, and did not provide lengthy elaborations of plot. Moreover, he seemed to reign free of the tensions of thematic constraint.

On the other hand, Bābā's bardic vocation reflected an elementary

[7] The proposed characterization of Bābā's activities in terms of three vocational types is approximate. His profile does not conform fully to any single ideal type, but embodies basic aspects of each. Moreover, to speak of Bābā's "accomplishments" does not reflect an implicit or explicit judgment on the literal truth value of his claims. His declamations are neither counted nor discounted as being literally true. Of interest here is a cultural rather than psychological or metaphysical phenomenon. Bābā's idiosyncratic portrayal of events, derived from selective appropriation and creative synthesis of cultural sediment deposited over millennia, reflects a significant cultural dynamic that allows the epics to perdure.

[8] Albert B. Lord, *The Singer of Tales* (New York: Atheneum, 1974), p. 118.

instinct for the numinous that is characteristic of an archaic and less literarily complex oral tradition. Albert B. Lord's observation on aboriginal bardic recitation aptly describes Bābā's compositional orientation:

> Its symbols, its sounds, its patterns were born for magic productivity, not for aesthetic satisfaction. If later [in the history of epic development] they provided such satisfaction, it was only to generations which had forgotten their real meaning. *The poet was sorcerer and seer before he became "artist"* [emphasis added]. His structures were not abstract art, or art for its own sake. The roots of oral traditional narrative are not artistic but religious in the broadest sense.[9]

Through Bābā such an archaic oral tradition was exposed in its nakedness.

In spite of a journalist's accusation that "his speech does not have the faintest touch of intellectualism or spiritualism" (p. 23), Bābā spoke with a bardic authority and specificity derived from intense involvement in the narrative materials. His cultural vocabulary was immense, encompassing references to Sanskritic literature, Hindu and Muslim folklore, and anomalous historical figures. Bābā expertly distinguished among various kinds of spirits including *bhūtas*, *pretas*, *jinns*, *pitṛs*, *naugajas*, *sayyeds*, *rākṣasas*, *śaktis*, and *piśācas*. His foes included combatants from Duryodhana's army, [Aurangzeb's chief] Maḥbūb Khān's [*sic*] army, as well as the Britishers' army. Bābā named as helpers the benevolent spirits of epic heroes such as Bhīṣma [*sic*], Duryodhana, Rāma, Balarāma, Hanumān, Garuḍa, Jaṭāyu, Kumbhakarṇa, Kubera, Hiḍimba, Yamarāja, and numerous unspecified epic characters. Three more helpers were the good spirits of Sir Edmund Hillary, Abraham Lincoln, and Jesus Christ. To top it off, this gigantesque epic reconstitution was conducted under the guidance of a cross-cultural array of divine powers: the traditional Hindu divinity Viṣṇu, the folk goddess Manśā Devī, and the Persian Qudrat [nature, fate].[10]

India's cultural lore so permeated Bābā's experience that the distinction between art and life was moot. It not only provided material for the

---

[9] Ibid., p. 67.

[10] Our records indicate that Bābā named "Bhīṣma" instead of "Bhīma." However, judging from the context it is probable that "Bhīma" was intended, for of the hero Bābā stated:

> "Yesterday also I mentioned that in the battle of Kurukṣetra, only Bhīṣma [*sic*] survived. All others died. And this devotee of Īṣvara I invite at the time of my daily offering [*havana*]." (p. 86)

Although Bābā recalled numerous figures, those with whom he seemed to have the closest relationship were Viṣṇu, Manśā Devī, and Hanumān. He did not specify the roles

telling of tales, but largely shaped his life story and world view. On a basic level, Bābā imitated traditional themes in conceiving his own biography. This simple epic identification is reflected in several details noted by Bābā: (a) His daughter was called "Satyavatī," namesake of Vyāsa's mother and grandmatriarch of the Kauravas and Pāṇḍavas. (b) As the Pāṇḍavas stored their weapons in the Śamī tree, so Bābā declared, "On top of the tree are [my] weapons." (p. 90) (c) When asked whether he would be reborn, Bābā answered, "my next birth will be without conception. . . . At that time, my head will be sacrificed. . . . It will be as it was done with Babarbhān [Babhruvāhana (?)] of the *Mahābhārata* [because Viṣṇu will ask for my head]." (p. 112) (d) Bābā's nights as well as his days were emboldened by epic themes and characters. Once Bābā dreamed that some "bad characters" carried away his wife intending to assault her. This oneiric situation reflects the epic accounts of Duḥśāsana and Duryodhana insulting Draupadī, and Rāvaṇa abducting Sītā. As Bhīma redeemed Draupadī and Hanumān delivered Sītā in the epics, so in Bābā's dream Bhīma and Hanumān descended to protect his wife.

Bābā's relationship with epic characters redounded beyond such descriptive echoes, however. As the archaic bard was a seer, so Bābā's poetic expression involved more than mimicry. His bardic research conferred the gnostic ability to distinguish between true and false narratives. Upholding a version of the *Rāmāyaṇa* that contradicted the traditional brahmanical view of Hanumān's *brahmacarya* status, Bābā believed that Hanumān had a wife (a fish) who conceived a son after swallowing a drop of the monkey's perspiration fallen when he crossed the ocean in search of Sītā. He based his claim that Hanumān was not *brahmacarya* on authority derived from two ecstatic experiences: (a) Bābā met Hanumān's fish-wife when the couple came to his *havana*, and (b) he personally conferred with Tulsīdās on details of the epic. Bābā noted that sometimes great falsehoods were perpetrated in transmission of the epics due to the self-interest of high-caste people who had only superficial

---

of many, and certainly not every character named is easily or necessarily identifiable. Of the three westerners mentioned, Bābā only specifically reported having communicated with the spirit of Lincoln. He said:

> "[Y]ou had Abraham Lincoln as a president, and he has brought his spirit here. . . . [He told me] there is a law in India that letters should not be given." (p. 85) . . . [At one point] Ma[nśā] told me that the British ruled the whole world. They engulfed the whole world, and there was only one crore of believers. All the rest were atheists [ie., not supporting traditional values]. Only three [were believers, namely] Jesus Christ, Abraham Lincoln, and Hillary." (p. 88)

knowledge. Intuiting that the absence of an ecstatic connection with epic characters (or authors!) leads to a degeneration of narratives into enfeebled and fanciful stories, he proclaimed:

> What a great falsehood that Hanumān is without a wife! All this has been mentioned in the texts. Hanumān-jī comes to my *havana* with his wife. This has not been mentioned in the Vālmīki *Rāmāyaṇa*. . . . I asked Tulsīdās if it was true. He replied, "Someone before me wrote it like that." Traditionally this [fact of Hanumān's conjugal relationship] does not occur in Vālmīki's *Rāmāyaṇa*. This has been added by high-caste people. . . . We are *śūdras*, but we still have power. (p. 107)[11]

Bābā's words wielded authority because, as seer, he had access to ecstatic sources of knowledge. In the telling of tales, he did not just repeat epic events willy-nilly. Bābā spoke of what he saw.

Bābā also had access to ecstatic sources of power. At times, epic characters emerged from their narrative lives to alter the turn of events in Bābā's own, and readily permeated the barriers of his mental states. Characters who visited Bābā during his daily offerings [*havana*][12] moved into his dreams, and again into wakefulness. For instance, when Bābā awoke from the dream [*sapanā*] of his wife's abduction, Viṣṇu simultaneously emerged. The divinity appeared before him in person [*sākṣāt*] and issued an empowering directive. Bābā described this hierophanic encounter:

> He [Viṣṇu] said in clear words, "Now look, you have been tested. The rest of your life you should spend performing *bhajan*. You are a true devotee. All my powers are with you." (p. 91)

Bābā was initiated by Viṣṇu and his status as *bhakta* and shaman was confirmed by the post-oneiric communication. Thus, Bābā's bardic activity was ecstatically enhanced to embrace aspects of shamanic practice—all in the context of devotion to Viṣṇu.

III. *Bābā as Shaman: Healing with Divine Weapons*

As shaman, Bābā extended the bardic function of reconstituting epic history—that is, of imaginatively enlivening epic characters and bringing

---

[11] There is confusion in the account here. Bābā does not seem to know much about Vālmīki, whereas he might have been more familiar with the *Rāmāyaṇa* of Tulsīdās. The point is, Bābā believes himself to be in touch with the living truth of the epics.

[12] *Havana* consists of lighting a fire and making offerings to a deity. Typically, faggots of mango, pipal and other auspicious trees are burnt. Offerings include grains, leaves, flowers, various roots, and ghee. The ashes from Bābā's *havana* were collected and immersed into his tube-well.

them into his midst. He created (might we say) "new history" and actualized original events by himself participating in the narrative action. Whereas typically a bard would not disturb the basic parameters of a narrative framework, a shaman prevails upon spirits and heroes to directly impact on the human condition.[13] Bābā governed his narrative subjects to a degree exceeding that of the bard as he marshalled an army of good spirits and harnessed their power to heal the sick. His intimate bardic familiarity with epic heroes issued in the shamanic means of enlisting their help to fight malevolent spirits that inflict human ills.

Although Bābā was no more a professional shaman than bard, his self-styled eclectic vocation clearly embodied prototypical shamanic elements. Bābā's profile resembles the portrait of a shaman drawn by Mircea Eliade:

> Here [among the Eskimos], as in so many other cultures, he alone is a shaman who, through mystical vocation or voluntary quest, submits himself to the teaching of a master, successfully passes through the initiatory ordeals, and becomes capable of ecstatic experiences that are inaccessible to the rest of mankind.[14]

Typically, a shaman receives two kinds of instruction in the course of initiation. One is ecstatic in which knowledge and power are bestowed through dreams, visions, trances, and so on. Another involves the transmission of traditional cultural lore, including the names and functions

---

[13] As narrative recitation is employed frequently in the course of shamanic healing, it is useful to distinguish between the vocations of shaman or sorcerer and bard. (The terms shaman and sorcerer are used often without distinction. Here "shaman" is preferred due to the rich connotations given to the term by Mircea Eliade in his classic work, *Shamanism: Archaic Techniques of Ecstasy*.) As Albert B. Lord does not examine the role of the archaic bard *as "sorcerer,"* his discussion is of limited use in probing the relationship between narrative recitation and healing—which is the vocation proper to a shaman (sorcerer). In general, the shaman is involved more with the healing arts, and less with the poetic arts. Shamanic recitations are designed specifically to produce therapeutic effects whereby the psychological or physiological disposition of the hearer/patient is altered. Claude Levi-Strauss (in "The Effectiveness of Symbols") analyzes the therapeutic dynamics of narrative recitation. Discussing the role of a poetic text in a shamanic rite to facilitate difficult childbirth he observes that

> "[t]he technique of the narrative thus aims at recreating a real experience [in the patient] in which the myth merely shifts the protagonists [from the poetic to the psychological and physiological contexts]."

Claude Lévi-Strauss, *Structural Anthropology*, trans. Claire Jacobson and Brooke Grundfest Schoepf (New York: Doubleday & Co., Inc., Anchor Books, 1967), p. 189.

[14] Mircea Eliade, *Shamanism: Archaic Techniques of Ecstasy*, trans. Willard R. Trask (New York: Pantheon Books, 1964), p. 297.

of spirits, tribal mythology, a secret language, shamanic techniques, and so on.[15]

Bābā received both traditional and ecstatic types of instruction. Although his traditional education was not transmitted in the context of a formal shamanic initiation, over the years Bābā vociferously digested vast amounts of the cultural lore generally available to him. Moreover, ecstatic experience was a consistent and potent feature of Bābā's vocational development, as through many dreams and visions he was granted knowledge and power. Viṣṇu, who served as Bābā's main ecstatic guide, issued a shamanic mandate whereby he was appointed the task of healing, and endowed with the means by which to enlist epic heroes as helpers. Thus empowered with a shamanic vocation, Bābā's bardic relationship with the epic narratives was extended.

The overriding context in which Bābā's vocation as a shaman gained coherence was the "ritual of battle" of the *Mahābhārata*, in which he employed the various weapons granted by Viṣṇu through ecstatic initiation.[16] He explained:

> When I was curing people, I was destroying the powers of Kurukṣetra. The army of Duryodhana was being brought in by the thousands. I started cutting the [evil powers of Kurukṣetra] to pieces. (p. 85)

Doing the work of Viṣṇu, Bābā fostered *dharma* in the world by exorcising and vanquishing malevolent spirits. He trapped them in an invisible *yantra* situated in the palm of his hand. (This invisible *yantra* was graphically portrayed, however, in mock-up photographs for sale at the healing festival. (p. 115)) Once attracted into the *yantra*, as to a magnet, Bābā put the trouble-makers into an invisible box. (p. 101) Before deciding to destroy them, he gave them a chance to do something good, such as "cure our children." (p. 87) For example, the spirit of Maḥbūb Khān's wife, Razīā, turned good after performing penance in Bābā's fields for one month. If the spirits reformed, Bābā released them from imprisonment.

In addition to the *yantra* and prison box, Bābā commandeered numerous other supernatural weapons such as the *daṇḍa*, *triśūla*, *gadā*, and spear.[17]

---

[15] Ibid., p. 13.

[16] Alf Hiltebeitel explores implications of the epic war as "ritual" in, *The Ritual of Battle: Krishna in the Mahābhārata* (Ithaca: Cornell Univ. Press, 1976).

[17] Bābā's expertise on weapons is noteworthy. For example, he spoke eloquently of one called "*kalkha*:"

> "This *kalkha* is a very powerful weapon. In my childhood, I saw a big earthen pot flying through the air like an atom bomb. It was in the air and smoke was coming out of it. I said to Pradhān-jī, though I was small at that time, 'Where will

One of the most effective was Viṣṇu's *cakra*, with which Bābā cut bad spirits to pieces before throwing them into his (also invisible) oven [*bhaṭṭhi*] to burn up. The *cakra* was activated when Bābā practiced his devotions, engaged in epic recitation, and circled his right index finger. He noted:

> My relatives thought that I was mad [and declared], "There is something wrong with Bhagavān-jī's mind. He is always in Muslim *pūjā* and *jñāna*, and moving his finger in circles." There were only four boys who knew [what I was doing]. Reciting the *Rāmāyaṇa* and *Mahābhārata*, I cut down the gathering of Kurukṣetra. (pp. 85–86)

Viṣṇu's *cakra*, thus empowered by recitation and *bhakti*, enabled Bābā to cut down thirty-six crores of spirits from Rakistan [*sic*] and fifty-nine crores from Pakistan. (p. 87)

Numerous epic protectors were also among Bābā's weapons, as shamanic spirit helpers. (p. 90) He declared:

> I have been given so many "automatic" [*sic*] weapons. For example, the *kalpavṛkṣa*—the flower of *kalpavṛkṣa*—that is on the *loṭā* [offering pot at the *havana*]. No [ordinary] person can see it. It is invisible. Only the *yogī* and *mahayogī* can see it. We [also] have hundreds and thousands of weapons that protect our house [including Gaṇeśa, Hanumān, Kumbhakarṇa and Vikramāditya]. (p. 89)

Gaṇeśa, Hanumān, and others served to protect Bābā, while the two birds Garuḍa (Viṣṇu's vehicle) and Jaṭāyu (king of vultures) more actively participated in his thaumaturgical exploits. Bābā explained:

> So, the magic *cakra* continues cutting and cutting, and all these spirits get into the oven. If I order them [Garuḍa and Jaṭāyu] to assume the form of vultures and eat [the bad spirits that magically were made to assume the form of snakes] up they will obey my orders. (p. 90)

Bābā occasionally referred to the superior effectiveness of his weapons. Of his *yantra*, for instance, the healer declared unequivocally,

---

> this ball strike?' He said, 'This is *gola* [round thing].' I said, 'This is not *gola*, it is an earthen pot. This is used for killing others.' There was a big brick kiln. Near the kiln was a potter. This earthen pot hit that potter. It was moving up and down [flying]. This is *kalkha*. It moves with the heart of a goat or sheep." (p. 95)

According to local folk tradition the *kalkha* returns to strike and kill its sender if unable to attack the enemy. It may also happen that a third person knowing the tantric art may divert this *kalkha* to any direction at will. Here, Bābā may be suggesting that he possesses tantric powers. (One Sanskrit scholar in Roorkie suggests that the term "*kalkha*" is not of Sanskritic origin, but is a corrupted [*apabhraṃśa*] form derived from some regional dialects of the seventh or eighth century.)

> There is such an "automatic" [*sic*] *yantra* we heard of that Paramātman used to wave in his hand. But no one has performed the kind of miracle [that I did] in which forty dumb people spoke. No *muni* or *ṛṣi* has such a palm. Here forty dumb people have spoken. History proves that no one [else] is able to cure dumbness. (p. 109)

Bābā also claimed that his oven was more effective than the spirit gravestones [*pretaśilā*] used by others in his region. Whereas stones merely pacify potentially harmful spirits, Bābā's oven completely destroys them.[18]

Bābā's synergistic embodiment of the functions of bard, shaman, and *bhakta* exerted exceptional influence over numerous epic characters and spirits. This eclectic vocation, imaginatively amalgamated from the north Indian cultural respository, allowed Bābā to deal with malevolent spirits in a manner superior to many other traditional methods. Bābā's bardic vocation enhanced his shamanic vocation, as without narrative command of the epics he would have no knowledge of weapons or helpers. Yet, without *bhakti*, or devotion, he was powerless to employ them.

IV. *Bābā as Bhakta: Healing through Faith and Devotion*

The Bābā of Sahāvalī might be viewed as a bard who reconstituted epics for those who lent ears and imaginations. He might be viewed as a shaman who, with a toehold in various cosmic realms, diagnosed and cured ills caused by malevolent spirits. Above all, however, in the eyes of others and in his own, Bābā was a *bhakta*. The people who flocked to Sahāvalī may have known generally that from an early age Bābā "was greatly interested in reciting the *Rāmāyaṇa*," for this fact was noted in his biography (p. 2); but they would not have been privy to the astonishing details of his epic involvement. Fundamentally, Bābā was considered to be a Viṣṇu *bhakta*, as both pamphlets and photographs for sale at the *melā* billed him thus. Himself recognizing the primacy of *bhakti*, Bābā declared: "I have done alot of 'research' [*sic*] [on the epics and spirits]. Otherwise, I am supposed to be doing *bhajan*." (pp. 95–96)

Bhakti was the key to Bābā's success. As Viṣṇu's disciple, the *bhakta* had access to divine guidance not so much through shamanic techniques of ecstasy such as drumming and dancing, but through traditional Hindu devotional methods. Communication with Viṣṇu was effected principally

---

[18] In Hardwar is a kind of spirit graveyard called "*thān*" [*sthāna*] where powerful and troublesome spirits are buried under special carved or painted spirit rocks [*pretaśilā*]. When potentially harmful spirits of the dead are properly installed and given offerings, they will not get out from under the stones and bother anybody.

by means of *bhajan* and *pūjā*. As the fruit of such devotions came dreams and visions of Viṣṇu. From Viṣṇu came weapons that Bābā used to deal with spirits—rather than more typical shamanic props such as the mask, drum, horse, mirror, and so on. And with weapons came the power to shape the living history of the battle of Kurukṣetra. Through participation in epic history, topologically transposed into the spirit realm of contemporary Āryāvarta, Bābā participated in Viṣṇu's work of restoring *dharma* to the world, manifest in the restoration of health to the faithful.

Though Bābā may not appear to be a conventional *bhakta* in the sense that Caitanya (d. 1533) was a *bhakta*, for example, their spiritualities share a common structure: For Caitanya the earthly Vṛndāvana was transformed into the divine Vṛndāvana through the power of *bhakti*. For Bābā, the epic Kurukṣetra with its telluric history was transformed into the spectral Kurukṣetra with its thaumaturgic history through the power of *bhakti*. In spite of the fact that Bābā was transported to a gruesome battlefield, while Caitanya was transported to a paradisal landscape, Viṣṇu was present to both of them. Bābā's Kurukṣetra and Caitanya's Vṛndāvana are both abodes of Viṣṇu, and both Vaiṣṇavas promote the deity's *dharma* as they participate in a history topologically transposed.

As *bhakti* was at the heart of Bābā's vocation, it was also the key to his patients' success. To be healed, the sick needed faith that Bābā was a channel of Viṣṇu's power, and that the well water was made into nectar through the influence of Manśā Devī.[19] Bābā did not expect that all of the thousands who came to see him in Sahāvalī village would be healed. He estimated that 50 percent of the people benefited from his healing. The 50 percent who did not respond to treatment were either curiosity seekers who were "not aware of my powers," or people of weak conviction who moved into rows more than once to get a double blessing, lacking faith that one was sufficient. (p. 107)[20] Bābā explained:

---

[19] Both Viṣṇu and Manśā Devī were directly involved in the genesis of the nectar-water miracle cure, and gave Bābā the authority to administer it. According to his biography, Bābā used to pour the water offered during prayers to Kubera, Lord of Wealth, into his tube-well. With that well water Bābā first cured a boy of high fever whose mother dreamed that the *bhakta* of Īśvara [Bābā] alone could heal her son. (p. 8) After this success, through the mediumship of this daughter, Bābā requested permission of Manśā Devī to serve the world with the healing water. At first, the goddess did not allow it; but after curing another patient with the water, by the grace of Viṣṇu, the *bhakta* repeated his request to Manśā Devī. She granted his wish, and blessed him. Viṣṇu also appeared in person and told the *bhakta* that "besides serving his family, he could serve the troubled people of the world." After that Bābā "began curing troubles with blessing and water." (p. 8)

[20] Bābā's observation that those with faith can be healed concurs with what Claude Lévi-Strauss observed in "The Sorcerer and His Magic." Noting (after W.B. Cannon) that physiological disturbances in individuals afflicted by spells or spirit possession are

> Those who have full confidence [*viśvās*] are cured.... Patients are tired of doctors [and lose faith]. Those who are theist and believe in God are cured. (p. 108)

In response to treatment, a handful of the faithful wrote Bābā letters of appreciation, and one wealthy patron provided funds to build a road into Sahāvalī. Yet, among all the thousands, Bābā said that "only twelve people offered *bhaktidān*" and became his disciples. (p. 108)[21] In the attitude of these twelve, however, is embedded a clue to the more general success of Bābā's exploits. *Bhakti* motivated both the healer and the healed. The faithful did not need to understand the technology of weapons, and the habits of spirits and epic heroes. They needed to know that Bābā was faithful to his tradition. Bābā, too, was convinced of his own fidelity. A newspaper claimed that Bābā could cure neither himself (who had leg pain and pyorrhea) nor his nephew (who sought traditional medical attention)—much less those afflicted with polio, dumbness, and so on. Bābā answered these charges saying, "Viṣṇu Bhagavān has given me directions to cure the ailments of the world. If I get busy curing myself, how will I serve the people?" (p. 28) As a devotee, Bābā expressed willingness to sacrifice even his own health in order to promote Viṣṇu's work in the world. In the final analysis, Bābā conceived that all his efforts and success stemmed from *bhakti*.

V. "*No Basis in Reality for these Things*"–*True or.....?*

Local journalists accused Bābā of throwing people into the jaws of death (not having cured even a simple headache), promoting the threat of disease by amassing huge crowds under unsanitary conditions, disrupting

---

quelled in the course of exorcism, he states:

> "There is, therefore, no reason to doubt the efficacy of certain magical practices. But at the same time we see that the efficacy of magic implies a belief in magic. The latter has three complementary aspects: first the sorcerer's belief in the effectiveness of his techniques; second, the patient's or victim's belief in the sorcerer's power; and, finally, the faith and expectations of the group, which constantly act as a sort of gravitational field within which the relationship between sorcerer and bewitched is located and defined."

Lévi-Strauss, *Structural Anthropology*, p. 162.

[21] In claiming to have twelve disciples is Bābā identifying with Jesus who also, according to tradition, had twelve disciples? As Bābā often thematically identified with the Indian epic heroes, he might easily appropriate details of other heroic lives (as they become culturally available) into his personal story.

the agricultural life of the community, and making money hand-over-fist through commission from his lackeys who sold bottles, photographs, mustard oil, rosewater, and pamphlets. One newspaper cynically reported that when questioned about the *darśana* given to him to Viṣṇu, Bābā "was evasive and said: 'If it was not a miracle, then why are patients from Israel coming here?' " (p. 23)

A booklet distributed with the December 1983 issue of *Srjan* bore the quizzical title "The Story of Sahāvalī's Water Bābā: How True? How . . . . . ?" Under a section called "Unbelievable and debatable points" the following observations were made:

> Several debatable points are raised that cast a question mark over the entire miracle story of Kanval Dās. For example, in Bābā's own words, "[My] elder brother Ami Cand (deceased) is at present a *pīr* in Gujarat and his name in this incarnation is Alāuddīn. [His] entire ghost family helps [my family]." . . . Is this possible? Can people from one family come back after death to the same family and become a part of Kanval Dās's story? Whereas we also hear that Kanval Dās's daughter Satyavatī claims to get personal *darśana* of Manśā Devī. (p. 60)

Several more "debatable points" were raised in our interviews with Bābā that, indeed, "cast a question mark over the entire miracle story of Kanval Dās"! Did Bābā really see Viṣṇu before his very eyes [*sākṣāt*]? Did Bābā really have a *yantra* in his palm with which he trapped *bhūtas*? Was Bābā correct in declaring that Hanumān has a wife? Do the evil spirits of slain members of Duryodhana's army continue to linger in contemporary Āryāvarta?

A still larger question looms: How might the "truth value" of Bābā's anomalous claims be judged? Though their assessments of his work were diametrically opposed, both the journalists and the faithful judged Bābā's credibility on the basis of the literal truth value of his statements. Those who figured that his claims were false discredited Bābā as a charlatan, while those who figured that his claims were true came to Sahāvalī for nectar-water. Now, it would be hasty if not foolish to accept the florid output of Bābā's fertile imagination as literal, historical fact. Yet, it would be too simple to decide, along with "progressive" journalists, that Bābā was a fraud with no trace of spiritualism.

In principle, it would be a legitimate interpretive enterprise to examine the structure and content of Bābā's states of consciousness, seeking insight into the psychological (or even metaphysical) authenticity of his claims. However, to engage in such analysis with respect to Bābā's account would be irresponsible mainly for two reasons: (a) there is an insufficient body of evidence, and (b) the evidence at hand is too haphazard, harboring many potential inconsistencies.[22] For a study of the "psychological" or "mystical" nature of Bābā's experience to be fruitful, the text must be complete and coherent enough to provide evidence of probable cause and effect relationships between his ritual activity and the extraordinary experiences claimed. This is not to discount the possibility that Bābā had certain authentic and transformative religious experiences. It is, however, to insist that a responsible analysis of the literal—or metaphorical—or symbolic—"truth" of his claims would require a more extensive, informative, and integrated body of materials.

There are other perspectives from which the phenomenon of Sahāvalī's Water Bābā fruitfully might be analyzed, though they may not decisively preclude the possibility of the literal truth of his claims. Bābā's activities might be interpreted in light of psychopathology, sociology, or economics, for instance. Thus, on the basis of information at hand one plausibly might consider his claims to be evidence of megalomaniacal raving, the social climbing of a downtrodden *śūdra*, or the cunning of an indebted villager. Yet, such interpretations would neglect the *positive and peculiar* value of this *śūdra*'s audacious activities. To judge Bābā's motives as based in mere lunacy or ambition would be to undermine his particular genius and its cultural value. One can hear many mad ravings and witness countless cases of social or financial ambition that are void of the color, genius, and social impact of Bābā's activities.

To capture the positive and peculiar value of Bābā's creative vision one might, instead, consider the cultural ingenuity reflected in it. Bābā was an exceptional character insofar as he embodied a tremendous portion of his great and little Indian tradition accumulated over millennia. Permeated by traditional symbols he had an uncanny ability to absorb, transmit, and promote the stuff of his culture in a way that most people never even dream of—be they mad or sane. As a repository and harbinger of culture Bābā proved to have tremendous public appeal, such that

[22] The hostile news media tirelessly pointed out discrepancies between what Bābā reportedly claimed and what they had discovered through investigation. For instance, whereas Bābā claimed that water from his tube-well could heal, the journalists claimed that it could kill, etc. (p. 49) Within Bābā's own account (gleaned from our interviews), inconsistency was less of a problem than the haphazard character of the exchange. Perhaps unfortunately, we did not elicit a more exacting account from our informant. Yet, considering his personal style and mentality, it is unlikely that Bābā could have been persuaded to render his views in a strictly systematic fashion. Overall, Bābā was cooperative, but maintained the force of his idiosyncratic and authoritative personality throughout. For instance, he had us turn off the tape recorder when "nothing important" was happening, and would not relinquish the letters from former patients because "Abraham Lincoln" had advised him not to.

thousands came to him by train, bus, tonga, bicycle, foot, and the strength of others who carried them in arms. He captured the imagination of the masses, and (whether they liked it or not) the imagination of modernists whose self-appointed task was to purge folk India of superstitious elements. The progressive journalists and outraged public might have been able to ignore Bābā alone, but they could not ignore the overwhelming impulse of the thousands who sought to be part of what was engendered in Sahāvalī village.

VI. *Conclusion*

The cultural tenacity of sacred places is well-attested in the history of religions. Despite intensive revalorization ensuing from exogenous influence and indigenous development, sacred places persistently maintain sanctity and significance.[23] Such topographic tenacity was evidenced in the village of Sahāvalī, whose connection with the Mahābhārata war bespeaks the power of a sacred place to capture the imagination of people after untold generations, in spite of numerous, culturally mitigating influences. Living on the land of ancient Āryāvarta, Bābā envisioned himself as a principle protagonist in the battle of Kurukṣetra topologically transposed, while thousands who came to Sahāvalī found a place made sacred by its Viṣṇu *bhakta* who had a toehold in epic history.

Over millennia Āryāvarta was permeated by uncharted cross-cultural influences that variously have nourished or sapped the vitality of traditional sacrality. How did Bābā weather the impact of such plenitude without losing sight of ancient stories? And how were uncounted folk (to

---

[23] Apt are Mircea Eliade's observations on the tenacity and religious value of sacred places:

> "... a sacred place involves the notion of repeating the primeval hierophany which consecrated the place by marking it out, by cutting it off from the profane space around it. ... That the Australian aboriginals went on visiting their traditional secret places was not because of any pressure of economic circumstances.... What they sought from these places was to remain in mystical union with the land and with the ancestors who founded the civilization of their tribe. The need the aboriginals felt to preserve their contact with those scenes of hierophany was essentially a religious one .... And these centres were only with the greatest difficulty robbed of their importance—they were passed on like an heirloom from tribe to tribe, from religion to religion. The rocks, springs, caves and woods venerated from the earliest historic times are still, in different forms, held as sacred by Christian communities today."

Mircea Eliade, *Patterns in Comparative Religion*, trans. Rosemary Sheed (New York: Meridian, 1958), pp. 368–369.

the dismay of modernists) summarily entranced by his traditional production? What factors adventitiously coalesced to produce the spectacle that endured for four months at Sahāvālī, where "Kurukṣetra" was once again overwhelmed by multitudes engaged in a ritual of battle?

Surely, Bābā's sheer proximity to Kurukṣetra promoted some familiarity with the epics, and his fertile imagination prompted a feeling of affinity for their spirited characters. Yet, how is it that Bābā so fully embraced the tempestuous martial epic themes in spite of predominant social tendencies favoring loving devotion to peaceful embodiments of divinity? As a low-caste *camār* Bābā might have lacked interest in the Mahābhārata war. Typically in western Uttar Pradesh, members of his *jāti* identified with peaceful saints such as Raidās, whereas *rājputs* of the region take Rāma and other *kṣatriya* heroes for role models.[24]

Moreover, how is it that throngs gravitated from near and far to participate in an event deemed sacred ostensibly by force of little more than rumor? Certainly, a turbulent regional history may have nourished a deep collective affinity for impetuous themes of battle and conflict. And the embedded Indian propensity for devotion, coupled with an archaic attraction to sacred water (from whatever cultural or psychic depth they come) may have drawn the multitude to seek Bābā's *darśana* and healing nectar-water. Yet, the Āryan, Mogul, British, and international touristic influences that seeped into Bābā's region over centuries might have dimmed the radiance of the epics irrecoverably, and paled the face of ancient tradition.

What accounts for the persistence of the Indian epics such that the battle of Kurukṣetra could be preserved by virtue of its topological transposition in Sahāvalī village? Of the numerous and diverse complementary influences, one was selected for particular inspection in this essay: the culturally creative genius of Sahāvalī's Water Bābā.

Bābā was not unique. If he was unique, not only the *fate* but also the *content* of the Indian epics would have been sealed long ago. Without the likes of Bābā the epics might have perished or petrified in the face of history. Due to the unleashed imagination of such bold characters, heroic tales have thrived over millennia despite awesome and torrential winds of cultural change. While Bābā was not unique, his talent was rare. The intensity with which this cultural enthusiast immersed himself in Āryāvarta afforded nothing less than a boon to the epic heroes of Kurukṣetra.

---

[24] J. Michael Mahar, personal communication of June 1987.

The case of Sahāvalī's Water Bābā suggests that (true to Oldenberg's observation echoed by Rice) "the Mahābhārata is the strongest link between old and new India, the India of the Āryan and of the Hindu."[25] What should not be forgotten is that this link exists only as long as there are psyches sufficiently creative to amalgamate the old and the new. The epics are sustained in the midst of a radically evolving India because there are folk with skill enough to weave together sundry strands of cultural lore. The battle of Kurukṣetra thus was preserved in topological transposition because Bābā's imagination was formidable enough to sustain the vocations of bard, shaman, and *bhakta*—each delitescent in the ground of India.

For the Bābā of Sahāvalī the epics were indeed "the music and color of life." If Stanley Rice could hear the new tale of Kurukṣetra he would be reassured that the epics still are "living and throbbing in the lives of the people of India"—though he might be discomfited with the turns of Bābā's imagination. After noting the pervasive influence of the epics on Indian life, Rice bemoaned an overloading of the Indian epics that became "swollen by ... inventions," declaring that

> the portentious volumes are enough to damp the spirit of the most ardent who, starting off gaily upon their journey are soon faced by the deserts of Levitical doctrine and the morasses of primitive speculation interesting only to the antiquarian.[26]

Yet, as Bābā was not a *brāhmaṇa* and had no "Levitical doctrine" to promote, perhaps the spirit of Stanley Rice would not be damped by hearing of the battle of Kurukṣetra topologically transposed after all. And if he would judge Bābā's ramblings to be an overwhelming "morass of primitive speculation" devoid of any religious value or contemporary interest, we would only ask in the spirit of Bābā: "If it was not a miracle, then how has a worldwide public come to hear of it?"[27]

Bibliography

Baines, Jervoise A. *Ethnography: Castes and Tribes*. Strassburg: Verlag von Karl J. Trübner, 1912.

Bhattacharyya, Narendra Nath. *The Indian Mother Goddess*. 2d ed., rev. New Delhi: Manohar, 1977.

---

[25] Rice, *Tales from the Mahābhārata*, p. 9.

[26] Ibid., p. 11.

[27] The on-site research of V. Urubshurow was supported by a fellowship award from the American Institute of Indian Studies, with funds provided by the Smithsonian Institution.

Eliade, Mircea. *Patterns in Comparative Religion*. Translated by Rosemary Sheed. New York: Meridian, 1958.

——. *Shamanism: Archaic Techniques of Ecstasy*. Translated by Willard R. Trask. New York: Pantheon Books, 1964.

Hiltebeitel, Alf. *The Ritual of Battle: Krishna in the Mahābhārata*. Ithaca: Cornell Univ. Press, 1976.

Lévi-Strauss, Claude. *Structural Anthropology*. Translated by Claire Jacobson and Brooke Grundfest Schoepf. New York: Doubleday & Co., Inc., Anchor Books, 1967.

Lord, Albert B. *The Singer of Tales*. New York: Atheneum, 1974. Originally published by Harvard University Press, 1960.

Mani, Vettam. *Purāṇic Encyclopedia*. Koṭṭayam, Kerala: n.p., 1964; reprint ed., Delhi: Motilal Banarsidass, 1984.

Rice, Stanley. *Tales from the Mahābhārata*. London: Selwyn & Blount, 1924.

Singh, T.R., Mahar, J.M., and Urubshurow, Victoria. "Bābā Project: Material Collected during 1983–1984." Unpublished manuscript.

ARTHAŚĀSTRA CATEGORIES IN THE *MAHĀBHĀRATA*: FROM *DAṆḌANĪTI* TO *RĀJADHARMA*

BRAJ M. SINHA

Introduction

Historians of Hindu political ideas have incessantly emphasized the Machiavellian orientation of the *Mahābhārata* by suggesting that the *Mahābhārata* maintains unqualified allegiance to the *Arthaśāstra* political categories.[1] However, it is important to recognize that in the *Śāntiparvan* of the *Mahābhārata*, a new conception of *rājadharma* emerges which attempts to synthesize the *daṇḍanīti* categories of *Arthaśāstra* with the *rājadharma* notion of the *Dharmasūtras*.

It is true that the *Mahābhārata* accords a very important place to the *Arthaśāstra* categories in its speculations pertaining to the nature of *rājadharma*. However, it is inappropriate to suggest that there is, in the *Mahābhārata*, the wholesale incorporation of the *Arthaśāstra* categories.[2] On the contrary, Bhīṣma in the *Śāntiparvan* has taken a very bold step in attempting to provide a comprehensive conception of *rājadharma* in which the *daṇḍanīti* categories of the *Arthaśāstra* tradition is combined with the *dharma* categories of the *Dharmasūtras*. The present paper attempts to bring out the implications of the attempted synthesis for a comprehensive understanding of the *Mahābhārata* conception of *rājadharma* as it relates to the conduct of the Righteous King (*dharmarāja*).

The original impetus for the symbiotic categories in the *Mahābhārata* can be understood only if one keeps in mind the chasm that had occurred in the pre-Kauṭilyan and Kauṭilyan *Arthaśāstra* tradition between *daṇḍanīti* and *rājadharma*.[3] It is apparent that both, the *Arthaśāstra* and the *Mahābharata*, are concerned with the art of statecraft in a monarchical state. However,

---

[1] See U.N. Ghoshal, *A History of Indian Political Ideas* (London: Oxford University Press, 1966); Trevor Ling. *The Buddha* (London: Temple Smith, 1973).

[2] U.N. Ghoshal, *op. cit.*, p. 73; T. Ling, *op. cit.*, p. 144.

[3] Both Kauṭilya in his *Arthaśāstra* and Kāmandaka in his *Nītisāra* allude to this gradual development of the science of polity, i.e. *daṇḍanīti* in the direction of its autonomy by freeing it of its connection with the restraining categories of the sacred knowledge, i.e. *trayī*. This is the position attributed to the *Arthaśāstra* School of Uśanas, who is listed as the last and probably the latest teacher of the pre-Kauṭilyan *Arthaśāstra*. *Vide*, *Kauṭilya Arthaśāstra*, Book I, Chapter II; *Kāmandakīya Nītisāra*, II.1–5.

while the *Arthaśāstra* confines itself exclusively to the investigation of the phenomenon of the State as the wielder of coercive authority (*daṇḍa*), the *Mahābhārata* deals with the same as an incident in a comprehensive scheme of duties of the King in terms of the *dharma* categories of the *Dharmasūtras*.

The specific objective of the *Mahābhārata* synthesis of the *Arthaśāstra* tradition of *daṇḍanīti* with that of the *dharma* categories of the *Dharmasūtras*, is to infuse in the structure of statecraft an element of ethics that can only be characterized as universal. The *daṇḍanīti* of the *Arthaśāstra* tradition is subjected to the restraint of the universal principles of *dharma*. There emerges a new conception of *kṣatriyadharma* (dharma of the ruling classes), which according to the *Mahābhārata*, is seen to be the very foundation of all *dharmas*.[4] Thus, in the *Mahābhārata*, there takes place a metamorphosis not only of *daṇḍanīti* categories of *Arthaśāstra*, but also *dharma* categories of the *Dharmasūtras*.

The significance of this new development in the Hindu political theory can be understood and appreciated in a larger context with reference to similar developments in the Buddhist notion of *cakravartin* as the *dharmarāja*.

The notion of *cakravartin* as the Ruler, who is an embodiment of *dharma*, has been seen as the most significant contribution of Buddhism to political thought in India. One of the most articulate expounders of this position is Trevor Ling who perceives in the *cakravartin* ideal, a real departure from the Hindu notion of King.[5] Ling's basic contention is that the linking of *cakravartin* with *dharma* and *saṃgha* in Buddhism is an attempt to provide a structural basis for the transformation of State into an ethical category. State is the institutional framework within which universal ethics become possible, precisely because the political structure is seen integrally linked with the structures of dharma.[6]

The present paper is an attempt to offer a comparative analysis of the notion of *cakravartin* in Buddhism and the idea of *dharmarāja* in the *Mahābhārata*. The innovative character of these notions in the two traditions stands out only in contrast with the machiavellian notion of State that one discerns in the *Arthaśāstra*. The two notions, emerging in both the traditions concurrently, mark a new beginning in the Indian political thinking that offers a different model of Ruler by relativizing the absolutism and autocratic character of the State. With this development, the emphasis on the *daṇḍanīti* (coercive authority of the State) takes

---

4 *Mahābhārata*, 64.19–29.
5 T. Ling, *op. cit.*, pp. 140–147.
6 *Ibid.*

backstage; thus enabling the emergence of State as an ethical category based on the universal principles of *dharma.*

The earliest statement to the effect that the Hindu conception of State is fundamentally different from the Buddhist conception, and that the basis of this difference is the respective understanding of Kingship in relation to *dharma* category was made by Paul Masson-Oursel.[7] He sees a basic antithesis between the Brahmanical and the Buddhist perspectives on *dharma* and its bearing on the two approaches to Kingship. According to Masson-Oursel, the Hindu conception, as delineated in the *Smṛti* literature, looks at *dharma* in a particularistic context of the *varṇa dharma*, and thereby reinforces a social divisiveness that prevents the emergence of "a political spirit". The implication of this position from the point of view of political theory, according to Masson-Oursel, is this: that the Hindus failed to develop a notion of Universal State. On the contrary, the Buddhist political theory, built on the principle of the universality of *dharma*, successfully undermines the particularistic ethical structure of the Hindu *varṇa dharma.* Moreover, the Brahmanical notion of King, Masson-Oursel argues, tends to be conservatist, since the King is the custodian and preserver of the eternal social order, i.e. the objective realm of *varṇa dharma.* The Buddhist King, according to Masson-Oursel, not only causes *dharma* to reign, but in significant ways functions as an innovator, or revolutionary, for he contributes to the ongoing dynamic structure of *dharma*, which, true to the early Buddhist notion of flux, is not seen to be a fixed order.

U.N. Ghoshal has pursued his argument in a somewhat similar fashion.[8] Ghoshal maintains that *dharma* in the Brahmanical literature connotes the comprehensive law of the social order which contains the King as only another element of the total structure. The Buddhist notion of *dharma*, according to Ghoshal, is primarily to be understood as carrying the connotation of righteousness. By identifying righteousness as the central connotation of *dharma* in the Buddhist canonical literature, Ghoshal is able to suggest the impossibility of any compromise by the Buddhist canon on the ethical basis of the character of State, since the King both governs by and is governed by *dharma*, the principle of righteousness. It is this

---

[7] Paul Masson-Oursel *et al.*, *Ancient India and Indian Civilization* (New York: Barnes and Noble, 1967) pp. 93–95; cf. U.N. Ghoshal, *op. cit.*, p. 73.

[8] It is interesting to note that Ghoshal's earlier work, *A History of Hindu Political Theories*, does not reflect this bias towards Buddhism vis-a-vis *Mahābhārata.* See U.N. Ghoshal, *A History of Hindu Political Theories* (London: Oxford University Press, 1927), p. 117. He, however, here too makes the claim that in the *Mahābhārata* and the *Manusaṁhitā*, the *Arthaśāstra* element is preponderant, "though it is occasionally transmuted and softened by contact with the prevailing religious and ethical ideas" (p. 116).

centrality of *dharma* that prevents the developments within the Buddhist tradition from being comparable to the *Arthaśāstra* understanding of State in which the principle of righteousness is not the sole criterion governing the fundamental structure of State. Thus writes Ghoshal:

> In its political aspect the Brahmanical *dharma* stands particularly for the whole duty of the King (*rājadharma*) which from the first is conceived in sufficiently elastic terms to provide for the needs of Kingdom and to permit in Manu and still more in the *Mahābhārata* (after Bhīṣma) the wholesale incorporation of the *Arthaśāstra* categories and concepts relating to the branches of the King's internal and external administration. On the other hand the Buddhist *dharma* in its relation to the King involves the application of the universal ethics of Buddhism to the State administration, this principle being even extended, . . . to the concept of the World Ruler (*chakravartin*).[9]

It is this position of Ghosal, that Ling[10] buys wholesale; lock, stock and barrel. Ghoshal is a perceptive and meticulous scholar of Indian political ideas and rightly deserves to be identified by Ling as "one of the most outstanding of historians of Indian political thought".[11] Ling, in his evaluation of Ghoshal's interpretation of the Buddhist notion of State totally agrees with his ideological Guru, A.L. Basham who has already gone on record to suggest that Ghoshal's work *A History of Indian Political Ideas* "is the most scholarly and comprehensive work on the subject ever to have been written".[12]

It is not my intention here to somehow undermine the towering personality and significant contributions of Ghoshal to the study of Indian political ideas. However, the time has come for Indological scholarhip to apply the tools of the sociology of knowledge to the Indological studies to raise the question of the possibility that caste, class and other categories of socio-cultural affiliations of the early pioneers of indological study have significant implications. On the indigenous scene of Indological studies, the cultural conditioning of the scholars seems to determine the direction of their scholarhip. One has only to skim through the literature to identify that phase of scholarship where Brahmanical stock tends to elevate the Hindu conceptions to the point that fails to see any significant contribution having been made by the Buddhists to Indian political theories. As a interesting example of this is provided by the London-trained disciple of A.L. Basham, Bhasker Anand Saletore, a Maharastrian Brahmin, the

---

[9] U.N. Goshal, *op. cit.*, p. 73.
[10] T. Ling, *op. cit.*, p. 144.
[11] *Ibid.*
[12] A.L. Basham, as cited in T. Ling, *op. cit.*, p. 258, n. 60.

retired Director of National Archives, Government of India. In his otherwise perceptive work *Ancient Indian Political Thought and Institutions*, he writes:

> It may be safely maintained that, so far as the ancient Indian political thought relating to kingship is concerned, the positive contribution of the Buddhists to it was practically nil.[13]

If I have touched a hornet's nest, I need not apologize, since it is completely intentional, and not incidental. The ideological context of Indological scholarhip deserves serious attention.

Ghosal fares no better than Saletore in expressing a biased opinion by downplaying the positive contributions of Hindu political thought as contained in the *Mahābhārata*. Our analysis will clearly demonstrate the falsity of his arguments when he affirms that there is in the *Mahābhārata*, an unqualified acceptance of the *daṇḍanīti* elements of the *Arthaśāstra* without any attempt to develop a comprehensive theory of the nature and function of State as embodied in the person of the King.

Rājadharma in the Mahābhārata

It is important to recognize that Bhīṣma in the *Śāntiparvan* of *Mahābhārata* is very much concerned with the transmutation of the *Arthaśāstra* categories by synthesizing them with the *dharma* categories of *Dharmasūtras*. It is my contention that this attempted synthesis by Bhīṣma goes far beyond what is implied in Ghoshal's observation that there is "in the *Mahābhārata* the wholesale incorporation of the *Arthaśāstra* categories".[14] Ling reads and interprets this to suit his contention that there is a fundamental opposition between the conception of *rājadharma* in the *Mahābhārata* and in the *Nikāyas* and the *Jātakas*.[15]

To recognize the far reaching consequences of the *Mahābhārata* synthesis, we need to trace certain developments within the *Arthaśāstra* tradition itself. According to Kauṭilya, the most significant representative of the *Arthaśāstra* tradition, traditionally there were four sciences (*vidyās*), namely: the Vedic canon (*trayī*); logic (*ānvīkṣikī*); the politics (*daṇḍanīti*); and economics: the art of agriculture, cattle horticulture, and commerce (*vārttā*).[16] At least three of the *Arthaśāstra* schools preceding Kauṭilya tended

---

[13] B.A. Saletore, *Ancient Indian Political Thought and Institutions* (Bombay: Asia Publishing House, 1963) p. 326.

[14] U.N. Ghoshal, *op. cit.*, p. 73.

[15] T. Ling, *op. cit.*, p. 144.

[16] *Kauṭilya Arthaśāstra*, Book I, Chapter II.

to reject the claims of all the four branches of the sciences which evidently gave due weight to both the sacred and secular branches of knowledge.[17] The school of Manu rejects the claim of *ānvīkṣikī*, for this is seen to be merely a branch of the Vedas. However, offorts of the other two radical schools are more devastating. The *Arthaśāstra* system of Bṛhaspati rejected not only the *ānvīkṣikī*, but *trayī* (i.e. *Vedas*) as well. This prince of the materialist school of thought concedes only to *daṇḍanīti* and vārttā the status of valid forms of science (*vidyās*). This in itself was an extreme swing in the opposite direction from the position of the *Dharmasūtras*, for according to the *Dharmasūtras*, *rājadharma* was held to be part and parcel of the canonical scheme of things. However, Bṛhaspati's position seeks to recognize *daṇḍanīti* as the only valid basis of *rājadharma*. The apex of this extreme secular vision of *daṇḍanīti*, divested of any constraints of *dharma* categories, is reached in Uśanas (Śukra) who took the bold step of proclaiming *daṇḍanīti* to be the only science. The basic orientation of *daṇḍanīti*, so conceived in the early *Arthaśāstra* tradition, seems to be the immediate context of the scathing criticism of the *kshattivijjā* in the Buddhist *Nikāyas* on the ground of its utter disregard for the universal principles of *dharma* as the fundamental ethical categories.[18]

The purpose of this analysis is to suggest that the *Mahābhārata* synthesis of the *Arthaśāstra* tradition of *daṇḍanīti* with that of the *dharma* categories of *Dharmasūtras* is precisely an attempt to infuse in the structure of statecraft the element of ethics that can only be characterized as universal. The ethics of *rājadharma* is seen in the *Mahābhārata* as the fundamental ethical principle in which all ethical categories of particularistic *dharmas* are grounded.

This synthesis of the *dharma* and *daṇdanīti* categories probably was occasioned by the need to alleviate the negative effects of the separation of the *daṇḍanīti* and *rājadharma* in the pre-Kauṭilyan and Kauṭilyan Arthaśāstra. To realize the fuller significance of this we must have a comparative perspective on the *Arthaśāstra*'s notion of the duties of a King and that of the views of the canonical *Dharmasūtras* on this subject. A careful reading of the texts makes it abundantly clear that both are concerned with the art of government in a monarchical State. *Arthaśāstra*, however, confines itself exclusively to the investigation of the phenomena of the State, while the conception of *rājadharma* in the *Dharmasūtras* deals with the same as an incident in a comprehensive scheme of duties deriving their source from the external Vedas. Hence, while the canonical writers

---

[17] *Ibid.*; also *Kāmandakīya Nītisāra*, II.1–5.

[18] For the context and implications of this criticism, see the following discussion in this paper.

of *Dharmasūtras* mention only the rudiments of public administration, the political writers are able to treat their subject on a vastly enlarged canvas.

Secondly, it must be noted that since *Arthaśāstra* is independent of the sacred canon, and is the product of the independent schools and individual teachers, it lacks the positive character attaching to the *rājadharma* by virtue of the latter's association with the great concept of *dharma* as the universal principle of ethical conduct.

Yudhiṣṭhira anticipates the essential principles of *rājadharma* in his very first query addressed to Bhīṣma.[19] According to Yudhiṣṭhira, *rājadharmas* are the refuge of all creatures; and not only the threefold end of life, but salvation itself depends upon them.[20] There are echoes of the *Nikāyas* conception of a righteous King and the socio-political and cosmic significance of such a righteous King.[21] The *Mahābhārata*, contrary to the *Arthaśāstra* postulations, categorically declares the fulfillment of righteousness to be the bounden duty of the King.[22] *Dharma* is the fundamental principle of human conduct. The King upholding *dharma* is the very epitome of ethical conduct. The creatures are grounded in the King. The King who rightly upholds *dharma* is indeed a King.[23]

How far removed the *Mahābhārata* notion of *rājadharma* is from the *Arthaśāstra* injunctions to the King becomes abundantly clear in the passages describing the significance of the principle of righteousness in state administration and public policy. Thus the text declares:

> Righteousness is called *dharma*. The sages, O King, have declared that *dharma* restraints and sets bounds to all evil acts of men. The Lord created *dharma* for the advancement and growth of creatures. For this reason, a King should act according to the dictates of *dharma* for benefiting his subjects. For this reason also, *dharma* has been said to be the foremost of all things. Disregarding lust and wrath, observe then the dictates of righteousness. Among all things that conduce to the prosperity of Kings, righteousness is the foremost.[24]

The supreme ethical significance of the principle of *dharma* is the fundamental *raison d'être* of a King who is governed by, and governs by the principle of *dharma*. The righteous King is not simply pursuing his own personal *dharma* and seeking his own personal salvation as Ling would want us to believe. On the contrary, the righteous King in the *Mahābhārata* is

[19] *Mahābhārata*, XII.56.3–7.
[20] *Ibid*.
[21] Please refer to the discussions in the following section dealing with parallel developments in Buddhist political thought in India.
[22] *Mahābhārata*, XII.90.3–5, 13–15, 27.
[23] *Ibid*.
[24] *Mahābhārata*, XII.91.3.

precisely the righteous King of the Buddhist canons and *Jātakas*. The righteous King is the very foundation of social, moral and cosmic order. When the King ceases to be righteous, neglecting his *rājadharma*, untold miseries afflict his kingdom: there is cold in the hot season, and vice versa; there is drought as well as heavy rain; diseases overtake the people; comets fall towards the earth; inauspicious planets appear. Righteous pursuit of *rājadharma*, on the other hand, destroys all evil consequences in this world just as the rising sun dispels unholy darkness.[25]

Lest it be construed that the above portrayal of the *rājadharma* simply implies exaggerated importance of the King and provides a sacred basis for the autocratic power of the King that the *Arthaśāstra* prescribes, I would argue precisely the opposite being the case here. It is not the particular duties (*dharma*) of the King belonging to *kṣatriya* classes that are being lauded here to ensure people's unqualified allegiance to the King. Rather, beyond the functional value of *rājadharma* for the maintenance of social and cosmic order, there is clear affirmation of the universal principles of *dharma* having deep and significant ethical implications. Instead of putting the interests of the King and the State above all interests, i.e. the way of *daṇḍanīti* of the *Arthaśāstra*, the *Mahābhārata* makes *dharma rāja* subservient to the interests of all. The scope of *rājadharma* is expanded to include virtues far beyond the compass of particularistic *varṇa dharma of kṣatriya* of casting away life in battle, protecting the realm, and preventing the intermixture of *varṇa*. *Rājadharma* comprises compassion for all creatures, knowledge of ways of the world, and relieving the distressed and the oppressed. While Kauṭilya specifically describes the objective of the *daṇḍanīti* of the *Arthaśāstra* to be the acquisition and protection of the land,[26] *Mahābhārata* declares that those misdirected towards the pursuit of worldly objects without restraints are men of the nature of beasts.[27]

Transmutation of Arthaśāstra Categories and the Notion of Rājadharma in Early Buddhism

The significance of the Buddhist understanding of a righteous king can only be appreciated in the wider context of the infusion of the *dharma* principle in public administration and policy. As indicated earlier, it is my contention that the Buddhist *Nikāya* and *Jātaka* literature on the one hand and *Dharmasūtra* and the Hindu *Smṛti* literature on the other hand, were

---

[25] *Mahābhārata*, XII.63.6.
[26] *Arthaśāstra*, Book 1, Chapter I.
[27] *Mahābhārata*, XII.69.3.

dealing with the specific phenomenon of the state autocracy and the supremacy of the principle of expediency in state administration and policy. The classical expression of this principle is found in the *Arthaśāstra* of Kauṭilya. However, Kauṭilya's *Arthaśāstra*, though the oldest extant document available to us, is either an attempt at regeneration of the ancient *Arthaśāstra* tradition, which Kauṭilya himself laments was waning, or a final refined culmination of an even coarser form of the *Arthaśāstra* principles, propounded and propagated by his predecessors.[28]

This tradition of the principle of state administration and public policy was prevalent during the *Nikāya* period and was referred to by the Buddha as the *khattivijjā* (*kṣatriya* science) for which the Master is reported to have nothing but contempt. This *khativijjā* corresponds much more closely to the early *Arthaśāstra* conception of *daṇḍanīti* and is certainly a synonym for the *rājavidyā* of later times. The *Dīgha Nikāya* recognizes *khattivijjā* as a low art (*tirachcchhānavijjā*) practised by individuals thriving on wrongful occupations (*michchhājiva*). This is the science by which false ascetics and Brāhmaṇas earned their livelihood by counselling the kings in state administration. Thus the *Brahmajālasutta* distinguishes the perfect Buddha from these false ascetics and Brāhmaṇas.[29]

The question that may be raised at this point is: in what way is the perfect Buddha different form the false ascetics and Brāhmaṇas engaged in counselling the King in state administration and policy? This is all the more significant as there exist well-known instances of the Buddha himself having played the role of royal counsellor to the contemporary monarchs. Indeed, the Buddha maintained active and close association with the royal courts of his time. Both Bimbasāra, the powerful King of Magadha, and Pasendi, the ruler of the kingdom of Kosala, were his lifelong supporters and friends.[30] As we gather from the *Kosala Saṁyutta* section of the *Saṁyutta Nikāya*, Pasendi visited the Buddha frequently and constantly sought his counsel. The discourses dealing with the Buddha's counsel to the royalty do not merely contain the basic principles of Buddhist teachings in terms of personal piety. There is clear evidence of instruction pertaining to state administration and public policy.[31]

In this respect, then, the Buddha was no different than the false ascetics and the Brāhmaṇas involved in similar enterprises of royal counselling.

---

[28] For details of the debate as to the authorship and date of the *Kauṭilya Arthaśāstra*, see R.P. Kangle, *The Kauṭilya Arthaśāstra* (Bombay: University of Bombay, 1965).

[29] *Brahma-Jāla Suttanta*, *Dīgha Nikāya*.

[30] See T. Ling, *op. cit.*, p. 141.

[31] *Ibid.*

What distinguishes the perfect Buddha from the other two is precisely the deprofessionalization of this art of royal counselling, which is a central assumption of the *Arthaśāstra*, as well as a clear emphasis on the principle of *dharma* as the fundamental basis of such counselling. It is even more important to realize that several canonical *suttas* bring to our notice the sad plight of a state that is run by a King who does not seek advice from a counsellor who is well versed in the principle of *dharma*.[32] On the other hand, a King listening to and following the *dharma* counsel of the wise ones not only gains wisdom but also brings good fortune to his realm, is one of the significant themes of the well-known *Sīhanāda Sutta*.[33]

What distinguishes the practitioners of *khattivijjā* from the perfect Buddha and the wise counsellers of the kings is precisely the element of the *dharma* principle which is the touchstone of wholesome state administration and public policy. It is this that accounts for classification of *khattivijjā* under the category of low arts (*tirachchhānavijjā*) and its practice as a wrongful occupation (*michchhājiva*). That this concern with the unscrupulous character of the *Arthaśāstra* elements was at the root of the Buddha's rejection of this art is even more clearly evident in a later *Jātaka* story which conveys an unqualified censure of this art. These stories, in a striking manner, bring out the non-dharmic character of the *khattivijjā*. The *Mahābodhi-Jātaka* tells us about a King with five ministers, one of whom professed the belief in *khattivijjā* which involved the teaching that one may accomplish one's goal even by killing one's parents. An ascetic, who was requested by the King to assist in the administration of justice, was falsely accused by the five ministers of treason. Subsequently, when the ascetic had occasion, he demonstrated to the King the untruthfulness of his ministers, and the falsity of the doctrines that they professed. The ascetic explicitly rebuked the fifth minister, the follower of the *khattivijjā* for the unethical and immoral doctrine professed and practised by him. The text admonishes that the practitioners of this science are: "poor simple fools that think themselves wise" in preaching that "a man may kill his parents, or elder brother, children, and wife, should occasion justify and need of it arise".[34]

In a similar vein, the *Mahā-Ummagga-Jātaka* censures the mysterious and senseless doctrine of *kṣatriya* (*khattiyamāyā*) that suggests that one should rescue one's distressed self by any means gentle or severe.[35] The *Mahā-*

---

[32] *Ibid.*

[33] *Sīhanāda Suttanta, Dīgha Nikāya.*

[34] *Mahābodhi Jataka*, No. 528.

[35] *Mahā-Ummagga-Jātaka*, No. 546.

Sutasoma-Jātaka mentions the virtuous King repudiating the *khattidhamma*; the duties pursued by *khatti* doctrine, being opposed to morality. The prince here maintains that those who are versed in *khattidhamma*, and live by it, are destined to suffer in hell.[36]

The passages conveying these trends in Buddhist political thought are very significant for our purpose. There are two implications that I would like to suggest here. First, in the Buddhist canon the *khattivijjā* is not seen as a haphazard, sporadic and diffused science. In the *Mahābodhi-Jātaka*, *khativijjā* is already conceived at par with such philosophical systems as theism (*issarakāranavāda*), determinism (*pubbekatāvāda*) and nihilism (*uchchhedavāda*).[37] *Khattivijjavāda*, consists of a systematized body of knowledge, specialization in which entitles one to become the counsellor of the King in the matters of state administration. For all practical purposes, this is the science that may be identified with the *Arthaśāstra* tradition which as we know, is primarily the science of polity, which places the interest of state and inter alia of King, above all other interests. Evidently, the censure and condemnation of this science is on the grounds of its creed of unbridled selfishness and ruthless cruelty. Thus, *khattivijjā* stands for that brand of politics, the science of polity, which can only be an antithesis of ethics, i.e. code of conduct governed by the highest ideal of *dharma*.

What could be the immediate context for this extreme injunction against the science of politics? One does not need to delve too deep to see in this the Buddha's ethics reacting in a very strong way against some of the extreme tendencies of *Arthaśāstra* statecraft which affirms the interest of the state and the King above all other interests, and enjoins that all other interests must be sacrificed to this end. The conflict between the two perspectives is rooted in the fundamental difference between the two standards or two sets of thought. The *Arthaśāstra* tradition, i.e. the tradition of *khattivijjā*, is inspired by the avowed end of ensuring the security and prosperity of the state and the King. To this end it is willing to condone and even justify breaches of morality. However, the early Buddhist perspective, committed as it is to the principle of *dharma* in all spheres of human endeavor, politics being no exception to that, affirmed the unqualified supremacy of the universal ethical principles, even over the affairs of the State. This point is well understood, and has definitely provided a clue to the extreme onesided injunction against the *khattivijjā*, both in the *Nikāyas* and the *Jātakas*. This has been duely noted by a host of scholars, among whom both Ghoshal and

[36] *Mahā-Sutasoma-Jātaka*, No. 537.
[37] *Mahābodhi Jātaka*, *op. cit.*

Ling stand out in their comprehensive treatment of this dimension of the Buddhist contribution to the Indian polity.

However, what appears as problematic is the apparent contradiction between this perspective on the *khattivijjā* and *khattidhamma* on the one hand and the *Aggañña Suttanta*'s closing statement where the Master is reported to have said:

> I too Vāsettha, say:
> The Khattiya is the best among this folk
> Who put their trust in lineage.[38]

It is equally intriguing that in almost all instances of the *Jātaka* story, words of severe condemnation of the *khattivijjā* and *khattidhamma* is put into the mouths of the princes and kings themselves, who see a fundamental incongruity between the way of the universal *dharma* and the particular *dharma* of the *kṣatriya* concerned with the ultimate security of the interests of the State and the person of the King.

It is my contention that here and indeed elsewhere Buddha sought to transform the fundamental orientation of the *kṣatriyadharma.*[39] In a significant way Buddha, who is identified with *cakravartin* and the *dharmarāja*, as indeed we will shortly recognize, Yuthisthira, the Hindu *dharmarāja*, represents a significant moment in the *kṣatriya* conscience and *kṣatriya* consciousness. Both in the Buddhist *Nikāyas* and *Jātakas*, on the one hand and in the *Mahābhārata* on the other, this conflict in the *kṣatriya* conscience is resolved by removing the *kṣatriyadharma* from its particular context of the specific *varṇa dharma* and raising it to the level of universal *dharma*, where *kṣatriya dharma* is seen as the very epitome of the universal *dharma*, *the* fundamental source of all *dharmas*. Of course, the *kṣatriyadharma* itself, in both the cases, have to undergo a significant metamorphosis, before it can really become the true *rājadharma*, *dharma* of the *rājā*, "the one who pleases", the unqualified adherence to which is what makes a *dharma-rāja.*[40]

The Buddhist conception of *dharmarāja* is formulated in the canonical text of *Añguttara Nikāya* where the question is asked as to who is the King of the righteous King. The explicit answer given there is that it is the *dhamma* itself.[41] The formula is further amplified in the *Jātakas* giving detailed

---

[38] *Aggañña Suttanta, Dīgha Nikāya.*

[39] See Braj M. Sinha, "Religion as Violence: An Early Buddhist Perspective", *ARC: Journal of the Faculty of Religious Studies*, Vol. XIII, No. 2, 1986.

[40] *Mahābhārata*, XII.63.24; *Dīgha Nikāya*, XXVII.

[41] *Añguttara Nikāya*, III.

descriptions of the King that ruled by the *dhamma*. The *Jātakas* are replete with stories telling us how the *dhamma* King (*dhammarāja*) practised *dhamma* in personal piety as well as in conducting the public affairs of the state. All these stories identify the *dharmarāja* as one who shunned the four wrong courses of life comprising of excitement, malice, delusion and fear.[42] The royal duties (*rājadhamma*) practised by them consisted of alms giving, morality, liberality, straightforwardness, refraining from anger and from injury, forbearance and refraining from confrontation. The well-known ten stanzas relating to the practice of righteousness (*dasadhamma-chariyā-gāthā*) by the King presents a strikingly different conception of the *kṣatriya* than the one professed by the specialist of the *khattivijjā* cited earlier. Here the ten principles of righteous behaviour by a *dhammarāja* consist of: righteousness towards the mother and father, the wife and the son, relatives and ministers, draught animals, the realm, recluses and Brāhmaṇas, birds and beasts.[43] Allusions to the ten *rājadhamma* are to be found in several of the *Jātaka* tales, including *Tesakuya-Jātaka*; *Cullahamsa Jātaka* and *Mahāmsa-Jātaka*, just to mention a few.[44] Through all these *Jātaka* tales the point is brought forth in unequivocal terms that what makes a state a righteous state is the total and uncompromising application of the principle of *dharma* to all aspects of state administration and public policy.

It is equally important to be reminded that the *Nikāyas* and the *Jātakas* never tire of emphasizing the immense social, political, and above all cosmic significance of the King's righteousness. The *rājadharma*, i.e. *dhamma* of the *kṣhatriya*, acquires a paradigmatic importance. The most powerful statement to this effect is made in the *Aṅguttara Nikāya*. To paraphrase the passage:

> When Kings become unrighteous, the King's officers (*rājayuttas*) also become unrighteous, this being so the *Brāhmaṇas* and the mass of ordinary householders (*gahapatis*), the townsfolk and the villagers in their turn become unrighteous; this being so the sun and the moon, the stars and the constellations go wrong in their courses; days and nights, months, seasons and years are out of joint; the winds blow wrong; the *devas* being annoyed do not bestow sufficient rain. This being so, the corps ripen in the wrong season and consequently men are short lived, ill favoured, weak and sickly. Conversely, when kings become righteous, all the reverse consequences follow.[45]

---

[42] See *Jātakas*, No. 521, 533, 534, 540, etc.

[43] *Rohanta-Miga-Jātaka*, No. 501.

[44] It is important to note that these *Jātaka* tales, though of later origin than the *Nikāya* literature, continue in significant ways the early Buddhist vision of the *rājadhamma*.

[45] *Aṅguttara Nikāya*, II.

The above view of the tremendous significance of the political righteousness is reflected in several of the *Jātaka* stories.

Mahābhārata: A Comparative Perspective

The central thrust of this portrayal of the Buddhist conception of the *dhammarāja* is to recreate for us the context in which we can appreciate the developments within the *Mahābhārata*. There simply is no denying the fact that the ideal of *dharmarāja* in the *Nikāyas* goes a long way in repudiating the central thrust of *Arthaśāstra* categories which probably were the governing themes of most of the little princely states, and to a great extent of the contemporary empires. That this idealistic and onesided theme of the *dhamma* rule was not seen as an easily accessible doctrine and to a great degree somewhat bewildered the *kṣatriya* rulers is obvious by the prominence of the doctrine and repeated reinforcements through tales in which Kings want to be instructed in this new science of polity. That both its boldness and its idealism, with significant disregard of the pragmatics of the statecraft, made it too difficult and opaque, is evident from many of the *Jātaka* stories designed to remove the doubt and inculcate an attitude of righteousness among its listeners, the Kings who sought to understand the principle of *rājadhamma*.

Reminiscent of the *Nikāyas* and the *Jātakas*, the *Mahābhārata* also seeks to reverse the class hierarchy of *brāhmaṇas* and the *kṣatriyas*, and beyond that causes the *kṣatriya dharma* to undergo a metamorphosis by freeing it of its particularistic context of the *varṇa dharma*. This enables the *Mahābhārata* to establish the *kṣatriyadharma* not in accordance with the particularistic framework of *varṇa dharma*, but on the universal principle of social and moral law. It is the universalization of the *kṣatriya dharma* that also accounts for the countervailing notion of *rājadharma* contrasted with the *Arthaśāstra* conception of *daṇḍanīti* in the *Śāntiparvan* which, in a very significant way, is resonant with the *Nikāya* and *Jātaka* conceptions.

The *daṇḍanīti* of *Arthaśāstra* tradition, corresponding to the *khattivijjā* of the *Nikāyas* and *Jātakas*, is subjected to the restraint of the universal principles of *dharma*. There emerges here a new conception of *kṣatriyadharma*, a conception that is far more noble than any previous body of Hindu literature had suggested. This metamorphosis of *kṣatriyadharma* is the need of the hour; nothing less than this will satisfy the anguished cry of the Yudhiṣṭhira. Only this transformed character of *kṣatriyadharma* can qualify it to be the fountainhead of all *dharmas*. In a manner reminiscent of the Buddha's statement in the *Nikāyas*, *kṣatriyadharma* now is declared to be supremest of all, nay the very foundation of all *dharmas*. The *dharmas* of the four orders (*varṇas*) we are told, are established upon the *dharma* of the *kṣatriya*. *Kṣatriyadharma*, the text tells us, flowed from the Primeval Deity (*Puruṣa*), and then came other *dharmas*, which are, as it were, its appendages: all other *dharmas* are included in this *dharma*, and therefore it is declared to be the highest.[46]

It is my contention that this is not an isolated phenomenon where the tenets of the politics and the statecraft was seen to be in conflict with the principles of *dharma*. The *Mahābhārata* in a very significant way presents to us the general context in which the *kṣatriya* ruling class seeks resolution of its own conflict of conscience. Yudhiṣṭhira, the *kṣatriya* prince, called *dharmarāja* in the *Mahābhārata*, is the epitome of that tension. In this particular situation the tension is clearly perceived between the *Arthaśāstra* principles of statecraft that Bhīṣma is laying down for Yudhiṣṭhira and the *dharma* categories of conduct, that Yudhiṣṭhira operating within the framework of the *Smṛti* tradition of *Dharmasūtras* holds dear to his heart. His anguish, as we all know, is borne of the tension between the *kṣatriya dharma* in its particularistic context, and what he perceives to be the universal principles of *dharma*. As R.C. Zaehner points out in a somewhat oblique way, Yudhiṣṭhira "has no quarrel with the ten commandments which sum up what is obligatory on all men, irrespective of class and caste for these are in accordance with his own nature-fortitude, patience, self-control, not to steal, purity, control of the senses, insight, wisdom, truth, and the avoidance of anger. What he protests against, time and time again, is the *dharma* peculiar to the warrior class particularly as it applies to kings."[47] In effect Yudhiṣṭhira wants to reject the particularistic claims of the *kṣatriya dharma*. This much is known. It is also a common knowledge that in the *Śāntiparvan* of the *Mahābhārata* one finds the Machiavelli of *Arthaśāstra* raising its head again and again. What is intriguing, however, is that Bhīṣma's answer always leaves Yudhiṣṭhira perplexed and bewildered, still probing; for him the conflict is not resolved. And what is equally intriguing is that our modern scholars have failed to see the other strain of the *Mahābhārata* polity, which constantly seeks to counterbalance the *Arthaśāstra* categories by resorting to the universal principles of *dharma* as the foundation of the *Mahābhārata* notion of *rājadharma*.

---

[46] *Mahābhārata*, XII.64 & 65.

[47] R.C. Zaehner, *Hinduism* (London: Oxford University Press, 1966) p. 116.

SNAKES, *SATTRAS*, AND THE *MAHĀBHĀRATA*

CHRISTOPHER MINKOWSKI

ABBREVIATIONS

AB	Aitareya Brāhmaṇa
ĀGS	Āśvalāyana Gṛhyasūtra
ĀpGS	Āpastamba Gṛhyasūtra
ĀpŚS	Āpastamba Śrautasūtra
Ārṣ	Ārṣeyakalpa
ĀŚS	Āśvalāyana Śrautasūtra
AV	Atharva Veda Saṃhitā
BGS	Baudhāyana Gṛhyasūtra
BP	Bhāgavata Purāṇa
BrP	Brahmāṇḍa Purāṇa
BŚS	Baudhāyana Śrautasūtra
GP	Garuḍa Purāṇa
HGS	Hiraṇyakeśī Gṛhyasūtra
HŚS	Hiraṇyakeśī Śrautasūtra
Hv	Harivaṃśa
JB	Jaiminīya Brāhmaṇa
JUB	Jaiminīya Upaniṣad Brāhmaṇa
KB	Kauṣītakī Brāhmaṇa
KGS	Khādira Gṛhyasutra
KS	Kāṭhaka Saṃhitā
KŚS	Kātyāyana Śrautasūtra
LŚS	Lāṭyāyana Śrautasūtra
MBh	Mahābhārata
MP	Matsya Purāṇa
MŚS	Mānava Śrautasūtra
PB	Pañcaviṃśa Brāhmaṇa
PGS	Pāraskara Gṛhyasūtra
R	Rāmāyaṇa
RV	Ṛgveda Saṃhitā
RV Khila	Ṛgveda Khila
SāB	Sāmavidhāna Brāhmaṇa
ŚB	Śatapatha Brāhmaṇa
ŚGS	Śāṃkhāyana Gṛhyasūtra
ŚŚS	Sāṃkhāyana Śrautasūtra
SV	Sāmaveda Saṃhitā
TĀ	Taittirīya Āraṇyaka
TB	Taittirīya Brāhmaṇa
TS	Taittirīya Saṃhitā
VāmP	Vāmana Purāṇa
VāP	Vāyu Purāṇa
VP	Viṣṇu Purāṇa
VS	Vājasasaneyī Saṃhitā

In an article that will appear elsewhere I discuss the frame stories of the Mahābhārata, the embedding structure that they presume, and the Vedic ritual structures that may be their inspiration.[1] This article is intended to complement that more theoretical one with a consideration of the specifics of Janamejaya's *sarpasattra* or snake sacrifice, its Vedic precedents, and its connection with the Bhārata story. In examining these specifics, more global considerations arise, having to do with continuities between Vedic and epic, with snake lore, with the thematics of the Mahābhārata and with the history of its formation. I will argue that Janamejaya's *sattra* is an artfully chosen frame story and that it appropriately foreshadows the wider theme of the epic that it introduces.

Janamejaya's Sarpasattra

The story of Janamejaya's *sattra* belongs to the Āstīka *parvan* of the Mahābhārata's first book (1.45–53).[2] The events of the Āstīka *parvan*, the curse of Kadrū (1.18), the death of Parikṣit (1.36–40), and the birth of Āstīka (1.33–44), culminate in the story of the snake *sattra*, which begins with Janamejaya learning that his father Pariṣkit was killed by the serpent Takṣaka. Seeking revenge, Janamejaya asks his priests whether they know a rite that would enable him to propel Takṣaka and his relations into blazing fire (1.47.4). The priests reply that there is a rite that will accomplish such a task, created by the gods especially for Janamejaya (*tvadartham devanirmitam*), known as the *sarpasattra*, and described in the Purāṇic lore (*purāṇe kathyate*) (1.47.6). Janamejaya is the only man eligible to sponsor this rite, and the priests have the training to perform it (1.47.7). Janamejaya agrees and orders the priests to prepare (1.47.8–9). As they are laying out the sacrificial enclosure one *paurāṇika* descries an omen that, because of a Brahmin, the sacrifice will be halted before completion (1.47.13–5).

Janamejaya orders that no strangers be allowed to enter and begins his rite. The priests, wearing black, begin their necromantic oblations, and snakes begin falling in large numbers into the sacrificial fire (1.47.16–25). Takṣaka, feeling the pull of the fire, finds a hiding place in Indraloka (1.48.14–18), but the other snakes are not so well favored by Indra. Many of them are destroyed. Āstīka, the son of the Brahmin

[1] "Janamejaya's *sattra* and Ritual Structure", JAOS 109.3 (1989) 401–20. I am greatly indebted to David Pingree for his advice and ideas in preparing this work.

[2] All references are to the Critical Edition of Sukthankar et al.

Jaratkāru and the snake woman Jaratkāru, goes to the *sattra* to try to save the snakes (1.48.24–49.24).

Āstīka enters in spite of the guards and sings an ornamental *stuti* in *triṣṭubh* meter, praising Janamejaya and his *yajña*, and likening him to gods, sages, and kings as legendary Yajamānas (1.50). Janamejaya wishes to give a boon to Āstīka, against the advice of his priests, who warn him to wait until Takṣaka is safely incinerated (1.51.1–3). Janamejaya urges the priests to finish the rite, and when he learns that Indra is protecting Takṣaka, he orders the priests to force Indra into the fire as well (1.51.4–11). Indra abandons Takṣaka, who begins to plummet toward the flames, and the priests allow Janamejaya to give Āstīka his boon (1.51.12–15).

By his Brahminic power, Āstīka dramatically stops Takṣaka in midair and requests from Janamejaya that the *sarpasattra* be halted (1.51.16–20). Janamejaya reluctantly agrees and concludes the rite, distributing *dakṣiṇā*, performing the *avabhṛtha*, and sending the priests home (1.53.7–14).

It is at this snake sacrifice that the Bhārata story, the story of Janamejaya's ancestors, is first narrated by Vaiśaṃpāyana in the intervals between the ritual actions. Both of these story traditions, the telling of the Mahābhārata and the boon of Āstīka, belong to the *sarpasattra* legend, and it is not made clear how they interact, except that at the end of the Mahābhārata, the *sūta* at 18.5.26–7 describes how Vaiśaṃpāyana finished his narrative; Janamejaya marveled; the priests stopped their rite; and Āstīka was pleased at saving the snakes. Presumably we are to understand that Vaiśaṃpāyana finished his story before Āstīka's intervention.

Why should this story about snakes and rituals serve as the introduction to an epic about cousins at war? First of all, there is the question of tradition and continuity. The *sarpasattra* is nothing new. It is not the invention of a late redactor of the epic. In fact it has more Vedic precedent than the Bhārata story itself.

Vedic Sarpasattra

There is a ritual antecedent to the Mahābhārata's snake sacrifice in the *sarpasattra* described in the Pañcaviṃśa Brāhmaṇa and in the *śrautasūtras*.[3]

---

[3] PB 25.15; BŚS 17.18; ĀpŚS 23.14.18–9; MŚS 9.5.4.37–9; ŚŚS 13.23.5–8; KŚS 24.4.50; ĀSS 12.5.1–5; LŚS 10.20.10–2; Also BGS 3.10; Ārṣ 11.8f–10b. Devayājñika on KŚS cites the lost Kāṭhaka *sūtra*, which provides the same details as ĀpŚS.

But this is not a rite that draws snakes into the fire. Rather, it is made up of the ordinary ritual components of *sattras*, i.e. Soma sacrifices. As are all *sattras*, it is subject to unusual rules. Only Brahmins are eligible to perform it; there is no separate Yajamāna or sponsor; no *dakṣiṇā*, or sacrificial fee, is given.[4] Thus it is different from Janamejaya's *sattra*, he being a Kṣatriya who pays substantial *dakṣiṇās*.

The *sarpasattra* is to last for one year. Like some other year-long rites it is arranged symmetrically around a *viṣuvat* or central day. In the PB version, for example, the rite begins with an Atirāta Soma sacrifice. Then for six months are performed Agniṣṭomas which use two different sets of Sāmaveda *stotras* on alternate days.[5] On the *viṣuvat* day itself a standard Agniṣṭoma is performed, only using for the *stotras* the *sarpasāmans* (Araṇyageyagāna 2.a.1–3).[6] After the *viṣuvat* day the Agniṣṭomas are performed in reverse order for six more months.[7] The rite concludes with another Atirātra.[8] Other schools follow the same structure but with variations.[9]

The distinctive characteristic of the *sarpasattra* is that it is *daśadaśī*, "done by tens and by tens".[10] This means that at all three Soma pressings only 10 verses of Sāmaveda are sung in the *stotras*, rather than the 9, 15, 17 or 21 verses typically recited in an Agniṣṭoma.[11] At the same

---

[4] See Harry Falk, "Zum Ursprung der Sattra-Opfer", ZDMG Suppl. VI (1985) 275–81. I am indebted to Stanley Insler for this reference.

[5] Ārṣ. 11.8f–9a.

[6] The *sarpasāmans* are Araṇyageyagāna 2.a.1.1–10 and are based on RV 3.51.1. (=SV 1.374); 7.32.16 (=SV 1.270); 9.75.1 (=SV 1.554); 9.97.58; 1.84.10(=SV 1.409). Inserted in the verses in Araṇyageyagāna are, among other expressions, *prasarpa, sarpa, utsarpa*. See below for more on this wordplay.

[7] i.e. before the *viṣuvat* ababab . . . , after the *viṣuvat* bababa. . . .

[8] Because PB 25.15.3 mentions the Abhigara and Apagara, the praiser and reviler, who appear properly only in a Mahāvrata, the question arises in Sāyaṇa's commentary on PB whether this mention is injunctive of a performance of a Mahāvrata, which would mean that the *sattra* as a whole should be modelled on the Gavāmayana *sattra* with its much more complex structure. The answer is that since the Ārṣeyakalpa 11.8f–10b has spelled out the format of the rite exactly, there is no need for such inferences. Similarly LŚS 10.20.10–2 and Agnisvāmī's commentary there; also noticed in Devayājñika on KŚS 24.4.50

[9] Āśvalayana prescribes alternating Goṣṭoma and Ayuḥstoma rites, with a Jyotiṣṭoma for the *viṣuvat* day. Kātyāyana (according to Karka and Yājñikadeva) prescribes alternating Virāṭ sacrifices with the *trivṛt* Agniṣṭoma rite that is performed on the second day of a Kausurabinda 10-day *sattra*. Baudhāyana alternates days of 10 *stomas* with days of 12 *stomas*. Āpastamba, Mānava, and Śāṃhkāyana are roughly equivalent to Pañcaviṃśa Brāhmana.

[10] PB 25.15.1; ĀpSS 23.14.9; ŚSS 13.23.7; BŚS 17.18 (*daśadaśa*); MSS 9.5.4.37; Kāṭhaka sūtra as cited in Devayājñika on KŚS 24.4.50, *sarvo daśadaśī saṃvatsaro dvādaśī visuvānt sarpāṇām ayanam*.

[11] BŚS alternates 10-*stoma* days with 12-*stoma* days as noted above.

time, the *viṣuvat* day is to be a 12-*stoma* day,[12] while the Atirātras at beginning and end are to be 16-*stoma* days.

The *sattra* is *daśadaśī* because of the wordplay with the bite verb *daṃś* (*daśati*). Baudhāyana ŚS 17.18 makes this connection explicit, *sa yad daśadaśeti tasmāt sarpā daṃśukā daṃśuvīryāḥ*, "because (it was performed) by tens and by tens, therefore serpents (have become) biters (*daṃśuka*) and wondrously brave (*daṃśuvīrya*).[13]

As for results, the predicted benefits of the *śrauta sarpasattra* are all beneficial, and far from the apocalyptic effects of Janamejaya's *sattra*. The Pãncaviṃśa Brāhmaṇa promises that the performers of this rite get a firm support in these worlds (25.15.2), that just as snakes slough their old skin, so do the performers conquer death and attain a splendor as if of the Ādityas (25.15.4).[14] Āpastamba ŚS promises the same splendor and also the prevention of old age (23.14.8). Mānava ŚS urges this rite on those desiring the wealth produced by all *sattras*, those desiring immortality and those desiring heaven (9.5.5.39). Baudhāyana ŚS 17.18 declares that the *sarpasattra* wins worlds, sons, and cattle, and, more to the point, that whoever performs it will not be harmed by snakes.

More significant is the aetiology provided for the *sarpasattra* by the Pañcaviṃśa Brāhmaṇa and Baudhāyana ŚS.[15] Both texts list the original performers of the inauguratory snake *sattra*. As it turns out, the first offerers of the *sarpasattra* were the snakes themselves, who, as noted above, became venomous by completing it. Below are given the three versions of this list as found in PB 25.15.3; BŚS 17.18; and BGS 3.10.

Priest	*PB*	*BŚS*	*BGS*
Gṛhapati	Jarvara	same	Jīrvara
Brahman	Dhṛtarāṣṭra Airāvata	same	Datta Tāpasa
Udgātṛ	Pṛthuśravas Dauresravasa	same	P. Dūreśravas
Prastotṛ	Glāva	same	same
Pratihartṛ	Ajagāva	same	Ajagara
Hotṛ	Datta Tāpasa	same	Vāruṇa
Maitrāvaruṇa	Śitipṛṣṭha	same	same

[12] So PB, ĀpŚS ŚŚS, ĀŚS, MŚS, Kāṭhaka and comms. on KŚS.
[13] This wordplay of *daśa* and *daśati* is, so to speak, an old joke. See below.
[14] Similarly ĀŚS prescribes the rite for those who desire splendor (*prakāśa*).
[15] Also it appears in BGS 3.10 and is referred to in MŚS.

Brāhmanācchaṃsin	Takṣaka Vaiśaleya	same	T. Vaiśālika
Neṣṭṛ	Śikha	same	same
Potṛ	Anuśikha	Atiśikha	Atiśikha
Acchāvaka	Aruṇa Aṭa	Aruṇa Ahya	Cakra
Āgnīdhra	Timirgha Daureśruta	Cakra and Piśaṅga	Piśaṅga
2 Adhvaryus	Arimejaya Janamejaya Kautustau	same	Dhṛtarāṣṭra Airāvata
Grāvastut	Arbuda	same	same
Subrahmanya	Ajira	Ajira Māheya	Ahira Maheya
Unnetṛ(s)	Cakra Piśaṅga	Sāṇḍa	Ṣānda
Abhigara	Ṣaṇḍa		
Apagara	Kuṣaṇḍa		
Dhruvagopa		Paśukra	Paśago
Sadasya		Uparīti Tārkṣya	Upanīti Tārkṣya
			Dhurimejaya Kaustuka Janamejaya[16]

The listing here of names that are prominent in the Bhārata epic, especially Dhṛtarāṣṭra, Janamejaya, and Takṣaka, prompted Caland to conclude that the vedic *sarpasattra* was the prototype for the epic one.[17] It is clear that in the passage from ritual to epic text, however, important transformations have taken place. In specific terms, the list of officiants has changed from reptilian to human; the serpent patriarchs are replaced with Brahmin *ṛṣis*.[18]

Hotṛ	Caṇḍabhārgava descendant of Cyavana
Udgātṛ	Kautsārya Jaimini
Brahman	Sārṅgarava
Adhvaryu	Bodhapiṅgala

---

[16] These last two are Adhvaryus according to the kha ms. in R. Shama Sastri's edition. The reading of BGS is apparently corrupted, so that familiar names are garbled and switched.

[17] Caland on PB 25.15.3.

[18] MBh 1.48.4–10. There are many variants in the names listed in the critical apparatus.

Sadasyas Vyāsa, Śamaṭhaka, Uddālaka, Śvetaketu, Asita Devala, Nārada, Pārvata, Ātreya, Kuṭighata, Vātsya Śrutaśravas, Kahoḍa, Devaśarma, Maudgala, Śamasaubhara.

Curiously, the four main priests are hardly found elsewhere in Vedic or epic texts,[19] while the *sadasyas* are well-known Vedic *ṛṣis*. As for the snakes, of those named in the Vedic passages only two appear at the epic *sarpasattra*, but that, ironically, is because they are consumed in its flames.[20] Dhṛtarāṣṭra Airāvata appears as a snake from the Atharva Veda onwards.[21] Takṣaka Vaiśaleya and Arbuda Kādraveya are also well known as snakes even in the Vedic period.[22] Janamejaya appears as the name of a snake in the Mahābhārata (2.9.10). On the other hand, he appears as a Yajamāna in the Brāhmaṇas.[23]

As for the site of the snake *sattra*, there is significance in its Vedic location and in its epic relocation. Baudhāyana ŚS 17.18 states that the original *sarpasattra* took place at Khāṇḍava Prastha. In the epic, of course, Khāṇḍavaprastha is another name for Indraprastha, the city that the Pāṇḍavas built on the site of the Khāṇḍava forest, the erstwhile home of Takṣaka. Krishna and Arjuna burn down the Khāṇḍava forest in a manner that appears unusually cruel, by preventing the wild animals, including snakes, from escaping the flames (1.214–223). Takṣaka is only saved by being away in Kurukṣetra. His son is saved by the special intervention of Indra, who is regularly Takṣaka's protector, but his wife is killed by Arjuna (1.218.4–9).

These events, the burning of Khāṇḍava Prastha, the slaughter of his people, his mate, and the near death of his son, establish a basis for a personal vendetta between Takṣaka and the Bhārata clan. The existence

---

[19] Caṇḍa appears in a list of Bhārgavas, MP 195.24; Śārṅgarava appears once, VP 41.73.

[20] Cakra and Piśaṅga, MBh 1.52.5;15.

[21] AV 8.10.22; JUB 4.26.15; MBh 1.3.142; 1.41.13; 1.52.13; 2.9.9; 4.2.14; 5.101.15; 8.24.72; 16.6.14; Hv 3.88; 6.23; BP 5.24.31; BrP 3.7.34; VāP 69.71; MP 6.40; 10.20; VP 6.8.95.

[22] Takṣaka—AV 8.10.29; 8.14.14; and Kauśika Sūtra on AV 4.6; 5.13; 6.12; JB 2.284; in the MBh Takṣaka is ubiquitous—see S. Sörenson, *An Index to the Names in the Mahābhārata* (New Delhi: Motilal Banarsidass, 1963) 672–3; BP 1.12.27; 1.18.21 5.24.29; 9.22.36; 12.11.35; BrP 2.17.34; 3.7.32; MP 6.39; 8.6; 10.19; VāP 39.54; 50.23; 54.91; VP 1.17.28; 2.10.7; etc. Arbuda—RV 2.11.20; 2.14.4; 8.3.19; 8.32.3; 8.32.26; AB 6.1; KB 29.1; ŚB 13.4.3.9; JB 1.345; 2.222; 3.374; ĀŚS 10.7; MBh 2.19.9; vanishes in Purāṇas.

[23] ŚB 13.5.4. 1–3; 11.5.5.13; AB 7.27; 7.34; 8.11; 8.21.

of this vendetta would explain why Takṣaka exerts all his powers to kill Parikṣit; he is not simply the neutral medium for the working out of a sage's curse.

In the Vedic literature the Khāṇḍava forest is not infrequently named as the site for *sattras*.[24] That Krishna and Arjuna raze this forest reveals the same process of transformation from ritual to epic, aetiological myth becoming apocalyptic narrative, that is seen in the epic generally. Thus a Vedic *yajña* that has only beneficial effects, (even if its original performance made snakes venomous,) turns into a destructive holocaust in the epic.

There appear to be two causes for this transformation. The first is that the Mahābhārata version is also drawing on non-*śrauta*, *abhicara* traditions. The black clothing, the non-Vedic provenance of the rite asserted by the epic (MBh 1.47.6), the rite's efficacy being unique for Janamejaya, and the malicious effects all suggest the influence of sorcery.[25] The second cause for the transformation of the *sarpasattra* is motivated by the differences in genre and expectation that separate ritual texts from epic ones. Moreover, the *sarpasattra* in the Mahābhārata forms the opening chapters of an epic that has as its dominating theme vengeful, apocalyptic practises, as shall be discussed below.

In the Mahābhārata the site for the *sarpasattra* is specified as Takṣaśilā (18.5.29). Why should Janamejaya hold his *yajña* at Takṣaśilā? Janamejaya's choice is apparently based on the similarity in names: Takṣaśilā as *takṣakasya śilā*, the rock of Takṣaka. In the Mahābhārata there is only the suggestive statement that Janamejaya conquered Takṣaśilā, and while he was away Utaṅka was duped by Takṣaka.[26] Purāṇic traditions, however, identify Takṣaśilā with Takṣa, the son of Bharata.[27] The historical sources notice large numbers of snakes and snake worshippers in the area.[28]

---

[24] PB 25.3.26; JB 3.168; TĀ 4.1.1.

[25] On *abhicāra* and its relation to *śrauta* practise see Hans-Georg Turstig, "The Indian Sorcery called *abhicāra*", WZKS 29 (1985) 69–117.

[26] 1.3.19; 1.3.179. Utaṅka then incites Janamejaya to perform the *sarpasattra*. MBh 3.*387 found only in Northern recension mss. lists as an abode of Takṣaka the Vitastā river. But the Vitastā does not flow through Taxila. For more on this question see O.P. Bharadvaj, "Janamejaya Pārikṣita and Two Ancient Traditions of Kuruksetra", *Studies in the Historical Geography of Ancient India*, Delhi: Sandeep, 1986, pp. 121–8.

[27] R 7.101.1; BrP 3.63.191; VāmP 88.190.

[28] Onesikratos, the least reliable of those who traveled with Alexander, mentions two snakes, one 80 cubits, the other 140 cubits (Strabo 15.1.28). For other accounts, see J. Fergusson, *Tree and Serpent Worship* (London: India Museum, 1868) 44–7.

Vedic Snake Lore

In creating the epic *sarpasattra* the "author" of the Mahābhārata was drawing on a vast repertory of snake lore, both Vedic and extra-Vedic. It would be impossible to give a complete description of snake lore in Indic literature here.[29] I will limit myself to some of the more prominent features of snake lore in the Vedic literature.

In general terms snakes were regarded in the Vedic period just as they were in later periods, as fearsome, potentially dangerous creatures. At the same time snakes were treated as semi-divine beings who required and received ritual propitiation.[30] Individual snakes, however, were regarded as contributors to the Vedic tradition, most notably Arbuda Kādraveya, who served as the original Grāvastut priest, and is traditionally listed as the *ṛṣi* of RV 10.94, the opening hymn of the Grāvastut's recitation.[31] According to Pañcaviṃśa Brāhmaṇa, just as Arbuda sloughed his old skin by these verses, so can a man slough off mortality using them.[32]

Aside from Indra, who because of killing Vṛtra is described in the Ṛgveda as a snake-killer (ahihan, RV 2.13.5; 2.19.3), the most celebrated bane of the snakes is the white horse of Pedu, Paidva, (RV 1.117.9; 1.118.9; 9.88.4). In Atharvaveda 10.4 the horse of Pedu is called on to beat down the snakes with his hooves.[33]

In the *śrauta* sacrifices the propitiation of snakes is performed with the *sarpanāma* verses: *námo astu sarpébhyaḥ, yé ké ca pṛthivī́m ánu....*[34] These verses are used in the Agnicayana, in placing the golden man in the footprint of the horse, to mark the place where the *cayana* will be built.[35] Among the oblations made on the fifth layer of the *cayana* are the *sarpāhutis*, offerings to the directions and the snakes associated with each

---

[29] For more detail see "Serpent-Worship", *Encyclopedia of Religion and Ethics* 11.399–423; Fergusson, *Tree and Serpent Worship*; J.Ph. Vogel, *Indian Serpent Lore* (London: Probsthain, 1928). For a comparative study see M. Lurker, *Adler und Schlange* (Tubingen, 1983), for a psycho-biological study, Balaji Mundkar, *Cult of the Serpent* (Albany, 1983).

[30] A.A. Macdonell, *Vedic Mythology* (Strassburg: Trübner, 1897) 152–3.

[31] AB 6.1; KB 29.1; ĀŚS 5.12; ŚŚS 7.15.

[32] PB 4.9.4; 9.8.8; also JB 1.3.45; 2.222.

[33] AV 10.4.3, *áva śveta padā jani* . . . , is used extensively in ritual, both in Kauśika Sūtra as described below and in the Śrāvaṇā rite, (also described below), in a variant form *ápa śveta padā jahi*. . . .

[34] TS 4.2.8.3; MS 2.7.15; VS 13.6–8; KS 16.15; ŚB 7.4.1.25ff; RV Khila 2.14.10; ĀpŚS 16.22.4; MŚS 6.1.7.

[35] The verses are also employed in a *gṛhya* rite in what appears to be a more intrinsic use. See below.

of those directions (TS 5.5.10.1–5).[36] In TB 3.1.1.6–7, in a description of the Nakṣatreṣṭi, the rite in which the 28 constellations are reverenced, a *homa* to the *sarpa*s is prescribed for bringing the *āśreṣa* constellation under control, for the *āśreṣa*s are the constellation of the serpents.[37] The *sarpasāman*s have already been mentioned in their *śrauta* use. They are also used in making an amulet to ward off snakes.[38]

The *sarparājñī* (or *sārparājñī*) verses are linked to snake lore less apparently. Consisting of RV 10.189.1–3,[39] the verses are used for establishing the sacred fires at the Agnyādhāna.[40] The *ṛṣi* is traditionally listed as *sarparājñī*, the queen of serpents, identified with the earth, but the verses make no mention of snakes. An alternative *śrauta* application of these verses is in the Daśarātra, the Soma rite that lasts ten nights. On the tenth day, after the priests creep back (*tataḥ sarpanti*, AB 5.23) from the performance of the *patnīsaṃyāja*s into the *sadas*, the Hotṛ recites the *sarparājñī* verses.[41] There is, therefore, the suggestion of two old jokes, both paronomastic, the tenth (*daśama*) day of the ten day rite (*daśarātra*) evocative of *daś* (*daśati*), and the acknowledged wordplay of the creep root *sṛp* (*sarpati*) with *sarparājñī*.[42]

In *gṛhya* rites the snakes are propitiated in the Śravaṇā, the Sarpabali, and the Āgrahāyaṇī rites.[43] There is great diversity in the practises followed and the *mantra*s recited, many of which are unique to the *gṛhyasūtras*. In general, the Śravaṇā rite is a *homa* performed in a fire established on the full moon day of Śrāvaṇa.[44] A *bali* or offering on the earth is made to the snakes every day until the full moon of Mārgaśīrṣa, when the *homa* of Āgrahāyaṇa is performed.[45]

---

[36] ĀpŚS 17.20.14; MSS 6.2.6; BSS 10.49.

[37] TB 3.1.4.7.

[38] SāB 2.3.3.

[39] With variation also found at AV 6.31.1–3; VS 3.6; TS 1.5.3.1; MS 1.6.1; KS 7.13; AB 5.23; KB 27.4; ŚB 2.1.4.29.

[40] In different schools either the Āhavanīya, Dakṣināgni, or Gārhapatya is established with this *mantra*. ŚB 2.1.4.29; KŚS 4.9.4.14–5; ĀpŚS 5.11.6; 5.13.6; 5.16.2; etc.

[41] ĀŚS 8.13.6; AB 5.23; KB 27.4; ŚŚS 10.13.26; ĀpŚS 21.10.5.

[42] Creeping was once perhaps the characteristic manner of approaching all *sattras*. On their originally secret performance and *upa* + *sṛp*, see Harry Falk, "Zum Ursprung der Sattra-Opfer", 277.

[43] ŚGS 4.15, 17–8; ĀGS 2.1,3; PGS 2.14, 3.2; KhGS 3.2ff; HGS 2.16–7; ĀpGS 18.5–20.19. See M. Winternitz, "Der Sarpabali", *Mitteilungen des Anthrop. Ges. in Wien* 18 (1888) 25–52, 250–64.

[44] July-August, when the snakes become more troublesome, and people begin to sleep on cots.

[45] Preparatory to redescending to sleeping on the earth.

In the Pāraskara, Āśvalayana, Āpastamba, and Hiraṇyakeśī versions of this rite the *sarpanāma* verses are recited. In the Baudhāyana version (BGS 3.10), one recites the list of priests at the original *sarpasattra* (BSS 17.18) as a *mantra*. Thus the "myth" of the Vedic *sarpasattra* itself takes on a ritual efficacy in warding off snakes.

In the Atharvaveda a typology of snakes is suggested in several *sūktas*, where the black, striped, and white are distinguished, as are the *pṛdāku* (adder), the *svaja* (viper, cobra), the *ratharvī* (?), and the *kasarṇīla* (?).[46] The Kauśika Sūtra prescribes the use of these and other *sūktas* in charms for driving away snakes or else for curing the venom of snakebite.[47] Kauśika 28.1–4 prescribes the use of AV 4.6 in case of snakebite, and in this connection the verses are to be recited after making obeisance to Takṣaka.

In short there is a vast body of snake lore in Vedic literature, much of it intended for the practical application of reducing the danger of poisonous snakebite, a danger as real as ever in India today. That this lore existed as a discrete element of the Vedic canon is suggested by the descriptions of the pāriplava of the Aśvamedha. The fifth day of the ten day cycle of stories and verse was devoted to a recounting of the *sarpavidyā*.[48] The text of the *sarpavidyā* is not provided in the *śrauta* texts. The commentators, who appear not to have had access to a continuous commentatorial tradition, suggest that *sarpavidyā* is the same as *viṣavidyā*, and that the *sarpavidyā* must therefore refer to charms against snakebite.[49] In making this identification, the commentators are linking the ritual *sarpavidyā* with the vast network of Indian snake lore, the science of how to avoid harm from snakes, which escapes the limits even of Sanskrit literature.

But I would like to suggest that the *sarpavidyā* also included a narrative component. That is, in addition to charms against snakes, the *sarpavidyā*

---

[46] AV 6.56; 10.4; 12.3.55–60

[47] Kauśika 28.1–4 (on AV 4.6); 29.1–14 (on 5.13); 24.24ff (on 12.1); 29.28–9 (on 6.12); 32.20ff (on 10.4); 50.17–22 (on 6.56).

[48] ŚB 13.4.3.9. ĀŚS 10.7.5; ŚŚS 16.2.13–5; P. Dumont, *L'Aśvamedha* (Paris: 1927) nos. 195–7.

[49] Gārgya on ĀŚS 10.7.5 states that a *sarpavid* is one who knows the *kāśyapīya* charms against venom. Varadattasuta on ŚŚS 16.2.15 equates *sarpavidyā* with the *gāruḍī* or *kaṅkanīyā* lore. The sage Kaśyapa is the father of the snakes and is endowed with the knowledge of the cures of their bites, (MBh 1.18.13; also 1.39.1–20). NCC 4.148–9 lists a Kāśyapīyasaṃhitā, a medical treatise on the cure of poisons through *mantras*. It is also called the Gāruḍapañcākṣarī, and appears, therefore, to overlap with the well-known *gāruḍī vidyā*, the science of warding off or curing snake bite, found in GP 19. I can find no references to a *kaṅkanīyā vidyā*.

also included stories about snakes. This can be argued purely from the narrative content of the recitations on the other days of the *pāriplava*.[50] I further suggest that the Mahābhārata became the repository for that narrative snake lore. Certainly it cannot be disputed that the Mahābhārata provides us with the most extensive collection of stories about snakes that we have in Sanskrit literature.

Snake Lore in the Mahābhārata

A majority of the sustained snake tales are collected in the Pauṣya, Puloman, and Āstīka chapters of the Ādi *parvan*. In the Pauṣya *parvan*, Utaṅka is robbed of his earrings by Takṣaka. He travels to Nāgaloka, praises the snakes, retrieves his earrings, but subsequently urges Janamejaya to destroy all of the snakes in a snake sacrifice (1.3.80–195). In the Puloman *parvan* a poisonous snake kills the wife of the Bhārgava Ruru. He revives her, but makes a practise thereafter of killing all snakes he happens on (1.8–9). Ruru nearly kills a sage trapped by curse in the body of a lizard (*ḍuṇḍubha*), (which curse was provoked by frightening a fellow sage with a snake). The lizard discourages Ruru's genocidal program, and reminds him of Janamejaya's *sarpasattra* and Āstīka's intervention (1.10–11). Ruru has never heard the story of Āstīka and goes off in search of a narrator. In the Āstīka *parvan* the Kadrū and Vinatā story is told, including the wager on the color of Uccaiḥśravas' tail, the curse of Kadrū's sons, the birth of Garuḍa and his quest for the Soma (1.14–40),[51] the story of Śeṣa (1.32), the churning of the ocean (1.15–7), and the machinations of the snakes to obtain the birth of their savior, Āstīka (1.33–44). Thus all three *parvans* lead by different paths to the story of the *sarpasattra*.

Other snake lore is spread throughout the epic. It would not be possible to list all of it here.[52] There are descriptions of the Nāgaloka, Bhogavatī (5.101).[53] Lists of serpents are given in various places: the serpents born of Kadrū (1.31), the serpents killed in Janamejaya's *sattra*

---

[50] ŚB 13.4.3. See R.D. Karmarkar, "The Pāriplava at the Aśvamedha", ABORI 33 (1952) 27–40. On the eighth and ninth days the *itihāsaveda* and the *purāṇaveda*, respectively, are recited.

[51] Another version of the story is told in the late-Vedic Suparṇādhyāya. For bibliography see Gonda, *Vedic Literature* (Wiesbaden: Harrassowitz, 1975) 47–8. It is evident that the Āstīka *parvan* of the Mahābhārata becomes the repository for this earlier narrative tradition.

[52] See E.W. Hopkins, *Epic Mythology* (Strassburg: Trübner, 1915) 23–9; Vogel, *Indian Serpent Lore*, 47–92; Sörenson, *Index*, 492–4.

[53] Also 1. App. 72.

(1.52), the snakes who attend on Varuṇa (2.9), the snakes in Bhogavatī (5.101), the snakes who welcome Śesa back from incarnation as Balarāma (14.4.14–5).

The Mahabharata also records technique for curing snakebite. Kaśyapa learns the *viṣahaṇī vidyā* from Brahmā (1.18.11).[54] In the *tīrthayātrā* sections pilgrimage spots associated with snakes are listed, e.g. Sarpadevī (3.82.14). A visit to the *tīrtha* Maṇināga renders a pilgrim impervious to snakebite (3.82.92). Similar claims are made for Nāgadhanvan, the home of Vāsukī (9.36.29–32). Furthermore, *mantras* to cure snakebite are used in the Mahābhārata.[55] Most pertinent for this study are the *mantras* cited in the Āstīka *parvan* (1.53.21–2), where Āstīka is called on to protect the reciter from snakes. Similarly RV Khila 2.1.5–6[56] uses the memory of Āstīka and Janamejaya's *sattra* itself as a charm against snakebite. Thus the story about the *sarpasattra* takes on a ritual application in the same way that the "story" of the Vedic *sarpasattra* in PB 25.15 and BŚS 17.18 is reused as a *mantra* in the Baudhāyana *gṛhyasūtra* version of the Sarpabali.

Snakes and Kurus

Why should so much snake lore be collected in the Mahābhārata? Since it is a book about everything, it is perhaps not surprising to see some description of serpents as of many other creatures. But there are more particular reasons for the inclusion of the snake lore, especially at the beginning of the epic.

To begin with, it is clear that the Kuru dynasty has a long and close association with serpents. There is, first of all, a systematic overlapping of snake names with Kuru and Bhārata names. Thus we encounter serpents named Dhṛtarāṣṭra, Janamejaya, Dhanaṃjaya, Kauravya, Dilīpa, and Nahuṣa.[57] Moreover, there are accounts of dynastic links between Kurus and snakes. Arjuna is carried off to the world of the Nāgas by Ulūpī, a Nāga princess (1.206), on whom he fathers a son Irāvant (6.86.5ff). Ulūpī later saves Arjuna's life, and revives his son Babhrūvāhana (14.79–81). The serpent Āryaka recognizes in Bhīma his grandson's

---

[54] He is subsequently bribed by Takṣaka so that he will not use it on Parikṣit 1.39.1–20.

[55] *saṃjīvana maṇi* 14.82.2; and 8.27.83 which cites from AV 10.4.9.

[56] =MBh 1*463.1–5, found in most Northern mss.

[57] Dhṛtarāṣṭra 1.41.131; Janamejaya 2.9.10; Dhanaṃjaya 1.31.5; Kauravya 1.31.13; Dilīpa 5.101.15; Nahuṣa 1.31.9.

grandson (*dauhitradauhitra*) (1.App.72.10–11).[58] Furthermore, there are episodes describing the interaction of Kurus with snakes. Nahuṣa becomes one (5.11–17; 13.103); Arjuna marries one (1.206); Yudhiṣṭhira argues *dharma* with one (3.175–8);[59] Janamejaya employs one as *purohita* (1.3.10–16).

There is also a dynastic vendetta, begun by Arjuna who kills Takṣaka's wife (1.218.1–11); Takṣaka's son Aśvasena, barely escaping the Khandava fire, tries to kill Arjuna by becoming one of Karṇa's arrows. Arjuna is saved only by Krishna and kills Aśvasena (8.66.1–24). Takṣaka kills Parikṣit, Arjuna's grandson (1.45–6). Janamejaya, Parikṣit's son tries to kill Takṣaka (1.47–53). Āstīka ends the vendetta (1.53).

It is natural enough that the great story of the Bhārata war would attract other story traditions about those heroes, especially considering the genealogical preoccupations of the Sanskrit epic. Then again, the ritual setting is customary for recounting genealogy and the feats of ancestors. The Aśvamedha allows time in the *pāriplava* for the king to hear bards tell stories of ancient kings and of the Yajamāna as well.[60] Aśvalāyana *gṛhyasūtra* 4.6.6 prescribes the recitation of Itihāsa and Purāṇa at a ceremony to expiate the loss of an elder, a rite to which the *sarpasattra* of Janamejaya can be likened, in that it is for the sake of a father's death.

But it can further be argued that the Mahābhārata version of the *sarpasattra* belongs in the epic. It makes sense, artistically and thematically, to begin with it. Embedding the epic in an apocalyptic rite that only some survive prefigures the theme of the epic as a whole: the passing of an age, the eradication of a race, the survival of a few. Parikṣit is the sole survivor of the bygone era in the following age. He was saved by the intervention of Krishna. That he should be killed by Takṣaka, who is then saved from another holocaust by another intervention, this time by Āstīka, makes the two story traditions interlock. Moreover, it is Takṣaka's son, Aśvasena, who is saved by intervention from another genocidal fire, that of the Khāṇḍavadāha, only to be killed on the battlefield at Kurukṣetra.

The *sarpasattra* is not the only apocalyptic rite in the Mahābhārata:

---

[58] There is also some parallel between Kadrū producing 1000 snake eggs, (vs. Vinatā's two) (1.14.5–15) and Gāndhārī's abortion that becomes 100 sons (vs. Kuntī's three) (1.107).

[59] None other than Nahuṣa.

[60] Dumont *L'Aśvamedha*, nos. 160ff.

Parāśara undertakes a Rākṣasa *sattra* in order to avenge the death of his father at the hands of a Rākṣasa, but is halted by Atri before all Rākṣakas are destroyed (1.172). Baka Dālbhi undertakes a rite to turn the kingdom of Dhṛtarāṣṭra to dust, but this rite is also halted (9.40.1–25).

In fact the Bhārata war is itself depicted as a sacrifice of weapons (*śastrayajña*), with Krishna serving as Brahman and Adhvaryu.[61] The apocalyptic rite is thus an organic component of the Mahābhārata's thematics.

Few would dispute that the Mahābhārata has the passing of the heroic age as its main theme. M. Biardeau sees in the Mahābhārata an enactment of the Purāṇic eschatological myth of the *pralaya*.[62] If one follows this thinking one discovers that there are two survivors of the full-scale mythological *pralaya* mentioned in the Mahābhārata, Mārkaṇḍeya, who figures prominently in the Vana *parvan* (3.17–207), and Śeṣa, the snake who holds up the world, whose name, "remainder", underscores his position as survivor.[63]

On the Formation of the Epic

It is possible, therefore, to see how the *sarpasattra* became the frame story for the Mahābhārata, that is, by thematic attraction. By this means the snake lore found in the Pauṣya, Puloman, and Āstīka *parvans* was brought into the epic as well, for it forms part of the *sarpasattra* myth cycle. These three *parvans* converge on the *sarpasattra*, as does the story of the narration of the epic.

In keeping with these claims about the formation of the opening chapters of the Mahābhārata it is necessary to re-examine a widely held view of the growth of the Mahābhārata, namely the theory of "Bhṛguization" advanced by V.S. Sukthankar. The major portion of Sukthankar's study, "The Bhṛgus and the Bhārata",[64] is devoted to collecting all the story material from the Mahābhārata about the members of the Bhṛgu race, Bhṛgu, Cyavana, Aurva, Ruru, Jamadagni, and others, but especially Rāma Jāmadagni or Paraśurāma. Sukthankar then makes

---

[61] 5.139.29–53. Similarly 7.80.22–3; 9.59.25; 12.99.12–13. The notion is central to Hiltebeitel's study of the epic; *The Ritual of Battle* (Ithaca: Cornell, 1976).

[62] M. Biardeau, "Études de Mythologie Hindoue IV, BEFEO 63 (1976) 203–217.

[63] Biardeau, "EMH I", Publications de l'EFEO 128, Paris, 1981, 170. Also S.S. Dange, "Śesa—the Cosmic Serpent", *Purāṇa* 7.1 (1965) 144–9.

[64] "The Bhṛgus and the Bhārata: a Text-Historical Study", ABORI 18 (1936–7) 1–76.

some conclusions about the history of the Mahābhārata, among them that "there is a conscious—nay—deliberate weaving together or rather stitching together of the Bhārata legends with the Bhārgava myths",[65] that a Bhārgava influence shaped the epic in its formative period,[66] and that this influence is tendentious, conscious, and self-serving.

The theory of "Bhṛguization" has apparently been embraced by epicists generally,[67] in recent years most notably by Goldman.[68] There are two presuppositions of Sukthankar's theory, however, that are troubling. The first is that there existed at the time of the formation of the Mahābhārata a group of Bhārgavas who had a distinct, clan-based ideology and mythology, and who succeeded in taking over the redaction and transmission of the Mahābhārata. The second is that the Bhṛgu story material has no connection with the Bhārata story, that it is "entirely foreign to the plan of the original saga of the Bhāratas",[69] and that its inclusion in the epic can only be attributed to "ulterior motives".[70]

As to the first presupposition, neither Sukthankar nor any subsequent proponent of this theory, so far as I have been able to discover, has presented any epigraphical, textual or other historical evidence independent of the epic that demonstrates the existence of a distinct Bhārgava movement.

As to the second, there is a demonstrable connection between the Bhṛgu myth cycle and the Bhārata story, and that is the thematic parallel: the passing of an age, the extermination of a race, intervention and survival. This is evident in the Paraśurāma story itself, which takes place at the end of the Tretayuga, and where the Kṣatriya race is eradicated twenty-one times before Paraśurāma is persuaded to stop (3.115–7). In the Aurva story, which takes place at the close of the

---

[65] Sukthankar 70.

[66] ibid. 71.

[67] F. Weller, "Who were the Bhṛguids"? ABORI 18 (1936–7) 286–320, A.P. Karmarkar, "Dr. V.S. Sukthankar's Theory of the Bhṛguisation of the Original Bhārata and the light it throws on the Dravidian Problem", ABORI 20 (1939) 21–4, N.J. Shende, "The Authorship of the Mahābhārata", ABORI 24 (1943) 67–82, R.N. Dandekar, "The Mahābhārata", ABORI 24 (1943) 67–82, R.N. Dandekar, "The Mahābhārata: Origin and Growth", *University of Ceylon Review* 12.2 (1954) 65–85.

[68] "Akṛtavraṇa vs. Srīkṛṣṇa as Narrators of the Legend of Bhārgava Rāma . . . ", ABORI 53 (1970) 161–73, "Vālmīki and the Bhṛgu Connection", JAOS 96.1 (1976) 97–101, *Gods, Priests, and Warriors* (New York: Columbia Univ., 1977). And yet the value of Goldman's own work on the Bhṛgus, especially *Gods, Priests, and Warriors*, does not rest on the validity of Sukthankar's claims about Bhrguization.

[69] Sukthankar 70.

[70] ibid. 67.

Kṛtayuga, the Kṣatriyas of the world are blinded by Aurva, who then undertakes to destroy the whole world by *tapas* before he is stopped by the intervention of his ancestors (1.169–71).

Other apocalyptic practises fill the epic—the burning of the Khāṇḍava forest (1.214–25), the Rākṣasa rite of Parāśara (1.172), Ruru's vow to kill all the snakes in the world (1.8–12), Ayodhyan Parikṣit's plan to kill all the frogs in the world (3.191), Aśvatthāman's unleashing of the all-consuming *brahmāstra* (10.13), and so on.

In all these stories the same thematic elements are discernible, the intention of causing total annihilation, then intervention and survival. They bear on the main story of the Bhāratas, which must always have had epochal themes. It lacks sensibility to maintain that they bear no relation.

Furthermore, more precedent needs to be adduced for the notion that a popular epic is subject to the kinds of manipulation suggested by the theory of Bhṛguization. What collective audience would readily accept the reworking of their favorite stories so that they were freighted with an unfamiliar ideology? Neoplatonic allegorical interpretations of Homer had no impact on the "effective history" of the Iliad and Odyssey. Why should we assume that in India a distinct group could take hostage the product of an entire culture, an epic, moreover, that itself suggests a history of conforming to the interests of its listeners?

I have no doubt that the Bhārgava story cycle fits together as a mythological system, as Goldman has shown. No doubt its origins were separate from the Bhārata story. I suggest only that, based on what we know now of the dynamics of traditional oral narrative, we reconsider the process that brought the Bhṛgu material into the Mahābhārata, and that we lay aside what amounts to a conspiracy theory of epic composition.

The motif of eradication of snakes by fire is not unique to the Mahabharata or even Indic literature. Winternitz has already remarked on the comparable folklore and folk practise in Central Europe, where legends of the incineration of snakes in ritual fires were once current.[71] The larger themes of the Mahābhārata, the passing of an age and the extinction of a race, are shared by other epic traditions.[72] But in the artful rendition of the Mahābhārata story, the story of snakes and the story of heroes are made to interlock and to complement each other.

---

[71] "The Serpent Sacrifice Mentioned in the Mahābhārata", JBBRAS 2.1 (1926) 74–91.

[72] See for example, Hiltebeitel, *Ritual of Battle* 299–335.

KṚṢṆA: IN DEFENCE OF A DEVIOUS DIVINITY

BIMAL KRISHNA MATILAL

I. *The Enigma*

Kṛṣṇa is an enigma in the *Mahābhārata*. He represents the most confusing kind of moral enigma not only in the epic, but also in the whole of Hindu ideal of dharma. In the icons, he is represented as the Dark Lord, an attractive appearance with a face bearing an enigmatic, mysterious and mischievous smile, the smile, very much unike the famous smile found in the icons of the Buddha. The Buddha's smile, in striking contrast with that of Kṛṣṇa, is straightforward, it radiates with compassion, calmness and peace, it strikes confidence in the minds of the viewers. The ethical doctrine of the Buddha is also straightforward. It is novel, but non-complex. The ethical doctrine of Kṛṣṇa by contrast is different, sometimes it appears to be just the opposite.

Kṛṣṇa is a riddle, a paradox. If anything, he appears to be a devious diplomat. Why should he, as he does, claim to be the Supreme Being, the Ultimate Reality, the Inner Controller of every being? If he is God, then God must be a great diplomat, greatly devious, in whom diplomacy was the other name of duplicity and fraud. Western Indologists, by and large, have been very critical of Kṛṣṇa's ethics and politics. The following may sum up the opinion of the majority of Western Indologists as well as some West-inspired Indian Indologists.

> "A bizarre figure"! A Yādava chieftain who looks and acts not uncommonly like a mortal—and a very ordinary mortal at that—and who has the incredible effrontery to say that he is a god! A cynic who preaches the highest morality and stoops to practice the lowest tricks, in order to achieve his mean ends! An opportunist who teaches an honest and godfearing man to tell a lie, the only lie he had told in his life! A charlatan who declares himself to be the god of gods, descended from the highest heaven for establishing righteousness on earth, and advises a hesitating archer to strike down a foe who is defenceless and crying for mercy"![1]

---

[1] The extract is from p. 95 of V.S. Sukthankar's posthumous publication, *On the Meaning of the Mahābhārata*, Bombay 1975, where the source was not mentioned.

Such opinion about Kṛṣṇa is not simply restricted to Western Indology, the Jains and the Buddhists were also highly critical of the ethics of Kṛṣṇa.

In fact, the author of the Mahābhārata himself supplied a strikingly candid list of the misdeeds perpetrated by Kṛṣṇa through the mouth of dying Duryodhana. When Duryodhana was struck down by Bhīma in an unlawful manner (it was *de facto* hitting below the belt breaking the ethical code of the mace-fight), and was dying, he took Kṛṣṇa to task for his questionable part in the battle of Kurukṣetra. In a way Duryodhana was right. According to him, Kṛṣṇa broke the moral code of Dharma in more ways than one, whenever he found it suitable for ensuring victory for the Pāṇḍavas. Duryodhana called Kṛṣṇa, son of a slave for his father Vāsudeva was sort of a slave of King Kaṃsa.

Duryodhana continued to point out, that it was Kṛṣṇa who advised Arjuna to place Śikhaṇḍin in front while attacking Bhīṣma, knowing that the grandsire would not fight Śikhaṇḍin and would let himself be mortally wounded without resistance. It was Kṛṣṇa again who prevailed upon Yudhiṣṭhira to utter that deadly lie which finally led to the killing of the great warrior and revered teacher Droṇācārya. Even the death of Karṇa was brought about by Arjuna who attacked him in a cowardly manner when the former was engaged in lifting his chariot-wheel from the mud in which it got stuck. And it was Kṛṣṇa who persuaded Arjuna to kill the invincible Karṇa in this manner. It was Kṛṣṇa again who instigated Sātyaki to butcher Bhūriśravas when his right arm had been cut off. Thus the misdeeds of Kṛṣṇa were well-known and that they cannot be justified on moral grounds was, on the surface, very obvious to any religious believer in traditional India. Can any of these be defended?

The contradictions in Kṛṣṇa's activities as well as in his professed ethical doctrines are self-evident. The Hindu believers were not unaware of them, but still they had been undaunted by such contradictions. The list of contradictions supplied in the above extract stands out, no matter what. But still a tradition that is just about 2000 years old has unconsciously believed that these contradictions must have either some deeper significance, or some plausible explanation. In fact, Kṛṣṇa is not a god, but *the* God for the Hindus, and yet he is very different from the God of Judeo–Christian tradition, or the Allah of Islam. I am not suggesting that there are many gods in the worlds today, but obviously there are many conceptions of God which have been around and well-entrenched in world religions.[2] So we may ask, what was the Hindu

---

[2] For an earlier comment on the different conceptions of God in the Indian tradition, see my *Logical and Ethical Issues of Religious Belief*, Calcutta, 1982, pp. 23–41.

conception of God that was enshrined in the Kṛṣṇa of the *Mahābhārata*?

Let us select a typical case of almost unpardonable violation of the moral principal by Kṛṣṇa from the story of the *Mahābhārata*. In many cases, Kṛṣṇa unquestionably appears to be the person who "preaches the highest morality and stoops to practice the lowest tricks to achieve his mean ends". It is indeed a mystery how a moral hero or a god who should be impartial and whose behaviour should be morally irreprehensible, can perpetrate such acts. However, let us take Kṛṣṇa to be a human being with superior intellect and with a superior sense of justice, fairness and moral responsibility. Then we may begin to understand the puzzle a little.

The battle of Kurukṣetra is the focal point of the *Mahābhārata*, and certainly Kṛṣṇa played a very important role in this battle. He did not fight, but certainly the battle was won by the Pāṇḍavas because of Kṛṣṇa's presence on the Pāṇḍava side, because of his support and advice. He was the supreme manipulator, who did not shoot a single arrow or use a single weapon to kill anyone, but all the main characters were killed by his superior strategy through behind-the-door manipulation. Kṛṣṇa as we have seen above had something to do with the killing of each of the following heroes: Bhīsma, Droṇa Karṇa and Duryodhana. And each time it was through a means that violated the well-known moral codes of any battle between Kṣatriyas. Duryodhana was absolutely right in his accusation of Kṛṣṇa. Even the author of the *Mahābhārata* agreed, and we are told that Duryodhana after his death ascended to heaven before the Pāṇḍavas.

II. *The Just War?*

The battle of Kurukṣetra was described as a *dharmayuddha*. But in what sense was it a *dharmayuddha*? How should we translate the expression "*Dharmayuddha*"? The word "dharma" is an enigmatic term. According to standard interpretation "*dharmayuddha*" can be translated as "the war of righteousness". It has the resonance of the concept of the "just war" in Christian tradition. The first verse of the Bhagavad-Gītā describes the battle-field as "Dharmakṣetra"[3]—the field where the seeds of moral merit/demerit are sown in order to bring forth the harvest of *Karma* or just desert. But what exactly is the point of the imagery? Sometimes, a war is described as a case of "just war", when it is undertaken with a view to protect certain moral and religious values. Was the battle of

---

[3] The first line runs as follows: *dharmakṣetre kurukṣetre samavetā yuyutsavaḥ*". See *Bhagavad Gītā*, any edition.

Kurukṣetra an example of this kind of "just war"? This has no easy answer. It is a very simplistic assumption that the world can be divided into black and white, that whenever a war, or even a just war breaks out, the two opposite sides would represent unalloyed good and unalloyed evil. In actual cases, it is almost impossible to decide that one side fights for the just cause while the other side represents the absolute evil. Good and evil, right and wrong, are never given in their unalloyed states—a fact, which along with the other well-known questions about whether such values are relative or absolute, situational or universal makes it almost impossible for us to give any uncontroversial verdict of moral judgement. Thus it is that I find it impossible to agree with those who wish to interpret the battle in the Epic as an allegory of the battle between good and evil. All we can say that the Pāṇḍava side was the "preferred" side, preferred by the author or authors and readers alike, while the Kaurava side was not so. There was greatness on both sides, both tried to maintain a set of moral principles and projects, a set of values and virtues. And there were many evil acts perpetrated by both sides, both stooped to meanness, to devious and devilish strategies, to conquer. But perhaps one side was more abrasive and more arrogant than the other. And if we put the immoral acts and wickedness of both sides, the Pāṇḍavas and the Kauravas, on the weighing scales, it may be that the latter will not be heavier than the former, except perhaps for a couple of greatly grotesque, grossly unjust acts by Duryodhana. The world in fact cannot be divided into black and white, but it contains only innumerable shades of grey areas. The epic represents the world exactly as such—paradoxically there was more realism in the epic than some of our present-day realistic novels. The situation actually presents us with what Isaac Levi[4] has called "Hard Choices" under unresolvable moral dilemmas.

If the *Mahābhārata* imparts a moral lesson, it emphasizes again and again, the ever-elusive character, the unresolved ambiguity of the concept of *dharma*. Kṛṣṇa's role was not to resolve the ambiguity but to heighten the mystery, which offered only temporary glimpses of the human and moral realities lying behind the stories, myths, allegories and illustrations.

I believe the battle was called *dharmayuddha* in a technical sense. One technical sense of this many-faceted word *dharma* is this. It means the code of conduct agreed upon and observed by a particular group or

[4] Isaac Levi, *Hard Choices*, Cambridge, 1986.

community. *Dharma* (in this sense) is what one should or should not do in a particular domain of human behaviour. In the beginning of the battle of Kurukṣetra, in the *Bhīṣma-Parvan*, we get a long list of *Dharmas* comprising the code of conduct of each Kṣatriya when they are engaged in a battle with the adversary. Both sides agreed to fight a war on the basis of fairness by observing a number of familiar rules and practices on humanitarian grounds. Nobody, for example, should fight and kill a person who is running away from the battlefield, nobody should attack an unarmed and defenceless person, and so on and so forth—rules that are very similar to that of the war conventions prevalent in any civilized society today. Fighting must be between equals, a charioteer should fight another charioteer, horsemen should fight horsemen. It may be that this battle was called *dharmayuddha* because both sides agreed to observe this *dharma*.[5]

It is of course clear that most of these rules were violated at different crucial moments of the war, and on the Pāṇḍava side Kṛṣṇa undoubtedly was instrumental in the decision to violate the norms. Hence, he seemed to be the devious manipulator, without whose help, the battle would not have been won by the Pāṇḍavas.

Suppose Kṛṣṇa was playing the role of the omnipotent lord. What could have happened? Was it possible for him to end the battle of Kurukṣetra in one day? An omnipotent lord could have done it. After all, he wanted the Pāṇḍavas to win. At every stage, we see him very unsure and concerned about the outcome of the battle. He knew about the superior strength of the rival side, and hence was afraid that the fight might be lost. Therefore he was planning and plotting all the time to avoid disasters for the Pāṇḍavas. This certainly does not testify to the fact of his being the omnipotent lord. Nor does the trickery which he frequently resorted to on behalf of the Pāṇḍavas, prove his God-like moral superiority.

Take the case of Kṛṣṇa's advice to Yudhiṣṭhira to tell a lie—the only lie he had told in his life—the lie that was calculated to kill the great teacher and fighter Droṇa.[6] This was perhaps one of the darkest deeds of

---

[5] See the "Bhīṣma-Parva", of the *Mahābhārata*, critical edition, Poona. I have discussed this issue in my *Yukti, Niti O Dharma* (in Bengali), Calcutta, 1988, pp. 13–16.

[6] Yadāśrauṣaṃ Droṇam ācāryam ekaṃ
Dhṛṣṭadyumnenābhyatikramya dharmam
Rathopasthe prāyagataṃ viśastam
tadā nāśaṃse vijayāya Sañjaya, verse 143 1.1.143.
"I did not hope hope for victory, O Sañjaya, when I heard that the teacher, Droṇa, was slaughtered by Dhṛṣṭadyumna. Dharma was thus violated for Droṇa at that time was sitting in his chariot unarmed."

our "dark Lord" Kṛṣṇa. One question that is not often asked is this: Kṛṣṇa was almost as venerable to the author or the story-tellers as he is to us today, but then why did he (or they) not, using the unbounded freedom of any story-teller or narrator, formulate the story in such a way that would have made Kṛṣṇa a patently obvious moral hero without such glaring blemishes in his character? Why this deliberate attempt at mystifying the issues, if this is what it is? I believe the answer is not very obvious, but there are implicit hints scattered all over the text, hints that might be collected and put together in such a way as would dissolve a greater part of the mystery. In fact there may be alternative ways of interpreting the text that we have received in the tradition and hence I would suggest only one such possible alternative which may not seem to be improbable at all.

III. *Truth and the Question of Survival*

Droṇa was a great hero, venerable teacher of both the Kauravas and the Pāṇḍavas but his behaviour had not always been ideal.[7] He was, to be sure, instrumental in bringing about the inglorious death of the boy warrior Abhimanyu, who was killed being attacked jointly by seven great warriors including Droṇa. And Droṇa was the ring-leader of the inglorious Seven! So he had already violated the *dharma* i.e. the moral code of warfare. It was highly immoral to kill a boy who was fighting most heroically all alone against the seven formidable adversaries.

It is interesting to note here another earlier episode in the *Ādiparvan* for it has implications for moral lessons or moral teachings of the Kauravas and the Pāṇḍavas. Droṇa was a Brahmin teacher, but he was an expert in archery and the art of warfare. He was appointed by Dhṛtarāṣṭra as the teacher of all the princes, the Kauravas and the Pāṇḍavas. He was apparently appointed to teach the art of warfare, how to fight and kill, but not any moral lessons or war ethics. Once Bhīṣma, the grand-father, wondered: who was taking care of the moral lessons to be imparted to the princes, the Kauravas and the Pāṇḍavas when they were growing up? He first thought it was the duty of Droṇa. So he approached Droṇa and enquired whether the latter was teaching moral lessons to the princes, along with the lessons in archery. Droṇa answered in the negative. When Bhīsma insisted further, Droṇa went to the paymaster Dhṛtarāṣṭra and asked. Dhṛtarāṣṭra said that Droṇa's

---

[7] See Droṇa-Parva of the *Mahābhārata*, critical edition, Poona.

appointment was solely for the purpose of teaching archery, and the art of fighting and killing, and he should not bother about teaching any moral lesson. This apparently satisfied Droṇa. This also throws some light upon the character of Dhṛtarāṣṭra—a fact we should recall when we analyse the character of the blind king as well as his characteristic repentance in the Ādiparva.

The episode unveils at least two facts. (a) The princes did not have any formal teaching in morality and ethics. The Pāṇḍavas probably received it from Bhīṣma, to whom Kauravas did not pay any heed. (b) Droṇa himself did not have much regard for moral lessons. His behaviour was generally within the bounds of morality, but sometimes he transgressed them. One may be reminded here of the story of Ekalavya, in which Droṇa's behaviour was abominable.

Briefly, the story is this. Ekalavya belonged to the lower caste, but he wanted to be one of the best archers of his time. He approached Droṇa, the most well-known teacher of archery at that time, but the latter refused because Eakalvya was born in a lower caste and Droṇa's brahminical background found it undignified. In other words, Droṇa lacked the generosity, open-mindedness and other moral virtues which a proper Brahmin (a sage like Gautama in Chāndogya Upaniṣad, for example) should have possessed. It is well-known that sage Gautama did not reject Satyakāma (who came to study under him) when the latter said that he was the son of his unwed mother and hence he was unable to tell his father's name or his family name. Gautama embraced the child with affection, accepted him as a student and decided that he must qualify as a Brahmin for his exemplary virtues, such as truthfulness. But Droṇa was no Gautama. Being rejected, Ekalavya went to a secluded place in the forest, created an image of Droṇa and, accepting that image as his guru for ritualistic initiation as well as inspiration, started learning archery all by himself! He was later discovered by Droṇa and his pupils (the princes) who went to forest one day on a hunting expedition. Droṇa saw to his utter surprise that Ekalavya's self-taught archery had been so good that he could excel Arjuna, his most favourite pupil. He played one of the dirtiest tricks upon young Ekalvya, who still claimed Droṇa to be his *guru* (in archery) in absentia. Droṇa claimed his *guru-dakṣiṇā* (present for the teacher after the completion of the training) from Ekalavya. He asked the latter to cut off his right thumb and make a present of it to his adopted guru, Droṇa, which Ekalavya did immediately by showing his exemplary courage, integrity and truthfulness. Of course, this meant the end of Ekalavya as an archer. In the background of such adorable self-sacrifice, Droṇa's heartlessness and total absence of any moral sensitivity in his character had been shown in sharp relief. Tradition justly condemned Droṇa and glorified Ekalavya who excelled not only in physical strength or archery but also in moral virtues. Let us now return to the battle of Kurukṣetra.

On the fifteenth day of the battle Droṇa became almost irresistible in his attempt to kill the entire army of the Pāṇḍavas and obtain victory for the Kauravas. Kṛṣṇa saw it in the beginning: If Droṇa could not be stopped that day, battle would end in another way. What could not have been done by strength apparently, was accomplished through a trick. And it was Kṛṣṇa's trick. Bhīma killed an elephant called Aśvatthāmā and proclaimed that he had killed Aśvatthāmā (which was also the name of Droṇa's only son). Kṛṣṇa saw a chance. He knew about Droṇa's love for his son and realized that the news of his son's death would have at least temporarily made him vulnerable. But the son was not dead. Droṇa ignoring the rumour continued to fight. He also started killing a number of Pāṇḍava soldiers while they were running away from the battlefield. So the moral code of dharma was again broken and the *Dharmayuddha* turned into an *Adharmayuddha*. Some celestial sages, who were watching the battle, approached Droṇa in their subtle bodies and took him to task for stooping to meanness and violating the ethical code of warfare. Instead of setting an example of greatness, the conduct of the great *ācārya* became again abominable. Being scolded by the celestial sages Droṇa paused for a moment. Kṛṣṇa was looking for this opportunity. Droṇa wanted to know whether the rumour about the death of his son was true. If Yudhiṣṭhira told him he would have believed it. Kṛṣṇa already had convinced Yudhiṣṭhira that since the life of everybody on the Pāṇḍava side was at stake and the dream of final victory would certainly be shattered, Yudhiṣṭhira would have to make a compromise and tell a *tactical* lie. The trick worked and Droṇa was killed.

Why do we feel quite embarrassed and upset about this rather sordid affair? There was plenty of such affairs described in the epic from the beginning to the end, and both sides had their share to contribute. But why is this particularly painful for us? I believe the answer lies in the fact that the two most important and presumably venerable characters are involved—one is Kṛṣṇa, who is supposed to be an incarnation of the Lord and presumably the upholder of justice, morality and dharma, and the other is Yudhiṣṭhira, who is also Dharma incarnate, who is not supposed to deviate from his high and lofty ideal of truthfulness. And yet it is a classic case of backsliding. Yudhiṣṭhira's lie was not even a "white lie", it was the "darkest of the dark",—deliberately lying to deceive his teacher and thereby ensuring the opponent's death and victory for his own side. It was a deliberate lie calculated to regain his throne. What can be a more selfish goal than this? And Yudhiṣṭhira was persuaded to take this course! I believe this exposes one of the fatal weaknesses in Yudhiṣṭhira's own character. The author's characterization became more lively by the portrayal of such paradoxicality and conflict of values. Yudhiṣṭhira was not a simple, lifeless, abstract painting of Dharma. He represented a human prince who had all the adorable virtues but had some serious flaws in his character—he had a vice, he was addicted to gambling. He did his utmost to protect the Dharma-morality and the ideal of truthfulness, but also failed, like all humans, on one or two crucial occasions. Lying on this occasion was such a case and he lost his moral reward. It was Arjuna who said at that time that this act of lying would be an indelible blemish in Yudhiṣṭhira's noble character.

It would be wrong to construe from this that the ideal of truthfulness should therefore be compromised sometimes in this way. For the ideal had not been compromised at all. The story-teller leaves no doubt in our mind that there had been an almost unpardonable violation of a very noble principle (truth-telling) here. Yudhiṣṭhira had to suffer accordingly. The weakness of the will once more got better of even Dharmarāja Yudhiṣṭhira.

In fact Yudhiṣṭhira lacked firmness, which must be an essential characteristic of a moral hero. Yudhiṣṭhira suffered from such weakness. This is also illustrated by his weakness for gambling. On the other hand, he had the stubbornness of a tragic hero. This is shown by his stubbornness in gambling, even when he was losing one stake after another.

IV. *The Divine Attributes*

How about Kṛṣṇa? He was the manipulator. To use the terminology of Pāṇini's grammar, he was the *prayojaka kartā*. He had the moral responsibility for almost all the important decisions of the Pāṇḍavas. One may argue that although it was emphasized that "*yato dharmas tato jayaḥ*" ("victory belongs to the party where *dharma* belongs), it was actually the case that "*yataḥ Kṛṣṇaḥ tato jayaḥ*", i.e. victory belonged to the party where Kṛṣṇa belonged.

> upaplavye Maharṣir yo Kṛṣṇadvaipāyano'–bravīt
> yato dharmastato Kṛṣṇo yataḥ Kṛṣṇaḥ tato jayaḥ
>
> (*Mahābhārata* 9.61. 30)
>
> (Kṛṣṇa Dvaipāyana, during the disaster said "Where there is *dharma* there is Kṛṣṇa, and where there is Kṛṣṇa there is victory")

Here Kṛṣṇa bears the entire responsibility. But the story-teller does not make Kṛṣṇa, the alleged Lord of the universe, an omnipotent being, and bring about this victory through his magical or supernatural power. Apparently this is the biggest mystery. If we can have a reasonable explanation of this mystery, we can find answers to most of our puzzlement about Kṛṣṇa's doings.

According to the received doctrine, God is supposed to be omnipotent and He should also see that justice is done in the end. But Kṛṣṇa in the *Mahābhārata* did not always claim to be omnipotent. Apart from certain inspired speeches (e.g. in the *Gītā*) he acknowledged his human limitations. He admitted before the hermit Utaṅka how powerless he was to stop the devastating war, and restore friendship between the two warring families. For as he said, the war was inevitable, and he had no power to stop the inevitable.

Kṛṣṇa's own admission that he did not have any power to stop the battle or devastation either of the Kauravas or of the Yādavas (his own race) is an important evidence to show that the Hindu conception of God does not always include the attribute of Omnipotence. I believe this constitutes an important difference between Judaeo-Christian theology and Hindu theology. Words such as *Īśvara* or *Bhagavān* are often used to denote what is called "God" in the Western tradition, but these words do have a number of meanings in the Indian tradition. God in Hindu theology is not always a creator God—that is, he is not a Creator *ex nihilo*. Nor is the Hindu God always a personal being. In the case of Kṛṣṇa or Rāma, he is of course conceived as a personal being, in fact a human being with all possible human virtues and vices. Of course, it has been claimed that Kṛṣṇa (or Rāma) was mightier than anybody else, had intelligence superior to that of anybody else, but this is hardly equivalent to the claim of omnipotence or even omniscience.

Omnipotence is not an important concept in Indian philosophy of religion. It has been generally pointed out that the problem of evil was not regarded by the philosophers of India as a serious flaw in the Hindu conception of God. Some Indologists have argued that the problem of evil was not important for Indians because evil was not real but an illusion. In other words this attitude was connected with the transfictional approach to the reality of the Indian philosophers in general. This may be so. However, there is another line of explanation. I believe, the problem of evil never posed a serious threat to the concept of Theos in India because the attribute of Omnipotence was never seriously emphasised. For the problem of evil becomes a serious problem if the problems of the two attributes of God are jointly emphasised in the context: Omnipotence and perfect goodness of God. We might also add Omniscience to the list. As we have seen, the concept of Kṛṣṇa as God does not include omnipotence. He was mightier than anybody else but he was not omnipotent.

The concept of God however must include a reference to morality and justice. This is even true of the dominant Hindu conception of God. In this respect, as we all know, the character of Kṛṣṇa comes under serious criticism. Examples of Kṛṣṇa's violation of ordinary moral principles are too numerous. Let us see briefly how he defended this move once. At the final stage of the battle, when Bhīma and Duryodhana were locked in a mace-fight, Arjuna asked Kṛṣṇa about the relative strength of the two combattants, and the possible outcome. Kṛṣṇa replied in no uncertain terms that while Bhīma was physically stronger than Duryodhana, the latter was a better mace-fighter than the former and then added:

> If Bhīma fights according to Dharma (approved ethical code of conduct), he will not win. Hence he should kill Duryodhana by breaking the moral rule (*anyāyena*).
>
> (*Mahābhārata*, 9.57.4.)

Kṛṣṇa continued to justify this breach of ethical conduct. He said that we had heard that the demons were defeated by the gods in a deceitful fight (*māyayā*). Similarly Virocana was defeated by Indra by unlawful means, and Vṛtra was defeated in a similar manner. Besides, Bhīma had already promised to break the thigh of Duryodhana by the stroke of his mace. Hence there was no other way but to resort to this deceitful means for destroying Duryodhana. For Kṛṣṇa was confident that a fair battle at that time would steal the victory away from the Pāṇḍavas. Kṛṣṇa said that Yudhiṣṭhira "had done it again". By agreeing to accept the outcome of the duel between Bhīma and Duryodhana as the final decisive factor of the entire battle of Kurukṣetra, Yudhiṣṭhira had put the prospect of final victory in grave danger; Kṛṣṇa had no illusion about it. He said:

> "Having won the battle, he is now throwing it away".
>
> (*Mahābhārata* 9.57.10)

It is significant to note that Kṛṣṇa gave two different sets of arguments to justify Bhīma's unlawful killing of Duryodhana. To pacify Balarāma He said that Bhīma took a vow of breaking Duryodhana's thigh during the fatal and deceitful gambling match where innocent Draupadī was publicly humiliated for no fault of her own. To the Pāṇḍavas, however, he gave the other reason. In a lawful battle, Bhīma would have been defeated by the superior technique of Duryodhana and hence the whole battle of Kurukṣetra would have been decided in favour of the Kauravas. I shall further expand the nature of Kṛṣṇa-logy or Kṛṣṇa's divinity by first referring to the story of Utaṅka.

The Utaṅka episode is interesting in itself.[8] The encounter between Kṛṣṇa and Utaṅka took place, after the devastating battle was over. Kṛṣṇa was apparently going back from Hastināpura to Dvārakā. On his way, in the desert of Rajasthan, he met the great hermit Utaṅka and accepted his hospitality for the day. Utaṅka regarded Kṛṣṇa as an *avatāra* of Lord Viṣṇu. He was also unaware that the great battle had already taken place, and everybody had died except a few fortunate warriors. He therefore asked Kṛṣṇa in confidence whether the Lord had been able to settle the quarrel between the two families, and had been successful in avoiding the devastating war. When the good hermit learned what had happened, he was visibly upset and accused Kṛṣṇa of all the evil doings. He insisted that Kṛṣṇa must have the full responsibility for all the evils of the war, simply by letting it happen when he could have stopped it. Kṛṣṇa then answered that it was unstoppable, even by Kṛṣṇa himself. It was impossible to stop something in the middle. The process of devastation started much earlier, started by both sides through their enmity, greed, jealousy and hatred. It was true that the Kauravas wanted to take over the whole kingdom by getting rid of the Pāṇḍavas by hook or by crook. But it was again the Pāṇḍavas who were abrasive and arrogant enough to insult Duryodhana and the Kauravas in the *Sabhāparva*. The root of hostility was too deep to be uprooted at a later time, but Kṛṣṇa did whatever he could and tried his best to see that justice was done towards the end. A god does not have to be omnipotent, but he could be noble enough to see that justice is done in the end. It is significant to know that after Duryodhana's fall, Kṛṣṇa greeted King Yudhiṣṭhira with a long speech, which was interspersed with the expression "*Diṣṭyā Vardhase*" ("luckily you have achieved the victory)". It was a plain admission that the Pāṇḍavas won against all odds because of luck, not through the omnipotence of Kṛṣṇa.

V. *The Force of Evil and Human Freedom*

Western philosophers and theologians have pondered throughout the ages over the intelligibility of the divine attributes, such as omnipotence, omniscience and perfect goodness. St. Thomas and St. Augustine are well-known for their formulation of these attributes in a faultless manner. In recent times, Anthony Kenny, Peter Geach, A. Plantinga, Nelson Pike and others of the analytical tradition have discussed these issues to

---

[8] See Āśvamedhika-Parva of the *Mahābhārata*, critical edition, Poona.

connect them with the contemporary problems of philosophy. Many old issues have been revived but several new dimensions have been added to them. I find some of these issues are strikingly relevant to our discussion of Kṛṣṇa in the Mahābhārata.

Recent discussion about the concept of God was triggered off by a paper written in 1955 by J.L. Mackie called "Evil and Omnipotence". The discussion rolled on, and Mackie in his posthumous writing, *The miracles of Theism*, modified his earlier formulation. Instead of calling his formulation of the problem of evil a genuine paradox, he described it as an undecidable question. There is no need to rehearse the well-known arguments here. Geach (1973) and Kenny (1970) both have agreed that the strictly philosophical notion of omnipotence is not essential for Western Theism.[9] The notion of *Almighty*, in the sense of having power over all things would be enough, according to these philosophers, to be compatible with Western theology. We may follow a similar move in defining Kṛṣṇa's power. In fact, in Kṛṣṇa-theology (or should we say Kṛṣṇalogy?) we need to modify the notion of creator-God, following such Hindu philosophical systems as the Sāṃkhya and the Nyāya-Vaiśeṣika.

According to the Sāṃkhya school, the material world was never created but it evolved out of some unmanifest material form, the abode of all potentialities. Hence there is no Creator God. In fact in one section of the early Sāṃkya the category of God was declared as redundant. In Sāṃkya-Yoga system however, God was accepted as one, who was not the creator but the goal of the Yoga practices. In other words one can seek the help of such God and thereby achieve success or *siddhi*. The God of the Yogins (and Kṛṣṇa has sometimes been called Yogeśvana) is supposed to have the highest form of all adorable qualities of humans. He is perfectly good but he does not have to be omnipotent. Hence the conception is free from apparent incoherence. In fact the God of the Yoga system does not do anything on his own, but it is said that we can get something done or accomplished and proceed towards our ultimate goal if we resort to him through meditation or other practices.

The Nyāya-Vaiśeṣika conception of God is different. He can be called the Creator God but in a different sense. Since the material atoms are eternal entities and so are the human souls we cannot say that God has created them. However, it is at God's will that the atoms come together to create the gross universe where human beings have embodied exis-

[9] Geach, P.T. *Providence and Evil*, Cambridge, 1977; Kenny, A. *The God of the Philosophers*, Oxford, 1979.

tence and act freely. Although they act freely, i.e., they can choose between what is morally good and bad, they have to act under the constraint of the circumstances in which they are born. Birth and environment are not under their control. This conception of God seems compatible with the Kṛṣṇalogy of the Mahābhārata. Bhīṣma at the Rājasūya sacrifice of Yudhiṣṭhira selected Kṛṣṇa as the best of men and hence worthy of worship by all. He listed all the adorable virtues of Kṛṣṇa on that occasion.

There is another important divine attribute which the epic literature ascribes to Kṛṣṇa as the godhead. The Purāṇa literature usually speaks of three complementary aspects of the ultimate deity, the creator (personified in Brahmā), the preserver or protector (Viṣṇu), the destroyer (Rudra-Śiva). This trinity is not relevant for our purpose. What is important to note is that God is also the destroyer and in this aspect he is identified with Kāla or Mahākāla or Time. In the *Gītā*, Kṛṣṇa says "I am the Kāla and as Kāla I destroy the world".

Time or Eternity has often been regarded in Hindu religious literature as the great destroyer of everything, sometimes identified with the supreme deity. In the Vedas, there is an entire hymn devoted to Time where it was emphasised that everything originates in time, persists in time as well as perishes in time. In other words Time not only creates everything but also destroys everything. In the epic literature, Kṛṣṇa has often been identified with the destructive aspect of Time. As God, He cannot make the world a better place overnight where every being will forget their enmity and hatred towards each other and live in perfect peace and harmony. For every creature is free to perform his own Karma and thereby create his own destiny in which God should not intervene. But when the earth is full of hatred and enmity and sin, when Justice is at the risk of being trampled over for ever, when disasters after disasters imperil the very existence of being then the will of God may intervene in whatever way it can. This is called the theory of Hindu God, or Kṛṣṇalogy, that has been expounded in the third and fourth chapters of the Gītā.

Kṛṣṇa as Kāla is passionless, free from any human virtues. Here, if not anywhere else, end justifies the means. He told Arjuna that as Kāla He had already destroyed (was going to destory) all the kings of the Kauravas and the Pāṇḍavas. Next He would destroy His own Race the Yādavas. All these were needed to release the burden of sin. People with their freedom had acted following their instincts and thereby a "sad mess" had been created. Hence it was time to let loose the destructive power of the divinity. He, acting as the inner manipulator of every being, would bring about the intended destruction. Therefore He described himself as Kāla. Kāla is also identified sometimes with Yama, the God of

Death. We should remember that in the Rāmāyaṇa also the Kālapuruṣa appeared towards the end, to have a secret counsel with Rāma, which marked the beginning of the end of the Rāma story.

VI. *Justice*

In fact, it was an uphill task for anyone who would try to see that justice was done in the end. When the two sides were lined up for battle, it was clear that the Kauravas represented the stronger side by all counts. The Pāṇḍava side was weaker by comparison. On the other hand, it was the Pāṇḍavas who were deprived of their kingdom for thirteen years through trickery and fraud. But above all, the unprovoked insult inflicted upon the defenceless Draupadī in public was the last straw. This particular incident could be regarded as a turning point of the moral balance in the story. This was uncalled for and unprovoked and it was an unparadonable offence on the part of the Kauravas. From that point onwards, as I have already noted, it seems, the balance of justice tilted in favour of the Pāṇḍavas.

It has already been noted that the Pāṇḍava side was comparatively weaker. The weaker side can defeat a stronger side only with the help of a strategy, and strategies cannot always be restricted to fair and just means. There is a touch of realism here. Idealism would have demanded that the good be the victorious over the evil by following the ideally constructed strategies, which should always be fair. But our story-teller preferred realism. Our world is really an imperfect world, and this is all we have. Our story-teller's conception of God was not that of an Almighty Deity. Through the Utaṅka episode, our story-teller consciously raised the question of Omnipotence but rejected it in favour of realism, contingencies of situation (moral luck) and fatalism. Courses of certain events cannot be stopped. All that Kṛṣṇa was able to do was to salvage justice at the end of the battle. So the paradox became more and more underscored. In order to save justice towards the end, many unjust and immoral acts were perpetrated. But what kind of justice was this? A sense of justice that kills all other senses of justice? A policeman in hot pursuit of a criminal overturns many vehicles and kills many innocent people—a very common sight in modern T.V. But is this right? I believe that this is the ultimate puzzle. A puzzle that is realistic enough; for we even see it today all around us, but it is too frustrating to yield a solution.

Apart from the above puzzle there are several intricate problems that can be connected with the incident in the *Mahābhārata*. Let us articulate at least one of them. Yudhiṣṭhira's problem was one of moral integrity. He maintained a very high profile as far as dharma or morality was concerned. He never told a lie in his life. So one would expect him to be telling the truth always. But at Kṛṣṇa's advice, he lied to save his life. Hence there was a visible crack in his otherwise impeccable honesty and moral integrity. But how about Kṛṣṇa? What was his justification for giving this advice to Yudhiṣṭhira? He obviously compromised his moral integrity by choosing to give this advice. Was he acting as a utilitarian consequentialist? Perhaps not. For a consequentialist opts even for a little bit of well-being or happiness (that is, utility) when he violates a well-established moral principle.

For the consequentialist, the consequence must produce more well-being or more happiness. One can obviously produce an argument by which it will be shown that Kṛṣṇa as a moral agent gave up the principle of moral integrity (assuming that moral integrity is an excellence or value) in order to ensure victory for the right side, that was the Pāṇḍavas, or negatively, to avoid disastrous consequences of the defeat of the side which was more *just* than the other. The unpardonable humiliation of the defenceless Draupadī by Duryodhana has already been mentioned. That was also the reason Kṛṣṇa gave to Balarāma, when the latter became extremely angry seeing that Bhīma resorted to unlawful means to defeat and kill Duryodhana. So one may say that Kṛṣṇa as a moral agent gave up moral integrity to avoid a total miscarriage of justice in the end. But this consequence can hardly be measured in terms of happiness or even well-being. Anybody who has read the *Mahābhārata* can testify to the fact that the conclusion of the war contributed to nobody's happiness in particular. It did not contribute even to the well-being of the Pāṇḍavas. For this, one can simply read the laments of Yudhiṣṭhira after the war. Therefore, the outcome of this apparently deviant behaviour of Kṛṣṇa cannot be explained in the consequentialist's terms. On the other hand, could we argue that if Kṛṣṇa as well as Yudhiṣṭhira maintained his moral integrity, and did not stoop to this devious means of lying to Droṇa (and thereby leading the great teacher to his own doom), would the world have been a better place or would it have contributed to the general well-being of humanity? We cannot answer affirmatively here, for our inherent sense of justice would have suffered a set back and our very trust in the moral order of the Universe would have been impaired. For at least the story-teller made us increasingly aware how far the Kauravas went in their wickedness and immoral actions.

VII. *Good vs. The Best World*

Why do we feel embarrassed and definitely shocked at the conduct of Yudhiṣṭhira and Kṛṣṇa on this occasion? It is because our expectations were high, as far as the Pāṇḍavas and Kṛṣṇa were concerned. Had Duryodhana been involved we would not have thought it to be irregular. But from Kṛṣṇa we expected something better.

There may be another way of looking at this issue. Let us regard Kṛṣṇa as a moral agent here. It was his duty to uphold *dharma* which also included justice, at any cost. The exact nature of *dharma* has remained ever elusive, for it was never spelled out fully. Various stories in the *Mahābhārata* illustrate the point underlying the ever-elusive nature of *dharma*. Of course, *dharma* is mostly represented as a set of rigid moral principles or a rigid moral code of a given society. It was something like the honour code of a given community. It is assumed that to breach the code, is to lose one's honour and one's place in the social order, circumscribed by that moral code. But this rigidity can sometimes be challenged by a proper agent who has proven to be superior to others in the community both in talents and intelligence as well as in leadership qualities. This only acknowledges the possibility of what is called today "a paradigm shift". Sometimes it is possible for a leader to transcend or breach the rigid code of conduct valued in the society, with the sole idea of creating a new paradigm that will also be acknowledged and esteemed within that order. Our Kṛṣṇa might be looked upon as a leader of that sort. It may be that he created new paradigms for showing limitations of such a generally accepted moral code of truth-telling and promise-keeping. Sometimes situational constraints and the risk of the loss of the greater good might influence a rational agent to transgress certain valued principles. In this case one might say that a threat posed by Duryodhana's victory and the consequential loss of the chance for the restoration of justice, might have influenced Kṛṣṇa's decision to follow the devious course. All these are speculations, but I claim that they are not entirely absent from the moral concerns of the Indian people who have loved the epic for about two millenia. Certainly these speculations are not at all foundationless. The available evidence found in the tradition of the great epics of India lends support to such speculations. I believe the moral consciousness of the people found its expressions through such portrayal of dilemmas throughout the epic literature and the different versions of the epic stories at different times.[10]

I shall conclude this discussion by introducing a thought experiment. Suppose there is a divine creator who is also omnipotent and omniscent

[10] For other ethical issues connected with the moral dilemmas, see my "Moral Dilemmas: Insights from Indian Epics" in *Moral Dilemmas in the Mahābhārata* (ed. Bimal Krishna Matilal), I.I.A.S., Shimla, and Motilal Banarsidass, Delhi, 1989.

in some acceptable and coherent senses of these terms. Suppose also that he is about to create a world where the pre-existent matter and human souls would be the ingredients. How much choice is left to the creator under the circumstances to create an entirely new world? Suppose there are three possibilities—W_1, W_2 and W_3. W_1 stands for a world as science sometimes is said to conceive it. There is no value, no justice. Things happen mechanically following the scientific rules, properties of matter, and those who suffer and enjoy are only rational beings. There is no standard for good and evil. It is an amoral world.

W_2 stands for a world, which is much like that of ours. There is good as well as evil. There is human rationality; sometimes justice is done, sometimes evil forces try to suppress justice. But there is this persistent belief that good will win at the end.

W_3 stands for another world, which we can call the perfect world or the best of all the possible worlds. There is no evil. Or evil has no power over the good. Everybody is happy. But in such a way the meaning of happiness is perhaps lost. Or, nobody understands what unhappiness is.

Now, if a divine creator is faced with the choice of creating a world like any one of this, which particular one would He select? For various reasons into which I do not wish to go into here, I suggest that he would select W_2 i.e. world no. 2. Whether there is a creator God or not, whether Kṛṣṇa was a devious deity or not, this is the kind of world we have got and hence if justice can be salvaged in the end the creator will fulfil His promise.*

* I wish to thank The British Academy for funding the preliminary research for preparing this article.

REPETITION IN THE *MAHĀBHĀRATA*[1]

A.K. RAMANUJAN

(*1*)

No Hindu ever reads the *Mahābhārata* for the first time. And when he does get to read it, he doesn't usually read it in Sanskrit. As one such native, I know the Hindu epics, not as a Sanskritist (which I am not), but through Kannada and Tamil, mostly through the oral traditions. I've heard bits and pieces of it in a tailor shop where a pundit used to regale us with *Mahābhārata* stories and large sections of a sixteenth century Kannada text; from Brahmin cooks in the house; from an older boy who loved to keep us spellbound with it (and the Kannada *Arabian Nights* which he was reading in the Oriental Library) after cricket, in the evenings, under a large neem tree in a wealthy engineer's compound; from a somewhat bored algebra teacher who switched from the binomial theorem to the problems of Draupadī and her five husbands. Then there were professional bards who "did the Harikathā Kālakṣepam", redeeming the time with holy tales (and not always holy ones). They were invited into a neighborhood by a group or a wealthy man, and they would recite, sing and tell the *Mahābhārata* in sections night after night, usually under a temporary canopy (*pandal*) lit by petromax lanterns, with a floating audience sitting on rugs on the street and on the verandas of houses that lined the street now turned into a makeshift auditorium. They sang songs in several languages, told folktales, sometimes danced, quoted Sanskrit tags as well as the daily newspaper, and made the *Mahābhārata* entertaining, didactic and relevant to the listener's present.

The *Mahābhārata* provides materials and allusions to every artistic

[1] This essay on the *Mahābhārata* was originally written in 1968 and presented to Victor Turner's Seminar on Comparative Epic at the University of Chicago. I had thought that the paper was suggestive but needed extensive reworking, so I did not venture to publish it. I venture to do so now, twenty years later, urged and encouraged by the responses of *Mahābhārata* scholars like Alf Hiltebeitel, David Shulman, Narayana Rao, and Arvind Sharma—to all of whom I'm indebted. I have changed very little in the original paper, except that I've added new references. Other and better scholars have independently anticipated and explored some of the notions expressed in this early essay. Such corroborations are both a pain and a pleasure. I've added several of these references to the essay.

genre—from plays to proverbs, from folk performances to movies and TV. Indeed, the *Mahābhārata* and the *Rāmāyaṇa* have appeared as serials, week after week in popular Tamil weeklies. C. Rajagopalachari, the veteran statesman, who was dedicated to bringing traditional wisdom into modern politics, retold them in Tamil, and later translated them into English. When they were published by Bharatiya Vidya Bhavan, they became, and probably still are, the most-read paperback renditions in English of the epics. The *Mahābhārata* also occurs in various sizes and in many languages—from proverbs like "Whatever you say, Kunti's children have no kingdom" (Kannada: *antu intu kunti makkaḷige rājyavilla*) to one-or two-hour versions, to the South Indian Sanskrit redaction which has 100,000 stanzas. Then there are "translations", transpositions truly, into the many Indian mother tongues, extensions into active cults and local communal performances where Draupadī or the Pāṇḍavas possess the actors and members of the audience. Two of these possession cults, the Pāṇḍavlīla in Himachal Pradesh (Sax 1987) and especially the Draupadī cult (Hiltebeitel 1987) in Tamilnadu, have been studied in some detail.

Thus a text like the *Mahābhārata* is not a text but a tradition. It used to be every poet's ambition to write a *Rāmāyaṇa* or the *Mahābhārata*. Subramanya Bharati's best narrative poem is a Tamil reworking of Draupadī's vow (*Pāñcāli Capatam*), where Draupadī's public dishonour at the hands of the villain Duḥśāsana represents the plight of all women in a male society and it also represented the British oppression of "Mother India". The poem has recently become popular with street-theatre troupes in Tamilnadu who use it as their script. Several years ago, K.V. Puttappa won national honors for his *Rāmāyaṇa Darśanam* in Kannada, as V.S. Khandekar's Marathi novel *Yayāti* did. Recently Bhairappa, a well-known Kannada novelist, has written a long novel on the *Mahābhārata* story, giving it ethnographic interpretations. Two of the best modern plays, to mention only two, are Girish Karnad's *Yayāti* in Kannada and Dharam Vir Bharati's *Andhāyug* in Hindi, both inspired by the epic. So was Shyam Benegal's Hindi film *Kaliyug*.

The size of the *Mahābhārata* appalls non-Indian readers. It is said to be eight times the size of the *Odyssey* and the *Iliad* put together. "What is here may be elswhere. But what is not here is nowhere else", says a verse in praise of the text. Another such verse says, "The whole world is Vyāsa's leftovers"—he has tasted, chewed and digested whole worlds. Both the *Bhagavad Gītā* and the story of the Goose That Laid the Golden Eggs are in its maw.

Yet the main, complex, many-storied plot of this enormous epic is remembered and recalled in great detail by most traditional Hindus. Such recall is possible because it is a *structured* work. In a largely oral traditon, one learns one's major literary works as one learns a language—in bits and pieces that fit together and make a whole in the learner's mind, because they are parts that reflect an underlying structure. Later tradition calls the *Mahābhārata* an *itihāsa* " that's the way it was" or a "history", not a *kāvya*, "poem", denying it structure and composition. Yet the great Sanskrit aesthetician, Ānandavardhana, treats the main epic story as a poem with a coherent central mood, all its parts and plots and characters cohering into a final sense of *śānta rasa* or "tranquillity" (Tubb 1985).Whether we agree with that description or not, it is clear that Ānandavardhana saw it not as an unstuctured monster but as a well-formed whole. Recent Indian and Western scholars have talked of hundreds of interpolations in the text; they see the work as a "loose-leaf file of palm leaves" with a knot (*grantha*) that holds the leaves together, to which anything at all could be, and was, added by anyone at all at different times. The name Vyāsa, they point out, indicated an "editor", a "compliler", not an author. Yet all these descriptions belie and deny the native's sense of its unity, its well-plotted network of relations. Only the "epic" is what's known everywhere in the regional languages, what the native speaker and listener remembers vividly and without fail. The so-called Brahminical "pseudo-epic", which is not "pseudo" but an integral part of the Sanskrit epic, and the many discourses (including the *Gītā*) are not recited as part of the story in the oral traditions or in the endless reworkings and abridgements in the mother-tongues, in oral and written traditions.

The present attempt is to explicate a "native intuition", the intricate sense of structure and unity in this ten-mile monster of a work. I use "intuition" not in any occult sense, but as linguists use it—the sense that every native speaker has of the grammar of his mother tongue which makes him speak grammatically and judge what is or is not grammatical.

(*2*)

I'd suggest that the central structuring principle of the epic is a certain kind of repetition. One might say that repetition or replication is the central principle of any structuring. What occurs only once does not allow us to talk of structure. *Einmal ist keinmal*—it's as if what happens once doesn't happen at all. Students of narrative like Propp, Levi-Strauss, Dumézil, and J. Hillis Miller have made this idea a commonplace. Indian artworks, like the Hindu temple, or the decads (*pattu*) of Tamil classical or bhakti poetry, or the rāgas of Karnatak music, are built on the principle of interacting structures of repetition and elaboration and variation. Not only are there repetitive phrases, similes, and formulaic descriptions that the students of oral poetics (Parry, Lord, et. al.) have taught us to recognize, but incidents, scenes, settings, and especially relationships are repeated. Let us look at one large overarching example of replicated relationships.

Here is a genealogical chart of the main characters.

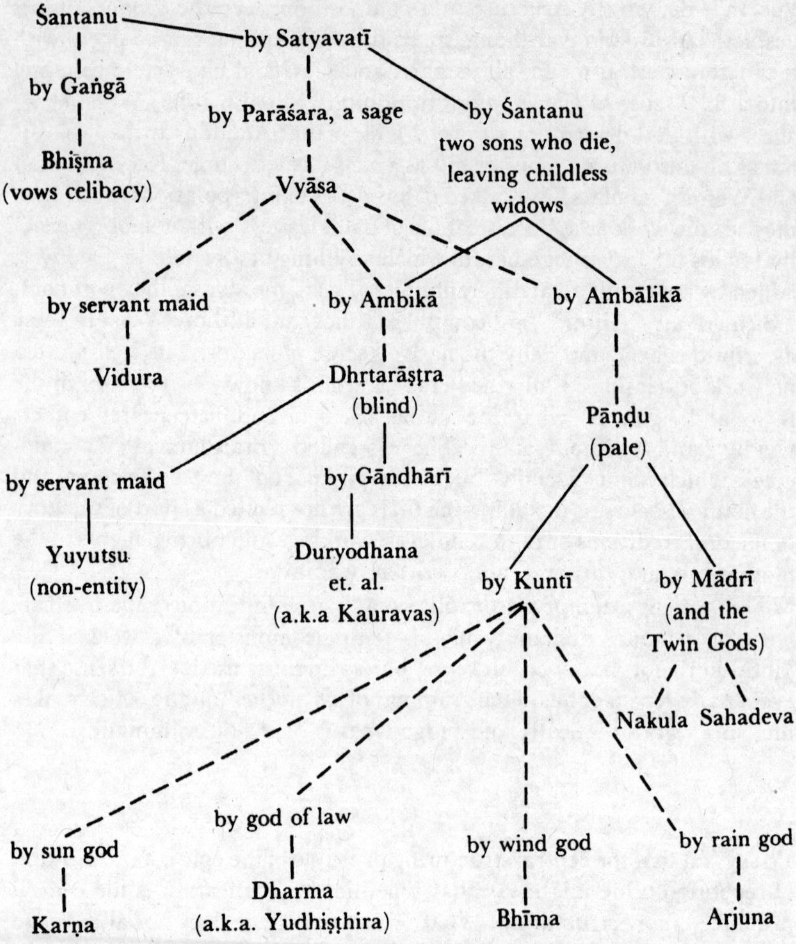

The chart is redrawn from the regular kinship diagram to show the double espousal and the double parentage of the major characters. Certain patterns of repetition may be noted:

1. Śantanu, as well as Satyavatī, has a human and a supernatural lover. Śantanu has goddess Gaṅgā on whom he begets Bhīṣma; and by human Satyavatī he has two sons. Satyavatī has had a liaison with

Parāśara, a sage with supernatural powers (and a very human lust) and she has a son Vyāsa by him. Vyāsa, too, is a sage with supernatural powers. He is the author of the *Mahābhārata* as well as the ancestor of the Pāṇḍavas and Kauravas.

Śantanu and Satyavatī's two sons (Citrāṅgada and Vicitravīrya) die childless, leaving two widows, Ambikā and Ambālikā. At Satyavatī's behest, sage Vyāsa begets two sons on them, Dhṛtarāśtra the Blind and Pāṇḍu the Pale. Thus each of these two widows too has a supernatural and a human lover.

At this point, there is a clear division. Dhṛtarāṣṭra's progeny by Gāndhārī is entirely human. But Pāṇḍu, cursed by a sage to die if he makes love, permits his wives Kuntī and Mādrī to invoke gods and get sons by them. Thus Kuntī and Mādrī too have supernatural and human lovers—actually Kuntī almost overdoes it, trying it once before marriage and three times after. Like Satyavatī, her virginity too is returned to her by her supernatural, premarital lover.

Thus, for three generations, practically every major male character, from Bhīṣma to Sahadeva, has a human and a supernatural parent. The only exceptions are the Kaurava brothers. When we reach the third generation, we have two sets of cousins, the Kauravas whose parents are entirely human and the Pāṇḍavas, fathered by the gods. That's when the battle is joined.

2. Bhīṣma, Vyāsa, Vidura, Dhṛtarāṣṭra, Pāṇḍu, and finally Karṇa are all born to their mothers before they were married or after they were widowed. The two legitimate sons born to Śantanu and Satyavatī die childless. Bhīṣma takes an oath of celibacy and abdicates his right to the throne; Vyāsa and Vidura are celibate sage figures. Dhṛtarāṣṭra is blind. Pāṇḍu is born pale and, after a brief reign, earns a curse which makes sex a mortal act, and unmans him. Thus, beginning with Bhīṣma's self-chosen celibacy and abdication, the succession totters, oscillating from brother to brother (Dhṛtarāṣṭra and Pāṇḍu) and from cousin to cousin (Pāṇḍavas and Kauravas). The war books also show the fortunes of war similarly vacillating between victory and defeat.

3. Not only are relationships (like Satyavatī's past and Kuntī's past) repeated to make patterns, and patterns of patterns. The appearance of certain characters and settings punctuates the continuity of narrative with patterns of repetition. For instance, Gaṅgā as a goddess and as a river appears several times: she is the mother of Bhīṣma, and the river carries/fosters Karṇa when he is abandoned by Kuntī, his mother. So both men are called Gāṅgeya, "son of Gaṅgā". The river is the setting of the great war, and it is on its banks that Dhṛtarāṣṭra gets a vision of all the war dead.

4. Fires occur over and over again. Duryodhana conspires to burn the Pāṇḍavas in a house of lacquer, but in their stead a hunter woman (*Niṣāda*) and her five sons die—as later in Aśvatthāmā's rampage, the Pāṇḍavas' own five sons die as surrogates for the Pāṇḍavas. Kṛṣṇa and Arjuna destroy a forest (*Khāṇḍava*) and all its denizens by fire, as an offering to the fire god, Agni.

5. A minor character like Durvāsas appears in the life of Kuntī as well as Draupadī. And Kālidāsa, when he reworks the Śakuntalā story from the *Mahābhārata*, brings Durvāsas into her life as well.

6. Whole situations like the heroes' exile and disguise are replicated. Such replications can be simultaneous, suffered by several characters at different times, like the Pāṇḍavas living in exile and disguise in Virāṭa's court; or successive, at different stages of the same lives, like the Pāṇḍavas who disguise themselves as brahmins after the first attempt on their lives, and later as different kinds of professionals in Virāṭa's court. Or the repetitive events may be concentric, or nested, as in the inset story of Nala who too lives in exile and disguise. Lastly, life lived incognito is personified in Karṇa whose destiny is governed by the fact that neither he nor most others around him know who he is—a situation that gives rise to many poignant ironies and reversals.

Such repetitive elements foreshadow later events and recapture earlier ones. Two major examples will do to make the point. Draupadī is outraged first in Dhṛtarāṣṭra's court with the elders' connivance and the husbands looking on, unmanned and helpless. When she is molested again in Virāṭa's court, abetted by the queen, her husbands are helpless because they have to lie low in disguise. But the episode is given a different ending. This time Bhīma does not put his anger aside. He beats her molester Kīcaka to a pulp and kills him—exactly foreshadowing what he would later do to Duḥśāsana, the first molester. The death of Kīcaka too is part of a series. For, in the epic, only five men were known to be equal to each other in strength, in the art of wielding a mace, and in wrestling: Jarāsandha, Kīcaka, Śalya, Bhīma and Duryodhana. Jarāsandha was killed early in the epic: Kṛṣṇa arranges that. Now Kīcaka is killed, later Śalya—so that Bhīma and Duryodhana alone are left for the final combat. The serial elimination of equals, like the gradual amassing of weapons by Arjuna and Karṇa, the two sworn opponents, is part of the epic progression.

One of the major instances of repetition concerns the *Bhagavadgītā*.[2]

---

[2] See Dumézil (1968), p. 93, van Buitenen (1978), pp. 15–16, and Shulman (1985), p. 262, for discussions regarding the opening chapter of the *Gītā* as an inversion of the Uttara episode, of the *Virāṭaparvan* as a "carnival".

Scholars have debated whether the *Gītā* belongs in the epic at all; editors have called it an interpolation. But to the native reader, it belongs incontrovertibly; artistically and structurally, it is firmly in place. Its central incident—a warrior suffers a failure of nerve, an attack of cowardice, before battle, but he is then counselled and urged into battle—occurs at least five times in the epic. But the most ironic parallel incident occurs immediately before the big battle scenes, as a comic scene in *Virāṭa Parvan*.

When Duryodhana hears of Kīcaka's death, he at once suspects the Pāṇḍavas' presence in the Virāṭa court. He lays siege to Virāṭa's country to smoke out the Pāṇḍavas. (If they are discovered in the year of living incognito, they would have to go back to the forest for 12 years again). Then, as Virāta's army gets ready for battle, Uttara the crown prince, darling of the palace women, boasts that if only he had a proper charioteer he would take on the Kauravas and rout them. Draupadī, who is disguised as a servantmaid, slyly suggests that Bṛhannaḍā, who is really Arjuna disguised as a eunuch dancing-master, knew Arjuna well and was his charioteer. After some ironic play on this situation, and after protesting that he, a mere dancing-master, couldn't really wear armour or mount a horse, Arjuna/Bṛhannaḍā agrees. Uttara then ostentatiously prepares for battle, patronizes Arjuna, then gets into his chariot. As Arjuna drives it between the contending armies, Uttara is overwhelmed by the array of shining spears, the trumpeting war-elephants and the dazzling host of warriors. He loses nerve and runs from the battlefield. Arjuna follows, catches him by the scruff of his neck and asks him, "Who do you think you are"? When Uttara falls at his feet and asks Arjuna to save him from certain death in battle, Arjuna relents. He then retrieves, with Uttara's help, his divine weapons (left on a tree before the five brothers entered service with Virāṭa). He asks Uttara to be his charioteer while he fights the battle. As he strings his divine bow Gāṇḍīva and strums it, Uttara is dazzled by his erstwhile eunuch dancing-master, now changed into a commanding hero. Uttara asks hims who he really is. Arjuna reveals his true identity. He recites his ten sonorous names: Phalguna, Savyasācī, Dhanañjaya, etc. Then, as Uttara is still amazed, he amazes him further by riding into the thick of battle and beating off the enemies.

The very next book opens with Arjuna in the chariot with Kṛṣṇa as the charioteer. When Arjuna's chariot moves between the two armies, Arjuna is conscience-stricken at the sight of his cousins, elders, and teachers whom he may have to kill. He loses his nerve and his appetite for battle. Then Kṛṣṇa asks him the same question that Arjuna asks of Uttara, "Who do you think you are"? and reminds him of his true nature as a Kṣatriya whose duty is here and now, to take part in battle. Kṛṣṇa further tells him that the real war is being fought by him, Kṛṣṇa, not Arjuna. Thus Kṛṣṇa, who began as a non-combatant and a charioteer, is seen to be the true war-maker, and Arjuna the warrior only a *nimitta*, an excuse and an instrument. At the end, Kṛṣṇa reveals his blinding, terrifying, cosmic form as Time the devourer of all, and he also describes himself in a hundred ways (just as Arjuna recites his ten names earlier). As in the earlier Uttara episode, here too several reversals take place between Actor/Agent, Charioteer/Warrior, Eunuch/Potent male. As victory earlier is falsely attributed to Uttara's efforts, now it is attributed to Arjuna's prowess. The former episode tells of the growing-up of Uttara, as the *Gītā* episode depicts the growing-up of Arjuna. What seems like a playful rehearsal in the *Virāṭa Parva* becomes earnest in the *Udyoga Parva.* Uttara's cowardice and Arjuna's self-revelation are physical, as Arjuna's cowardice and Kṛṣṇa's self-revelation are metaphysical.

As one rereads or remembers such episodes in the *Mahābhārata*, one is reminded of Henry James on Flaubert's careful *mots juste*, designed and planted in his novels with infinite care. Though the *Mahābhārata* has qualified in the eyes of many as "a loose baggy monster" (Henry James' phrase about 19th century novels), a second look at the foreshadowings and recapitulations make one think of Flaubert, except on an epic scale. Henry James spoke of how the elements in Flaubert were

> . . . always so related and associated, so properly a part of something else that is in turn part of something other, part of a reference, a tone, a passage, or page, that the simple may enjoy it for the least bearing and the initiated for the greatest.

(*3*)

This may be the place to talk briefly of the many substories (*upākhyāna*) that participate in and intensify the repetition of events. To give only two examples: just when Bhīṣma decides to give up his sexual and political life so that his father may marry again, th story of Yayāti is told as a kind of model and precedent. Puru transfers his youth to his aged father Yayāti and thereby earns merit. Such appropriate reminiscence speaks of a kind of mythic imprinting, motivating present action (Ramanujan 1972; 1983). To cite another instance, one of many, when Yudhiṣṭhira is despondent, having lost everything at dice, now exiled in a forest, a sage tells him the story of Nala. Nala, too, has gambled away a kingdom and lost it to a brother, has even lost his wife in the forest, is bitten by a serpent which turns out to be literally a blessing in disguise—

for it turns his body ugly and unrecognizable until his exile ends. But, in the end, the story restores him to his wife, gives him skills in dice so that he wins back his kingdom. As he listens to this story, Yudhiṣṭhira sees that his plight is not singular and that he is only a half-finished story, with him still in exile (Ramanujan 1980).

Thus, these scores of tales that seem to interrupt the main action have a narrative function. They are performative, i.e. they too are acts, not merely explanations. They add the vector of past and precedent to present and future. They are "bovariste" as the French would say. (Madame Bovary's fantasies and later actions are molded by the cheap romances of her youth—a process aptly called "bovarisme" by Gaultier). They also help in amassing repetitive networks and density, to make the heroes' lives not singular but representative, tokens of a type.

(*4*)

Many of these features are also replicated in the local texture of significant passages. Many waves of many amplitudes meet here—as in a harmonic series. A passage like the description of the first contest between Arjuna and Karṇa is only one among many. It is one node of the larger rhythms of the epic. Before reading the rest of this page, the reader might want to refresh his memory of the following passage I'm going to discuss: pp. 276–282, in van Buitenen's translation of the *Ādiparva* (1973).

> When the day came, the king and his councilors arrived, preceded by Bhīṣma and Kṛpa, the first of the teachers and they entered the royal stand that, decked with gold leaf, was screened off by pearl-studded lattice and paved with beryl. Then the great lady Gāndhārī came out, and Kuntī, O victorious king, and all the king's women with their maids and retainers; and excitedly they stepped up on their platforms as the wives of the Gods ascend Mount Meru. And the whole fourfold society of brahmins, barons, and the others came hurriedly from the town and assembled to watch the weapons trails of the princess. There was a crowd there like an ocean, rippling in waves with the music that was played, and the people's curiosity.
>
> Then the teacher himself arrived with his son Aśvatthāman, dressed in white clothes and wearing a white brahmins' thread, anointed with white ointments, white-haired, white-bearded; and he entered the middle of the arena, as the Moon enters with Mars the sky that is cleared of rain clouds. Mighty Droṇa made an offering such as suited the day, and had brahmins who knew the spells recite Vedic lines as a blessing. Then, as the sacred sounds that blessed the day subsided, men entered the arena carrying all kinds of weapons and gear.
>
> Thereupon, the powerful bulls of the Bharatas descended with their

bows, armour, and belts tightened, the quivers fast. Headed by Yudhiṣṭhira, the mighty princes from the eldest onward each gave a superb and marvelous exhibition of weaponry. Some of the spectators ducked their heads, afraid that the arrows might land on them, while others boldly kept looking, wonder-struck. They hit the targets with their arrows, and nimbly let go while they drove past with horses. And watching that army of princes wield their bows and arrows, the crowds were astounded, as though they were watching a castle in the air. Their eyes wide with wonder, the men there wildly cheered them by the hundreds and thousands: "Bravo! Bravo"! The powerful princes did their courses with the bow, over and again, on chariot, elephant, or horseback, and in hand-to-hand combat. Then they seized hold of their swords and shields and, brandishing their arms, ran through the courses of swordsmanship all over the terrain. The spectators watched the deftness, skill, flamboyance, balance, and firmness of grip of them all as they used their shields and swords.

Now Suyodhana and the Wolf-Belly descended, as always in high spirits, clubs in hand, like two single-peaked mountains. The strong-armed princes buckled their armour, hell-bent on showing off their masculine prowess, like two huge rutting bull elephants joining battle over a cow. They circled each other, sunwise and widdershins, with their sparkling clubs, like two bulls in rut. Vidura described to Dhṛtarāṣṭra, and Kuntī to Gāndhārī, all the exploits of the princes.

Vaiśaṃpāyana said:

When the Kuru prince and Bhīma, strong among the strong, had taken up their position in the arena, the crowd split into two factions, each partial to its own favorite. "Hurray for the champion, the prince of the Kurus"! they shouted, or "Hurray for Bhīma"! and the wildly rising cheers of the onlookers echoed widely.

The wise Droṇa Bhāradvāja looked at the arena that was like a stormy sea, and he said to Aśvatthāman, his beloved son, "Stop those two champions, highly trained as they are, or else there will be a riot in the arena over Bhīma and Duryodhana"! The son of the guru halted the two as they raised their bludgeons like two violent seas that are whipped by the tempest of Doomsday.

Droṇa entered the court of the arena, stopped the music band that raised the din of a thundercloud, and began to speak: "Now watch the Pārtha, the greatest of armsmen, son of Indra and the match of Indra's younger brother, whom I love more than my own son"! Thereupon the young man, whose happy entrance had been blessed by his teacher, entered with bow and full quiver, with wrist guarded and finger guards tied on; and so, wearing a golden cuirass, Phalguna made his appearance like a rain cloud with a golden sun, iridescent as the rainbow aglow with lightning, red like twilight. There was a huge commotion all over the arena, and the musical instruments and the conches exploded into sound. "There is the magnificent son of Kuntī"! "There goes the middlemost of the Pāṇḍavas"! "There is the son of great Indra, the safeguard of the Kurus"! He is the greatest of armsmen, he is the greatest of the upholders of the Law, of morality, the supreme treasury of the wisdom of morals"! And when Kuntī heard these words beyond compare that the spectators voiced, her breasts became damp with tears that commingled with milk. His ears filled with the uproar, Dhṛtarāṣṭra, the best of men, happily turned to Vidura and asked, "Steward, what is that uproarious outcry like the roaring of a stormy sea that has suddenly risen from the arena as though to rend the skies"?

Vidura said:

Phalguna Pārtha has descended, great king, the son of Pāṇḍu, wearing his armour; and hence this commotion!

Dhṛtarāṣṭra said:

How lucky am I, and favored am I, and protected am I, sage, by these fires of the Pāṇḍavas that were kindled from the block of Pṛthā!

Vaiśaṃpāyana said:

When the rising theatre had somehow calmed down, the Terrifier began to exhibit the skill with weapons he had learned from his teacher. With the *āgneya* he created fire, with the *vāruṇa* water, with the *vāyavya* wind, with the *pārjanya* rain; with the *bhauma* he entered earth, with the *pārvata* he brought forth mountains. With the disappearing weapon he made it all vanish again. One instant he stood tall, the next squat, then was up in front on the chariot yoke, then again in the middle of the chariot, and the next instant had jumped to the ground. Trained to high excellence, the favorite of his guru hit and shot through fragile targets, and tiny ones, and hard ones, with different makes of arrows. While an iron boar was moved about, he loosed into its snout five continuous arrows as though they were one single one. The mighty archer buried twenty-one arrows in a cow's hollow horn that was swaying on a rope. And in this and other fashions he gave an exhibition of his dexterity with the long sword as well as the bow and the club.

When the tournament was almost over and the crowd had thinned and the music stopped, there came from the area of the gate the sound of arms being slapped, like the crash of a thunderbolt, which betokened greatness and prowess. "Are the mountains rending? Is the earth caving in? Is the sky filling up with clouds that are heavy with rain"? Such, overlord of the earth, were the thoughts of the arena that instant. All the spectators looked toward the gate.

Droṇa, surrounded by the five Pāṇḍava brothers, shone like the moon in conjunction with the constellation of the Hand. The proud one hundred brothers, joined by Aśvatthāman, surrounded Duryodhana,killer of his enemies, who had risen to his feet. And he, brandishing his club, encircled by the brothers who kept their weapons ready, stood there like the Sacker of Cities of olden times surrounded by the hosts of the Gods at the Slaughter of the Dānavas.

Vaiśaṃpāyana said:

The people, eyes popping with wonder, made way, and Karṇa, victor of enemy cities, entered the spacious arena like a walking mountain, wearing his inborn armour and his face lit by his earrings, with his bow and tied-on sword—Karṇa, scourge of the hosts of his foes, of the wide fame and wide eyes, who had been born by Pṛthā as a maiden to the sting-rayed Sun, of whom he was a portion. His power and might were like the regal lion's or bull's or elephant's, and he was like sun, moon, and fire in brightness, beauty, and luster. Tall he stood, like a golden palm tree, this youth with the hard body of a lion. Innumerable were the virtues of this magnificent son of the Sun.

The strong-armed champion glanced about the circle of the stands; then, with none too great courtesy, bowed to Droṇa and Kṛpa. The entire crowd was hushed and stared at him, and a shudder went through the people as they wondered who he was. With a voice rumbling like a thunderhead, the eloquent brother, son of the Sun, spoke to his unrecognized brother, son of Pāka's Chastiser: "Pārtha! Whatever feat you have done, I shall better it before the eyes of all these people. Don't be too amazed at yourself"!

He had not finished speaking, eloquent king, when the people all about rose like one man, like a pitcher heaved from the well. Pleasure flooded Duryodhana, O tiger among men, and abasement and anger pervaded the Terrifier instantly. Droṇa gave his permission, and the powerful, pugnacious Karṇa accomplished every feat that the Pārtha had achieved. Wereupon Duryodhana and his brothers embraced Karṇa; and he joyously said to him, "Welcome, strong-armed hero! Good fortune has brought you here, you who know how to humble pride. Take your pleasure of me and the kingdom of the Kurus"!

Karṇa said:

Then enough of everything else! I choose to be friends with you. And I want a duel with the Pārtha, Bhārata!

Duryodhana said:

Enjoy all pleasure with me, show your friends your favour, and set your foot on the heads of your ill-wishers, scourge of your foes!

Vaiśaṃpāyana said:

But the Pārtha thought himself insulted, and he said to Karṇa, who stood like a mountain in the midst of the crowd of his brethren, "The worlds that are set aside for uninvited intruders, and for uninvited prattlers, those worlds you shall attain, Karṇa, when I have done killing you"!

Karṇa said:

The stage is open to all, so what of you, Phalguna? Barons are those who are the strongest. Law obeys might. Why abuse, which is the whimpering of the Weak? Talk with arrows, Bhārata, until before your teacher's own eyes I carry off your head with mine!

Vaiśaṃpāyana said:

Droṇa gave his permission, and the Pārtha, sacker of enemy cities, was embraced by his brothers and rushed to the other to fight. Duryodhana and his brothers clasped Karṇa, and he stood there ready for battle, holding his bow and arrows.

Then the sky became overcast with lightning-streaked, thunderous, rainbow-attended clouds that laughed with lines of cranes. And seeing how Indra of the golden horses fondly down upon the stage, the Sun carried off the clouds that came too close. Now the Pāṇḍava could be half seen, hidden by the shadow of the clouds, and Karṇa appeared in a nimbus of bright sunlight. The sons of Dhṛtarāṣṭra stood by Karṇa; and Droṇa Bhāradvāja, Kṛpa, and Bhīṣma stood by the Pārtha.

The arena was divided, the women took their sides; but Kuntibhoja's daughter, who knew the issue, fell in a faint. Vidura, who knew all the Laws, brought the fainting woman back to consciousness by splashing her with water in which sandalwood had been sprinkled. When her breath had returned, she stared at her two sons, clad in their armour; but however much grieved, she did not interfere.

As the two champions raised their large bows, Śāradvata said to them, for he was experienced in the conduct of duels and knew all the Laws, "This is the youngest son of Pāṇḍu born from Pṛthā, a scion of Kuru, who will engage in a duel with you, sir. You too must now tell the names of your mother, your father, and your lineage, and of the barons whose scion you are. When he has learned them, the Pārtha shall fight you, or mayhap not".

At his words Karṇa hung his head in shame, and his face faded like a lotus that has been showered by the rains.

Duryodhana said:

Master, in the scriptures it is ruled that there are three ways for one to be a king: to be born one, to become a champion, or to lead an army. If Phalguna refuses to fight with anyone who is not a king then I shall anoint him to the kingdom in the country of the Angas!

Vaiśaṃpāyana said:

That very instant the warlike Karṇa was consecrated by Vedic brahmins with roasted rice grains, flowers in golden pitchers, and enthroned on a golden stool, to rule the kingdom of Anga; and the mighty hero was endowed with fortune. He received a royal umbrella and a yak-tail fan; and when the wishes for victory had died down, the bulllike king said to King Kaurava, "What can I give that matches this gift of a kingdom? Tell me, tiger among kings, and I shall do it so, my liege"! "I want your eternal friendship"! replied Suyodhana. And upon his word Karṇa answered, "So shall it be"! Joyously the two embraced and became greatly happy.

Vaiśaṃpāyana said:

Then, his upper cloth awry, sweating and trembling, Adhiratha entered the stage, swaying on his feet, held up by a stick. When Karṇa saw him, he let go of his bow and moved by his reverence for his father he greeted him with his head, which was still wet with the water of the consecration. Nervously, the chariot driver covered his feet with the end of his *dhoti* and said to Karṇa, who was crowned with success, "Ah, my son"! Trembling with love, he embraced him and kissed his head, and with his tears he once more sprinkled the head that was still damp from the consecration to the Anga kingdom.

When Bhīmasena Pāṇḍava saw Adhiratha, he decided that Karṇa was the *suta's* son and burst out laughing. "Son of a *sūta*", he said, "you do not have the right to die in a fight with a Pārtha! You better stick to the whip that suits your family. You have no right to enjoy the Anga kingdom, churl, no more than a dog has a right to eat the cake by the fire at a sacrifice"! At these words a slight tremor started in Karṇa's lower lip, and he sighed and looked up to the sun in the sky. But Duryodhana leaped up from amidst his brothers, like a rutting elephant from a lotus pond, and he said to Bhīmasena fo terrible deeds, who stood his ground, "Wolf-Belly, you have no right to speak such words! Might is the father of barons, and even the least of barons deserves a fight. The origin of both barons and rivers are surely obscure. Fire that pervades all creatures springs from water. The thunderbolt that slew the Dānavas was made from a bone of Dadhīca. The blessed lord God Guha is a complete mystery: he is said to be the son of Fire, or the Pleiads, or Rudra, or the Ganges. Men born from baronesses are known to have become brahmins. Our teacher was born from a trough, Master Kṛpa from a reed stalk. And the princes all know how you yourselves were born. How could a doe give birth to his tiger who resembles the sun, with his earrings and armour and celestial birthmarks? This lordly man deserves to rule the world, not just Anga! He deserves it by the power of his arms and by me who shall obey his orders. Or else, if there be a man who will not condone my action, let him, on chariot or on foot, bend the bow"!

There was a great uproar in the entire arena, mixed with cheers; then the sun went down. Duryodhana, holding Karṇa by the hand, his way lighted by the flames of torches, left the arena. The Pāṇḍavas, Droṇa, Kṛpa, and Bhīṣma, O lord of the people, all went to their own dwellings. The people departed, some hailing "Arjuna"! others "Karṇa"! others again "Duryodhana"! And when she had recognized the king of Anga by his birthmarks as her own son, Kuntī's hidden pleasure grew with love. Duryodhana's fear of Arjuna also diminished rapidly when he had found Karṇa, O king of the earth. That hero himself, who had mastered the labour of weaponry, flattered Duryodhana with the most coaxing words. And at that time even Yudhiṣṭhira thought that no archer on earth was Karṇa's equal.

The entire scene, where Droṇa is displaying the martial skills of his young disciples to the Kaurava assembly, foreshadows the later war. As the young men arrive, buckled in armour, showing off their prowess, Vidura describes it all to blind Dhṛtarāṣṭra, and Kuntī to blindfolded Gāndhārī: as, later, Sañjaya describes the war to Dhṛtarāṣṭra. The old father's blindness is always kept in view.

All the parents and parent-figures are present here: the blind Dhṛtarāstra, the heroic but ineffective Droṇa and Bhīṣma, Kuntī, the mother of both Arjuna and Karṇa (who become sworn enemies before her very eyes, in this scene), and then, as a late arrival, the charioteer and foster-father of Karṇa, and also the true fathers of the two young antagonists, the Sun-God and the Rain-God. These onlooking presences enlarge the scene from earth to heaven, deepen the present with the ironic poignancies of the ever-active past (like the heroes' births).

Protagonist and antagonist are matched for life beginning with this scene: Bhīma and Duryodhana, Arjuna and Karṇa. And their fortunes oscillate. This oscillation is dramatic in the case of Karṇa's rising and falling fortunes in the course of this one scene—which is paradigmatic of all of his life. These oscillations are echoed not only in the shouts of the crowd but in the heart of Kuntī who alone knows the identity of Karṇa. When she hears the shouts of praise for her Arjuna, "her breasts became damp with tears that commingled with milk". When Karṇa gets ready for battle with Arjuna, Kuntī, "who knew the issue, fell in a faint". "When her breath had returned, she stared at her two sons, clad in armour, but, however much grieved, she did not interfere". But we know that before the very last battle of Arjuna and Karṇa, she, who has held her secret in silence till then, does interfere. By revealing herself and his identity then to Karṇa, she brings him inevitably closer to his defeat and death.

To return to the contest: we begin by seeing Arjuna display his skills, his mastery over the elements, fire, water, winds, rain, earth; he shoots with different kinds of arrows fragile targets, tiny ones, hard ones, and shoots five arrows into the mouth of a moving iron boar. These feats have many resonances but I'll pick out only one. Arjuna shoots five arrows here exactly as he does later when he wins Draupadī—it's as if he is not alone in these acts but he is all five brothers.

Just as he finishes his display, we hear the sound of arms being slapped, "like the crash of a thunderbolt", and Karṇa enters. The attention of the spectators shifts to Karṇa. His beauty and prowess and sun-like luster are fully described. He challenges Arjuna and calls him Pārtha, son of Pṛthā or Kuntī—without knowing that he, Karṇa, is also a Pārtha, son of Pṛthā.[3]

---

[3] In this passage, as elsewhere, the repeated epithets and names play a crucial role. Arjuna is called Pārtha (son of Pṛthā or Kuntī), Kaunteya (son of Kuntī), Pāṇḍava, son of Pāṇḍu, Bhārata ("descendant of Bharata"), Kaurava, a scion of the Kurus, etc. Each of these epithets highlights and describes an aspect of the hero, often ironically. Several play on the irony of this apparent difference and deeper kinship with Karṇa to whom all the lineage and matronymic names ("Kaunteya") apply as well, though no one present knows it. The irony reaches a climax here when Bhīma taunts Karṇa, laughing at his low birth: "Son of a *sūta*, you do not have the right to die in a fight with a Pārtha"! I've already commented on Arjuna's recital of his ten names to Uttara in the act of self-revelation. The *Gītā* too uses several names for Arjuna and Kṛṣṇa in significant ways: e.g., Paraṃtapa, "chastiser of foes", reminds him of his duty as a warrior. Each of these epithetic names, here and in the Purāṇas, summarize the history, index the actions and relations of the character. The agent here is a sum of his actions, a point of intersection for multiple relationships. Acts constitute the actor.

When he challenges Arjuna, the crowd rises "like a pitcher heaved from the well". Pleasure floods Duryodhana who offers Karṇa friendship—one that lasts throughout the epic. When Arjuna and Karṇa are about to begin the contest, "the Sun carried off the clouds that came too close", reminding us of the divine fathers. Arjuna is "hidden by the shadow of the clouds", and Karṇa appears "in a nimbus of bright sunlight". The arena is divided, the women take sides.

It's then that Karṇa is asked to name his father and mother. He hangs his head in shame (Arjuna is called Pārtha again here), and his face fades "like a lotus showered by the rains", suggesting the rivalry of the parent gods, sun (friend to lotuses) and rain.

Duryodhana quickly interferes, instantly crowns Karṇa a king with royal insignia, raising him up again. At the height of this good turn, enters an old man, swaying on his feet, held up by a stick, Karṇa's lowborn (foster-) father, moved by his son's good fortune, his tears mixing with the water of his son's consecration. Now Bhīma calls him the son of a chariot-driver and shames him further. Throughout, there is also a rivalry of explanations—what qualifies a man, might or birth? Here too the argument vacillates and is inconclusive, like the contest itself. The crowd itself is divided in its opinions and it cheers for Arjuna now and for Karṇa again. Kuntī too oscillates from grief to hidden love and pleasure as she recognizes Karṇa, now king of Aṅga, by his birthmarks.

Such oscillation of fortune, outcomes, rights and wrongs, and emotions within characters in characteristic of this epic's movements, enacted even in the texture.[4]

---

[4] Four outstanding images recur throughout to describe the war between the cousins: (1) encounter between the gods and demons; (2) a forest of trees felled by some natural calamity; (3) man as a sacrificial beast, the war as a sacrifice, and the end of a battle as the dying sacrificial fire; (4) universal dissolution in the ultimate fire. These images extend the human time-span into mythic time, magnify the significance of the action and its terror. Furthermore each is embodied in some important incident within the action: (1) Kṛṣṇa beheading Śisupāla; (2) the Khāṇḍava forest decimated by a fire, devouring tree, bird and beast; (3) the sacrifices undertaken (the Aśvamedha, the Rājasūya, and the bizarre vengefulness of genocide in the Snake Sacrifice); (4) fires, beginning with the fire-trap set for the Pāṇḍavas, the Khāṇḍava fire mentioned above, and the forest fire in which Dhṛtarāṣṭra, Gāndhārī and Kuntī die, and lastly, the fiery terror of Time in the *Gītā* when Kṛṣṇa is seen as the agent of universal dissolution. I may add that each of these should be seen as a *leitmotiv*, subordinated to the total human action, not as a central overarching theme. Madeleine Biardeau (1987) sees the epic as an extended sacrifice, and Alf Hiltebeitel (1976) sees Kṛṣṇa as a form of "Śiva, destroyer of all". While each of these emphases is truly illuminating, their overemphasis seem to me to underrate the architectonic complexity of the *human* action of the epic.

(5)

The dubeity and oscillation of fortunes, outcomes and emotions are fully matched by the legal or legalistic ambiguities, arguments and counter-arguments that precede and succeed *every* major act—Karṇa's rights in the above passage, Kṛṣṇa's rights to receive the first honors at the sacrifice, arguments regarding whether five brothers could marry one woman, the rightness of the dicing game, whether Draupadī could be rightfully wagered, whether Arjuna came out of the life to be lived incognito before the contracted thirteenth year, and so on. It is not *dharma* or right conduct that the *Mahābhārata* seems to teach, but the *sūkṣma* or subtle nature of *dharma*—its infinite subtlety, its incalculable calculus of consequences, its endless delicacy. Because *dharma-sūkṣmatā* is one of the central themes that recur in an endless number of ways, the many legal discussions are a necessary part of the action.

Related to this ambiguity is the ineradicable mixture of good and evil in each of the main characters. The Pāṇḍavas, with Kṛṣṇa, who are "the good guys", manage to kill every Kaurava hero, Bhīṣma, Droṇa, Karṇa, and Duryodhana, by foul means. And the Kauravas, especially Duryodhana and Karṇa, are not just villains, but heroic and honest warriors despite everything. Neither is ever underestimated or underdescribed. Also, the major Pāṇḍava heroes are tested and found wanting in the one virtue around which their ego, their character, and their great fame are built. Yudhiṣṭhira, famed for his truth-telling, tells a lie to kill Droṇa and is at once taken down several notches—this virtuous man's chariot which always moved inches above the ground now has to come down to earth and run on it like any other defective mortal's. Arjuna, the greatest and best equipped of warriors, loses nerve and morale in the first moment of battle.[5]

---

[5] Folklore and later *Mahābhāratas* continue these tests and question Draupadī's chastity also. For instance, both the Tamil Bhārata of Villipputtūrār, the Kannada one by Kumāravyāsa, and a Tamil chapbook tell the episode in the *Vanaparva* (third *sandhi*), the Forest Book. In the Kannada *Bhārata*, Draupadī sees a beautiful mango on a tree in a sage's garden and covets it. Bhīma fetches it. The brothers soon learn that it is a fruit grown specially for the sage who wakes up from his *tapas* only once in six moths, when he breaks his fast with this single fruit in the garden. To forestall his anger, they wish somehow to restore the fruit to its place in the tree. As only Kṛṣṇa can accomplish such a deed contrary to nature, they summon him. He does arrive and says that the fruit would return to its stalk only if each of the five brothers and Draupadī reveal their deepest desire. The five brothers say nothing surprising or shameful—for instance, Bhīma and Arjuna desire fame and battle, and Yudhiṣṭhira speaks of oneness. With each revelation, the fruit rises magically toward the stalk from which it was plucked. When it is Draupadī's turn, she says that women desire all handsome men, even brother, father and

Yet amid all these doubts, arguments and ambiguities, one thing is certain—everyone's destruction. Through all the oscillations, there is a single unrelenting direction—the destruction of the Kuru race. The pervasive ambiguity here is not a structural uncertainty. In the short range, what seems doubtful in outcome, in the long range leaves no doubt at all about the outcome—which is neither winning or losing, but nothing less than total destruction. Both Draupadī and Gāndhārī, the two queens on opposite sides, are left childless.

Part of this relentlessness is the way pairs of enemies grow up together or apart: Bhīṣma and Śikhaṇḍin, Droṇa and Dhṛṣṭadyumna, Bhīma and Duryodhana, Arjuna and Karṇa. Vows and weapons gather towards the moments of battle. And as Arjuna gathers weapons from Śiva and others, Karṇa too gathers them. But the latter also gathers curses and forfeits, all because he does not know who he is, i.e. a Kṣatriya as well-born as Arjuna. When he finally comes to know who he is, he is denuded further by his promises to Kuntī. In fact, his tragedy is not caused by a "fatal flaw" but a fatal virtue—his generosity that makes him give away the armour and earrings of immorality to Indra, his rival's divine father, and that makes him promise Kuntī that he would kill none of the Pāṇḍavas but only Arjuna and that he would not use the same weapon twice.

With each day of the war, there is a further decimation until Aśvatthāmā kills all the Pāṇḍava children with his ultimate weapon, a burning arrow that cannot be withdrawn, which reaches into the wombs of the Pāṇḍava women to kill their foetuses (a terrifying prophecy of the nuclear threat, as Peter Brook sees it), while Kṛṣṇa hides the Pāṇḍavas. Only one foetus in Uttarā (wife of Abhimanyu) is revived from still-birth, leaving the Pāṇḍavas one lone descendent. He is Parīkṣit, who by his discourtesy to a sage, earns a curse, and is killed by a snake. So his son vows vengeance and performs a sacrifice for the universal destruction of serpents—during which the text comes full circle, for the *Mahābhārata* itself gets told to this grandson, sole survivor. And the epic begins with the snake sacrifice.

---

son. But the fruit does not go back to the stalk, and Kṛṣṇa insists that she tell the truth about herself. She then reveals that though she has five husbands, she has six in her heart—a suggestion that she desires Karṇa as well, though she doesn't know that he is the sixth. In the Tamil chap-book, *Pāṇṭavar Vanavāsam*, this desire for Karṇa is made explicit. She says she had seen Karṇa at her bride-choice before Arjuna won her with his feat of archery, had mistaken him for Arjuna and desired him for her husband. Thus, Draupadī the chaste wife is also shown up as having lewd desires. In Kumāravyāsa, she says, "Women are chaste only when men are not available". See the recent essay by Shulman (1989) for further discussion of this episode. I'm indebted to David Shulman for the references to Villipputtūrār and the Tamil chapbook.

(*6*)

It's time to step back and sum up the conception of action in the epic and how the replications are part of a total world-view.

1. The relentless march of each character towards his death is accompanied by the suggestion of infinite regress in motivation, often into previous lives. Yet, what's presented in "close-up" and in dramatic terms is the present life.

Sage Vasiṣṭha has cursed the divine Vasu brothers to be born as mortals and suffer the thousand ills that such flesh is heir to. Gaṅgā saves the first seven from mortal lives by drowning them at birth. But the eighth drowning is interrupted by Śantanu who knows nothing of the curse and the release that Gaṅgā is attempting. He saves the eighth child *for* mortal strife, and he is Bhīṣma. Then the central act of Bhīṣma's life, his vow of celibacy, uncoils the rest of the action, including his refusal to marry Ambā, who vows vengeance and commits suicide to be reborn as Śikhaṇḍin, who alone can face and kill Bhīṣma. Thus a prenatal curse and an early noble deed together fire the life that leads relentlessly to war and death.

2. Many characters undergo similar experiences, as we have seen, for example, in the kinship diagram with its repetitious patterns (e.g. Satyavatī and Kuntī) in relations, settings, acts, etc., or in the inset tales like the Nala story wherein what happened to Yudhiṣṭhira (dice game, loss of kingdom, exile) happens also to Nala.

3. Thus the experiences are not bound to one character. It's as if action is released from character. Furthermore, the same man undergoes an experience more than once—e.g. living incognito, or engaging in the dice game, almost rehearsing it once and playing it for real a second or third time—like a neurotic's compulsions to repeat, or certain "autonomous complexes". It's as if there's a kind of autonomy of action. Once set into motion, the act chooses its personae, constitutes its agents.

4. Characters usually know what they are doing and still do it. Counsellors advise Yudhiṣṭhira against the dice game, giving him reasons, quoting texts. But he still accepts the invitation to the game. The Pāṇḍavas are told that Draupadī is born out of a sacrifice chiefly to wipe out the Kuru race, but then they still marry her.

5. No action goes unrecorded, unjudged, unexpiated—whatever be the motives or the total character of the person. Bhīṣma, for his own good reasons, rejects Ambā's offer of marriage and so must die at her hands. Yudhiṣṭhira yields to casuistry and tells a single lie. So he must visit hell at least briefly. No action is withdrawn from consequence. Kuntī's early indiscretion by which she gives birth to Karṇa and

abandons him, dogs her and Karṇa. Even Kṛṣṇa dies of Gāndhārī's curse that he be killed by a lowborn hunter in an unknown place.

6. Not only action, not even a passion in the mind can pass unpurged or fade without expression and consequence in the world outside the self. Action, once it begins in thought and feeling cannot be repressed. (Hence, Patañjali's yoga aphorism: *Yogaścittavṛttinirodhaḥ* "Yoga is the stilling of the waves of the mind"). That's why when Dhṛtarāṣṭra is angry with Bhīma and embraces him, Kṛṣṇa pushes an iron image into the blind old king's embrace. Dhṛtarāṣṭra crushes the effigy in an upsurge of repressed anger and that expressive vengeful act purges him of his grief and rage. Gāndhārī's anger too must find expression: as her sight (through the blindfold) lights on Yudhiṣṭhira's toes they begin to smolder and burn. And she curses Kṛṣṇa with an obscure and ignoble death. As the passions already are a form of action with consequences, mere self-control is not enough: they should not arise at all: hence Patañjali's second aphorism quoted above. The *Gītā*'s ideal man is therefore a *sthitaprajña* "the man with the steadied mind"; ideal action is *niṣkāmakarma* "the act without desire". For once the passions come into being, they issue in actions. They'll get themselves enacted. So, says the *Gītā*, act without thought of results or attachment.

7. Hence, the dramaturgic notions of action issuing from character, character transformed by action in some direct way, do not fit here. Characters do not change here. The usual kind of expectation of character change, of growth and maturation, is disappointed. Arjuna, after the obviously mind-blowing experience of the *Gītā* and the vision of the Cosmic Kṛṣṇa, does not become a different man. He gains just enough perspective to return to battle and to remain himself. The only change in a character usually is one of knowledge, a shift from ignorance to knowledge. Uttara sees Arjuna in his true form, but does not lose his natural cowardice. Arjuna sees the true form of Kṛṣṇa and is restored to the action that is true to his "nature" (*svabhāva*).

8. Furthermore, thanks to the replications, patterns of action are not confined to single characters: similar things happen to Satyavatī and Kuntī, to Yudhiṣṭhira and Nala, in the past and in the present. Thus the notion of "character" as something finite (etymologically "engraved", "fixed") crumbles as it opens into other lives and partakes of their patterns.

9. The chain of causation, central to the notion of karma, is structured so that one undergoes the same experience one has caused. If Māṇḍavya thrusts a blade of grass in a fly as a child, later he is impaled on a stake. Pāṇḍu kills a sage in a sexual act, so he dies in the act of sex. The structure repeats itself, except that the subject (Pāṇḍu) of the first act

becomes the object in the second. Curses, boons, and the consequences of past acts cannot be withdrawn—they have an autonomy independent of character. Action thus becomes prior to actors. Knowledge of precedent and legal advice do not prevent disastrous action—Yudhiṣṭhira gambles after hearing all the arguments against dice as a breeder of disputes. And the Pāṇḍavas marry Draupadī after learning that she has been born out of a sacrifice to root out the Kauravas.

(7)

In view of this way of thinking, the cast of characters can be divided into watchers and actors: Vidura (the god of Dharma reborn in a servant-maid's womb) and Vyāsa, the ancestor of all and the watcher/narrator of the whole epic, and Sañjaya in the battle scenes, watch all the action. Bhīṣma and Droṇa, after their initial actions, interfere very little—they can only watch the inexorable unrolling of events. Such watching and witnessing is part of the silence and failure of the elders in catastrophic scenes like the dice-game or the disrobing of Draupadī. The entire cast of dramatis personae seems to illustrate the ancient conception that the self has two aspects, a watching one (*sākṣin*) and an active one:

> Two birds, twin images
> in plumage,
> friends, ever inseparable,
> cling to a tree.
>
> One eats the fruit,
> eats of the sweet and eats
> of the bitter,
> while the other watches,
> watches without eating.
>
> Buried in the bole
> of the self-same tree
> one suffers, engulfed
> in his impotence.
>
> Yet as he watches the watching
> bird, the adorable one, and sees
> the sweet bitter glory
> as His alone,
> he rises, free
> from grief.

freely rendered from
Muṇḍakopaniṣad, III

We said earlier that characters were not quite "fixed", or "finite" as they are open to past lives as well as other lives around them. In another way too their status as characters is changeable: they tend to act as individuals sometimes, as representing classes and values at others, and at other times as part of one composite unit. Others (e.g. Goldman 1980) have noticed the composite character of Indian heroes like Rāma and Lakṣmaṇa. In this epic, the Pāṇḍavas act as one person vis-à-vis Kuntī, Draupadī and the Kaurava cousins. As noticed earlier, both in the early exhibition of skills and in winning Draupadī, Arjuna shoots five arrows into the target. He represents all five as warriors in the first instance and as suitors to Draupadī. The *Mahābhārata* says that Yudhiṣṭhira was the root and his brothers the branches of one tree. At another level, Yudhiṣṭhira, centrally concerned with ethical issues, stands for Brahminical values and the others for the Kṣatriya. Bhīma accuses him more than once of acting like a Brahmin, not a Kṣatriya. This pair is the focus of a central division and conflict in classical Indian society. Bhīma and Arjuna, frequently mentioned together as Bhīmārjuna, are clearly warriors. Bhīma is further distinguished by his physical power and Arjuna by his art and skill. Nakula/Sahadeva, the twins, are the "maintenance" men, like the Vaiśyas. As Dumézil points out, here is an Indo-European tri-partite society. Their true natures are hinted at when they

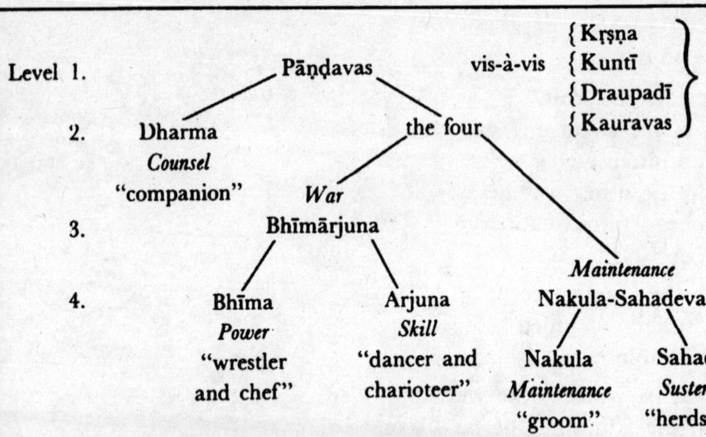

Level 1. Unity of the Five Pāṇḍavas
2. Dharma vs. Karma
3. Tripartite (Indo-European, à la Dumézil)
4. The five heroes individuated by the poet.

choose their disguises in Virāṭa's court: Yudhiṣṭhira as a brahmin counselor; Bhīma as wrestler and chef (he's also known for his enormous appetite and called Wolf-Belly, *vṛkodara*); Arjuna as an artful dancer and later as a charioteer; Nakula as a caretaker of horses and Sahadeva as a herdsman of cows. As Oscar Wilde says, "Give a man a mask, he will tell you the truth".

The five heroes are also individuated by the poet (especially the first three) by separate episodes for each—ex. Yudhiṣṭhira's dice-game, Bhīma's romance with the domoness Hidimbā, Arjuna's with Ulūpī and Urvaśī, and his special relation with Kṛṣṇa. They also have special foibles, as revealed in their deaths. These various relations at different levels may be summed up as in the diagram on page 440.

(*8*)

While I was contemplating the form of the *Mahābhārata*, I happened to browse in the section on crystallography in the *Encyclopedia Britannica*. I found that the following sentences offered apt analogies for what I've been talking about.

> All crystals have at least this kind of order, which can be described as a periodic repetition of their atomic chemical motif by translations. (p. 852) Repetition can be defined by translation, rotation, and by reflection . . . or combinations of these simple devices. (p. 858)

On the *Mahābhāratas* in different languages, appearing in different sizes:

> When a crystal is placed in contact with a solvent, it dissolves in such a way as to be consistent with its symmetry. (p. 858)

Crystallographers also speak of crystal growth in steps wherever there is a "dislocation", which makes for both order and growth, an open-ended system. When one compares the many *Mahābhāratas* or other works based on the epics, the way new incidents are added only in certain places where there seems to be a need for them, one thinks of such an analogy with crystal growth. Of the scores of instances, I shall cite only one. The way Yudhiṣṭhira loses evrything in dice seems to many readers a little incredible. Others (like van Buitenen) have offered ingenious, somewhat extra-textual explanations of why the dicegame was necessary—e.g., it is because it was part of the Rājasūya sacrifice, the sacrifice that Yudhiṣṭhira performs. There are other good reasons given in the Sanskrit text: for one, Śakuni says, "Invite Yudhiṣṭhira to a dice game. He loves to play dice but doesn't know how". Lest there should still be any doubt regarding the absolute certainty of Śakuni's victory, both later and folk-*Mahābhāratas* tell a story about Śakuni's past. Śakuni and his brothers were once cruelly imprisoned by Vicitravīrya in the generation before Dhṛtarāṣṭra. Part of the cruelty consisted of giving all six brothers only one plate of food, just enough to feed only one, each day. As they were all starving, tantalized by these morsels, they decided to give it to the cleverest of them, so that he could survive and take revenge. The test: to thread a bone without a needle. Śakuni, clever Śakuni, threads it by tying a thread to an ant and baiting it with a grain of rice. So the brothers give Śakuni the daily plate and starve to death. Śakuni makes dice out of his dead brothers' bones and waits for a chance to take revenge against the Kauravas. The dead men's anger in the dice makes sure that Yudhiṣṭhira will win at no throw and will lose kingdom, brothers and himself, and lead to a total war of destruction. Such a story adds one more past and one more motive to the action. That's a characteristic "growth step" for the *Mahābhārata*.

> Surprisingly, many of the most important properties of the crystal are one of the few odd places in which the crystal goes wrong. Many crystals could not have grown at all without having imperfections in them. (p. 866)

References

Bharati, Subramanya (Pārati, Cuppiramaṇiya), *Kavitaikaḷ* (Poems), Madras: Pūmpukar, 1976.

Biardeau, Madeleine, *Le Mahābhārata*, I & II, Paris: Flammarion, 1987.

Dumèzil, Georges, *Mythe et Epopée*, I, Paris: Editions Gallimard, 1968.

Goldman, Robert P. "Rāmaḥ Sahalakṣmaṇah: Psychological and Literary Aspects of the Composite Hero of Vālmiki's Rāmāyaṇa", *Journal of Indian Philosophy*, Vol. 8, No. 2, June 1980.

Hiltebeitel, Alf, *The Ritual of Battle*, Krishna in the *Mahābhārata*, Ithaca: Cornell University Press, 1976.

——, *The Cult of Draupadī*, I, Mythologies: from Gingee to Kurukṣetra, Chicago: University of Chicago Press, 1988.

Rajagopalachari, C., *The Mahābhārata*, Bombay: Bharatiya Vidya Bhavan (in Tamil: *Makāpāratam*, Vānoli patippakam, 1973).

Ramanujan, A.K., "Is There an Indian Way of Thinking"? Conference on the Hindu Persons, sponsored by the SSRC/ACLS Joint Committee on South Asia, 1980; reprinted in *Contributions to Indian Sociology*, (n.s.) 23, 1 (1989).

——, "The Indian Oedipus", in Alan Dundes and Lowell Edmunds (eds.), *Oedipus: A Folklore Casebook*, Garland Press, 1983; revised version of "The Indian Oedipus," in *Indian Literature*, ed. A. Potdar, Simla: Indian Institute of Advanced Study, 1972.

Sax, William, "The Pāṇḍava Līlā", typescript, 1987.

Shulman, David D., *The King and the Clown in South Indian Myth and Poetry*, Princeton: Princeton University Press, 1985.

——, "On Fate and Being Human in the Sanskrit Epic: The Riddle of Nala" (typescript), 1989.

——, "The Yakṣa's Questions" (typescript). Seminar on Enigmatic Modes, Jerusalem. 1989.

Tubb, Gary, "*Śāntarasa* in the *Mahābharata*", *Journal of South Asian Literature*, vol. xx, no. 1, Winter, Spring 1985 (issue devoted to the *Mahābhārata*, guest editor: Arvind Sharma).

van Buitenen, J.A.B. (tr.), *The Mahābhārata*, vol. I, Chicago: University of Chicago Press, 1973.

Venkatesa Ayyangār, M., *Bhāratatīrtha* (in Kannada).

HIMALAYAN VARIATIONS ON AN EPIC THEME

JOHN LEAVITT

For the several thousand years that we have any information about, the tide of tradition has flowed across the South Asian subcontinent, giving forth stories. These stories were (are) told to suit local needs for amusement, explanation, or connection with the past or the gods; but sometimes stories have stuck to each other and grown into more extensive, complex, and fixed wholes, crystallizations (Ramanujan's term, this volume) out of the intergenerational flow of tellings. The growth of a large body of fixed discourse, an epic or a collection of hymns, may be encouraged by the development of techniques such as writing, oral-formulaic composition, or the disciplines of memory; once in existence, such a textual monument changes the flow-pattern of stories around it. These continue to develop and change, but they will begin to draw on, refer to, and feed back into a text that is now a continuing point of reference.

My use of a liquid metaphor to characterize the history of tradition in South Asia is not, of course, original.[1] It reproduces a South Asian metaphor, since many collections of poems or stories are called *sāgara*, 'ocean', the most famous being the Sanskrit tale-collection the *Kathāsaritsāgara*, literally 'the Ocean of Streams of Story'. The oceanic metaphor also has the virtue of highlighting the continual process of interchange between levels of tradition, between fixed text and folk text. While such interchange takes place in all parts of the world, it is particularly marked in South Asia, to the point of requiring rethinking of a whole series of Western assumptions. Western scholars have generally accepted a dichotomy between a literate tradition made up of written and therefore permanent texts meant to be read privately and an oral tradition of spoken and therefore ephemeral and public texts. This neat lining-up of oppositions—written/oral = fixed/fluid = lasting/ephemeral = private/public—is reorganized in surprising ways in some of the most important textual

[1] The importance of patterns of flowing and liquidity in many aspects of South Asian conceptualization has been most consistently and convincingly argued by McKim Marriott. See, for instance, Marriott 1989.

corpuses of South Asian tradition. Three cases: First, the Vedas, the central texts of Hinduism, have been passed down for thousands of years in a virtually fixed form not through writing, which has played the role of an after-the-fact aid, but through prodigious feats of syllable-by-syllable memorization in one generation after another. Second, the great epics, the *Mahābhārata* and the *Rāmāyaṇa*, were composed essentially in an oral formulaic mode,[2] woven together around central narrative frameworks, and transmitted as structured masses of story. While writing may have contributed to their formation, here too it has primarily served as an aid to oral performance—and a variable and impermanent aid at that, due to the short lifespan of the writing materials available through most of South Asian history.[3] Finally, in South Asia much of the folk tradition has developed in interaction with the oral and written classical tradition, and the prestige of writing is such that illiterate tale-tellers often claim written sources for their stories. As often as not, these sources are either vaguely remembered from several generations in the past or are mysterious, legendary, or lost books that no one can quite get a copy of any more.

Thus central to South Asian tradition are cases that violate our expectations about literacy and orality: fixed and frozen bodies of oral material that have lasted longer than anything written; writing as an ephemeral aid to oral performance; an orality that co-exists with literacy and often claims written origins. Rather than an oral or a literate civilization as such, South Asia is a civilization of fixed orality, of writing for reading aloud, and at the same time an oral civilization of the phantom book.

This is not to say, however, as many have, that all aspects of classical and folk traditions in South Asia are manifestations of a single underlying pattern. The continual interchange between levels of tradition has led, in my view, not to a single cultural monad (Marriott 1976) in which all variation is to be seen as "the local working-out of (a general) idea" (Dumont 1957: 25), but, on the contrary, to a situation so complex that scholars have a hard time conceptualizing it. In most parts of South Asia, multiple traditions continue to coexist and influence one other,

---

[2] As Sheldon Pollock puts it (1986: 37), "the *Rāmāyaṇa*, in the form we have it, must represent the culmination of a long tradition of heroic song." The most ambitious effort to analyze the Sanskrit epics in terms of oral-formulaic theory is that of Grintser (1974). For discussions of the oral nature of the Sanskrit epic, see Ingalls and Ingalls 1985; O'Flaherty 1978, 1988; Pollock 1984.

[3] On orality and literacy and on fixity and fluidity in South Asian literature, see O'Flaherty 1988, especially the section "Fixed and Fluid Texts in the East" (pp. 56–63).

without any one clearly dominating: rich and coherent oral literatures continue to flourish cheek by jowl with orthodox oral and literate traditions, to draw on the latter, and to overlap with them in subject matter while maintaining their autonomy. Thus within a couple of square kilometers in the Central Himalayas, some Brahmans may be chanting to an audience from a copy of the Hindi *Rāmāyaṇa*, other Brahmans in a nearby house may be studying the Sanskrit *Rāmāyaṇa* among themselves, in the village center a Hindi *Rām Līlā* may be going on, while in a third house a local bard may be singing an orally composed epic in the regional language telling of the deeds of Lord Rām—here portrayed as a kind of village chief who slays demons in a familiar landscape, and whose deeds may not be found in any written text.

One way to begin to come to grips with this extraordinary complexity is to focus in on the vicissitudes of particular bits of tradition, particular themes. This is what I will be attempting here by presenting several variations on one theme from the *Mahābhārata*, the story of the hero Bhīma's killing of a demon and his marriage to the demon's sister. I will be comparing the Sanskrit version with variations that are told for particular occasions in the village life of the Kumaon hill region in northern India: first a translated retelling published in a scholarly work on the region, then a performance of the story in its ritual context. In both cases, I will be seeking to show ways in which differences in the stories' content may be seen as responses to differences in their contexts of telling.[4]

Classical and Folk Mahābhāratas

The *Mahābhārata* clearly illustrates this contiguity, interweaving, and autonomy of traditions. It exists both in a relatively fixed written form and in many oral folk forms that diverge more or less widely from the written version. The written version itself is not an individual composition but the end-product of centuries of oral transmission, crystallizing out between the fourth century B.C. and the fourth century A.D. Like the *Iliad* and the *Odyssey*, it is a written text that retains clear marks of its oral composition. And the written text itself has only recently and

---

[4] For a discussion of similar issues in the analysis of a Himalayan version of an international folktale, see Leavitt 1981. On the worship of Hiḍimbā in South India, see Hiltebeitel 1988: 212–215.

partially, with the introduction of printing, become an object in and for itself, a book for reading in the Western sense. Through most of its history, it existed in "a fairly small number of hand-written transcripts, fatefully fragile, that assisted word of mouth" (van Buitenen 1973: xxviii). Since its crystallization between the fourth century B.C. and the fourth century A.D., the *Mahābhārata* has provided material for regional and local traditions all over the subcontinent and wherever Hindu civilization has had an influence. Vernacular versions of the epic have generally remained autonomous while developing according to specific cultural dynamics alongside and in interaction with the continuing transmission of the Sanskrit version.

Commentators are always marvelling at the bulk of the *Mahābhārata*, and it was long the fashion to decry its shapelessness, to consider it a simple repository of all kinds of folkloric and religious accretions around an original and straightforward narrative core. More recent scholarship, on the other hand, without denying the syncretistic nature of the epic's development, has concentrated on its overall structure, whether as a manifestation of more ancient patterns (Dumézil 1968), in light of its Hindu context (Biardeau and Péterfalvi 1986), or through noting repetitions that weave the epic together, often in surprising ways (Ramanujan, this volume). In this, contemporary Western scholarship is in line with traditional Hindu views (Ramanujan, this volume; Tubb 1985). What is most striking about the *Mahābhārata* would seem to be not its enormity and diversity in themselves, but the coherence that the text imposes on this enormity: while it may indeed be a repository for the odds and ends of Indic tradition, the *Mahābhārata* possesses mechanisms for weaving these together and incorporating them into a coherent whole—mechanisms that may have been furthered by writing, but that do not depend on it.

The *Mahābhārata* also, of course, exists in many regional and folk versions. In the Central Himalayas, folk versions of the epic are performed in single episodes. These fragments of epic material are made to serve a wide variety of functions, including ritual, healing, and entertainment. This is to say that folk *Mahābhāratas* participate in a set of occasions regulated not primarily by textual considerations as such, but by social and cultural ones more generally: they depend on occasions of storytelling, serve the ritual goals of a performance, provide justifications for social institutions or explanations of the landscape. This complex and changing symbolic economy, provoking the telling of stories of many kinds, existed before the forging of the Sanskrit *Mahābhārata*, and indeed provided its varied source material; it continues to develop alongside and around the epic, drawing on and feeding back into it over the centuries.

The Hiḍimbā Story in the Sanskrit Mahābhārata

The story of Bhīma and Hiḍimbā in the *Mahābhārata* is found in the *Ādiparvan* (*Mahābhārata* 1.139–143),[5] immediately after the five Pāṇḍava brothers, the heroes of the epic, escape from the burning of the Lacquer House in which their enemies the Kauravas had sought to trap them. It is retold much more briefly in the *Vanaparvan* as part of the Pāṇḍavas' wife Draupadī's narration of their adventures up to then (3.13.85–100). I'll be giving an extremely abridged version of the main rendition, selecting bits from the van Buitenen translation (1973: 294–301) and adding some explanatory material in brackets. I have not bothered to note omissions, since doing so would have meant separating nearly every two phrases with ellipsis points. The reader can easily refer to the original; here I have simply pulled narrative phrases out of the mass of descriptive and intensifying material that makes up the major part of the Sanskrit text.

> While [the Pāṇḍavas] were sleeping [in a wood], a Rākṣasa by the name of Hiḍimba was living not very far from the wood. He was hungry and looking for flesh when he happened to see them. Then [he] said to his sister, "Kill all those humans and bring them to me." The Rākṣasī hurriedly went to the spot where the Pāṇḍavas were lying. No sooner had she seen Bhīmasena than the Rākṣasi fell in love with him. "That swarthy, strong-armed, lion-shouldered, lustrous, conch-necked, lotus-eyed man is the right husband for me! I won't follow my brother's outrageous orders. If I don't kill them I'll be pleasured for years without end!" She took on a beautiful human shape and approached Bhīmasena, and smilingly she said to him, "Where have you come from and who are you? This desolate jungle is haunted by Rākṣasas, and a wicked Rākṣasa lives here. He is my brother, and he sent me from sheer wickedness. But I chose you for my one and only husband."
>
> The lordly Rākṣasa Hiḍimba descended from his tree and went down to the Pāṇḍavas. [Bhīmasena challenges him.] They set upon each other with all their might. Their great noise awakened the bulls among men, and they and their mother saw Hiḍimbā [the demon's sister] standing before them. [The other Pāṇḍavas try to help Bhīma, but he rejects their efforts. Arjuna warns him to kill the Rākṣasa before dawn, "the grisly hour when Rākṣasas become stronger."] Bhīma tossed up the body of the terrible Rākṣasa and spun it around over a hundred times. [After some taunting from Arjuna,] Bhīma became very indignant. He strangled [Hiḍimba] to death like a sacrificial animal. [Bhīma thinks it would be wise to kill Hiḍimbā as well, but she and Yudhiṣṭhira persuade him to marry her instead.] She took

---

[5] References are to the Critical Edition of the *Mahābhārata*, V.S. Sukthankar, ed., Poona: Bhandarkar Oriental Research Institute, 1933–1966.

> Bhīma and strode up above. On lovely mountain peaks she took on a superb body, and she made love to the Pāṇḍava. The Rākṣasī gave birth to a son by the powerful Bhīmasena. He was a terrifying sight [but appeared human because] Rākṣasas assume any shape they want. The shiny child bowed and touched his father's feet and his mother's, and his parents gave him a name: Ghaṭotkaca, Shiny-as-a-Pot. This Ghaṭotkaca was devoted to the Pāṇḍavas, and they loved him. Then Hiḍimbā said to Bhīma that the time of their life together had run out; and she went her own way. Ghaṭotkaca promised his father that he would come to them whenever he was needed. For he had been created by Māghavat for power's sake, so that he might destroy the great-spirited Karṇa, whose prowess was unmatched.

The story stands as an independent unit with its own internal structure, the story of a remarkable meeting, battle, marriage, and birth. Historically, the marriage of a hero with a demoness is found elsewhere in Indo-Iranian mythology, and Dumézil (1968: 64) sees evidence for the existence of a Hiḍimbā-like story predating the formation of the *Mahābhārata* as a whole. In the form we now have it in, however, certain elements of the story lead out of the episode itself and serve to bind it into the overall *Mahābhārata* narrative.

Three such elements stand out. First of all, the very fact of the odd marriage between a prince and a demoness serves to point up the special traits of this particular prince. Bhīma is a clearly defined character: he is the biggest, strongest, fiercest, least thoughtful, most short-tempered of the Pāṇḍavas; indeed, his very name means "frightful" or "fierce". Because of this, since demons are defined by these very qualities, Bhīma is the most "demonic" of the Pāṇḍavas, something this marriage serves to highlight. The centrality of Bhīma's character to the *Mahābhārata* as a whole has been stressed by Georges Dumézil (e.g., 1968: 63–65), who sees him as representing the ferocious "berserker" aspect of the warrior function, in opposition to his brother Arjuna, the courtly or knightly warrior. For Dumézil, the Hiḍimbā episode exemplifies this "demonic" side of Bhīma's character:

> Unlike Arjuna, whose good fortunes link him to honorable women, Bhīma unites himself with a rākṣasī, Hiḍimbā, and gives her a son (an excellent one, by the way), just as [the Iranian hero Keresāspa, who in many respects corresponds to Bhīma] lets himself be seduced by a demoness (Dumézil 1968: 64, citing Wikander 1947: 38).

A second and more obvious way in which this episode connects into the narrative as a whole is in the loose end provided by the birth of Ghaṭotkaca, the formidable kinsman and ally of the Pāṇḍavas, who will play an essential role in the great battle of Kurukṣetra toward which the whole multilayered narrative is made to build. As we have seen, this is quite explicit in the text, which, foreshadowing the story of Ghaṭotkaca's death in the *Droṇaparvan* (*Mahābhārata* 7.149–155), tells us that Ghaṭotkaca was created by Indra (Māghavat) to serve as a means of nullifying the power of Karṇa, the most dangerous enemy of the Pāṇḍavas. More specifically, Ghaṭotkaca will represent such an enormous threat that Karṇa will finally decide to use his one irresistible weapon against him, instead of saving it, as he had intended, to kill Arjuna. The weapon, a magic lance, was given to Karṇa by Indra, and it can only be used once. In the *śloka* foretelling this outcome (*Mahābhārata* 1.143.38), which ends the selection given above, van Buitenen translates *śaktihetor*, "because of" or "for the sake of *śakti*", as "for power's sake". In this context, however, *śakti* is used not only for power in general, but specifically for Karṇa's magic lance, and it is in this latter sense that Péterfalvi translates the phrase: "because of the magic lance (*śakti*)" (Biardeau and Péterfalvi 1986: I, 142).

A third linking of this episode into the overall narrative structure of the epic also derives from the fate of Ghaṭotkaca. He was born to counter Karṇa's "power" by serving as a substitute victim for it—a kind of sacrifice. This too is part of a major theme of the epic as a whole, since a whole series of sons of the Pāṇḍavas die on the field of battle, apparently as sacrificial counterparts for the deaths of their enemies (Biardeau 1979).

In all of these ways, the story of Bhīma and Hiḍimbā, which at first glance seems an independent adventure, is linked into the structure of the *Mahābhārata* as a whole. This kind of linking is, I think, typical of a long, relatively fixed text that has developed its own internal imperatives, its own tendencies toward structuration. We shall see that folk versions of this story operate very differently, responding to a very different set of imperatives.

The Regional Cycle: Mahābhārat *in the Central Himalayas*

The Central Himalayan region, which covers the mountainous portion of the Indian state of Uttar Pradesh, lies along the chain of the Himalayas between Nepal to the southeast and the state of Himachal Pradesh to the northwest. The region includes zones of high mountains, of less rugged hills and valleys, and of flat land along the foot of the mountains. The central hill and valley zone has always formed the civilizational nucleus for the region. The people of this zone, called Paharis or mountain people, formed the core population of the two kingdoms of Garhwal and Kumaon, which were overthrown by the Nepalis in the late eighteenth century, and were soon after that incorporated, for the most part, into British India. The population of this region is mainly Hindu, mainly rural, mainly poor but not starving. Economically and politically, the region is peripheral to the North Indian scene; no longer independent kingdoms, Garhwal and Kumaon now form the mountainous part of a state dominated by the enormously larger population of the North Indian plains.

Historically, the people of the central hill and valley zone have been fairly, but only fairly, open to influence from the plains, which was slowed down by the malarial jungle at the bottom of the hills and by the ruggedness of the outer ranges. As a result, the hill population, not only in the Central Himalayas, but in much of Himachal Pradesh and much of Nepal, speaks languages related to the great Indo-Aryan languages of North India, but distinct from them and forming a distinct Pahari language family. The dominance of Hinduism indicates the relative openness of this region to the plains, but the kind of Hinduism practiced, centered primarily on local divinities and heroes, is an indicator of its relative isolation. Both of these factors—language and religion—are of central importance in understanding the nature of Central Himalayan oral literature.

The linguistic situation in Kumaon—which is the sub-region that I will be discussing—is highly complex (as are most linguistic situations in South Asia). Before the Nepali and British conquests, Sanskrit was the language of orthodox ritual, and the regional Pahari language, now called Kumaoni, with its various dialects and registers, the dominant language of village, bazaar, and court. The British introduced administrative Hindustani, and Hindi, the official language of the state of Uttar Pradesh, is today the language of administration, education, broadcasting, most publishing, including all newspapers, and much of urban life. Sanskrit has retained its place in orthodox ritual. Kumaoni remains the major language of everyday interaction, especially in rural areas, where the people have been massively illiterate until very recently; and it is the language of an extraordinarily rich and vibrant tradition of bardic performance.

Versions of the *Mahābhārata* exist in all three languages. Copies of all or part of the Sanskrit text, especially the *Bhāgavad Gītā*, are common, particularly in Brahman families. Mass-published Hindi versions and translations are widely available, although there is neither a popular Hindi version of the *Mahābhārata* nor a public performance tradition based on the epic, both of which are the case for the *Rāmāyaṇa*. Finally, the oral tradition in Kumaoni includes an enormous mass of *Mahābhārata*-related material. But to give an idea of this material requires a clearer distinction between traditions related to the Pāṇḍavas, on the one hand, and the Kumaoni use of the word *mahābhārat* on the other.

In folk literature, toponymy, and local historical traditions, the Pāṇḍavas have a special link to the Central Himalayan region, which is where the *Mahābhārata* tells us they came at the end of their lives. The association is particularly strong with Garhwal, and in Garhwal the Pāṇḍavas are considered both ancestors of some living clans and still active, still present in the region. In Garhwal, Pāṇḍava-worship has developed into an elaborate cult, the *Pāṇḍav Līlā*, that involves controlled possession by the heroes of their devotees (Berreman 1963: 381–385; Sax, this volume). This strong link between the Pāṇḍavas and this region led Gerald Berreman to postulate that rather than being borrowed from Sanskrit literature, the Pāṇḍavas "may well be indigenous objects of worship in these hills who have been universalized to become part of the literary tradition of Hinduism" (1963: 382).[6]

Pāṇḍava-worship is less developed in Kumaon than in Garhwal, but here too the heroes are important in landscape and legend; one of the most important lakes in the region, for instance, is called Bhīmtāl, "Bhīm's Lake." In Kumaon, the stories of the Pāṇḍavas are sung by semi-professional bards as ballads or sung epics. The bards classify them as *mahābhārat*, but it is important to note that this use of the term refers not just to the Sanskrit epic, but to a genre of bardic performance: *mahābhārat* includes the whole set of ballads that are derived from classical epic or Puranic sources. *Mahābhārat* present regional versions of the stories of orthodox Hindu gods and heroes such as Rām, Kṛṣṇa, Śiva, and so forth (Gaborieau 1974, 1975; P. Jośī 1971: 6–8; Pāṇḍey 1962: 171–179). *Mahābhārat* versions are thus distinct from the orthodox versions of the stories, which are retold by Brahmans and in performances, such as the *Rām Līlā*, which are not a particular preserve of the bards—who are usually of low caste and of very limited formal education. As one bard put it when I asked him whether Rāvaṇ figured in his *mahābhārat* version of a story of Rām, "That's in books, that comes in the *Rām Līlā*. Rāvaṇ and so forth, that comes in the *Rām Līlā*." At the same time, *mahābhārat* is equally distinct from the other genres of oral literature that the bards perform, which tell primarily of regional divinities and heroes. Ballads of regional gods are performed as part of nocturnal possession rituals of healing and blessing called *jāgar* or 'vigil'; ballads of non-divinized heroes are sung at fairs and to inspire work in the fields at highly labor-intensive points in the agricultural cycle.[7] These are all

[6] Even if it is true that the Pāṇḍavas originated in the hills—and it is not clear how one is to tell this—there has been a great deal of feedback from the Sanskrit epic onto the hill representations of the heroes.

[7] On indigenous and scholarly definitions of oral *genres* in Kumaoni, see Gaborieau 1974; Leavitt 1985; Pāṇḍey 1962.

distinct from the many folktales and fables that circulate among the population as a whole.

Mahābhārat is performed not primarily for entertainment, but either as an adjunct to *jāgar*, in which case it is seen as an additional offering to the regional god, who likes hearing these stories of the great Hindu gods and heroes, or as rituals in their own right, meant to bring blessings on the family sponsoring them. *Mahābhārat* are generally said to be stories of *avatārs*, but here again the term has a greater extension than it has in classical literature: these *avatārs* are not descents of Viṣṇu to earth, but rather divine beings who have acted on earth. Rām, Kṛṣṇa, Śiva, the Pāṇḍavas, and often the Goddess are all *avatārs* in this sense (cf. Gaborieau 1975: 150–151). Unlike the *jāgar*, *mahābhārat* performance as ritual does not involve possession, and, while it is meant to bring blessings and control demonic forces in general, it seems less focused than the *jāgar* on dealing with specific illness or trouble.

While *mahābhārat* seem clearly derived from epic and Puranic models, these regional versions have usually been transformed—sometimes drastically—through a period of oral transmission. In an essay on Kannada folklore, A.K. Ramanujan (1986: 64–67) asks, "What happens when classical myths are borrowed and retold by folk performers?" He offers four ways in which such myths are transformed, all of which fit Kumaoni *mahābhārat*. First of all, these stories "appear mostly in bits and pieces" in the folk tradition. This process of fragmentation, as I argued at the beginning of this essay, seems to be a result of the great difference in the requirements of village performance from those of a relatively integrated fixed text. Ramanujan continues by pointing out "three kinds of striking changes in the folk form." First, the gods and heroes are domesticated, that is, made more like the people who are telling and listening to the story. Ramanujan cites Rāma's runny nose in a Kannada version of his story; compare this to Bhīm's prodigious urination in the version below. Second, "the folk renditions *localize* the pan-Indian epics and myths," that is, they re-set them in localities familiar to the story's audience. Finally, "folk renditions tend to *contemporize* the action." All three of these processes serve to bring the events of the story nearer to those who are telling and hearing it, whether in time, space, or the nature of the protagonists—all are processes, if I may coin a term, of *proximation*. Both fragmentation and proximation make sense in a context of ritual performance, since the first allows the story to be used in internally coherent pieces in performances, and the second heightens the pertinence of the performances for those who take part in them. I will be drawing on these concepts to orient the discussion of Himalayan variants of the Hiḍimbā story.

Mahābhārat stories about the Pāṇḍavas may be found in a few books on

Kumaoni folklore, where they are generally arranged in a way that follows the chronology of the Sanskrit *Mahābhārata*, forming a kind of cycle of stories within the *mahābhārat* genre (K. Jośī 1971: 89–95; Pāṇḍey 1962: 172–174). These stories show a high degree of proximation to contemporary rural life in Kumaon. The Pāṇḍavs and the Kauravs, for instance, live in two villages with their respective mothers; the cause of their enmity is a fight between the Pāṇḍavs' cat and the Kauravs' chicken.

The longest such set of retellings is found in U.D. Upādhyāy's book in Hindi, *A Literary and Cultural Study of the Folk Ballads of Kumaon* (1979), which includes a version of the Hiḍimbā story which I present in translation below. Upādhyāy's version has passed through three filters before reaching us: it is a retelling rather than an attempt to reproduce the actual telling; it is retold in prose from a sung original; it is a translation into Hindi of a story originally performed in Kumaoni. My own translation, of course, is a fourth filter. While Upādhyāy's book offers discussions of many aspects of these ballads, it does not give information about their singers or their region of origin within Kumaon.

Upādhyāy's version (1977: 279–281) sets the Hiḍimbā story during the period of the Pāṇḍavs' dwelling in the forest. The Pāṇḍavs arrive in a part of the forest in which there is nothing to eat. Here is an abridged translation (for a full translation, see Leavitt 1988):[8]

> Bhīmsen said to his family members, "Around here there aren't any fruits or flowers . . . So I am going away to look for food, and I'm going to put you people in some safe place . . ." Bhīm made a tree-house in a tall tree and settled his family in it and went away looking for food. Going, going, Bhīm came to Hiḍambā's house. Hiḍambā challenged Bhīm to play at swinging with her. "If you win at swinging, then I will go with you; if I win, then you'll stay in my house. . . ." At that time Hiḍambā was pregnant and her months were almost fulfilled. Bhīm and Hiḍambā started playing on the swing. Sometimes the swing would brush one edge of the sky, sometimes it would brush the other. Sometime's Bhīm's side was on the point of winning and sometimes Hiḍambā's side. Finally, when the swing was at its highest on Bhīmsen's side he gave it one extra push upwards. With this great jerk of the swing, Hiḍambā's womb fell [i.e., she gave birth], and Hiḍambā lost the swinging game. Out of Hiḍambā's womb fell

[8] Like most modern Indo-Aryan languages, Kumaoni has lost Sanskrit final -a, and this principle has been extended to Sanskrit loanwords. So, for instance, Sanskrit Bhīma gives Kumaoni Bhīm. At the same time, in Kumaoni the differences between b and v (with v sometimes being pronounced like English w or a very short u), and between s and ś, are not phonemic, and pronunciation tends to fluctuate by position. So from Sanskrit Śiva we have Kumaoni Siv, Sib, or Siu, from Pāṇḍava Kumaoni Pāṇḍav or Pāṇḍab.

> a child; he tied his umbilical cord around his waist and started to fight with Bhīmsen. Bhīm knocked him down playfully. Both Bhīm and Hiḍamba [the child] went into Hiḍambā's house.

This first section of the story already gives a good deal of information. It is evident, first of all, that we are not dealing with a parallel oral tradition that has grown up independently since ancient times. The names alone indicate close and fairly recent interaction with the Sanskrit *Mahābhārata*, and the story clearly seems to be derived from the epic. Significant divergences from the Sanskrit version are, however, already evident. The meeting with the demoness has been elaborated to become a contest. The role and importance of the son, on the contrary, have shrunk drastically. He is no longer Bhīm's son at all, but the result of some earlier *amour* of the demoness's; and once Bhīm has established friendly relations with him, he disappears from the story. This severs what the Sanskrit text presents as the main link between the Hiḍimbā episode and the *Mahābhārata* narrative as a whole, and so represents a major step in the isolating of this episode, part of the general fragmentation of the epic discussed above. This dual pattern of elaboration of the internal elements of the story and weakening of its links to the epic as a whole will keep recurring in the two Kumaoni versions being considered here. We should note, however, that the disappearance of Ghaṭotkaca is not universal in Kumaon. Under the name Ghāṭku, he continues to be an important figure in some parts of the region, with temples dedicated to his worship (Atkinson 1884: 807). We may, then, presume that in other parts of Kumaon the link between this story and Ghaṭotkaca's career remains part of the tradition. This is simply to say that the fragmentation of the epic is not uniform, but depends on local histories of transmission.

> Meanwhile, Hiḍambā's brother Kinkar Dānu [i.e., Kinkar the Dānava, the demon] went into the jungle where the Pāṇḍavs were . . . Kinkar Dānu saw the Pāṇḍavs up in the tree, and he decided to steal them away . . . Calling to the Pāṇḍavs from below, the demon said, "Hey ascetics! There is a *pūjā* at my house, I've come to invite you all . . ." The Pāṇḍavs said, "But we're up in this inaccessible tree, how can we get down"? The demon set a ladder up against the tree and underneath it he spread a net. All the Pāṇḍavs came down . . . and Kinkar Dānu shut them all up in the net and headed for home.
>
> Meanwhile, Bhīm was remembering his family. Bhīm went back to that jungle to look for them . . . He saw that the tree-house was empty . . . Lamenting, Bhīm wandered all around the forest.
>
> Kinkar Dānu took the net with the Pāṇḍavs in it to a temple of the Goddess [Kālī] in order to sacrifice them . . . The demon brought the net . . . into the temple and tied it up tight. In his heart, his very heart, he was delighted, thinking, "Today when she gets such powerful offerings, the

> Goddess will be filled with power [to grant me blessings]." The demon asked each of the Pāṇḍavs who or what could save them at such a time. Each told of his own weapon, which now was far away. Only Draupadī said, "Now if Bhīmsen is a warrior at all, then he will save us." The demon burst out laughing: "Bhīm is like a fly, what can he do?"

In the Sanskrit version, the demon comes to see what is going on, and the fight takes place there in the wood. Here a whole new theme is added: the demon captures the rest of the Pāṇḍavas and takes them home to sacrifice to his patron goddess—it is, of course, appropriate for bloodthirsty demons to practice blood sacrifice to Kālī. The purpose here, as in blood sacrifice practiced by humans instead of demons, using buffaloes, goats, or chickens instead of people as victims, is to strengthen and please the goddess, who in turn will grant blessings.

> Meanwhile Bhīm, weeping, weeping, came back to Hiḍambā's house and . . . explained the whole situation. Hiḍambā told Bhīm of her brother's evil deed . . . Bhīmsen went to that Goddess temple, took on the form of a flower-bug, and hid in a basket of flowers. Bhīm was brought into the temple along with the flowers and he quietly started to eat the materials and offerings for the *pūjā*. When it was time for the six Pāṇḍavs to be killed, Bhīm took on a gigantic form and burst the roof of the temple. The six Pāṇḍavs escaped, and Bhīm and the demon started to fight.
>
> Bhīm came out of the temple dragging the demon along behind him . . . For seven days and seven nights there was a ferocious battle. Bhīm started to feel tired and pinched by hunger . . . In his heart, his very heart, he remembered Queen Hiḍambā. Suddenly Hiḍambā was there, and . . . together [they] put an end to the demon. All the Pāṇḍavs stayed at Hiḍambā's house for some time, then they went back to the jungle.

Three areas of divergence from the Sanskrit *Mahābhārata* stand out in this story. All represent both an elaboration of the internal structure of the tale and a weakening of its links to the Pāṇḍava-epic as a whole.

The first area of divergence has to do with the plot and narrative setting. In the Sanskrit *Mahābhārata*, the Hiḍimbā story takes place immediately after the escape from the Lacquer House, and so is bound up in a highly structured series of events. Here, however, the incident with Hiḍambā has been made part of the Pāṇḍavas' period of forest dwelling (Book Three of the Sanskrit text). This shift decontextualizes the episode, since the forest dwelling is here treated as an amorphous period without overall narrative structure, during which one adventure simply follows another. At the same time, some of the elaborate plot-line that surrounds the Hiḍimbā episode in the Sanskrit version has here been incorporated into the episode itself. The battle between Bhīm and the demon, a straightforward fight in the Sanskrit *Mahābhārata*, here develops into a story of abduction, incarceration, imminent slaughter, and escape—a reversal of the syntax of the Sanskrit narrative, in which the meeting with the demoness *follows* the Pāṇḍavas' escape from entrapment and murder in the Lacquer House.

The second area of divergence has already been noted: the folk version loses interest in the son while greatly developing both the meeting with the demoness and the battle with her brother. The shift in interest is reflected in the use of names in the two versions. In the Sanskrit text the demoness and her brother share a single name, each being simply the masculinization or feminization of the name of the other, while the son has a memorable name of his own. It seems to me that this pattern is a key to the balance of the story as a whole, whose narrative elements fall into two parts: first, Bhīma marries/destroys Hiḍimbā/Hiḍimba, allying himself with a tractable demon while eliminating an incorrigible one, and at the same time replacing her brother as Hiḍimbā's lord and master; this leads to the birth of Ghaṭotkaca, a figure fated to save Arjuna, making the whole story one more example of Bhīma's service to his brothers. In the Kumaoni version, it is the son who has to share a name with his mother; he is a kind of smaller double of hers. The two main parts of the story are now, the namings suggest, first the subduing/marrying/adopting of Hiḍambā/Hiḍamba, then the complicated struggle with her brother—a brother who has now earned a name of his own. The subduing and destruction of demons is now the whole story, contained in itself. And this is of great importance, since much of Kumaoni folk religion is dedicated to the controlling of demonic forces, and it is the gods celebrated in *jāgar* and *mahābhārat* who are called upon to control them. How dangerous demons are depends on whether they are brought under control or allowed to run wild; properly subdued and fed, demons can, as this story shows, be extremely helpful—especially in fighting other demons.

A third area of divergence, closely related to the other two, is in the character of Bhīma himself. In the Sanskrit *Mahābhārata* he is the biggest, strongest, and fiercest of the brothers, as well as the least clever, and through the length of the epic Bhīma's physically strong and headstrong character is contrasted with those of his brothers—Yudhiṣṭhira is wise and cautious, Arjuna the "parfit gentil knyght," and so forth. In the folk version, while Bhīm is strong indeed, he is also clever and possessed of magical powers of transformation. These changes of character are necessary in Bhīm's role as a subduer of demons. Here it is not his rugged charm that brings the demoness into his power, but his victory in a struggle with her; and while it is his strength that ultimately defeats her brother, it is his cleverness and magical skills that get him to the temple on time. What we are seeing, I think, is Bhīma's transformation into the all-round divine hero of Kumaoni ritual narration, a figure charged with controlling demons, who must at least match them in strength and sorcery while beating them in brains—demons being notoriously and fatally stupid.

In all of these areas of divergence from the Sanskrit epic, the process of fragmentation, of isolating the folk text, is accompanied by one of internal elaboration. Both of these processes are set in motion by the requirements of ritual narration, which is meant to bring blessings and the control of demonic forces for a specific group of participants.

The elaborations and alterations that are evident in this multiply-filtered generic retelling of the story are, as we shall see, even more pronounced, more exuberant, in a version collected from a bard in performance.

Mahābhārat *in Performance*

In 1982 I had the opportunity to participate in and record a series of *mahābhārat* performances in pargana Kuṭaulī in northern Nainītāl District, an area that is culturally and linguistically part of central Kumaon. The singer was the bard Kamal Rām Ārya, who is well known in this area, particularly since his late father, who was his mentor, was considered the area's finest bard. Kamal Rām himself maintains that his ballads are derived from a book call the *Ḍhol Sāgar*, "the Ocean of Drumming;" he's never actually seen the book himself, nor has any other bard that I was able to meet.

Kamal Rām performed a series of *mahābhārat* over several nights. The stories sung were of the *avatār*s of Rām, Kṛṣṇa, Śiva, and the Pāṇḍavs. During a conversation after the performance of the Rām *avatār*, Kamal Rām told a prose version of this Pāṇḍav story, and I will be drawing on this from time to time to supplement the material presented here.[9]

A translation of the entire performance of the Pāṇḍav *avatār* would be far too long for this space. The bard uses several oral styles in performance, some of which involve a great deal of repetition, including periods of singing certain lines over and over again. We will have to make do with a retelling of the narrative in the ritual, illustrated with translated excerpts from the sung performance.[10] In the translations, a

---

[9] This story was told in mixed Hindi and Kumaoni prose, with the Kumaoni taking over as the teller got more involved in the telling. It been published in an English translation (Leavitt 1988). Here I have corrected some mistakes in that translation.

[10] Final vowels, especially -a, are often added in bardic chanting. I have sometimes shown this in the translation for the sake of the rhythm: Pāṇḍav or Pāṇḍava.

slash (/) is used to indicate breaks in the bard's chanting marked by a long note held by an assistant or members of the audience; ellipsis points (. . .) indicate the omission of material.

The bard begins with the chanting of *sandhyā*, literally "evening," a kind of evensong that opens the performance of both *jāgar* and *mahābhārat*, both of which are done at night. While each bard performs *sandhyā* in his own way, all *sandhyā* evoke the swinging fall of evening and invoke regional divinities to be present and attend the performance. He sings slowly and deliberately:

> Oh, listen, Bhagvān, at evening time, oh evening time /
> At evening time, Narāyaṇ, we take your name /
> Narāyaṇ, at evening time, evening time has come swinging /
> Evening has swung, at evening time, oh Narāyaṇ, we take your name, Mother Evening has swung in Uttarākhaṇḍ / . . .
> At evening time what work is being done, Bhagvān? At evening time, ho, in the falling evening /
> At evening time, Narāyaṇ, the little bird of the nest has gone into the nest / . . .
> At evening time what work is being done, Bhagvān? The child of the lap is sitting in the lap / . . .

Thus far, we have the general setting of an evening ritual, using formulas that are identical to those Kamal Rām sings in all his *sandhyās*, and similar to formulas used by other bards. The bard orients the participants in space and time, locating them and describing the activities associated with evening time.

Uttarākhaṇḍ, literally "the northern section" or "region," is the name for the hill region including both Kumaon and Garhwal. Narāyaṇ, Bhagvān, and, later, Isvar are all general divine names; the ritual is being addressed to all the gods, but particularly the gods sung about in *mahābhārat*.

From this point on, the *sandhyā* is aimed specifically at the presentation of *mahābhārat*, the stories of *avatārs*, rather than any other kind of ritual:

> At evening time where has evening swung? To those houses, Bhagvān, where there are such *avatārs* /
> At evening time in those houses, Narāyaṇ, what work is being done at evening time? /

The bard then describes the cleaning and preparations of the house for the performance and moves on to the blessings associated with houses where *mahābhārat* is performed. He contrasts houses that have a "Lakṣmī-woman," i.e. a good mother described as preparing for the *mahābhārat*, with those that have "a woman of evil signs." Where the Lakṣmī-woman dwells is the dwelling of the goddess Lakṣmī, and so of prosperity and happiness; where dwells the woman of evil signs—presumably one who does not encourage the hiring of bards to do *mahābhārat*—Lakṣmī flees fifty-two *kos* away.[11]

The bard then names the various *avatār*s whose stories have already been sung to us:

> I have sung for you ['caused you to hear'], Narāyaṇ, lords, the Śiva *avatār* /
> After singing you the Siva *avatār*, I sang you the Rām *avatār* /
> Whoever hears the Rām *avatār* goes to the heavenly world, to Rām's world /
> Whoever hears the Siva *avatār*, whoever hears it goes to Siva's world /
> I have sung you the Kṛṣṇa *avatār*, I've sung it to you /
> Whoever hears the Kṛṣṇa *avatār*, lords, he goes to dwell in Baikunṭha /
> Today I will sing you, Bhagvān, the Pāṇḍav *avatār* /
> In those houses where, Narāyaṇ, there are such *avatār*s at evening time /
> In those houses, Narāyaṇ, from one comes ten million, from five come fifty /
> In those houses is the dwelling of Laksamī, in those houses fears stay far away /

At this point, without a change in melody or rhythm, the bard shifts from *sandhyā* into the narration of the *mahābhārat* story. He begins:

> There were, Narāyaṇ, at shady Jainti homestead, there were, Narāyaṇ, the five Pāṇḍava brothers /
> There were the five Pāṇḍava brothers, Arjun, Nakul, Sahadev, Bharata /
> Bhīm Singh Pāṇḍava, they were at shady Jainti /
> The five Pāṇḍava brothers, Narāyaṇ, they were men of might, the five Pāṇḍava brothers /
> Their mother was Kunthā at shady Jainti homestead, the five Pāṇḍava brothers /
> So mighty was Bhīm Singh Pāṇḍava, at shady Jainti homestead /
> He wielded a twenty-two *piṛ* sword, Bhīm Singh Pāṇḍava, ho the five Pāṇḍava brothers / . . .

---

[11] I have not attempted to translate weights and measures.

> [Arjun's] wife was named Dropadī, in their house, Bhagvān, was the Lady Dropadī / . . .
> One day the Pāṇḍavas' mother said, Dharmavāṇī Kunthā, / . . .
> "Since your, our fathers' deaths in our shady Jainti homestead, Pāṇḍavas, Bhīm Singha, /
> We have not performed your fathers' *sarād* [the ancestral rites, Sanskrit *śrāddha*]. Let's do it," said Kunthā, "our fathers' *sarad*." /

What is most evident here is an even greater degree of proximation compared to the Sanskrit text. The Pāṇḍavs are here typical rural Kumaoni brothers of the warrior caste, living at their homestead with their mother and the wife of the eldest, here Arjun. As in such a household, the mother tends to be the boss.

But the greatest factor of proximation in this version is the hero's name. The Sanskrit Bhīmasena, one of the forms of Bhīma's name, changed to the modern form Bhīmsen in Upādhyāy's retelling. Here, however, the bard has heard the name as Bhīm Singh. "Singh," from Sanskrit *siṃha*, 'lion', comes in the second place, that of the caste marker, in all Kumaoni names of men of the warrior caste. "Bhīm Singh," then, is a perfectly normal and in fact extremely common Kumaoni man's name.

The bard goes on to tell how Mother Kunthā sends her sons off to find their family priest, the Brahman Baṛu Josi. Another striking bit of proximation: the priest lives in another village, presumably a village of Josi Brahmans. Since the small villages of upland Kumaon, such as those of the bard's area, are usually inhabited by a single patriclan, intercaste cooperation is also intervillage interaction. And Josi is one of the most common Brahman clan-names in Kumaon (see, for instance, the two Jośīs cited in the references below).

The Pāṇḍavs go to the priest's house and ask for his help, but Bhīm Singh insults him, and he refuses to come with them. This *acār*, "excessive behavior" (Sanskrit *atyācāra*) is typical of Bhīm Singh's character, and the word will be used in relation to him throughout the performance.

The Pāṇḍavs return home, and Mother Kunthā roundly chastises Bhīm Singh, who informs her of the Brahman's curse. She sends him back against his will to apologize to the Brahman and beg him to come. Bhīm does so, returns home, and tells his mother to make ready for the *sarād*.

At this point Dropadi goes to the spring to draw water. But there is someone at the spring already: the Iron-Devil Demon, *Luvāsuri Daint* (Sanskrit *daitya*), who puts on Brahman's clothes and sandalwood on his forehead. He tells Dropadi that he is the family Brahman, come to do the *sarād*, and she bows down to him and guides him back to shady Jainti homestead. Mother Kunthā welcomes him, but Bhīm Singh is suspicious. He says that this is no pandit, and his mother chides him again for his rudeness. Bhīm Singh points out some of the "Brahman"'s demonic traits: he has shifty eyes and "so much filth on his body you could dig it with a hoe" (*kuṭāuv khodan maila*). The demon, realizing that he'd better get rid of the perspicacious Bhīm Singh, says that to do the *sarād* he needs sesame seeds from the Garden of Death (*kavābāri tīla*), and that only Bhīm Singh can do the job. Bhīm accepts this task and departs.

> Bhīm Singh got halfway on his road, halfway on his road Bhīm Singh Pāṇḍava /
> Bhīm Singh got halfway on his road, and there Bhīm Singh fell into rolling, rolling sleep /
> At shady Jainti homestead, Narāyaṇ, the demon said, "Oh five Pāṇḍava brothers, / . . .
> We'll do our work when Bhīm Singh gets back / . . .
> Listen, Pāṇḍavas," said the demon, "bring me a pot full of water /
> I will give you *darsan* [a religiously-marked vision] of your fathers," said, Narāyaṇ, the Iron-Devil Demon /

The brothers bring the pot and the demon tells them to look into it. They gaze at their own reflections, thinking them the images of their ancestors.

> Behind them the "honorable pandit" (*paṇḍit jyū*) pulled out, Narāyaṇ, he pulled out his Iron-Devil net /
> He threw it over them, he threw the Iron-Devil net over the five Pāṇḍava brothers /
> He threw the Iron-Devil net over Mother Kunthā too, he threw the net over Dropadi too /
> The demon tied up the net, the demon threw the net over his shoulder and hit the road /
> The five Pāṇḍava brothers, Narāyaṇ, and the sixth Dropadi, were all locked up (*bandūrai*) /

The demon mocks the Pandavs in the net on his back; Dropadi says that if only her *divar* (husband's younger brother) Bhīm Singh were there he'd fix things, but of course he's not. She breaks her necklace and throws golden jewels from it onto the ground to mark their way.

The relationship between a *bhauji* (elder brother's wife) and her *divar* (husband's younger brother) is highly marked in Kumaon, as it is in other parts of North India. Ideally, it is one of easy affection and familiarity, often involving teasing of the *divar* by the *bhauji* and reciprocal devotion on his part.

Bhīm Singh comes back to shady Jainti homestead; he laughs in anger to see his family gone.

> "Oh Mama," he said, "The demon has taken Mama. I told you so, Mama, oh Mama Kunthā /
> I told them it was inauspicious to do our fathers' *sarād*. Well, so be it," said Bhīm Singh Pāṇḍava /

Bhīm Singh goes to the altar and eats all the heaps of food that had been prepared for the ceremony.

> Bhīm Singh said, "I'm not going, I'm not going," said Bhīm Singh, "to look for the five Pāṇḍava brothers, I'm not going to look for them." /
> Bhīm Singh in shady Jainti homestead, Bhīmi Pāṇḍava spread out his golden bed, Bhīm Singh Pāṇḍava /
> When Bhīm Singh was in his golden bed, Bhīm Singh went to rolling, rolling sleep / . . .

Bhīm thinks better of his decision, however, and sets out to look for his family, particularly for his *bhauji* Dropadi. He follows the trail of jewels that Dropadi dropped to mark their way.

The five Pāṇḍava brothers are now in the Demon Fortress (*daintigaṛh*), tied up in the Iron-Devil net.

> In the middle of the road, Narāyaṇ, what work was being done, oh in the middle of the road? /
> That Iron-Devil demon, Bhagvān, he had two, he had two little sisters /
> Two sisters, whose names were, Narāyaṇ, oh my Bhagvān, /
> Hiṛmā and Khiṛmā were their names. What work had the demons done in the middle of the road? /

Hiṛmā is a predictable Kumaoni transformation of the name Hiḍimbā, showing greater divergence from it than does Upādhyāy's form Hiḍambā. This repeats the pattern of divergence we saw with the progression from Bhīmasena through Bhīmsen to Bhīm Singh and is evidence for considering the Upādhyāy version an intermediate one between the Sanskrit text and this version.

> (Hiṛmā and Khiṛmā) had spread out a twenty-two hand wide cloth, and over it they had written a sign, at the Demon Fortress /

> They had cut a woman's skirt (*ghàgari*), Bhagvān, the demons had made everything ready /
> They had written on the sign, "Whoever is the son of a living mother, he will jump over my twenty-two-handspan cloth. /
> Whoever is the son of a dead mother, he will cross over walking on my skirt." /
> The demons had set up a game of dice, Narāyaṇ, a game of dice /

Any male traveller on the road has to choose between attempting a superhuman leap or accepting the double insult of being called the son of a dead mother and having to tread on a woman's skirt. This is a deceptive dice game: the losing stake is beautifully decorated, the winning stake is filthy and unappealing.

> Going going Bhīm Singh Pāṇḍava arrived there, ho Bhīm Singh Pāṇḍava /
> Bhīm Singh saw the twenty-two-span cloth, Bhīm Singh did this *acāra*, Bhīm Singh /
> Bhīm Singh did his Eastern Leap, Bhīm Singh leapt over the twenty-two-span cloth /
> The demon's little sister said, "My *bhin* (elder sister's husband) Bhīm Singh has come! Come on, *bhin*, come on," she said.

In a variation on the already-established theme of affinal bonding, the demoness—presumably as part of the deception—calls Bhīm Singh "elder sister's husband," a highly honorific title. This appears to be a way of luring him into the dice game, which, it has been arranged, he will lose. Bhīm Singh not only accepts this kinship appelation, but turns it to his own advantage: he calls the demoness "wife's younger sister" (*sàì*), putting her in a relationship of service to him: a wife's younger sister does what her older sister's husband asks. He asks for some water. The demoness tells her servant girl (literally, "orphan," a term of abuse) to go and get it, but Bhīm Singh says that he will not drink water from an "orphan"'s hands; the demoness has to go herself. In her absence, Bhīm Singh sits himself down at the winning stake, the one disguised with mud and filth. The demoness returns with the water, asks him what he's doing sitting in the mud, and he says, "Forget the water, let's throw dice!"

> Bhīm Singh threw fives and sixes, Bhīm Singh, ho Bhīm Singh Pāṇḍava /
> Bhīm Singh won everything of the demons', he won the house, the demons' house /

The two demon sisters Hiṛmā and Khiṛmā, Bhīm Singh, Bhīm Singh made them his own /
Bhīm Singh said, "I'm going, I'm going, *sài*, I'm going", he said, "to the Demon Fortress /
Now you tell me, tell me, my *sài*, /
Tell me where are Mother Kunthā, my *bhauji* Dropadi, the five Pāṇḍava brothers?" /

The sisters tell him that his family has been kidnapped by the Iron-Devil Demon and that they will be sacrified in the temple of Kālikā the following night. Bhīm Singh sets out for the demon's fortress.

On the road there was a blacksmith. What work was the blacksmith doing, Bhīm Singh Pāṇḍava? /
The blacksmith was carrying a trident, carrying it, that Blackie Blacksmith (*kaiyā lvār*) /
Bhīm Singh said, "Hey, Blackie Blacksmith, that trident, Blackie, where are you taking it?" /
Blackie Blacksmith joined his hands [in respectful greeting]; what did Blackie Blacksmith say? /
"Oh our master," he said, "is having a *pūjā* to Kālikā in the Kālikā Temple /
Narāyaṇ, there will be a Kālikā *pūjā* and she'll be getting a sacrifice of Panu birds." /
Bhīm Singh said, "Oh Blackie Blacksmith, buddy, what will you get paid?" asked Bhīm Singh Pandava /
Blackie Blacksmith said, "Oh great king, I'll get a leg," he said, Narāyaṇ, Bhīm Singh Pāṇḍava /
Bhīm Singh grabbed hold of Blackie Blacksmith, beat him to bits, twisted his leg around and stuck it in his mouth /

This is how sacrificial goats are treated: after the goat is killed, its head with one leg in its mouth is offered in the temple. "Panu birds" is an obvious pun on Pāṇḍav.

Bhīm Singh then meets a basketmaker who says he will get a back from the sacrifice, so Bhīm tears off the basketmaker's back and leaves him there with his back in his mouth. Finally, Bhīm meets a flower-gardener picking flowers and filling a basket with them. These are flowers, he says, that he is providing for his master's sacrifice of Panu birds.

Bhīm Singh seized his mother's truth (*sat*), he seized his *bhauji*'s truth /

> Bhīm Singh, my Bhīm Singh changed his shape, he changed to the shape of a fly, Bhīm Singh Pāṇḍava /
> Bhīm Singh changed his shape to that of a fly, Bhīm Singh went inside a flower /
> The flower-gardener took up his basket and carrying, carrying it went to the Demon Fortress /

At the fortress, the *pūjā* is underway. Suspecting that Bhīm Singh might be hiding in a flower, the demons are weighing every flower that arrives; any that seem heavier than usual they are tossing into a pot of boiling oil. But when they weigh the flower with Bhīm Singh in it, it's as light as can be. They take that flower into the Kālikā temple and put it right on top of the *ling*, the phallic symbol of Lord Śiva.

> The demons in Demon Fortress, the demons were so happy in Demon Fortress /
> Bhīm Singh did such an *acāra*, Bhīm Singh Pandava, in Demon Fortress, ho Bhīm Singh Pandava /
> Bhīm Singh had to piss, Bhīm Singh Pāṇḍava did such an *acāra* /
> Bhīm Singh from the top of Kālikā's *ling*, Bhīm Singh pissed /
> This made the demons so happy, the demons said, "Our Kālikā is very delighted," /
> The demons said, "Today Mother Gangā has come here! Demons, come on and take a bath!" /
> Now the Iron-Devil Demon took hold of his net, he brought the Iron-Devil net /

The demon asks the Pāṇḍavs who will save them now. They reply that since he has captured them, no one can save them. Only Dropadi says that if her *divar* Bhīm Singh were there, he'd save them. The demon replies that Bhīm Singh is like a fly (speaking more truth than he intends). Hearing this, Bhīm Singh gets angry in his flower.

> Bhīm Singh's forearm hairs, Bhagvān, stood up from his forearms, Bhīm Singh Pāṇḍava /
> The hairs on his waist, Bhīmi, Bhīm Singh Pāṇḍava, stood up from his waist /
> Oh Bhīm Singh's buttery throat, Bhīm Singh Pāṇḍava, sprang up hundred-maund goosebumps /
> Struck by anger, Bhīm Singh suddenly stood up, Bhīm Singh Pāṇḍava /

Bhīm Singh takes on his true form, gets out his sword and starts slaughtering demons. This is one of the bard's periods of fast repeating of sung lines:

> Oh Bhīma, now Bhīma was waging battle, he was waging battle /
> Oh Bhīmiyā, he started looking at his Eastern Thorn (his sword), his Eastern Thorn /
> Oh Bhīma, he was waging battle, he was waging battle /
> Oh Bhīma, he was waging battle, he was waging battle /

The bard then continues in a fast, clipping prose:

> Oh that Bhīm Singh was giving battle, Isvar my father. For every head he cut off a hundred demons were born. He was drowning in a river of gore (*ragat ki gangā*). And Bhīm Singh was getting sleepy. And Bhīm Singh Pāṇḍav was getting hungry, hungry, he was getting thirsty, thirsty. In golden dreams, Bhīm Singh went to Mother Kunthā. "Look here, Mother Kunthā. I'm drowning in a river of blood. I'm drowning in a river of gore. I'm hungry-hungry, I'm thirsty-thirsty." Then Mother Kunthā gave forth a stream of milk [from her breast]. From this stream of milk Bhīm Singh had a milky feast... Then Mother Kunthā said, "Oh Bhīmi," she said, "you won't be able to stop the demons' heads (from growing) the way you're doing it. Press a black bumblebee (*bhāvar*) under your heel. Oh Bhīmi, throw a white bumblebee up into the sky," she said.

The bard goes back to singing as he tells of Bhīm Singh doing this. In his prose version of the story given several days earlier, he explained that this stopped the reproduction of demons; here he moves right on to the next thing. Bhīm Singh picks up the net, tosses it over his shoulder, and goes back to shady Jainti homestead.

Having reached this point in the story, it is time for the bard to bring the audience directly into the narrative action: it's time to cut the demon's web and led the Pāṇḍavs out. The bard asks for a knife and a brass plate with some rice and a small clay lamp on it. He has constructed a little net out of string, and each person present comes forward, passes his or her hand over the flame, and cuts part of the net with the knife. The bard sings, over and over again, variations on the following:

> I have cut, I have cut today, oh I have cut the Iron-Devil net /
> I have cut the Iron-Devil net, I have opened it up for the Pāṇḍavas /
> For the five Pāṇḍava brothers I have opened, I have opened what was shut up / . . .

As each person comes up, cuts the net, and offers a little money on the brass plate, the bard modifies his song, names the person, and says that he or she has cut the net and released the Pāṇḍavas. When this ritual has been completed, the bard closes the performance:

> Oh gods, the Pāṇḍav *avatār* is complete, it is complete / . . .
> Oh Bhagvān, the net has been cut, they have been released from the net, released from the net /
> Oh Bhagvān, from one come twenty-one, from five come fifty, from five come fifty / . . .
> Oh Bhagvān, the Pāṇḍav *avatār* is complete, the Pāṇḍav *avatār* /
> Hail! (*jay hō*!)

This is not the place for attempting a rigorous analysis of this tale, one which would take account, among other things, of its manipulation of kinship relations, the bloodthirsty piety of its demons, and its streams of urine, blood, and milk. Some things, however, can be said. While I cannot tell how typical or idiosyncratic this version of the story is, there is one overwhelming difference between it and those we looked at earlier: this version was presented as part of a ritual. In Kamal Ram's own view, this ritual performance was the "real" one, and he considered his prose retelling of it—which, after all, conveyed only information, not benediction—unworthy of the tape it took to record it.

Some of the striking characteristics of the version presented here are directly determined by this ritual context. This is most obvious for the framing elements that open and close the performance. These consist largely of reiterations of the effectiveness of the performance itself: where the *mahābhārat* is heard is the dwelling of Lakṣmī, there will be happiness and increase. Insofar as these parts of the performance contain references to other stories, they are to other similar rituals, other recitations of *avatār*s, not to other parts of a longer connected narrative. These framing elements of the ritual replace the strictly narrative frames of the Sanskrit text, which tell how one character told the story to another character who recited it to a third, and so forth.

Within the telling of the tale itself, we find again the three areas of divergence from the Sanskrit text that we noted for the Hindi prose version; here, these divergences go farther in the same direction.

1. I noted earlier that themes of incarceration and escape that precede the episode in the Sanskrit version were found inside it in the Upādhyāy version. Here these themes have grown more evident: the Pāṇḍavs are caught in an iron net, and the whole point of the ritual is to let them out again. And now the isolation of the episode is even greater: it begins and ends not with the Pāṇḍavs between two adventures, as in the Sanskrit text, nor while they are, exceptionally, drifting through the forest, as in the Upādhyāy version, but at home. This is a base situation of absolute normalcy from which any adventure is equally possible. Such a fixed,

stable opening and closing point, typical of folktales around the world, effectively seals off this episode from any longer connecting narrative.

2. The demon son, the main link to the overall narrative in the Sanskrit *Mahābhārata*, has disappeared altogether. Hiḍimbā is doubled again, but this time by a little sister with more or less the same name whose function in the story is not at all evident. On the other hand, this version shows an even greater elaboration of the agonistic game-playing between Bhīma and the demons. It is richly complicated with multiple disguises, transformations, tricks and counter-tricks, all of which lead to Bhīm Singh subduing or destroying demons.

3. The rounding-out of Bhīm Singh's character that typified the Upādhyāy version progresses in this one. Bhīm Singh is now both the youngest—this was specified in the prose retelling—and the most intelligent of the Pāṇḍavs: the bard calls him *antarjānī*, "knower of what is inside (hidden)." He sees through the demon's Brahman disguise when no one else in his family does, and his absence is what allows the demon to trick and capture them. He outwits demonesses and sneaks his way into the sacrifice just before his family is slaughtered, where he urinates all over the demons, who in contrast reveal their stupidity by taking it for holy water.

This version of the story also brings out a new aspect of Bhīm Singh's character by insisting on his *acār*, his excessive behavior, both bad and good. First of all, as in both the other versions, he is excessively strong, and in Kumaoni folk literature this also means that he is an excessive eater, drinker, and sleeper. More specifically, the deeds described as *acār* include both his troublemaking at the beginning of the story and his wonderworking at the end of it.

We observed in discussing Upādhyāy's version of the story that the new facets of Bhīm's personality all serve to make him an adequate controller of demons, a central role of divinities in Kumaoni lore. This ritual version of the story allows us to go farther and say that some degree of *excessiveness*—the very trait that characterizes demons—is also necessary for a Kumaoni divinity to be able and disposed to deal with demons. Such divinities, typically the regional divinities of the hills, are usually dangerous and somewhat demonic themselves, and the *jāgar* ceremony is specifically designed to bring them under control by inducing them to possess a human medium and dance. The aim is focused relief of some trouble, often a demonic one.

Now Bhīm Singh, like the other protagonists of *mahābhārat*, is not this kind of possessing god,[12] and his *mahābhārat* is not performed to cure a

[12] The exception here is the Goddess, who participates in both categories and does possess people.

specific illness or a run of devilish back luck. Yet the general blessings that *mahābhārat* are supposed to bestow involve telling of a divine hero controlling and destroying demons; and some of the stylistic devices Kamal Rām uses for no obvious reasons other than aesthetic ones in fact serve specific purposes in *jāgar*. The periods of loud sung repetition of lines, for instance, are used in *jāgar* for the possessed oracle to dance to. The principles of the two *genres*, in other words, seem to parallel each other, with the *jāgar* representing a more "concentrated" form of processes that are also at work in *mahābhārat*. Here again, *mahābhārat* performance shows linkages not into a narrative universe as such, but into the ideological and practical universe of Kumaoni folk religion.

Conclusion

It would be foolhardy to make any hard and fast claims on the basis of three variants of a tale. At the same time, however, the comparison of these texts does reveal clear patterns which might merit further investigation.

We noted earlier that the differing forms of the names Hiḍimbā and Bhīmasena suggest that this version has diverged more widely than has Upādhyāy's from their common source. Whatever the reason for this pattern—a longer period of oral transmission, a bard's lesser exposure to the classical version, his more active imagination, or any number of other factors—it is repeated in the structure of the stories themselves. The Sanskrit text and the Kumaoni performance represent opposed poles along a couple of dimensions: the first is relatively fixed while the second is relatively fluid; the first is bound up in a larger narrative context while the second, a separate narrative unit, is bound up in a specific situational context, in this case a ritual one. The version published by Upādhyāy is intermediate on both scores: it is a fixed retelling of what we must presume to have been a far more fluid original; and it has been situationally de-contextualized and narratively recontextualized as one of a series of Pāṇḍav stories, either by the author or his bardic informants. The three versions thus progress from the dominance of an intratextual context to that of an extratextual one. Two mutually reinforcing processes are at work shifting the texts themselves from one kind of context to the other: a process of increasing fragmentation, that is, of separation of the episode from the rest of the epic; and a process of increasing proximation and internal elaboration, both of which tend to increase the pertinence and power of the story for those helping to realize it in a ritual meant to affect their lives directly.

It remains to be seen whether other variants bear out this interpretation and whether these processes can be seen at work more widely. My effort here has been to chart the patterning in one small set of narrative variations, an eddy in the ocean of story.

Appendix

Kumaoni texts of a few of the excerpts from the *Mahābhārat* performance by Kamal Rām presented here.

* * *

First excerpt, beginning: "Oh, listen Bhagvān, at evening time. . ."

suṇā bhagvānō, sandhyā bakhat mẽ ho sandhyā bakhata /
sandhyā bakhat, naraiṇo, tumara nām lhinū̃ hō /
naraiṇo, sandhyā bakhat māja jhuli ai ge ho sandhyā bakhata /
sandhyā jhuli ge, sandhyā bakhat, īhō naraiṇo, tumar nām lhinū̃,
mātā, jhuli sandhyā ge uttarākhaṇḍā mājā /. . .
sandhyā bakhat ke kām hai raī, bhagvānō, sandhyā bakhat mẽ hō paṛaṇi sandhyā /
sandhyā bakhat, naraiṇo, ghole ki caṛi ho gholai phaiṭi rai cha /. . .
sandhyā bakhat mẽ kyā kām hai raī, bhagvānō, godi ko bālak hō godi bhaiṭi rau cha /. . .

* * *

Second excerpt, beginning "At evening time where has evening swung?"

sandhyā bakhat mẽ sandhyā kā̃ jhuli ge cha? jin gharō̃ mẽ, bhagvānō, yasa-yasā avatārā /
sandhyā bakhat mẽ un gharō̃ māja, naraiṇo, kyā kām hai rī̃ hō sandhyā bakhata /

* * *

Excerpt beginning "There were, Narāyaṇ, at shady Jainti homestead . . ."

chiyā bhagvāno syoi jainti bāra chiyā, chiyā naraiṇo pāncai bhai pāṇḍavā /
pāncai bhai pāṇḍava chiyā arjun, nakul, sahadev, bharatā /
bhīm siṅh pāṇḍava chiyā hō syoi jaintī mājā /
pānc bhai pāṇḍav, naraiṇo, baladhāri chiyā hō pāncai bhai pāṇḍavā /
uneri mātā holi kunthā syoi jainti bār hō pāncai bhai pāṇḍavā /
yasa baldhārī chiyā bhīm siṅh pāṇḍab hō syoi jaintī bārā /

baīs-baīsa pīṛai kā kuṛkā lagaũ chī bhīm siṅh pāṇḍav hō pāncai bhai pāṇḍavā /. . .
uneri patnī kā nāma chiyo dropadī hō, un ghara bhagvānō, uneri holi ho dropadī nārī /. . .
ēkā dinā pāṇḍavō̃ ki mātā kunā hō dharmavaṇī kunthā /. . .
"tumārā hamārā pitarō̃k jaiyā batiḳ hamar syoi jainti bār mẽ hō pāṇḍab bhīm siṅhā /
tumārā pitarō̃ ko sarād ni hai rayo, karanū̃," kunai kunthā, "pitarai sarāda." /

* * *

Excerpt beginning "The demons in Demon Fortress. . ."

daintā daintī gaṛa ho mājā, daint ituk khusī hai rī̃ daintī gaṛā mājā /
bhīm siṅha yas acārā, bhīm siṅha pāṇḍava dainti gaṛ mẽ hō bhīm siṅhā pāṇḍavā /
bhīm siṅh kaī pesāb lagi ge cha, bhīm siṅh kaī, bhīm siṅha pāṇḍavā, yas acār bhīm siṅhā /
bhīm siṅh lai kālikā ki liṅga mali bai, bhīm siṅh hō pesābai kari hai cha /
daint ituk khusī hai gayā, daint kunī̃, "hameri kālikā hō bhautai prasannai hai ge cha!" /
daint kunī̃, "āj gaṅgā māī ai ge cha! daintiyā āvā, isnāṇ kari lhiyā!" /
āb luvāsuri daint jāvai kaī pakaṛi lāyo, luvāsuri jāl hō lāi bhalā gayā /

* * *

Closing excerpt:

īrē dēvō, pāṇḍav avatārā pūraṇ hai ga hō, pūraṇ hai ga hō /
īhō bhagavān, jāla kaṭi bhera nirjālā hai ga hō, nirjālā hai ga hō /
īhō bhagavān, ēka ki ekāis, pā̃co ki pacāsa, pā̃co ki pacāsa /
īhō bhagavān, pūraṇ hai gayo pāṇḍav avatārā, pāṇḍav avatārā /
jay hō!

Acknowledgements

Field research in India was sponsored by the American Institute of Indian Studies and the U.S. Office of Education and carried out under the supervision of the Department of Anthropology, University of Delhi.

I am grateful to Kamal Ram Arya for performing the original material presented here, to Indra Singh Negi for his invaluable guidance in collecting and interpreting it, and to Lynn M. Hart, Margaret Lock, Richard Lock, Wendy Doniger O'Flaherty, and Bruce Owens for their help and advice. I would also like to acknowledge my gratitude to Madeleine Biardeau and Charles Malamoud, whose seminar at the Ecole Pratique des Hautes Etudes offered a glimpse into the depths of coherent complexity of the *Mahābhārata*.

References

Atkinson, E.T. 1884. *The Himalayan Districts of the North-Western Provinces of India.* Volume two. Allahabad: Government Printing Office. [Gazetteer of the North-West Provinces and Oudh, 11.]

Berreman, Gerald D. 1963. *Hindus of the Himalayas: Ethnography and Change.* Berkeley: University of California Press.

Biardeau, Madeleine. 1979. Compte rendu du séminaire "Religions de l'Inde." *Annuaire de l'Ecole Pratique des Hautes Etudes, Ve section—Sciences religieuses* 87: 145–171.

Biardeau, Madeleine, and Jean-Michel Péterfalvi. 1986. *Le Mahābhārata.* Two volumes. Paris: Flammarion.

Dumézil, Georges. 1968. *Mythe et épopée, 1. L'idéologie des trois fonctions dans les épopées des peuples indo-européens.* Paris: Gallimard.

Dumont, Louis. 1957. Village Studies. *Contributions to Indian Sociology* 1: 23–41.

Gaborieau, Marc. 1974. Classification des récits chantés. La littérature orale des populations hindoues de l'Himalaya central. *Poétique* 19: 313–332.

——1975. La transe rituelle dans l'Himalaya central: Folie, avatār, méditation. *Puruṣārtha* 2: 147–172.

Grintser, P.A. 1974. *Drevneindijskij epos: Genezis i tipologija.* Moscow: Glaznaja Redaicija Vostočnoj Literatury.

Hiltebeitel, Alf. 1988. *The Cult of Draupadi, 1. Mythologies: From Gingee to Kurukṣetra.* Chicago: University of Chicago Press.

Ingalls, Daniel H.H., and Daniel H.H. Ingalls, Jr. 1985. The *Mahābhārata*: Stylistic Study, Computer Analysis, and Concordance. *Journal of South Asian Literatures* 20(1): 17–46.

Jośī, Kṛṣṇānand. 1971. *Kumāū̃ kā lok sāhitya: Paricayātmak sangraha.* Bareilly: Prakash Book Depot.

Jośī, Prayāg. 1971. *Kumāū̃nī lok gathāẽ.* Dehra Dun: Jugal Kiśor.

Leavitt, John, 1981. Himalayan Versions of "The Three Golden Sons": The Effect of Context on Narrative Content. *Journal of Indian Folkloristics* 4: 1–17.

—— 1985. *The Language of the Gods: Discourse and Experience in a Central Himalayan Ritual.* Doctoral dissertation, the University of Chicago.

—— 1988. A *Mahābhārata* Story from the Kumaon Hills. *Himalayan Research Bulletin* 7(2): 1–12.

Marriott, McKim. 1976. Interpreting Indian Society: A Monistic Alternative to Dumont's Dualism. *Journal of Asian Studies* 36: 189–195.

—— 1989. Constructing an Indian Ethnosociology. *Contributions to Indian Sociology* (n.s.) 23: 1–39.

O'Flaherty, Wendy Doniger, 1978. Review of J.A.B. van Buitenen, ed. and trans., *The Mahābhārata. Religious Studies Review* 4(1): 19–28.

—— 1988. *Other People's Myths: The Cave of Echoes.* New York: Macmillan.

Pāṇḍey, Trilocan: 1962. *Kumāū̃ kā lok-sāhitya.* Almora: Sri Almora Book Depot.

Pollock, Sheldon J. 1984. The *Rāmāyaṇa* Text and the Critical Edition. *In* Robert J. Goldman, ed. and trans., *The Rāmāyaṇa of Vālmīki: An Epic of Ancient India*, Volume one, pp. 82–89. Princeton: Princeton University Press.

—— 1986. (ed. and trans.) *The Rāmāyaṇa of Vālmīki: An Epic of Ancient India*. Volume two. Princeton: Princeton University Press.

Ramanujan, A.K. 1986. Two Realms of Kannada Folklore. *In* Stuart H. Blackburn and A.K. Ramanujan, eds., *Another Harmony: New Essays on the Folklore of India*, pp. 41–75. Berkeley: University of California Press.

Tubb, Gary. 1985. *Śāntarasa* in the *Mahābhārata*. *Journal of South Asian Literatures* 20(1): 141–168.

Upādhyāy, Urbā Datt. 1979. *Kumāū̃ kī lok-gāthāõ kā sāhityik aur sāṃskṛtik adhyāyan.* Bareilly: Prakash Book Depot.

van Buitenen, J.A.B. 1973. *The Mahābhārata: Book One*. Chicago: University of Chicago Press.

Wikander, Stig. 1947. Pāṇḍavasagan och Mahābhāratas mytiska förutsättningar. *Religion och Bibel* 6: 27–39.

LIST OF CONTRIBUTORS

VIDYUT AKLUJKAR
Asian Studies
University of British Columbia
Vancouver, BC
Canada V6T 1W5

B.N. SUMITRA BAI
157 Kamakshi Hospital Road
12th Main, 10th Cross
Saraswathipuram
Mysore 570023
India

MADHAV M. DESHPANDE
Asian Languages and Cultures
University of Michigan
Ann Arbor, MI 48109–1285
U.S.A.

JOHN DUNHAM
Department of Indian Studies
University of Melbourne
Parkville Vic. 3052
Australia

JAMES L. FITZGERALD
Department of Religious Studies
University of Tennessee
Knoxville, TN 37996
U.S.A.

EDWIN GEROW
Reed College
3203 S.E. Woodstock Blvd.
Portland, OR 97202
U.S.A.

DAVID L. GITOMER
Department of South Asian Languages and Civilization
University of Chicago
Chicago, IL 60637
U.S.A.

ALF HILTEBEITEL
Religious Studies
George Washington University
Washington, DC 20052
U.S.A.

DANIEL H.H. INGALLS
The Yard
Hot Springs, VA 24445
U.S.A.

DANIEL H.H. INGALLS, JR.
The Yard
Hot Springs, VA 24445
U.S.A.

RUTH KATZ
Department of Religion
Florida State University
Tallahassee, FL 32306
U.S.A.

KLAUS KLOSTERMAIER
Department of Religion
University of Manitoba
Winnipeg, Manitoba
Canada R3T 2N2

JOHN LEAVITT
Département d'anthropologie
Université de Montréal
Montreal, Quebec
Canada

BIMAL KRISHNA MATILAL
The Oriental Institute
University of Oxford
Pusey Lane
Oxford OX1 2LE
U.K.

BARBARA STOLER MILLER
Department of Oriental Studies
Barnard College
Columbia University
606 West 120th Street
New York, NY 10027
U.S.A.

CHRISTOPHER MINKOWSKI
Wolfson College
Oxford OX1 2JD
U.K.

INDIRA V. PETERSON
Mount Holyoke College
South Hadley, MA 01075
U.S.A.

A.K. RAMANUJAN
Department of South Asian Languages and Literature
University of Chicago
Chicago, IL 60637
U.S.A.

WILLIAM SAX
Department of Philosophy and Religious Studies
University of Canterbury
Private Bag
Christchurch 1
New Zealand

T.R. SINGH
Head
Department of Sociology
B.S.M. College
Roorkee
U.P.
India

BRAJ M. SINHA
Department of Religious Studies
University of Saskatchewan
Saskatoon, SK
Canada S7N 0W0

MARY CARROLL SMITH
Religion Department
Vassar College
Poughkeepsie, NY 12601
U.S.A.

BRUCE M. SULLIVAN
Department of Humanities and Religious Studies
Northern Arizona University
Flagstaff, AZ 86011
U.S.A.

GARY A. TUBB
Department of Sanskrit and Indian Studies
Harvard University
Cambridge, MA 02138
U.S.A.

VICTORIA URUBSHUROW
School of Religious Studies
The Catholic University of America
Washington, DC.20064
U.S.A.

ROBERT J. ZYDENBOS
157 Kamakshi Hospital Road
12th Main, 10th Cross
Saraswathipuram
Mysore 570023
India

INDEX